BILLY THE KID'S
Writings, Words & Wit

BY GALE COOPER

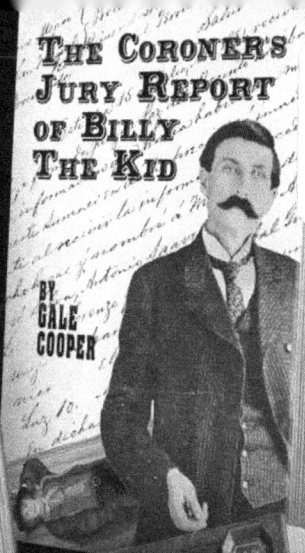

THE CORONER'S JURY REPORT OF BILLY THE KID

BY GALE COOPER

THE LOST PARDON
OF BILLY THE KID: AN ANALYSIS

BILLY AND PAULITA

GALE COOPER

BILLY THE KID'S
Writings, Words & Wit

BY GALE COOPER

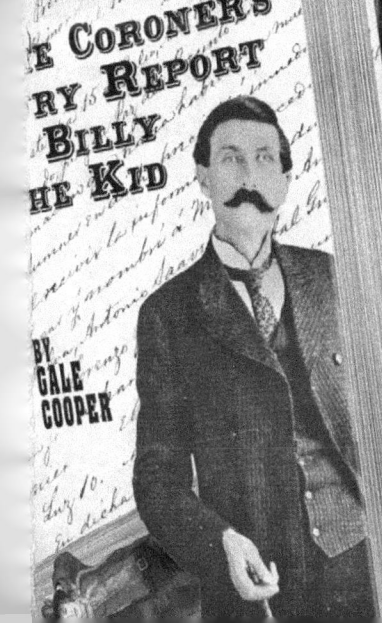

THE CORONER'S JURY REPORT OF BILLY THE KID

BY GALE COOPER

THE SANTA FE RING
VERSUS BILLY THE KID
BY GALE COOPER

WHO'S TE BLAMEY? 'TWAS HIM!

"BILLY THE KID"

THE LOST PARDON
OF BILLY THE KID: AN ANALYSIS

GALE COOPER

THE SANTA FE RING VERSUS BILLY THE KID BY GALE COOPER

WHO'S TE BLAMED 'TWAS HIM!

"BILLY THE KID"

THE CORONER'S JURY REPORT OF BILLY THE KID

BY GALE COOPER

BILLY THE KID'S Writings, Words & Wit

BY GALE COOPER

BILLY THE KID'S Writings, Words & Wit

BY GALE COOPER

WITH NEWLY AUTHENTICATED BILLY THE KID LETTER

BILLY AND PAULITA

GALE COOPER

THE LOST PARDON OF BILLY THE KID: AN ANALYSIS

THE LOST PARDON OF BILLY THE KID: AN ANALYSIS

GALE COOPER

THE SANTA FE RING VERSUS BILLY THE KID BY GALE COOPER

WHO'S TE BLAMED 'TWAS HIM!

"BILLY THE KID"

THE CORONER'S JURY REPORT OF BILLY THE KID

BY GALE COOPER

GALE COOPER'S
REAL BILLY THE KID HISTORY

THE YOUTUBE TALKS

❧ ● ☙

BY
GALE COOPER

GELCOUR
BOOKS

OTHER BILLY THE KID BOOKS
BY GALE COOPER

THE HISTORY

BILLY AND PAULITA: THE SAGA OF BILLY THE KID, PAULITA MAXWELL, AND THE SANTA FE RING

BILLY THE KID'S WRITINGS, WORDS, AND WIT

THE LOST PARDON OF BILLY THE KID: AN ANALYSIS FACTORING IN THE SANTA FE RING, GOVERNOR LEW WALLACE'S DILEMMA, AND A TERRITORY IN REBELLION

THE SANTA FE RING VERSUS BILLY THE KID: THE MAKING OF AN AMERICAN MONSTER

THE CORONER'S JURY REPORT OF BILLY THE KID: THE INQUEST THAT SEALED THE FAME OF BILLY BONNEY AND PAT GARRETT

THE HOAXES

CRACKING THE BILLY THE KID IMPOSTER HOAX OF BRUSHY BILL ROBERTS

BILLY THE KID'S PRETENDER JOHN MILLER

CRACKING THE BILLY THE KID CASE HOAX: THE STRANGE PLOT TO EXHUME BILLY THE KID, CONVICT SHERIFF PAT GARRETT OF MURDER, AND BECOME PRESIDENT OF THE UNITED STATES

THE COLD CASE BILLY THE KID MEGAHOAX

THE BILLY THE KID'S BAD BUCKS HOAX: FAKING BILLY BONNEY AS A WILLIAM BROCKWAY GANG COUNTERFEITER

BLANDINA SEGALE, THE NUN WHO RODE ON BILLY THE KID: SLEUTHING A FOISTED FRONTIER FABLE

For the real Billy Bonney
and his fellow fighters
against the Santa Fe Ring

COVER AND BOOK DESIGN
BY GALE COOPER

ISBN: 978-1-949626-33-9 HARDCOVER
ISBN: 978-1-949626-32-2 PAPERBACK

LIBRARY OF CONGRESS CONTROL NUMBER:
2021902727

GELCOUR BOOKS
Albuquerque, New Mexico

ORDERING THIS BOOK:
Amazon.com, BarnesandNoble.com, bookstores

WEBSITE:
GaleCooperBillytheKidBooks.com

YOUTUBE:
Gale Cooper's Real Billy the Kid

Printed in the United States of America
on acid free paper

CONTENTS

ANNOTATED BIBLIOGRAPHY

AUTHOR'S FOREWORD

This book presents my YouTube talks titled "Gale Cooper's Real Billy the Kid." They distill my revisionist history books about Billy the Kid, the Lincoln County War, and the Santa Fe Ring.

Conventional history is a tale of how the West was won, amidst triumph of law and order, against outlaws like Billy the Kid. My revisionist version tells how the West was stolen by corrupt and racist invading Anglos, from its Hispanic land grant holders, against the backdrop of genocide of Native Americans. In New Mexico Territory, those invaders founded the political cabal of the Santa Fe Ring. And Ring-named Billy the Kid, was actually teenaged Billy Bonney, one of the many unsung anti-Ring freedom fighters vilified by the Ring.

In New Mexico Territory, the 1870's flared with grass-roots uprisings against the Santa Fe Ring. All were crushed. The last and bloodiest was 1878's Lincoln County War, which made Billy Bonney a hero. But reality was buried by these criminal victors under the Ring's outlaw myth propaganda.

Adding to injustice was Territorial Governor Lew Wallace, who replaced his Ringite predecessor. In fact, his self-protective shielding of the Ring allowed it to flourish. And his self-serving betrayal of his pardon bargain with Billy Bonney, sealed Billy's fate as the last Regulator killed by the Ring. Wallace covered-up his hypocrisy with his own outlaw myth of Billy the Kid.

And the outlaw myth was expanded by Billy's killer, Pat Garrett, in his 1882 ghostwritten book: *The Authentic Life of Billy the Kid.*

Modern historians merely plastered their newly researched information onto the antique armature of those outlaw myths of Billy the Kid.

My talks, like my books, declare the truth at last, singing out for the unsung brave men and women who fought the Santa Fe Ring and paid the martyr's price, but deserve history's applause.

Gale Cooper, M.D.
Sandia Park, New Mexico

METHODOLOGY

PERIOD DOCUMENTS: Original errors of spelling, grammar, and punctuation are retained in quoted period documents.

AUTHOR'S COMMENTS: Notes are inserted for author's input within documents.

ON SCREEN: The "on screen" direction from the original videos is retained, but with a Figure number for the provided illustration.

ACKNOWLEDGMENTS

Overriding is my debt to Billy Bonney, whose cause, courage, intelligence, and joie de vivre are my inspiration.

Historical bedrock is from books by Frederick Nolan on Billy the Kid, the Lincoln County War, and John Henry Tunstall. As valuable is Leon Metz's Pat Garrett biography and Jerry (Richard) Weddle's book on Billy Bonney's early adolescence.

Collections used were at the National Archives' Civilian Records Branch, Justice Department, and Department of the Interior; the Indianapolis, Indiana Historical Society's Lew and Wallace Collection; the Santa Fe, New Mexico, Fray Angélico Chávez Historical Library; the Las Cruces, New Mexico State University Library's Rio Grande Historical Collections' Herman B. Weisner Papers, ca. 1957-1992; the Albuquerque, University of New Mexico Center for Southwest Studies, University Library, Catron Papers; the State of New Mexico Office of Cultural Affairs Historic Preservation Division; the Office of the New Mexico State Historian; the Silver City Museum and Library; the Midland, Texas, Nita Stewart and J. Evetts Haley Memorial Library and Historical Center; the Canyon, Texas Panhandle-Plains Historical Museum; and the Morgantown, West Virginia & Regional History Center at West Virginia University Libraries' Stephen B. Elkins Papers.

Billy Bonney's unique Spencerian penmanship was discussed with Mott Media; David Sull; and the Iowa, Ames Historical Society's curators, Dennis Wendell and Sarah Vouthilak..

INTRODUCTION TO THE YOUTUBE TALKS

Did you know that most of what you've seen, read, or heard about Billy the Kid is untrue? My name is Gale Cooper. I'm a medical doctor and forensic psychiatrist. My specialty is murder case consultation for the defense. For 20 years, I've used my expertise to uncover the real Billy the Kid. Researching over 40,000 pages of archival documents and books, I've written the revisionist history. It's shocking. It's liberating. And I've written books demolishing the hoaxes hijacking the history. My talks will share with you what I've found. Cover-ups, misinformation, and fakery - to use Old West lingo - will bite the dust.

LECTURE:
MY ADVENTURES WITH BILLY THE KID
MAY 24, 2019

Today I thought I'd tell you all about my adventure with Billy the Kid, because he changed my life in a very strange way. This story starts in July of 1998 when I had a completely different life. I was living in California. My education had put me on a trajectory, which I was following. I was educated in Smith College, graduated Summa Cum Laude, and went to Harvard Medical School. And that was my trajectory. I did all my training there, internship, residency, and then moved to California to practice. In July of '98, this was my life. I had a Beverly Hills practice. I had a big house in a place called Bell Canyon in San Fernando Valley. I had stables with miniature horses. And here's the important thing. I was doing consultation in high profile murder cases. And that was my life. That's what I expected that I'd be doing.

On my way home from the office, one day, I went through Sherman Oaks and decided to stop at a Barnes and Noble bookstore, just to get a book. And I didn't see anything I wanted. I was on my way out, and I looked at the sale table; and there was a book, $5, Pat Garret's *The Authentic Life of Billy the Kid*. I figured $5! I've heard of Billy the Kid, and he was an outlaw boy who was killed by a Sherriff when he was young. That's all I knew. Well, I went home. And I tend to be a speed reader. So, in about an hour, I completed the book - about a 275 page book. And I - being a consult in murder cases - I read between the lines. And I said, "There're parts of this story that don't fit together. Pat's leaving out things."

Here's what caught my eye. Billy, when he was put in jail, escaped in April of 1881. At that point, he was the most hunted man in the country, and he had two choices. He was completely bicultural and bilingual, and could've - he was 150 miles away -

he could've gone to old Mexico, and lived the rest of his life. He was 21 years old. He could've ridden 150 miles northeast to Fort Sumner and near certain death. Pat didn't write about that or why it happened. I said to myself: "Twenty-one years old, it's got to be a girl."

And so I got on the internet and looked up Billy the Kid. And the first thing I saw was the Billy the Kid Outlaw Gang. And the president of it was a woman named Carolyn Allen. So, I called her - she left her phone number - and I said, "Was there a girl involved?" She said, "Paulita Maxwell. the richest heiress in New Mexico Territory. The heiress to the Maxwell Land Grant: the two million acre grant in northern New Mexico and southern Colorado. And she was a young teenager then; and she was Billy's secret lover." Now here was Billy, a homeless boy. In terms of the books on him, violent, and an outlaw. How did this happen? This was such a strange love story. And, in addition, she said, when I asked her more, that behind it all was something I'd never heard of. And you'll see if any of you have heard of it: the Santa Fe Ring. Does that ring a bell?

Behind it was the Santa Fe Ring. And she said that "it's never been written, but Billy was involved not only with Paulita, but with the freedom fight." And, all of the sudden, the concept of this unusual star-crossed romance, and Billy not being an outlaw, but being part of a freedom fight, was absolutely fascinating to me.

So, this woman had a whole library of Billy the Kid books. I got all the titles, bought them, read them quickly, and I sold everything I had. I sold my practice, my big house, my stable. My life completely changed within a few months - this was mid-July when I saw the book. By July 28th, I flew to New Mexico to travel to all the historic sites, where some of you may have been: Fort Sumner, where Billy's buried; Lincoln town, which is still preserved like it was in his day; Silver City, where he lived for a while.

And I moved here by April of '99 to the Sandia Mountains to write about him. Ultimately, I read 40,000 pages of archival documents and books, and made a whole new view of the history Billy the Kid.

Behind me, these are some of the books that I ended up writing about him, because what happened was the victors got to write the history. Ultimately, in this freedom flight, the Santa Fe Ring won. So, guess who was their outlaw? The most charismatic individual in the freedom fight: Billy. Except he exceeded the Ring's expectations. He was merely outlawed so they could get rid of him. In fact, he's the one, by being so memorable, that's dragged the Ring right into the present. So all of us can take a look at what happened in those days.

And I'll give you an idea of what I learned, and then some more strange turns. But first, I'll tell you the strangest thing of all. That was mid-July of '98, and I knew none of his history. If I left on July 28th, and calculated back, it was around July 14th that I found that book. The day Pat Garrett shot Billy in 1881 was July 14th! Whatever that means in terms of the currents of fate that pick us up and move us along, it's hard to know, but I have become the person who spoke for all the freedom fighters as well as Billy of that period. Because here's what was really going on in New Mexico.

This wasn't a shoot-'em-up outlaw story of some random frontier boy. And there were many of those kind of violent outlaws. This was a time in the 1870's of massive upheaval in New Mexico, which again, has been so suppressed that many of you may not even know that it had occurred. The Santa Fe Ring began in 1866 when two profiteering attorneys named Thomas Benton Catron and Stephen Benton Elkins, college friends from Missouri, moved here to take advantage of easy picking: the land grants. When the Treaty of Guadalupe Hidalgo was made in 1848, the Hispanic people living here, as part of the agreement, were allowed to keep their land. And some of the holdings were massive - like the Maxwell Land Grant, with Paulita Maxwell's family, of two million acres. They came purposefully to cheat the people out of their land.

And by 1866, soon after they arrived, they already had a foothold with the objective of infiltrating all parts of the power structure: the executive, the legislative, and the judicial branches, and law enforcement. By the early 1870's - and no one had put this together - there was starting to be uprisings, pushback. There weren't a lot of Anglo people, and the ones being terribly victimized were the Hispanic people, but there was still a pushback that had never been described.

By 1872, the legislature rose up against the appointment that the Ring was doing of judges, to be able, not only to control the outcome of cases and protect their cronies, but to terrorize people with malicious prosecution. It was a horrible thing. They were suppressed by the military. The Governor at that time, Marsh Giddings, brought in the military onto the legislative floor to quash them. That was 1872.

In 1876, in Silver City, was the Grant County Rebellion. Nobody put this together. They made a Declaration of Independence and were going to secede from New Mexico to get away from the Santa Fe Ring. They were managed to be pressured out of leaving. There was not bloodshed yet. 1877 was the Colfax County War in the old Maxwell Land Grant, where the Ring had taken over the grant, cheating Lucien Maxwell, Paulita's father, out of ownership of the Grant. After that, he moved and made Fort Sumner. There the settlers had an uprising from 1875 onward, and there was bloodshed.

Then came the Lincoln County War, 1878 - just the next year-that made Billy famous. By that point, the Santa Fe Ring- it's the end of the '70s - was a terrorist organization.

And let me now overlap Billy's life, because his life trajectory intersected the Ring when it was at its most lethal. Billy was born in New York City, an illegitimate child of an Irish mother, whose last name isn't known. Her name's Catherine. His name was William Henry McCarty. She was a washerwoman. She moved, for unknown reasons, to Indiana where she took up with a man named William Henry Harrison Antrim, who wanted to be a miner. She moved with Billy and her older son, Josie, and William Henry, to Silver City. It was '73. Billy was a 13½ year-old boy then, and had his minimal education, where you can see the product in this letter. He probably had less than a year of schooling. At that time, his brilliance wouldn't have been noticed by anyone. What would've been noticed was his violence and his hair-trigger temper. He was a difficult child, and known to the local people, and starting a little bit, we'll see, with it.

In the next year, his mother died of tuberculosis, and his venal stepfather, Antrim, kicked him and his brother out of the house. At 14½, he was homeless. At that point, he became a real juvenile delinquent. He was stealing; and escalated with an adult accomplice, in 1875, to burglary and robbery, for which he was put in jail. Well, the sentence would've involved 10 years of hard labor.

He escaped through the chimney, being very inventive; and made it to Arizona, where he continued on his path of delinquency: stealing horses, again with an accomplice, military horses and saddles, culminating horribly in August of 1877 - this was in Bonita, Arizona - of murdering a blacksmith who had aggressively attacked him. And poor Billy probably thought his life was in danger. But, by then, Billy's obsession with guns had advanced, and he shot the man dead. He would've been hanged in Arizona, because that would've been no excuse: of not knowing the man was unarmed.

He made it back, escaping to New Mexico Territory, and followed his path downward, becoming part of the Jessie Evans gang: a terrible gang, which was really Ring-affiliated enforcers, who did rustling and murdering for the Ring.

This would've been Billy's life, but something very strange happened. That was September of '77. In October, he got hired as a ranch hand by a young British man named John Henry Tunstall, who had come - naïve about the Ring - but with all kinds of dreams of making his family's mercantile empire from England expand in the United States. He had a store already in Lincoln town. He befriended a local attorney named Alexander McSween, who happened to be fighting the Santa Fe Ring; and he was making cattle ranches.

Well, the Ring didn't take any competition. They certainly didn't take exposure which was going on. Within 4½ months, Billy would have understood that. Tunstall was murdered horribly, his horse killed; there was mutilation involved. And Billy would've been in the group of ranch hands riding with Tunstall. None of them saw it. Tunstall had been separated. But this trauma of the first good and honest person he'd ever been exposed to, completely transformed this boy into, surprisingly, a political zealot. And this is the part that hasn't been told.

What happened in the immediate aftermath, is the local sheriff, William Brady, who was part of the Ring, made no effort to capture the murderers. And Billy, among others, was appointed a deputy to serve arrest warrants, since the sheriff wouldn't. At that point, the people organized themselves as the Regulators, which harked back to the Revolutionary War, when pre-revolutionary North Carolinians called themselves Regulators to deal with the corrupt control that was going on.

Well, things escalated badly. The Regulators tried to make arrests. There were killings involved; and the Governor outlawed their group. And that was when the Governor was a pure Ring appointee: Samuel Beach Axtell. That was the beginning of what became the Lincoln County War. The fighting escalated until July, that July. And again, strangely on July 14th, Billy would have only three more years to live.

July 14th, 1878 began the Lincoln County War, where the Regulator's side - which was primarily Hispanic - took over the town, hoping to end the Ring domination. Instead, the powerful Ring brought in the military, crushed the group, killed the leader, Alexander McSween, who had been Tunstall's friend; and the freedom uprising was over in the most brutal way. Not only the murder, they burned down the house. If you were ever in Lincoln town, there's still just a bare lot where the McSween house was. But Billy managed to escape.

Well, the logical thing, at that point, for everybody was to leave the Territory. This was clearly a lost cause. And they did. The ones who weren't killed left. Billy didn't. He stayed. And he had fought in his own way. And how he came up with this at the age of 18 is inexplicable.

The Governor - who had outlawed them, had done other corrupt things - was removed and replaced by Lew Wallace. Lew Wallace became everybody's hope. He was, at that point, writing *Ben-Hur*. He came in as the new Governor and the new hope. And Billy wrote him the letter, which you have. This was March 13th, of 1879, in which Billy said that he had indictments against him for the murders that had occurred during the Lincoln County War. The murders being of the Sheriff, who had killed Tunstall, and members of his posse. The Regulators had killed them. Billy wasn't the only one indicted, the Regulators were indicted as a group for that. And Billy, meanwhile, had witnessed another Ring murder and offered an exchange deal.

The audacity of this homeless boy, who was outlawed, writing to the Governor of New Mexico in the best handwriting he could, on the best stationery he could find - I did a whole book just on his writings - saying, "I've heard you have $1,000 offered for my body (and he had the audacity) which I take to mean as the witness against those who killed Attorney Chapman." He was wheeling and dealing with the Governor and saying: "I'll do it if you give me a pardon. I'll testify." And the Governor took him up on it. But Billy had a tragic fate. And the Governor - even after Billy testified - the Governor reneged under Ring pressure. It's hard to imagine the danger of this organization that controlled everything.

There was nowhere to turn. Lew Wallace, to pardon Billy the Kid, would've had to give up his entire - he was an ambitious man - his entire political future; and he wouldn't do it. So, he let Billy go to his death. At that point, the Ring saw Billy as a real risk. With his bi-culturalism, he'd already arguably brought in the Hispanic people to the Lincoln County War. He could do it again. He was only - at that time, he was 19. And they had to kill him. These are people who were the two heads of the Santa Fe Ring: Catron stayed in New Mexico, Elkins was in Washington, holding very high offices.

They brought in the Secret Service - one of only 40 operatives in the country - to kill Billy. It was probably ... And you're hearing brand new history, because you're not gonna find it in history books except mine, putting this story together. And I've read all the documents, all Secret Service reports. The objective was to end the last of those opposing the Ring.

The operative, named Azariah Wild, assisted in making Pat Garret, the Sheriff, to kill Billy. He also made him a Deputy U.S. Marshal. He paid for posses. He paid for informers. Billy was so protected in New Mexico - he was the hero, freedom fighting hero of the people. He would not have been able to be captured if it had not been for the Secret Service's back-up. Ultimately, he was probably one of the first political murders of the Secret Service.

They captured ... Pat did capture Billy in Stinking Springs, along with some of the people who were with him; after killing his two companions, the only Regulators left over: Tom O'Folliard and Charlie Bowdre. And if you've ever visited the Fort Sumner grave, those are the two other people buried with Billy. Within days of each other, Pat and his posse killed those two, and then he captured Billy. He only captured him rather than killing him, because he killed Charlie instead, who was accidentally wearing Billy's sombrero, and he mistook him.

Well, Billy was taken to jail in Santa Fe, and still wrote letters to Lew Wallace pleading for his pardon, to no avail. Went to Mesilla for his hanging trial, where the judge - obviously was a Ring judge - and he didn't have any option for anything but hanging.

In those days, first degree murder automatically meant hanging. And the attorney who was backing him all along, from the time of his pardoning, Ira Leonard, was probably threatened by the Ring and withdrew from the case. So, Billy was left alone with a court-appointed attorney, and was obviously sentenced to hang. He was then taken to jail in Lincoln town. And some of you may have seen the old courthouse-jail. And he made one of the most famous jailbreaks in history.

He came on April 21st of 1881. He was to be hanged on May 13th. On April 28th, he had two guards, 24-hour guards. He was hand and leg shackled and chained to the floor. He escaped. It was like a Houdini escape. It's never been known who helped him. He must have had an accomplice. And it's thought that he had an accomplice who left the gun in the outhouse. And Pat was still letting him use that, rather than a chamber pot. And he killed the one deputy guard who refused to be tied; then shot the other guard, who ran back to the courthouse, from an upstairs window. Then, here was the point that I started my story. He had a choice in front of him: to go to Mexico 150 miles away, to got to Paulita 150 miles away. He went to Paulita.

And the culmination was part of the tragedy that originally inspired me: where was he killed? Well, the Maxwells had a mansion in Fort Sumner. Lucien Maxwell, when he bought the town, converted the old officer, commanding officer's quarters, into their mansion. Paulita's brother, Peter, betrayed him. Had Pat Garret waiting in the bedroom. Billy had been hiding out in Fort Sumner. And he must have gotten the message a little before midnight, on July 14th, of 1881, that the patrón wanted to see him. He went into the dark bedroom, and was killed. And then Paulita, they have said, was pregnant with his child. She would've been 17 at the time. And this was the story that made me want to change my life for it.

Well, that puts us now in 2003. I had finished my draft of my novel, and I was ready to publish and maybe move on, maybe Montana, Wyoming. I liked the West by then. Suddenly, front page of the *New York Times* - and I tell you when fate catches you up in its current, it's a fast current - June 5th, 2003, front page of the *New York Times*: Governor Bill Richardson announces that he's investigating Billy the Kid. You may have - some of you - seen that. He claimed that Pat Garrett never killed Billy, Billy wasn't buried in his grave. And it was the largest historic forensic hoax ever instituted.

And he's arguably the only Governor that was poised to give his state's iconic history to another state - that being Texas - for a political donor who believed in an old-timer named "Brushy Bill" Roberts. "Brushy Bill" was part of a whole group of old-timers in the first half of the 20th century, who claimed - because they had nothing else in life - to be part of famous history. And there were several who claimed to be Billy the Kid, who survived the Pat Garrett shooting.

Now, Billy himself had a Coroner's Jury Report. The townspeople - 200 townspeople had a vigil. They loved him. They recognized him. It goes on and on how many identifications he had, but, irrespective, Governor Richardson had his path. So, I just assumed - here I'm an outsider coming to write a novel - that the people out in Fort Sumner and Silver City, where the mother is buried, would just stop this silliness. And that's their tourism; and it's the reality of the history.

In fact, when I called around, no one dared do anything at all. It was just me. I came here to write a novel, and suddenly, I was facing head-on the Santa Fe Ring myself. All by myself, and absolutely terrified, because I'd just written a whole book about how horrible they were.

And so, for the first, what I did - leaving terror out - what I did was when I found that no one was doing anything, I hired the Kennedy Han Law Firm, a very prominent law firm at that time; and with a real firebrand, Mary Han, heading it. And you may have all heard in the news subsequently, like 2010, that Mary was claimed to have committed suicide, when many people thought she was murdered. She was willing to fight the very dangerous fights. And so she took my case. And in the courts, in 2003 and 2004, we blocked the exhumations of Billy The Kid and his mother.

This was the plot that Richardson had backed. They were going to dig up Billy and his mother, compare the DNA, say it didn't match. Therefore, Billy couldn't be her child. Therefore, Pat killed somebody else and put the innocent victim in the grave. The catch to it was, which I saw right from the *New York Times* article, that these are tourist markers. These aren't real graves. Billy is not right there. If you stand and want to give your respects, he's somewhere, but not there. And the mother is in no way buried in Silver City where her grave marker is, which is in the new part of the cemetery. This was a complete hoax.

Okay, 2003, 2004 I won. I blocked the exhumations of Billy and his mother. All of a sudden, coming here to write a book, I'm part of saving the history. It was completely unexpected. So, then I thought it was over. I kept myself anonymous. A very great journalist named Jay Miller, proxied articles that I wrote exposing all this. And I thought: it's over. Not when you're dealing with hoaxers. And not when you're dealing with someone who doesn't like to lose, like Bill Richardson.

And what they then claimed is - remember I told you that Billy was shot, and they had a vigil in the town? Well, when they had their vigil, they laid him out on an old carpenter's bench. So, the hoaxers - who were ... I'm thinking it was strange, because it re-repeated the original Santa Fe Ring structure - the ones who were carrying on the hoax were the Lincoln County Sheriff's Department - Pat Garret's old Sheriff's Department. And they claimed that they found the carpenter's bench on which Billy had been laid out, and that it had his blood on it. So, they didn't need to dig up anyone, because it had DNA.

Well, it turns out I was their nightmare, because if you recall, I'm a forensic expert. I was doing forensic psychiatry. By then, I'm arguably the world's expert on Billy the Kid. And, most of all, I'm passionate enough that I was willing to fight. So, I continued fighting. And they continued persisting. They finally dug up some bodies in Arizona - another old pretender, like "Brushy Bill" - just to get something done. They had already made a documentary about their case, trying to legitimize it.

At that point, that took them to court in an open records case in 2007. I said, "Okay, you say you've dug up bodies, you have DNA. Give it to me. You're public officials." They had made the mistake of thinking if they structure their case like a real murder investigation against Pat Garrett, they could do exhumations. They forgot that that made them public officials - meaning public records. So, this being the modern Santa Fe Ring, for seven years I fought them in court. They would not give the records, obviously, because they were fake.

Finally, after five sets of attorneys who abandoned my case - because the Ring is very powerful - unexpected to them, I had 2½ months before a major hearing. I brought all the law books from the law library that were relevant, speed read through them, and took the case myself and won. At that point that was not good, but there was no way out of it. So, the only thing they managed to do was make a special change to the law to remove all penalty: to remove all penalties to my wrongdoers.

At that point in the statute - it's called IPRA, The Inspection of Public Records Act - they owed me almost a million dollars in damages. It's a per day accrual. The high courts - after the Appellate Courts, then it's up to the Supreme Court - they removed all penalty for violating open records; so, they wouldn't have to give me penalty that my people had accrued. So, I became an expert on the Santa Fe Ring in a way that you can't by reading books.

You have to live with a system that's completely rigged to understand the history of Billy the Kid, and what all those people fought and died for. And what I've now dedicated myself to making clear to people, that something amazing happened in New Mexico. That a small number of people rose up against an impossible political machine, and gave their lives, and believed they could win. They believed enough in democracy. And that, to me, deserved a voice. And that's what I'm trying to give them. That's the story.

TALK 1:

THE REAL HISTORY OF BILLY THE KID
OCTOBER 21, 2020

This talk summarizes for you my revisionist history of Billy the Kid. Other talks will fill in details. Key is my identifying the pivotal role of New Mexico Territory's land-grabbing, racist, murderous, political cabal known as the Santa Fe Ring. As I've written: "Past authors' leaving out the Santa Fe Ring from the history of Billy the Kid and the Lincoln County War, was like writing about the Civil War and leaving out slavery." The real history of Billy the Kid took place against the backdrop of New Mexico Territory's crushed freedom fights against Ring tyranny. The Lincoln County War of 1878 was the last and bloodiest. The Ring won only by treasonous use of the military to murder citizens. And teenaged Billy emerged as the people's hero. The triumphant Ring hid in history's shadows. But Billy's posthumous fame kept the light shining, and the truth could not be escaped. Here's what really happened.

In a New Mexico Territory night, moonlit almost bright as day, the 21 year old, homeless youth, Billy Bonney, with trusting stockinged feet, approached the porticoed, two story, Fort Sumner mansion of the Maxwell family, at about a quarter to mid-night.

That day, July 14, 1881, was the third anniversary of the start of the six day Lincoln County War Battle, which had left him branded as the outlaw, "Billy the Kid." But, to himself, he was a freedom fighter: the last Regulator and that bloody War's only participant to be convicted and sentenced to hanging.

That July night, he intended to cut a dinner steak from the side of beef hanging, at the patrón's generosity, on the mansion's north porch. But first he would check with that patrón and town owner, Peter Maxwell, at his south porch's corner bedroom.

Asleep in that mansion was Billy's secret lover, Maxwell's sister, Paulita, seventeen. Also there, was a never-emancipated Navajo slave, Deluvina; purchased as a child by Peter's and Paulita's fabulously wealthy, deceased father, Lucien Bonaparte Maxwell. Then, the family lived in Cimarron, a New Mexico Territory town in Colfax County, which Lucien had founded on his and his wife's almost two million acre land grant, that he named after himself.

That was before Lucien was cheated in the sale of that Maxwell Land Grant by unscrupulous lawyers, Thomas Benton Catron and Stephen Benton Elkins, who used the profits to propel their Santa Fe Ring. As Billy knew, their corrupt collusion of public officials still held New Mexico Territory in a stranglehold. Billy, as a hero in the failed Lincoln County War freedom fight of 1878, had fought that Ring. If he was thinking about his mortal danger, he knew its source was that Ring. If he thought about injustice, its focus would have been his promised pardon withheld by departed Territorial Governor, Lew Wallace.

That July of 1881 day was 2½ months since Billy's jailbreak escape from his scheduled May 13th hanging. He knew that Lincoln County Sheriff Pat Garrett would be in pursuit. Garrett had captured him on December 22, 1880 at Stinking Springs for his hanging trial. And, in convicted Billy's April 28, 1881 escape from Garrett's Lincoln jail, he had shot dead Garrett's deputy guards: James Bell and Robert Olinger. Garrett would kill him on sight.

When first tracking Billy in late 1880, Garrett had shot dead Billy's friends, Tom O'Folliard and Charlie Bowdre - missing Billy only by accident in two consecutive ambushes: at Fort Sumner and Stinking Springs. In fact, at the Stinking Springs capture of Billy and his companions, Garrett killed Bowdre by mistaking him for Billy: the target for which the Santa Fe Ring had made him a sheriff.

Billy had recklessly chosen return to Fort Sumner to be near Paulita, instead of fleeing to Old Mexico, the natural choice given his bi-culturalism. But he trusted the Maxwell family's protection, as well as affection of the townspeople he had known since late 1877. It would take betrayal to bring his death.

Billy's whole life had been trauma-filled. Possibly illegitimate, he was a second son, born on November 23, 1859, in New York City, as Henry McCarty. Raised in Indiana and Kansas with his brother, Josie, by his mother, Catherine, he became "Henry Antrim," in 1873, when she married a William Henry Harrison Antrim after they moved to New Mexico Territory. Antrim became a miner; and the family lived in Silver City. Antrim was a rejecting parent, evicting Billy at 14½ to homelessness when Catherine died of tuberculosis in 1874. But Billy's longing for a father remained; and he sometimes used the name "Antrim" for himself.

In Silver City's school, Billy learned Spencerian handwriting. He also became fluent in Spanish, and was equally comfortable in Anglo and Hispanic sub-cultures in those racist times.

By 1875, 15 year old Billy spent his last year in Silver City doing petty thievery, and butcher shop and hotel work; while fights with local boys revealed his violent temperament.

By that September, Silver City Sheriff, Harvey Whitehill, arrested him for burglary, and laundry and revolver robbery; his adult accomplice, Sombrero Jack, having escaped. Facing 39 lashes to his back and 10 years hard labor - Territorial statutes making no provision for juveniles - Billy made his first dramatic escape: through the jail's chimney. He then fled westward to Arizona Territory's little town of Bonita.

In Arizona, as Henry Antrim, Billy again combined work – as a cook in a small hotel - with crime: stealing military blankets, saddles, and horses; while fatefully developing shootist skills. In 1876, jailed at local Fort Grant's guardhouse with his adult accomplice, John Mackie, he escaped through a roof ventilation space. But he defiantly stayed in Bonita, betting on his rustling charges being dropped on a technicality: his first demonstration of risky behavior for his longing to have a "home."

On August 17, 1877, Billy's life again changed horrifically. His argument at Bonita's Atkins Cantina with a bullying blacksmith named Frank "Windy" Cahill, escalated to his fatally shooting that unknowably unarmed man. Billy escaped on a stolen horse. The Coroner's Jury declared him - as Henry Antrim - guilty of murder, though in absentia; ignoring self-defense. So, at 17, Billy was almost hanged. He fled back to New Mexico Territory with a newly created alias: "William Henry Bonney" or Billy Bonney. "Bonney" was possibly his mother's maiden name.

In New Mexico Territory, by the next month of September, 1877, Billy attached himself to the familiar sociopaths in Jessie Evans's murderous and rustling Santa Fe Ring-affiliated gang.

And since all Ringites ended up immune to prosecution and profited financially, intelligent and energetic Billy, unknown to history, would have likely had a wealthy and long life.

But Billy had a conversion. He met a kind, rich newcomer: British John Henry Tunstall, a Ring competitor. By the next month, October of 1877, Billy left Jessie Evans's gang and became Tunstall's youngest ranch hand. Tunstall's men affectionately nick-named this teenager "Kid." Tunstall became the lost father found; even gifting him, under the Homestead Act, with a ranch on the Peñasco River in partnership with another employee, half-Chickasaw, Fred Waite. That was likely Billy's proudest and most optimistic moment.

Billy had stumbled into a noble cause: ending Ring oppression. His gunman skill now elevated him to a protector of the good. His hair-trigger temper became vehemence for justice. And the town of Lincoln, as well as Tunstall's ranch on the Feliz River, became home. But Billy's tragic destiny was unrelenting. After only 4½ months, this idyllic time ended with Tunstall's Ring murder.

The setting was Lincoln County, the largest county in the United States - bigger than combined Massachusetts, Connecticut, Vermont, Rhode Island, and Delaware - making up the southeast quarter of the nearly square territory.

Its county seat, Lincoln, site of the future Lincoln County War Battle, had already sustained Ring abuses through the mercantile monopoly of the so called "House": a huge, two-story adobe, general store run by its successive local Ring bosses - Emil Fritz, Lawrence Murphy, James Dolan, and John Riley - for special secret partner, Ring boss, Thomas Benton Catron. They bled cash-poor Mexicans and Anglo homesteaders with usurious credit. Redress was impossible, since law enforcement and courts were Ring-controlled. Terror reigned. In 1875, when local rancher, Robert Casey, defeated Lawrence Murphy in a Lincoln election, he was killed the same day. Three weeks later, Lincoln's anti-Ring, Mexican community leader, Juan Patrón, was shot by John Riley; though accidentally surviving as a limping cripple.

Hope began in late 1876 with arrival of British merchant, John Tunstall; persuaded to settle in Lincoln by resident attorney, Alexander McSween, a Ring opponent; but once legal counsel to "The House," and aware of its abuses. Tunstall planned to beat the Ring by fair mercantile and ranching competition. But that inadvertently put him in direct competition with boss Catron's personal, secret, monopolistic plans for Lincoln County: use of

"The House" for beef and flour contracts to Fort Stanton and the Mescalero Indian Reservation; a Pecos River cow camp fronted by The House;" and take-over of dying Lawrence Murphy's huge ranch, which he made into his Carrizozo Land and Cattle Company, under management of his brother-in-law, Edgar Walz.

By 1877, Tunstall built - just a quarter mile northeast of "The House" on Lincoln's single street - a general store containing his Lincoln Bank. He made Catron's cattle competitor, cattle king John Chisum, that bank's president. And he founded two cattle ranches to wrest from "The House" its beef contracts. He even exposed Ringite Lincoln County Sheriff William Brady's embezzlement of tax money to buy rustled cattle for Catron's cow camp and Carrizozo ranch. So, Tunstall and McSween qualified for the Ring's hit list.

Ringmen preferred to kill with guise of legality. So they entangled Tunstall in fabricated criminality, starting with false prosecution of Alexander McSween, then attorney for the estate of "The House's" partner, Emil Fritz, who died intestate in 1874, but had two local siblings and a life insurance policy. The Ring seized on that policy. In 1877, McSween obtained its $10,000 proceeds from the dishonestly withholding New York City insurance company, minus $3,000 to the collections firm - leaving $7,000 minus his fees. Knowing that "the House" was going bankrupt from Tunstall's competition, and was desperate for that money from Fritz's local heirs, he retained it while seeking other heirs in Germany.

In December of 1877, McSween left on business to St. Louis with his wife and John Chisum. The Ring pounced, declaring McSween an absconding embezzler of the Fritz insurance policy money. Ring boss Catron, then U.S. Attorney, the Territory's highest legal position, issued McSween's warrant for apprehension in Las Vegas, New Mexico. Chisum was jailed too in retaliation for backing Tunstall. On February 4, 1878, McSween had his hearing in Mesilla under Ringite District Judge Warren Bristol (later Billy's hanging judge), who indicted him for embezzling. The intent was McSween's incarceration and murder in Lincoln by its Ringite Sheriff, William Brady. But McSween was saved by an honorable Deputy Sheriff, Adolph Barrier, from his Las Vegas arrest site, who knew Ring risk and kept him in protective personal custody.

But Judge Bristol had set other traps for assassination of McSween and Tunstall. Bristol's indictment did two things. First, he set McSween's bail at $8,000, with approval only by Ringite District Attorney William Rynerson. So, Rynerson refused all bondsmen to leave McSween open to Sheriff Brady's fatal seizing at any time.

The second was Tunstall's trap. Bristol attached McSween's property to the sum of $10,000 - falsely deemed the embezzled total - as surety if he was convicted at April's Grand Jury. Then Bristol made the strategic lie: that Tunstall was in partnership with McSween. That enabled attaching Tunstall's property also. And Bristol empowered Sheriff Brady to do the attachment inventories. This harassment was intended to provoke Tunstall and his men to violence to justify Tunstall's killing in so called "self-defense."

But John Tunstall merely responded that any man's life was worth more than all he owned. Hardened Billy, with Tunstall just three months, must have been overwhelmed by this novel idealism.

So the Ring urgently grasped the property attaching to fake justified killing - knowing that the April Grand Jury would likely exonerate McSween, ending the opportunity for prosecution-related killing of Tunstall.

So, on February 18, 1878, when Tunstall sought to transfer his fine horses, which were immune to the attachment, from his Feliz River ranch to Lincoln, Sheriff Brady lied that it was theft of attached property, and sent his posse of Deputies, Ring rustlers, and Jessie Evans's outlaw gang after him and his men, including Billy. Tunstall, becoming isolated, was murdered, his horse slain; with both corpses hidden and mutilated. This martyrdom, coupled with more Ring outrages intended to terrorize the citizens into submission, instead triggered the Lincoln County War.

Because Sheriff Brady refused to arrest Tunstall's murderers, anti-Ring Justice of the Peace John "Squire" Wilson issued warrants for James Dolan and Brady's other possemen. For service, Wilson appointed Billy and Fred Waite as Deputy Constables under Town Constable Atanacio Martinez. Billy had already given Wilson an affidavit as to his first-hand knowledge of Tunstall's murderers. But Brady shielded them by illegally casting Billy, Waite, and Martinez into Lincoln's pit jail. And he confiscated and kept Billy's Winchester '73 carbine - likely a gift from Tunstall.

Next, "Squire" Wilson defied the Ring by deputizing Tunstall's foreman, Dick Brewer; who, in turn, made Tunstall's men, including just-released Billy, his possemen to serve those murder warrants. Billy, now 18, was still a lawman.

Meanwhile, Attorney Alexander McSween, in mortal danger from Brady and the Ring, went into hiding with Deputy Sheriff Barrier; mostly in the nearby Hispanic town of San Patricio.

By March of 1878, Dick Brewer's posse had captured Tunstall murder possemen, William "Buck" Morton and Frank Baker. Morton was foreman of Catron's Pecos Cow Camp. Baker was in Jessie Evans's gang. They were shot attempting escape. Billy was in the firing group.

At that point, including "Windy" Cahill, Billy Bonney was now involved in three killings.

The Ring hit back. Ringite Governor Samuel Beach Axtell, by illegal proclamation, removed Wilson's Justice of the Peace powers to retroactively outlaw Dick Brewer's posse; then declared Sheriff William Brady to be Lincoln County's only law enforcer.

Enraged, Tunstall's men named themselves "Regulators" after America's pre-Revolutionary War freedom fighters. Included were Tunstall's men - Billy; Dick Brewer, Fred Waite; John Middleton; Jim "Frenchie" French; farmers, George and Frank Coe; and homesteader, Charlie Bowdre - and Chisum's cattle detective, Frank MacNab. Brewer was made leader. Only one month after Tunstall's death, Billy was being schooled in politics of revolution.

Sheriff Brady's next chance to assassinate McSween was April 1, 1878, when McSween returned to Lincoln for his Grand Jury embezzlement trial. That morning, to save him, Regulators with carbines, and Billy with a revolver, ambushed Brady and his three deputies from behind an adobe corral wall at Tunstall's store, as those lawmen walked east on Lincoln's sole street to meet McSween. Brady and Deputy George Hindman died. Recklessly, Billy, with Jim French, ran out to retrieve his confiscated Winchester '73 carbine from Brady's body. Both got leg wounds from firing surviving deputy, Jacob Basil "Billy" Matthews. But Billy regained his symbol of father-figure Tunstall. (It is likely the carbine held in Billy's famous tintype two years hence.)

Three days later, on April 4, 1878, Deputy Dick Brewer, seeking Tunstall's stolen horses, led Billy, John Middleton, Fred Waite, Frank Coe, George Coe, and Charlie Bowdre to Blazer's Mill - a privately owned, way station and grist mill within the Mescalero Indian Reservation. Accidentally encountered was

Tunstall murder posseman, Andrew "Buckshot" Roberts, for whom they had a warrant. Roberts fired his Winchester carbine at Bowdre, who shot him in the belly. Roberts's bullet hit Bowdre's belt buckle, ricocheted, and wrenched George Coe's revolver, mutilating his trigger finger. Another Roberts shot penetrated Middleton's chest; though Middleton survived. Then Roberts killed Brewer, later dying himself from Bowdre's wound. Billy had not fired a shot. Roberts had demonstrably resisted arrest murderously, necessitating self-defense response. But Ring boss Catron, as U.S. Attorney, seized on this killing to file his federal indictment against the Regulators, including Billy, claiming the murder site was the Mescalero Reservation, under his federal control, to personally guarantee their hanging.

Billy's murder involvement now totaled six men; though only "Windy" Cahill was demonstrably by his hand.

At the April, 1878, Lincoln County Grand Jury, McSween was exonerated for embezzling. But the Regulators, including Billy, were indicted for the Brady, Hindman, and Roberts killings.

McSween bravely continued his anti-Ring fight, backed by the Regulators; though John Chisum had dishonestly reneged on paying them. Fighting injustice sufficed. And Billy, their hot-headed fearless zealot, was becoming an inspiration - with McSween as his new father substitute.

McSween's lawful tactic was seeking high-level intervention to expose Tunstall's Ring assassination, because murder of a foreign citizen could elicit a Washington, D.C. investigation. He filed a complaint with the British ambassador and President Rutherford B. Hayes, accusing U.S. officials of murdering Tunstall. In response, investigating attorney, Frank Warner Angel, was sent by the Departments of Interior and Justice. Arriving in New Mexico Territory on May 4, 1878, Angel took 39 depositions. Billy, volunteering for one, risked his life and entered the national stage.

Public optimism of Ring defeat grew further when the Lincoln County Commissioners appointed neutral John Copeland as the Sheriff replacing Brady. He even deputized Regulator, Josiah "Doc" Scurlock, to recover Tunstall's stolen horses. Still a lawman, Billy was on Scurlock's posse. And Wilson, ignoring Axtell's proclamation, continued as Justice of the Peace.

Optimism was short-lived. On April 28, 1878, new Regulator leader, Frank MacNab, was murdered in ambush by Ringite Seven Rivers rustlers. By May 28th, because John Copeland forgot to post his tax collecting bond, Governor Axtell, by another proclamation, removed him and appointed as Sheriff, Ringite George Peppin, Brady's deputy, present at Brady's killing.

War fervor built, with Regulators and Mexicans calling themselves "McSweens." Billy's affiliation with local, firebrand youth, Yginio Salazar, and Billy's closeness to Hispanic residents of nearby San Patricio and Picacho, had arguably brought them all into the McSween alliance. By April 30, 1878, McSweens were skirmishing with Ring partisans, known as "Murphy-Dolans."

McSween again hid, sometimes at John Chisum's South Spring River Ranch, and often in San Patricio. Sheriff George Peppin first unsuccessfully brought Fort Stanton troops there to kill him. Then, on July 3, 1878, in terrorist revenge, Peppin brought John Kinney's Ring-rustler gang from Mesilla. They massacred men, women, and children, and destroyed their farm animals and property. In response, on July 13th, the "Regulator Manifesto" was sent to Catron's brother-in-law, managing his Carrizozo ranch. It threatened retaliation against Catron himself. Signed only "Regulator," it was likely created by Billy.

The Lincoln County War's culminating Battle began the next day: July 14, 1878. McSween, with 60 men - Regulators and Hispanic residents of San Patricio and Picacho - occupied Lincoln. Reflecting McSween's intended peaceful victory was that his wife, Susan, and her sister, with five young children, remained in his double-winged house; along with the sister's attorney husband's law intern, Harvey Morris.

McSween's men took strategic positions in houses throughout the mile-long town, most of whose residents had fled. When Seven Rivers rustlers and John Kinney outlaws joined James Dolan and Sheriff George Peppin, Billy; Yginio Salazar; Tom O'Folliard; and San Patricio men - José Chávez y Chávez, Ignacio Gonzales, Florencio Chávez, Francisco Zamora, and Vincente Romero - rushed to McSween's house, joining guard, Jim French.

Though Ring men occupied south foothills, they were held at bay for five days by shooting McSweens, now winning. But Alexander McSween had not realized that Fort Stanton's new Commander, Lieutenant Colonel Nathan Augustus Monroe Dudley, was beholden to the Ring. McSween was also reassured by the Posse Comitatus Act, passed the month before in

Washington, D.C., baring military intervention in civilian disputes.

On July 16th, Dudley began his illegal invention. He sent to Lincoln, for so called "fact-finding," 9th Cavalry Private Berry Robinson, who was almost hit in gunfire. On July 18th, James Dolan used Ringite Lincolnite, Saturnino Baca, McSween's tenant, to lie that his wife and children were at risk from McSween.

The next day, July 19th, violating the Posse Comitatus Act, Dudley marched on Lincoln with 39 troops - white infantry, black 9th Cavalry, and white officers - two ambulances; a howitzer cannon; and a Gatling machine-gun, that period's most terrifying weapon. Panicked McSweens - except for those in his besieged house - fled north across the nearby Bonito River. Dudley himself threatened McSween with razing his house if any soldier was shot. He then left three soldiers there to inhibit its defenders' shooting from it, and ordered three more to accompany Sheriff Peppin as a shield. Next, by death threat, Dudley forced Justice of the Peace Wilson to write arrest warrants for McSween and his men as attempting murder of Private Robinson to feign reason for his intervention. Then he encamped at the east side of Lincoln.

Empowered by the troops, Sheriff Peppin's outlaw posseman set fire to McSween's house's west wing. His family was evacuated after Dudley refused McSween's wife's plea to save her husband.

By nightfall, the McSween house conflagration left all trapped in the east wing. At 9 p.m., escape was attempted into fire-lit shooting Ringites. With Billy ran law intern, Harvey Morris, whom he saw fatally shot. And before Billy escaped across the Bonito River, at the property's rear, to rescue by fellow Regulators, he witnessed Dudley's treasonous crime: three of his white soldiers, imbedded with the assailants, fired a volley at those escaping. Arguably, they had even killed Morris.

Then shot dead were Alexander McSween, Francisco Zamora, and Vincente Romero. Yginio Salazar survived with two bullets in his back. Symbolizing horror, McSween's starving, yard chickens ate his corpse's eyeballs. Again was Ring murder and mutilation in Lincoln County to gain treacherous victory. And the freedom fight was lost.

The last hope was for Investigator Frank Warner Angel's report. But people were unaware of Ring influence in Washington, D.C. Angel, after documenting crimes of Governor S.B. Axtell, U.S. Attorney Catron, and Sheriff Brady's posse, was apparently forced to deny that U.S. officials were involved in Tunstall's murder; though Catron had to resign as U.S. Attorney. Ring-protecting President Hayes instead scapegoated Governor Axtell, replacing him with Civil War General Lew Wallace. But Angel secretly sought justice by preparing for Wallace a notebook listing Ringites, and giving him an exposé on the Santa Fe Ring, printed in 1877.

Though most Regulators fled the Territory, 18 year old Billy stayed and carried out the "Regulator Manifesto's" threatened retaliatory rustling with Tom O'Folliard and Charlie Bowdre - who had relocated to Fort Sumner with his wife Manuela. For his stolen stock, Billy used non-Ring outlets: Pat Coghlan in the western part of the Territory; and Dan Dedrick. Dedrick was a counterfeiter and rustler owner of Bosque Grande, a ranch 12 miles south of Fort Sumner. With his two brothers, he also owned a livery stable in White Oaks, a town about 45 miles northwest of Lincoln. That livery was another stock outlet for Billy. Billy also sold rustled horses in Tascosa, Texas; where he wrote a subsequently famous, bill of sale to a friendly doctor named Henry Hoyt, for an expensive sorrel horse - likely dead Sheriff Brady's. Billy also got money by gambling. He was again a homeless drifter. That would now be permanent.

Amidst public hope, on October 1, 1878, new Governor, Lew Wallace, took office. A high-achieving elitist, he was the son of an Indiana governor; a Civil War Major General; an Abraham Lincoln murder trial prosecutor; author of best-selling novel, *The Fair God*; and was writing *Ben-Hur A Tale of the Christ*. He had sought an exotic ambassadorship, like to Turkey, not governorship of backwater New Mexico Territory. So, to dispatch with Lincoln County's so called "troubles" without confronting the dangerous Santa Fe Ring, a month after arriving, he issued a general Amnesty Proclamation. But it excluded those already indicted. Billy had been indicted for the Brady, Hindman, and Roberts killings.

There were more sources of hope. The new Sheriff, George Kimbrell - appointed to replace Sheriff Peppin, who had resigned - was anti-Ring. And McSween's intrepid widow, Susan, had brought to Lincoln an attorney named Huston Chapman to charge Commander Dudley with the Lincoln County War Battle's murder of her husband and arson of her home.

In that atmosphere of legal scrutiny, local Ring boss, James Dolan, made peace overtures, first to Susan McSween, then to Billy - a proof of that teenager's acknowledged Ring threat. Billy and his Hispanic compatriots could instigate another uprising - as Thomas Benton Catron feared.

The Billy-Dolan peace meeting was fatefully scheduled on the February 18, 1879 anniversary of Tunstall's murder. It ended in calamity. As James Dolan; Billy; Jessie Evans and Jessie's new gang member, Billy Campbell; and Billy's Regulator friends, Tom O'Folliard and Josiah "Doc" Scurlock, walked Lincoln's dark street after the meeting, they encountered Chapman. Dolan and Campbell fired point-blank, killing him, then setting fire to his body. Billy was again an eye-witness. And again there was murder and mutilation in Lincoln County.

Chapman's murder forced Governor Wallace to go to Lincoln - after procrastinating for five months after arriving. Once there, he avoided Ring confrontation, using the Ring's concoction that the Lincoln County War had been caused by vague trouble-making "outlaws and rustlers." The Ring had also given Wallace a list of Regulators as the "outlaws," with Billy as "the Kid."

Focus on Billy - likely through James Dolan - made Wallace offer the astronomical reward of $1,000 for that 19 year old. Billy responded with a pardon plea letter, on March 13, 1879, offering Wallace his eye-witness testimony against Chapman's murderers in exchange for annulling his Lincoln County War indictments. It was Billy's bold and calculated risk to negate Ring power over himself.

His articulate letter, in his personalized Spencerian script, led to his March 17, 1879, nighttime meeting with Wallace in Justice of the Peace Wilson's Lincoln house. Evidence indicates that anti-Ring Wilson had also covertly backed Billy's plea. And Billy believed Wallace agreed to his pardon bargain.

To avoid assassination before testifying, Billy requested, from Wallace, sham arrest. (He'd already seen Ring murders of John Tunstall, Alexander McSween, Harvey Morris, Francisco Zamora, Vincente Romero, and Huston Chapman.) He was kept in the home of his Lincoln friend, Juan Patrón, the town Jailer. Wallace, housed next door, interviewed him and got his additional letter - intimately signed just "Billie" - about Lincoln County War issues.

Billy fulfilled his pardon bargain the next month by testifying in the Grand Jury. He got indictments of Chapman's killers, with James Dolan and Billy Campbell for first degree murder, and

Jessie Evans as accessory. But Ringite District Attorney William Rynerson, colluding with Judge Bristol, had Billy's trial venue for his indictments switched from Lincoln to Doña Ana County to guarantee a hanging verdict. Still Wallace issued no pardon.

By that April of 1879, Alexander McSween's widow, Susan, retained Attorney Ira Leonard, murdered Chapman's office-mate from Las Vegas, New Mexico Territory, to prosecute Dudley. So reprobate Dudley, likely advised by Catron, his attorney for his past court martials, got defamatory affidavits from Ringites to ruin her credibility. And he requested a military Court of Inquiry, where he would be defended by Catron's law firm member, Henry Waldo. And, on April 25th, the Ring tried unsuccessfully to assassinate Ira Leonard to stop the case.

Wallace, after removing Dudley as Fort Stanton's Commander, testified against him in the 1879 Court of Inquiry, though avoiding confronting the Ring. Billy, again risking his life, testified also, for his own anti-Ring agenda. He devastatingly reported the three white soldiers firing a volley at him and escaping others: meaning officers; meaning under Dudley's orders; meaning violating the Posse Comitatus Act and justifying court martial, and even hanging for treason. Billy's courage made Ira Leonard take him as client.

By July of 1879, the biased Court of Inquiry cleared Dudley. And Billy, with no pardon and imminent transport to Mesilla for a hanging trial, exited his bogus jailing.

The Ring recouped. By October of 1879, Susan McSween lost her civil trial against Dudley in Mesilla, to which her venue had been changed by Judge Bristol. That month, Bristol also voided James Dolan's Chapman murder indictment based on no witnesses daring to appear for a trial. Dolan, certain of immunity, had even taken over Tunstall's store. Tunstall's Feliz River ranch had been given by the Ring to Dolan, Riley, and Rynerson; and Billy's Peñasco River ranch had gone to Jacob Basil "Billy" Matthews, head posseman for Tunstall's murder. And there was a more subtle Ring victory: Wallace's humiliating loss in the Court of Inquiry made him shun Lincoln County "troubles" and Billy's pardon.

Billy's future killer, Patrick "Pat" Floyd Garrett, had arrived in New Mexico Territory's Fort Sumner in 1878. Born to an Alabama plantation family, relocated to Claiborne Parrish, Louisiana, when 9½ - and Billy was just born - he had even been willed a slave. After the Civil War, he had drifted to Texas, where he possibly murdered a black man, before becoming a buffalo hunter, from 1876 to 1878, with two partners and a kid named Joe Briscoe. Garrett fatally shot Briscoe, but successfully claimed self-defense. On the range, he never met fellow buffalo hunter, John William Poe; but later, his, Poe's, and Billy's histories would merge on the night of July 14, 1881.

In Fort Sumner, tall Garrett met transient kid, Billy Bonney, gambling at Hargrove's or Beaver Smith's Saloons. They were given townspeople's nicknames, "Big Casino" and "Little Casino," for their poker playing and height discrepancies.

The original Fort Sumner was built in 1865 by the U.S. government on desert flatlands east of the Pecos River for soldiers guarding Bosque Redondo: a concentration camp for 3,500 Navajos and 400 Apaches; until their scandalous starvation forced release of the Navajos to their homeland in 1868; the Apaches having already escaped. In 1870, Fort Sumner was purchased by Lucien Bonaparte Maxwell, one of the Territory's richest men. Converting it into a town around the parade ground, and using its thousands of acres for sheep raising, he settled there with his wife, Luz Beaubien; daughters, including Paulita; and son, Peter. Retained was the military cemetery for his family. It would receive Billy's body, to lie beside Garrett's earlier shooting victims: Billy's Regulator pals, Tom O'Folliard and Charlie Bowdre. Maxwell died in 1875, leaving the town to his wife and son, Peter; who became the family's ruin through mismanagement. But when Pat Garrett and Billy Bonney gambled there, Fort Sumner thrived.

Lucien Maxwell's wealth came from marrying Luz Beaubien, an heiress of the almost two million acre Beaubien-Miranda Land Grant, and by buying its shares from her siblings. In 1870, he sold it as the Maxwell Land Grant; but was cheated by his attorneys, Thomas Benton Catron and Steven Benton Elkins, who resold it for double the money. That profit fortified their Santa Fe Ring, as they enriched themselves with railroads, banks, and mines. Catron eventually owned six million acres - more than anyone in U.S. history. In the Lincoln County War period, he was Billy's lethal enemy, with the Ring branding Billy as the murderous outlaw "Billy the Kid" to justify his extermination. By 1912's New Mexico statehood, Catron became one of its two first senators.

In 1878, before the Lincoln County War, Pat Garrett and Billy Bonney led separate lives, though connected by Fort Sumner's Gutierrez sisters: Juanita, Apolinaria, and Celsa. Billy befriended

Celsa, married to her cousin, Saval Gutierrez, a Maxwell sheep herder. Billy's July 14, 1881 death walk would start at their house. Garrett married Juanita, who soon died of a possible miscarriage. In 1880, he married Apolinaria, with whom he had eight children. It was a double marriage with his Fort Sumner, friend, Maxwell's foreman, Barney Mason, later a spy assisting Garrett's capture of Billy.

In New Mexico Territory, Garrett had struggled with unemployment. At Fort Sumner, he drove a wagon for Peter Maxwell; helped a local hog raiser, Thomas "Kip" McKinney; and bartended at Hargrove's Saloon. Then came 1880 and the opportunity of his life. For Lincoln County's November election, the Ring needed a compatible Sheriff. To qualify, Garrett moved with his wife, Apolinaria, to that county's town of Roswell; adding, as a boarder, an unemployed journalist named Ashmun "Ash" Upson. In 1882, Upson would ghostwrite Garrett's book about killing Billy the Kid.

By 1880, the Ring's outlaw myth propaganda had advertised Billy's gunman reputation. That almost achieved his killing on January 3, 1880 at Fort Sumner's Hargrove's Saloon. A Texan bounty hunter named Joe Grant tried to shoot him in the back. Saved by Grant's gun's misfiring, Billy retaliated fatally. Obvious self-defense, that killing was not legally pursued.

Billy was now linked to killings of seven men: Frank "Windy" Cahill, William Brady, George Hindman, Andrew "Buckshot" Roberts, William "Buck" Morton, Frank Baker, and Joe Grant.

That 1880, when Billy's now-famous tintype picture was taken in Fort Sumner, Billy may have heard first whispers of his outlaw myth as a rustler and murderer. The Ring was setting its trap for eliminating him, since he refused to flee, and was impossible to kill or capture with his partisan backing.

Apparently using Santa Fe Ring "co-boss" Stephen Benton Elkins's Washington, D.C., connections, the Chief of the Secret Service, James Brooks, was contacted for what would arguably be one of that agency's first political murders. Formed in the Civil War as a branch of the Treasury Department to combat counterfeiting, the Secret Service could pursue other crimes at its discretion, and could provide funding for informers and posses.

The scheme involved co-ordination of Catron's Lincoln minions. James Dolan initiated the investigation by reporting receipt of four counterfeit $100 bills from local counterfeiters at his Lincoln store (Tunstall's prior store which he had taken over). The Operative would then be fed information by Dolan himself; by Catron's brother-in-law, Edgar Walz, at his Carrizozo ranch; and by Ringite U.S. Attorney Sidney Barnes. And, by 1880, the Ring was confident that Governor Lew Wallace's only mission was protecting himself, and would not pardon Billy or interfere with killing him. So Billy and remaining Regulators, Charlie Bowdre and Tom O'Folliard, would be presented as murderous rustlers linked to the counterfeiting gang. The only missing piece was an Operative who was adequately gullible.

By September 11, 1880, Secret Service Special Operative Azariah Wild was sent to Lincoln, and proved an ideal dupe by lazy reliance on his Ringite informers. Though Wild initially recognized that the counterfeit bills Dolan got were from a youth named Billy Wilson, who was linked to the counterfeiter, Dan Dedrick, reputed to have a printing press, he was duped into thinking Billy was involved. In fact, Billy occasionally used Billy Wilson for his anti-Ring retaliative rustling, along with a "Dirty Dave" Rudabaugh, and past Regulators, Tom O'Folliard and Charlie Bowdre. And Billy used Dan Dedrick and the White Oaks livery stable as an outlet for his rustled stock.

Wild also was tricked into believing that Billy was in the country's largest counterfeiting and rustling gang. By that December, 1880, came the Ring's *New York Sun* article, using Wild's leaked reports for "Outlaws of New Mexico, The Exploits of a Band Headed by a New York Youth, War Against a Gang of Cattle Thieves, Murderers, and Counterfeiters." Now Billy was alias "the Kid." The Ring had launched his national outlaw myth.

But the Ring's plot almost backfired when Azariah Wild was told by Attorney Ira Leonard that his client, Billy Bonney, would testify *against the counterfeiters* in exchange for the pardon not granted by Lew Wallace. It was obvious that in Billy's dealings with Dan Dedrick, he had become aware of the activities. Billy had even gifted Dedrick his tintype, which became famous. And, as with his prior pardon bargain for testifying against Ringites, Billy was willing to convict people doing reprehensible crimes.

On October 8, 1880, Wild wrote in his daily report to Chief James Brooks that he himself would arrange a pardon for Billy in exchange for that testimony. But Wild confided that pardon plan to his Ringite handlers, who convinced this dupe that Billy, staying in Fort Sumner, was actually the leader of the fictional, so called "rustling-counterfeiting gang!" So, in his report for October 14, 1880, Wild wrote that he would arrest Billy at the meeting for the pardon bargain. But Billy was cautious. He held up the stagecoach carrying Wild's mail, and read that report, and avoided the meeting. So another pardon chance was lost.

The Ring, determined to eliminate Billy, expanded the scheme to getting a Lincoln County Sheriff willing do it. The current Sheriff, George Kimbrell, who had assisted in Billy's sham arrest for the pardon bargain, was a McSween-side sympathizer.

The Ring chose Pat Garrett. Secretly, Wild worked with him to form a dragnet to capture Billy and his so called "rustler-counterfeiter gang;" while, for the upcoming sheriff's election, Garrett was advertised as a law-and-order man to new gold-rush settlers in White Oaks, unaware of Lincoln County War issues, but a third of Lincoln County's voters.

In the November 2, 1880 election, Pat Garrett got 358 votes to Kimbrell's 141. Wild, convinced by his Ring contacts that Kimbrell protected the so called "Kid gang," also gave Garrett Territory-wide power for the capture by appointing him Deputy U.S. Marshall. Unaware, Billy would have thought wrongly that Garrett's lawman authority was limited to Lincoln County, not Fort Sumner's San Miguel County, where he stayed.

And unaware of his locally publicized "outlawry," Billy still brought stolen horses to the Dedricks' White Oaks livery.

On November 22, 1880, a White Oaks posse ambushed Billy, Tom O'Folliard, Billy Wilson, Tom Pickett, and "Dirty" Dave Rudabaugh at nearby Coyote Spring, shooting dead two of their horses before Billy's group escaped. Five days later, that posse attacked them again at the way station ranch of "Whiskey" Jim Greathouse, 45 miles northeast of White Oaks; accidentally killing one of their own men, Jim Carlyle, but blaming Billy.

That accusation prompted Billy's only letter of 1880 to Governor Lew Wallace. On December 12th, he wrote, denying his outlawry and murdering of Jim Carlyle. He even described his Robin Hood role of aiding the downtrodden. Wallace never answered. Instead, on December 22nd, he placed a Las Vegas *Daily Gazette* newspaper notice: "Billy the Kid: $500 Reward." He would repeat it in the *Daily New Mexican* on May 3, 1881, after Billy's jailbreak. His betrayal of the pardon bargain was complete.

By December of 1880, dreadful days began for Billy. Deputy U.S. Marshall Pat Garrett, backed by Azariah Wild, had assembled Texan posses to ride after Billy, since New Mexicans, to whom he was an anti-Ring hero, refused. Garrett's first ambush was on December 19, 1880, when Billy, Tom O'Folliard, Charlie Bowdre, Billy Wilson, Tom Pickett, and Dave Rudabaugh rode into Fort Sumner. O'Folliard was shot dead. The rest escaped.

Billy's group tried to flee the Territory in a snowstorm; but stopped, about 16 miles from Fort Sumner, on December 21, 1880, at a rock-walled, windowless, shepherds' line cabin at Stinking Springs. There, Garrett ambushed them the next morning, killing Charlie Bowdre, whom he mistook for Billy, his intended victim. The rest surrendered. It would be 6 months and 22 days before Garrett succeeded in his mission to kill Billy.

And Azariah Wild, his own mission completed, left the Territory, unperturbed that he had found no masses of counterfeit bills, no counterfeiting-rustling gang, and had not even sought Dan Dedrick's alleged printing press.

Garrett transported his prisoners by train, via Las Vegas, New Mexico, to the Santa Fe jail. Billy was held there from December 27, 1880 to March 28, 1881, because the Ring, fearing Billy's rescue, awaited completion of the railroad to Mesilla for transport. But Billy nearly escaped anyway by tunneling out with fellow prisoners.

From his cell, in 1881, Billy wrote four unanswered letters to Governor Wallace, pleading for his pardon: writing on March 4th: "I have done everything that I promised you I would, and you have done nothing that you promised me." On March 2nd, he had threatened: "I have some letters which date back two years and there are Parties who are very anxious to get them but I will not dispose of them until I see you." Hypocritical Wallace never got over that audacity or his own guilt, reworking the pardon obsessively till the end of his life in vindictive fictionalized articles on the outlaw "Billy the Kid."

Billy's first Mesilla murder trial, under Ringite Judge Warren Bristol, began on March 30, 1881, with jurors unaware of Lincoln County War issues, and without the Lincolnites daring to be witnesses for his defense. Attorney Ira Leonard represented him for past U.S. Attorney Catron's June 21, 1878 federal indictment, Case Number 411, the United States versus Charles Bowdre,

Josiah Scurlock, Henry Brown, William Bonney alias Henry Antrim alias the Kid, John Middleton, Steven Stevens, John Scroggins, Frederick Waite, and George Coe for the murder of Andrew "Buckshot" Roberts. It was first because the Ringites likely considered it air-tight. Also, pardon would require the U.S. President, not Governor Wallace.

But, surprising everyone, Ira Leonard got it quashed as invalid, since the federal government had no jurisdiction over Blazer's Mill, the murder site; because private property, like it, was under Territorial jurisdiction. Its being surrounded by the federally-controlled Mescalero Reservation was irrelevant.

Remaining were only the Brady and Hindman Territorial indictments; and, though Billy been firing in the group of Regulators, he had only a revolver lacking accurate range.

But, suddenly, Ira Leonard withdrew, likely after a Ring threat. That was disastrous for Billy. He got Ring-biased, court appointed attorney whose name was Albert Jennings Fountain, who considered him an outlaw, along with co-counsel John D. Bail, a Ringite Catron friend.

On April 8th and 9th of 1881, was Billy's Brady murder trial. His Spanish-speaking jury, given no translator, heard only prosecution witnesses - including James Dolan. After Judge Bristol's biased instructions (with translator) made Billy's mere presence equal to firing the fatal shot, the jury found him guilty of first degree murder - its sole punishment being hanging. On April 13th, Judge Bristol set Billy's hanging date for May 13th, to limit time for appeal. Billy was to be hanged in Lincoln by its Sheriff, Pat Garrett.

From the Mesilla jail, Billy wrote to Attorney Edgar Caypless - conducting his replevin or recovery case against Garrett's posseman, Frank Stewart, for stealing his racing mare at Stinking Springs - hoping to get money from her sale to pay for an appeal.

Ironically, the new Lincoln jail, where Billy was incarcerated to await hanging, was in the past "House," which Catron, its owner, had sold to Lincoln County for its courthouse, with second floor as jail.

On April 21, 1881, Billy arrived to Sheriff Garrett's custody. For Billy's 24 hour guard, Garrett deputized a White Oaks man, James Bell, and a Seven Rivers man, Bob Olinger. Garrett's further precaution was shackling Billy at wrists and ankles, with securing to a floor ring - all to guarantee his hanging death.

But, on April 28th, with Garrett away collecting White Oaks's taxes, Billy escaped. He either used a revolver hidden in the outhouse, or seized Bell's. A likely accomplice was caretaker, Gottfried Gauss: Tunstall's past cook, and witness to the Ring's Lincoln County War atrocities. Billy shot Bell dead as the man fled down the jail's stairway to sound alarm.

Deputy Bob Olinger, across the street at the Wortley Hotel, lunching with jail prisoners, either heard the shot or was directed to the ambush. Billy waited at the second-floor jail's east window, and killed him with his own Whitney double-barrel shotgun.

Billy then spent hours using a miner's pick, supplied by Gauss, to break his leg chain to enable riding; while gathered loyalist Lincoln townspeople, in passive resistance, did nothing to stop Billy. Billy finally rode away on a pony supplied by Gauss.

As of that April 28, 1881 escape, Billy was involved in the killing of nine men; James Bell and Robert Olinger adding to Frank "Windy" Cahill and Joe Grant as Billy's only provable victims.

Of the dead, Billy would have said that Cahill's and Grant's killings were in self-defense; that he was a legal posseman at the group shooting of escaping, arrested, Tunstall murderers, William "Buck" Morton and Frank Baker; that his gun lacked range to hit Sheriff William Brady or Deputy George Hindman, and their killings by the Regulators were to save Alexander McSween from murder by them; that he had not shot Andrew "Buckshot" Roberts - a Tunstall murderer and murderer of Dick Brewer - who fired at his group, and was killed solely by Charlie Bowdre in self-defense; and that Deputy James Bell, after refusing to be tied, had tried to run for help, so was killed to save himself from unjust hanging (and Bell had been on the White Oaks posse, and possibly killed Jim Carlyle, then falsely accused him).

Only Seven Rivers rustler, Bob Olinger, would have been admittedly hated as being in each Lincoln County War period crime - Tunstall's murder, Frank MacNab's ambush murder, and the War's skirmishes and Battle. Billy's rage was so great, that he smashed apart Olinger's shotgun to throw it down on his corpse, delaying his own escape.

That count of nine killed men - with only four certain - remained as Billy's final true tally.

Billy's escape route was across the Capitan Mountains to the Las Tablas home of Yginio Salazar. He next went south, possibly intending to go to Old Mexico, and visited rancher friend, John Meadows. But he then reversed northeast to Fort Sumner and Paulita, where he hid in the Maxwells' sheep camps, confident of protection by the Maxwells and townspeople.

Garrett's two deputies for the pursuit of Billy to Fort Sumner - John William Poe and Thomas "Kip" McKinney - did not know Billy. Poe, a buffalo hunter, past Deputy U.S. Marshall in Texas, a cattle detective, and recent White Oaks settler, had met Garrett during the Wild-assisted tracking of the so called "Kid gang." McKinney knew Garrett from their 1878, hog farming days. And they were unaware of the Santa Fe Ring, the Lincoln County War freedom fight, or Billy's role; knowing only outlaw myth propaganda.

Once in Fort Sumner, Garrett, doubting Billy's presence as too foolhardy, was urged by Poe to stay. On July 14, 1881, Poe, a stranger to the townspeople, did reconnaissance in the town; and also checked with Sunnyside postmaster, Milnor Rudulph, seven miles to its north. Poe became convinced Billy was nearby.

That night, Poe, Garrett, and McKinney planned an ambush in Peter Maxwell's bedroom, with Maxwell as traitor. Unknown accomplices likely directed Billy to Maxwell's bedroom, where Garrett waited, with Poe and McKinney outside to kill Billy if he managed to escape through the door to the porch.

Near midnight, Billy proceeded from the converted barracks house of Celsa and Saval Gutierrez, carrying their butcher knife across the parade ground to cut a dinner steak in light of the almost-full moon, hovering in huge moon illusion at the horizon.

Billy first went toward Maxwell's bedroom; but seeing Poe on the porch, asked in Spanish who he was, then entered.

Inside, to Peter Maxwell, in bed as decoy, Billy asked again in Spanish who was there, possibly sensing Garrett in the darkness. Garrett quickly fired two shots; the first was fatal. In terror of Billy's retaliation, Maxwell ran out to the porch, almost getting shot by Poe, primed for back-up killing. Then Garrett returned to the room with Poe and McKinney, and made sure Billy was dead.

The townspeople held a night vigil for Billy's body in their carpenter's shop. The Coroner's Jury, the next day on July 15, 1881, had Peter Maxwell as witness. As its intimidating President was Postmaster Milnor Rudulph, a Ringite who had helped take over the Legislature in 1872 to block anti-Ring bills. The Coroner's Jury Report, in Spanish, was written by Fort Sumner's Justice of the Peace Alejandro Segura, and sent to the District Attorney of the First Judicial District: Ringite William Breeden, T.B. Catron's close friend and also Territorial Attorney General. The frightened juryman had no alternative but to sign the conclusion; stating: "[O]ur verdict is that the deed of said Garrett was justifiable homicide and we are unanimous in the opinion that the gratitude of all the community is due to the said Garrett for his deed and he is worthy of being rewarded."

Ring terrorism was now complete. Silence fell for a generation before any dared contradict the Santa Fe Ring's outlaw mythology of Billy the Kid. And the Santa Fe Ring's pivotal role in the history was buried along with Billy Bonney, until I came along.

TALK 2:

GALE COOPER'S BILLY THE KID BOOKS; THE HISTORY AND THE HOAXES
OCTOBER 29, 2020

This talk summarizes my Billy the Kid books. Their intent – like my intent in these talks - is to arm you with powerful evidence. The books have complete archival documents, and bibliographies with my thousands of sources. And their facts will immunize you to charlatans hoaxing Billy Bonney.

As I discussed in my talk summarizing the history, New Mexico Territory's 1870's flared with grass-roots rebellions against the land-grabbing, political cabal known as the Santa Fe Ring. In that decade, Ringites were infiltrating Territorial government and law enforcement, and creating mercantile and ranching monopolies. The 1878 lost Lincoln County War, the last and bloodiest uprising, was made famous by its teenaged hero, Billy Bonney, demonized by the Ring as "Billy the Kid."

The freedom fights may have been crushed, and the freedom fighters reduced by Ring propaganda to mere outlaws, but the voices of the anti-Ring fighters lived on in their depositions, court testimonies, petitions to the President, pamphlets, newspaper articles, and letters. And speaking through time, is Billy Bonney himself, as he confronted the Ring by his letters, deposition, pardon seeking, court testimonies, and interviews.

The history books are my novel, *Billy and Paulita*; and my non-fiction books: *Billy the Kid's Writings, Words, and Wit*; *The Santa Fe Ring Versus Billy the Kid*; *The Lost Pardon of Billy the Kid*; and *The Coroner's Jury Report of Billy the Kid*.

Billy and Paulita, **subtitled** ***The Saga of Billy the Kid,
Paulita Maxwell, and the Santa Fe Ring***, was my first book
revealing the real history. I described its inspiration in my lecture
titled "My Adventures With Billy the Kid" - now on my playlist.
My goal was bringing to life the star-crossed romance of Billy
Bonney and young heiress, Paulita Maxwell, against the backdrop
of the lost Lincoln County War freedom fight against the Santa Fe
Ring. For it, I not only did extensive research, but also recreated
the scenes at their historic sites, and interviewed descendants of
historical characters. Though Billy is killed by the Ring at the end,
he triumphs by completing his hero journey, as he wanted: free till
the end.

Billy the Kid's Writings, Words, and Wit gives all known
communications of Billy Bonney. They demonstrate his brilliance,
literacy, pursuit of justice, and unquenchable ironic humor. Most
grew out of the Lincoln County War freedom fight and his
subsequent outlawing by the Santa Fe Ring.

Included is analysis of his uniquely modified Spencerian
handwriting. There is his complete deposition to Washington,
D.C., Investigator Frank Warner Angel about witnessing the
murder of John H. Tunstall. His pardon plea letters to Governor
Lew Wallace include reproductions of all the originals. And there
is Wallace's interview of him. Discussed is Billy's expurgated,
1879, Grand Jury testimony against the murderers of Attorney
Huston Chapman. Present is his entire testimony for the
prosecution in the Court of Inquiry for possible court martial of
Fort Stanton Commander N.A.M. Dudley. There is Billy's letter to
Attorney Edgar Caypless about appealing his death sentence. And
there are his newspaper interviews, taunting his unjust
prosecution and withheld pardon.

A bonus is my authentication of a new Billy the Kid letter to
Governor Lew Wallace about Lincoln County War matters.

All show that Billy was a freedom fighter, not an outlaw.

The Santa Fe Ring Versus Billy the Kid, **subtitled** ***The
Making of an American Monster***, presents, for the first time
ever, the unvarnished villainous history of New Mexico's Santa Fe
Ring, begun in 1866 by attorneys Thomas Benton Catron and
Stephen Benton Elkins.

As to "the making of an American monster" subtitle, it refers
to the rise to power of the moral monstrosities in the Ring, as well

as the Ring's manufacturing of the monster outlaw, Billy the Kid, as cover-up.

Traced through their whole criminal careers are Ring co-bosses, Catron and Elkins, as well as their Lincoln County War minions, all untouched by justice.

And portrayed for the first time - with some named by me - are New Mexico Territory's crushed freedom fights against the Ring. Santa Fe's 1872 Legislature Revolt tried to pass bills stopping Ring take-over of the judiciary. The 1876 Grant County Rebellion attempted secession to Arizona to escape the Ring. The 1877 Colfax County War had Maxwell Land Grant settlers fighting the Ring's illegal seizure of their land. And the 1878 Lincoln County War, which Billy Bonney made famous, had citizens pitted against the Ring and the military.

Also featured are unsung anti-Ring fighters – adding to those of the Lincoln County War. There are Ring-murdered Colfax County War leader Reverend Franklin Tolby, firebrand petitioner and pamphleteer Mary Tibbles McPherson, journalist Raymond Morley, and New Mexico Territory Governor Miguel Otero.

Revealed also is the Ring's expansion through the 19th century by briberies, vote-fixings, malicious prosecutions, defamations, and murders of opponents. It all worked. No Ringite was ever punished for their crimes. And Ring boss Catron was appointed as one of the first two senators at New Mexico's 1912 statehood. And, in 1921, Catron County was created, branding the state's map, to this day, with injustice.

Provided are complete texts of the 19th century communications, secret Ring cipher codes, petitions, exposés, pamphlets, legal papers, and newspaper articles.

Added is the modern Santa Fe Ring's 21st century, profiteering Billy the Kid Case hoax, which hijacked Billy's history. It is also exposed in my book, *Cracking the Billy the Kid Case Hoax.*

The Lost Pardon of Billy the Kid, subtitled ***An Analysis Factoring in the Santa Fe Ring, Governor Lew Wallace's Dilemma, and a Territory in Rebellion,*** explains why New Mexico Territory Governor Lew Wallace denied Billy Bonney's promised pardon. Key is the role of the Santa Fe Ring. And my psychological analysis of Wallace adds perspective.

Presented also is Billy's lost second pardon chance through the Secret Service, again blocked by the Ring.

Provided are texts of original communications, legal papers, and newspaper articles.

Included are hoaxes recycling Billy's pardon request. I also debunked them in my books about the Brushy Bill Roberts imposter hoax and the Billy the Kid Case hoax.

The Coroner's Jury Report of Billy the Kid, subtitled *The Inquest That Sealed the Fame of Billy Bonney and Pat Garrett,* gives the history of William H. Bonney's July 15, 1881 Coroner's Jury Report documenting his killing by Sheriff Pat Garrett on July 14, 1881.

It sealed a fateful moment in Old West history. And it marked the Santa Fe Ring's elimination of the last Regulator.

Presented is a certified copy of this three page, Spanish language Report, as well as its translation. Its storage is traced from its recipient, District Attorney of the First Judicial District, William Breeden, to its 20th century rediscoveries in Santa Fe public records.

This book is fatal to the Billy the Kid imposter hoaxes of men, like Brushy Bill Roberts and John Miller, who claimed to be surviving Billy the Kid by denying that Billy was killed by Pat Garrett, and by lying that this Report did not exist.

My hoaxbusting books cover the main 20th and 21st century hoaxes which hijacked Billy the Kid history. They are: *Cracking the Billy the Kid Imposter Hoax of Brushy Bill Roberts; Billy the Kid's Pretender John Miller; Cracking the Billy the Kid Case Hoax; The Cold Case Billy the Kid MegaHoax; The Billy the Kid's Bad Bucks* Hoax; and *Blandina Segale, the Nun Who Rode on Billy the Kid.*

Cracking the Billy the Kid Imposter Hoax of Brushy Bill Roberts demolishes this elaborate hoax that has endured from the mid-20th century to the present. It claimed that Brushy Bill, as Billy the Kid, survived Pat Garrett's shooting on July 14, 1881, because Garrett shot Brushy's fictional partner, named Billy Barlow, instead. And it lied that the Coroner's Jury Report of Billy the Kid did not exist.

In actuality, Oliver Pleasant Roberts, self-named "Brushy Bill," was born in 1879, and was not even two at Billy Bonney's 1881 killing. He was mentally ill, vocationally disabled, and cared for by his family and wives. Billy the Kid was just one of his multiple delusional personas. But he was promoted by a huckster named William V. Morrison, a salesman who impersonated an attorney. Morrison failed in his 1950, profiteering, publicity stunt to get a modern New Mexico governor's pardon for Brushy as Billy. But after Brushy died, Morrison continued the hoax with a 1955 book titled *Alias Billy the Kid*, written with a fellow hoaxing author named C.L. Sonnichsen.

This book exposes the error-filled prompting sources used by Brushy Bill, Morrison, and Sonnichsen to create his Billy the Kid persona. Proved is Brushy's lack of any special knowledge and his fatal errors. Referenced are also Brushy's family members who revealed him as an imposter.

Later Brushy Bill hoaxes, to the present, are also debunked. They evolved with ever-increasing fakery, as their authors surreptitiously added Billy the Kid history, discovered after Brushy's day, by forging Brushy's original transcripts to fake his so-called "special knowledge" of Billy the Kid.

Covered too is the 21st century, forensic DNA hoax to fake Brushy as Billy, which is also debunked in my book, *Cracking the Billy the Kid Case Hoax*.

Billy the Kid's Pretender John Miller debunks a minor, early 20th century, Billy the Kid imposter named John Miller, who claimed that Sheriff Pat Garrett killed his Native American partner, mistaken for him as Billy.

This hoax was continued by a Helen Airy in her 1993 book titled *Whatever Happened to Billy the Kid?* In it, Airy hid that Miller was born in 1850, almost a decade before Billy Bonney, making him no kid in the Lincoln County War, and not 21 on July 14, 1881. Also hidden is that Miller's knew no Billy the Kid history. For proof, Airy just cited Miller's friends, saying he told them he was the Kid.

This hoax is noteworthy only because it was recycled in the early 21st century in the gigantic Billy the Kid Case hoax, claiming that DNA would prove that John Miller or Brushy Bill Roberts had been Billy the Kid. The DNA claims were fake, but that did not stop the hoaxers from digging up John Miller for bogus DNA matching for a planned, profiteering, TV documentary.

I also exposed the John Miller hoax in my book, *Cracking the Billy the Kid Case Hoax*.

Cracking the Billy the Kid Case Hoax, subtitled *The Strange Plot to Exhume Billy the Kid, Convict Sheriff Pat Garrett of Murder, and Become President of the United States* debunks arguably the biggest historic-forensic hoax ever perpetrated. It tried to fake that Billy the Kid imposter, Brushy Bill Roberts, was Billy the Kid. For filler, it added Billy the Kid imposter, John Miller. At stake was the real history of Billy the Kid.

Ironically, this hoax, begun in 2003, was done by the modern Santa Fe Ring - again trying to destroy the real Billy the Kid, as had the original Ring. Colluding in this caper were New Mexico's unscrupulous publicity-seeking Governor; profiteering New Mexico lawmen; the historian of the U.S. Marshals Service; a state-funded university professor as official historian and creator of their 2004 hoax-promoting TV program; the Governor's Brushy-believing political donor, as so-called "lawyer for Billy the Kid;" an editor of a glossy Old West magazine; and New Mexico press. Their forensic expert for their fake DNA investigation was notorious Dr. Henry Lee.

Their self-named "Billy the Kid Case" claimed that Sheriff Pat Garrett didn't kill Billy the Kid on July 14, 1881, but, instead, viciously murdered an innocent victim to fill the Fort Sumner grave, so Billy could escape. Real, filed, Sheriffs Department murder cases were opened against Garrett, to justify exhuming Billy the Kid and his mother, Catherine Antrim. Intended was faking their DNA mismatch to make-up that Garrett's innocent victim was in Billy's grave, not Billy. Then Brushy Bill was to be awarded a posthumous governor's pardon as Billy the Kid for having led a long and law-abiding life. Kept secret was that the graves were just tourist markers, without valid DNA!

Billy the Kid DNA was also faked from an old carpenter's bench, as an excuse to dig up Billy the Kid imposter, John Miller for fake matching. But since Miller's Arizona grave was unmarked, the adjoining corpse was dug up also. His name was William Hudspeth. These multiple felonies were concealed by the hoaxers and colluding Arizona public officials. And kept secret was that the carpenter's bench had yielded no DNA at all to match with anyone!

Provided are the texts of all the hoax documents and press.

This book is also my memoir of fighting the Santa Fe Ring. I saved real Billy the Kid history by court cases blocking the exhumations of Billy and his mother, then by my open records litigation which got the hoaxers' faked and forged DNA records. And I got first-hand experience of fighting a dangerous rigged system. It added to my admiration and sympathy for the 19th century, anti-Ring, freedom fighters – including Billy Bonney.

The Cold Case Billy the Kid MegaHoax, subtitled ***The Plot to Steal Billy the Kid's Identity and Defame Sheriff Pat Garrett as a Murderer*** debunks the re-run of Billy the Kid imposter hoaxes of Brushy Bill Roberts and John Miller - with new hoaxes added - in a 2018 book titled *Cold Case Billy the Kid.*

The fakery - which hides the Coroner's Jury Report of Billy the Kid proving his killing - makes-up that Billy's alleged "death" was really a cold case murder, because Sheriff Pat Garrett killed an innocent victim instead of him, and was never prosecuted for that crime. Multiple fake investigations are offered to claim that history was wrong.

The writers were in the earlier Billy the Kid Case hoax, which they now hid, while recycling its fake Dr. Henry Lee forensics. They also used so-called "Dr. Lee's reports," which were apparently the forgeries created for my open records litigation in the Billy the Kid Case. So my book, *Cracking the Billy the Kid Case Hoax* also applies to this rerun.

Provided are the all the documents exposing the hoaxing.

The Billy the Kid's Bad Bucks Hoax, subtitled *Faking Billy Bonney as a William Brockway Gang Counterfeiter* debunks a new Billy the Kid hoax, appearing in 2010 and 2015 articles, and in the 2018 book titled *Cold Case Billy the Kid.*

This hoax made-up a satanically evil Billy the Kid rustler, who was in alliance with New York City counterfeiter William Brockway. This Billy also despicably murdered a freight driver who dared report him as a counterfeiter to the Secret Service.

The writers were Billy the Kid Case hoaxers in the early 2000's, making-up that Sheriff Pat Garrett never killed Billy the Kid. I debunked that hoax in my book, *Cracking the Billy the Kid Case Hoax.*

This hoax's m.o. was to use obscure, National Archive documents about Billy the Kid's late 1880 pursuit by Secret Service Special Operative, Azariah Wild; and unrelated, obscure, Secret Service documents about pursuit of counterfeiter, William Brockway. Text was also lifted, out of context, from Pat Garrett's 1882 book, *The Authentic Life of Billy the Kid.*

To fake the connection of Billy Bonney and Brockway, these sources were misstated. The hoaxers' obvious bet was that no one would check the originals. I did. Further fake evidence was a random counterfeit bill gotten from the National Archives. Pretended was that it came from Azariah Wild's investigation, and proved Billy was a counterfeiter.

Billy the Kid's murdering a freighter was lifted from outlaw myth press. But the freighter's being an informer on Billy was made-up for this hoax. In truth, that freighter, named Sam Smith, was killed by Apaches, months before Azariah Wild's Secret Service investigation, and had nothing to do with Billy the Kid or Wild.

Included in the book are the actual documents about which the hoaxers lied to fabricate their so-called "evidence."

Blandina Segale, the Nun Who Rode on Billy the Kid, subtitled ***Sleuthing a Foisted Frontier Fable*** presents the earliest and weirdest Billy the Kid imposter hoax as perpetrated by a Sisters of Charity of Cincinnati frontier missionary nun, named Blandina Segale, who impersonated being a participant in Billy the Kid history, in articles, and in a 1932 book titled *At the End of the Santa Fe Trail*. In her day, dime novel-style publications were her only available sources - like Pat Garrett's 1882 *The Authentic Life of Billy the Kid* and Walter Noble Burns's 1926 *The Saga of Billy the Kid*. So she lifted their tell-tale falsehoods to build her lies about her faked Billy the Kid. And she added her own spin with an evil, Colorado, highwayman, outlaw Billy the Kid, who scalped people for revenge - though real Billy was not in Colorado, nor was he a highwayman, nor was he a scalper! But impersonating a heroine, Blandina saves people from this scary Billy by bringing out his better side with her spiritual powers. Her lies are made more intriguing by the fact that she is currently in the running for sainthood.

Using her quotes, I demonstrated the sources from which she lifted them to create her hoax. And I hypothesized about her psychological need to create her fantasies.

My talks to follow will give you these books' specifics about the real Billy Bonney and about the hoaxers hijacking him!

TALK 3:

BILLY THE KID'S CHAMPIONS
OCTOBER 30, 2020

This talk introduces the real Billy Bonney through his championing contemporaries.

As I discussed in my talk summarizing Billy's history, years of Santa Fe Ring terrorism, culminating in his killing, yielded a generation of frightened silence. Indeed, Regulators who stuck with Billy - Charlie Bowdre and Tom O'Folliard - were, not coincidentally, buried beside him in Fort Sumner. And their killings by Pat Garrett were just months before his.

But, unanticipated by the Ring, killing Billy just sealed his fame. And the Ring's Billy the Kid outlaw myths didn't fool everyone. Billy's growing public intuitively sensed more to the story. And since Billy's fame began when he was alive, he even ridiculed the fables. On December 12, 1880, he wrote to Governor Lew Wallace about a newspaper article calling him a murderer with an outlaw gang. He stated: "The gentleman must have drawn very heavily on his imagination."

Billy's champions confirmed that this cocky, teenaged, freedom fighter was fearless, brilliant, literate, bi-cultural, charismatic, and a natural leader.

John Henry Tunstall, Billy's admired employer, was quoted by Billy's fellow Regulator, George Coe, in his 1934 autobiography titled *Frontier Fighter*. Coe wrote: "Tunstall seemed really devoted to the Kid. One day, I was in Lincoln, and I asked him about Billy. 'George, that's the finest lad I ever met,' he said. 'He's a revelation to me every day and would do anything to please me. I'm going to make a man out of that boy yet. He has it in him.'"

Gottfried Gauss was part of Billy's Lincoln County history from Billy's October of 1877 arrival as a John Tunstall ranch hand - and Gauss was Tunstall's cook - to Billy's April 28, 1881 Lincoln jailbreak, when Gauss was the courthouse-jail's caretaker.

Gauss's experience of Santa Fe Ring crimes - from Tunstall's murder, through the Lincoln County War - left him allied with Billy and bitterly anti-Ring. He may have been Billy's jailbreak accomplice, by leaving a revolver for him in the outhouse.

On March 1, 1890, Gauss was interviewed for the *Lincoln County Leader* about Billy's great escape. He implied the enabling role of Lincolnites, who even shook hands with escaping Billy. And Gauss might have directed Billy's guard, Deputy Robert Olinger, to the courthouse-jail's east side, where Billy waited for him with a shotgun at its second story window.

Gauss was quoted: "I was crossing the yard behind the courthouse, when I heard a shot fired, then a tussle upstairs in the courthouse, somebody hurrying downstairs, and deputy sheriff Bell emerging from the door running toward me. He ran right into my arms, expired the same moment, and I laid him down, dead. That I was in a hurry to secure assistance, or perhaps to save myself, everybody will believe.

"When I arrived at the garden gate leading to the street, in front of the courthouse, I saw the other deputy sheriff Olinger, coming out of the hotel opposite, with the four or five other county prisoners, where they had taken their dinner. I called to him to come quick. He did so, leaving his prisoners in front of the hotel. When he had come up close to me, and while I was standing not a yard apart, I told him that I was just after laying Bell dead on the ground in the courtyard behind. Before he could reply, he was struck by a well-directed shot fired from a window above us, and fell dead at my feet.

"I ran for my life to reach my room and safety, when Billy the Kid called to me: 'Don't run, I wouldn't hurt you -   I am alone, and master not only of the courthouse, but also of the town, for I will allow nobody to come near us. You go,' he said, 'and saddle one of Judge (Ira) Leonard's horses, and I will clear out as soon as I have the shackles loosened from my legs.' With a little prospecting pick, I had thrown to him through the window, he was working for at least an hour, and could not accomplish more than to free one leg. He came to the conclusion to wait a better chance, tie one shackle to his waist-belt, and start out. Meanwhile I had saddled a small skittish pony belonging to Billy Burt (the county clerk), as there was no other horse available, and had also, by Billy's command, tied a pair of red blankets behind the saddle ...

"When Billy went down the stairs at last, on passing the body of Bell he said, 'I'm sorry I had to kill him but I couldn't help it.' On passing the body of Olinger he gave him a tip with his boot, saying, 'You are not going to round me up again.' And so Billy the Kid started out that evening, after he had shaken hands with everybody around, and after having a little difficulty in mounting on account of the shackle on his leg, he went on his way rejoicing."

Attorney Ira Leonard was anti-Ring. He was Billy's best friend in a high place. In 1879, he volunteered as Billy's lawyer. He was impressed by Billy's fulfilling his pardon bargain's Grand Jury testimony for Governor Lew Wallace, against Ringite killers of his office mate, Attorney Huston Chapman. And, he was impressed by Billy's testimony in the military Court of Inquiry against past Commander N.A.M. Dudley for illegally intervening in the Lincoln County War Battle.

Leonard also kept Wallace informed about Billy's Grand Jury testifying. In April 20, 1879, he wrote about courtroom pressure by Ringite District Attorney William Rynerson; stating: "I will tell you Governor that the prosecuting officer of this District is no friend to the enforcement of the law. He is bent on going for the Kid and ... is proposed to destroy his testimony and influence ... He is a Dolan man and is defending him by his conduct all he can."

By late 1880, Ira Leonard tried himself, though unsuccessfully, to get Billy a pardon through Secret Service Operative Azariah Wild, during Wild's Territorial counterfeiting investigation. And Leonard represented Billy in 1881 in the first of his Mesilla hanging trials, until forced from Billy's defense by an apparent Ring death threat.

Cousins Frank and George Coe were Lincoln County homesteading farmers, when 17 year old Billy met them. In the Lincoln County War, they became his fellow Regulators. And they fled Lincoln County after it was lost. Years later, they flaunted having been freedom fighting soldiers.

As an old-timer, on August 3, 1926, Frank Coe wrote about Billy in an unpublished letter to a William Steele Dean. He emphasized Billy's bi-culturalism, and above-average height (5 feet 6 was average), belying myths calling Billy short. Coe wrote: "[He was] 5 feet 8 inches, weight 138 pounds stood straight as an Indian, fine looking a lad as I ever met. He was a lady's man, the Mex girls were all crazy about him. He spoke their language well. He was a fine dancer, could go all their gaits, and was one of them. He was a wonder, you would have been proud to know him." Remember that. It's real Billy: "He was a wonder, you would have been proud to know him."

Frank Coe, interviewed about Billy for the *El Paso Times* of September 16, 1923, called the Regulators soldiers. He stated: "He was brave and reliable, one of the best soldiers we had. He never pushed his advice or opinions, but he had a wonderful presence of mind; the tighter the place, the more he showed his cool nerve and quick brain." Frank added Billy's shootist reputation; stating: "He never seemed to care for money, except to buy cartridges with; then he would much prefer to gamble for them straight. Cartridges were scarce, and he always used about 10 times as many as any one else."

George Coe, as an old-timer, published his 1934 *Frontier Fighter*. The subtitle is: *The Autobiography of George Coe Who Fought and Rode With Billy the Kid*. So it proclaimed the freedom fight. Coe emphasized Billy's charisma and intelligence. He wrote: "Billy came down to the Dick Brewer Ranch on the Ruidoso. He was the center of interest everywhere he went, and though heavily armed, he seemed as gentlemanly as a college-bred youth. He quickly became acquainted with everybody, and because of his humorous and pleasing personality grew to be a community favorite. In fact, Billy was so popular there wasn't enough of him to go around. He had a beautiful voice and sang like a bird. One of our special amusements was to get together every few nights and have singing. The thrill of those happy evenings still lingers – a pleasant memory – and tonight I would give a lot to live through one again. Frank Coe and I played the fiddles, and all of us danced, and here Billy, too, was in demand."

George also gave a telling anecdote about Billy's teasing bravado which occurred in April of 1878, during Lincoln County War skirmishes. It shows how this teenager inspired grown men. And it foreshadowed Billy's undaunted and ironic press interviews, three years later, after his unjust Mesilla hanging trial. Coe wrote: "We made a big bonfire, and sat around swapping lies and bragging ... Then we talked about riding into Lincoln and setting in short order all the difficulties that were troubling the people there. We were a brave band, as we told it. Our guns, which formed the most important part of our possessions, had been placed carelessly around, against nearby trees. Billy sized up the situation, and, looking for a little fun and excitement with an inexperienced bunch of greenhorns, he slipped about five or six cartridges out of his belt and tossed them into the fire. In less than a minute they began to go off, and such a mad dash for tall timber you have never seen ... I looked back as I ran, and there stood the Kid, with his arms folded, perfectly unconcerned ... He said, 'Well, you're a damn fine bunch of soldiers. Run like a bunch of coyotes and forget to take your guns. I just wanted to break you in a little before we met the enemy, and, boys, I'm sure proud of your nerve.' "

About Lincoln County War fighting, George quoted Billy's militant fervor, seen also in Billy's later writings. George wrote that Billy said about their adversaries: "As for going out and giving up to that outfit, we'll die first." That matches Billy's equally bellicose and brave words in his letter, the next year, to Governor Lew Wallace: "I am not afraid to die like a man fighting, but I would not like to be killed like a dog unarmed."

Ygenio Salazar, Billy's younger friend, as an old-timer, was quoted in Walter Noble Burns's 1926 *The Saga of Billy the Kid.* Ygenio said: "Billy the Kid' ... was the bravest fellow I ever knew. All through the three-days' battle (note that it was actually six days) he was as cool and cheerful as if he were playing a game, instead of fighting for his life."

Henry Hoyt was a medical doctor, working as a mail rider, when he met Billy in Tascosa, Texas, three months after the lost Lincoln County War. Billy and fellow Regulators, Charlie Bowdre and Tom O'Folliard, were doing petty rustling against Ringmen targets, as forewarned in Billy's "Regulator Manifesto" letter of July 13, 1878.

Billy, liking Hoyt, gifted him with a fine sorrel horse, which was apparently Dandy Dick, dead Sheriff William Brady's, stolen from the ranch of T.B. Catron or Charles Fritz, a Ring sympathizer. Billy wrote Hoyt a Bill of Sale to confirm his ownership. Noteworthy is that Billy, then 18 and unknown, impressed Hoyt so much that he saved it. And based on knowing Billy, he published his 1929 memoir, *A Frontier Doctor.*

In it, Hoyt noted Billy's intelligence and bi-culturalism. He wrote: "After learning his history directly from himself and recognizing his many superior natural qualifications, I often urged him, while he was free and the going was good, to leave the country, settle in Mexico or South America, and begin all over again. He spoke Spanish like a native; and, although only a beardless boy, was nevertheless a natural leader of men. With his poise, iron nerve, and all-around efficiency properly applied, he could have made a success anywhere."

In the 1920's, Hoyt learned that Lew Wallace's family had Billy's letters; and, on April 27, 1929, by letter, he contacted the grandson, Lew Wallace Jr. He enclosed a photocopy of Billy's tintype and his Bill of Sale. On its back, Hoyt wrote: "He was a remarkable character, a natural leader of men, and was largely forced into the life of an outlaw by his circumstances over which he had no control."

John Meadows was a rancher in New Mexico Territory from early 1880. As an old-timer, he capitalized on his friendship with Billy. In 1931, he made a pageant called "Days of Billy the Kid in Story, Song and Dance." It was printed in the *Roswell Daily Record*. And from August, 1935 to June, 1936, the "Alamogordo News" printed his reminiscence articles. They became a posthumous 2004 book titled *Pat Garrett and Billy the Kid as I Knew Them: Reminiscences of John P. Meadows*.

Meadows stated about Billy in *Reminiscences*: "I will indicate that the man who is generally chronicled as having turned outlaw really had some excellent traits along with some of his bad ones. I don't know how many he had killed - in fact, I don't know that he had killed any - and I didn't care ... I liked him right off the reel, and I do to this day, though it has been fifty years since Pat Garrett captured him by killing."

John Meadows also gave a clue as to how Billy got respect from the older men. Meadows wrote: "When he was rough, he was as rough as men ever get to be, yet he had a good streak in him."

Meadows also partly filled-in the gap between Billy's Lincoln jailbreak and his Fort Sumner killing. He wrote that Billy first came to his ranch on the Peñasco River in early May. That implied Billy's sensible plan of heading southward to Old Mexico, where his bi-lingual skills and Hispanic affinities were a natural fit.

Meadows also reported that Billy had told him then about the Deputy James Bell shooting. Meadows quoted: "I did not want to kill Bell, but I had to do so to save my own life. It was a case of have to, not of wanting to."

Meadows also claimed that Billy told him he had a letter from Governor Lew Wallace about the pardon promise. Though Meadows's rendition of the bargain was wrong - based on "standing trial" instead of "testifying in a trial" - the fact of an agreement letter's existence repeated Billy's own claim by letter to Wallace from the Santa Fe jail. Meadows wrote: "He had a letter which he showed me from the governor, Lew Wallace, which said that if he came in and stood his trial and was convicted, the governor would pardon him." Sadly, that letter is lost.

Billy's March 2, 1881 jail letter to Wallace had stated: "I have some letters which date back two years and there are Parties who are very anxious to get them but I will not dispose of them until I see you."

A.P. "Paco" Anaya, Billy's Fort Sumner teenaged friend, had his manuscript about Billy published posthumously, in 1991, as *I Buried Billy*. In it, about Billy's bi-culturalism, Anaya stated: "Billy liked better to be with Hispanics than with Americans."

Tantalizing is that Billy's bi-culturalism was common knowledge. "Teddy Blue" Abbott, a roving cowboy about Billy's age, had merely heard about him in 1878; and published, in 1955, as an old-timer, *We Pointed Them North: Recollections of a Cowpuncher*. Abbott wrote: "The Lincoln County troubles was still going on, and you had to be either for Billy the Kid or against him. It wasn't my fight ... it was the Mexicans that made a hero of him."

"Teddy Blue" Abbott, thus, was one of the first strangers to capture the star quality of this teenager, who symbolized the freedom fight of Ring-oppressed people. And unbeknownst to Abbott, he had picked-up on what Ring boss Thomas Benton Catron knew: that Billy and his Hispanic compatriots were primed for another uprising against his Santa Fe Ring. Boss Catron knew that Billy had to die.

Future talks will let Billy speak for himself, through his many and varied communications.

TALK 4:
BILLY THE KID'S UNIQUE SPENCERIAN HANDWRITING
FROM BOOK: *BILLY THE KID'S WRITINGS, WORDS, AND WIT*
NOVEMBER 1, 2020

This discussion begins my talks on Billy Bonney's own communications. They're from my book, *Billy the Kid's Writings, Words, and Wit*. Featured here is Billy's personally modified, Spencerian handwriting.

Because of the popularized outlaw myths of Billy the Kid, it surprises people that he was highly literate. In fact, one of his mid-20th century imposters, named Brushy Bill Roberts, even claimed to match Billy by being illiterate himself! So telling you about Billy's handwriting helps to understand the real Billy the Kid.

Billy benefited from mid-19th century America's goals of universal literacy and standardized penmanship.

In the century before, people wrote with a trimmed quill feather. By the early 19th century, that design was translated into a long wood or bone holder, with a pointed tip called a nib. The nib was a hollow steel half-cylinder, with a split tip. Eventually, the nib's ink flow was improved by a hole above the split, and side slits.

One needed skill to use this pen. It required frequent dipping in ink. And ink splattering was a risk.

In Billy Bonney's day, ink was made from gallotannic acid. It resulted from the gall wasp's laying her eggs on oak trees. The trees encapsulated the growing larvae in swellings filled with gallic and tannic acid, called oak galls. Those colorless acids were harvested from the galls. Color came from adding sulfate of iron and dyes like indigo. That made iron-gall ink. That's what Billy used.

Over time, iron-gall ink oxidized to rusty brown. And its acid could eat through paper. So luck of good preservation kept for posterity Billy's written words.

As to paper, in Billy's day, America led pulp paper production. Though its availability in remote New Mexico Territory was often limited. The pulp came from rags, ground wood, or a mixture of both. It was spread by hand, pressed, bleached, dried, and cut. As will be seen in a later talk about my authenticating a new Billy the Kid letter, this process resulted in each paper batch having unique pulp and fiber patterns, like fingerprints.

The man who created standardized penmanship in the 19th century was a calligrapher named Platt Rogers Spencer. He made a business empire from his instructional texts and copy books with his legible, standardized, cursive writing style – called, after himself, Spencerian. After Spencer's 1864 death, his sons continued the manuals as the Spencerian Authors. Billy Bonney's education before he arrived in New Mexico Territory is unknown. But from the age of 13 ½ to 14 ½, he was in Silver City's public school, and would have been taught the Spencerian writing method.

The fact that all Billy Bonney's known writings are in Spencerian cursive style, is a boon to authenticating his writings. As will be seen, he uniquely modified the Spencerian alphabet for a bolder look in his own communications.

Learning Spencerian style was demanding on students. It involved the whole body, as illustrated in the teaching manuals.

On screen are the proper positions for Spencerian writing. **[FIGURE 1]** Before putting pen to paper, required was assuming a proper position at a desk. That position is illustrated in Spencer's sons' 1874 book titled *Theory of Spencerian Penmanship.*

One sat at the desk with straight posture, stable foot positioning, writing hand's forearm flat on the desk surface, and pen properly held. The intent was to make the entire arm a sliding unit. That gliding was used to form the Spencerian alphabet. Important to note, is that a desk was therefore necessary. That will later have implications for analyzing Billy's handwriting when he was on the run or in jail, and lacking proper writing facilities.

FIGURE 1: Writing positions (From H.C. Spencer. *Theory of Spencerian Penmanship.* 1874. Courtesy of the Ames Historical Society.)

On screen is the proper holding of the pen for Spencerian handwriting. **[FIGURE 2]** As Spencer taught, the objective was to control the gliding penmanship. Here are Platt Rogers Spencer's 1857 obsessive details: "Take the pen between the first and second fingers and the thumb, observing 1st, that it crosses the second finger on the corner of the nail; 2nd, that it crosses the fore finger forward of the knuckle; 3rd, that the end of the thumb touches the holder opposite the lower joint of the fore finger; 4th, that the top of the holder points towards the right shoulder; 5th, that the wrist is above the paper, and the hand resting lightly on the nails of the third and fourth fingers; 6th, that the point of the pen comes squarely to the paper."

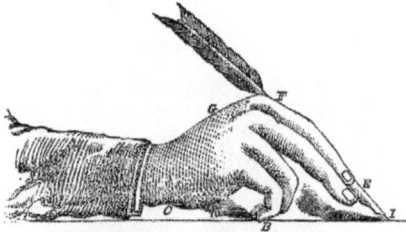

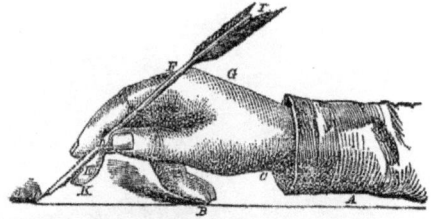

FIGURE 2: Holding the pen (Platt Rogers Spencer. *Spencerian Penmanship*. 1857.)

This much complexity needed practice. Spencer's manuals had drills for pen holding and alphabet formation. He divided the alphabet's shapes into what he called elements. They were ovals, curves, and lines. And they all slanted rightward, at exactly 52 degrees.

Here are some Spencerian practice exercises from 1874.

On screen are Spencerian writing exercises. **[FIGURE 3]** Rote was essential to Spencer's system. The exercises were done on chalkboard or paper to practice underlying principles of the alphabet's design and slant, until they became automatic.

That all this rigmarole was necessary to achieve the Spencerian look, is proved by Billy's handwriting changing in the Santa Fe jail - where he could not assume the correct position. And he was distressed enough about his poor writing to explain its reason to one of his attorneys, named Edgar Caypless, in an April 15, 1881 letter from the Mesilla jail. Billy stated: "Excuse bad writing. I have my handcuffs on." To put Billy's inculcated Spencerian perfectionism in perspective, realize that he had a bigger problem on April 15, 1881: he had just been sentenced to hang!

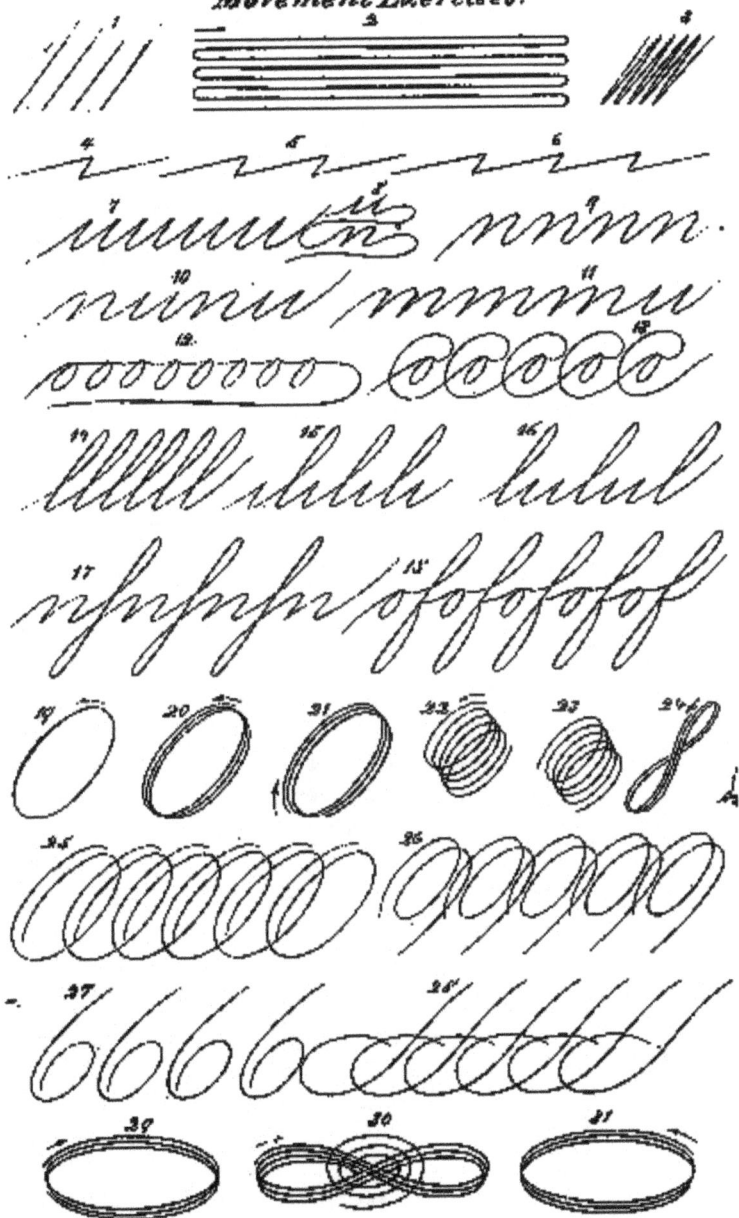

FIGURE 3: Spencerian writing exercises (From H.C. Spencer. *Spencerian Key to Practical Penmanship*. 1874. Courtesy of the Ames Historical Society.)

Here is a comparison of Billy's Spencerian handwriting, with and without proper writing facilities.

On screen is the comparison of Billy's letter of March 13, 1879 to Lew Wallace, and his January 1, 1881 letter **[FIGURE 4]** to Wallace from the Santa Fe jail. **[FIGURE 5]** As can be seen, Billy's letter of March 13th had proper Spencerian slant, as opposed to his January 1st one from the Santa Fe jail. There he wore handcuffs and had no proper writing desk, so lost the slant. Nevertheless, as will be seen, examination of his individual alphabetical letters, as well as his typical spelling and punctuation errors, show all the letters to be by him.

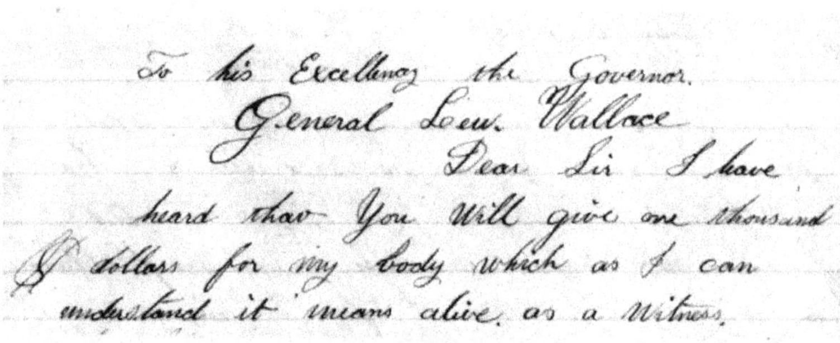
To his Excellency the Governor.
General Lew. Wallace
Dear Sir I have
heard that You will give one thousand
$ dollars for my body which as I can
understand it means alive as a Witness.

FIGURE 4: Billy Bonney's March 13, 1879 letter to Governor Lew Wallace. Fray Angélico Chávez Historical Library, Santa Fe, New Mexico. Lincoln County Heritage Trust Collection

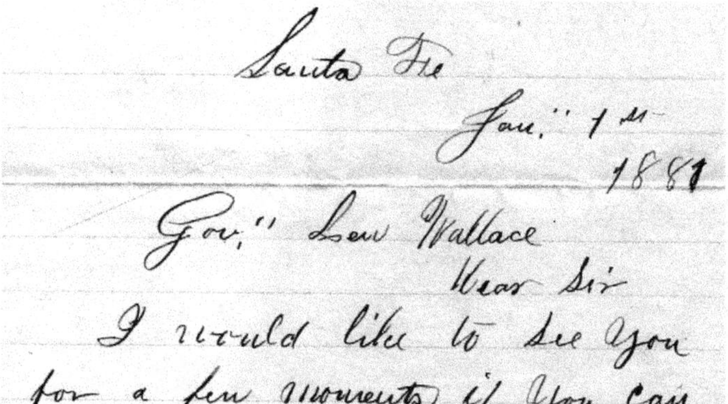
Santa Fe
Jan." 1st
1881
Gov." Lew Wallace
Dear Sir
I would like to See you
for a few moments if You can
Spare time

FIGURE 5: Billy Bonney's January 1, 1881 letter to Governor Lew Wallace. Indiana Historical Society, Lew Wallace Collection

Spencerian lower case letters look much like today's cursive lettering. But the upper case letters don't. They had ornate loops and flourishes. Since Billy personalized his Spencerian script, here is a comparison of standard Spencerian capital letters with Billy's modifications of them.

On screen is the comparison of Spencerian capital letters with Billy's modifications to their right. **[FIGURE 6]** Billy rejected the fussy calligraphic excesses of the Spencerian method's capital letters, as can be seen by comparing Spencerian capital letters and Billy's bolder versions. As to the Spencerian style's simpler lower case letters, Billy used them outright and maintained their rightward slant.

A	*A*	APPENDIX 7: December 12, 1880, Letter to Governor Wallace (Analla) *Analla*
B	*B*	APPENDIX 7: December 12, 1880, Letter to Governor Wallace (Bonney) *Bonney*
C	*C*	APPENDIX 5: March 20,, 1879, Letter to Governor Wallace (Commanding) *Commanding*
D	*D*	APPENDIX 3: March 13, 1879, Letter to Governor Wallace (Dear) *Dear*
E	*E*	APPENDIX 3: March 13,1879, Letter to Governor Wallace (Excellency) *Excellency*
F	*F*	APPENDIX 2: October 24, 1878, Hoyt Bill Of Sale (F. Hoyt) *F. Hoyt*
G	*G*	APPENDIX 3: March 13, 1879, Letter to Governor Wallace (General) *General*
H	*H*	APPENDIX 1: June 8, 1878, Deposition to Frank Warner Angel (H. Bonney) *H. Bonney*
I	*I*	APPENDIX 3: March 13, 1879, Letter to Governor Wallace (I remain) *I remain*
J	*J*	APPENDIX 3: March 13, 1879, Letter to Governor Wallace (J.J. Dolan) *J. J. Dolan*
K	*K*	APPENDIX 3: March 13, 1879, Letter to Governor Wallace (Kid Antrim) *Kid Antrim*

$\mathscr{L}$	$\mathscr{L}$	APPENDIX 5: March 20, 1879, Letter to Governor Wallace (Lincoln) *Lincoln*
$\mathscr{M}$	$\mathscr{M}$	APPENDIX 5: March 20, 1879, Letter to Governor Wallace (Mountains) *Mountains*
$\mathscr{N}$	$\mathscr{N}$	APPENDIX 11: March 27, 1881, Letter to Governor Wallace (New) *New*
$\mathscr{O}$	$\mathscr{O}$	APPENDIX 7: December 12, 1880, Letter to Governor Wallace (Officer) *Officer*
$\mathscr{P}$	$\mathscr{P}$	APPENDIX 4: March 20, 1879, 1880, Letter to "Squire" Wilson (P.S.) *P.S.*
$\mathscr{Q}$	———	NONE (Q)
$\mathscr{R}$	$\mathscr{R}$	APPENDIX 7: December 12, 1880, Letter to Governor Wallace (Respect) *Respect*
$\mathscr{S}$	$\mathscr{S}$	APPENDIX 4: March 20, 1879, 1880, Letter to "Squire" Wilson (Soldiers) *Soldiers*
$\mathscr{T}$	$\mathscr{T}$	APPENDIX 4: March 20, 1879, Letter to "Squire" Wilson (Thursday) *Thursday*
$\mathscr{U}$	———	NONE (U)
$\mathscr{V}$	$\mathscr{V}$	APPENDIX 7: December 12, 1880, Letter to Governor Wallace (Vegas) *Vegas*
$\mathscr{W}$	$\mathscr{W}$	APPENDIX 4: March 20, 1879, Letter to Governor Wallace (Watch) *Watch*
$\mathscr{X}$	———	NONE (X)
$\mathscr{Y}$	$\mathscr{Y}$	APPENDIX 7: December 12, 1880, Letter to Governor Wallace (Yerbys) *Yerbys*
$\mathscr{Z}$	$\mathscr{Z}$	APPENDIX 7: December 12, 1880, Letter to Governor Wallace (Zuber) *Zuber*

FIGURE 6: Billy Bonney's modified Spencerian capital letters

Spencerian penmanship also used calligraphic shading of alphabet letters by increasing nib pressure to let out more ink. Billy tried shading just once - on his Bill of Sale for a horse to a Henry Hoyt. He failed. He almost blotted the capital B-B of the horse's brand that he was illustrating.

Billy did use Spencerian embellishments in his signatures They evidence his practice, experimentation, and artistic goals. Here are his signatures. On screen is Billy's signature on the Hoyt Bill of Sale. **[FIGURE 7]** It is the most famous of Billy's signatures. It is from his October 24, 1878 Bill of Sale to Henry Hoyt. For it, Billy cleverly joined his middle initial "H" - for Henry - with the "B" of Bonney. It is not a natural fit. Trying to do it yourself, shows the cleverness of his design.

FIGURE 7: October 14, 1878 Hoyt Bill of Sale signature

On screen is another of Billy's attempts at a fancy signature. It is on his March 20, 1879 letter to Justice of the Peace John "Squire" Wilson. In it he joined the "W" – for William - the "H" – for Henry – and the "B" – for Bonney. But he lost the rightward slant. **[FIGURE 8]**

FIGURE 8: March 20, 1879 letter to Justice of the Peace John "Squire" Wilson

On screen are some of jailed Billy's signatures. They are more awkward because of his handcuffs and poor writing facilities. Examples here are his letters to Governor Lew Wallace of January 1, 1881 **[FIGURE 9]** and March 27, 1881 from the Santa Fe jail. **[FIGURE 10]** Though his personal Spencerian alphabet is maintained, he looses the correct Spencerian slant.

FIGURE 9: January 1, 1881 Santa Fe jail letter

FIGURE 10: March 27, 1881 Santa Fe jail letter

So Billy mastered Spencerian penmanship. And his sophisticated vocabulary proved his high intelligence. But his writings betray his limited formal education. He had a few, repeating, grammatical errors and misspellings. Ultimately, they help to authenticate his writings.

Billy apparently didn't know that all letters are dated. But he was a quick learner. His first pardon bargain letter to Governor Lew Wallace is undated - though it is thought to be from March 13, 1879. Two days later, he saw the March 15, 1879 date on Lew Wallace's answer to him. So he added the March 20, 1879 date to his response to Wallace. And he dated all his letters after that.

Billy also never learned that sentences start with a capitalization. So all his letters have that tell-tale error, except when the word was automatically capitalized, like someone's name. Along with that error, is his rather frequent omission of periods at sentences' ends. And he never used a question mark.

Billy also added emphasis by capitalizing words he wanted to stress.

Billy also made a few, consistent spelling errors; though his overall spelling was excellent. He even correctly spelled "indictments" in his March 13, 1879 letter to Lew Wallace. He seems to have misspelled when sounding out words. So for Billy Campbell - one of John Tunstall's murderers - he spelled his last name C-A-M-U-L in his December 12, 1880 letter to Wallace. He also used E-N-I-M-I-E-S for "enemies" in his March 20, 1879 letter to Wallace. And he spelled murdered as M-U-R-D-E-R-D-E-D in his March 13, 1879 letter to Wallace.

But, since Billy was so smart, he remembered his wrong spellings and reused them. So they help to confirm his authorship of letters. So A-N-N-S-E-R for "answer" is three times in his March 13, 1879 letter to Wallace; and is also in his jail letters to Wallace, two years later, on March 4, 1881 and March 27, 1881.

As we will see in another talk, Billy's personalized Spencerian handwriting, along with his few, consistent, grammatical and spelling errors, helped me to authenticate a new Billy the Kid letter.

In upcoming talks, we'll see what Billy actually wrote about.

TALK 5:
BILLY THE KID'S FIRST WRITINGS
FROM BOOK: *BILLY THE KID'S WRITINGS, WORDS, AND WIT*
NOVEMBER 4, 2020

This talk is about two, first known writings of Billy Bonney, known as Billy the Kid. The information comes from my book, *Billy the Kid's Writings, Words, and Wit*. Billy's personalized Spencerian handwriting was the subject of a previous talk. And the background of New Mexico Territory's freedom fights against the deadly Santa Fe Ring, into which Billy's writings fit, is in my talk titled "The Real History of Billy the Kid."

The writings add to the understanding the real Billy Bonney.

Billy's known words, written by him or transcribed by others, sought justice: first for his boss, John Tunstall, murdered by the Santa Fe Ring; then against other Ring criminals during the Lincoln County War; then for his own pardon as a freedom fighting Regulator in that War. Though Billy was teenaged and penniless, his writings show that he believed his words could prevail against politicians and military brass.

Billy's known writings are a "Regulator Manifesto" letter; a bill of sale to a Henry Hoyt for a horse; two pardon negotiation letters to New Mexico Territory Governor Lew Wallace; one pardon negotiation letter to Justice of the Peace John Wilson; one additional pardon bargain letter, newly identified by me; one pre-capture letter to Governor Wallace; four pardon plea letters to Wallace from the Santa Fe jail; and one letter to his Attorney, Edgar Caypless, about appealing his hanging sentence.

As I discuss in other talks, Billy's words were also recorded by others. There is his deposition to Presidential Investigator Frank Warner Angel about the Ring murder of John Tunstall. There are his quotes remembered by his championing contemporaries as old-timers. There is his interview on Territorial outlawry, as recorded by Lew Wallace during their pardon bargain meetings. There is record of his testimony for the prosecution in a Lincoln County Grand Jury against Ringite murderers of Attorney Huston Chapman. There is his testimony in the military Court of Inquiry for possible court martial of past Fort Stanton Commander N.A.M. Dudley for intervention in the Lincoln County War Battle. And there are his brash and witty interviews with reporters, both after his capture and after his hanging sentence.

But there are lost words also. Lost is Billy's transcript of his Grand Jury testimony for his Lew Wallace pardon bargain. Lost is his letter for a second pardon option, sent to Secret Service Special Operative Azariah Wild for exchanging his testimony against counterfeiters. And there may be others awaiting discovery.

The first of the writings which I attribute to Billy Bonney, is controversial as to his authorship. It is a letter claimed to be by his fellow Regulator, Charlie Bowdre. But only its copy exists. So its handwriting is unknown. And it is signed just "Regulator."

Dated July 13, 1878, the day before the start of the great Battle of the Lincoln County War, it was written just 10 days after the Ring's terrorist massacre of McSween-side Hispanic residents of San Patricio. And Billy was especially close to them. I named it the "Regulator Manifesto." It magnificently declares the Regulators' stand against Santa Fe Ring boss, Thomas Benton Catron. And it foreshadows Billy's post-war retaliatory stock rustling against Ringites.

The letter was addressed to Ring boss, Catron's, brother-in-law, Edgar Walz. Walz managed Catron's huge, Lincoln County, cattle ranch.

Edgar Walz apparently found the Manifesto either sufficiently alarming or incriminating to give it to Fort Stanton's Ring-loyalist Post Adjutant, Second Lieutenant 9th Cavalry Millard Fillmore Goodwin.

Goodwin, in turn, took legal precautions to make its so-called "true copy." He had it certified by Ringite, past Justice of the Peace, David Easton; by the copyist, a Thomas Blair, Captain 15th

Infantry;" and by himself. But that established only that it was an accurate copy. It had nothing to do with who authored it.

This copy is in the Washington, D.C., National Archive Records of the Adjutant General's Office.

Its attribution to Charles Bowdre came in the 20th century. It was by early Billy the Kid historian, Maurice Garland Fulton. Fulton claimed that Edgar Walz identified the handwriting. But there is no evidence that Walz knew Bowdre's handwriting. It seems more likely that Walz simply gave a Regulator name which he knew. If, however, it was actually Bowdre's writing, I would venture that Billy dictated it to him.

The wording matches Billy's known literary skill and melodrama. For example, on March 20th, 1879, he wrote to Governor Lew Wallace: "I am not afraid to die like a man fighting but I would not like to be killed like a dog unarmed." And on April 16, 1881, after his hanging sentence, he told a *Mesilla News* reporter: "If mob law is going to rule, better dismiss judge and sheriff and let all take chances alike." He added: "I think it hard that I should be the only one to suffer the extreme penalty of the law."

And it is noteworthy that Thomas Benton Catron's stock in Edgar Walz's care, would, by late 1878, and through 1880, become one target of Billy's retaliative rustling, as threatened in that "Regulator Manifesto."

The "Manifesto," like a soldier's report, was headed, "In camp, then dated July 13th, 1878. It stated:

"Mr. Walz. Sir: - We are all aware that your brother-in-law, T.B. Catron sustains the Murphy-Kinney party, and take this method of informing you that if any property belonging to the residents of this county is stolen or destroyed, Mr. Catron's property will be dealt with as nearly as can be in the way in which the party he sustains deals with the property stolen or destroyed by them.

"We returned Mr. Thornton the horses we took for the purpose of keeping the Murphy crowd from pursuing us with the promise that these horses should not again be used for that purpose. Now we know that the Tunstall estate cattle are pledged to Kinney and party. [Note that John Kinney was the Ring rustler, who did the San Patricio massacre with his gang.] If they are taken, a similar number will be taken from your brother [meaning brother-in-law]. It is our object and efforts to protect property, but the man who plans destruction shall have destruction measured on him. Steal from the poorest or richest American or Mexican, and the full measure of the injury you do, shall be visited upon the property of Mr. Catron. This murderous band is harbored by you as your guest, and with the consent of Catron occupies your property. Regulator"

For the three years of life left to him, Billy would live true to this manifesto, and true to its bi-cultural commitment: I repeat: "It is our object and efforts to protect property, but the man who plans destruction shall have destruction measured on him. Steal from the poorest or richest American or Mexican, and the full measure of the injury you do, shall be visited upon the property of Mr. Catron."

Billy would refer again to his Robin Hood role in his December 12th, 1880 letter to Governor Lew Wallace. He wrote: "Several instances I have recovered stolen property when there was no chance to get an officer to do it. One instance for Hugo Zuber Postoffice Puerto de Luna. Another for Pablo Analla same place."

The second earliest writing of Billy Bonney is a Bill of Sale for a horse. And his authorship is undisputed. After the Lincoln County War's defeat, teenaged Billy became a petty rustler and gadfly harassing Ringmen. One location Billy used for stock disposal was Tascosa, Texas. There, on October 24, 1878, he wrote, and had legally witnessed, a Bill of Sale for an expensive horse to a Henry Hoyt, a medical doctor, then working as a mail rider.

This document is legally sophisticated. It reflects Billy's experience of legal maneuvering. By its writing, Billy had been exposed to John Tunstall's and Alexander McSween's malicious prosecution by the Santa Fe Ring for a fake embezzling case about the Emil Fritz life insurance policy proceeds. Billy had been legally deputized to arrest Tunstall's Ring murderers. He had been briefly jailed illegally by Ringite Lincoln County Sheriff William Brady. He had seen Tunstall's murderers shielded by the Ring. He would have rejoiced at McSween's Grand Jury victory in the embezzling case. And he would have been privy to McSween's legal complaint about Tunstall's murder to the British

Ambassador and the President. And Billy had himself given an eye-witness affidavit on Tunstall's murder; as well as a formal deposition to Presidential Investigator Frank Warner Angel about that murder.

The Hoyt Bill of Sale was written about three months after Billy's "Regulator Manifesto" and the lost Lincoln County War Battle. It epitomized Billy's retaliative anti-Ring rustling in action.

Riding with past Regulator friends, Charlie Bowdre and Tom O'Folliard - and initially with Regulators, Josiah "Doc" Scurlock and John Middleton, who soon left the Territory - Billy was adhering to the "Regulator Manifesto" and rustling from Catron's ranch. Another rustling target was the ranch of Ring-biased Charles Fritz, brother of deceased Emil Fritz.

The Bill of Sale yields a riddle: Why did Hoyt keep it? The horse was merely a gift from a scruffy teenager. If the horse was originally stolen, that was common. And Hoyt often got horses for his mail rider job. The answer came in Hoyt's April 27, 1929 letter to Lew Wallace's grandson about the document. Hoyt stated about Billy, then 18: "He was a remarkable character." So Billy stood out: charismatic, brilliant, audacious, and bi-cultural. The Bill of Sale was a great souvenir for the young doctor!

By 1929, Hoyt's intuition paid off: based on owning that Bill of Sale, and knowing Billy, he wrote his book, titled *A Frontier Doctor*.

The Hoyt Bill of Sale, as reflecting the "Regulator Manifesto's" threat of retribution, seems to be Billy's taunt. And it reveals much about him: from handwriting, content, and signature. The horse in question is called a "sorrel," which is a flashy chestnut. Hoyt states in his book that its name was "Dandy Dick." That name says it all.

Dandy Dick had belonged to hated and killed, Tunstall murdering, Ringite Sheriff, William Brady. After Brady's Regulator killing, the horse would have been at Ringman ranches of T.B. Catron or Charles Fritz. One can say that stolen Dandy Dick was, for Billy, "spoils of war."

A Bill of Sale, Billy knew, was needed to protect Hoyt. But it teasingly gave away the horse's audacious theft, while mocking its foul master by providing its precise brands. In this document, Billy began the cocky irony that would persist in his writings as rage's substitute.

Dramatically, Billy used correct legalize. Besides giving date, location, and buyer, he worded a contract. One can only guess how he learned. But Exhibits provided by Alexander McSween to Frank Warner Angel, for his own deposition on John Tunstall's murder, have the wording Billy used. It was: "Know all persons by these presents." Possibly Billy, privately reading over his own deposition at the Lincoln courthouse prior to signing it, found and read McSween's.

Also legal is Billy's getting signed witnessing by a George J. Howard and a James E. McMasters. They were the owners of the store and saloon where the document was apparently written.

As to its penmanship, it is Billy's personalized Spencerian style. It is also his only attempt at Spencerian shading. Though his pen caught and spread ink at the B-B brand.

In addition, after his Angel deposition's more awkward signature on June 8, 1878, Billy must have practiced. The Bill of Sale has a clever and beautiful innovation. He is now "W standing alone, with united "HBonney." The H and B are joined with very clever, intertwined artistry.

Here is the Hoyt Bill of Sale.

On screen is the Hoyt Bill of Sale. Billy headed it precisely as "Tascosa Texas, Thursday October 24th 1878." **[FIGURE 11]** He wrote: "Know all persons by these presents that I do hereby sell and deliver to Henry F. Hoyt one sorrel horse branded BB on left hip and other indistinct branded on shoulders for the sum of Seventyfive $ dollars in hand received. W HBonney

This is a correct and meticulous contract. Billy confirmed both selling and delivering the horse. And he must have asked Hoyt for his middle initial. The sum is legally written as a dollar sign and the word "dollars." The brands are noted. And Billy's adding the so-called "other indistinct" brand is teasing, since rustlers blurred past brands, then added their own. So Billy may be saying that local Ring boss James Dolan, who is thought to have given the horse to Brady, may have stolen it! Also playful is the astronomical price of seventy-five dollars, for this horse given as a gift to likeable Hoyt. And, after the traumas of the Lincoln County War, Billy's resilience comes through. Still a boy, he shows that he is powerful enough to give accomplished Hoyt a great horse.

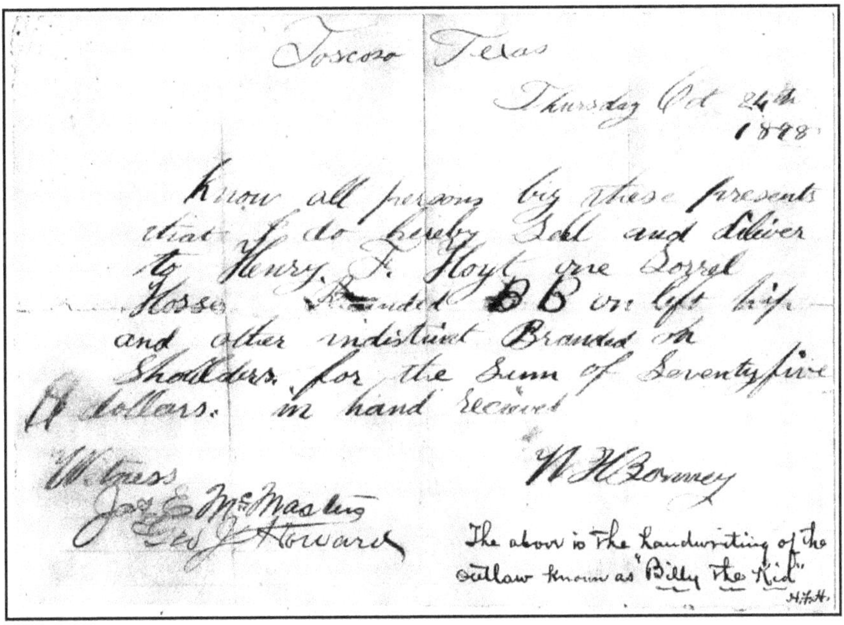

FIGURE 11: Hoyt Bill of Sale. From Panhandle-Plains Historical Museum, Canyon, Texas

That this outlaw life-style was not what Billy wanted, is evidenced by his next letters - only 4½ months away - to Governor Lew Wallace, in which he proposed to risk all to re-enter society free of his Lincoln County War murder indictments. That would free him from the Santa Fe Ring's hold on him by hanging trials if he could be caught.

Those next letters were about the pardon bargain he offered to Governor Lew Wallace. Like his "Regulator Manifesto" and Hoyt Bill of Sale, they were still in the realm of legal negotiation.

I will discuss them in later talks. And they will also contribute to analysis of the pardon bargain itself in talks about my book, *The Lost Pardon of Billy the Kid.*

TALK 6:
BILLY THE KID'S
PARDON BARGAIN LETTERS
FROM BOOK: *BILLY THE KID'S WRITINGS, WORDS, AND WIT*
NOVEMBER 5, 2020

This continues my talks from my book, *Billy the Kid's Writings, Words, and Wit*. This one is about Billy Bonney's famous letters, written in 1879, bargaining for a pardon from New Mexico Territory's Governor, Lew Wallace. Two went to Wallace, and one to Justice of the Peace John "Squire" Wilson. I also authenticated a third letter to Wallace. It's in another talk. And the pardon bargain itself is discussed with my book, *The Lost Pardon of Billy the Kid*.

As background, after the Santa Fe Ring's Lincoln County War atrocities, Ring-shielding President Rutherford B. Hayes merely scapegoated Ringite Territorial Governor Samuel Beach Axtell, by replacing him with Civil War General, Lew Wallace. Unaware of President Hayes's sell-out, New Mexico Territory's citizens hoped for a new era of justice. No one imagined that Wallace himself intended to avoid confronting the dangerous Ring. His strategy was pretending that Lincoln County's troubles had been caused by general outlawry. He would then capture and hang outlaws. Soon after his October 1, 1878 arrival, the Ring helpfully gave him an outlaw list. Of course, they were mostly anti-Ring Regulators. Billy, as "the Kid," was number 14.

Wallace, however, procrastinated. He didn't even visit Lincoln County. On November 13th, 1878, he simply issued an Amnesty

Proclamation for everybody involved in the War, hoping that would settle things. It did not.

Susan McSween, the intrepid widow of Attorney Alexander McSween, the Ring-murdered leader of the freedom fighting faction in the Lincoln County War, took action herself. She hired a Las Vegas, New Mexico, attorney, named Huston Chapman, to prosecute Fort Stanton's Ringite Commander, Nathan Augustus Monroe Dudley, for intervening illegally in the Lincoln County War Battle, to enable the murder of her husband and arson of her home.

But when Attorney Huston Chapman came to Lincoln to meet with Susan McSween, he was murdered on the night of February 18, 1879. The killers were local Ring boss, James Dolan, with his outlaw henchmen, Billy Campbell and Jessie Evans. Added was Dolan's sadistic setting fire to Chapman's body. Billy was an eye-witness, having been present with Dolan to negotiate local peace.

In response to that latest Ring atrocity, Lew Wallace merely increased his efforts to capture his fictional outlaws with Fort Stanton's troops and Lincoln County's current Sheriff, George Kimbrell. Ringites, apparently, red-flagged anti-Ring zealot Billy as an exceptionally bad outlaw. So Wallace offered the astronomical reward of $1,000 for that teenager. That's $10,000 in our day. Then Wallace reluctantly left Santa Fe to come to Lincoln in March of 1879.

In Lincoln, Wallace faked activity by interviewing locals about rustling. Meanwhile, brave Susan McSween hired murdered Chapman's office mate, Attorney Ira Leonard, to continue her case against Dudley. Wallace was about to crash into a wall of reality.

Just then, on what is thought to be March 13, 1879, Wallace got a lucky break. It was a letter from Billy Bonney, the outlaw he knew from the Ring's list as "the Kid." Billy offered to testify as an eye-witness against Huston Chapman's murderers in exchange for a pardon for his Lincoln County War indictments. And it revealed an amazing boy.

One should remember that Billy was born to the generation growing up with the Civil War's promise of equality for all. And even the Revolutionary War, just a century before, was still a vivid inspiration of democracy. In fact, the Lincoln County War freedom fighters had first named themselves Regulators, after pre-Revolutionary War insurgents. So Billy, just three months into being 19, wrote his letter not as a suppliant, but as the equal to any man. In this case, the man was the Governor of the Territory.

Billy blithely dispensed with Wallace's huge dead or alive reward as merely a measure of his worth as a witness to Chapman's murder! And he turned the tables of power. He offered the bargain. Wallace could take it or leave it. He would testify, in exchange for a pardon, for what he called his "Lincoln County War indictments." He left out that they were for the murders of Sheriff William Brady, Deputy George Hindman, and Andrew "Buckshot" Roberts. The issue was that they were in the context of War, not wanton killings. And he needed to be rid of them, not just for his own sake, but because his enemies could use them to kill him. Unsaid, is that they would hang him! And, obviously, if he was killed, he couldn't testify.

To be noted is Billy's correct legalize. He asked not for a pardon, but for the annulment of his indictments - which he calls anully. That is the correct term before sentencing. Pardoning comes after sentencing. And he added character references from quote, "good citizens." He also alluded to the Lincoln County War freedom fight, by stating that his peace meeting with James Dolan was to, quote: "lay aside our arms."

An added touch was that the letter, in his best Spencerian handwriting, was on fine paper. As will be seen in a later talk, that gave me clues about Billy's secret backers.

And, since Billy was a traumatized youth, still in search of a father figure, even included unconsciously in this letter is that longing. So Billy explained that the name "Antrim," which he was sometimes called, was actually just his stepfather's name. He was still available for adoption!

To be noted also, is that, in later life, hypocritical betrayer Lew Wallace would lie that he had made-up the pardon bargain himself to capture the outlaw, Billy the Kid.

Here is Billy's letter.

On screen is Billy's March 13th, 1879 letter to Lew Wallace. **[FIGURE 12]** Billy, wrote, with his characteristic lack of capitalizing at start of sentences and capitalizing words for emphasis, as follows: "To his Excellency the Governor, General Lew Wallace, Dear Sir I have heard that You will give one thousand $ sign dollars for my body which as I can understand it means alive as a witness. I know it is as a witness against those that murderd Mr Chapman. if it was so as that I could appear at

To his Excellency the Governor.
General Lew. Wallace
                    Dear Sir I have
heard that You Will give one thousand
dollars for my body which as I can
understand it means alive. as a Witness,
I know it is as a witness against those
that Murdered Mr Chapman. if it was so
as that I could appear at Court, I could
give the desired information. but I have
indictments against me for things that
happened in the late Lincoln County War
and am afraid to give up because my
Enimies would Kill me, the day Mr Chapman
Was Murdered I Was in Lincoln. at the request
of good Citizens to meet Mr J. J. Dolan
to meet as Friends. So as to be able to lay
aside our arms and go to Work, I was present
When Mr Chapman Was Murdered and know
who did it and if it were not for those
indictments I would have made it clear before now

If it is in your power to Anully
those indictment I hope you will do so
So a to give me a chance to explain.
please Send me an answer telling me what
You can do You can Send answer by bearer
I have no Wish to fight any more indeed
I have not raised an arm Since Your proClamation

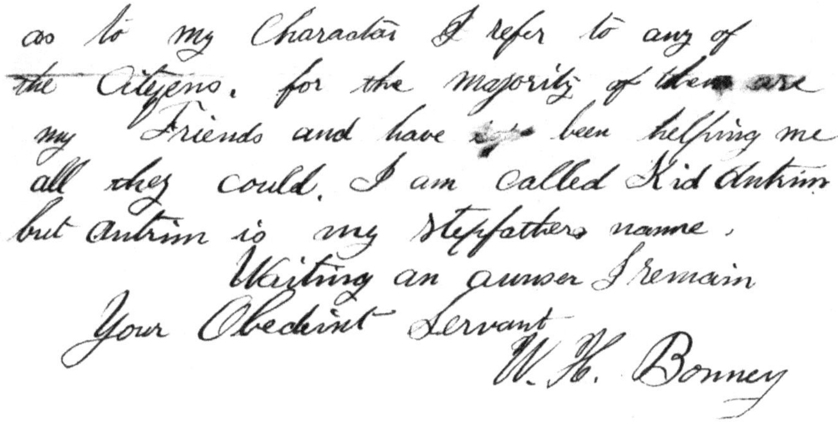
as to my Charactar I refer to any of
the Citizens. for the majority of them are
my Friends and have been helping me
all they could. I am called Kid Antrim
but Antrim is my stepfathers name.
Waiting an annser I remain
Your Obedient Servant
W. H. Bonney

FIGURE 12: Billy Bonney's March 13, 1879 letter to Governor Lew Wallace. Fray Angélico Chávez Historical Library, Santa Fe, New Mexico. Lincoln County Heritage Trust Collection

court, I could give the desired information. but I have indictments against me for things that happened in the late Lincoln County War and am afraid to give up because my Enimies would Kill me the day Mr Chapman was murderded I was in Lincoln, at the request of good citizens to meet Mr J.J. Dolan to meet as Friends, so as to be able to lay aside our arms and go to Work. I was present when Mr Chapman was murderded and know who did it and if it was not for those indictments I would have made it clear before now if it is in your power to Anully those indictments I hope you will do so so as to give me a chance to explain. please send me an annser telling me what you can do You can send annser by bearer

"I have no wish to fight any more indeed I have not raised an arm since your proclamation. As to my Character I refer to any of the Citizens. for the majority of them are my Friends and have been helping me all they could. I am called Kid Antrim but Antrim is my stepfathers name.

"Waiting an annser I remain Your Obedient Servant W.H. Bonney"

Wallace's answer came on March 15th, 1879. He set a meeting in Justice of the Peace John "Squire" Wilson's Lincoln house at 9 o'clock p.m. on the 17th. And he responded to Billy's concern about being killed by his enemies, by promising to make him safe. Wallace told Billy he could trust him. And he told Billy to keep the meeting secret.

No description exists of the March 17th Billy-Wallace meeting, with "Squire" Wilson as witness. But Billy came away believing that Wallace agreed to his pardon bargain.

But circumstances changed almost immediately. For the Chapman murder, Wallace had arrested James Dolan, Billy Campbell, and Jessie Evans. He jailed them in Fort Stanton, apparently ignoring that it was a Ring stronghold. So two days after Wallace's meeting with Billy, on the 19th, Campbell and Evans were allowed to escape. That led to Billy's concern that the pardon bargain would be canceled for less defendants to testify against. Resulting was a letter flurry on March 20th among Billy and Wallace, with "Squire" Wilson, as go-between.

To be noted, is that Wallace was then in Fort Stanton. Wilson was in Lincoln. And, though Billy gave his address as San Patricio, it was unlikely that he actually give away his hide-out. As will be seen in a later talk, he might have been hiding in Lincoln itself.

On March 20th, Billy first wrote to Wilson. And, as an incorrigible tease, he made fun of Wallace's letter of the 15th telling him to keep their meeting secret. So he called Wallace "you-know-who."

This is Billy's letter.

On screen is Billy's letter of March 20th, 1879 to Justice of the Peace John "Squire" Wilson. **[FIGURE 13]** It stated: "San Patricio, Thursday 20th 1879, Friend Wilson. Please tell You know who that I do not know what to do, now as those Prisoners have escaped. So send word by bearer. a note through You it may be that he has made different arrangements if not and he still wants it the same to Send William Hudgins as Deputy, to the Junction tomorrow at three Oclock with some men you know to be all right. Send a note telling me what to do   WHBonney   P.S. do not send Soldiers"

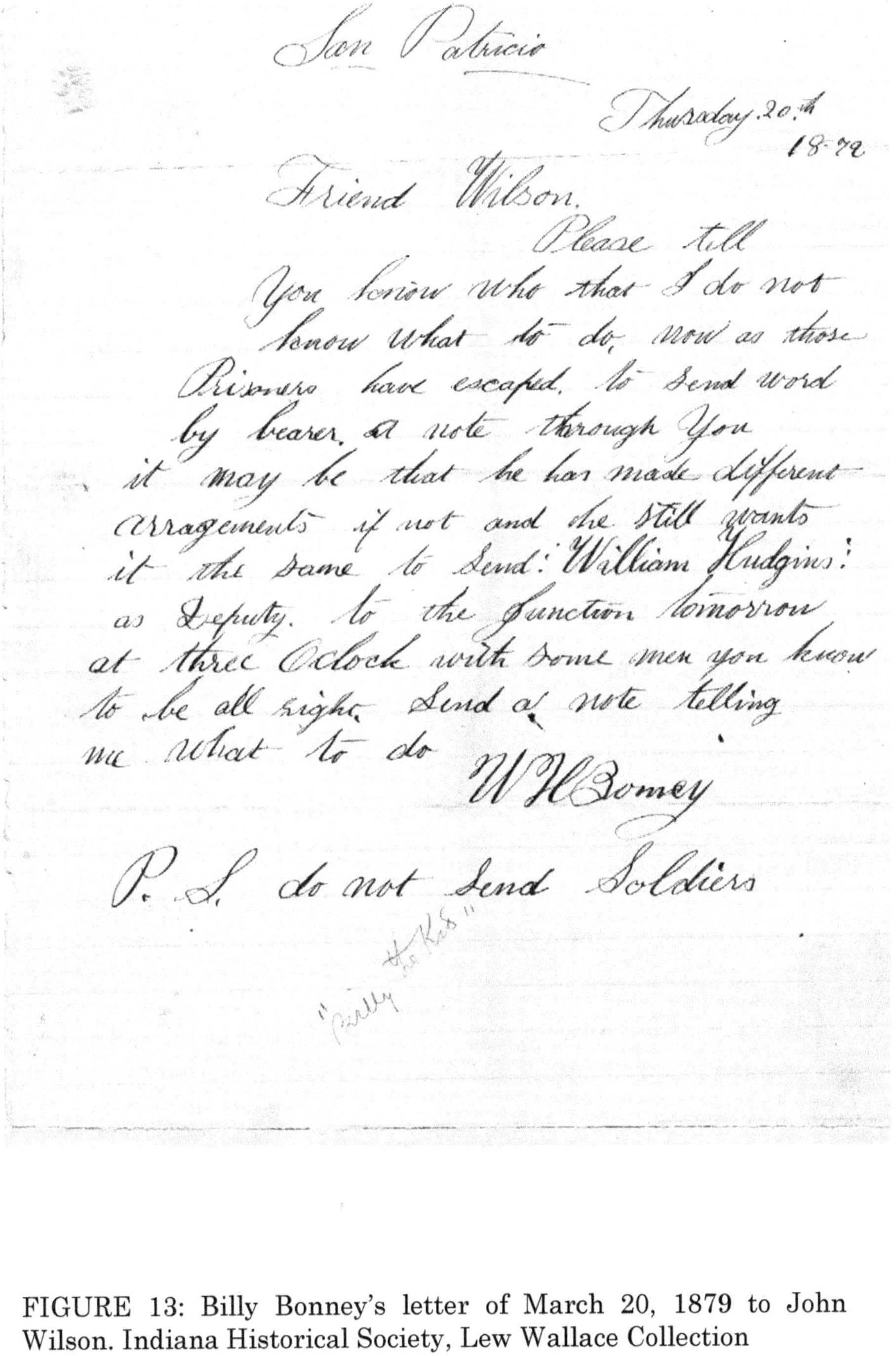

FIGURE 13: Billy Bonney's letter of March 20, 1879 to John Wilson. Indiana Historical Society, Lew Wallace Collection

Wallace responded to Billy's letter. As was his custom, he kept his draft. It stated that the prisoners' escape made no difference to their arrangements. And with ominous slyness, he crossed out: "I will comply with my part if you will with yours." Of course, Billy could not know that Wallace's betrayal of him was in the works. And Wallace agreed to Billy's plan for his sham imprisonment, so he could be housed safely until his testifying.

Billy responded. Here is his second letter to Wallace that day.

On screen is Billy's second letter to Lew Wallace on March 20th, 1879. **[FIGURE 14]** He wrote: "San Patricio, Lincoln County, Thursday 20th 1879, General Lew. Wallace: Sir. I will keep the appointment made. but be Sure and have men come that You can depend on I am not afraid to die like a man fighting but I would not like to be killed like a dog unarmed. tell Kimbal [that was Sheriff Kimbrell] to let his men be placed around the house and for him to come in alone: and he can arrest us. all I am afraid of is that in the Fort we might be poisoned or killed through a window at night. but You can arrange that all right. tell the Commanding Officer to watch Lieutenant Goodwin he would not hesitate to do anything there Will be danger on the road of Somebody Waylaying us to kill us on the road to the Fort. You will never catch those fellows on the road Watch Fritzes. Captain Bacas ranch and the Brewery they Will either go to Seven Rivers or to Jicarillo Mountains they will stay around close untill the scouting parties come in. give a spy a pair of glasses and let him get on the mountain back of Fritzes and watch and if they are there there will be provisions carried to them. it is not my place to advise you, but I am anxious to have them caught, and perhaps know how men hide from Soldiers, better than you. please excuse me for having so much to say, and I still remain Yours Truly, W H. Bonney, P.S. I have changed my mind Send Kimbal to Gutieres just below San Patricio one mile, because Sanger and Ballard are or were great friends of Camels [meaning Billy Campbell] Ballard told me – today is crossed out - yesterday to leave for you were doing everything to catch me. it was a blind to get me to leave tell Kimbal not to come before 3 oclock for I may not be there before"

San Patricio
Lincoln County
Thursday 20th 1879

General Lew Wallace;

Sir, I will keep
the appointment I made.
but be sure and have men come
that You can depend on I am not
afraid to die like a man fighting
but I would not like to be killed
like a dog unarmed, tell Kimbal
to let his men be placed around
the house. and for him to come in
alone; and he can arrest us. all I am
afraid of is that in the Fort we
might be poinined, or killed through
a window at night. but You can
arrange that all right. tell the
Comanding Officer to watch) Let Goodwin
he would not hesitate to do anything
there will be danger on the road of
Somebody Waylaying us to kill us on the
road to the Fort.

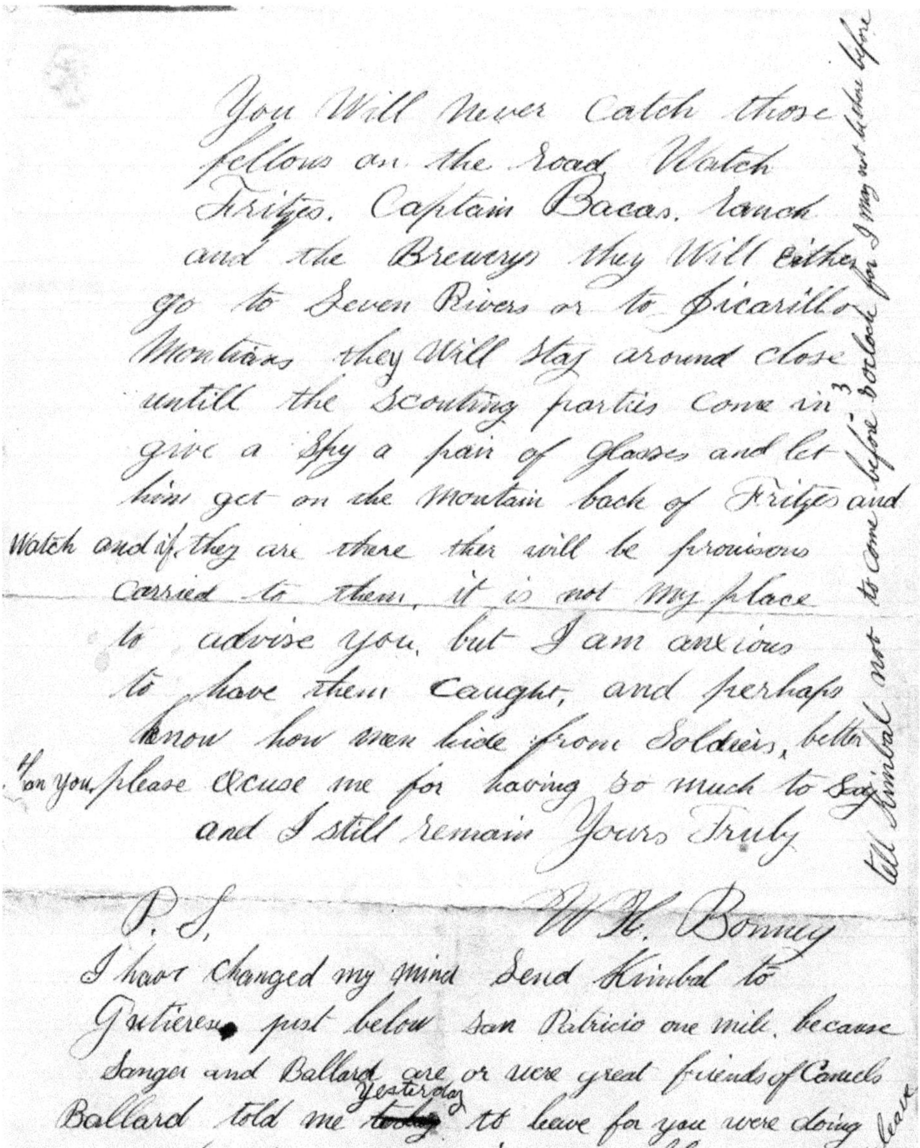

You Will never Catch those
fellows on the road Watch
Fritzes, Captain Bacas, ranch
and the Brewerys they Will either
go to Seven Rivers or to Jicarilla
Montains they Will Stay around close
untill the Scouting parties come in
give a Spy a pair of glasses and let
him get on the mountain back of Fritzes and
Watch and if they are there ther will be provisions
carried to them. it is not my place
to advise you, but I am anxious
to have them caught, and perhaps
know how men hide from Soldiers, better
than you. please excuse me for having so much to say
and I still remain Yours Truly

W. H. Bonney

P.S.
I have changed my mind Send Kimbal to
Gutierez just below San Patricio one mile, because
Sanger and Ballard are or were great friends of Camels
Ballard told me ~~today~~ yesterday to leave for you were doing
everything to catch me. it was a blind to get me to leave

tell Kimbal not to come before 3 oclock for I may not be there before

FIGURE 14: Billy Bonney's letter of March 20, 1879 to Lew Wallace. Indiana Historical Society, Lew Wallace Collection

These dangerous plans required Billy trusting Wallace. Arrest was what Billy had avoided for the past year, knowing he was a Ring target. And he believed he'd be incarcerated in Fort Stanton, a Ring stronghold. He referred specifically to Ringite Lieutenant, Millard Filmore Goodwin, who was possibly one of the white officers shooting at him and others during their escape from the burning McSween house in the Lincoln County War Battle.

Billy also realistically warned about his being assassinated on the way to a Fort Stanton incarceration. This is important to remember, because, in two months, he would bravely chose to testify against its treasonous Commander, N.A.M. Dudley, for his own anti-Ring agenda, not for the pardon bargain. Thereby he risked that dangerous transport from Lincoln to the Fort for two days of testifying in the military Court of Inquiry.

Billy's letter also displays his literary skill. He wrote: "I am not afraid to die like a man fighting but I would not like to be killed like a dog unarmed." Note his reference to being a fighting Regulator soldier.

And cocky Billy also tried to enlist Wallace in that fight for justice; including giving that past Civil War General advice on how to capture the escapees! And he provided correct information that Charles Fritz, brother of Emil Fritz, the founder of the Ring's Lincoln mercantile monopoly, called "The House," might shelter Billy Campbell and Jessie Evans. Billy identified another Ringite as "Baca." That was Saturnino Baca, the Hispanic traitor in the Lincoln County War Battle. And when Billy referred to quote "arresting us" for the sham jailing, he meant his friend and fellow Regulator, Tom O'Folliard, who was to accompany him.

Billy's wry humor also came through. He wrote, quote, "it is not my place to advise you," even though much of his letter did just that. And he added that, quote: "perhaps [I] know how men hide from Soldiers, better than you." That was a not too subtle reference to Wallace's having unsuccessfully sent soldiers to capture him as an outlaw.

Billy's overwrought excitement about this new father-figure was evident even to him. He apologized in the letter's end for, quote: "having so much to say." And he signed formally as W.H. Bonney. That was William Henry Bonney, his alias.

His postscript was a hectic addition of precautions. And he made clear that their plans might not be as secret as Wallace thought, since Billy Campbell's friend had already tried to trick him into leaving, instead of staying and testifying. So Billy well knew that everything depended on Wallace's honoring their bargain. And Billy's not wanting Sheriff Kimbrell to show up early in San Patricio to arrest him, was another clue that he might not have been there when he wrote the letter.

Billy believed he made a pardon bargain with Wallace. He also believed that, in Wallace, he had found an ally to fight the Ring. With that optimism, he was sham arrested on March 21st, 1879, only four days after meeting Wallace face-to-face. And Billy had an unexpected boost to safety. His anti-Ring Lincoln friend, Juan Patrón, the town Jailor, offered to keep him in his home, instead of putting him in dangerous Fort Stanton. And the key defendant was still in custody: local Ring boss, James Dolan.

As will be seen in subsequent talks, incarcerated Billy's Lincoln next-door neighbor was Lew Wallace. Soon added to Billy's words was Wallace's interview of him. It will be discussed in my talks about my book, *The Lost Pardon of Billy the Kid*. And there was an additional letter Billy wrote to Wallace for the pardon bargain. It was unknown until I authenticated it. That will be in a talk of its own.

TALK 7:

AUTHENTICATING A NEW BILLY THE KID LETTER

FROM BOOK: *BILLY THE KID'S WRITINGS, WORDS, AND WIT*

NOVEMBER 12, 2020

This talk is about my authenticating a new Billy the Kid letter. It's from my book, Billy the Kid's Writings, Words, and Wit.

For decades, a mysterious, handwritten, letter fragment was known to be in the vast collected papers of past New Mexico Territory Governor Lew Wallace. Those papers had been donated in the first half of the 20th century. They became the Lew Wallace Collection in the Indiana Historical Society in Indianapolis.

The fragment is a two-sided, single page. It is signed just Billie. It's spelled B-I-L-L-I-E, not B-I-L-L-Y!

When I began to research Billy the Kid, I got its typed, two page copy. On top, was the copyist's brief commentary. It was dated May 14th, 1947. I got it from the papers of early Old West researcher, Herman Weisner. They are in the Rio Grande Historical Collections of New Mexico State University at Las Cruces. But Weisner had merely photocopied this unknown copyist's work.

The commentary indicated that the copyist had seen the original fragment. It said: "Page torn from notebook about 8 by 9, ruled, black ink, two sides. Pencil notation in different handwriting at top of sheet. Handwriting resembles, but is not identical, with letters signed Bonney." In parentheses was 1880. So that copyist believed it was not a Billy the Kid letter, and that its date was 1880.

The Indiana Historical Society was ambivalent. The fragment was kept in the Lew Wallace Collection's archival box for 1880. Billy the Kid's known letters were kept in a special vault. And the 1880 date was just a guess by a past Indiana Historical Society archivist, and included a question mark.

The mystery deepens. Robert Mullin, an early Billy the Kid historian, had the same copy in his papers in the Midland, Texas, Nita Stewart Haley Memorial Library. But he had scrawled on its top: "Important, Billy's letter."

So disputed authorship kept the fragment in limbo.

As a novice Billy the Kid researcher, I ignored the "Billie" letter fragment based on the copyist's note. But 11 years later, when analyzing Billy's letters for my book, *Billy the Kid's Writings, Words, and Wit*, I became intrigued by its content. I decided to check its handwriting myself.

The fax arrived from the Indiana Historical Society. It took my breath away. It was obviously by Billy Bonney. Contrary to the copyist's opinion, its Spencerian penmanship perfectly matched Billy's handwriting in his March, 1879 pardon bargain letters to Lew Wallace and to Justice of the Peace John "Squire" Wilson. But the archivist's 1880 dating misled the copyist. Billy's 1880 and 1881 letters were written when he was on the run or in jail. He had no desk to properly write Spencerian style. So the script was cramped.

And the ragged left margin, called mistakenly by the copyist "torn from notebook," would ultimately assist in confirming the place and date of that letter's writing.

But what about its signature? It was B-I-L-L-I-E, not B-I-L-L-Y. My sleuthing began.

As to the Billie signature, Billy Bonney used many names. By birth, he was Henry McCarty. As a stepson, he was Henry Antrim. And he invented William Henry Bonney, in 1877, as an alias. And his other known signatures used Bonney and just: W.H., W., W$\underline{m}$, or "William" itself.

Intriguingly, Billy's name, with an I-E, is in a diary entry by a Sallie Chisum. She was cattle king, John Chisum's, pretty niece. Amusingly, she kept a diary listing presents from her many suitors - including Billy. She called him Willie, as W-I-L-L-I-E. She wrote: "Indian Tobacco sack presented to me on the 13 of

August 1878 by William Bonney. Two candy hearts given me by Willie Bonney on the 22 of August."

Also, Billy may have always spelled Billy with an I-E. In his December 12, 1880 letter to Governor Lew Wallace, he cited a Billy Wilson. He spelled it B-I-L-L-I-E.

So, discovery one was that Billy the Kid spelled his name as B-I-L-L-I-E!

Next came frustration. What if the fragment's missing front page or pages had accidentally gotten mixed in with other Lew Wallace Collection papers? So I went to Indianapolis. For weeks, I turned every one of its thousands of pages. The missing front was not there.

On a long-shot, I then went to Bloomington. There, Lew Wallace's literary papers are in the Indiana State University's Lilly Library. I turned very page of all his original manuscripts - including *Ben-Hur* – looking for the missing front. It was not there.

I had to give up.

So historical analysis of this "Billie" letter depended entirely on clues in it. Little did 1 anticipate that it held new insight into Billy's pardon negotiations, his thoughts on the Lincoln County War, and his possible secret allies. And, I'm pleased to say, that after my authentication, it is now in the vault with Billy Bonney's other letters.

The fragment is in excellent condition. It measures 8 inches wide x 9 ¾ inches long. It has a ragged left side, which made the copyist guess it was torn from a notebook. Its other three edges are sharply cut.

Its fancy, medium weight paper is off-white. It has faint blue, horizontal guidelines, leaving a top margin bigger on the back than the front. The handwriting, however, starts high on both sides - as if not wasting paper.

On the front side's upper left corner is a small embossure of a "lady's head."

The writing is dark brown. That's typical of aged, oxidized, iron-gall ink. And the signature is merely B-I-L-L-I-E.

For handwriting comparison, I'll show you an excerpt from a known Billy letter and the "Billie" letter fragment.

On screen, is an excerpt from Billy's March 13th, 1879 pardon bargain letter to Lew Wallace **[FIGURE 15]**, and an excerpt from the "Billie" letter fragment. **[FIGURE 16]** As you can see, Billy's uniquely modified Spencerian script is in both.

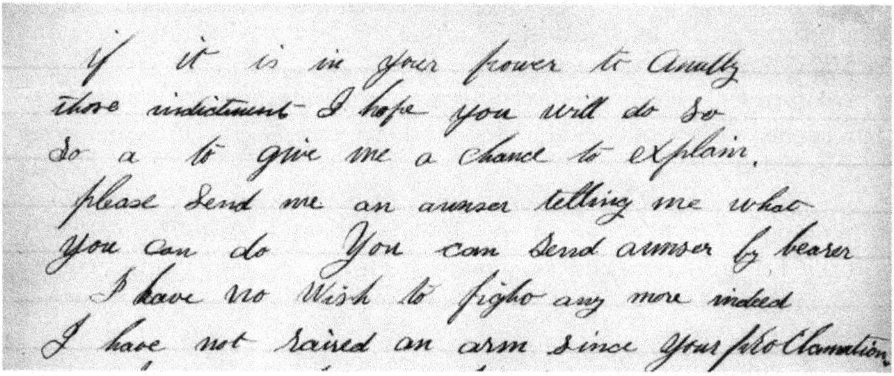

If it is in your power to Anully
those indictment I hope you will do so
so a to give me a chance to explain.
please send me an annser telling me what
you can do You can send annser by bearer
I have no wish to fight any more indeed
I have not raised an arm since your proclamation

FIGURE 15: Billy Bonney's letter of March 13, 1879 to Lew Wallace. Indiana Historical Society, Lew Wallace Collection

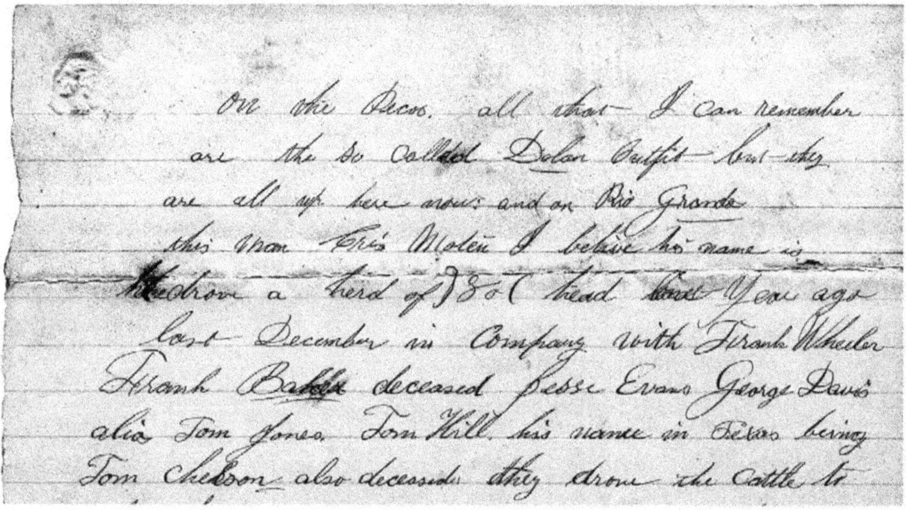

On the Pecos. all that I can remember
are the so called Dolan Outfit but they
are all up here now and on Rio Grande
this man Cris Moten I believe his name is
drove a herd of 800 head one year ago
last December in Company with Frank Wheeler
Frank Baker deceased Jesse Evans George Davis
alias Tom Jones Tom Hill his name in Texas being
Tom Chelson also deceased they drove the cattle to

FIGURE 16: "Billie" letter fragment. Indiana Historical Society, Lew Wallace Collection

I also compared penmanship of specific words in the fragment and in Billy's known letters. The words were: "JJ Dolan," "John Chisum," "Seven Rivers," and "Wallace." They matched.

I also compared the fragment's "Yours respectfully" closing to Billy's "Yours respect" in his known letters. They matched.

Here is the comparison of the "Billie" letter's signature with Billy's writing of the B-I-L-L-I-E name for Billy Wilson in his December 12th, 1880 letter to Lew Wallace.

On screen is the name "Billie Wilson" from Billy's December 12th, 1880 letter to Lew Wallace. **[FIGURE 17]** Its B-I-L-L-I-E matches the fragment's "Billie" signature.]

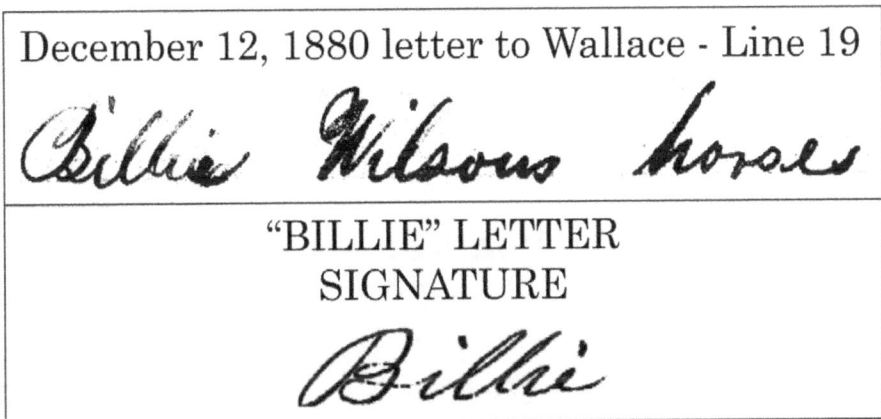

FIGURE 17: Comparison of "Billie" in December 12, 1880 letter to Lew Wallace with "Billie" signature in the fragment.

Billy also had tell-tale grammatical errors in his known letters. He didn't capitalize sentences' starts. He capitalized words for emphasis.

Here's the "Billie" letter fragment showing those same errors.

On screen is the "Billie" letter fragment showing Billy's no capitalizations at sentences' starts, and capitalizing words for emphasis. **[FIGURE 18]**

NO CAPITALIZATION AT
SENTENCE START

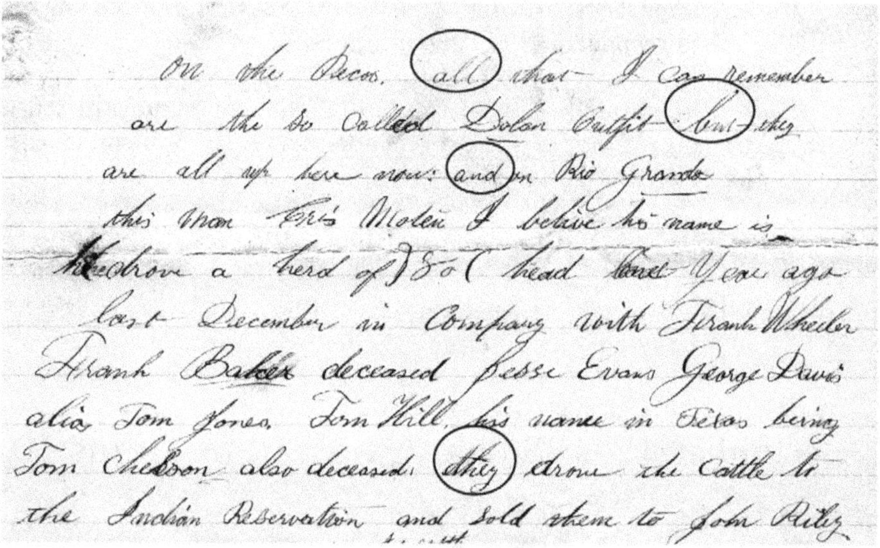

CAPITALIZATION OF WORDS
FOR EMPHASIS

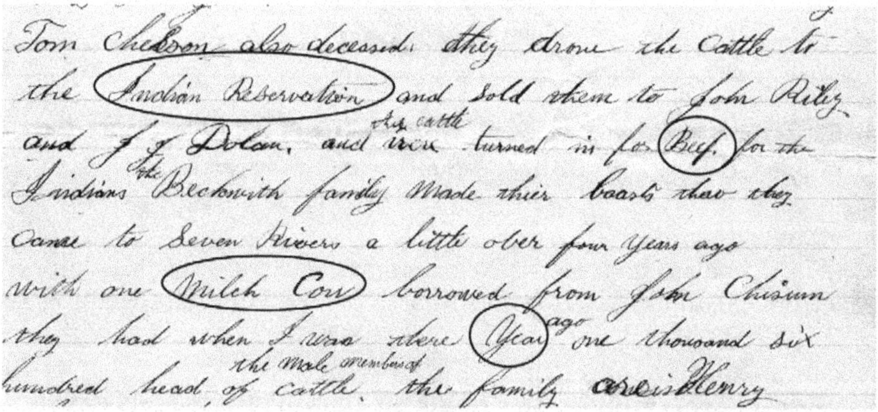

FIGURE 18: Comparison of "Billie" in December 12, 1880 letter
to Lew Wallace with "Billie" signature in the fragment

Billy had excellent grammar and a sophisticated vocabulary. But he wrongly used "seen" as the past tense of "see" - instead of "saw." He does that in his May 28th, 1879 Dudley Court of Inquiry testimony about seeing those killed in the Lincoln County War Battle. He said, "I seen five killed, I could not swear to who killed them, I seen some of them that fired."

That "seen-saw" error appears twice in the "Billie" letter fragment. It appeared as, quote, "when I seen them last," and quote, "I afterwards seen some of the cattle."

The "Billie" letter fragment's embossed "lady's head" is also a clue.

Luckily, the Indiana Historical Society has a superlative conservation department. One of its experts worked with me to compare the fragment to the few other "lady's head" stationery letters I had found when searching the Lew Wallace collection for the missing front. Two were by Billy himself. The others were by people in Lincoln.

The expert told me that because 19th century paper was hand-made, each batch had unique pulp fiber patterns, like fingerprints. And paper was not only cut into single sheets. It was also cut as a double sized sheet. That was folded into what was called a folio - like a greeting card.

The expert concluded that all the "lady's head" stationery users' sheets - including Billy's two known letters - were from the same batch as the fragment itself!

What about the folio format? The fragment's torn left margin, which made the copyist mistakenly call it "torn from a notebook," actually came from tearing apart a folded folio, leaving the ragged left margin - as if you tore a greeting card in half. As a bonus, one of the "lady's head" letters by a Lincoln user was still a folded folio. That left the possibility that the fragment's missing front could have been a whole folio. That meant four more pages. What a loss to history!

Then came the "lady's head" embossure. From the 1850's through the 1880's, stationery was embellished on its upper left margin by a stamping machine. Merchants could buy a machine - like modern notary stamps - to decorate blank stationery.

Here is the "lady's head" embossure on the "Billie" letter fragment.

On screen is the "lady's head" embossure on the "Billie" letter fragment. **[FIGURE 19]** Its stamping isn't sharp. That means it's a folio's second page. The first page was sharpest.

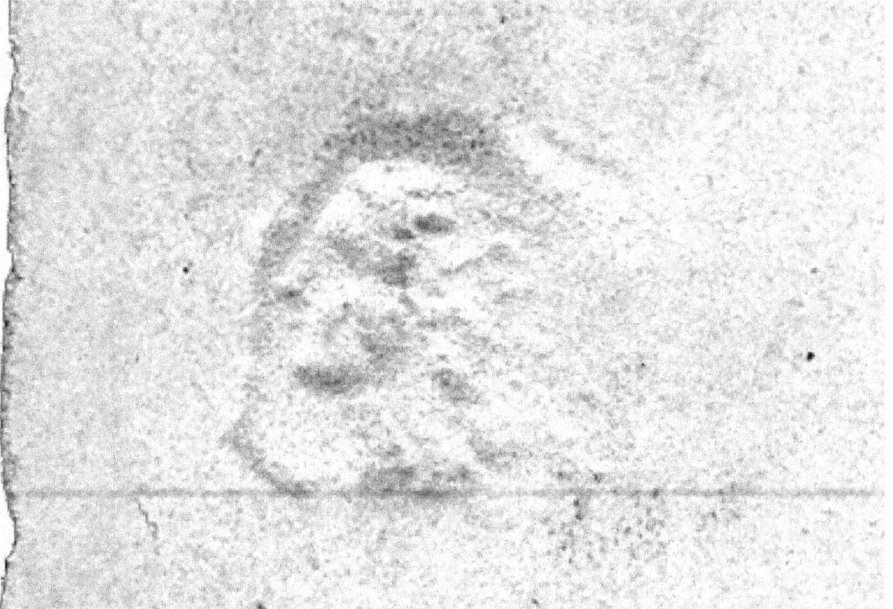

FIGURE 19: Enlarged "Lady's head" stamp from the "Billie" letter fragment

Important for authenticating and dating the "Billie" letter fragment was my discovering that two of Billy Bonney's known signed letters, both dated March 20th, 1879, were on the same "lady's head" stationery. They were to Justice of the Peace John "Squire" Wilson and to Governor Lew Wallace for his pardon bargain.

Furthermore, all the "lady's head" stationery users wrote from Lincoln in just a 4 month time-frame of March to June of 1879.

Besides Billy, they were all anti-Ring. They were Billy's jailor, Juan Patrón; Justice of the Peace John "Squire" Wilson, who lent his home for the Billy-Wallace meeting; George Taylor, the assistant to Billy's attorney, Ira Leonard; and Deputy Sheriff Robert M. Gilbert, who had been on Ring- murdered John Tunstall's Coroner's Jury.

But who was the embossed lady? Did she have special meaning to the users?

The most perfect "lady's head" embossure is on a letter of March 29th, 1879 by Juan Patrón to Governor Lew Wallace. Here she is.

On screen is the crisp "lady's head" embossure on Jailer, Juan Patrón's March 29th, 1879 letter to Lew Wallace. **[FIGURE 20]** She has a classical profile. She has a rod, topped by a drooping cap. She's not recognizable to most modern viewers.

FIGURE 20: Enlarged "Lady Liberty" stamp from Juan Patrón's letter of March 29, 1879 to Governor Lew Wallace

But in Billy's day, she was obvious. Her cap is the give-away. The "lady's head" is "Lady Liberty," holding her liberty cap on a pole.

Her image goes back to the Roman Empire. There, the conical Phrygian cap symbolized freedom, because liberated slaves wore it.

That symbol of freedom was adopted in 18th century, revolutionary France as goddess Liberty. In 1775, a Jean-Michel Moreau painted her as a Roman with a Phrygian cap topping her war pike. By 1790, in France, that cap was called the "liberty cap."

The "Lady Liberty" symbol also came to the United States by the late 18th century. It was used on coins and other public venues through the 19th century. Mostly in profile, she wore the liberty cap, or held it on a pike, like in revolutionary France.

"Lady Liberty" on the "Billie" letter fragment is that revolutionary image. And its users were indeed fighting for liberty from the Santa Fe Ring.

Then we come to the "Billie" letter fragment's content. It adds to the authentication by showing special knowledge that only Billy would have. As to its recipient, it appears to be a follow-up to Billy's interview with Governor Lew Wallace on March 23, 1879. He was then in their pardon bargain's sham jailing in Juan Patrón's house.

Referenced were Lincoln County War incidents. There is the 1878 Regulator killings in March of Frank Baker. There is the April killing of Andrew "Buckshot" Roberts. It was one of the indictments for which Billy sought pardon. There is July's house arson and killing of Alexander McSween. The fragment also has the phrase, quote: "places I mentioned." That implies adding to Billy's prior Wallace interview.

As such, the fragment is unique among Billy Bonney's letters. It is less a pardon plea, and more a sharing of Billy's insights. How frustrating to think that its missing front could have had Billy's full description of the Lincoln County War!

Here's my commentary on the "Billie" letter fragment's content.

On screen is the "Billie" letter fragment. **[FIGURE 21]**

On the Pecos. all that I can remember are the so called Dolan Outfit but they are all up here now: and on Rio Grande this man Cris Moten I beleive his name is drove a herd of 780 head one year ago last December in Company with Frank Wheeler Frank Baker deceased Jesse Evans George Davis alias Tom Jones. Tom Hill, his name in Texas being Tom Chedron, also deceased. they drove the Cattle to the Indian Reservation and sold them to John Rilzy and J J Dolan, and were turned in for Beef, for the Indians the Beckwith family made their boasts that they came to Seven Rivers a little over four years ago with one Milch Cow borrowed from John Chisum they had when I was there one year ago one thousand six hundred head of cattle. the male members of the family are Henry beckwith and John Beckwith Robert Beckwith was killed the time McSweens house was burned. Charles Robert Olinger and Wallace Olinger are of the same gang. their cattle ranch is situated at Rock Corral twelve miles below Seven Rivers on the Pecos. Potton and Pierce are still below them forty miles from Seven Rivers there are four

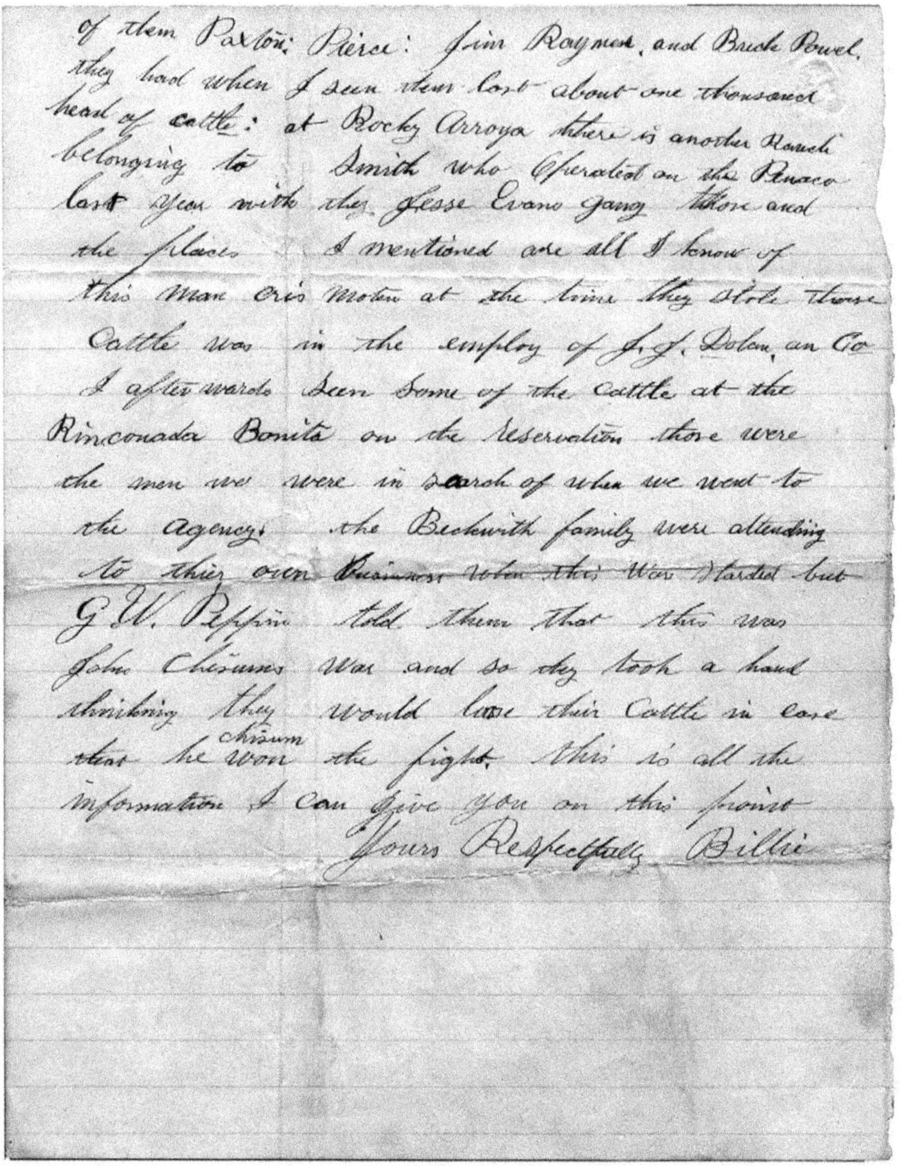

of them Paxton: Pierce: Jim Raymer, and Buck Powel.
they had when I seen them last about one thousand
head of cattle: at Rocky Arroya there is another Ranch
belonging to   Smith who Operated on the Penaco
last year with the Jesse Evans gang there and
the places   I mentioned are all I know of
this Man Cris Moten at the time they stole those
Cattle was   in the employ of J. J. Dolan, an Co
I afterwards seen some of the cattle at the
Rinconada Bonita on the Reservation those were
the men we were in search of when we went to
the agency;   the Beckwith family were attending
to their own business when this war started but
G. W. Peppin   told them that this was
John Chisum's war and so they took a hand
thinking they   would lose their cattle in case
   he chisum
that he won the fight. this is all the
information I can give you on this point
              Yours Respectfully Billie

FIGURE 21: "Billie" letter fragment. Indiana Historical Society.
Lew Wallace Collection

It starts; quote: "on the Pecos." That ends a sentence. But known is that "on the Pecos" were Lincoln County's participants in strife. There was cattle king, John Chisum, who betrayed his alliance with John Tunstall by refusing aid to Alexander McSween in the Lincoln County War. Chisum even broke his promise to pay the Regulators' wages. "On the Pecos" were also Ringite Seven Rivers rustlers. They were the McSween side's murderous opponents in the Lincoln County War.

Billy continues: "all that I can remember are the so called Dolan outfit, but they are all up here now." This show's Billy's special knowledge. By 1879, James Dolan and his henchmen lost the Pecos Cow Camp. They went bankrupt in 1878 from competition with John Tunstall. Intriguingly, Billy underlined Dolan. And Dolan was the Santa Fe Ring boss in Lincoln County.

Billy continues: "and on the Rio Grande this man Cris Moten, I believe his name is, he drove a herd of 80 head one year ago last December in company with Frank Wheeler." That "Cris Moten" is possibly "Dutch Chris." And the "Rio Grande" adds to Billy's description of a rustler gang in his interview with Lew Wallace on March 23rd, 1879. There, he said: "in the direction of the Rio Grande. Frank Wheeler ... and Dutch Chris are supposed to have used this trail taking a bunch of cattle over."

Billy continues listing rustlers; stating: "Frank Baker deceased, Jesse Evans, George Davis alias Tom Jones, Tom Hill, his name in Texas being Tom Chelson also deceased." Baker is underlined. Baker's "deceased" is snide. He was actually killed by the Regulators - including Billy - when escaping arrest for John Tunstall's murder. So Billy was listing Ring outlaws relevant to the Lincoln County War: Jessie Evans's boys. They were Frank Baker, George Davis, and Tom Hill. All were involved in murdering Tunstall. And Jessie Evans was also involved in murdering Attorney Huston Chapman. Billy also knew the obscure fact that Tom Hill was dead. He knew Hill from riding with Jessie Evans's gang in September of 1877. Unrelated to Lincoln County War issues, Hill had recently been shot dead in a stock theft gone wrong.

Billy continues: "They drove the cattle to the Indian Reservation and sold them to John Riley and JJ Dolan. And the cattle were turned in for Beef for the Indians." This amazing statement shows Billy's insider's knowledge of the outlaw dynamics of the Santa Fe Ring. Key was that the Ringites rustled cattle to meet beef contracts for the Mescalero Indian Reservation and for Fort Stanton. Tunstall was murdered because he was making legitimate cattle ranches to compete for those beef contracts.

Billy continues: "The Beckwith family made their boasts that they came to Seven Rivers a little over four years ago with one milch cow borrowed from John Chisum. They had, when I was there a year ago, one thousand six hundred head of cattle." This is Billy's joke. He calls rustling "borrowing." So the Beckwith's big herd came from borrowing. In fact, like the other Seven Rivers boys, they stole from John Chisum's giant herd of 80,000 cattle.

Billy continues: "The male members of the family are Henry Beckwith and John Beckwith. Robert Beckwith was killed the time McSween's house was burned." This is Billy's insider's knowledge of the Lincoln County War Battle. Robert Beckwith - underlined by Billy - was killed on July 19th, 1878 in friendly fire. He was about to serve fake arrest warrants on Alexander McSween at his burning house. At that moment, Sheriff Peppin's Ringite posse fired at McSween. They killed Beckwith too.

Billy continues: "Charles – there's a blank - Robert Olinger, and Wallace Olinger are of the same gang. Their cattle ranch is situated at Rock Corral twelve miles below Seven Rivers on the Pecos." Billy was very clear about the Olinger brothers, Robert and Wallace. Their rustling gang was the Ringite Seven Rivers boys.

Billy continues: "Paxton and Pierce are still below them forty miles from Seven Rivers. There are four of them Paxton, Pierce, Jim Raymen, and Buck Powel. They had when I seen them last about one thousand head of cattle." Billy is reporting on another rustler gang. And he is making his seen-saw grammatical error.

Billy continues: "At Rocky Arroya there is another Ranch belonging to – there is a blank for the first name - Smith who Operated on the Penasco last year with the Jesse Evans gang." So Billy links this Smith to Jessie Evans. That means Ring-related rustling.

Billy continues: "Those and the places I mentioned ..." This use of "mentioned" implies a past conversation. It is likely Billy's Wallace interview on March 23rd, 1879 about outlawry.

Billy continues that the mentioned things, quote: "are all I know of this man. Chris Moten at the time they stole those Cattle was in the employ of J.J. Dolan and Co." Billy links Chris Moten to James Dolan's mercantile business, named J.J. Dolan and Company.

Billy continues with insider information. He stated: "I afterwards seen some of the cattle at the Rinconada Bonita on the reservation. Those were the men we were in search of when we went to the Agency." This is Billy's eye-witness description of the Regulators going to privately owned Blazer's Mill. It was within the Mescalero Indian Reservation. Billy calls it the "Agency" because Indian Agent Frederick Godfroy had his office in a building there. The Regulators encountered Tunstall murder posseman, Andrew "Buckshot" Roberts. He was at that building's post office. He was killed resisting arrest. Billy also confirmed that Chris Moten's rustled cattle ended up fulfilling James Dolan's beef contract through "the House" to the Mescalero Indian Reservation.

Billy continues: "The Beckwith family were attending to their own business when this War started, but G.W. Peppin told them that this was John Chisum's War and so they took a hand thinking they would loose their cattle in case that he Chisum won the fight." This is again Billy's insider information. The Seven Rivers ranchers feared that Chisum would take back his rustled cattle. And Ringite Sheriff George W. Peppin was recruiting anti-McSween fighters for the Lincoln County War. Note that Billy said, quote "he Chisum." He may have picked up that legalize when giving his deposition to Investigator Frank Warner Angel, on June 8th, 1878, about John Tunstall's murder.

Billy continues: "This is all the information I can give you on this point." That clipped conclusion matches Billy's upcoming testimony in the Dudley military Court of Inquiry. Billy said then; quote: "When I escaped from the house - meaning McSween's burning house - three soldiers fired at me from the Tunstall store, outside corner of the store. That's all I know in regards to it."

The fragment is signed: "Yours Respectfully Billie," as B-I-L-L-I-E.

Can we date the "Billie" letter fragment? For clues, we have Billy's known dated letters on the "Lady Liberty" stationery, dated letters by others using it, and its content.

As seen, the letter fragment's Spencerian handwriting matches Billy's three, signed, pardon bargain letters in March of 1879. That points to writing in that month.

And before Billy went into his sham jailing for the pardon bargain, he wrote his two "Lady Liberty" stationery letters on March 20th, 1879; after having been in "Lady Liberty" stationery-user "Squire" Wilson's house three days earlier. That was when he met with Governor Wallace. He might have gotten the paper then.

And, after Billy's sham jailing, on March 21st, at Juan Patrón's home, the "Billie" letter fragment was written on the second folio page of a letter which Patrón wrote to Lew Wallace on March 29th on that folio's first page.

By June, the "Lady Liberty" paper ran out. Its users switched to different stationery.

The "Billie" letter fragment's content adds clues. It follows-up Billy's March 23rd, 1879 interview with Wallace. And it said "mentioned," referring to a prior conversation. And it adds to that interview. And, with Wallace housed next door to Juan Patrón's house, delivery was easy.

So I dated the "Billie" letter fragment to the day after Wallace's interview with Billy at Patrón's house. That made it March 24th, 1879.

The fragment was in Wallace's collected papers. Apparently, when he left Lincoln in May of 1879, he took it, with Billy's other letters, and his interview notes with Billy. So Wallace, living out of a suitcase in Lincoln, may have accidentally lost its front pages.

Does the "Billie" letter fragment reveal more about the real Billy Bonney?

As to the B-I-L-L-I-E spelling, we've seen that Billy used Willie, as W-I-L-L-I-E, when wooing Sallie Chisum. Was Billy now wooing Governor Wallace? In March of 1879, Wallace came to Lincoln after Huston Chapman's murder. He interviewed Lincolnites about outlawry. All believed he sought justice against the Santa Fe Ring. So the "Billie" letter fragment adds to Billy's Wallace interview about general Territorial outlawry. It adds Lincoln County War issues. Billy was wooing Wallace to the freedom fighter side. And Billy was on a life-long search for a father-figure. So his presenting himself as just Billie, like a child, indicates that Wallace was now chosen. That makes more cruel Wallace's betrayal of the pardon bargain - as we shall see in a later talk.

But can more be extrapolated?

All the "Lady Liberty" stationery users were anti-Ring. Billy may have gotten that stationery for his two, known, March 20th, 1879, pardon bargain letters from Justice of the Peace Wilson, in whose house he met with Wallace on the 17th. And the "Billie" letter fragment used the back half of the folio split by Juan Patrón for his own letter to Wallace on March 29th. Billy was there in his sham jailing. Obviously, Patrón gave him the paper.

That led me to a revisionist history conclusion. At least Wilson and Patrón were helping their Lincoln County War hero, Billy, with his pardon quest. They gave good paper for impressive letters. Possibly they helped him strategize the bargain. They lent their homes to him: Wilson for his meeting with Wallace, Patrón for his sham jailing. And don't forget that the month before, on February 18th, the Ring assassinated the man who brought hope: Attorney Huston Chapman. Billy was going to testify against the killers. That would make the "Lady Liberty" stamp a secret declaration of freedom.

And, since the "Lady Liberty" paper was only in Lincoln, that's where Billy may have been hiding with his friends. Not in San Patricio, as his March 20th letter to Lew Wallace had stated.

Limited supply of "Lady Liberty" paper grants one more leap. It may have come from Ring-murdered John Tunstall's Lincoln store. He may have embossed its "Lady Liberty" there, knowing full well who she was. So Tunstall's symbol of his fight against the Ring may have lived grandly on.

The "Billie" letter fragment is, thus, a tantalizing part of Billy's pardon bargaining with Governor Lew Wallace. It will also be discussed when I talk about my book, *The Lost Pardon of Billy the Kid*.

TALK 8:
BILLY THE KID'S TESTIMONIES
FROM BOOK: *BILLY THE KID'S WRITINGS, WORDS, AND WIT*
NOVEMBER 17, 2020

This talk is about Billy Bonney's legal testimonies exposing Santa Fe Ring criminals. Its information comes from my book, *Billy the Kid's Writings, Words, and Wit*. As I discuss in other talks, in that time-frame, he also wrote letters seeking justice.

Billy's testimonies prove he was a political zealot. In 1878, he risked Ring arrest to come to Lincoln for a deposition to Presidential Investigator, Frank Warner Angel, about John Tunstall's murder. In 1879, for his pardon bargain with Governor Lew Wallace, he risked transport to a hanging trial, to testify in Lincoln County's Grand Jury against the Ringite murderers of Huston Chapman. The next month was his own anti-Ring agenda. He risked Ring assassination to testify in the military Court of Inquiry against past Fort Stanton Commander N.A.M. Dudley for intervening in the Lincoln County War Battle.

Billy's deposition of June 8th, 1878 resulted from the Santa Fe Ring's biggest blunder. It was murdering John Tunstall, a British citizen. That forced investigation by President Rutherford B. Hayes to satisfy England's ambassador, Sir Edward Thornton. Alexander McSween had reported that the killing was done by U.S. officials.

So, in May of 1878, 2½ months after Tunstall's murder, Investigator Angel was sent to New Mexico Territory. If Ring-biased Hayes's motive was cover-up - as is likely - he picked the wrong man. Angel was diligent and honest. He deciphered the role of the Ring in his several month stay. He sympathized with the

McSween side. He amassed evidence. He took 39 depositions. Billy's was one.

By his deposition, 18 year old Billy had endured Ring and Regulator confrontations. John Tunstall and Alexander McSween were falsely prosecuted. Tunstall was assassinated. He was illegally arrested by Sheriff William Brady. Tunstall murderers, Frank Baker and William "Buck" Morton, were killed fleeing arrest. Sheriff Brady and Deputy George Hindman were killed to stop their murdering McSween. Tunstall murder posseman, Andrew "Buckshot" Roberts, was killed resisting arrest. In that April's Grand Jury, he, and other Regulators, were indicted for Brady's, and Hindman's, and Roberts's deaths.

Added were Billy's losses. Tunstall, his first real father figure, was lost. Lost was the Peñasco River ranch Tunstall had gifted him. Lost was a life of peace. In 36 days the Lincoln County War Battle would erupt.

Billy's 1,533 word deposition has his first recorded words. It showed his excellent recall and meticulous descriptions.

It was legally witnessed by anti-Ring Justice of the Peace John "Squire" Wilson. Wilson had already participated in Tunstall's Coroner's Jury Report. He had written arrest warrants for Tunstall's killers. He had deputized Tunstall's employees, Billy and Fred Waite, under Town Constable Atanacio Martinez to serve the murderers' warrants. He had deputized Tunstall's foreman, Dick Brewer, to capture those murderers. But Wilson had been thwarted. Ringite Governor S.B. Axtell shielded Tunstall's murderers by his illegal proclamation voiding Wilson's powers and outlawing Tunstall's deputized men. So, justly angry, Wilson now heard and notarized the boy's deposition. By the next year, as covered in another talk, Wilson covertly helped Billy when new hope came to Lincoln County in the form of new Governor, Lew Wallace.

Noteworthy also is Billy's hiding his grief and anger, which must have been intense that June 8th day, as he recounted Tunstall's assassination.

I'll read and comment on the excerpted deposition. Its entire transcript is in my book, *Billy the Kid's Writings, Words, and Wit.* I'll read selected portions. But I'll keep the deposition scrolling in silence through the skipped parts for those who want to read them. On screen is the legal transcript of Billy Bonney's June 8th, 1878 deposition to Investigator Frank Warner Angel in Lincoln. **[FIGURE 22]** I'll read selected portions.

Territory of New Mexico }

County of Lincoln }

William H. Bonney being duly
sworn, deposes and says, that he is a resident of
said County, that on the 11th day of February
A.D. 1878 he in company with Walt. A. Waun-
mann and Fred. T. Waite, went to the ranch of
J. H. Tunstall on the Rio Feliz, that he and said
Fred. T. Waite at the time intended, to go to the Rio
Penasco to take up a ranch, for the purpose of farming
That the cattle on the ranch of said J. H. Tunstall
were thraughtthe County of Lincoln, known to be
the property of said Tunstall; that on the 13th of
February A.D. 1878 one J. B. Mathews claiming
to be Deputy Sheriff came to the ranch of said
J. H. Tunstall in company with Jesse Evans,
Frank Baker, Tom Hill and Rivers, (known
outlaws who had been confined in the Lincoln County
jail and had succeeded in making their escape)
John Henry, George Hinman, Roberts and
an Indian alias Ponceano the latter said to be
the murderer of Bennito Cruz, for the arrest of
the murderers of whom (Bennito Cruz) the Governor of
this Territory offers a reward of $500. — , Before
the arrival of said J. B. Mathews, deputy Sheriff, and
his posse, having been informed that said deputy
sheriff and posse were going to round up all the cattle
and drive them off and kill the persons at the ranch,

any arrive, run off and kill the persons at the ranch,
the persons at the ranch cut portholes into the
walls of the house and filled sacks with earth, so
that they, the persons at the ranch, should they be
attacked or their murder attempted, could defend

themselves. This course being in anywise necessary as the
sheriffs posse was composed of murderers, outlaws
and desperate caracters none of whom had any interest
at stake in the County, nor being residents of said
County. That said Mathews when within about 50
yards of the house was called to to stop and advance
alone and state his business, that said Mathews
after arriving at the ranch said that he had come
to attach the cattle and property of A. A. McSween,
that said Mathews was informed that A. A. McSween
had no cattle or property there, but that if he had he,
said Mathews could attach it. That said Mathews
said that he thought some of the cattle belonging to
R. M. Brewer, whose cattle were also at the ranch
of B. H. Tunstall, belonged to A. A. McSween, that
said Mathews was told by said Brewer that he
Mathews, could round up the cattle and that he,
Brewer would help him. That said Mathews said
that he would go back to Lincoln to get new instructions
and if he came back to the ranch, he would come back
with one man. That said Mathews and his posse were
then invited by R. M. Brewer to come to the house
and get something to eat.

Deponent further says that Robert A. Widenmann

told R. C. Brewer and the others at the ranch, that he
was going to arrest Frank Baker, Jesse Evans and
Tom Hill, said Widenmann having warrants for
them. That said Widenmann was told by Brewer and
the others at the ranch, that the arrest should not be
made, because if it was made they, all the persons
at the ranch would be killed and murdered by
J. J. Dolan & Co. and their party. That Jesse Evans

advanced upon said Widenmann, said Evans swinging at his gun and catching it cocked and pointed
directly at said Widenmann. That said Jesse Evans
asked said Widenmann whether he, Widenmann,
was hunting for him, Evans, to which Widenmann
answered that if he was looking for him, he, Evans,
would find it out. Evans also asked Widenmann
whether he had a warrant for him; Widenmann
answered that that was his (Widenmann's) business.
Evans told Widenmann, that if he ever came to arrest
him (Evans) he, Evans would pick Widenmann as
the first man to shoot at, to which Widenmann
answered that that was all right, that two could play   two could play at that
at that game. That during the talking Frank Baker
stood near said Widenmann, swinging his pistol
on his finger catching it full cocked pointed at said
Widenmann. — The persons at the ranch were
R. C. Brewer, John Middleton, G. Causs McCarty,
R. A. Widenmann, Henry Brown, F. P. Waite
Wm McClaskey and this deponent. O. B. Mathews, after

eating at a ranch for Lincoln with Robt Henry and Ponce and the rest of the party saying they were going to the Rio Peñasco. Deponent started for Lincoln with Robt. A. Widenmann and F. T. Waite and arrived at Lincoln the same evening and again left Lincoln on the next day, February the 14th, in company with the above named persons, having heard that said Mathews was going back to the ranch of said R. H. Tunstall with a large party of men to take the cattle and deponent and Widenmann and Waite arrived at said ranch the same day.— Deponent states that on the road to Lincoln he heard said Mathews ask said

Widenmann whether any resistance would be offered if he, Mathews returned to take the cattle, to which said Widenmann, answered that no resistance would be offered if the cattle were left at the ranch but if an attempt was made to drive the cattle to the Indian Agency and kill them for beef as he, said Mathews had been heard to say would be done, he said, Widenmann, would do all in his power to prevent this.

Deponent further says, that on the night of the 17th of February A.D. 1878 R. H. Tunstall arrived at the ranch and informed all the persons there, that reliable information had reached him that R. B. Mathews was gathering a large party of outlaws and desperadoes as a posse and that said posse was coming to the ranch, the mexicans in the party to gather up the cattle and the balance of the posse to kill the persons at the ranch. It was thereupon decided that all persons at the ranch one was overrun and and was all persons at the ranch excepting G. Gauss, were to leave and Wm McCloskey was that night sent to the Rio Penasco, to inform the posse who were camped there, that they should come over and round up the cattle, count them and leave a man there to take care of them, and that Mr. Tunstall would also leave a man there to help round up and count the cattle and help take care of them, and said McCloskey was also ordered to go to Martin Martz, who had left Tunstall's ranch when deponent, Widenmann and Waite returned to the town of Lincoln on the 13th of February, and ask him said Martz to come to the ranch of said Tunstall and aid the sheriffs posse in rounding up in a counting the cattle and to stay at the ranch and take care of the cattle.

Deponent left the ranch of said Tunstall in company

with J. H. Tunstall, R. A. Widenmann and R. M. Brewer, John Middleton and F. T. Waite, said Tunstall, Widenmann, Brewer, Middleton and deponent driving the loose horses, Waite driving the wagon. Said Waite took the road for Lincoln with the wagon, the rest of the party taking the trail with the horses. Deponent says that all the horses which he and party were driving, excepting 3 had been released by sheriff Brady at Lincoln that one of these 3 horses belonged to R. M. Brewer, and another was traded by Brewer to Tunstall for one of the released horses.

Deponent further says, that when he and party had travelled

... [illegible] ..., ... [illegible] and party was going to within about 3½ miles from the Rio Ruidoso. He and John Middleton were riding in the rear of the balance of the party and just upon reaching the brow of a hill they saw a large party of men coming towards them from the rear at full speed and that he and Middleton at once rode forward to inform the balance of the party of the fact. Deponent had not more than barely reached Brewer and Widenmann who were some 100 or 200 yards to the left of the trail when the attacking party cleared the brow of the hill and commenced firing at him, Widenmann and Brewer. Deponent Widenmann and Brewer rode over a hill towards and other which was covered with large rocks and trees in order to defend themselves and make a stand. But the attacking party, undoubtedly seeing Tunstall, left off pursuing deponent and the two with him and turned back to the cañon in which the trail was. Shortly afterwards we heard a two or three separate and distinct shots and the remark was then made by Middleton that they, the attacking party would have killed Tunstall. "Dick of Taos", in the meantime joined deponent and Widenmann and Brewer. Deponent then made the best of his way to Lincoln in company with Robt A. Widenmann, Brewer, Waite and Middleton stopping on the Rio Ruidoso in order to get men to look for the body of ob. H. Tunstall—

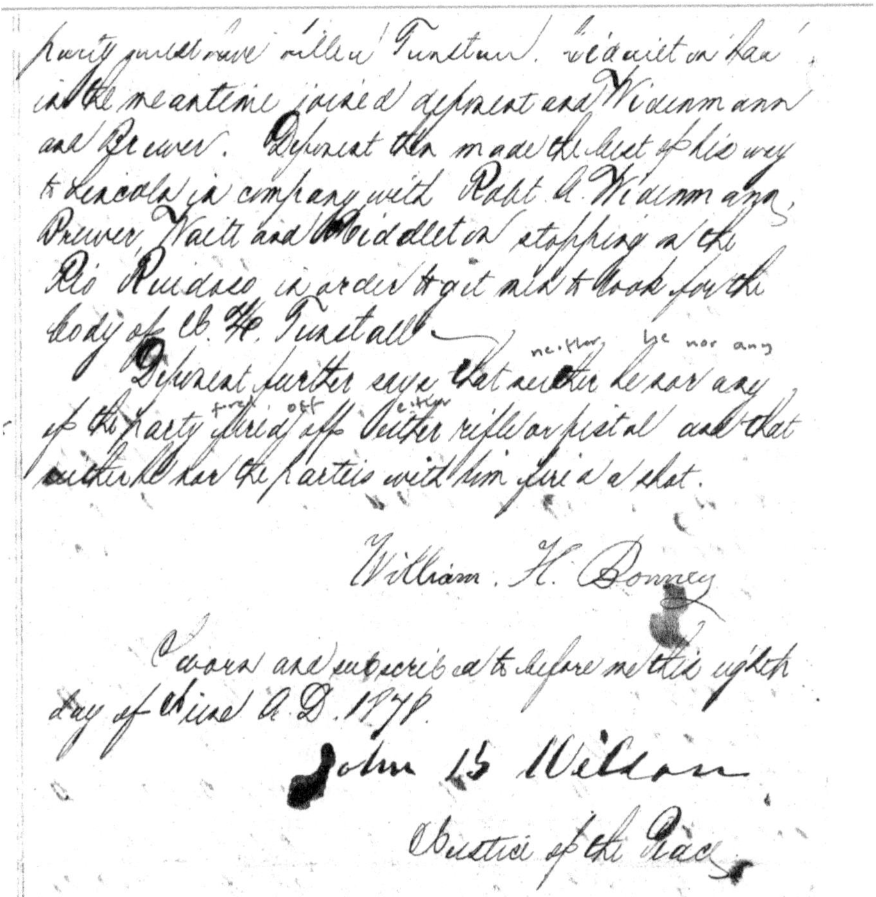

Deponent further says that neither he nor any of the party fired off either rifle or pistol and that neither he nor the parties with him fire a shot.

William. H. Bonney

Sworn and subscribed to before me this eighth day of June A.D. 1878.

John B. Wilson

Justice of the Peace

FIGURE 22: Billy Bonney's June 8, 1878 Deposition to Frank Warner Angel. National Archives

It began: "William H. Bonney was duly sworn, deposand says, that he is a resident of said [Lincoln] county, that on the 11th day of February A.D. 1878 he in company with Robert A. Widenmann and Fred T. Waite went to the ranch of J.H. Tunstall on the Rio Feliz, that he and said Fred Waite at the time intended to go to the Rio Peñasco to take up a ranch for the purpose of farming."

Note that Billy began his deposition with his proudest achievement. He anticipated having a ranch on the Peñasco River in partnership with fellow Tunstall employee, Fred Waite. It would have been under the Homestead Act. As a British citizen, John Tunstall did not qualify. But he intended to give his employees ranches. Their confederation along the Peñasco River would end the Ring's Lincoln County economic stranglehold. And Billy knew that Tunstall was murdered for that dream.

Billy continued: "That the cattle on the ranch of said J.H. Tunstall were throughout the County of Lincoln, known to be the property of said Tunstall."

Note that Billy addressed the Ring's lie that Tunstall was in partnership with McSween, to attach both their properties. It became the excuse to murder Tunstall.

Billy continued: "that on the 13th of February A.D. 1878 one J.B. Matthews claiming to be Deputy Sheriff came to the ranch of said J.H. Tunstall in company with Jesse Evans, Frank Baker, Tom Hill and [first name left out] Rivers, known outlaws ..."

Note that Billy's point was that the Ring used outlaws as terrorist enforcers. Eventually they would murder Tunstall.

Billy continued: "Before the arrival of said J.B. Matthews, Deputy Sheriff, and his posse, having been informed that said Deputy Sheriff and posse were going to round up all the cattle and drive them off and kill the persons at the ranch, the persons at the ranch cut portholes into the walls of the house and filled sacks with earth, so that they, the persons at the ranch, should they be attacked or murder attempted, could defend themselves, this course being thought necessary as the sheriffs posse was composed of murderers, outlaws, and desperate characters none of whom has any interest at stake in the County, nor being residents of said County."

Note that Billy emphasizes both the danger and criminality of the Ring side.

Billy continued: "That said Matthews when within about 50 yards of the house was called to stop and advance alone and state his business, that said Matthews after arriving at the ranch said that he had come to attach the cattle and property of A.A. McSween, that said Matthews was informed that A.A. McSween had no cattle or property there, but that if he had he, said Matthews could take it ... That said Matthews said that he would go back to Lincoln to get new instructions ..."

Note that Billy, aware of the fake partnership claim, again denies that Tunstall's cattle were McSween's. Matthews had failed to provoke hoped-for violence to justify killing. So he needed new instructions from local Ring boss, James Dolan.

Billy continued: "The persons at the ranch were R.M. Brewer, John Middleton, G. Gauss, M. Martz, R.A. Widenmann, Henry Brown, F.T. Waite, William McClosky and this deponent. J.B. Matthews after eating started for Lincoln ... Deponent started to Lincoln with Robert A. Widenmann and F.T. Waite and arrived at Lincoln the same evening and again left Lincoln on the next day, February the 14th in company with the above named persons, having heard that said Matthews was going back to the ranch of said J.H. Tunstall with a large party of men to take the cattle, and deponent and Widenmann and Waite arrived at said ranch the same day ... Deponent further says that on the night of the 17th of February A.D. 1878   J.H. Tunstall arrived at the ranch and informed all the persons there that reliable information had reached him that J.B. Matthews was gathering a large party of outlaws and desperados as a posse and the said posse was coming to the ranch ... to kill the persons at the ranch."

Note that Billy established mortal risk from Sheriff Brady's posse.

Billy continued: "It was thereupon decided that all persons at the ranch excepting G. Gauss, were to leave and William McClosky was that night sent to the Rio Peñasco to inform the posse who were camped there, that they could come over and round up the cattle ..."

Note that Billy emphasized Tunstall's pacifism. It gives insight as to how Tunstall converted Billy from a violent delinquent to a rebel with a cause.

Billy continued: "Deponent left the ranch of said Tunstall in company with J.H. Tunstall, R.A. Widenmann, R.M. Brewer, John Middleton, F.T. Waite, said Tunstall, Widenmann, Brewer, Middleton and deponent driving the loose horses ... Waite took the road for Lincoln with the wagon, the rest of the party taking the trail with the horses. Deponent says that all the horses which he and party were driving, excepting 3 had been released by Sheriff

Brady at Lincoln that one of these 3 horses belonged to R.M. Brewer, and the other was traded by Brewer to Tunstall for one of the released horses."

Note that Billy is establishing that the horses were immune to attachment.

Billy continued: "Deponent further says, that when he and the party had traveled to within about 3 miles from the Rio Ruidoso he and John Middleton were in drag in the rear of the balance of the party and just upon reaching the brow of a hill they saw a large party of men coming towards them from the rear at full speed and that he and Middleton at once rode forward to inform the balance of the party of the fact. Deponent had not more than barely reached Brewer and Widenmann who were some 200 or 300 yards to the left of the trail when the attacking party cleared the brow of the hill and commenced firing at him, Widenmann and Brewer."

Note Billy's meticulous observations, even in life-threatening events. A year later, this would yield his fatal testimony against Ringite Commander N.A.M. Dudley in his Court of Inquiry for his treasonous Lincoln County War Battle intervention.

Billy continued: "Deponent, Widenmann and Brewer rode over a hill towards another which was covered with large rocks and trees in order to defend themselves and make a stand. But the attacking party, undoubtedly seeing Tunstall, left off pursuing deponent and the two with him and turned back to the caño in which the trail was. Shortly afterwards we heard two or three separate and distinct shots and the remark was then made by Middleton that they, the attacking party must have killed Tunstall. Middleton had in the meantime joined deponent and Widenmann and Brewer. Deponent then made the rest of his way to Lincoln in company with Robert. A. Widenmann, Brewer, Waite and Middleton stopping on the Rio Ruidoso in order to get men to look for the body of J.H. Tunstall. Deponent further says that neither he nor any of the party fired off either rifle or pistol and that neither he nor the parties with him fired a shot."

Note that Billy emphasizes that Tunstall's murder was in cold blood.

Billy signed as "William H. Bonney." This is his first known signature.

Hopeful Lincoln citizens, including Billy, had no way of knowing that Attorney Frank Warner Angel's investigation was a sham. It's likely that Angel himself did not know, until forced into a conclusion covering-up the Ring. In his report of October 4th, 1878, Angel lied. He stated: "After diligent inquiry and examination of a great number of witnesses, I report that the death of John H. Tunstall was not brought about through the lawless and corrupt conduct of United States officials in the Territory of New Mexico."

Billy Bonney's next legal testimony risked his life again. Again, it was against the Santa Fe Ring. It fulfilled his pardon bargain with Governor Lew Wallace. He testified in April of 1879's Lincoln County Grand Jury against Huston Chapman's murderers - James Dolan, Billy Campbell, and Jessie Evans. And he got Dolan and Campbell indicted for first degree murder, and Jessie Evans for accessory to murder.

The transcript is lost, a likely Ring expurgation. But Billy's testimony was confirmed in newspapers and by his attorney and friend, Ira Leonard.

On May 10th, 1879, the *Grant County Herald* wrote: "At the recent term of court in Lincoln, about 200 indictments were found. Among them, Col. Dudley and George W. Peppin for burning McSween's house, Dolan and Campbell for the Chapman murder, in which the Kid is the principal witness."

On April 20, 1879, Attorney Ira Leonard reported to Governor Lew Wallace. He described testifying Billy's harassment by Ringite District Attorney William Rynerson. Leonard wrote: "I tell you, Governor, the District Attorney here is no friend to law enforcement. He is bent on going after the Kid. He proposes to destroy his evidence and influence and is bent on pushing him to the wall. He is a Dolan man and is defending him in every manner possible."

Billy's next testimony was the following month. He was still in his pardon bargain's sham jailing. This time it was for his own anti-Ring agenda. He testified against past Commander N.A.M. Dudley in the May to July of 1879, Fort Stanton, Court of Inquiry for his possible court martial. The complaint was by Alexander McSween's widow, Susan, accusing Dudley of the Lincoln County War Battle's murder of her husband, Alexander, and the arson of her home.

Billy knew his risk. He had written to Governor Wallace two months earlier, on March 20th, 1879, when his incarceration at Fort Stanton was possible for the pardon bargain. He wrote: "all I am afraid of is that in the Fort We might be poisoned or killed through a Window at night."

Billy's testimony was devastating. When escaping the burning McSween house with others, he had seen three of Dudley's white soldiers fire at least one volley at them. Volley meant firing in unison. That meant under Dudley's orders. White meant officers. Billy also saw law intern Harvey Morris shot down. Possibly, he was killed by them. Based on Billy's testimony alone, Dudley should have been court martialed, and even hanged, for treasonously murdering citizens in violation of the Posse Comitatus Act.

On May 28th and 29th of 1879, Billy was transported the nine miles from Lincoln to the Fort Stanton courtroom. The three Judges were Colonel Galusha Pennypacker, Captain Henry Brinkerhoff, and Major Nathan Osborne. The prosecutor was Captain Henry Humphreys, with co-counsel Ira Leonard. For the defense was Henry Waldo. The Court was rigged. Chief Judge Pennypacker was Dudley's best friend from Fort Union. Waldo had been in Ring boss T.B. Catron's law firm. And Catron himself had represented reprobate Dudley for his past court martials.

Billy's two day transcript reveals his precise mind and iron nerve. Brutal Attorney Henry Waldo had just reduced testifying Susan McSween to utter confusion. He would humiliatingly destroy Lew Wallace's prosecution testimony too. Billy's questioning focused on Dudley's July 19th, 1878 Lincoln County War Battle intervention. It was with his black cavalry, white infantry, white officers, a howitzer cannon, and a Gatling machine gun, to aid Ringite Sheriff, George Peppin, who was losing to the McSween side.

Billy had been in the besieged, and eventually burning, house of Alexander McSween. Present too were other freedom fighters; McSween's wife, Susan; her sister, and her sister's five young children. Noteworthy, is that overwhelmed McSween relied on 18 year old Billy to review his letters to and from Dudley.

I'll comment on excerpts from the transcript. The full transcript is in my book, *Billy the Kid's Writings, Words, and Wit.* One should note that Attorney Ira Leonard, present throughout, saw Billy's brave testimony, and became his loyal attorney.

On screen is Billy from 1880, likely looking much the same as at his testimony. **[FIGURE 23]**

FIGURE 23: Billy the Kid tintype

On May 28th, 1879, his first day of testimony, he responded to the military prosecutor's questioning as follows:

"Question. What is your name and place of residence?

"Answer. My name is William Bonney. I reside in Lincoln.

"Question. Are you known or called Billy Kidd [spelled K-I-D-D], also Antrim?

"Answer. Yes Sir." Note Billy's misunderstanding. He knew only his nicknames "Kid" and "Kid Antrim."

"Question. Where were you on the 19th day of July last and what, if anything, did you see of the movements and actions of the troops in that city, state fully?

"Answer. I was in the McSween house in Lincoln, and I saw soldiers come from the post with sheriff's party, that is the sheriff's posse joined them a short distance below there, the McSween house. Soldiers passed on by and the men dropped off and surrounded the house, the sheriff's party. Shortly after, the soldiers came back with Peppin, passed the house twice afterwards. Three soldiers came and stood in front of the house, in front of the windows. Mr. McSween wrote a note to the officer in charge asking what the soldiers were placed there for. He replied saying that they had business there, that if a shot was fired over his camp, or at Peppin, or at any of his men, that he had no objection to blowing up, if he wanted, his own house. I read the note myself, he handed it to me to read. I saw nothing further of the soldiers until night. I was in the back part of the house. When I escaped from the house three soldiers fired at me from the Tunstall store, outside corner of the store. That's all I know in regards to it ..." Note the precision of Billy's testimony.

The testimony continued: "Question. Who escaped from the house with you and who was killed at the time, if you know, while attempting to make their escape?

Answer. Jose Chavez escaped with me, Vincente Romero, Francisco Zamora and McSween.

"Question. How many persons were killed in that fight that day, if you know, and who killed them, if you know?

"Answer. I seen five killed, I could not swear to who killed them, I seen some of them that fired.

["Question.] Who did you see that fired?

"Answer. Robert Beckwith, John Hurley, John Jones, those three soldiers, I don't know their names." Note that Billy was willing to say dangerous truth to bring down the Santa Fe Ring.

"Question. Did you see any persons setting fire to the McSween house that day, if so, state who it was, if you know?

"Answer. I did, Jack Long, and there was another man I did not recognize."

Henry Waldo then cross-examined Billy for the defense.

"Question. What were you, and the others there with you, doing in McSween's house that day?

"Answer. We came here with McSween.

"Question. Did you know, or had you not heard, that the sheriff was endeavoring to arrest yourself and others there with you at the time?

"Answer. Yes Sir. I had heard so, I did not know." Note Billy's unintimidated retort: he had heard about the fake arrest warrants, but he knew no proof of their validity.

"Question. Then were you not engaged in resisting the sheriff at the time you were in the house?"

Prosecution objected as to irrelevance and was upheld.

"Question. In addition to the names you have given, are you also known as the 'Kid?'

"Answer. I have already answered that question, Yes Sir, I am, but not 'Billy Kid' that I know of." Note that Billy refers back to the earlier questioning, and corrects his answer, stating that he is not known as "Billy Kid."

"Question. Were you not and were not the parties with you in the McSween house on the 19th day of July last and the days immediately preceding, engaged in firing at the sheriff's posse?" Note that Waldo is trying to portray Billy as a lying outlaw.

The Court objected as to irrelevance.

"Question. Whose name was signed to the note received by McSween in reply to the one previously sent by him to Col. Dudley?"

"Answer. Signed N.A.M. Dudley, did not say what rank, he received two notes, one had no name signed to it." Note again Billy's precise memory.

"Question. Are you as certain of everything else you have sworn to as you are to what you have sworn to in answer to the last proceeding question?

"Answer. Yes Sir." Note that Waldo could not faze Billy.

"Question. From which direction did Peppin come the first time the soldiers passed with him?

"Answer. Passed up from the direction of where the soldiers camped, the first time I saw him.

"Question. What direction did he come from the second time?

"Answer. From the direction of the hotel from the McSween house.

"Question. In what direction did you go upon your escape from the McSween house?

"Answer. Ran towards the Tunstall store, was fired at, and there turned towards the river.

"Question. From what part of the McSween house did you make your escape?

"Answer. The northeast corner of the house.

"Question. How many soldiers fired at you?

"Answer. Three.

"Question. How many soldiers were with Peppin when he passed the McSween house each time, as you say?

"Answer. Three.

"Question. The soldiers appeared to go in company of threes that day, did they not?

"Answer. All that I ever saw appeared to be three in a crowd at a time after they passed the first time." Note that Billy cannot be shaken by Waldo.

"Question. Who was killed first that day, Bob Beckwith or McSween men?

"Answer. Harvey Morris, McSween man, was killed first.

"Question. How far is the Tunstall building from the McSween house?

"Answer. I could not say how far, I never measured the distance. I should judge it to be 40 yards, between 30 and 40 yards." Note Billy's precision. He is willing to estimate distance, but denies formal measurement. Waldo can't rattle him.

"Question. How many shots did those soldiers fire, that you say shot from the Tunstall building?

"Answer. I could not swear to that, on account of firing on all sides, I could not hear. I seen them fire one volley." Note that this is Billy's precise and devastating answer. Billy even qualifies his counting shots by denying hearing, but by seeing the black power puffs coming in unison from the soldiers' rifles as a volley. Billy's observation should have led to Dudley's court martial. Waldo knew this. And, in his closing argument, he attacked Billy. This answer alone shows just how dangerous a gadfly Billy could be.

"Question. What did they fire at?

"Answer. Myself and Jose Chavez.

"Question. Did you not just now state in answer to the question who killed Zamora, Romero, Morris, and McSween that you did not know who killed them, but you saw Beckwith , John Jones, and three soldiers fire at them?

"Answer. Yes Sir. I did.

"Question. Were these men, the McSween men, there with you when the volley was fired at you and Chavez by the soldiers?

"Answer. Just a short ways behind us.

"Question. Were you looking back at them?

"Answer. No Sir.

"Question. How then do you know they were just behind you then, or that they were in range of the volley?" Note that Waldo thinks he can trip Billy up.

"Answer. Because there was a high fence behind, and a good many guns to keep them there. I could hear them speak." Note that Billy is untouchable.

"Question. How far were you from the soldiers when you saw them?

"Answer. I could not swear exactly, between 30 and 40 yards." Note that Waldo tried again, but Billy simply stuck to his original answer.

"Question. Did you know either of the soldiers that were in front of the window of McSween's house that day? If so, give it.

"Answer. No Sir, I am not acquainted with them ...

"Question. How do you know if you were making your escape at the time and the men Zamora, Morris and McSween were behind you that they were killed at that time? Is it not true that you did not know of their death or the death of either of them until afterwards?

"Answer. I knew of the death of some of them, I did know of the death of one of them. I saw him lying down there." Note that Waldo fails to make Billy overstate.

"Question. Did you see any of the men last mentioned killed?

Answer. Yes Sir, I did, I seen Harvey Morris killed first, he was out in front of me.

Question. Did you not then a moment ago swear that he was among those who were behind you and Jose Chavez when you saw the soldiers deliver the volley?

Answer. No Sir, I didn't think I did. I misunderstood the question if I did. I said he was among them that was killed, not behind me." Billy is unflappable.

The next day, May 29th, 1879, the Judges questioned Billy.

"Question. Were the soldiers which you say fired at you as you escaped from the McSween house on the evening of July 19th last, colored or white?

"Answer. White troops." Note that "white troops" meant officers. That further confirmed that they were under orders of Dudley. That made him responsible.

"Question. Was it light enough so you could distinctly see the soldiers when they fired?

"Answer. The house was burning. Made it almost light as day for a short distance all around." Note that day-like visibility was key to Billy's seeing shooting soldiers. This ended Billy's testimony.

On the 49th and last day of Dudley's trial, on July 5th, 1879, Henry Waldo gave his closing argument. It began the Santa Fe Ring's outlaw myth of Billy the Kid. That 19 year old could have toppled the Ring in a fair Court. Waldo lied wildly to deny Billy's seeing shooting soldiers. Here's Waldo's excerpted statement. It is complete in my book, *Billy the Kid's Writings, Words, and Wit.* Waldo said:

"Then was brought forward William Bonney, alias "Antrim," alias 'the Kid,' a known criminal of the worst type although hardly up to his majority, murderer by profession, as records of this Court connect him with two atrocious murders, that of Roberts and the other of Sheriff Brady. Both of them are cowardly and atrocious assassinations.

"There were warrants enough for him to the 19th of July last to have plastered him from his head to his feet, yet he was engaged to do service as a witness, and his testimony showed that his qualifications did not terminate with blood guiltiness. His testimony was brief, yet he signalized his opening sentences with a lie. He swears that members of the sheriff's posse fell in with the troops and came up to the McSween house ... It has been proven by competent and unimpeachable witnesses that this statement is without any foundation in fact. Sheriff Peppin, his Deputy Sheriff Powell, Deputy Sheriff Marion Turner, Milo Pierce, Robert Olinger, Joseph Nash, Andrew Boyle, J.B. Matthews, Lt. Goodwin, Captain Purington and Corporal Bugold, who brought up the rear of the column all swear that none of the posse was anywhere near the troops ..." Note that these lying Ringites were fighting the McSweens.

Waldo continued: "As to seeing the soldiers about the building, at the time of the escape of the men from the McSween house the evening of the 19th of July last ... "Kid" says that the soldiers stood at the outside corner of the building ... Now this story comes with its own reputation. In the first place, in the intense excitement of the moment, these men could not have had the coolness to select from a number of shots delivered at them, the firing of certain particular shots, to fix it in their minds, the men who did the firing. Besides, in the deceptive glare of the fire, it is very doubtful if any of the parties who were looking upon the space between those two houses could identify with any degree of certainty, particularly at such a time, the kind of clothes anybody wore. This difficulty would be enhanced in the case of the "Kid" ... looking from the center of the light out against the darkness, which is a circumstance of the greatest importance. While from the darkness to the wall objects are plainly discernable, the direct opposite follows when the conditions are changed ..." Note that Waldo is desperately lying. He says escaping Billy was not cool enough to observe shooting soldiers. He absurdly lies that the fire could light the building, but not shooting soldiers. He hides Billy's testimony that fire "made it almost light as day for a short distance all around."

Waldo continued: "Besides, it is clear the soldiers were not then present, the evidence of the Sergeant who testified that late roll call for the night was at dusk, or near as he can judge, about a quarter past eight, and that the men were then all there ..." Note that the escape was an hour later, ample time for the 3 soldiers to position for the shooting.

Waldo continued: "Besides, we must take into consideration that some of these men ... of the sheriff's posse ... were dressed with soldier jackets ... To all probability as they fled they may have seen some of these men who had soldiers' jackets and thought they were soldiers." Note this absurd lie that Peppin's possemen dressed as soldiers.

At 4:30 PM that same July 5th, 1879 day, Chief Judge Galusha Pennypacker, Colonel Dudley's best friend, delivered the three judges' decision. Pennypacker stated: "In view of the evidence adduced, Colonel N.A.M. Dudley is not guilty of any violation of law or of orders. And his act of proceeding to the town of Lincoln was prompted by the most humane and worthy motives and by good military judgment under exceptional circumstances. Proceedings before a Court Martial are therefore unnecessary."

This corrupt decision sealed Ring dominance in Lincoln County. And it fueled the Ring's determination to exterminate the teenager making a habit of giving devastating testimony against their members.

On June 17th, 1879, nineteen days before Dudley's exoneration, Billy walked out of his sham pardon bargain jailing. Wallace had not issued the promised pardon. And the Ring was about to transport him to Mesilla for a hanging trial.

As we shall see in talks about my book, *The Lost Pardon of Billy the Kid*, Billy still nursed hope for his pardon, as he returned to gambling and gadfly rustling.

TALK 9:

BILLY THE KID'S WIT

FROM BOOK: *BILLY THE KID'S WRITINGS, WORDS, AND WIT*

NOVEMBER 18, 2020

This talk is about Billy Bonney's unquenchable humor. Its information is from my book, *Billy the Kid's Writings, Words, and Wit*.

Billy Bonney stood out among his contemporaries for many reasons; one was his jaunty and ironic wit. That wit masked a lifetime of traumatic losses. But right down to his last known words, he never lost his ability to mock his fate. His wit had amused his cohorts enough to be recounted in their old age. Wit was Billy's weapon when captive, blasting truth through reporters' haze. Wit added to Billy's drama as the last freedom fighter against the Santa Fe Ring. And wit punctuated his dialogue to his Lincoln audience from the high courthouse balcony at jailbreak, when he announced that he was standing pat against the world.

By Billy's Stinking Springs capture, on December 22nd, 1880, he was famous. Locally, among his partisans, he was a bi-cultural freedom fighter. Nationally, via Santa Fe Ring outlaw myth propaganda, he was a murderer, rustler, and counterfeiter.

Facing his Mesilla hanging trials, then facing unjust sentence, Billy gave newspaper interviews in the shadow of a noose, but defiant with lively humor and sardonic truth.

We first see Billy's wit flashing in his pardon bargain letters to New Mexico Territory Governor Lew Wallace and Justice of the Peace John "Squire" Wilson. Those letters themselves are more extensively discussed in other talks.

Billy's March 13th, 1879, first letter to Wallace, bristles with cockiness bolstered by his allies' respect and his possible secret support by his Lincoln public official friends. Underneath all that, however, was this teenager's confidence that he was the equal to any man – governors included. So Billy jauntily preempted the lofty governor's intimidating dead-or-alive reward of a $1000 on his head, as an outlaw. He wrote: "I have heard that You will give one thousand dollars for my body, which as I can understand it, means alive as a Witness. I know it is as a witness against those that murdered Mr. Chapman."

On March 20th, 1879, in his letter arranging sham arrest for his Wallace pardon bargain, Billy wrote tongue-in-cheek to Justice of the Peace Wilson, as "Friend Wilson." As I described in my talk about authenticating a new Billy the Kid letter, Wilson was, indeed, Billy's secret "friend." He aided the pardon scheme, provided its fine stationery for its letters, and arranged Billy's meeting with Wallace in his house. Billy's letter to Wilson even playfully omits Wallace's name – making fun of Wallace's pompous letter telling Billy to keep their Lincoln meeting secret. Billy wrote: "Please tell You know who that I do not know what to do now ..."

That same March 20th, Billy teased Wallace in a letter by playing on Wallace's having unsuccessfully sent troops to capture him as an outlaw. Billy wrote: "perhaps [I] know how men hide from Soldiers better than you."

By Billy's December 12th, 1880 letter to Wallace, and no pardon, his wit became testy. He wrote: "I noticed in the Las Vegas Gazette a piece which stated that Billy 'the' Kid, the name by which I am known in the Country was the captain of a Band of Outlaws who hold Forth at the Portales. There no such Organization in Existence. So the Gentleman must have drawn very heavily on his Imagination."

In his March 4th, 1881 letter to Wallace from the Santa Fe jail, Billy's wit became snide, with his quote "patiently waiting" meaning its opposite. His other two letters had been ignored. He stated: "I guess they mean to Send me up without giving me any Show, but they will have a nice time doing it. I am not entirely without friends. I shall expect to see you sometime today. Patiently waiting ...." He then signed. And the irony of "not entirely without friends" taunted rescue.

Nearly being killed, did nothing to sober Billy's wit. On January 3rd, 1880, a Texas cowboy, and possible bounty hunter, named Joe Grant was tempted by Billy's gunman reputation. Grant aimed for his back in Fort Sumner's Hargrove's Saloon. His pistol misfired. Billy whirled. His bullet exploded Grant's brain. The *Las Vegas Daily Optic* quoted Billy. "It was a game of two, and I got there first."

By December 28th, 1880, captured Billy was interviewed in the Las Vegas jail on the way to the Santa Fe jail. The reporter was Lucius "Lute" Wilcox, city editor for J.H. Koogler's *Las Vegas Gazette.*" The article would be titled: "The Kid, Interview with Billy Bonney The Best Known Man in New Mexico." Billy simply teased and taunted any future hangman and his own fate. The reporter wrote: "Bonney ... was light and chipper, and was very communicative, laughing, joking and chatting with bystanders. 'You appear to take it easy,' the reporter said. 'Yes! What's the use of looking on the gloomy side of everything. The laugh's on me this time,' he said."

Billy also used this *Las Vegas Gazette* interview to sarcastically ridicule his Santa Fe Ring outlaw myth. The article stated: "He was the attraction of the show, and as he stood there, lightly kicking the toes of his boots on the stone pavement to keep his feet warm, one would scarcely mistrust that he was the hero of the "Forty Thieves" romance which this paper has been running in serial form for six weeks or more. 'There was a big crowd gazing at me wasn't there?' he exclaimed, and then, smiling, continued: 'Well perhaps some of them will think me half a man now; everyone seems to think I was some kind of an animal.' "

Also on December 28th, 1880, but already in the train at the depot, Billy was interviewed again for the *Las Vegas Gazette,* while awaiting departure to the Santa Fe jail. Billy's nonchalant banter adds ironic humor when one realizes that, during it, the train was being detained by a mob on the tracks, whose unclear intent was lynching or rescuing him. He said, "They wouldn't let me settle down; if they had I wouldn't be here today." The reporter added: "And he held up his right arm on which was the bracelet." Billy also joked about his Stinking Springs capture - concealing his grief of his friend, Charlie Bowdre's, killing, 6 days earlier, mistaken for him. He merely floated a silly dime novel escape fantasy about jumping his famous bay mare out of the rock-

walled, line cabin's doorway. It was obstructed by a horse, shot by
Pat Garrett. Billy said "If it had not been for the dead horse in the
doorway I wouldn't be here in Las Vegas. I would have ridden out
on my bay mare and taken my chances of escaping. But I couldn't
ride over that for she would have jumped back and I would have
got it in the head." About the deadly siege at Stinking Springs,
that had ended with surrender, Billy teased: "We could have
stayed in the house but there wouldn't have been anything gained
by that for they would have starved us out. I thought it was better
to come out and get a square meal - don't you?"

When the train finally started, for jail and certain hanging
trials, Billy avoided morbidity. He just joked. The reporter wrote:
"As the train rolled out, he lifted his hat and invited us to call and
see him in Santa Fe, calling out 'adios.' "

On March 29th, 1881, after three months in the Santa Fe jail,
Billy was transported by train and coach to Las Cruces. A crowd of
the curious waited. With Billy, were fellow captive Billy Wilson,
Attorney Ira Leonard - who had protectively accompanied Billy -
and their guards. Someone asked the group which was Billy the
Kid. Billy's cheeky response was reported in the April 3rd, 1881
Santa Fe Daily New Mexican's article, "Something About the Kid."
Billy put his hand on bald middle-aged Ira Leonard's shoulder. He
said, "This is the man!" He also mocked his outlaw myth. Billy
said: "At least two hundred men have been killed in Lincoln
County during the past three years, but I did not kill all of them."

In Mesilla, on April 15th, 1881, two days after his hanging
sentence, Billy was interviewed by a *Mesilla News* reporter. That
same day he had written a desperate letter to Attorney Edgar
Caypless about trying to sell his stolen bay mare for appeal
money. For the article, after recounting injustices of his hanging
trial, Billy made wry comments about "mob law." He topped them
with spoof "personal advice." He was quoted: "If mob law is going
to rule, better dismiss judge and sheriff and let all take chances
alike. I expect to be lynched in going to Lincoln. Advise persons
never to engage in killing." About Lew Wallace's pardon promise,
Billy said tersely: "Don't know that he will do it." And he worded
his own tragi-comedy: "I think it hard that I should be the only
one to suffer the extreme penalty of the law."

In darkness, on April 17th, 1881, Billy was secretly taken by wagon from the Mesilla jail. Feared was his rescue on his way to Lincoln's jail and to hanging. *Newman's Semi-Weekly* reported his departure. It had Billy's literal gallows humor. It stated: "On Saturday night, about 10 o'clock, Deputy U.S. Marshal Robert Olinger with Deputy Sheriff David Woods and a posse of five men ... started for Lincoln with Henry Antrim alias the Kid ... They stopped in front of the "Semi-Weekly" office while we talked to them ... [The Kid] appeared quite cheerful and remarked that he wanted to stay until their whiskey gave out, anyway. Said he was sure that his guard would not hurt him unless a rescue should be attempted and he was certain that it would not be done unless perhaps 'those fellows at White Oaks come out to take me,' meaning to kill him. It was, he said, about a stand-off whether he was hanged or killed in the wagon."

Billy was fondly remembered by his Lincoln County War cohorts as frenetically exuberant and an inveterate prankster.

George Coe, in his 1934 book, *Frontier Fighter: The Autobiography of George Coe Who Fought and Rode With Billy the Kid*, told about Billy's teasing the older Regulators in April of 1878. Coe wrote:

"We made a big bonfire, and sat around swapping lies and bragging ... Then we talked about riding into Lincoln and setting in short order all the difficulties that were troubling the people there. We were a brave band as we told it.

Our guns, which formed the most important part of our possessions, had been placed carelessly around against nearby trees. Billy sized up the situation and, looking for a little fun and excitement with an inexperienced bunch of greenhorns, he slipped about five or six cartridges out of his belt and tossed them into the fire. In less than a minute they began to go off, and such a mad dash for tall timber you have never seen ... I looked back as I ran, and there stood the Kid with his arms folded, perfectly unconcerned ...

"Well, you're a damn fine bunch of soldiers. Run like a bunch of coyotes and forget to take your guns. I just wanted to break you in a little before we met the enemy, and, boys, I'm sure proud of your nerve."

After Billy's jailbreak, he arrived at his friend, John Meadows's Peñasco River ranch, 42 miles to the south of Lincoln.

The most hunted person in the nation, Billy was still joking. Meadows's memories were posthumously printed in a 2004 book titled *Pat Garrett and Billy the Kid as I Knew Them.* In it, Meadows included the scene. He wrote: "He showed up at Tom Norris' and my ranch, on the Peñasco about four miles below where Elk now stands ... Tom Norris and I was in the cabin cooking some supper. Kid come up to the corner of the house and seeing there was nobody there but us two, whom he could trust, he stepped to the door and said, 'Well, I've got you, haven't I?' I said, 'Well, you have. So what are you going to do with us?' He said, 'I'm going to eat supper with you.' "

Billy's courage in the face of danger was famous among his admiring contemporaries. Less comprehended was his greater triumph. Facing injustice about to end his life at 21, he refused to yield to rage and sadness. But for a moment, in his December 28th, 1880 interview to the *Las Vegas Gazette* reporter, given from the train about to take him to the Santa Fe jail, he revealed pain. He said: "I don't blame you for writing of me as you have. You have had to believe others' stories, but then I don't know as anyone would believe anything good of me, anyway,' he said."

I'm here now for him and the other freedom fighters to set the record straight.

TALK 10:
THE SANTA FE RING'S EXISTENCE
FROM BOOK: *THE SANTA FE RING VERSUS BILLY THE KID*
NOVEMBER 19, 2020

This begins my talks on the Santa Fe Ring, the corrupt political cabal which seized New Mexico Territory's land, government, and economy. The information comes from my book, *The Santa Fe Ring Versus Billy the Kid: The Making of an American Monster*. The "monster" is the Ring. It's also their made-up monster: the outlaw, Billy the Kid, as cover-up.

Writing the history of Billy the Kid and the Lincoln County War, and leaving out the Santa Fe Ring, is like writing the history of the Civil War and leaving out slavery. Great evil propelled the events. Including the Ring is key to my revisionist history.

The Santa Fe Ring began as a racist, profiteering, land-grab scheme involving millions of acres. The 1848 Treaty of Guadalupe Hidalgo, which ended the Mexican-American War, had added 525,000 square miles of northern Mexico to the victorious United States. The Treaty promised citizenship and retained land ownership to its 75,000 Hispanic residents. Ultimately carved out, was almost square New Mexico Territory. It had 121,697 square miles. About 15 million acres were land grants.

Within two decades, Hispanic land grant holders became victims. This paralleled genocide of Native Americans to get their land. The Santa Fe Ring was the scheme of Missourian attorneys, Stephen Benton Elkins and Thomas Benton Catron. They used a loophole in the Treaty of Guadalupe Hidalgo. Grant holders had to prove ownership. Then they needed confirmation by Congress. Catron and Elkins pretended to represent them. Then they'd buy the land far below value, and resell it at great profit.

Hiding multi-million acre theft, needed complicit government. So Catron and Elkins took legislative and judicial positions, and made corrupt alliances. By 1873, Elkins became Territorial Delegate, and entangled Washington politicians for Ring protection. Opponents were destroyed by malicious prosecutions or murder. Legal redress was impossible. Catron and Elkins diversified to banks, loans, railroads, mining, mercantile enterprises, and ranching.

The burgeoning Ring tyranny precipitated Territory-wide uprisings in the 1870's. They are discussed in a separate talk. But by the 1878 days of the Lincoln County War freedom fight, Ring-biased President Rutherford B. Hayes covered-up Ring atrocities so well that his, and his responsible cabinetmen's, reputations remained unscathed.

The successful Ring took the victor's option of writing the history. So it called its opponents outlaws. And it denied its own existence. A quirk of history made these lies last. The Ring stayed in power to the present. And the oppressed citizenry stayed silent in learned helplessness. Billy the Kid history fell victim to this blight. Scholarly researchers in the 20th centaury meekly omitted the Ring. Fawning hagiographers of the original Ring bosses, Catron and Elkins, pooh-poohed its reality.

Twentieth century Ring-biased historian, Victor Westphall, in his 1973 book, *Thomas Benton Catron and His* Era, mimicked antique Ringites. He called the Ring a fantasy. He wrote: "[It was a] romantic imagination [of] ... a sinister organization with members dedicated to unqualified promotion of their own selfish interests ... accompanied by connotations of violence, deception, deceit, fraud, and other nefarious implications." Westphall blamed Democrats and fate. He wrote: "Thomas Benton Catron was present when the Republican party in New Mexico was organized in the winter of 1867 and when the epithet "Santa Fe Ring" was applied to its leaders. It was Catron's fate to become the acknowledged head of both party and ring ... While Catron was often assailed as leader of the Ring, he held that position by virtue of ability as a common spokesman for others interested in common goals."

Westphall used the Ring's own cover-up that it was not a formal organization. He wrote; quote: "There was no network of control in an organized sense; there was mutual cooperation ... for particular events or projects." Such evaded culpability by Ringites was satirized by 19th century cartoonist, Thomas Nast. He drew

"Boss" Tweed's Tammany Hall Ring as a circle of men, each pointing to the other, saying, " 'Twas him."

So step one for condemning the Ring, is exposing its existence.

First one needs to understand democracy. America's founding fathers anticipated tyranny's temptation. So they divided government into executive, legislative, and judicial branches, to monitor each other. It was called checks and balances. Unanticipated was take-over of all branches by one cabal. That was the Santa Fe Ring's brain-child.

Other criminal minds had hit on that formula. The 19th century Mafia also had fixed structure. For the Santa Fe Ring, "boss," Thomas Benton Catron, ran the Territory. Stephen Benton Elkins managed Washington, D.C. Their local sub-bosses exercised power; as in Lincoln County's mercantile and cattle ranching monopolies. Their "enforcers" were lawmen, judges, and district attorneys. "Associates" were hired thugs for rustling, terrorism, and assassinations. Secrecy was by cipher-code communication, expurgation of incriminating records, and denial of existence. The higher-ups evaded connection to their minions' crimes by claiming "plausible deniability." That meant: " 'Twas him, not me.' " The Mafia's growth spurt came from Prohibition. The Ring's came from stealing massive Hispanic land grants.

It was not until 1970, 104 years after Catron and Elkins began their Ring, that Congress defeated "plausible denial" by passing the Racketeer Influenced and Corrupt Organizations Act, or R-I-C-O, RICO. It enabled prosecution of all conspirators having the same criminal objective. It stated: "If conspirators have a plan which calls for some conspirators to commit the crime and others to provide support, the supporters are as guilty as the perpetrators." RICO ultimately pitted law enforcement against the Mafia underworld. But there was no one to prosecute the Santa Fe Ring. They were the law. They were the world. They encompassed the Territory and infiltrated the federal government. And, unlike the Mafia, no insider has ever broken ranks. Nevertheless, RICO's making supporters as guilty as perpetrators is key to condemning the Ring's monsters.

There was no doubt about the Ring's existence. It was well known to it its victims, and well publicized. From its early days, even national press compared it to "Boss" Tweed's New York Ring. An editorial in March 13th, 1876's *The Boston Daily Globe*" was titled: "New Mexico, A Sorry Showing for a Would-be State, Tweed's Disciples Preying on the Populace." It stated: "The Territorial Government, executive and judicial, is as closely an allied ring as ever inflicted itself upon a people. Its headquarters is at Santa Fe, and it includes among its members public officials of every grade, and is ably assisted in its operations by the judicial element of the Government and its official organ, the Santa Fe New Mexican [newspaper]. Justice in the Territory is a sad delusion. The probate judges always have a hand in the election of the juries, and completely control the cases before the courts."

In New Mexico Territory, October 27th, 1880's *Las Cruces Thirty-Four* newspaper wrote: "The Santa Fe Ring is the most corrupt combination that ever cursed any country or community. It has controlled the machinery of the Republican party in the Territory for the past twelve years. It has vilified, oppressed or otherwise sought to ruin every man who had the independence and hardihood to oppose its corrupt schemes. It has grown fat upon the prostitution of the party it controls. It has used its power in the courts to defend its criminal tools from merited punishment. It has retained its power by wholesale bribery and intimidation of voters. It has threatened innocent men with prosecution in the courts, should they dare to oppose it. It has promised indicted criminals immunity from punishment if they would assist it to retain its power. The people of this county and every county will be benefited by its overthrow."

Ring accusations against T.B. Catron continued into the 20th century. A December 11th, 1911 letter of a Bronson Cutting to a James Roger Addison stated: "Catron was the boss of the Territory from 1865 [it was 1866] to 1900 and is probably still the most unscrupulous man in the Southwest. His methods of wholesale assassination and blackmail are [notorious]. [H]e still runs the gang in this country."

Oppressed citizens became the Ring's risk. The Ring thwarted their rebellions by rigged elections, malicious prosecutions, terrorist threats, forced flight, troops, biased press, and murder. They were defeated. But they documented the Ring's existence. I'll let them speak.

In the tinder keg, grass-roots uprisings of the 1870's, contemporary reports and exposés by Ring adversaries and victims are profuse. I'll discuss the uprisings more in a talk of their own. But they are the 1872 Legislature Revolt, the 1876

Grant County Rebellion, the 1877 Colfax County War, and the 1878 Lincoln County War. And these fighters certainly reported that the Ring existed.

For the 1872 Legislature Revolt in Santa Fe, January 1872's Denver "Rocky Mountain News" decried the Ring's attack on antagonistic legislators. It called it, quote "unparalled in the history of western politics." Federal troops were brought into the legislature to aid in voiding anti-Ring legislation. The paper called the Santa Fe Ring "a political and economic clique."

The 1876 Grant County Rebellion generated a "Declaration of Independence," announcing intent to secede to Arizona Territory to escape the Ring. On October 7th, their *Grant County Herald* printed it. It stated: "[W]e consider the Territory of New Mexico badly governed owing to the fact that the chief power in the Territorial legislation rests in the hands of a selfish oligarchy, who designedly wield the same in their own selfish interest."

In 1877, the Colfax County War peaked. Mary Tibbles McPherson, the firebrand mother-in-law of the local anti-Ring newspaper's editor, sent her own charges to Washington against Ringites. On May 1, 1877, she submitted her "Charges Against New Mexican Officials, Together With Corroboration Evidence." It stated: "The undersigned in behalf of the people of the Territory of New Mexico herewith present the following charges." She charged U.S. Attorney, Thomas B. Catron; Judge Warren Bristol; Chief Justice Henry L. Waldo, Governor Samuel B. Axtell, and others unnamed with quote: "having conspired together to corrupt and defraud justice and defeat the ends thereof, both by fraudulent and illegal practices in their respective Districts and offices; and by procuring the passage of insidious legislative enactments tending to dismemberment, confusion, and centralization of power and designed to protect infamy, legalize crime, deprive its citizens of personal liberty, and the right of trial by jury; compass the revenues of the Territory and the property of all its citizens for purposes of private gain." And she requested; quote: "their removal from office."

In August of 1877, McPherson submitted her 31 page, typeset booklet, "In the Matter of Charges vs. Governor S.B. Axtell and Other New Mexico Officials" to the Departments of the Interior and Justice. It stated: "That there has existed in Santa Fe for several years past, a Ring, is now beyond question. That this Ring has, by its power and influence, controlled all the offices, revenues, and Courts of the Territory, - and that they have used this power to oppress, intimidate and plunder the people, cannot now be denied."

The 1878 Lincoln County War generated many responses confirming the Santa Fe Ring's existence.

Billy Bonney himself knew the Ring existed. On July 13, 1878, the day before the start of the Lincoln County War Battle, he wrote his "Regulator Manifesto" letter to Ring boss T.B. Catron's brother-in-law. Billy stated: "We are all aware that your brother-in-law, T.B. Catron sustains the Murphy-Kinney party ... Steal from the poorest or richest American or Mexican, and the full measure of the injury you do, shall be visited upon the property of Mr. Catron." He signed it as "Regulator."

John Henry Tunstall's letters to his British family documented the Ring. On April 27th, 1877, he wrote to his father: "Everything in New Mexico, that pays at all (you may say) is worked by a "ring."

Alexander McSween's February 23rd, 1878 letter to just-murdered Tunstall's father, John Partridge Tunstall; stated: "[Tunstall] understood well from the U.S. Attorney [that meant Catron] to the lowest magistrate, that there was a combination and determination to keep down independence. This combination is known as the 'Santa Fe Ring.' To the branch of the Ring down here he had become particularly obnoxious owing to the fact that he was acquiring so much land, and because I aided him."

Lilly Klasner, engaged to Bob Olinger when he was killed on April 28, 1881 by Billy Bonney in his famous jailbreak, had her manuscript published posthumously in 1972 as *My Girlhood Among Outlaws*. She wrote: "John [Chisum] suffered at the hands of the powerful Santa Fe Ring of those days. This ring, a group of politicians and businessmen, sought to control the courts and everything else in the state [she meant Territory] and to get their hands on as much resources of the state as possible to exploit in their own interests. In other words, they were greedy for personal gain and sought to obtain it by fair means or foul, most frequently the latter ... Thomas B. Catron – then United States District Attorney [was] commonly regarded as one of the most influential members of the Santa Fe Ring, if not its guiding spirit."

Cattle king, John Chisum, himself wrote a sarcastic account of the Santa Fe Ring, dated January 16th, 1878, while in false imprisonment by boss Catron in Las Vegas, New Mexico Territory. The Lincoln County War was six months in the future. Chisum wrote: "I know it is said by many of the citizens that there is a Ring at Santa Fe but as the Governor [that was Axtell] said in his last message there was no ring, and I am of his opinion. If there was a ring there would be some show for the people, as a Ring is not solid, and there would be some show to get through it, or to get on the outside or inside of it. But the thing they have got there is perfectly solid, it cannot be penetrated from neither side or end, and it is perfectly hard and solid and when this solid substance strikes a citizen, it goes right through him and leaves him in such a condition that he never recovers from it. It is so powerful that it don't only ruin citizens but sometimes it strikes whole counties."

David Shield, Ring-murdered Alexander McSween's brother-in-law, writing on July 30th, 1878 for a loan to Montegue Leverson, a Colorado friend of John Chisum, said: "I do not wish to place myself under any obligation to the ring or their clique and they control everything here."

Investigator Frank Warner Angel had written reports about the murder of John Tunstall for the Hayes administration. He was apparently forced to cover-up the Ring in his reports. But he took his own covert action for justice. He sent incoming Governor, Lew Wallace, a copy of Mary McPherson's August, 1877 printed booklet, which she had sent to President Hayes. It exposed the Santa Fe Ring, its members, and their crimes.

Angel also prepared for Wallace, a secret, handwritten notebook, listing Ringites. Here are some examples. Under "Newspapers," was; quote: " 'Las Vegas Gazette, Republican' – Favors the ring; 'Santa Fe New Mexican,' Ring paper, Republican; [and] 'The Independent,' 'Mesilla Independent,' 'Mesilla News,' Ring papers." Individuals were listed alphabetically. Here are some examples. "Dolan J.J. Lincoln Leader in Lincoln Co, trouble, Murphy party, Brave sharp - determined fellow – Badly mixed up with the ring ... Loud Lieut. Santa Fe, officious – Works for the ring – not reliable ... "Longwill Dr Santa Fe, Good Dr – but mixed up in Colfax Co trouble, Axtel man, ring man, do not rely on him .... Thornton W.T. Santa Fe, Catrons partner ...Walz E.A. Lincoln – a tool of Catron – a boy – not reliable."

Lew Wallace took office as Governor on October 1st, 1878. A little over a month later, on November 14th, 1878, he wrote secretly to his Civil War friend Colonel Absalom Markland. "I came here, and found a 'Ring' with a hand on the throat of the Territory. I refused to join them, and now they are proposing to fight me in the Senate. Ex [Territorial] Delegate Elkins is head-center in Washington."

Susan McSween, widow of Alexander McSween, who was murdered in the Lincoln County War, hired an attorney named Huston Chapman to prosecute Fort Stanton's Commander N.A.M. Dudley for her husband's murder and arson of her home. On November 29th, 1878, Chapman wrote to Lew Wallace. "The McSween men are willing to stand their trial in the proper courts of the territory, or to observe your proclamation [of Amnesty], provided, the other side or "ring" observe it."

After the Ring murdered Chapman, his office mate, Ira Leonard, took over the case against Dudley. He also became an advisor to Lew Wallace. Well aware of the Ring, he wrote the following to Wallace on May 20th, 1879: " [The Murphy-Dolan] party had for a long time uninterrupted sway in this County and could not brook opposition, and they were determined either by fair or foul means to have no opposition, and they resorted to every artifice in their power to accomplish that purpose. They were a part and parcel of the Santa Fe Ring that has been so long an incubus on the government of this Territory."

Cautious Pat Garrett did not name the Ring in his 1882 ghostwritten book, *The Authentic Life of Billy the Kid.* But he made clear that T.B. Catron backed the side fighting Alexander McSween. The book stated: "It is not the intention here to discuss the merits of the imbroglio [meaning the Lincoln County War] ... but merely to detail such events of the war as ... [Billy the Kid] took part in. The principles in this difficulty were on one side John S. Chisum, called the Cattle King of New Mexico, with Alexander A. McSween and John H. Tunstall as important allies. On the other side were the firm of Murphy and Dolan, merchants in Lincoln, the county seat, backed by nearly every small cattle owner in the Pecos Valley. This latter faction was supported by Thomas B. Catron, United States Attorney for the Territory, a resident of Santa Fe, one of the eminent lawyers of the Territory, and a considerable owner in the Pecos region."

Obviously, there was no doubt to those present in New Mexico Territory's 1870's that the Santa Fe Ring existed. Other talks will detail the 1870's brave, desperate, and lost freedom fights against it.

TALK 11:
UPRISINGS AGAINST THE SANTA FE RING

FROM BOOK: *THE SANTA FE RING VERSUS BILLY THE KID*

NOVEMBER 20, 2020

This talk is about New Mexico Territory's freedom fights. It's central to my revisionist history of Billy the Kid. The information is from my book, *The Santa Fe Ring Versus Billy the Kid: The Making of an American Monster.*

Democracy hung in the balance in New Mexico Territory in the 1870's, as citizens resisted the rapacious political cabal known as the Santa Fe Ring. Freedom fights blazed while the Ring escalated terrorism to defeat them. The Lincoln County War was last and bloodiest. Its loss meant tyranny's victory.

A separate talk will cover Ring co-bosses, Thomas Benton Catron and Stephen Benton Elkins. Noted here is that they founded their Ring in 1866, after coming to New Mexico Territory from Missouri. Their racist scheme was to steal Hispanic residents' huge land grants. Congress had left grant holders vulnerable by forcing proof of ownership and boundaries. Catron and Elkins, as their lawyers, tricked them into selling their land for a pittance, to themselves or to cronies. Catron and Elkins also infiltrated Territorial government to back these crimes. And they infiltrated judgeships to maliciously prosecute adversaries.

By the 1870's, their victims' sole recourse was rebellion. In 1872, was what I named the Legislature Revolt. In 1876, was the Grant County Rebellion. In 1877, the Colfax County War peaked. In 1878, was the Lincoln County War. All were crushed. Washington turned a blind eye. The Ring won. No Ringite was ever punished. But their victims left documentation that can still bring history's judgment.

The 1872 Legislature Revolt was first. Fittingly, it was in Santa Fe, in the legislature, the seat of democratic power.

The Republican Santa Fe Ring already controlled the Governors. By 1869, boss Elkins influenced President Ulysses S. Grant to appoint William Anderson Pile from Missouri. In his scandal-filled tenure, Governor Pile empowered Catron and Elkins as Attorney General and U.S. Attorney respectively.

In 1871, Grant made Marsh Giddings of Michigan Governor. A Ring loyalist, he taxed land grants to aid Ring take-overs by bleeding owners. With Catron, he started the Ring's ploy of calling opponents "outlaws." He precipitated the Legislature Revolt.

At the December 7th start of the 1871 to '72 legislative session, Democrats controlled the Council. They were poised to gain the House of Representatives. That would stifle the fledgling Ring. In December of 1871, they first passed bills for Silver City's incorporation and Grant County's public school system.

Then came the challenge. On December 30th, the Council and House passed, by large majorities, redistricting of Ring-biased judges. That attack centered on Judge Joseph G. Palen. He was the Ring's weapon for malicious prosecutions and shielding of cronies. He was to be transferred from Santa Fe's First Judicial District to remote Third Judicial District. That would also end his being the Supreme Court's Chief Justice. Subsequently, legislator, August Kirchner, sent an affidavit to the federal Judiciary Committee, stating that Catron and Elkins tried to use him to bribe legislators to leave Palen undisturbed.

On January 4th of 1872, Governor Giddings vetoed the Democrats' bills by lying that those legislators had no power to reassign judges.

On January 5th, to block Democrats over-riding Giddings's illegal veto, Ringites faked a Republican majority by adding names of four absent Taos legislators.

On January 9th, Ringites tried to end and void the session.

On January 10th, the four Taos men arrived. But the Ring dared not risk a real vote. So Ringite House Speaker, Milnor Rudulph, illegally ended the session. The Democrat majority objected. Rudulph adjourned the House. He walked out, taking 10 legislators with him. (Note that Ringite Rudulph, in 9 years, would be President of Billy Bonney's Coroner's Jury, dictating to the jurymen praise of Pat Garrett for killing him.)

That day, January 10th, 1872, began the Legislature Revolt. Outrage at Rudulph's illegal ending of the session to shield the Ring started it. Democrats claimed his leaving left a vacancy. So they elected, as Speaker, Silver City mine developer, John R. Johnson. They then directed the Santa Fe County Sheriff to arrest and bring back the departed legislators for a quorum. Arrested and returned were Milnor Rudulph and two others.

The next day, January the 11th, Ringites retaliated. Governor Giddings and Milnor Rudulph, still calling himself Speaker, declared "anarchy and rebellion."

The majority of legislators backed John Johnson. So Catron and Elkins bribed them to back Rudulph's House and to shield Judge Palen.

On January 12th, Giddings brought troops from Fort Marcy into the legislature. They seized Speaker Johnson. Chief Justice Palen called in Santa Fe's U.S. Marshal and his deputies. They escorted Milnor Rudulph to the Speaker's chair.

January of 1872's "Denver Rocky Mountain News" described the actions as; quote: "unparalled in the history of western politics. Federal troops had been stationed in the halls of the Territorial legislature to assure control by the Santa Fe Ring, a political and economic clique." And Council President Don Diego Archuleta, exposing the racist core of the Ring, cried futilely: "Before we submit to such despotic action on the part of the Executive, the Mexican people had better be placed upon reservations as the Indians are now. We had better resign our seats than to beg our rights of the newly fledged governor who seeks to overawe us, and force us to obedience to his despotic will by the presence of U.S. bayonets."

Next Catron, as Attorney General, filed writs of habeas corpus in the Supreme Court to free Rudulph and the two other arrested legislators. And he called an emergency Supreme Court session for their case. Fake Speaker Milnor Rudulph then suspended the legislature pending the Supreme Court's decision.

On January 22nd, the Supreme Court convened. Present were troops and the Sheriff for intimidation. The Court ignored its limited habeas corpus issue. Instead it declared null and void all Democratic legislation of the session. Republicans then passed a resolution expunging from the record and nullifying all proceedings of the Democratic legislators.

On February 28th, Giddings castrated the rebellious legislators. By a gerrymandering Proclamation, he halved their numbers from anti-Ring Grant, Doña Ana, and Lincoln Counties.

Ringites recognized the Legislature Revolt's danger. The next year, in 1873, writing to the Department of Interior, Giddings called the revolt "that terrible war" and "one of the most reckless revolutionary efforts made any where." And its successful suppression began the Ring's patterns of bribery; abuse of executive and judicial power; and using troops for terrorism. And never again would an uprising be called a revolution. Opponents became so-called "lawless outlaws." Opened was the door to murder.

In 1876 was the Grant County Rebellion. Formed in 1868, Grant County was named after Ulysses S. Grant. It occupied the southwestern corner of New Mexico Territory. To the west, it bordered Arizona Territory. Only 50 miles from the border was Silver City, its mining-rich county seat, founded in 1870.

The Santa Fe Ring clutched Grant County from its inception. Its district court in 1868 had boss Thomas Benton Catron himself as its District Attorney.

The Grant County Rebellion was rooted in simmering resentment going back to the 1872 Legislature Revolt. Its illegally voided acts had stopped Grant County's self-governing incorporation of Silver City, and its taxation to create a public school system. Silver City's John Johnson, the legal Speaker, had been manhandled by troops and cast out. And Governor Giddings had halved their legislators to hobble them.

It's possible that Billy Bonney himself heard anti-Ring grumblings when living in Silver City from 1873 to 1875. On August 8th, 1875, the *Grant County Herald* reported the wish to secede from the Territory to escape the Ring's "political vassalage."

The actual Grant County Rebellion intentionally coincided with the American Revolution's centennial. On September 16th, 1876, the *Grant County Herald* published "A Contemplated Political Change." A citizens' meeting was announced to discuss annexation to Arizona Territory.

At the October 4th Grant County Annexation Meeting, legislator John M. Ginn was elected Presiding Officer. An elected committee of five then authored the "Grant County Declaration of Independence." The independence was from the Santa Fe Ring.

A committee of eight was elected to write, for Congress, the memorial for annexation.

On October 7th, the *Grant County Herald* printed in full the "Grant County Declaration of Independence." It stated: "[W]e the citizens of Grant County here assembled, having met pursuant to said call, do hereby declare it is our earnest wish to join our political destinies with the neighboring Territory of Arizona and cease our political connection with the Territory of New Mexico ... and for taking this important step we assign the following as some of the principal reasons for the desired change." Included was, quote: "[We] have little or no voice in the enactment of laws which are necessary to our welfare, which we believe would be remedied by the liberal-minded people of Arizona ... [We] consider the Territory of New Mexico badly governed owing to the fact that the chief power in the Territorial legislation rests in the hands of a selfish oligarchy, who designedly wield the same in their own selfish interest, and ... we see no hope for relief in the near future." It ended: "Resolved: That it is the wish of the people of Grant County, as expressed through the persons here assembled, that the necessary steps to be taken at once to further that view herein expressed."

On November 7th, Grant County voted almost unanimously for annexation. On January 3rd, 1877, Arizona Territory's Governor A.P.K. Safford seconded the annexation.

Then national politics collided. November 1876's Presidential election was won by Republican Rutherford B. Hayes. Hayes, opposed Democratic Arizona's getting mine-rich Grant County. So, when the Arizona Representative introduced the Resolution for annexation to Congress, it was referred to the Committee on Territories, where it was killed. No one knew that Hayes was entangled with the Santa Fe Ring.

The rebellion deflated. Grant County retreated into non-intervention, as Ring rampages escalated in other parts of the rebelling Territory. That emboldened Ringite Governor Samuel Beach Axtell, in office for a year, to implement the Ring's growing brutality to stamp out resistance.

The next year, 1877, the Colfax County War peaked in the north. Its anti-Ring uprisings spanned 1873 to 1887 without a central battle, but with 200 people killed. But 1877 had an outburst of anti-Ring press exposés, petitions, and complaints to the Hayes administration. And the Ring perfected strategies for tyranny: assassination, malicious prosecution, shielding of its criminals by obstructing courts, and using troops against civilians.

As background, T.B. Catron and S.B. Elkins cheated Lucien Bonaparte Maxwell out of his 2 million acre Maxwell Land Grant in 1870. But its settlers remained. Catron and Elkins intended the land for mining, timber, coal, agriculture, grazing land, and railroad passageway over its Raton Pass. And they planned to sell land to new settlers. The Grant was immediately sold to their speculator friends. They, in turn, sold it to British investors as the Maxwell Land Grant and Railway Company. Ringite Governor, William Pile, assisted the filing. That 1870, Elkins also increased Catron's power by resigning as U.S. Attorney, so Catron could take the position.

On April 17, 1871, Governor Pile assisted Elkins by a Proclamation sending troops to evict Grant settlers resisting take-over of their land.

In 1872, the Grant was bought by Dutch investors. Elkins was President of their Board of Directors. Catron was their attorney. That year, Elkins used Ringite Governor Marsh Giddings to send troops against the settlers. To reduce their political power, the county seat was moved to Cimarron, where the Grant Company was headquartered.

In 1873, the Dutch Company hired 26 year old Raymond Morley from Iowa - Chief Construction Engineer of the Atchison Topeka and Santa Fe Railroad - as their Vice-president, to develop that train's route into New Mexico. He brought his wife, Ada McPherson Morley. They were housed in the company's headquarters, the Maxwell family's prior mansion. Surprisingly, Raymond Morley became anti-Ring. He sympathized with the Grant's settlers, whose rioting had become the Colfax County War.

In 1874, Morley, and his attorney friend, Frank Springer, founded the anti-Ring *Cimarron News and Press*. With local anti-Ring leader, Reverend Franklin J. Tolby, they anonymously exposed Catron, Elkins, Judge Joseph Palen, and Land Grant Company Directors Robert Longwill, and Melvin Mills, as Ringites in articles for *The New York Sun*.

By 1875, the Ring retaliated. It began with boss Catron's favorite tactic of malicious prosecution. He targeted Morley's wife Ada. In early 1875, her firebrand mother, Mary Tibbles McPherson had come from Iowa, and became inspired by Reverend Tolby. So she mailed an anti-Ring letter to Washington at Cimarron's post office. Scared of repercussions, Ada took it from the post office box. The Ringite postmaster reported Ada to Catron. As U.S. Attorney, he federally indicted her for mail theft. But he left her arrest in abeyance as torture.

Catron had bigger fish to fry. On September 14, 1875, Reverend Franklin Tolby, on horseback, was assassinated on a remote road - mirroring John Tunstall's Ring murder in three years. Catron's agents were the Grant Company Directors, Melvin Mills and Robert Longwill, who used local thugs for the crime.

Anti-Ring leadership was assumed by Tolby's assistant, Reverend Oscar P. McMains. He identified the killers. As would be repeated in Lincoln County's Tunstall murder, the murderers were shielded by the Ringite sheriff. But one of the two actual killers, exposed the plot. So he was murdered before testifying. And Ringite Governor S.B. Axtell sent troops into Cimarron to intimidate the outraged citizens. Killer, Robert Longwill, escaped to Santa Fe to Catron's protection. And the Ring launched an outlaw myth. November 16th, 1875's Ringite *Santa Fe Weekly New Mexican* reported "Anarchy in Cimarron." It wrote: "There seems to be an armed band of men in and about town bent on violence, lawlessness and ruling to suit themselves."

But Catron failed. His attack on Ada McPherson Morley did not stop her husband, Raymond Morley's, exposés. And her mother, Mary Tibbles McPherson, increased her efforts to expose the Ring. And the settlers kept on rioting.

On December 22nd, 1875, *The New York Sun* published an anonymous anti-Ring article about Reverend Tolby's murder. It exposed the Ring as organized crime. By Raymond Morley, it was titled: "The Territory of Elkins ... The Murder of the Reverend F.J. Tolby in New Mexico." It stated: "The political revolution which has taken place, and is still in progress in this Territory, is mainly attributed to the exposures of the Santa Fe Ring which have appeared in the "Sun," and which have created great consternation among our corrupt officials ... By means of libel suits, and still more effectual measures, the Ring has succeeded in intimidating the local press, with one or two exceptions; and so long as the courts are constituted as they are at present, it is absolutely unsafe for any man to actively oppose the corrupt scheme of the Ring. The nature of the means taken to harass those who show rebellious spirit has already been described in this correspondence ... On the 14th of September last, the Reverend F.J. Tolby, a minister of the gospel, generally respected and beloved, was brutally murdered on the highway while passing through a lonely canyon ... It is said that a few days before his death Mr. Tolby had a warm discussion with Judge Palen of the First Judicial District, one of the chiefs of the Ring ... At last ... the actual murderers were hunted down, and when it was found that they implicated the principal members of the Colfax county branch of the Ring as the instigators of the crime, the indignation of the people knew no bounds ... Their names are R.H. Longwill, Probate Judge; [and] M.W. Mills, member of the Legislature ... [T]he feeling against all persons who are supposed to be connected in any way to the operation of Elkins and Company is bitter in the extreme ... On the 10th of November a mass meeting of the citizens of Colfax county was held in the court house in Cimarron ... The Reverend O.P. McMains presided, and resolutions were adopted that the killing of Mr. Tolby was a deliberately planned assassination, in which the actual murderers were the tools of other parties, who ... planned the murder; and those who procured the murder are far more guilty, if possible, than the duped and hired tools, and that, if satisfactory evidence is found to discover and identify any such party or parties, there should not be permitted to them any loophole to escape the extreme penalty of the law. If a new election for Delegate to Congress could be held for tomorrow, Elkins would be defeated by such a tremendous majority that not even the tools of the Santa Fe Ring would dare attempt the job of counting him in."

By 1876, the Ring escalated repression. On January 14th, the Maxwell Land Grant Company, using Governor Axtell, petitioned to force settlers to buy or rent their land, with eviction for refusal.

The same day, Axtell abolished Colfax County's courts. He transferred them to distant and inaccessible Taos County. He also barred Colfax County citizens from being on Taos juries. Colfax County witnesses in litigation had to travel over a mountain range to Taos. Intended was obstructing Franklin Tolby's murderers' trials to snuff out the Colfax County War.

Within days, Raymond Morley; Frank Springer; businessman, Henry M. Porter, and rancher Clay Allison, requested a meeting with Governor Axtell in Cimarron. Frank Springer also went to Santa Fe to meet with Axtell to request that visit. Axtell's response, that January of 1876, heralded his Lincoln County War brutality and outlawing. Springer recounted: "He said there were bad men [in Cimarron] and that he intended to have them punished or compelled to leave the county, if it took all the troops in New Mexico."

The Ring was poised for murder. Morley, Springer, Porter, and Allison were next. In what became called the "Dear Ben Plot," in March of 1876, Axtell colluded with Ringite Second Judicial District Judge Benjamin Stephens. Stephens came to Cimarron with a telegram to lure the victims. He also had a secret telegraphed direction from Axtell. Stephens, knowing Morley, invited him to the local St. James Hotel. He gave him the lure telegram. It stated that Axtell was coming by that Saturday's coach for a secret meeting with him, Springer, Allison, and Porter about the Colfax County courts.

In fact, Axtell was not coming. The victims were to be met by Fort Union's troops, who would kill them. The twisted logic was that hot-headed Allison would react violently, and justify the shootings of all as self-defense.

But Morley was warned of the plot, likely by the telegraph operator, who got Axtell's secret telegraph to Benjamin Stephens. It was to "Dear Ben." It said: "Have your men placed to arrest him [that meant Clay Allison] and to kill all the men who resist you or stand with those who do resist you. Our man [that was Allison] signed the invitation with others who were at that meeting for me to visit Colfax – Porter, Morley, Springer, et. al. Now, if they expect me Saturday, they will be on hand. Send me letters by messenger, and do not hesitate at extreme measures. Your honor is at stake now, and a failure is fatal." Morley warned the others. So the plot failed.

Not included in the "Dear Ben plot" was actually the most dangerous of the Colfax County freedom fighters: the breathtakingly brave and bold Mary Tibbles McPherson. Sexist underestimation apparently spared her. Meanwhile, she wrote the most important documents in existence exposing the Santa Fe Ring. She stayed in Cimarron from 1875 through 1876. She then continued her anti-Ring fight in Washington D.C. Her writings remove any doubt that President Hayes and his administration knew about the Ring, its members, and its crimes. She demanded removal from office of U.S. Attorney Catron, Territorial Delegate Elkins, Governor S.B. Axtell, Judge Warren Bristol, and Chief Justice Henry Waldo. Had she succeeded, the Lincoln County War would not have happened. In fact, the 1878 Lincoln County investigations of Frank Warner Angel were structured to cover-up her proof that U.S. officials were behind murder. And when Angel covertly sought to pit new Governor Lew Wallace against the Ring, he supplied Wallace with McPherson's magnificent type-set booklet of 1877, covering everything.

Mary McPherson began her onslaught by attacking boss Catron. He was then maliciously prosecuting her daughter, Ada, for fake mail theft. On February 7, 1877, McPherson complained to Attorney General Alphonso Taft. She included the murder of Reverend Tolby. She titled her exposé: "Charges against Thomas B. Catron, U.S. Attorney, and Others." She wrote: "I wish to bring to your attention the sufferings of the people of New Mexico ... In searching out the assassins, the evidence pointed strongly to U.S. officials ... all US officers out there are in league together, and the people are the sufferers."

Catron himself fired back with a letter to Taft that she was, quote, a "crazy person," that outlaws had taken over Colfax County, and that Territorial courts were free of politics. As Ring head, that liar hissed: "It is utterly false that the U.S. officials in this Territory are in any manner engaged together so that the people are sufferers, or that there is any combination among them for any purpose whatever." McPherson's complaint was ignored.

Mary McPherson was next forced to use an attorney for her Washington complaints. On May 1, 1877, adding one, she submitted her "Charges Against New Mexican Officials, Together With Corroboration Evidence." It included a "Petition to Remove Judge Bristol" and two lists of "Charges Against S.B. Axtell, Governor of New Mexico." It had a cover letter to President Hayes and extensive evidence and charges.

She spelled out the Ring's organized crime. She asserted, quote: "[T]he United States District Attorney, Thomas B. Catron; Associate Justice Warren Bristol; Henry L. Waldo, Chief Justice; Samuel B. Axtell, Governor, and others of the said Territory, to them unknown, [have] conspired together to corrupt and defraud justice and defeat the ends thereof, both by fraudulent and illegal practices in their respective Districts and offices; and by procuring the passage of insidious legislative enactments ... It is in evidence that for several years these parties have been in collusion in a general plan having for its aim the centralizing of power, the reduction of large and valuable private Grants of land within the Territory to their personal use and benefit, by corrupt Territorial and Congressional enactments, and by passage of bills of attainment and de facto laws depriving the citizens of due process of law ... To accomplish these purposes this Ring so formed appears to have paused at nothing however difficult or questionable." McPherson's goal was to, quote, "respectfully request their removal from office."

On May 3rd, 1877, McPherson added to her complaint to Hayes. She got corruption's favored tactic: stonewalling.

On July 26th, 1877, McPherson made an open records request to Secretary of the Interior Carl Schurz. She wanted records pertaining to her "Charges vs. Governor S.B. Axtell in connection with the Santa Fe Ring; including S.B. Elkins, and Thomas B. Catron, as U.S. Attorneys of New Mexico."

Stonewalled, on August 23rd, 1877, she tried to contact Attorney General Charles Devens. She was stonewalled.

But her charges were forwarded to Ringite Governor Axtell. He denied them.

Unfazed, in August of 1877, Mary McPherson wrote the best contemporary exposure of the Santa Fe Ring. She dispensed with the attorney. It is a 31 page, typeset booklet. She titled it: "In the Matter of Charges vs. Governor S.B. Axtell and Other New Mexico Officials; Submitted to the Departments of the Interior and Justice." It could have prevented the Lincoln County War. And it heralded its atrocities.

For it, McPherson distilled her past complaints to expose the Ring: its fraudulent land grant grabs; its murder of Franklin Tolby; and its suppression of the settlers by removing their courts. She wrote: "That there has existed in Santa Fe for several years past, a Ring, is now beyond question. That this Ring has, by its power and influence, controlled all the offices, revenues, and Courts of the Territory, - and that they have used this power to oppress, intimidate and plunder the people, cannot now be denied." She accused Catron and Elkins of having, quote: "the Courts of New Mexico, manipulated by the Ring [to] get just such decisions as they wanted to complete this general land steal or 'partition' of other men's property among themselves!" She covered the Ring's malicious prosecutions, briberies, vote fixings, removal of Colfax County courts to shield Reverend Franklin Tolby's murderers, and criminal acts of Governor Axtell. She added the petition to remove Judge Warren Bristol. She concluded with truth that heralded the Lincoln County War revolution: "And if the Government allow [Ringmen] to retain their place and power,

148

in the face of this showing; it deserves to have its authority defied." She was stonewalled.

Unbeknownst to Mary McPherson, Ringites had no problem getting the ear of President Hayes. On June 11th, 1877, Territorial Delegate S.B. Elkins wrote to him in support of Governor Axtell. He called McPherson's charges "absolutely false." He added the Ring's all-purpose outlaw myth. He wrote: "[The charges] are proffered by irresponsible parties now residents who have no interest in the Territory and to satisfy a few bad people to whom I am informed the Governor gave offence in attempting to repress violence and murder ... [A]s a citizen of New Mexico deeply interested in her welfare and as a friend of your administration I beg to record my protest."

So nothing was done by the Hayes administration. The Colfax County War simmered on. Franklin Tolby's murderers went unpunished. By 1878, Elkins's and Catron's land-grab vision was realized. The Raton Pass of the Maxwell Land Grant along the old Santa Fe Trail was bought by the Atchison, Topeka, and Santa Fe Railroad to run its tracks from Colorado to New Mexico Territory.

So it was inevitable that on February 18, 1878, the Ring assassination of its adversary, John Tunstall, went unpunished. So it was inevitable that on July 19, 1878 - the last day of the Lincoln County War Battle - that the Ring's use of troops to murder Alexander McSween, Francisco Zamora, Vincente Romero, and Harvey Morris went unpunished.

By the end of 1878, President Hayes faked action for Lincoln County War atrocities by removing Governor Axtell. By 1879, Raymond and Ada Morley fled Cimarron and New Mexico Territory. On July 13th, 1882, removed Axtell was reinstated as New Mexico's Territorial Chief Justice by the Senate Judiciary Committee. And, by April 18th, 1887, by federal Supreme Court decree, the Ring achieved eviction of all Maxwell Land Grant settlers.

There was no justice whatsoever.

The Colfax County War clinched the Ring's blueprint for unbeatable organized crime: control the governor, legislature, courts, and law enforcement; conduct malicious prosecution for intimidation; use the outlaw myth to invalidate adversaries; remove legal redress to shield members from prosecution; enlist troops for suppression; hire thugs for assassinations; expurgate incriminating documents; and use Washington's protection.

But this perfect tyranny had an Achilles heal. It had to remain secret. The Ring almost achieved that too. The Legislature Revolt, the Grant County Rebellion, and the Colfax County War were forgotten.

But, in August of 1877, when Mary McPherson wrote her damning booklet on the Ring, a rough teenager, just renamed by himself as "Billy Bonney," dashed from Arizona Territory to New Mexico Territory on a stolen racehorse. He had just killed a bullying blacksmith in self-defense. By the next month, he was riding with Ring thug, Jessie Evans, and his boys, as just another gunman. But this kid was destined to drag the Ring into the glare of insatiable international curiosity about his life and his death, till their crimes could become common knowledge, till their condemnation was finally possible, and till the forgotten freedom fighters could be honored.

The Lincoln County War, which Billy Bonney made famous, will be in a talk of its own.

TALK 12:
THE RING AND LINCOLN COUNTY
FROM BOOK: *THE SANTA FE RING*
VERSUS BILLY THE KID
DECEMBER 14, 2020

This talk begins my revisionist history discussion of New Mexico Territory's Lincoln County War. It continues in Talks 13 to 17. The information is from my book, *The Santa Fe Ring Versus Billy the Kid: The Making of an American Monster*.

One can say that the Lincoln County War was caused by the Santa Fe Ring's most gruesome land-grab. And that War ended the 1870's Territory-wide anti-Ring uprisings. They're discussed in Talk 11. They were crushed with escalating brutality.

The 1872 Legislature Revolt was triggered by the Ring wanting to void acts stopping Ringite judges' power for malicious prosecutions. The 1876 Grant County Rebellion was triggered by the Ring's wanting to block that county's legislative power to oppose it. The Colfax County War was triggered by the Ring's wanting the Maxwell Land Grant settlers' land.

But what did the Ring want in Lincoln County? Key was who was doing the wanting. It was the Ring's Territorial boss: Thomas Benton Catron. He wanted Lincoln County for himself! At that time, it was the biggest county in the United States. It was 30,000 square miles, or 19,200,000 acres. It was bigger than combined Massachusetts, Connecticut, Vermont, Rhode Island, and Delaware. It was the southeast quarter of almost square New Mexico Territory. There, Catron sought mercantile and ranching monopolies, and supply contracts to its Fort Stanton and the Mescalero Indian Reservation.

And, after illegally defeating earlier anti-Ring uprisings with impunity, Catron was emboldened for take-over of Lincoln County. He would cause the Lincoln County War.

To cover-up Thomas Benton Catron as responsible for the horrors that followed, his Ring-denying hagiographer, Victor Westphall, in his 1973 book, *Thomas Benton Catron and His Era*, parroted the Ring's lie, as did 20th century historians. Claimed was that the Lincoln County War was a local conflict between the mercantile business of Lawrence Murphy and James Dolan, known as "The House;" and that of British newcomer John Tunstall and his ally, cattle king, John Chisum.

Apologist Westphall made-up that Catron's role was, quote "shrouded in mystery," and that, quote "at no time was he personally in the region." This is the so-called "plausible deniability" defense used by layered organized crime - like the Santa Fe Ring. As I discussed in Talk 10, by 1970, the Racketeer Influenced and Corrupt Organizations Act, or RICO, defeated it. It stated: "If conspirators have a plan which calls for some conspirators to commit the crime and others to provide support, the supporters are as guilty as the perpetrators." So RICO explains Catron's guilt in Lincoln County.

What follows is T.B. Catron's involvement - without having to set foot in Lincoln. Ironically, it is Westphall who provided Catron's economic links to Lincoln County. They translate into Catron's motive for eliminating John Tunstall.

Catron had been making monopolistic inroads in Lincoln County since his 1866 Territorial arrival, and founding of the Santa Fe Ring with co-boss Stephen Benton Elkins. He'd immediately dealt in military beef contracts. By 1868, Catron's records show receipts for merchandise signed by Lawrence Murphy. That linked Catron to Fort Stanton's beef suppliers, Emil Fritz and Lawrence Murphy, then operating its sutler store as L.G. Murphy and Company. At the Fort, were also Catron's future minions: store employee, James Dolan, and then-Major and future Lincoln County Sheriff, William Brady.

According to historian, Philip Rasch, Catron, as owning the First National Bank of Santa Fe, was the silent backer of L.G. Murphy and Company. In 1873, the business was expelled from Fort Stanton after ruffian James Dolan tried to kill a soldier.

Catron's backing built them Lincoln's huge, two story, general store and post office called "The House." On forty acres, it was nine miles from the Fort. It was the Ring's stronghold in Lincoln County. Its builder, George Peppin, became a Ring loyalist. Ultimately he was the Sheriff at the Lincoln County War.

Westphall also revealed Catron as silent owner of Dolan's supposed Pecos River Cow Camp. It held John Chisum's rustled cattle. Catron also controlled Mescalero Indian Reservation Agent, Frederick Godfroy, to guarantee acceptance of "The House's" stolen cattle, shoddy hay, and mealy flour for its supply contract.

Catron's direct contact to Agent Godfroy and Lincoln County was through his business agent, David Easton, housed in Blazer's Mill within the Mescalero Indian Reservation. Easton also managed "The House's" brewery for Catron. In the Lincoln County War, as a Justice of the Peace, David Easton served the Ring by writing false arrest warrants on May 30th, 1878 outlawing Alexander McSween and Regulators for malicious prosecutions.

Catron's minions replicated his political terrorism. They caused Lincoln County's real "troubles." "The House" oppressed cash-strapped locals with supplies sold on usurious credit, while underpaying them for their farming produce. In 1875, in Lincoln, local rancher, Robert Casey, was murdered by the Ring immediately after he won an election against Lawrence Murphy. A month later, Juan Patrón, Lincoln's anti-Ring Hispanic leader, was crippled in attempted assassination by "The House's" future partner, John Riley, Catron's cattle dealer.

By 1876, with Lawrence Murphy terminally ill, James Dolan, as local Ring boss, added John Riley as his partner, renaming the business J.J. Dolan and Company.

Westphall topped off Catron's Lincoln County interests by stating that his brother-in-law, Edgar Walz, was also his agent there. Walz ran Catron's Carrizozo Land and Cattle Company ranch. Catron got it from dying Lawrence Murphy to settle Murphy's debt to him. It was 20 square miles.

But, by 1877, it was Catron who had "troubles" himself.

In 1876, a British settler named John Henry Tunstall had arrived in Lincoln By 1877, he had built his own large general store, just a quarter mile east of "The House." It had Lincoln County's first bank. He made two cattle ranches along the west-to-east Feliz and Peñasco Rivers to control grazing land all the way to the north-to-south Pecos River by controlling the water. He used his employees, like Billy Bonney, to homestead land on the Peñasco River, after buying another ranch there from a Jacob Basil "Billy" Matthews. His fair dealings were bankrupting "The House." He had sights on "The House's" beef contracts to the Mescalero Indian Reservation and Fort Stanton. So, by 1877, Catron's goal of mercantile and cattle monopolies was threatened.

Tunstall was one of the few people in the Territory with considerable cash through his wealthy British father. So he could compete aggressively in the cash-poor Territory. In a fair market, he would have won. Magnifying risk to Catron's goals was high-minded Lincoln Attorney, Alexander McSween. He knew Ring crimes after working for "The House" from 1875 to 1876. He was inspiring Tunstall's anti-Ring fervor. So Tunstall's competitor was Thomas Benton Catron himself.

Tunstall and McSween exposed "The House's" Fort Stanton and Mescalero Indian Reservation supply scams. In 1878, their complaint triggered Department of Interior Investigator E.C. Watkins's investigation. It showed that Indian Agent Godfroy was giving Reservation supplies, like blankets, to supply "The House." He was getting rustled beef from outlaw John Kinney and his gang. Godfroy was also billing for 1,500 Apaches, while only a few hundred were actually there.

Catron was also having "troubles" with his cattle rustling victim, John Chisum. A cattle king, with herd of 80,000 along the Pecos River, he'd been empowered by Tunstall's business alliance, and had been made President of Tunstall's Lincoln Bank.

On January 12th, 1878, Catron emerged from his secret partnership with "The House," then going bankrupt from Tunstall's competition. Dolan and Riley mortgaged it to Catron, with its 40 acres. The transaction was done in Lincoln by Catron's law partner, William Thornton. Catron put his brother-in-law Edgar Walz, in charge of "The House." So when Tunstall was murdered on February 18th, "The House" was Catron's! This was no local mercantile competition!

To protect his Lincoln County schemes, Catron needed a beholden Governor. Through John Riley, he had loaned Governor Samuel Beach Axtell, $1,8000. That was half of Axtell's salary. It would guarantee his proclamations shielding Tunstall's Ringite murderers from prosecution.

So, by 1878, in place were Catron's enforcers. William Brady was Lincoln's first Sheriff. The District Attorney was William Rynerson. The Third Judicial District Judge was Warren Bristol.

The Seven Rivers rancher-rustler cattle suppliers were available for violence. Rustling outlaw gangs of Jessie Evans and John Kinney were available too. And only nine miles from Lincoln, was Fort Stanton, with its Ring-biased Commanders being first George Purington, then Colonel N.A.M. Dudley.

Crushing earlier uprisings, left Catron confident of his elimination tactics. John Tunstall, would have seemed easy. But Catron didn't anticipate Lincoln County citizens' resistance. It would make him resort to atrocities and treason to win.

And, as we shall see in other talks, Catron would not have guessed that he would encounter the most dangerous adversary yet to his schemes: a teenager named Billy Bonney.

TALK 13:
THE RING VERSUS JOHN TUNSTALL
FROM BOOK: *THE SANTA FE RING VERSUS BILLY THE KID*
DECEMBER 15, 2020

This talk continues my revisionist history of the Lincoln County War, as covered in Talks 12 to 17. The information is from my book, *The Santa Fe Ring Versus Billy the Kid: The Making of an American Monster.*

By the start of 1878, with escalating violence, Thomas Benton Catron, boss of the Santa Fe Ring, had snuffed out Territorial anti-Ring uprisings in the Santa Fe capitol; in Grant and Colfax Counties. By 1878, he was assured of cover-ups. His co-boss, Stephen Benton Elkins, was in Washington as Territorial Delegate. President Rutherford B. Hayes was complicit. By 1878, Catron was poised for take-over of 19,200,000 acre Lincoln County, the largest county in the United States. There he had mercantile and ranching presence, sub-bosses and agents, and loyal troops at Fort Stanton. That just three men challenged his monopoly must have seemed trivial.

The first, Alexander McSween, had almost become a Presbyterian minister. He'd worked as an attorney for Catron's local bosses, at their store called "The House," in the county's seat of Lincoln. He'd quit in 1876, disgusted by their abuse of government contracts to Fort Stanton and the Mescalero Indian Reservation. They rustled for beef, and sold inferior flour and hay. That year, he turned to private law practice in Lincoln. The second man was a young British entrepreneur, named John Tunstall. McSween convinced him to settle in Lincoln and make a store and ranches. The third was their ally: cattle king, John Chisum, victim of Ring rustling.

Catron recognized that elimination of Tunstall would eliminate the other two, since he provided cash from his wealthy father in London.

Catron's favorite attack was malicious prosecution. Assassination was a back-up.

In position at "The House" was savage hooligan, James Dolan. Its first owner, Lawrence Murphy, was Catron's front. In 1873, Dolan was a clerk at their original sutler store in Fort Stanton, known as L.G. Murphy and Company. Dolan got them kicked out. He tried to kill 9th Cavalry Captain James F. Randlett for exposing their corruption to the Adjutant General. Murphy and Dolan were arrested. But with Catron's apparent intervention, their charges were dropped. Randlett was charged instead!

In 1878, after Murphy retired, Dolan took over "The House." He made Catron's shady cattle dealer, John Riley, his partner in J.J. Dolan and Company. In 1875, rough Riley's attempted murder shooting of Lincoln's anti-Ring Hispanic leader, Juan Patrón, had left him a limping cripple. So Catron's lethal sub-bosses were in place.

Ringite enforcers were in place too. Fort Stanton's Major William Brady became Lincoln County's first Sheriff. "The House's" builder, George Peppin, got that office later by illegal Proclamation of Ringite Governor S.B. Axtell. The rest were District Attorney William Rynerson, and Third Judicial District Judge Warren Bristol.

In place also was a spy. Saturnino Baca was a Ringite Lincoln resident. Unsavory, in 1855 he'd married a 14 year old. In the Civil War, he served under Kit Carson, becoming a Captain. Later, at Fort Stanton, he participated in the Indian Wars' genocide of Apaches and Navajos. There he befriended the sutler store's Ringites. Discharged in 1867, he settled in Lincoln. He then worked with that store's owners, Emil Fritz and Lawrence Murphy, to monopolize supply of inferior hay to the Fort. In 1868, Baca, with Catron, Murphy, and Brady, got a bill passed forming Lincoln County. Lincoln was the county seat. Brady became its first Sheriff. Ringite Governor Robert Byington Mitchell made Baca a Probate Judge. In 1878, Baca was caught stealing 12,000 pounds of coffee, sugar, and other supplies from the Mescalero Indian Reservation. He was likely colluding with Agent Frederick Godfroy to supply "The House." In 1882, he murdered black Lincoln resident, George Washington, for eloping with one of his daughters. In 1878, he proved a traitor to his people in the Lincoln County War Battle.

The Lincoln County solution was not as easy as Catron and his minions thought. John Tunstall was a new type of Ring victim. His idealism, sweetness, fairness, and vulnerability of a blind eye made him tenderly beloved. He was a potential martyr in the making. Billy Bonney would be his ranch hand only 4½ months, before his murder. But it was enough to convert him from a dangerous delinquent to a rebel with a cause.

By 1877, Tunstall had built, on the northeast side of Lincoln's only street, a single-story building housing his store, bank, and personal apartment. It stood just a quarter mile east of "The House." He made John Chisum his bank's president. Under the Desert Land Act, he had gotten about 4,000 acres of ranchland along Lincoln County's Feliz and Peñasco Rivers. So he controlled miles of grazing land by access to its only water.

And McSween built a two-wing house next-door to Tunstall's store. There he and his wife, Susan, resided on one side. At the other, lived his brother-in-law and law partner, David Shield, husband of Susan's sister, Elizabeth, with their five children. There, McSween and Shield had a law office, with Shield's law student, Harvey Morris.

Historian Frederick Nolan's 1965 biography, *The Life and Death of John Henry Tunstall*, reprinted Tunstall's loving letters to his London family. They reveal his inability to comprehend the Ring's lethality. In June of 1876, he'd been pointed to New Mexico Territory by a California rancher; though warned by him about the Ring. Tunstall wrote to his family: "He says the politics are in the hands of a ring who control things as they like ... He says that as soon as I go there, everyone will know my business, that it is 'a rare field full of razors.' "

By March of 1877, Tunstall responded naively to his more realistic family's fears. He wrote: "As regards my getting shot, I don't expect it. There are two very prolific causes for shooting in this country, namely, drink and jealousy. I don't frequent the locality of the former ... and I don't make myself an object for the excitement of the latter ... I have a presentment that I shall not get killed." He added: "The whole of New Mexico is under the control of a ring composed of two or three lawyers ... and their practices and power throughout New Mexico are quite astonishing."

In April of 1877, to "Much Beloved Father," he prattled about "rings" as self-styled "adventurer." He thought a Ring was a way to do business. So gave his own plan. He wrote: "I propose to confine my operations to Lincoln County, but I intend to handle it in such a way as to get the half of every dollar that is made in the county by anyone."

So, guilelessly, Tunstall overlapped the Ring with his store, bank, ranches, and plans. And true to British proclivities, he bought fine horses, and became attached to them. That last idiosyncrasy would be the immediate cause of his death.

In the Colfax County War, the Ring had harassed settlers they wanted to expel by attacking their stock. Likewise, in September of 1877, Jessie Evans and his gang were used by the Ring to steal Tunstall's horses and mules. But, Tunstall, as he wrote to his family, was amused. He thought it was dime novel antics when Jessie (who ultimately killed him) raged that his three shots had all missed Tunstall's foreman, Dick Brewer. Tunstall merrily reported that the gang threatened to kill him, McSween, and Brewer because they were incited by people, quote: "whose business I have very nearly taken away." That meant "The House."

By November 7th, 1877, Tunstall encountered usual Ringite obstruction of justice to shield members. Jessie Evans and his gang had been arrested, but Sheriff Brady let them escape. Then Brady tried to incite Tunstall to violence, to kill him in faked self-defense. Brady accused Tunstall of aiding the jailbreak, then drew his gun. McSween intervened. But Brady gave away the Ring plan by blurting out to Tunstall: "You haven't long to run."

By late 1877, Catron rolled out malicious prosecution. His diabolically convoluted plot used as its hook Alexander McSween. McSween had been hired to collect a $10,000 life insurance policy of "The House's" first partner, Emil Fritz. He had died intestate in Germany in 1874. McSween represented the heirs, including Fritz's local siblings, Charles Fritz and Emilie Scholand. But the crooked policy holder refused payment, forcing litigation in New York to get the money. Legal fees depleted the sum to $7,000. McSween delayed payment to seek German heirs. And he awaited the Probate Court's decision on James Dolan's fraudulent claim that Fritz's estate owed "The House" $76,000.

McSween was unaware that the Ring controlled Charles Fritz by mortgage of his ranch near Lincoln. He was unaware that Dolan, District Attorney William Rynerson, and Judge Warren Bristol were poised to attack him. On December 21st, 1877, Charles Fritz's sister, Emilie Scholand, was manipulated by Dolan and Rynerson into filing an embezzlement complaint with Judge Bristol. It claimed that McSween had stolen the policy's money.

On December 25th, Catron, as U.S. Attorney, advanced the malicious prosecution. Knowing that McSween and his wife, Susan, along John Chisum, were leaving to St. Louis for business, he made-up that McSween was absconding with the embezzled money. He got a warrant from Bristol to arrest him. Vindictively, Catron also had Chisum arrested as reneging on loans. Both were jailed in Las Vegas by the San Miguel County Sheriff.

McSween was then transported back to Lincoln by honest and brave Deputy Sheriff Adolph Barrier. He knew McSween was in grave danger of Ring murder. So he kept him in personal custody as McSween awaited his hearing. But crafty John Chisum stayed in the remote Las Vegas jail to wait out the Ring's inevitable violence.

On January 18th, 1878, Tunstall joined the fray, in what he called a taxpayer's duty. He attacked the Ring in an editorial titled "A Tax-payer's Complaint." It appeared in January 26th's *The Mesilla Valley Independent*. He must have been amused that the real embezzler was a local lawman. He accused Sheriff Brady of embezzling tax money to buy cattle from Underwood and Nash, through James Dolan and John Riley.

It was dangerous to accuse Ringite Brady. It was more dangerous to identify rustlers, Underwood and Nash, as recipients. Nathan Underwood and Josiah "Joe" Nash worked with Ringite Seven Rivers rustlers, Milo Pierce and Lewis Paxton. In 1877, Chisum's men had caught Underwood and James Dolan herding Chisum's rustled cattle to Underwood's cow camp. Presumably, they were intended for Catron's Pecos Cow Camp for "The House's" government beef contract. Sheriff Brady shielded Underwood and Dolan from prosecution. So implied in Tunstall's complaint was that Chisum was feeding him evidence for a chain leading to Catron and his rustler-based sourcing of cattle.

On January 29th, James Dolan responded for the Ring in the *Mesilla Independent*. He made-up that Brady had missed the tax deadline because of sickness in the family. He added snidely that Tunstall, being no gentleman, was excluded from respectable circles, so was unaware of real circumstances.

Catron's biographer, Victor Westphall, in his 1973 book, *Thomas Benton Catron and His Era*, linked Catron to the "Tax-payers Complaint" as paying-off Brady's embezzled money. It revealed Catron's entanglement with the Indian Department and John Riley. Westphall wrote: "Catron had paid the money on behalf of Brady with proceeds of Indian Department vouchers made out to John H. Riley and forwarded to the First National Bank of Santa Fe for deposit."

Naïve Tunstall thought it was just an endurance game. On January 20th, he wrote home: "I won't give up or back down, as long as I can give another kick."

On January 31st, Tunstall, with 18 days to live, finished his last letter to his father as "Much Beloved Governor." He was about to travel to Mesilla for McSween's hearing; unaware it was a trap for him.

On February 4th, Alexander McSween, his law partner, David Shield, his protector Deputy Sheriff Barrier, and his supporters Tunstall and Justice of the Peace John "Squire" Wilson, left for the Mesilla hearing with Judge Warren Bristol. They were unaware of Colfax County's Mary McPherson's 1877 exposés of Bristol as a corrupt and dangerous Ring tool, who should be removed.

Victor Westphall, Catron's biographer, inadvertently revealed that Rynerson and Bristol were frontmen for Catron's malicious prosecution. Westphall also wrote that Catron was responsible for creating the embezzlement judgment issued by Bristol.

At the hearing, Bristol set the Ring's traps for McSween and Tunstall. To enable Sheriff Brady to take McSween into fatal custody, Bristol set bail of $8,000, with approval only by District Attorney Rynerson, who would refuse all bondsmen. That would leave McSween open to lethal jailing by Sheriff Brady. To ensnare Tunstall, Bristol lied that he was McSween's partner. That made Tunstall also responsible for McSween's debt. Bristol ordered property attachment of both men for the faked embezzled sum of $10,000. Brady was to do the attachments. It was a harassment plot to incite their violence to justify Brady's killing them in so-called "self defense."

Biographer Westphall revealed Catron was also part of the Bristol-Rynerson bondsman trap. He reported that Catron threatened José Montaño that if he became surety for McSween's bond, he would prosecute him as U.S. Attorney for cutting timber on public land."

On February 8th, Brady began attachments by ransacking McSween's Lincoln house. Next invaded were Tunstall's store, bank, apartment, and ranches. Outrageously, Brady's inventory sum far exceeded Bristol's required $10,000.

At the February 11th Tunstall's store inventory, furious Billy Bonney almost did the violence sought by the Ring. But he was stopped by fellow Tunstall employee, Fred Waite.

This torment didn't stop McSween's anti-Ring crusade. Knowing his innocence, he assumed he'd prevail in April's Grand Jury. So on February 11th, seven days before Tunstall's murder, he exposed James Dolan's, John Riley's, and Mescalero Indian Agent Frederick Godfroy's beef and flour frauds to Secretary of the Interior Carl Schurz. He wrote: " I suggest you send a detective here who will ferret this matter; he'll find things as I have stated them."

It was time for murder. To be repeated was the Ring's 1875 ambush killing of Colfax County War's anti-Ring leader, Reverend Franklin Tolby. Used were Catron's Lincoln minions. Sadistic District Attorney William Rynerson featured in the plot. In 1867, he'd murdered Chief Justice John P. Slough. Slough had just exposed Rynerson's Ring-rigged 1867 election to the legislature. Catron's co-boss, Attorney S.B. Elkins, had gotten Rynerson off on self-defense. In 1876, Ringite Governor S.B. Axtell had made Rynerson a District Attorney.

Rynerson revealed the plot in a February 14th letter to co-conspirators, John Riley and James Dolan. Tunstall had four days to live. Alexander McSween later found it, folded in Riley's pocket notebook, accidentally dropped in his house, after Riley came on the night of Tunstall's murder, to lie that he was not involved.

Freakishly seven foot, sadistic Rynerson wrote: "Friends Riley and Dolan ... If Mr. Weidman [that was Tunstall employee, Robert Widenmann] interfered with or resisted the Sheriff in discharge of his duty Brady did right in arresting him, And any one else who does so must receive the same attention. Brady goes into the store in McSween's place and takes his interest. Tunstall will have same right there he had heretofore but he neither must not obstruct the sheriff or resist him in the discharge of his duties. If he tries to make trouble the Sheriff must meet the occasion firmly [underlined] and legally. I believe Tunstall is in with the swindlers with the rogue McSween. They have the money belonging to the Fritz estate and they know it. It must be made hot for them all the hotter the better. Especially is this necessary now that it has been discovered that there is no hell.

It may be that the villain Green "Juan Baptista" Wilson will play into their hands as Alcade [meaning Justice of the Peace]. If so, he should be moved around a little. Shake that McSween outfit up till it shells out and squares up, and then shake it out of Lincoln. I will aid to punish the scoundrels all I can. Get the people with you. Control Juan Patron if possible. You know how to do it. Have good men about to aid Sheriff Brady, and be assured that I shall help you all I can, for I believe there was never found a more scoundrely set than that outfit."

This replicated 1876's Colfax County War's "Dear Ben plot." It is discussed in Talk 11. Carried out by Ringite Governor S.B. Axtell, it attempted murder of four Ring opponents in Cimarron. Axtell telegraphed his accomplice, Second Judicial District Judge Benjamin "Ben" Stephens: "Have your men placed to arrest him [that meant one of the victims] and to kill all the men [that meant the other opponents] who resist you or stand with those who do resist you ... do not hesitate at extreme measures. Your honor is at stake now, and a failure is fatal."

Only 56 days after Catron began his malicious prosecution of McSween and Tunstall, he got Tunstall murdered by Sheriff Brady and his posse - including the Jessie Evans gang. Brady, as obviously coached by Rynerson, falsely claimed that Tunstall was evading the embezzlement case's attachment by herding his (actually exempt) horses to Lincoln from his Feliz River ranch.

Catron's urgency to kill resulted from the upcoming convening of the Lincoln County Grand Jury. McSween would likely be exonerated. That would free Tunstall from legal harassments using the faked partnership.

On February 18th, 1878, while Tunstall herded the horses on a remote road from his Feliz River ranch toward Lincoln with his men, Brady's posse attacked. Separated from his fleeing men, Tunstall died on a lonely trail, just as had Franklin Tolby. His was an intentionally terrifying execution, with a coupe de grâce exploding his skull with a circumferential fracture. His face was bashed in. In perverted mockery, his hat was put on his likewise murdered horse's head. And, like Tolby's corpse, Tunstall's was hidden to delay pursuit of his killers.

The trauma to then 18 year old Billy Bonney was unimaginable. Collapsed after only 4½ months was his newfound "family," with his marvelous father figure and a future as a rancher on the Peñasco River. The next day, February 19th, Billy gave an eye-witness affidavit to Justice of the Peace John "Squire" Wilson, along with Tunstall's foreman, Dick Brewer.

Tunstall's Coroner's Jury Report was done on February 19th. The named murderers were Jessie Evans and his boys, Frank Baker and Thomas Hill; Deputy George Hindman; James J. Dolan; and William Morton.

To cover-up the murder as self-defense, Ringite Fort Stanton surgeon, Dr. Daniel Appel, wrote a fraudulent autopsy report. He attributed Tunstall's split skull to thinning by venereal disease. He fabricated that the disease caused Tunstall's insane shooting at possemen. McSween countered by a legitimate autopsy by Lincoln's Dr. Taylor Ealy.

But Catron was poised to repeat his 1875 obstruction of arrest of Franklin Tolby's Ringite killers. Sheriff Brady would refuse to arrest the murderers. After they were indicted by the Grand Jury, District Attorney William Rynerson would refuse to write arrest warrants.

There was no way that Catron could anticipate that the cataclysm he had unleashed would leave a teenager as his implacable enemy. And that teenager, Billy Bonney, whose life he had just destroyed, would transcend his own later killing, by another of Catron's minions, to ensure retribution in the light of his unbeatable fame.

Other talks will present Lincoln County's grass roots freedom fight that caught the complacent Ring by surprise as the Lincoln County War.

TALK 14:
REVOLUTION IN LINCOLN COUNTY
FROM BOOK: *THE SANTA FE RING VERSUS BILLY THE KID*
DECEMBER 19, 2020

This talk continues my revisionist history of the Lincoln County War. It's covered in Talks 12 to 17. The information is from my book, *The Santa Fe Ring Versus Billy the Kid: The Making of an American Monster.*

On February 18th, 1878, Territorial Ring boss Thomas Benton Catron succeeded in exterminating his Lincoln County mercantile, ranching, and banking competitor, John Henry Tunstall, who had also started exposing the Ring in the press.

By then, Catron was an old hand at eradicating competitors and at annihilating adversaries in anti-Ring uprisings of 1872 and 1876. The Colfax County War, ongoing since 1873, still simmered ineffectually. In 1875, Catron was behind assassinating its anti-Ring leader, Reverend Franklin Tolby, and behind shielding his murderers. He likely expected an identical rerun in Lincoln County.

In Colfax County, enraged and intellectual citizens had sent a flurry of exposés of Catron, his Ring, and their crimes to President Rutherford B. Hayes and his cabinetmen. The citizens were unaware that the Hayes administration was in Catron's pocket. Secretary of State William Evarts had even worked as an attorney with him and co-boss Stephen Benton Elkins in 1870 to cheat Lucien Bonaparte Maxwell out of his 2 million acre Maxwell Land Grant. So the exposés were ignored.

Catron was in for a surprise. His minions had done everything right. The responsible murderer, Sheriff William Brady, shielded his outlaw killers, while lying that they were not on his posse. He illegally imprisoned Town Constable Atanacio Martinez and his Deputies, Billy Bonney and Fred Waite, to block their serving murder warrants. He also immediately involved Catron as U.S. Attorney to request President Hayes's authorizing of troops to intimidate Lincolnites. And Governor S.B. Axtell issued an illegal proclamation to void Justice of the Peace John Wilson's arrest warrants for Tunstall's murderers, and to outlaw Wilson's legally deputized warrant servers – including Billy Bonney.

The surprise was that abused Lincoln County citizens did not withdraw into embittered silence, as had Colfax County citizens. Instead, they chose revolution.

Revolution had been foreshadowed in the 1876 Grant County Rebellion. Citizens wrote a "Declaration of Independence" from the Ring at the 1876 centennial of the American Revolution. But these citizens did not take up arms. In Lincoln County, they did.

The United States was born in revolution and declaration of its independence from England on July 4th, 1776. Still fettered by slavery, it was further liberated by revolution in its Civil War, almost a hundred years later.

Thomas Jefferson, as an author of the "Declaration of Independence," had opined in a January 30th, 1787 letter to fellow freedom fighter, James Madison, that a revolution "at least once every 20 years [is] a medicine necessary for the sound health of government." And Jefferson's call to rebellion in the first "Declaration" had led British citizens of the 13 colonies to victory. He wrote: "That whenever any form of government becomes destructive of these ends [meaning for freedom], it is the right of the people to alter or abolish it."

In his "Emancipation Proclamation," President Abraham Lincoln completed that declaration. He declared: "That on the first day of January, in the year of our Lord one thousand eight hundred and sixty-three, all persons held as slaves within any State ... shall be then, thenceforward, and forever free."

Slightly over a decade after slavery's end, revolutionary spirit in New Mexico Territory led to fighting Santa Fe Ring slavery. Jefferson, in that January 30th, 1787 letter to James Madison had anticipated such a crisis. He wrote that in United States government, quote: "the will of every one has a just influence." That was opposite to, quote: "governments of force: as is the case in all other monarchies [which] is a government of wolves over sheep."

By 1878, the wolves of force were unchecked in New Mexico Territory. But freedom was alive in recent memory. To common people, democracy held the vigor of its revolutionary victory of 1776, with sacrifice of 50,000 dead and wounded. And the Civil War, spilling blood of over 646,000 dead and wounded, had touched the lives of those now living.

Thomas Benton Catron had underestimated Lincoln County citizens and democracy's power when he had John Tunstall murdered. For them, July 4th, 1776's "Declaration of Independence" was vivid. It proclaimed: "[W]hen a long train of abuses and usurpations, pursuing invariably the same Object evinces a design to reduce them under absolute Despotism, it is their right, it is their duty, to throw off such Government, and provide new Guards for their future security."

Catron had bet on Lincoln County succumbing to his Colfax County tactics of malicious prosecutions and assassination. Instead, the Regulator movement arose. It had John Tunstall as a martyr. It had Alexander McSween as leader. In the wings it had a symbol of their militant zeal: teenaged Billy Bonney was about to enter the world stage.

Tunstall's employees named themselves "Regulators." The Mexican population joined the cause. The Ring would face a long overdue Hispanic uprising. And Territory-wide, that Hispanic majority could have broken the Ring by votes or combat.

But a critical vulnerability was isolation. Residents knew about Catron's Ring, but not its power or past uprisings against it. They wrongly believed in protection from President Hayes, unaware of his Ring loyalty and co-boss Stephen Benton Elkins's Washington influence. They never suspected local military alliance with the Ring. And they had no newspapers to give a voice to rebellion. But all was counterbalanced by their willingness to fight and to die for liberty and justice.

The original Regulators were 18th century American colonial, pre-Revolutionary War freedom fighters, extolled in song and dime novels. The Regulator movement began in North Carolina in 1771, before the "Declaration of Independence." Their fight mirrored Lincoln County's. It was against corrupt public officials and lawmen.

In North Carolina, public official elites conducted land-grabs. Poor homesteaders, working to purchase their land, relied on credit and payment by harvests. They were subjected to stolen land titles and usurious interest. Pious pacifist activists failed to get justice. By 1768, militant "Regulators" arose. They were inspired by 1765's Stamp Act protestors, the "Sons of Liberty," who opposed British taxation of stamped paper, like newspapers.

North Carolina's counterpart of New Mexico Territory's 1870's Ringite governors, was Governor William Tryon. He dissolved the legislature to block its delegates from attending New York City's Stamp Act Congress, which repealed the act.

Citizens believed it was government's duty to protect freedom. They believed fighting tyrant Tryon regulated government to that end. So they called themselves "Regulators."

Governor Tryon used troops to suppress them. Foreshadowing the Santa Fe Ring's outlawing of adversaries, Colonel Edmund Fanning called Regulators outlaws in "defiance of law and contempt of authority." Tryon wrote that the Regulators were "destroying the Peace of this Government, and the Security of its inhabitants." The final fight was May 16th, 1771's Battle of Alamance. There, 2,000 leaderless Regulators, lacking ammunition, met 1,100 British troops with six swivel guns and two brass cannons. Three Regulators, sent to negotiate peace, were taken prisoner by Governor Tryon. He shot one in sight of the others. Then Tryon's army rampaged, destroying farms and crops of Regulator leaders. Six Regulators were hanged in retribution at Hillsborough on June 19th, 1771.

Lincoln County Regulators may have heard North Carolina Regulators' freedom song. "From Hillsborough town the first of May, / March'd those murderous traitors. / They went to oppose the honest men, / That were called the Regulators."

Billy Bonney himself was being politicized. The day after Tunstall's February 18th, 1878 murder, he gave an eye-witness affidavit to Justice of the Peace John "Squire" Wilson, along with Tunstall's foreman, Richard "Dick" Brewer. They named the killers as Sheriff Brady's possemen; quote: "James J. Dolan, Frank Baker, Jessie Evans, George Davis, A.H. Mills, W.S. Morton, [William] Moore, George Hindman, [Frank] Rivers, Pantaleon Gallegos, divers other persons unknown." That yielded Wilson's February 19th arrest warrants for the murderers.

By June 8th, 1878, Billy gave his deposition on John Tunstall's murder to Investigator Frank Warner Angel. Justice of the Peace Wilson was witness. It's presented in Talk 8.

Key to comprehending real Lincoln County War history, is the lawman status and legality of those pursuing Tunstall's killers - including Billy Bonney. That added urgency to the Ring's illegal outlawing of them to cover-up their legitimacy, and to cover-up the illegality of Sheriff Brady's refusal to do so.

With Billy's and Brewer's affidavit, on February 20th, Justice of the Peace Wilson prepared arrest warrants. Sheriff Brady illegally refused to serve them. So Wilson took over based on, quote "there being then and there no officers to serve such warrant." He added: "[T]he undersigned, as directed by law, in such cases, specially empowered Richard H. Brewer to serve the same [warrants] endorsing such deputation." This enabled deputizing of Billy and Fred Waite as Deputy Constables under Lincoln Town Constable Atanacio Martinez to serve the arrest warrants.

Additionally lawful, was Attorney Alexander McSween's pursuit of justice for John Tunstall. He determined that murder of a British subject, like Tunstall, triggered federal investigation. On February 23rd, he filed a complaint with British Ambassador, Sir Edward Thornton. And for the remainder of his life - a mere 146 days before his own Ring murder – McSween never lost faith that legal justice would prevail.

With Justice of the Peace Wilson's arrest warrants, Special Constable Brewer, with Tunstall's men - including Billy - as his posse, on March 6th, apprehended Tunstall murderers, William "Buck" Morton [Catron's Cow Camp foreman], and Jessie Evans's gang member, Frank Baker. On March 9th, Morton and Baker were fatally shot attempting escape during transport to Lincoln's jail. Billy likely fired with the others. All claimed self-defense. Morton had grabbed the gun of posseman, William McClosky, and murdered him.

All this resistance led to Ring backlash by military intervention, obstructing of arrest warrants for Tunstall's murderers, and illegal Proclamation by Governor Axtell to remove Justice of the Peace Wilson and to make Sheriff Brady the only law enforcer. The Ring, thus, descended further into blatant and criminal tyranny.

On February 19th, the day after Tunstall's killing, Alexander McSween naively requested soldiers for protection from Fort Stanton's Commander, George Purington. He did not guess the Commander's Ring loyalty. He did not guess that Sheriff Brady himself colluded with Governor Axtell to get troops approved for suppression from New Mexico's District Commander, General Edward Hatch. So Purington sent to Lincoln First Lieutenant Cyrus Delaney and a 9th Cavalry squad to "The House." They enabled Tunstall's murderers, hiding there, to escape. Brady even led the cavalrymen to dead Tunstall's store to get hay for their horses.

Seeing that, McSween had Justice of the Peace Wilson issue an arrest warrant for hay theft against Brady. McSween and Wilson still thought law protected against the Ring.

On February 20th, Town Constable Atanacio Martinez and Deputy Constables, Billy Bonney and Fred Waite, accompanied by a Citizens' Committee led by Hispanic leader and Lincoln County jailor, Juan Patrón, went to "The House" to serve Wilson's warrants for Tunstall's murderers. So Sheriff Brady arrested Martinez, Bonney, and Waite. He had no legal basis. But, with Ringite hubris, he hissed that he had the power. He also confiscated Billy's Winchester '73 carbine - his prized possession from Tunstall. Then he threw them into Lincoln's pit jail. They were held until February 22nd, after Tunstall's burial. But Brady kept Billy's carbine.

Then boss Catron intervened. Brady had requested troops from him as U.S. Attorney. On March 3rd, it was Governor Axtell who telegrammed President Hayes, using the Ring's usual outlawing. Axtell wrote: "I am unable to enforce the law and to protect life and property in this Territory, and request assistance from the President." On March 9th, with a Fort Stanton escort, Axtell arrived in Lincoln to obstruct justice directly. That repeated his 1876 Colfax County removal of their courts to shield Reverend Tolby's Ringite killers from prosecution. That day, Axtell issued an illegal Proclamation removing Justice of the Peace Wilson to make his deputizings illegal. And he declared Sheriff Brady to be Lincoln County's only law enforcer. By the end of the year, it would get Axtell removed as Governor. But it would be too late. The Ring's murdering would be completed.

So do not miss this key point: Legally appointed officials - Wilson, Brewer, Billy Bonney, and other Tunstall men - were illegally outlawed, so the Ring could get away with murder.

But, once again, Catron and his minions met the unexpected. Resistance continued.

Montegue Leverson, a politically connected, Colorado friend of cattle king, John Chisum, seeking a New Mexico Territory governorship for himself, went to Lincoln to intervene. On March 16th, he wrote to Secretary of the Interior Carl Schurz, enclosing a letter to President Hayes blaming the Ring's public officials for Tunstall's murder. That truth became Hayes's future investigator's job to hide. Leverson stated: "[I]t is not likely that the British Government will allow the murder of one of its subjects by United States officials and their appointees, to pass without a rigorous investigation, and a demand of indemnity for the family of the murdered man." To be noted is that such reparations were commonly awarded. But the Ring ended up blocking reparations to Tunstall's family because awarding them admitted his murder was by U.S. officials. And Leverson was unaware that Hayes and Schurz were Ring-backing, and covered-up Mary McPherson's identical Colfax County exposés to them in 1877.

On March 24th, Sheriff Brady tried to apprehend or murder Alexander McSween, at John Chisum's South Spring River Ranch by using Fort Stanton troops as his posse. He used a county sheriff's option to conscript soldiers for peace-keeping or pursuit of a felon. But McSween was successfully hidden.

Truth and justice were closing in. It was time for the Ring to murder again. But Catron and his minions didn't anticipate that the citizens were watching their own clock. It was time for war!

In Talks 15 and 16, I'll present the revisionist history of the Lincoln County War and its final Battle.

TALK 15:
THE LINCOLN COUNTY WAR
FROM BOOK: *THE SANTA FE RING VERSUS BILLY THE KID*
DECEMBER 23, 2020

This talk continues my revisionist history of the Lincoln County War. It's covered in Talks 12 to 17. The information is from my book, *The Santa Fe Ring Versus Billy the Kid: The Making of an American Monster*. I also brought the Lincoln County War to life in my docufiction novel, *Billy and Paulita*.

One of America's great freedom fights has gone unsung, though its name appears in Billy the Kid history books. It's the Lincoln County War of 1878. It was a grass roots fight of past ranch hands of murdered John Henry Tunstall, Anglo homesteaders, and Hispanic townspeople. It only makes sense if you add in their adversary and the precipitant: the corrupt political cabal of the Santa Fe Ring.

For my revisionist history, I've divided the Lincoln County War into its months of skirmishing and its final six day battle. That clarifies the pattern of citizens' lawful attempts to get justice for John Tunstall's murder, countered by the Ring's escalating violence for suppression. So, contrary to conventional history, the outlaws and wanton murderers were Ring boss T.B. Catron and his minions, not the freedom fighting opponents.

Lincoln County citizens tried all legal remedies to arrest John Tunstall's murderers. All were blocked by Catron's lackey, Ringite Governor S.B. Axtell. To shield the murderers from arrest, Axtell's illegal Proclamation removed their Justice of the Peace and outlawed his deputizings. Axtell also made Lincoln Sheriff

William Brady the sole law enforcer. Everyone knew Brady was responsible for Tunstall's murder and had shielded his hitmen. There were just two possible responses: surrender or opposition. The people chose the latter.

When did the Lincoln County War start? Billy Bonney likely reflected contemporary consensus in his March 13th, 1879 letter to new Governor, Lew Wallace, when he began his pardon request. He wrote: "I have indictments against me for things that happened in the late Lincoln County War."

Those indictments, considered by Billy in the War, were for the April of 1878 Regulator killings of Tunstall's murderers: William Brady, George Hindman, and Andrew "Buckshot" Roberts. And the obvious precipitant of the War was Tunstall's Ring murder.

As to their adversaries, Billy cites the Ring in his July 13th, 1878 "Regulator Manifesto;" stating: "Mr. Walz. Sir: We are all aware that your brother-in-law, T.B. Catron sustains the Murphy-Kinney party." And everyone would have dated the War's end to the battle of July 14th to 19th, with the McSweens' defeat.

As to deaths in the Lincoln County War, Billy gave a cheeky response for an April 3rd, 1881 *Santa Fe Daily New Mexican* article titled "Something About the Kid." Aware of his outlaw myth press, he was in custody awaiting his Mesilla hanging trial. He stated: "At least two hundred men have been killed in Lincoln County during the past three years, but I did not kill all of them."

It would have been obvious to everyone after Tunstall's murder, that Alexander McSween would be next. When, could also be predicted. In April would be Lincoln County's Grand Jury. There, he would likely be exonerated for embezzling. The Ring would loose its excuse for his malicious prosecution. McSween had been hiding in San Patricio and at John Chisum's South Spring River Ranch. Aware of his risk, he tried to protect himself in his return to Lincoln to await his Grand Jury trial. In his buggy, he would take Chisum, Chisum's friend, Montegue Leverson, and his wife, Susan. He also requested a military escort from Fort Stanton, unaware it was a Ring stronghold. So the Ring knew his return date. And, of course, the escort never came.

The Regulators knew the date too. It was mid-day, Monday, April 1st, 1878. Ringite Sheriff Brady knew the date too. It was the day he had to murder McSween.

The morning of April 1st, the Regulators secretly gathered in the Tunstall store's corral, behind its adobe wall with its gate. They faced Lincoln's single street. The men had carbines. Billy had only a revolver.

The Regulators saw Brady walking Lincoln's single street eastward, brandishing Billy's confiscated Winchester '73 carbine. It was the direction at which McSween would arrive. With Brady were his armed Deputies: George Hindman, Jacob Basil "Billy" Matthews, George Peppin, and Jack Long.

At 9:00 a.m., the Regulators opened fire. Matthews, Peppin, and Long escaped. Brady and Hindman did not. Recklessly, Billy ran out, with Jim "Frenchie" French for cover, to retrieve his carbine from Brady's corpse. Billy Matthews, hiding in the Cisneros family house, opened fire. Billy and French got leg wounds. The Regulators then fled. They'd saved McSween's life. They'd fired the first shots of the Lincoln County War. And two Tunstall murderers were dead.

On April 3rd, Brady's past Deputy, Ringite George Peppin, tried to complete the Ring's mission. He falsely arrested McSween and his brother-in-law David Shield for allegedly murdering Brady and Hindman. He put them in Fort Stanton custody under Ringite Commander George Purington. But McSween's wife and Montegue Leverson stayed with McSween. Assassination would have been too obvious. The men were released.

The Regulators had ignored Governor Axtell's illegal March 9th, 1878 Proclamation removing their lawman appointments. They continued to serve Justice of the Peace John Wilson's warrants. Dick Brewer had one for Andrew "Buckshot" Roberts, a Tunstall murder posseman. The Regulators, seeking Tunstall's cattle, stolen by the Ring after his murder, chanced to meet Roberts on April 4th at Blazer's Mill. It was a way station, post office, and grist mill belonging to a Dr. Joseph Blazer, within the Mescalero Indian Reservation.

Refusing arrest, Roberts fired his carbine. His bullet struck Charlie Bowdre's belt buckle. It ricocheted to wrench George Coe's revolver, mutilating his trigger finger. In self-defense, Bowdre shot Roberts in the abdomen. Roberts then hit John Middleton non-fatally. Then he fatally shot Dick Brewer. So Roberts, a Tunstall murderer, had now killed another innocent man, and injured others. Billy fired no shot. Roberts died the next day.

By April 9th, citizens had hope. With Brady dead, their County Commissioners appointed local rancher, John Copeland, a non-Ringite, as Sheriff.

The April, 1878 Lincoln County Grand Jury, ignoring pressure of Ringite Judge Warren Bristol and District Attorney Rynerson, exonerated McSween of embezzling. It indicted Tunstall's murderers, including James Dolan. It also indicted Billy and other Regulators for the murders of Brady, Hindman, and Roberts. (Those indictments were later the reason for Billy's pardon proposal to Governor Lew Wallace).

The Ring responded to protect its own. Ringite District Attorney Rynerson refused to issue arrest warrants for Tunstall's indicted murderers. By letter, McSween dutifully reprimanded that murderous sadist, who saw him as a dead man walking.

That April, a new Fort Stanton Commander was brought in. Lieutenant Colonel Nathan Augustus Monroe Dudley was an alcoholic reprobate. From Colfax County's Fort Union, he was a beholden Ringite, already defended by T.B. Catron for two prior court martials. McSween and other Lincolnites naively believed he was their protector - until it was too late.

The Ring still had a problem. McSween was alive and kicking. On April 26th, he continued his anti-Ring campaign by reporting to President Rutherford B. Hayes that the Mexican and American citizens had united, to pledge their lives to protect each other and the laws.

On April 29th, the desperate Ring tried to murder McSween and the Regulators. Ringite Seven Rivers rustlers rode toward Lincoln. For guise of legality, they claimed to be a posse to arrest murderers of Brady, Hindman, and Roberts. In Lincoln, alerted Regulators waited secretly in Isaac Ellis's house in the town's east end to defend McSween.

New Regulator head, following Dick Brewer's murder, was Frank MacNab, John Chisum's cattle detective. He decided to scout for the attackers with Frank Coe. Near Ring-controlled Charles Fritz's ranch, they were ambushed by that "posse." MacNab was murdered. Coe was taken captive.

The next day, the "posse" came to Lincoln to kill McSween. Regulators in the Ellis house faced them. George Coe wounded

Seven Rivers rustler, Dutch" Charlie Kruling. Four others were killed. Commander Dudley, at overwhelmed Sheriff Copeland's request, sent Second Lieutenant George Smith and a squad to Lincoln. They took the 27 Seven Rivers men, whom Copeland had arrested, to Fort Stanton. Frank Coe was released.

McSween, still seeking a legal solution, went to San Patricio to report Frank MacNab's murder to its Justice of the Peace Gregorio Trujillo. Trujillo made arrest warrants for Sheriff John Copeland.

But the Ring saw the chance to renew malicious prosecution of McSween. Local boss, James Dolan, rode to Blazer's Mill, with George Peppin and Jacob Basil "Billy' Matthews, to swear out warrants to Catron's agent there, David Easton - then a Justice of the Peace. They were against McSween, William Bonney alias Henry Antrim alias Kid, and others unknown, for killing the four MacNab murderers and injuring "Dutch" Charlie Kruling. Noteworthy is that the Ring now saw Billy as enough risk to single out. But Easton immediately quit, fearing reprisal. That voided his warrants.

By May 4th, Commander Dudley revealed his Ring allegiance. That day, Sheriff George Copeland gave him Justice of the Peace Gregorio Trujillo's arrest warrants for MacNab's Seven Rivers murderers held at Fort Stanton. Their hearing was for May 6th. Instead, Dudley handed Copeland Easton's warrants for McSween and "the Kid," unaware that they were void. He ordered troops to take Copeland to San Patricio and force his arrest of them. It was a likely murder plot. But they were not found. Dudley then released the Seven Rivers murderers. None stood trial for Frank MacNab's murder. They became Sheriff George Peppin's murderous posse by that July's Lincoln County War Battle.

On May 19th, the Ring unfurled its usual outlaw myth to set-up military intervention. "House" partner, and Catron's cattle agent, John Riley, sent Commander Dudley a staged letter lying that the Regulators had stolen 2,000 of Catron's Pecos Cow Camp cattle, and had murdered one of his men there. Riley claimed that the recovered cattle were then taken to Catron's Carrizozo ranch.

Catron's biographer, Victor Westphall, in his 1973 book, *Thomas Benton Catron and His Era*, inadvertently revealed that Catron was behind that letter by quoting his May 30th letter to complicit Governor Axtell. It used the attack of the fake posse. It left out that the Regulators' response was in self-defense. Catron used his outlaw myth to get the Regulators disarmed, then killed by troops. He wrote: "I would most respectfully request that some steps be taken to disarm all parties carrying arms ... I am informed that the sheriff [John Copeland] keeps with his deputies large posses armed who are one of the factions only and who take occasion at all time to kill persons and take the property of the other faction whenever they get an opportunity. There is no power from what I can learn that can keep the peace in that county, except the military."

Unaware of impending doom, Lincolnites got false hope from the May 4th, arrival of an investigator from the Hayes administration: Attorney Frank Warner Angel. They were unaware that Ring-backing Hayes was scrambling to avoid an international incident with British Ambassador Edward Thornton after Tunstall's murder by public officials. By June 8th, Billy would risk his life to come to Lincoln to give Angel his deposition on Tunstall's murder. It's presented in Talk 8.

On May 28th, Governor S.B. Axtell issued his second improper Proclamation to stop Lincoln County's opposition. He removed neutral Sheriff John Copeland - in office just 49 days - with excuse of his not filing his tax collector bond on time. That was done to replace him with Ringite George Peppin, Brady's deputy and a Tunstall murder posseman. The Ring needed their lackey in place for murder.

On June 6th, Alexander McSween gave his deposition to Investigator Angel, 43 days before the Ring killed him. Though Angel took 39 depositions, McSween's was the longest. It was the best rendition of the Ring's control of "The House," its malicious prosecution of himself and Tunstall, and its intent to murder them both. It proved that U.S. officials had murdered Tunstall and had tried to murder him.

On June 21st, Catron, emerged to kill the Regulators himself by hanging. As U.S. Attorney, he wrote federal indictment Number 411, as the United States of America versus Charles Bowdre; Doc Scurlock; Henry Brown; Henry Antrim, alias Kid; John Middleton; Stephen Stevens; John Scroggins; George Coe; and Frederick Waite, for the murder of Andrew Roberts at federal property of the Mescalero Indian Reservation. That also meant that any pardon had to come from the President, not a governor.

Again, everything was in place for killing McSween and the Regulators. Then a problem arose. On June 18th, Congress passed the Posse Comitatus Act. It barred use of the military to intervene in civilian disputes. Its exception was protecting women and children. In fact, on March 24th, just before the restriction, Sheriff Brady had used Fort Stanton troops as his posse comitatus in attempt to kill McSween at John Chisum's ranch. And the Ring had already used troops as potential killers in the Legislature Revolt in 1872, and in the Colfax County War in 1875 and 1876. One can imagine Catron as feverishly strategizing ways around this blockade. There was one asset. In place was Ringite Lincoln resident, Saturnino Baca. He had a wife and many children. He was likely coached, in case the Ring wanted troops.

First Catron tried terrorism to end resistance. It revealed the Ring's racist core. Racism was central to Catron's and Elkin's 1866 scheme to rob Hispanic land grant owners of their land. Ringite Governor Marsh Giddings had used racism in his April 3rd, 1873 response to the Department of Interior about his suppressing the 1872 Legislature Revolt. He blamed it on Mexicans, as quote, "vilest of the vile" from the "slums of vice" in Santa Fe. Giddings complained: "Nearly all the people of the Territory are Mexican 86,000 out of 93,000." On May 28th, 1911, Catron wrote to his son Thom: "[I]t is the disposition of most all of the Spanish-American people to indulge in revolutions." As a New Mexico senator, Catron commented on the Spanish-American War for the February 10th, 1913 "Washington Times." He stated: "Mexicans ... were perfectly equal to starting five revolutions in five days." By July of 1878, Catron had figured out that the main resistance was Hispanic. San Patricio citizens had protected McSween and the Regulators since Tunstall's murder. It's conceivable that bi-cultural Billy Bonney had made the bridge. So racist Catron launched what he guessed would be the lethal blow to opposition. It would be struck by his Ringite Sheriff, George Peppin.

On June 28th, Sheriff Peppin had already used Fort Stanton's new Commander, N.A.M. Dudley with troops, in violation of the Posse Comitatus Act passed ten days earlier, to invade San Patricio in an unsuccessful attempt to kill Alexander McSween there.

Five days later, on July 3rd, Peppin returned to lead the Ring's massacre at San Patricio. The Hispanic people of that town,

12 miles from Lincoln, were to be punished unforgettably. With Peppin, as his posse, were Ringite rustler John Kinney and his gang from Mesilla. Men, women, children, and farm animals were slaughtered. Property was destroyed. No one was ever prosecuted. Fury remains to this day in the victims' descendants.

Catron's biographer, Victor Westphall inadvertently linked Catron to outlaw John Kinney as setting up the massacre. It was through Catron's law partner, William Thornton. Thornton defended Kinney for rustling. Catron's link was also through District Attorney William Rynerson. Westphall wrote: "If any Territorial official is to be charged with recruitment of the outlaw element, it must be District Attorney Rynerson."

But the Ringtites again miscalculated. Instead of causing withdrawal, the massacre at San Patricio guaranteed fighters. And it may have set the date: just 11 days later. Most of Alexander McSween's 60 men in the upcoming Lincoln County War Battle were from San Patricio and Hispanic Picacho. These fighters made that Battle the Territory's biggest Hispanic anti-Ring uprising.

Billy Bonney must have been enraged by the San Patricio massacre. On July 13th, 10 days after it, he challenged the Ring, in what I named the "Regulator Manifesto." Knowing that McSween planned to take a stand in Lincoln the next day, he wrote its anti-Ring declaration. It's signed only "Regulator." It's discussed in Talk 5. To T.B. Catron's brother-in-law, it stated, in part: "We are all aware that your brother-in-law, T.B. Catron sustains the Murphy-Kinney party ... Steal from the poorest or richest American or Mexican, and the full measure of the injury you do, shall be visited upon the property of Mr. Catron. This murderous band is harbored by you as your guest, and with the consent of Catron occupies your property."

Ring boss T.B. Catron had taken a tremendous risk of exposing himself and his Ring in his determination to crush Lincoln County's rebellion. Even teenaged ranch hand Billy Bonney knew about him and his criminal party. But conscienceless, megomaniacal, and now maddened by blood-lust revenge, Catron refused to stop. Catastrophe hung over the freedom fighters. Catastrophe also hung over Catron and his Ring.

The Lincoln County War Battle will be discussed in a talk of its own.

TALK 16:
LINCOLN COUNTY WAR BATTLE
FROM BOOK: *THE SANTA FE RING VERSUS BILLY THE KID*
DECEMBER 29, 2020

This talk gives my revisionist history of New Mexico Territory's Lincoln County War Battle. Talks 12 to 17 cover the Lincoln County War. The information is from my book, *The Santa Fe Ring Versus Billy the Kid: The Making of an American Monster.* The Lincoln County War is brought to life in my docufiction novel, *Billy and Paulita.*

The lost Lincoln County War Battle is one of the great tragedies in the history of American democracy. It was a tragedy made inevitable by unchecked greed of Santa Fe Ring organized crime. It was a tragedy made inevitable by Lincoln County's Anglo and Hispanic freedom fighters refusal to yield to tyranny. Its triumph of evil, murder, and treason, is a tragedy. Its being unsung to the present is a tragedy.

Ring boss, Thomas Benton Catron, and his minions took horrific revenge on citizens for their defiance during the Lincoln County War. It was in the final battle, from July 14th to 19th of 1878. By then, the Ring had assassinated John Tunstall, issued an illegal proclamation shielding his killers, killed Regulator leader Frank MacNab, tried repeatedly to murder Alexander McSween, and massacred at San Patricio. Now it sought extermination: using troops and weapons of war against civilians.

The six day Lincoln County War Battle began with naïve hope in one mile long, one street, Lincoln town on Sunday, July 14th, 1878. Its leader, Attorney Alexander McSween, was a pious idealist, personifying grass-roots Americans' confidence in law and government to yield justice. Though he'd lived through grim proof to the contrary, McSween rode optimistically into Lincoln that Sunday. He'd left the safe haven of cattle king, John Chisum's, South Spring River Ranch. He believed that confronting the Ring, at its Lincoln stronghold, would end in peace and in his prevailing.

Most townspeople had fled. There must have been an eerie silence that Sunday when McSween and his 60 primarily Hispanic men from San Patricio and Picacho rode into Lincoln. With them were Regulators, including new leader, Josiah "Doc" Scurlock, and 18 year old Billy Bonney. All called themselves McSweens.

McSween's confidence in peace had stifled alarm. So, in his double-winged adobe house - next door to murdered John Tunstall's store - remained his wife, Susan; her sister, Elizabeth Shield; and Elizabeth's five young children. Elizabeth's husband, Attorney David Shield, was away, not anticipating danger. And Shield's intern, Harvey Morris, was there. The McSween and Shield law practice was conducted from the house.

Still in Lincoln that day were also Ringite Sheriff George Peppin, his deputies, Billy Mathews and Jack Long, and Ring sub-boss James Dolan. Dolan's partner, John Riley, from his Lincoln mercantile business, J.J. Dolan and Company, was in Santa Fe strategizing with his actual employer for cattle acquisitions, Ring boss, U.S. Attorney T.B. Catron. They wanted to evade the Posse Comitatus Act, barring military intervention.

Remaining in town was also stubborn John "Squire" Wilson, ignoring being illegally removed from his Justice of Peace office that March 9th by Ringite Governor Samuel Beach Axtell. In martyred Tunstall's private apartment in his store, remained Dr. Taylor Ealy, who had taken part in Tunstall's gruesome autopsy; and Ealy's wife and two children. Across the street, in the house of McSween-side Jose Montaño, his wife and children remained. At the east end of town, McSween side's Isaac Ellis and his family were at home. And, to the east of Tunstall's store, stayed Ringite Saturnino Baca, in a house rented from McSween, with his wife and many children, poised to be a traitor to his people.

Heading to Lincoln was an outlaw hoard of about 60 - Seven Rivers rustler-ranchers and Mesilla's outlaw John Kinney and his gang - to become Sheriff Peppin's so-called "posse."

On that first day of the Battle, that McSween believed would be bloodless, his men took strategic positions along Lincoln's single street to hold the town. They occupied Tunstall's store, and the houses of José Montaño, Juan Patrón, and Isaac Ellis. Strategically useless, at the western end of town, were the Ring's "House" and hang-out, the Wortley Hotel.

McSween's more realistic men provisioned his house, including a keg of gunpowder for reloading ammunition. But McSween only permitted Regulator, Jim "Frenchie" French, into his house as a guard.

But when shooting Seven Rivers and Kinney men arrived that day, McSween accepted additional men from the Montaño house. They were Billy Bonney, Yginio Salazar and Tom O'Folliard. They were from San Patricio: Jose Chávez y Chávez, Francisco Zamora, and Vincente Romero. They were from Picacho: Ignacio Gonzales and Florencio Chávez.

Lincoln's terrain was ideal for defense. To the south were nearby, sparsely vegetated, high foothills, which would leave assailants exposed to McSweens' gunfire. To the north, behind McSween's house, was the Bonito River, blocking adversaries. Much pointed to victory.

By the Battle's second day, in McSween's house, his men had blockaded windows and cut defensive portholes in its adobe brick walls. McSween, with usual legality, sent by messenger, an eviction letter to his tenant, Saturnino Baca. Its grounds were that Baca was aiding men threatening his life. Baca was provisioning Sheriff George Peppin's men occupying an old stone tower in the middle of town.

Baca, the Ring stooge, got that letter to local Ring boss, James Dolan, at "The House," to fake that McSween threatened his wife and children. It was their pre-arranged excuse to circumvent the Posse Comitatus Act to get troops from Fort Stanton.

But that second day's only aggression was Deputy Jack Long's attempt to serve Catron's agent, David Easton's, invalid warrants on McSween and "the Kid." Easton wrote them after the Lincoln County War's April 30th skirmish. Regulators had responded in self-defense to Ringite Seven Rivers rustlers who came to Lincoln to kill McSween. But Easton's warrants were invalid, because he immediately quit as Justice of the Peace. Deputy Long retreated at warning shots. No warrants were served. McSween apparently stayed confident of victory.

Day three of the Battle proved that McSweens held the town. Commander Nathan Augustus Monroe Dudley, already twice court martailed, hesitated to violate the Posse Comitatus Act. So Ringite Sheriff George Peppin floated the Ring's usual outlaw myth. He wrote to Dudley: "Sir. If you could loan me a howitzer, I am sure that parties for whom I have warrants would surrender. We are being attacked by a lawless mob." Dudley took a tentative step. He sent to Lincoln 9th Cavalry Private Berry Robinson, for so-called "fact finding." A staged shot at Robinson, likely from "The House," caused his horse to throw him. Uninjured and remounted, he returned to the Fort. But Alexander McSween was now set-up for another malicious prosecution: attempted murder of a soldier.

Day four of the Battle had some action by Dudley. By Fort Stanton's telegraph, he was likely being instructed by T.B. Catron on evading the Posse Comitatus Act. The Private Berry Robinson "attack" provided ammunition. So Dudley sent Fort Stanton's Ringite Post Surgeon, Daniel Appel, to Lincoln. Married to Ringite Indian Agent Frederick Godfroy's daughter, Appel had written a fraudulent autopsy report on Tunstall, claiming he was insane from venereal disease, and attacked Sheriff Brady's possemen, who killed him in self-defense. With Appel went Ringite Captain George Purington, and five soldiers. It was called "fact finding." They questioned McSween about the Private Robinson shooting. They ignored his denial. And Sheriff Peppin used the cease-fire of troops' presence to get his men on the south foothills. That day had first casualties. From the Montaño house, Fernando Herrera, Regulator Charlie Bowdre's brother-in-law, fatally shot, with his Sharps Big Fifty buffalo rifle, Seven Rivers posseman, Charlie Crawford, 915 yards away on those foothills. And Ben Ellis, son of McSween-side Isaac Ellis, was wounded by Peppin's men shooting from the foothills. After that, carnage was solely by the Ring.

By day five of the Battle, since the south foothills were little advantage for the Ringites, McSween anticipated a near-bloodless victory. And charismatic Billy Bonney inspired all in McSween's house. Susan McSween later describing him as "lively." The Ringites too recognized that McSween's victory was neigh. So local boss, James Dolan, and outlaw posseman, John Kinney, paid Commander Dudley a visit at Fort Stanton. His saying no was not an option.

On day six of the Battle, Friday, July 19th, 1878, Commander N.A.M. Dudley marched on Lincoln. He was violating the June 18th Posse Comitatus Act by intervening as a partisan in a civilian conflict. He was endangering women and children in the McSween, Ealy, and Montaño houses. With terrorist intent, he brought into the tiny town 39 soldiers, a Gatling machine-gun, and a howitzer cannon; all sufficient to level it and kill everyone.

T.B. Catron's apologist biographer, Victor Westphall, in his 1973 book, *Thomas Benton Catron and His Era*, inadvertently confirmed Catron's role in Dudley's intervention. As U.S. Attorney, Catron set the stage during the Lincoln County War by using the outlaw myth to inform District Commander Edward Hatch about troops being needed in Lincoln County. Hatch informed army headquarters at Fort Leavenworth. Westphall also confirmed that Dudley was beholden to Catron for legally defending him in his court martials of 1871 and 1877.

Dudley personally threatened Alexander McSween with annihilation if any soldier was fired upon. He left three soldiers on McSween's property to inhibit shooting and enable besiegement. Furthermore, Dudley placed three soldiers with Sheriff Peppin as guards.

Dudley then panicked upon learning that David Easton's arrest warrants were invalid. So he coerced Justice of the Peace Wilson, by death threat, to write false arrest warrants for McSween and "the Kid," using the Private Robinson shooting as an excuse.

Dudley next pointed his howitzer cannon at José Montaño's house, and began its loading drill. Terrified McSweens fled from there, precipitating mass flight of their comrades in the town. Only those trapped in McSween's house remained. Dudley then berated Peppin for not capturing or killing the escapees.

After setting up camp, Dudley, likely drunk, with mocking obscenities refused Susan McSween's plea for protection. He then enabled the arson of the McSweens' house in attempt to incinerate those inside. But he let Susan and her sister and children depart.

At 9 p.m., the house's inmates tried escape. The raging fire, with added exploding gunpowder keg, had left them trapped in the east wing's north kitchen. In anticipation, Dudley embedded three of his officers at the next door Tunstall building, with Peppin's shooting outlaw possemen. Dudley's mission was death to all. While escaping, Billy saw the three soldiers fire at least one volley in unison at him and escaping others. He saw Harvey Morris shot dead. The soldiers might have been the murderers. Murdered also were Francisco Zamora and Vincente Romero. McSween was murdered by Peppin's possemen just as Seven Rivers rustler, Robert Beckwith, tried to serve him with the coerced Wilson warrant. Beckwith was killed in the friendly fire. Escaping Yginio Salazar was left with two bullets in his back for life. McSween's house was destroyed. The Lincoln County War Battle was lost by treachery. The War was over.

Never again in New Mexico would people dare to rise up against the organized criminality of the monstrous Santa Fe Ring. So the Ring never ceased to exist or to control.

On July 20th, the day after the Lincoln County War Battle, Alexander McSween's corpse was found in his rear yard, with its eyeballs eaten by his starving chickens. At the adjoining Tunstall store property, Sheriff Peppin's outlaw possemen, with soldiers' enabling presence, looted Tunstall's store.

By the next year, Billy's witnessing Dudley's using soldiers to kill civilians would yield his testimony against him in the Fort Stanton military Court of Inquiry.

The immediate response to the lost Lincoln County War was flight from the Territory by most of the Regulators; and frightened silence in Lincoln County. The Lincoln County War was the Ring's greatest triumph, not only by crushing mercantile, banking, and ranching competition; not only by exterminating opposition; but by using the outlaw myth to hide it as a freedom fight. It would also be the Ring's historical undoing by its creation of larger-than-life outlaw "Billy the Kid," guaranteeing that the Lincoln County War would not be forgotten.

And there was a final surge for freedom. Susan McSween, Alexander's widow, like Colfax County's Mary McPherson before her, refused to bow to Ring terrorism. The day after the Battle, she risked her life to return to Lincoln. She even tried to stop Peppin's outlaw possemen from looting Tunstall's store. And she was determined to prosecute Commander Dudley for the murder of her husband and arson of her home.

Hope for justice now rested with the reports by Investigator for the Departments of Justice and the Interior, Frank Warner Angel. He'd been in New Mexico Territory during much of the Lincoln County War. He knew the truth.

The Lincoln County War's aftermath and the Frank Warner Angel reports are in a talk of their own.

TALK 17:
LINCOLN COUNTY WAR AFTERMATH AND FRANK WARNER ANGEL REPORTS
FROM BOOK: *THE SANTA FE RING VERSUS BILLY THE KID*
DECEMBER 30, 2020

This talk continues my revisionist history of the Lincoln County War by discussion of its immediate aftermath. The information is from my book, *The Santa Fe Ring Versus Billy the Kid: The Making of an American Monster.*

On July 19th, 1878, the Lincoln County War was ended treacherously by the Santa Fe Ring. But there was a last attempt at justice. Susan McSween, Alexander McSween's widow, like the Colfax County War's Mary McPherson before her, took action. She intended to prosecute Fort Stanton's illegally intervening Commander N.A.M. Dudley for the murder of her husband and arson of her home.

She had bravely returned to Lincoln the day after the final Battle. There, she tried to stop looting of John Tunstall's store by Ringite Sheriff George Peppin's outlaw possemen.

Then, homeless, she relocated to Las Vegas, New Mexico Territory, to stay with her sister's family. There, she hired a local attorney, named Huston Chapman, to pursue Dudley. Presumably, her traumatized brother-in-law, Attorney David Shield, refused.

Chapman was one-armed from a childhood shotgun accident. He compensated by brashness. His father had founded Portland, Oregon's first newspaper: *The Oregonian.* He, like Susan, knew the case would risk their lives. Susan would also have met

Chapman's office-mate: Attorney Ira Leonard. Both men became intrinsic to Lincoln County's and Billy Bonney's fate.

Lincoln County citizens' post-war focus would have been on Frank Warner Angel, Investigator for the Departments of the Interior and Justice. He'd spelled-out his mission in his report of October 3rd, 1878 to Secretary of the Interior Carl Schurz. He wrote: "Under your instructions I visited New Mexico for the purpose of ascertaining if there was any truth to the repeated complaints to the Department as to fraud, incompetency, and corruption of United States officials." Angel could have broken the Santa Fe Ring. Angel could have changed New Mexico's history. Angel uncovered the Ring's atrocities in the Colfax County War where it murdered anti-Ring leader Reverend Franklin Tolby in 1875. There, the Ring's pocket Governor, S.B. Axtell, in 1876, had used troops to attempt murder of other anti-Ring leaders. Angel knew those unpunished crimes mirrored the 1878 assassinations of John Tunstall and Alexander McSween by Ringite U.S. public officials. Angel had the 1877 printed booklet by Colfax County's Mary McPherson. She named the Ringite public officials. They were Thomas Benton Catron, Governor Samuel Beach Axtell, and Judge Warren Bristol. She listed their crimes. They were malicious prosecutions, shielding of Ringite murderers, use of troops for terrorism and murder, and assassinations. They had repeated those crimes in the Lincoln County War.

Angel interviewed Ring victims. He took 39 depositions. On June 6th, Alexander McSween gave him his deposition, 43 days before his own Ring murder. Angel's longest deposition, it proved that the malicious prosecution and murder of John Tunstall were by U.S. public officials. McSween said, "The House" partners were backed by "all the power in Santa Fe." McSween made clear that behind it all was U.S. Attorney Thomas Benton Catron.

Two days later, on June 8th, Billy Bonney gave Angel his deposition on witnessing the harassment by Sheriff Brady's posse at Tunstall's Feliz River ranch. And he gave his eye-witness account of that posse murdering Tunstall.

Angel was in the Territory for five months. During it, the Lincoln County War occurred. He knew its horrors. He knew Tunstall was murdered by public officials. He knew McSween was murdered by public officials. He even wrote a secret notebook listing the Territory's Ring newspapers and Ringites. On July 13th, the day before the final Battle, Angel was in Las Vegas,

New Mexico, taking the deposition of Deputy Sheriff Adolph Barrier. Barrier had risked his life to protect Alexander McSween from Ring murder. He told Angel that he did it because; quote: "[J]ustice should be meted out to everyone without fear or favor." Angel would betray that ideal.

In my novel titled *Billy and Paulita*, I had Billy's fellow Tunstall employee, savvy half-Chickasaw Fred Waite tell him: "Lincoln County is a moral proving ground. Evil here's so powerful, it breaks people where they're weakest." Frank Warner Angel broke under pressure of Ring-backing President Rutherford B. Hayes, and likely professional ruin.

Ringites had obstructed Frank Warner Angel. He angrily documented it in his letters from his New York City office. They imply that, initially, he didn't realize his reports were to be cover-ups. On August 24th, Angel complained to Secretary of the Interior Carl Schurz about obstruction. Angel wrote: "I have had a very difficult and dangerous mission, and every obstacle thrown in my way by officials in New Mexico." By September 6th, Angel complained to Schurz that District Attorney William Rynerson was pressuring him to absolve Axtell. Angel wrote: "[Rynerson] is an appointee of Governor Axtell – a strong partisan – and his conduct in the Lincoln County troubles is open to censure ... [H]is interests are with the officials who have suffered the existing troubles to continue in New Mexico." So, in early September of 1878, Angel still blamed U.S. officials. By his October reports, he hid that.

By October of 1878, Angel was apparently forced by the administration to cover-up the Ring by denying U.S. officials were involved in murdering John Tunstall or causing Lincoln County turmoil. Evidence exists that he originally accused the Ring in his reports, and later edited that out. For example, his report about Governor S.B. Axtell's illegal transferring of Colfax County's courts to Taos in 1876, Angel wrote: "The juries were entirely taken from Taos County, manipulated by Pedro Sanches a ringite, and prejudiced by outside influence." Note this editing failure, where Angel mentions the Santa Fe Ring as "ringite" and "outside influence."

But Angel was no moral degenerate, like Ringites. He also turned over his research. Thus, he gave some future person the evidence to break the Ring.

But Angel did great damage. To shield the Ring, he blamed fictional outlaws for Lincoln County's "troubles." That backed the Ring's outlaw myth criminalizing opponents. And to allow President Hayes to fake action, Angel scapegoated Governor Axtell. Angel's reward, the month after his lying reports, was promotion to Assistant District Attorney of the Eastern District of New York State.

But Angel's conscience yielded covert anti-Ring action. When he learned that Civil War General Lew Wallace would replace removed Governor Axtell, he gave him his secret notebook naming Ringites. He gave him Colfax County's Mary McPherson's 1877 printed booklet naming the public official Ringites and their crimes. The information was enough to make Lew Wallace the one to break the Ring.

Angel's lying report on John Tunstall's murder, dated October 4th, 1878 was titled "In the Matter of the Cause and Circumstances of the Death of John H. Tunstall, A British Subject." It went to the Justice Department's Attorney General Charles Devens. Angel slyly wrote that it was claimed that Tunstall was McSween's partner. Angel's lying by innuendo that a partnership existed, was to justify Sheriff Brady's illegal attaching of Tunstall's horses. Angel blamed the murder itself on outlaws: Jessie Evans and his gang. He faked that their motive was an unnamed grudge. Angel concluded; "After diligent inquiry and examination of a great number of witnesses, I report that the death of John H. Tunstall was not brought about through the lawless and corrupt action of United States officials in the Territory of New Mexico."

To hide Territorial anti-Ring freedom fights, and to further obscure Tunstall's Ring murder, Angel cited vague "troubles" and the outlaw myth in his October 4th, 1878 report titled "In the Matter of the Lincoln County Troubles." It went to Attorney General Charles Devens. Angel made-up competing local factions to write: "The leaders of these parties have created a storm that they cannot control, and it has reached such proportions that the whole Territory cannot put it down ... lawlessness and murder are the order of the day."

On October 3rd, 1878, likely under coercion, Angel scapegoated Governor Axtell to hide the Santa Fe Ring in his report titled:

"In the Matter of Investigation of the Charges Against S.B. Axtell, Governor of New Mexico." It was written for Secretary of the Interior Carl Schurz. Its purpose was to fake that removing bad apple Axtell removed the cause of turmoil. Angel concluded: "[T]he continuations of the troubles that exist today in Lincoln County are chargeable to him." Hiding the Lincoln County War Battle, Angel continued: "Again we have an unusual number of murders, robbery and accompanied with arson ... after Kinney and his party have accomplished their mission of murdering McSween and robbing and stealing all they can." So Angel blamed the Lincoln County War just on outlaw John Kinney! His reprehensible fiction was to avoid blaming U.S. officials. Angel concluded: "It is seldom that history states more corruption, fraud, mismanagement, plots and murders, than New Mexico has been the theatre, under the administration of Governor Axtell."

Frank Warner Angel actually needed only one report on John Tunstall's murder. It was on Thomas Benton Catron. And Angel did write it. It became Catron's obsession.

Catron had first tried stonewalling Angel's investigation by refusing to turn-over documents. Then he denied all Angel's interrogatory questions. Furthermore, co-boss Stephen Benton Elkins intervened personally in Washington to shield Catron. But Angel gave the report to the Department of Justice. It resulted in Catron's resignation as U.S. Attorney on October 10th, 1878.

Catron's alternatives were official removal, Ring exposure, destruction of his Territorial influence and ambitions, and criminal prosecution. And the Report was never made public. In 1888, conniving Catron staged a fire in his law office to destroy other evidence of his causing the 1870's Territorial uprisings. In 1893, Catron got Elkins to destroy the report. And he subsequently denied that it existed. But he failed to destroy evidence of its existence, or of his attempts to destroy it.

The Catron report's existence was implied in an August 29th, 1878 letter to President Hayes from a supposed John C. Routt. It inadvertently confirmed that Angel's investigation was originally about, quote, "supposed misconduct of Governor Axtell and [U.S.] District Attorney Catron." The intent was to remove them. That meant the Ring knew that U.S. officials were being accused by Angel! The letter may have been by Catron himself. In the 1890's, he was caught writing so-called "anonymous" letters to newspapers to defame adversaries. This supposed John C. Routt wrote from Santa Fe: "I am here on a visit to my daughter and have more by accident than otherwise heard statements pro and con in relation to the causes of the recent troubles in this Territory and also in relation to the supposed misconduct of Governor Axtell and [U.S.] District Attorney Catron. I also learned that there is an effort being made to remove the said officers, and from all I can learn, in my judgment the charges against these officials have been made without good cause, and [without] the best people in and around Santa Fe ... It seems to me that this removal would have much influence to encourage the lawless conduct that has caused so much trouble in the Territory."

Catron's biographer, Victor Westphall, in his 1973 book, *Thomas Benton Catron and His Era*, revealed that Catron pressured Commander N.A.M. Dudley to give prejudiced affidavits for the Angel report. Dudley refused. Westphall wrote: "[Dudley] said he had refused to comply with Catron's insulting written demand at the time Catron's official conduct [as U.S. Attorney] was being investigated by Frank Warner Angel, that he go blind and certify to the United States attorney general [Charles Devens] that certain parties who had made affidavits against Catron were unreliable and unprincipled men."

It took a crisis for Catron and co-boss Elkins to do their own dirty work. But Angel's report on Catron risked everything. So Elkins intervened on September 24th, 1878, from his mansion in Deer Park, Maryland. He wrote to the report's potential recipient: Attorney General Charles Devens. Devens was no Ringite. But Secretary of the Interior Carl Schurz and Secretary of State William Evarts were Ring-biased. Apparently Elkins used them to influence Devens. And he came to Washington himself for secret lobbying. The result was apparently forcing Frank Warner Angel to hide that his mission had been to investigate Governor Axtell and U.S. Attorney Catron as U.S. officials involved in murdering John Tunstall and caused the Lincoln County "troubles." The negotiating was for Catron's resignation without blame. Elkins wrote to Devens: "I will be in Washington on Monday next, and if it would be agreeable to you to hear me, I would like to make a statement in Mr. Catron's behalf. With the testimony, and his answer, and the facts I know, I think it can be clearly established that only bitter political and personal enemies have assailed him and the charges are unfounded. I have written the President today."

The following year, on August 15th, 1879, Elkins wrote a letter to Catron from his mansion called Hallihurst, in Elkins [named after himself], West Virginia. He reminded Catron about saving his skin in regard to the Angel report. Known as "smooth Steve" to his political enemies, Elkins preferred honeyed persuasion to thug Catron's brutish assaults.

In the letter, Elkins used his favor to checkmate Catron in a dispute about their entangled crooked business dealings. That confirmed the report's existence. But it also showed how close Catron's unrestrained crimes of malicious prosecution, murder, and treason had brought him and the Ring to destruction. Elkins wrote: "About one year ago when your enemies were fighting you both in New Mexico and Washington, and your dismissal as U.S. Attorney was ordered, and an indictment talked of strongly, I let every other matter drop and devoted myself to your defense. I never exerted myself more in my life, and I have been assured by the authorities that, but for me and the fight I made, you would have been dismissed."

Catron's biographer, Victor Westphall, stated that, in 1892, the report resurfaced. Westphall wrote: "In 1892, Catron was running for Delegate to the United States Congress. Word came to him that his political opponents intended to secure a copy of Angel's report on the charges against him to use for political mudslinging."

So, by 1892, it was obvious that the report existed. On September 20th, 1892, Catron's past law partner, Frank W. Clancy, worried about it during Catron's (ultimately lost) campaign for Delegate, warning him: "From something I have heard, I believe the Democratic management is making an effort to get from Washington everything they can against you as U.S. Attorney and prepare to revive all the things urged against you before you resigned. I think you will better try to prevent their getting the information if you can ... Get Elkins to have obstacles put in their way."

So Catron wrote to Elkins, then Secretary of War, telling him to stop the Attorney General issuing a copy of the report to anyone. Elkins assured Catron that the attorney general would comply. The following year, 1893, Catron asked Elkins to destroy the report. Elkins replied that it, quote: "could not be found." That was apparently "smooth Steve's" confirmation of its destruction - instead of confessing to the crime in writing.

In 1880, Governor Lew Wallace had confirmed the existence of the Catron report. In a crossed-out letter draft on February 16th, 1880, he wrote to Secretary of the Interior Carl Schurz. It stated: "Mr. Catron is not unknown to fame in your department ... He also figures largely, I am told in the report of Mr. Angel, in which, as late U.S. District Attorney, he was admitted to a kind of head-centership of the famous old Santa Fe ring."

The outcome of Frank Warner Angel's faked reports was the untouched Ring's race to exterminate its last adversaries: that meant the remaining Regulators.

Colfax County War's anti-Ring fighter Raymond Morley was prophetic. He wrote to his wife, Ada, on August 15th, 1878, 27 days after the lost Lincoln County War Battle. He stated: "In the meantime the Ring seems more and more desperate. If I am a good guesser, the War in Lincoln is far from over. The Murphy party say they mean to kill or drive every McSween man from Lincoln." And the Ring most wanted to "kill or drive" away zealot Billy Bonney. He had just miraculously escaped being burned alive, executed by soldiers' volleys, or riddled with bullets of their Lincoln County Sheriff's outlaw gang.

At the July 19th, 1878 end of the Lincoln County War, Billy Bonney was 18 years, 7 months, and 27 days old. He had become the War's local hero. And his bi-culturalism made the majority of Lincoln County's citizens, who were Hispanic, his friends. Conceivably, the Ring saw him as a risk of instigating another uprising. In six months, local Ring boss James Dolan would offer him a peace meeting.

But, by that October of 1878, Billy was carrying out his "Regulator Manifesto," written on July 13th, the day before the Lincoln County War Battle. It stated: "Steal from the poorest or richest American or Mexican, and the full measure of the injury you do, shall be visited upon the property of Mr. Catron." Billy was doing revenge-rustling. Billy was also getting money by gambling in a circuit from Fort Sumner to Las Vegas.

But, as we'll see in future talks, fate was far from finished with Billy Bonney.

TALK 18:
SANTA FE RING BOSS
THOMAS BENTON CATRON
FROM BOOK: *THE SANTA FE RING VERSUS BILLY THE KID*
JANUARY 17, 2021

This is my revisionist history of the Santa Fe Ring's Territorial boss, Thomas Benton Catron. The information is from my book, *The Santa Fe Ring Versus Billy the Kid: The Making of an American Monster.*

Billy the Kid history needs the crimes of the Santa Fe Ring to make sense. And the Santa Fe Ring needs the crimes of boss Thomas Benton Catron to make sense.

To uncover Catron's crimes, I ignored his so-called "plausible deniability" of personal guilt by using henchmen to commit his wrongs. I used criteria of the Racketeer Influenced and Corrupt Organizations Act about criminal conspirators. They make an instigator, like Catron, as guilty as his perpetrators. And Catron's guilt is obvious. All the crimes benefited him, not the committers. All the victims were his opponents. All the perpetrators were his lackeys. Laid bare is Catron's responsibility for the rigged elections, briberies, malicious prosecutions, terrorism, murders, and false outlawing of opponents that made 19th century New Mexico Territory his fiefdom. He soaked its history in blood of anti-Ring opponents from 1867 to 1892. He almost penetrated the 20th century with attempted murders. His escaped prosecutions prove only his corrupt power. His wicked henchmen were spared punishment and gained life-long rewards. As will be seen, Catron's outrages in the Lincoln County War and in Billy the Kid history were not unique. They were his standard repertoire to destroy challengers.

On screen is Thomas Benton Catron. **[FIGURE 24]** He was a gluttonously bloated facsimile of robber baron cartoons by 19th century artist, Thomas Nast. His psychopathic, brutal, vindictive, and megalomaniacal personality set his Santa Fe Ring's style. His malignant cronyism infiltrated government, law enforcement, and business in his half century of unpunished rampage. He became America's largest landowner and a New Mexico senator. A state county has his name.

FIGURE 24: Territorial Ring boss Thomas Benton Catron. https://www.loc.gov/pictures/collection/hec/item/2016863601/ Title: Catron, Thomas Benton. Delegate From New Mexico, 1885-1897; Senator, 1912-1917. Collections: Harris & Ewing Collection

In 1866, with fellow lawyer, Stephen Benton Elkins, Catron founded the Santa Fe Ring.

On screen is Stephen Benton Elkins. **[FIGURE 25]** Elkins was Catron's co-boss in Washington, D.C., shielding the Ring on a federal level. Elkins was Catron's twin in physical appearance, greed, and conscienceless criminality.

FIGURE 25: Washington D.C. Ring boss Stephen Benton Elkins. https://www.loc.gov/pictures/collection/hec/item/2016856185/ Title: Elkins, Stephen Benton. Senator. Collections: Harris & Ewing Collection

Catron's biographer is Victor Westphall, in his 1973 book, *Thomas Benton Catron and His Era*. An apologist, Westphall parroted Catron's own cover-ups. As historically ignorant, he accidentally revealed damning truths.

Thomas Benton Catron was born on October 6th, 1840. At his Ring's start, he was 26. He was the fourth of nine children in a Lexington, Missouri, farm family. Its original German surname was "Kettenring." It wasn't the Hispanic "Catrón," as sometimes mispronounced in New Mexico. His "Thomas Benton" honored Missouri Senator Thomas Hart Benton. Senator Benton coined the racist and genocidal doctrine of "manifest destiny." It rationalized Anglo's right to seize North America from Native Americans and Hispanics.

In 1857, at Lexington's Masonic College, Catron met Stephen Benton Elkins, a year younger. In 1859, they were roommates in the University of Missouri. In the Civil War, Catron, then a Democrat, was a Confederate in the Missouri State Guard for four years. Elkins had brief Union service, then settled in New Mexico Territory. In 1864, Elkins was admitted to the law bar. He practiced in Doña Ana County's Mesilla. In 1865, when elected to the Territorial legislature's House of Representatives, he moved to Santa Fe.

In 1866, Elkins convinced Catron, studying law in Missouri, to join him. He accompanied Catron back, as both schemed. Biographer, Victor Westphall, stated; quote: "Oral tradition indicates that on their journey Catron and Elkins mutually resolved to seek a seat in the United States Senate [and to create] economic empires." Elkins inspired Catron to learn Spanish, like himself, for intended land-grab from Hispanic grant owners. On July 27th, 1866, Catron arrived in Santa Fe. In 12 years his and Elkins's Ring would control the Territory.

Catron became a Republican to ally with William Breeden, well-connected founder of the Territory's party. Five months after Catron's arrival, Breeden got Acting Governor William F.M. Arney to appoint Catron District Attorney for the Third Judicial District, and to appoint Elkins as Attorney General. The legislature protested Catron's appointment. It was ignored. Returned Governor Robert Byington Mitchell upheld Catron's appointment. And he promoted Elkins to U.S. Attorney. The circle of friends had begun. This was the Santa Fe Ring.

Catron, practicing law in Las Cruces, joined the bar in 1867.

In late 1868, Catron was elected to the Territorial House of Representatives. Ringite Governor Robert Byington Mitchell, on Elkins's recommendation, appointed Catron as Attorney General. Catron relocated to Santa Fe, becoming Elkins's law partner.

As Attorney General, Catron was Territorial prosecutor. And Elkins, as U.S. Attorney, was federal prosecutor. So by 1868, two years after Catron's arrival, the Ring could do malicious prosecutions against opponents Territorially and federally.

In 1869, William Anderson Pile, became the next Ringite Governor. In 1870, on Elkins's recommendation, Pile kept Catron as Attorney General. In Pile's corrupt administration, he and Catron were accused of destroying Territorial archives and conspiring to split offices with Democrats if the Territory became a state.

In 1870, came the Ring's big boost. Elkins and Catron, acting as attorneys for Lucien Bonaparte Maxwell, cheated him out of his 2 million acre Maxwell Land Grant. They resold it immediately for double the money to a syndicate of their friends. It became the Maxwell Land Grant and Railway Company. Additionally, they tricked Maxwell into founding the First National Bank of Santa Fe. Then they seized it by ruining him with their competing Second National Bank of Santa Fe. Money-lending through the banks added to Catron's power. And Catron kept for himself the Maxwell Land Grant's Aztec gold mine, the richest in the world.

Catron ultimately owned at least 34 land grants, as well as property in Mexico, California, Oregon, Colorado, Arizona, Kansas and Missouri. Ultimately, he was the largest individual landowner in the history of the United States, with up to six million acres.

Catron also had railroad interests. The Maxwell Land Grant's Raton Pass was used by the Atchison, Topeka, and Santa Fe Railroad for tracks from Colorado into New Mexico Territory. Catron was their attorney; as well as for the Southern Pacific; El Paso and South Western; and Denver and Rio Grande Railroads.

In 1871, President Grant appointed Marsh Giddings as Governor. He joined the Ring and escalated its tyranny.

In March of 1872, President Grant promoted Catron to U.S. Attorney. He held the title until his forced resignation in 1878, to cover-up his Lincoln County War crimes.

That 1872 was the tipping point. Anti-Ring rebellions began.

What I named the Legislature Revolt occurred that year when legislators passed acts redistricting Ring judges to stop their malicious prosecutions. Ringite Governor Marsh Giddings, using

Catron as U.S. Attorney, suppressed them with troops. And Catron also bribed them. And he convened the Supreme Court to void that session's anti-Ring acts. To end legislators' future power in rebelling Grant, Doña Ana, and Lincoln Counties, Catron and Giddings halved their representatives.

In 1873, the Colfax County War began. Original Maxwell Land Grant settlers resisted the Catron and Elkins-controlled Maxwell Land Grant and Railway Company's eviction attempts to get their land. That year, Elkins was elected Delegate to Congress, extending Ring influence to Washington, D.C. Catron was accused of fixing Elkins's election by over 600 malicious prosecutions to force voters to back Elkins in exchange for Catron's dropping their cases.

In 1875, Elkins was re-elected Delegate. Vote-fixing was alleged. And the Ring became lethal. Catron used two Ringite Maxwell Land Grant Company board members to hire thugs to murder the Colfax County War's anti-Ring leader, Reverend Franklin Tolby. Catron then tried to hang Tolby's successor, Reverend O.P. McMains, by a malicious prosecution murder case.

That 1875, Governor Giddings died in office. President Grant replaced him with Utah Territory's Republican Governor, Samuel Beach Axtell. Catron's agent, his cattle dealer, John Riley, then bribed Axtell with $1,800. (That was half of Axtell's salary.) In 1876, Axtell earned his money. He shielded Tolby's murderers from prosecution by illegally removing Colfax County's courts. And he tried to murder four other anti-Ring men with troops in Cimarron.

In 1876, was also the Grant County Rebellion. Secession to Arizona Territory was tried unsuccessfully to escape the Ring, called a "selfish oligarchy."

In 1877, the Colfax County War peaked. Firebrand, Mary Tibbles McPherson, on May 1st, spelled out the Ring's organized crime to President Hayes, unaware that he shielded the Ring. She wrote: "[T]he United States District Attorney, Thomas B. Catron; Associate Justice Warren Bristol; Henry L. Waldo, Chief Justice; Samuel B. Axtell, Governor ... [have] conspired together ... [F]or several years these parties have been in collusion in a general plan having for its aim the centralizing of power [and] the reduction of large and valuable private Grants of land within the Territory to their personal use and benefit ... To accomplish these purposes this Ring ... appears to have paused at nothing however difficult or questionable." She accused them of Tolby's murder.

Catron responded that she was a "crazy person;" and that outlaws had taken over in Colfax County.

Lincoln County became Catron's trouble-spot too. Catron was making mercantile and ranching monopolies there. That started at his 1866 arrival, when he got cattle as collateral on loans. He sold the beef to forts. By 1868, receipts show him allied with Lincoln County's Fort Stanton sutler store partner, Lawrence Murphy. Murphy, with partner Emil Fritz, held beef contracts for the Fort and the Mescalero Indian Reservation. Catron was a secret partner in their later Lincoln store, nicknamed "The House." Murphy, Fritz; and later partners, James Dolan and John Riley, were Catron's Lincoln County sub-bosses. In 1875, when rancher, Robert Casey, beat Murphy in a local election, he was murdered that day by a hitman. Catron tolerated no competition. These sub-bosses ran Catron's Pecos River Cow Camp. He also had his Carrizozo Land and Cattle Company ranch from 1878 to 1882, run by his brother-in-law, Edgar Walz. Dying Murphy left it to him to settle his debt. Its stock came from Seven Rivers rancher-henchmen, who rustled from cattle king, John Chisum's giant herd along the Pecos River.

In 1877, a rival appeared. New-comer, British John Tunstall, made his own general store, bank, and cattle ranches. So Catron did his usual malicious prosecutions. He made a fake embezzlement case against anti-Ring Lincoln attorney, Alexander McSween, about proceeds of a life insurance policy of "House" partner Emil Fritz. Through Ringites, District Attorney William Rynerson and Judge Warren Bristol, Catron lied that Tunstall was McSween's partner. That made Tunstall responsible for the money too. That enabled attaching both men's property using local Ringite Sheriff, William Brady.

When neither man yielded, Catron had Tunstall murdered on February 18th, 1878. It replicated his 1875 Colfax County murder of anti-Ring leader, Franklin Tolby. As with Tolby, Catron shielded the murderers. Governor Axtell was used to illegally outlaw arresting deputies, like Billy Bonney, and to empower only Sheriff Brady. Brady's job was to kill McSween next.

Unexpectedly, Tunstall's past employees fought back as the Regulators. That began the Lincoln County War. They killed Brady and his deputy, George Hindman, to save McSween's life. Later killed resisting arrest, was a Tunstall posse murderer named Andrew "Buckshot" Roberts. McSween was then exonerated of embezzling by the Grand Jury.

Responding lethally to opposition, Catron risked exposing himself and destroying his Ring. On April 28th, Catron used his Seven Rivers rustlers to try McSween's murder. They succeeded in killing Regulator head, Frank MacNab. On June 21st, Catron used his U.S. Attorney power to try to hang the Regulators by his federal indictment for their Roberts killing. On July 3rd, Catron used Ringite Sheriff, George Peppin and John Kinney's outlaw gang to massacre San Patricio's anti-Ring Hispanic backers of the Regulators. On July 14th, McSween, Regulators, and Hispanic backers took a stand in Lincoln. It became the six day Lincoln County War Battle. On July 19th, Catron used Fort Stanton troops, under Ring-beholden Commander N.A.M. Dudley, to aid loosing Peppin and his Seven Rivers and John Kinney outlaw posse. The troops enabled arson of McSween's house and murder of McSween and his defenders: Harvey Morris, Vincente Romero, Francisco Zamora, and near killing of Ygenio Salazar. Then Catron used his outlaw myth to cover-up the freedom fighting opponents as desperados.

By October of 1878, Catron faced a reckoning. Presidential Investigator Frank Warner Angel wrote a report incriminating him for Tunstall's murder and Lincoln County's turmoil. In Washington, co-boss Elkins negotiated keeping the report secret in exchange for Catron's resigning as U.S. Attorney. By July 20th, 1888, Catron further hid his 1870's criminality by a record-destroying fire in his law office. In 1893, he had Elkins destroy the report.

On October 1st, 1878, Ring-biased President Hayes, covering-up Catron's Lincoln County War crimes by scapegoating, replaced Governor Axtell with Lew Wallace. On November 14th, Wallace wrote to a Civil War friend, Absalom Markland: "I came here, and found a 'Ring' with a hand on the throat of the Territory. I refused to join them, and now they are proposing to fight me." Wallace responded self-protectively by not confronting the Ring and by issuing an Amnesty Proclamation for all non-indicted Lincoln County War participants.

In late 1878, Alexander McSween's widow, Susan, hired Attorney Huston Chapman to prosecute Commander Dudley for the murder of her husband and arson of her home.

In 1879, Catron got defamatory affidavits about her chastity to ruin her credibility. And he murdered again. He used local sub-boss, James Dolan and outlaw thugs to murder Chapman. When Susan got a new attorney, Ira Leonard, Dolan was used to try to murder him too. Catron then rigged Dudley's military Court of Inquiry for his acquittal with biased judges and with defense by his past law firm member, Henry Waldo.

Catron also represented in court all his indicted Lincoln County War murderers and arsonists. Colluding with Ringite Judge Warren Bristol, he got them pardoned by misstating Wallace's Amnesty Proclamation baring those indicted. And Catron gifted henchmen with murdered Tunstall's belongings. James Dolan got the store. Dolan, District Attorney William Rynerson, and John Riley got his Feliz River ranch. Catron was likely a silent partner. Chief Deputy of Tunstall's murder posse, Jacob Basil "Billy" Matthews, got Tunstall's Peñasco River ranch.

That 1879, the Lincoln County freedom fight lived on with gadfly zealot, Billy Bonney. He made a pardon bargain with Governor Wallace for annulling his wartime indictments for Brady, Hindman, and Roberts in exchange for testifying against Chapman's Ringite murderers. On his own, Billy also testified against Dudley in the Court of Inquiry.

By 1880, Billy was in Catron's sights. Billy had been in Catron's 1878 federal indictment against the Regulators. He then stood out by testifying against Ringites, like Chapman's murderers and Commander Dudley. So Billy's pardon request to Lew Wallace was blocked by Ring pressure. And through Catron or Elkins, a Secret Service Special Operative named Azariah Wild was assigned to the Territory in mid-September. Catron used his brother-in-law Edgar Walz and James Dolan to trick Wild that Billy led a rustling and counterfeiting gang. Wild empowered Sheriff-elect Pat Garrett, as a Deputy U.S. Marshal, to capture or kill him. While trying, Garrett killed Billy's companions, Tom O'Folliard and Charlie Bowdre. Garrett captured Billy on December 22nd, for a hanging trial in Mesilla. But Billy's April 28th, 1881 jailbreak, forced Garrett do the killing himself with a Fort Sumner ambush on July 14th, 1881.

Ringite Governor Lionel Sheldon, who replaced Lew Wallace, covered-up the anti-Ring rebellions. He wrote: "The desperado and thieving element has substantially disappeared." Billy became the Ring's outlaw myth symbol as their creation: "Billy the Kid."

Billy was the last of the anti-Ring freedom fighters. So Catron's malicious prosecutions, obsessive vendettas, attempted murders, and murders continued more brazenly.

Catron had continued cattle ranching. In 1882, he made the Boston and New Mexico Cattle Company. He partnered with Surveyor General Henry M. Atkinson, whom he used to inflate acreage of his purchased land grants.

By 1883, Catron killed again. His two victims replicated the Tunstall murder for desired ranchland. Since 1882, Catron was attorney for the American Valley Company ranch. It controlled three million acres of grazing land. But Alexis Grossetete and Robert Elsinger said the land was theirs. So on May 6th, 1883, they were murdered by "employees" of the company. Two so-called "employees" were professional gunmen hired days earlier. Another was company shareholder, John P. Casey's, brother. Catron paid one of the hitmen by a so-called "cattle purchase." Catron paid John Casey by a so-called "loan" of $6,000. That's over $154,000 today. Casey then sold his shares to Catron's Boston and New Mexico Cattle Company partner, Henry Atkinson. In 1885, Catron paid Atkinson to partner in the American Valley Company. The next year, Atkinson died, leaving Catron as owner. Biographer Victor Westphall admitted that people believed Catron murdered Grossetete and Elsinger. But no one was ever prosecuted.

In 1885, Catron used his Tularosa Land and Cattle Company to reward, with partnerships, his Lincoln County War murderers: John Riley and William Rynerson. It controlled water rights along the Tularosa River, and from the Mescalero Indian Reservation to 10 miles west of the town of Tularosa. In 1880, Catron had eliminated its competition by malicious prosecution of rancher, Pat Coghlan, in the Tularosa Valley. He accused him to the Secret Service of being in his fabricated Billy the Kid gang.

Catron's criminality colored his political career. To accusations of vote-fixing, he was elected to the Territorial legislature's House in 1868, and Council from the 1880's to 1909. As one of numerous examples, on July 23rd, 1890, Catron got a letter from a Francisco Gonzales y Borrego. Borrego's name, in two years, would become famous as Catron's hired assassin. As to vote-buying, Borrego wrote: "I have the honor to Report to you that I have two men that they have agreed to come to the Republican party but you know that they always want some money they want $10.00 each ... I will tell you that each one of them is worth 2 votes." Note that $10 is about $286 today.

In 1891, Catron tried another malicious prosecution for personal gain. On February 5th, shots were fired into a legislative meeting. Catron said it was an assassination attempt on him. He accused leaders of the Hispanic, anti-Ring, anti-land-grab Las Gorras Blancas or White Caps. But he failed to get them prosecuted. And it was rumored that he had been trying to assassinate rival legislators.

In 1892, Catron murdered again. The victim was Santa Fe Sheriff Francisco Chavez. A Democrat, he was Catron's political opponent and a rumored White Cap sympathizer. Catron's lackeys did the killing. They were his vote-fixer, Francisco Gonzales y Borrego; his brother, Antonio Gonzales y Borrego; Laurencio Alarid, Patricio Valencia; and Hipolito Vigil. (Vigil named Catron as the instigator, but was killed during capture.) Furthermore, victim Chavez had told people that he feared assassination.

And, as in Tolby's and Tunstall's assassinations, the murders were shielded. Ringite Santa Fe County Sheriff Charles M. Conklin refused to arrest them. Conklin was also rumored as Catron's accomplice in murdering Chavez.

It took until 1895 for arrests. It became the sensational "Borrego Case." Catron represented the murderers, with his law partner, Charles A. Speiss, as co-counsel. Biographer Westphall, blaming Democrats, wrote that the prosecutors tried harder to implicate Catron as the killer, than to convict the defendants.

The murder occurred on the night of May 29th, 1892. Catron was running for Delegate to Congress. Chavez voiced opposition. One of the prosecutors in the Borrego trial, Napoleon Bonaparte Laughlin, later wrote about the killing in a 1895 Supreme Court opinion. He stated: "[At] the time of [Chavez's] assassination ... he was the acknowledged leader of his party ... and the testimony given ... tended strongly to show that the primary motive for his assassination was ... an inordinate desire to remove him from the road of political preferment."

Biographer Westphall used Catron's plausible deniability alibi, by claiming Catron wasn't in town for the murder. But Catron knew the killers. He, Speiss, and the killers belonged to a violent Republican organization called the Knights of Liberty. And Francisco Gonzales y Borrego had murdered twice before. Catron had successfully defended him by self-defense. In fact, the Borrego case proved Catron's crime family loyalty to Ringites doing his dirty work.

Catron's major accuser was his past law partner, Democrat, William Thornton, now Governor. He owned the *Santa Fe Weekly New Mexican*. He knew Catron's criminality. In 1893, he had headlined an article: "Ex-Sheriff Chavez Assassinated Because of his Political Influence." It was Thornton who removed Ringite Sheriff Conklin for embezzling public funds. It was Thornton who replaced him with William P. Cunningham, a Democrat. On January 10th, 1895, 591 days after Francisco Chavez's murder, Sheriff Cunningham arrested his killers.

Thornton reported in his paper that, in the January 14th pre-trial hearings, a Juan Gallegos testified that Hipolito Vigil (the one killed during arrest) told him that Catron offered him $700 to kill Francisco Chavez, plus legal defense by Catron himself. (Note that in 1875, in the Colfax County War, gunslinger, Clay Allison also claimed that Catron offered him $700 to kill anti-Ring opponent Franklin Tolby.) Other eye-witnesses incriminated the four Borrego case defendants.

The 1895 trial's prosecutor was District Attorney Jacob H. Crist. During the trial, Catron and Speiss, bribed, intimidated, slandered, and kidnapped prosecution witnesses. Nevertheless, on May 29th, the defendants were sentenced to hang. Catron responded with his usual defamatory affidavits - here from jurors - attacking prosecutor Crist. But the judge rejected them.

In that July's plea bargaining, Laurencio Alarid and Patricio Valencia confessed that they and the Borrego brothers had murdered Chavez. But Catron remained untouched.

That 1895, Elkins became West Virginia's Senator. He tried to help Catron stop the defendants' hangings.

But Catron got caught for something. On August 20th, prosecutor Jacob H. Crist filed a complaint with the Territorial Supreme Court against Catron and Speiss for witness tampering. The Court appointed five attorneys to prepare charges. On August 31st, disbarment charges were filed. The tampered prosecution witnesses' transcripts showed horrifying pressures to make them recant testimony against the Borrego case defendants.

Catron's response was his usual outlawing. He called these prosecution witnesses, quote: "penitentiary convicts ... and disreputable characters, unworthy of credit or belief."

Behind the scenes, sociopath Catron defamed accuser Jacob Crist and pressured the Supreme Court Judges. He had Judge Humphrey B. Hamilton contacted by his friend, *Socorro Chieftain* publisher, W.S. Williams. To influence Judge Gideon Bantz, Catron used Elkins, whose wife was Bantz's cousin.

There was an obstacle. Supreme Court Chief Justice Thomas Smith was honest. And gone were the 1867 days when Ringite William Rynerson simply murdered anti-Ring Chief Justice John P. Slough. So Catron began a press campaign to ruin Smith professionally and personally.

He used *Albuquerque Daily Citizen* Editor, Thomas Hughes, whom he previously bribed for political backing. On October 9th, Hughes published an anonymous letter by Catron. Catron pretended to be a man protecting Catron by exposing bad Judge Smith. It was titled: "Is It Honesty or Partisanship?" It made-up that bad Smith colluded with one of the attorneys drawing up the charges, to cripple good Catron's efforts to help New Mexico's people. Then Catron added a diabolical twist. "Anonymous" claimed that the Bar Association vouched for Catron. So bad Smith was insulting the Bar Association by accusing Catron!

The next day, October 10th, Catron responded as himself to the anonymous letter. Complicit Editor Hughes printed it, with his own so-called response, which Catron wrote also. Catron's letter said his enemies were trying to hurt his disbarment case by saying he was "Anonymous." Hughes's response denied Catron as being "Anonymous." This was perjury.

That same October 10th, Catron sent Hughes a real letter. Catron told him that if he was charged with perjury, he should hide Catron's role. And he told him to destroy the letter.

Catron's biographer, Victor Westphall, spun his criminality as loyalty. Hughes was fined and jailed. Westphall wrote: "Tom Catron did not forget his promise to 'make up the difference' for Thomas Hughes forbearance in accepting quietly the jail sentence on behalf of Catron ... Catron responded with financial aid." On July 11th, 1896, Catron wrote Hughes a pay-off check for $350 from his First National Bank of Santa Fe. That's over $9,000 today.

Catron continued to attack Judge Thomas Smith. He got his usual fake affidavits to claim Smith had been bribed to reverse another judge's decision. Then he wrote another anonymous letter, for his friend, W.S. Williams's, *Socorro Chieftain*. It said Smith's uncles were an embezzler and a murder, and he was a drunkard and a homosexual.

It all worked. That October 25th, the corrupted Supreme Court vindicated Catron and Speiss. Traumatized Chief Justice Smith was absent, claiming illness. The majority opinion was by bribed Judge Humphrey H. Hamilton. He stated that, quote: "the low moral character and poor reputation for veracity of the prosecution witnesses rendered their testimony about tampering beyond belief." He ignored the *Albuquerque Daily Citizen* scandal.

But Judge Napoleon Bonaparte Laughlin dissented. He wrote that those witnesses were so credible that they got the Borrego case murderers a hanging sentence! He added that Catron's *Albuquerque Daily Citizen* attack on Chief Justice Smith itself merited disbarment.

So Catron got away with murdering Francisco Chavez and witness tampering. And he was immediately elected President of the Bar Association. He and his Ring were untouchable.

But Catron's vindictiveness was unsatiated. He tried to destroy Prosecutor Jacob Crist, dissenting Judge Napoleon Bonaparte Laughlin, and Governor William Thornton.

Catron pursued Prosecutor Crist with private detectives. They found an old, dormant, Colorado indictment for "larceny of household furniture." But there were no witnesses. Learning Crist was traveling to Arizona, Catron tried to have him arrested there. Then he backed off, realizing he risked disbarment again; this time for obvious malicious prosecution.

As to Judge Laughlin, on July 18th, 1896, Catron used his powerful Ringite ally, William J. Mills, in Washington, (later the last Territorial governor) to damage his career.

As to Governor Thornton, on September 5th, 1896, Catron wrote another anonymous letter to Editor Hughes for his *Albuquerque Daily Citizen*. He called Thornton dissolute "Poker Bill," and made-up that he caused the Borrego case convictions by tampering the court record.

Thornton, as rough as Catron, was unfazed. He printed the letter in his paper. He called Catron a coward hiding behind anonymity. And he accused him of the *Albuquerque Daily Citizen's* anonymous defamation of Chief Justice Thomas Smith.

Catron decompensated into a savage frenzy of letters. On September 16th, he accused Thornton of a trying to make him commit, quote, "some act of violence, which might give your adherents an opportunity to injure me physically." Don't miss this window into Catron's psychopathic mind. He blames his potential victim for forcing him to kill! And he projects his murderous urge onto Thornton, thinking that Thornton threatened him! Thornton, calling him venomous, published it.

Then, with deranged paranoia, Catron tried unsuccessfully to get President Grover Cleveland to fire Thornton as Governor for, quote, "[inciting] blood-shed;" though the bloody urge was his own. With crime boss loyalty, he then suggested, as replacement, one of Billy Bonney's killing team: John William Poe! Catron also wrote to Elkins to help in removing Thornton. It failed.

As slight justice, exposed Catron lost his 1896 run for Delegate to Congress, even with his usual vote-fixing. So he tried to get reappointed as U.S. Attorney, despite his 1878 forced resignation to hide his murdering John Tunstall. Elkins tried to pull Washington strings. But Catron was defeated, in part, by his victim, past Governor Lew Wallace, well aware of his evil.

On April 2nd, 1897, the Borrego case murderers were hanged. That made Francisco Chavez just the second Ring victim whose murderers (excluding Catron) got punished. And he was Catron's last known corpse in his 25 year killing spree. The others were John Potts Slough, Franklin Tolby, Robert Casey (whose hitman was hanged), Maxwell Land Grant settlers, John Tunstall, Frank MacNab, San Patricio massacre victims, Alexander McSween, Harvey Morris, Vincente Romero, Francisco Zamora, Huston Chapman, Tom O'Folliard, Charlie Bowdre, Billy Bonney, Alexis Grossetete, and Robert Elsinger. Accidental survivors were Colfax County's William Morley, Frank Springer, Henry Porter, and Clay Allison; and Lincoln County's Juan Patrón, Ygenio Salazar, and Ira Leonard. But that doesn't mean that Catron stopped trying.

Next on Catron's hit list was a ranching competitor in the Tularosa Valley named Oliver Lee. Catron did his usual malicious prosecution. Using Billy Bonney's betraying court-appointed Attorney, Albert Jennings Fountain, as co-counsel, Catron attacked Oliver Lee and his ranch hand, William McNew, for rustling and defacing brands. Convicting Lee would also sully Catron's political rival, Democrat Albert B. Fall, as Lee's friend and attorney.

Lee had come from Texas to the Tularosa Valley in 1884, making his Sacramento Cattle Company. He had a power base and gunmen ranch hands. One was James Gilliland.

On January 30th, 1896, Fountain and Catron got Lee and McNew indicted in Lincoln's courthouse. But Fountain got a threatening note, later found in his abandoned buggy on the road home. He and his young son, Henry, were believed murdered. Their bodies were never found. Catron, of course, accused Oliver Lee. Added was ranch hand James Gilliland. Hanging was Catron's favored killing, since it looked legal. And Catron knew the right man for the job. Pat Garrett had successfully led the Secret Service hunt for the factitious Billy the Kid gang. Then, after Billy's jailbreak, he had efficiently killed him.

Garrett, on hard times because of alcoholism, abrasive personality, and business failures, was brought from Uvalde, Texas. He was to be made Doña Ana County Sheriff. If he got Lee and Gilliland convicted, he'd get $8,000. That's about $248,000 today.

Garrett had ambushed Billy Bonney near midnight, and had called it self-defense. So on the night of July 12th, 1898, at Oliver Lee's property at Wildy Well, Garrett ambushed presumably sleeping Oliver Lee and James Gilliland on a adobe house's flat rooftop. They were awake. They shot dead his posseman. Garrett retreated. Lee and Gilliland, later surrendered.

On May 21st, 1899, Ringite Attorney Sidney Barnes (one of Billy Bonney's Mesilla trial prosecutors) reported to Catron about coercing local rustlers to be witnesses for the prosecution.

In their 1901 trial, Lee and Gilliland were declared innocent. Garrett's dead posseman was considered a self-defense killing. Oliver Lee subsequently succeeded in business, and was twice elected to the legislature. He escaped Catron's lethal clutches.

Next attacked by Catron was his political enemy, Miguel Otero, seeking Governorship after William Thornton. Murder was out of the question. On May 2nd, 1897, Catron sent to President William McKinley his henchmen, Henry Waldo and John Riley, to block the appointment. Of Catron, Otero had written: "It was inevitable that we should conflict. He was dictatorial and absolutely ruthless in his methods." Otero was confirmed that June 2nd.

To block Otero's reappointment, Catron filed charges against him to President McKinley and Vice-president Theodore Roosevelt. They were his usual defamatory affidavits and sexual scandalmongering. Elkins helped. But Otero was reappointed.

Catron then met personally with President Roosevelt. He accused Otero of stealing military equipment and having a ring. There was no third term. But Otero said he'd refused one.

Catron then got Herbert J. Hagerman appointed Governor. For payback, he wanted to be appointed Attorney General, apparently to maliciously prosecute Miguel Otero. He was not appointed. Next, Catron and Elkins got Ring friend, George Curry, appointed Governor for two terms; followed by Ring friend, William J. Mills. So Catron prevailed.

Catron's goal was state senatorship. On November 15th, 1911, he requested legislators' backing. The press claimed he bribed them. Biographer Westphall quoted his son, Charles C. Catron, inadvertently implying bribery. On June 3rd, 1921, after Catron's death, Charles wrote: "My father probably spent over a million dollars in following up his hobby [of politics]." If the spending was that 1911, it was today's $27 million. If one starts with Catron's bribes of legislators in the 1872 Legislature Revolt, it's much more with today's inflation.

Elkins died January 4th, 1911, missing the statehood resolution signed by President William Howard Taft that August 21st. New Mexico became the 47th state on January 6th, 1912. On April 2nd, Catron was sworn in as senator, along with Albert Fall. Catron held office till 1917.

On May 15th, 1921, at 80, Catron died in bed. It was 79 days after still-existing Catron County was carved out in New Mexico, on February 25th, to honor this monster.

His eulogy was written by a George W. Prichard. He gushed: "Hypocrisy was never laid at his door ... He did not cherish animosity toward an enemy ... Those who had the hardest things to say of him knew the least about him." For the *Santa Fe New Mexican*, an E. Dana Johnson added: "He was frankly a 'practical politician;' the appellation 'boss' complimented instead of offending him."

Omitted were Thomas Benton Catron's real achievements: he was a serial murderer, who never got caught. He created the criminal syndicate of the Santa Fe Ring: an American fiefdom, insulated from exposure or prosecution; so perfect that it exists to the present.

And T.B. Catron invented the outlaw myth of Billy the Kid to cover-up his own outlawry. It would be fitting if his most famous victim, Billy Bonney, hero of New Mexico's grandest freedom fight against him, finally set the record straight. That's the purpose of my talks.

TALK 19:
SANTA FE RING MINIONS
FROM BOOK: *THE SANTA FE RING VERSUS BILLY THE KID*
JANUARY 19, 2021

This talk gives my revisionist history of Santa Fe Ring members in Billy the Kid history. The information is from my book, *The Santa Fe Ring Versus Billy the Kid: The Making of an American Monster.*

Santa Fe Ring boss Thomas Benton Catron's minions, from henchmen to hitmen, called each other "friends." Unlike the Mafia, members took no oaths, though they became Masons. They were united by secret guilt for Catron's depraved plots. They were united by Catron's pay-offs. They were united by shielding from prosecution. Billy Bonney knew the injustice. In his April 16th, 1881 *Mesilla News* interview, after his hanging sentence, he said: "I think it hard that I should be the only one to suffer the extreme penalty of the law."

To demonstrate the injustice, I'll present their crimes, their life-long rewards from Catron, and their sanitized obituaries.

In Lincoln County, Catron's minions went back to his 1866 Territorial arrival. He engaged in money-lending and military beef contracts.

On screen are Fort Stanton's sutler store partners, who later built the Lincoln general store called "The House." **[FIGURE 26]** From left to right, they are clerk, James Dolan, Emil Fritz, unnamed clerk, and Lawrence Murphy. Fritz, Murphy, and Dolan served Catron's Lincoln County mercantile and ranching monopolies.

FIGURE 26: Partners in "The House." Courtesy of the Palace of the Governors Photo Archives (NMHM/DCA). Personnel of L.G. Murphy and Company. 1872-1873? Negative Number HP.2012.22.5; 104912

On screen is Emil Fritz, co-founder of the sutler store with its government contract frauds. **[FIGURE 27]** He died in 1874. Catron used his life insurance policy proceeds for a malicious prosecution embezzling case against anti-Ring Alexander McSween and John Tunstall. In fact, McSween's honest delay in paying local heirs was merely diligent seeking of other heirs in Germany.

FIGURE 27: Emil Fritz. Courtesy of the Palace of the Governors Photo Archives (NMHM/DCA). Brevet Lieutenant Colonel Emil Fritz. 1866. Negative Number: 023137

Fritz was born on March 3rd, 1832 in Germany. He had 10 siblings. He emigrated to America in the 1840's. He entered the military, and came to New Mexico Territory with General James H. Carleton's Column. He re-enlisted in Fort Sumner, then served at Fort Stanton. He then made its sutler store with fellow soldier, Lawrence Murphy. In 1874, he died in Germany.

On screen is Lawrence G. Murphy, co-founder of the corrupt sutler store with Emil Fritz, that became Lincoln's general store nicknamed "The House." **[FIGURE 28]** Catron's attempted mercantile monopoly through it contributed to John Tunstall's murder and the Lincoln County War.

FIGURE 28: Lawrence G. Murphy.
https://commons.wikimedia.org/wiki/File:Lawrence_Murphy.jpg

Born about 1831 in Ireland, Murphy graduated college, and came to New Mexico Territory. In 1861, he joined the army at Fort Union, serving under Kit Carson in the Navajo Wars. In 1865, he served under General James H. Carleton in Fort Sumner. In 1866, he mustered out with other Carleton soldiers, William Brady and Emil Fritz. Murphy and Fritz made the Fort Stanton sutler store as L.G. Murphy and Company. They employed Brady, and a James Dolan. In 1873, the business was expelled after Dolan tried to murder a soldier exposing their corruption, with Murphy as possible accomplice. With Catron's backing, they built a Lincoln store nicknamed "The House." Murphy and Fritz cheated local farmers with usurious loans and underpaying for produce. In 1874, when Fritz died, Murphy made Dolan his partner. In 1875,

Murphy was possibly behind the hitman murder in Lincoln of his political rival: rancher, Robert Casey. Murphy later left politics after being caught embezzling Lincoln County taxes. In 1876, he got Frederick Godfroy appointed as Mescalero Reservation Indian Agent to collude in his supply scams. In 1877, he retired. On October 20th, 1878, he died. Catron took over his Carrizozo ranch to settle Murphy's debt to him. Murphy's Masonic Lodge's tribute was by Ringite Henry Waldo, from Catron's law firm. It stated: "[He] was recognized and beloved ... as a man of unblemished honor and integrity ... [H]e held a position of prominence and influence in the Territory."

On screen is James J. Dolan, a violent sociopath and multiple murderer. **[FIGURE 29]** His Lincoln store, J.J. Dolan and Company, backed by Catron, was known as "The House." It was bankrupted by John Tunstall's competition.

FIGURE 29: James J. Dolan. William A. Keleher Collection. Center for Southwest Research, University Libraries, University of New Mexico. ZIM CSWR Pict Colls PICT 000-742
https://econtent.unm.edu/digital/collection/keleher/id/48/rec/2 and
https://www.pinterest.com/pin/397864948328207441/

In 1878, Dolan, with others, was involved first in murdering Tunstall, then in murdering Lincoln County War anti-Ring fighters, including Alexander McSween. He recognized Billy Bonney's threat to the Ring, and tried to enlist him in a February 18th, 1879 so-called "peace meeting." In 1879, he murdered Attorney Huston Chapman, and tried to murder Attorney Ira Leonard, in attempt to stop their prosecution of Ringite Commander N.A.M. Dudley for his Lincoln County War intervention.

Dolan was born on May 22nd, 1848, in Ireland, coming to America as a child. In the Civil War's Union Army, he was discharged at Fort Stanton, and worked in its L.G. Murphy and Company sutler store as a clerk. In 1873, he got the business expelled by trying to murder a soldier exposing its corruption. The store relocated to Lincoln as "The House." In 1877, he assumed control after Emil Fritz's death and Lawrence Murphy's retirement. He partnered with Catron's cattle broker, John H. Riley, to form J.J. Dolan and Company. In 1877, he murdered a Hilario Jaramillo as a possible favor to "The House's" builder, George Peppin; who then married Jaramillo's widow. In 1878, when "The House" went bankrupt, he mortgaged it and its 40 acres to Catron. In 1878 and 1879 were Dolan's murders of Tunstall, Lincoln County War opponents, and Huston Chapman. He was indicted for the Tunstall and Chapman murders.

Dolan was rewarded by Catron. He got Tunstall's store and ranch. The ranch was renamed the Feliz River Cattle Company, in partnership with other paid-off Ringites: John Riley and William Rynerson. Dolan was president and general manager. In 1883, he was elected Lincoln County Treasurer. In 1888 he was elected to the Territorial Senate. In 1889, he became receiver of the U.S. Land Office in Las Cruces. He died on February 26th, 1898. His March 2nd *Santa Fe New Mexican* obituary declared: "He was a man whose personal integrity was without blemish, whose word was as good as his bond, and whose geniality, generosity and other manly qualities attracted to him many friends. His death is generally deplored as a loss to the territory."

Dolan's profuse letters to Catron concern loans, politicking, and using Catron as an attack dog. On June 11th, 1895, he wrote: "You no doubt have noticed that cowardly slanderous article against me, published in the *Santa Fe New Mexican* of the 3rd instant ... [I]f there is any way to punish the outfit, I want you to do it."

On screen is John H. Riley, Catron's cattle dealer, an attempted murderer, and partner in "The House's" J.J. Dolan and Company. **[FIGURE 30]** He was in District Attorney William Rynerson's "Friends Riley and Dolan plot" to kill John Tunstall. During the Lincoln County War, he was in Santa Fe as liaison to Catron.

FIGURE 30. John H. Riley. William A. Keleher Collection. Center for Southwest Research, University Libraries, University of New Mexico. ZIM CSWR Pict Colls PICT 000-742
https://econtent.unm.edu/digital/collection/keleher/id/152/rec/5

Riley was born on May 12th, 1850, in Ireland. He emigrated to America with his family in 1862. In 1865, he worked as a Colorado railroad contractor. In New Mexico Territory, he clerked for a beef contractor near the Mescalero Indian Reservation, and had a ranch near Fort Stanton, and may have met Catron in 1866 through these businesses. In 1875, he tried to murder anti-Ring Hispanic leader, Juan Patrón, in Lincoln. In 1877, he became a partner in "The House." In 1878, he was involved in Tunstall's murder and the Lincoln County War murders of freedom fighters.

Riley was rewarded - along with James Dolan and William Rynerson - by getting Tunstall's Feliz River ranch, named by them the Feliz Cattle Company. He also partnered with Charles Fritz's son, Emil Fritz, in a ranch. He was Assessor of Doña Ana County. With Catron, he co-owned the American Cattle Company, Tularosa Land and Cattle Company, the Terra Amarilla Land Grant, and the Santa Teresa Land Grant. He died in 1916. His February 25th obituary in "The Deming Graphic," stated: "John H. Riley [was] a pioneer of the Southwest ...[H]e was the owner of large cattle interests in Lincoln county in the early eighties and through the receiving a large beef contract from the government he became the butt of a bitter feud that figured prominently in what is remembered as the Lincoln County War, in which he and his friends were victors. His fortune is estimated at $250,000." That's almost $6 million today.

Riley's letters to Catron often included James Dolan and William Rynerson. On February 5th, 1890, he described attacking their political rival by defamatory affidavits and harassment. He wrote: "I today mailed Senator Edmunds my affidavit corroborated by Dolan against Fiske – Rynerson writes me he is making it hot for him ... Do all you can to down him but do not let it appear as coming from you."

On screen is Edgar A. Walz, Catron's wife's brother. [FIGURE 31] During the Lincoln County War period, he managed Catron's Carrizozo Land and Cattle Company ranch and "The House" in Lincoln after Catron took possession. In 1880, working with James Dolan, he tricked Secret Service Operative Azariah Wild into thinking Billy Bonney headed a huge rustler-counterfeiter gang, and should be captured or killed.

Walz was born in Minnesota on March 3rd, 1859. In 1876, he moved to New Mexico Territory. In 1878, Catron put him in charge of his ranch and Lincoln store. Later, Walz started businesses while begging Catron for money. His *New York Times* obituary stated: "[H]e left home as a lad to seek his fortune in the Southwest. He established himself in the cattle business and for years managed a large ranch in New Mexico."

Walz's letters show access to Ringite heights through Catron. His June 8th, 1897 letter asked Catron to get Ring co-boss, S.B. Elkins, to invest $15,000 in his hotel company. That's over $466,000 today.

FIGURE 31. Edgar Walz. "Edgar A. Walz. *The San Francisco Examiner*. December 25, 1891. Page 26. www.newspapers.com

David M. Easton was Catron's business agent, stationed within the Mescalero Indian Reservation to work with Indian Agent Frederick Godfroy to defraud government contracts for "The House." During the Lincoln County War, as Justice of the Peace, he wrote false arrest warrants against Alexander McSween and Billy Bonney.

Easton was born in Pennsylvania on September 3rd, 1846. He joined the military in 1865 and deserted in 1870. After the Lincoln County War, he was in the legislature, worked in dry goods, and was a postmaster. He died on April 21st, 1917. The October 21st, 1881 *Rio Grande Republican* had written: "David M. Easton is one of the pioneers of this district ... He is favorably known in the Territory."

Easton's letters to Catron match those of Catron's other begging lackeys and affidavit fakers. On April 8th, 1889, he wrote:

"I would like your assistance in obtaining for me some employment by which I can be able in time to pay you what I owe ... Riley and Rynerson both promised me that they would see that I 'was taken care of' ... As to the Affidavit I gave regarding their Desert Land Entries, it was in their favor ... [I]t directly and flatly contradicted every witness."

On screen is Saturnino Baca, a Lincoln resident and murderer, who betrayed the Hispanic cause of the Lincoln County War. [FIGURE 32] He aided the fatal intervention by Commander N.A.M. Dudley in the final battle by lying that he needed protection for his wife and children from Alexander McSween. That made Baca responsible, with others, for the murders of Alexander McSween, Vincente Romero, Harvey Morris, and Francisco Zamora, and arson of McSween's home.

FIGURE 32. Saturnino Baca. Robert N. Mullin Collection. Haley Memorial Library and Research Center. Midland, Texas. RNM.IV.A.14.2

Baca was born on November 11th, 1830, in the Territory. In the Civil War, he became a Captain. Serving in Fort Stanton, he met its Ringite veterans at its sutler store. In 1867, after discharge, he settled in Lincoln. In 1868, he used Catron, among others, to pass a bill forming Lincoln County. In 1871, a Fort Stanton complaint documented his conspiracy with Emil Fritz and Lawrence Murphy to supply inferior hay to Fort Stanton. In 1878, he was caught stealing hundreds of pounds of coffee, sugar, and other supplies from the Mescalero Indian Reservation, likely for the "The House." That year, he helped defeat the Lincoln County War freedom fighters. In 1882, he murdered black Lincoln resident, George Washington, who had eloped with one of his daughters. In 1897, he was on the New Mexico Board of Prison Directors. In 1909 he was Master at Arms of the New Mexico legislature. Baca died on March 7th, 1925 in Lincoln. In 1961, a Tom Charles, in an essay titled, "The Father of Lincoln County," called him "one of Lincoln County's most loved citizens." It stated that Baca, Murphy, and Brady were, quote: "citizens seeking establishment of better law and order in southeastern New Mexico."

Baca's March 28th, 1892 letter to Catron shows confident cronyism as he requested help for a Francisco Baca's reimbursement for "Indian depredations." He added imperiously: "Please let me know if the claim has been allowed, or what shape it is in."

Catron's Ring enforcers in the Lincoln County War period carried out his malicious prosecutions, terrorism, murder, and obstruction of justice.

On screen is Samuel Beach Axtell, the Ring-bribed Governor from 1875 to 1878, who assisted Catron's crushing of the anti-Ring uprising in Lincoln County. **[FIGURE 33]** His illegal proclamation outlawing the Regulators - including Billy Bonney – was to block arrest of John Tunstall's Ring murderers. Axtell also replaced non-Ring Sheriff, John Copeland, with Ringite George Peppin. All that contributed to the Lincoln County War murders of Alexander McSween and his men.

Born on October 14th, 1819, in Ohio, Axtell became a lawyer. He was a District Attorney in California. In 1874, he was appointed by President Ulysses S. Grant as Governor of Utah. In 1875, he was transferred to New Mexico Territory to replace deceased Governor Marsh Giddings. In Colfax County, in 1875

FIGURE 33. Governor Samuel Beach Axtell.
https://catalog.archives.gov/id/526813

and 1876, he shielded from prosecution Ring murderers of anti-Ring leader Franklin Tolby by illegally removing the courts. He also plotted murders of other anti-Ring opponents there. In 1878, he shielded Tunstall's Ringite murderers and contributed to the Lincoln County War. After the War, he was scapegoated by removal as Governor to hide boss T.B. Catron as the responsible U.S. official. In 1882, with Ring bosses, S.B. Elkins's and T.B. Catron's, backing, he was appointed Chief Justice, serving to 1885. He died on August 6th, 1891. On August 13th, the *Santa Fe New Mexican* ran his Supreme Court eulogy by fellow Ringites, William Breeden and Henry Waldo. It stated: "[D]uring his service as Chief Justice of this court and his prior service as Governor of the Territory, [he] endeared himself to the members of the bar and other citizens of the territory by his sterling qualities, his high sense of justice ... and his zeal in the public service."

On screen is Warren Bristol. **[FIGURE 43]** As Third Judicial District Judge in 1878's Lincoln County War period, under Catron's direction and with District Attorney William Rynerson, he conducted malicious prosecutions of Alexander McSween and John Tunstall. He also indicted Billy Bonney and other Regulators for the killings of William Brady and George Hindman. With Rynerson, he changed Billy's trail venue to Doña Ana County to insure a hanging. In 1881, he was Billy's judge in Mesilla, manipulating the jury to get the first degree murder verdict.

FIGURE 34: Third Judicial District Judge Warren Bristol. Courtesy of the Palace of the Governors Photo Archives (NMHM/DCA). Warren Bristol. 1890? Negative Number: 007008.

Bristol was born on March 19th, 1823, in New York state. He became a lawyer. In 1850, he became a District Attorney in Minnesota. From 1866 to 1870, he served in the Minnesota legislature. In 1872, he was appointed by President Ulysses S. Grant as Associate Justice of the New Mexico Supreme Court and District Attorney of the Third Judicial District, encompassing Lincoln, Doña Ana, and Grant Counties. He aided Ring plots to outlaw opponents for malicious prosecutions during the anti-Ring uprisings in the 1870's. In 1877, Colfax County War activists petitioned President Hayes for his removal for corruption. In 1878, in Lincoln County, his malicious prosecutions contributed to Ring murders and the Lincoln County War. He served as District Attorney for a little over 12 years, resigning in 1884 to practice law in Deming. He died there, on January 12th, 1890. January 14th's *Santa Fe Daily New Mexican* gave his Supreme Court testimonial by Ringites, T.B. Catron, Chief Justice S.B. Axtell, and Judge Simon Newcomb. It stated: "In the judicial opinions ... he has built for himself a monument which will not soon crumble, resting ... upon established principles of justice and equity."

On screen is William L. Rynerson, a murderer. **[FIGURE 35]** As a District Attorney, he orchestrated Catron's malicious prosecutions and murders in Lincoln County. He authored the February 14th, 1878 "Friends Riley and Dolan" letter plot for murdering Tunstall and McSween. He helped Governor Axtell write the improper Proclamation removing Lincoln County Sheriff John Copeland and replacing him with George Peppin. In 1878, he blocked arrest of Tunstall's killers after they were indicted by the Grand Jury. For the 1879 Grand Jury, he blocked arrest of Huston Chapman's killers, and tried to discount Billy Bonney's eye-witness testimony against them. There he colluded with Judge Bristol to change Billy's trial venue from Lincoln County to Doña County to ensure his hanging sentence. In 1881, he assisted District Attorney Simon Newcomb (his law partner) and Judge Bristol in Billy's Mesilla hanging trial. He possibly threatened Billy's lawyer, Ira Leonard, to make him withdraw; to be replaced with Rynerson's friends: court appointed Attorney Albert Jennings Fountain and co-counsel John D. Bail. They ensured the first degree murder verdict.

Born on February 22nd, 1828 in Kentucky, Rynerson attended college in Indiana. In 1852 he went to California for the gold rush; remaining to study law. In Union service, with Carleton's

FIGURE 35: District Attorney William L. Rynerson.
https://commons.wikimedia.org/wiki/File:The_California_column_(
IA_californiacolumn00pett).pdf

California Column, he came to Las Cruces. Mustering out in
1866, he stayed there, making mining claims. In 1867, he was
elected to the legislature's Council. When anti-Ring Supreme
Court Chief Justice John Potts Slough declared the voting rigged,
he murdered him. Represented by Ring boss, U.S. Attorney S.B.
Elkins, Rynerson got off on "self-defense." He served in the

legislature till 1870. That year, he was admitted to the bar. Ringite Governor William Pile made him Territorial Adjutant General. In 1871, he and other campaigning Republicans were accused of attempting to murder Democrat candidates' relatives. The resulting clash, called the Mesilla Riot, killed nine. In 1872, Rynerson joined Catron and Ringite John D. Bail (Billy Bonney's future hanging trial co-attorney) in a Silver City mining law suit. In 1874, with help of Elkins as Delegate to Congress, he litigated unsuccessfully to take over the Mesilla Land Grant. In 1876 and '78, Ringite Governor S.B. Axtell appointed him District Attorney for the Third Judicial District, covering Doña Ana, Grant, and Lincoln Counties. In 1878, he was key to the Ring's malicious prosecutions and murders in the Lincoln County War period. In the 1880's, he ranched near Las Cruces. In 1882, with law partner, Simon Newcomb, he got the county seat transferred from Mesilla to Las Cruces, so his land there could be bought for its courthouse and jail.

Rynerson was rewarded. In 1884, with John Riley and James Dolan, he became a partner in Tunstall's stolen Feliz River ranch, renamed the Rio Feliz Land and Cattle Company. In 1889, he partnered in Catron's and John Riley's Tularosa Land and Cattle Company. He died, on September 26th, 1893. His September 30th *Rio Grande Republican* obituary stated: "Expressions of regret are heard on every side on account of this sudden death of one of our best citizens."

Rynerson's letters to Catron showed him as his business partner, loan recipient, and political agent. On November 11th, 1888, he wrote on behalf of himself and John Riley about political strategizing: "I notice what you say in relation to having mutual understanding in regard to appointments in this Territory ... Riley and I were talking over this ... If we are united we will succeed ... We have, like you, had a hard fight against the enemy."

On screen is William Brady, a Lincoln County Sheriff. **[FIGURE 36]** He was exposed in 1878 by John Tunstall as embezzling county taxes to buy rustled cattle for "The House." He murdered Tunstall with his outlaw posse, shielded the murderers, and attempted to kill Alexander McSween.

Brady was born on August 16th, 1829 in Ireland; emigrating to America in 1851. He joined the army, serving until 1861. That year, he joined the Second New Mexico Volunteer Infantry. Serving as a Major at Fort Stanton, he met sutler store

FIGURE 36: Lincoln County Sheriff William Brady.
https://commons.wikimedia.org/wiki/File:Brady-William-J-
1872.jpg

proprietors, Emil Fritz and Lawrence Murphy. In 1869, he became
Lincoln County's first Sheriff. In 1878, he implemented Tunstall's
murder. He was killed on April 1st by the Regulators to prevent
his murdering Alexander McSween that day. An April 13th *Las
Vegas Gazette* article about his killing; stated: "We are loath to
believe that Sheriff Brady had been in any way connected to the
death of Tunstall. He had ever borne the reputation of an honest
man and good officer."

On screen is Jacob Basil "Billy" Matthews. **[FIGURE 37]** He was Sheriff William Brady's Chief Deputy for the malicious prosecution property attachment of John Tunstall's ranch. He then led the Tunstall murder posse. When the Regulators' ambushed Brady, he was present, and likely in the plot to murder Alexander McSween that day. During the Lincoln County War, he attempted ambush killings of Regulators, Billy Bonney and Charlie Bowdre, and participated in the final battle.

FIGURE 37. Jacob Basil "Billy" Matthews.
Ancestry. Web. 30 Dec. 2020
https://www.ancestry.com/family-
tree/person/tree/6998202/person/-1185255992/facts

Matthews was born on May 5th, 1847 in Tennessee. In the Union Army, he was discharged in 1865. In 1867, he mined in New Mexico Territory, and settled in Lincoln County. In 1874, he made a Peñasco River ranch without full title, but fraudulently sold it to John Tunstall in 1877. He used the money to buy into secret partnership in "The House." In 1878, he was involved in murdering Tunstall and in the Lincoln County War. He was indicted, with others, for its murders. In 1879, Catron got him pardoned by misuse of Governor Lew Wallace's Amnesty Proclamation. In 1892, he and James Dolan became directors of the Peñasco Reservoir and Irrigation Company. In 1894, he moved to Roswell as manager of the Pecos Irrigation and Improvement Company. In 1898, with past Seven Rivers rustler, Buck Powell, he unsuccessfully made an Arizona ranch. He then was appointed by President McKinley as Roswell's postmaster, serving six years. He died there on June 3rd, 1904. His June 4th *Santa Fe New Mexican* obituary, calling him a stock raiser and postmaster, added: "He was an honest man and his word was as good as his bond in every transaction, public or private. He was an exemplary citizen."

Matthews was rewarded by getting Tunstall's stolen Peñasco River ranch. He named it the Peñasco Cattle Company.

Matthews stayed in contact with Catron. His August 31st, 1892 letter stated: "I congratulate you upon your nomination [for Territorial Delegate], and you can rest assured that I will give you all the support that is in my power."

On screen is George W. Peppin, the builder of "The House." [FIGURE 38] He was a Deputy in the Tunstall murder posse. He was in the Regulators' ambush of Sheriff Brady, and was possibly in the plot to murder Alexander McSween that day. He was made Lincoln County Sheriff by improper Proclamation of Ringite Governor S.B. Axtell. He was a multiple murderer and arsonist in the Lincoln County War. He led its massacre at San Patricio. He led the outlaw posse in its final battle. In it, he colluded with Fort Stanton Commander, N.A.M. Dudley for illegal intervention. He colluded with Dudley to burn down the McSween house to incinerate its freedom fighting occupants. He used his posse to murder those escaping. He enabled looting of dead Tunstall's store. The next year, he gave a false affidavit defaming Susan McSween's chastity to sabotage her litigation against Commander Dudley.

Born in Ohio in 1843, Peppin came to the Territory with Carlton's column. He mustered out in Mesilla in 1864. Settling in Lincoln, he was the builder, for the Ring, of Lincoln's general store, called "The House." In 1877, Peppin may have been involved in James Dolan's murder of Hilario Jaramillo, so he could marry

FIGURE 38: Lincoln County Sheriff George W. Peppin.
https://www.pinterest.com/pin/397864948328207476/

Jaramillo's widow. In 1878, he was active in all Lincoln County
Ring atrocities. In 1885, he was made director of a school board. In
1893 he was Lincoln jailor. He was also a Deputy to Ringite
Sheriff George Curry. He died on September 18th, 1904. His
September 23rd *Capitan News* obituary stated: "The history of
Lincoln county would be extremely partial that did not give the
deceased the important role in the conduct of its affairs, for Mr.
Peppin was one of the oldest settlers in the county ... Mr. Peppin
was a good citizen, a true friend and kind husband and father."

On screen is Nathan Augustus Monroe Dudley. **[FIGURE 39]**
As Fort Stanton Commander, he was active in the Lincoln County
War. On June 28th, 1878, Sheriff George Peppin used him and his
troops to raid San Patricio in a failed attempt to murder
Alexander McSween. On July 19th, he violated the Posse
Comitatus Act by intervening for the Ring in the Lincoln County
War Battle. He was treasonously responsible for that Battle's
murders of Alexander McSween, Harvey Morris, Vincente
Romero, and Francisco Zamora, arson of the McSween home, and
looting of Tunstall's store.

FIGURE 39: Fort Stanton Commander Lieutenant Colonel
Nathan Augustus Monroe Dudley.
http://www.arlingtoncemetery.net/namdudley.htm

On February 18th, 1879, he was a co-conspirator in murdering Attorney Huston Chapman, who intended to prosecute him for murder and arson. In his 1879 military Court of Inquiry, Dudley was represented by Catron's past law firm member, Henry Waldo. In that rigged court, he was cleared, despite Billy Bonney's eye-witness testimony of his officers shooting to kill civilians in the final battle.

Born on August 20, 1825 in Massachusetts, Dudley began his army career in 1855, as a First Lieutenant in the 10th Infantry, where he was involved in massacring Sioux Indians in Nebraska, and plundering their village for artifacts for the Smithsonian Museum. In 1857 to 1858, he was in Utah's Mormon War against Brigham Young. In 1862, becoming a Colonel in the Civil War, with his 30th Massachusetts Infantry regiment, he burned down a plantation of a suspected Rebel around women and children – foreshadowing his later enabling of murderous arson of the McSween home. After the Civil War, he was transferred to the 3rd Cavalry. In 1871, he was court martialed and found guilty of drunkenness on duty at Arizona Territory's Camp McDowell. In 1877, he was court martialed again as Commander of Fort Union, for drunkenness on duty and trying to force a marriage between the raped post chaplain's daughter and her rapist. Catron represented him, yielding no punishment. On April 5th, 1878, he got command of Fort Stanton. He then used his troops to murder anti-Ring fighters in Lincoln. In 1879, he was involved in the Huston Chapman murder. New Governor, Lew Wallace, removed him as Commander. But he prevailed in his corrupt military Court of Inquiry. In 1880, he was returned to Command at Fort Union. Until his retirement in 1889, he was in campaigns against Native Americans. He died on April 29th, 1910, in Massachusetts. He was buried in Arlington National Cemetery. His May 3rd obituary in Washington's *The Evening Star* said he was, quote, a "retired veteran of the Civil War ... Later in his career he was engaged in many exciting campaigns against hostile Indians."

On screen is Henry Waldo, from Catron's law firm. **[FIGURE 40]** He defended Commander N.A.M. Dudley in his rigged Court of Inquiry covering-up his Lincoln County War crimes. Waldo furthered the outlaw myth of Billy the Kid in that court to diminish Billy's testimony against Dudley.

Waldo was born on January 16th, 1844 in Missouri. He grew up with future Ring co-boss, Stephen Benton Elkins. In 1864 he

FIGURE 40: Attorney Henry Waldo. Courtesy of the Palace of the Governors Photo Archives. Judge Henry L. Waldo. 1900? Negative Number: 013118.

was admitted to the California bar and became a District Attorney. In 1873, he joined the Elkins and Catron Santa Fe law firm after Elkins left to Washington as Territorial Delegate. In 1875, he made his own firm with Ringite William Breeden. From 1876 to 1878 he was Chief Justice. Ringite Governor S.B. Axtell appointed him Attorney General. He served to 1881. In the 1880's, as Director of the New Mexican Printing and Publishing Company, he printed the Ring's mouthpiece, *The Santa Fe New Mexican*. His law partner, William Breeden, was President. He was also director, attorney, or president of multiple railroad companies. He died on July 10th, 1915. His August eulogy in *The Santa Fe Magazine,* stated: "[H]is great dignity, integrity of purpose and unimpeachable character enabled him to deal with political officials and bosses of whatever party without fear or favor."

Waldo's letter of February 18th, 1866 shows his adulation of Elkins, calling him "[m]y most loved friend." He wrote: "I am stimulated by your example – I do not expect to emulate it in all aspects, but I can feebly imitate it."

John D. Bail, appointed by Judge Warren Bristol, as co-counsel of Albert Jennings Fountain, represented Billy Bonney in Mesilla after his attorney, Ira Leonard, withdrew after a likely threat. Their job was to guarantee Billy's hanging sentence.

Bail was born in Ohio, on July 4th, 1825. In 1844, he entered the army, serving in the Mexican-American War. In 1849, in Illinois, he was admitted to the bar. In the Civil War, he was on the Union side. He then moved to New Mexico Territory. His law practice was in Mesilla, then Silver City. He twice served in the legislature's House, and once in the Council. He was involved with Catron in legal cases, politicking, and money-lending. He died on June 20th, 1903. His obituary in the 1904 "Minutes of the New Mexican Bar Association" claimed: "[He] was personally recognized as a man of sterling honor and uprightness."

Catron's firm's December 28th, 1888 letter shows that Bail worked with them. It requested: "Can you give us any information in regard to A.M. Connor, whom we are informed is living in Silver City? As to whether he has any property subject to execution."

On screen is Patrick "Pat" Floyd Garrett, a multiple killer. [FIGURE 41] He is the best known participant in Billy the Kid history. He bridged the Ring's enforcers and thug assassins, by getting a lawman's title. In 1880, after being backed by the Ring for Lincoln County Sheriff to pursue Billy Bonney, he joined Secret Service Operative Azariah Wild - also engaged by the Ring for that task. Wild made him a Deputy U.S. Marshall, with money to pay spies. In ambushes, Garrett accidentally killed Tom O'Folliard and Charlie Bowdre. In the December 22nd ambush at Stinking Springs, he captured Billy. After a hanging sentence in Mesilla, Billy escaped his Lincoln jail. Garrett finally succeeded in killing Billy in a Fort Sumner ambush on July 14th, 1881.

Garrett was born on June 5th, 1850 in Alabama. His family moved to a Louisiana plantation when he was three. In 1868, he

FIGURE 41: Lincoln County Sheriff and Deputy U.S. Marshal Patrick Floyd "Pat" Garrett.
https://commons.wikimedia.org/wiki/File:PatFGarrett.JPG

went west, possibly killing a black man in Texas. In 1876, as a buffalo hunter, he murdered a teenager in his group, named Joe Briscoe. Though his partner called it malicious, Garrett got off on self-defense. Depressive, alcoholic, and unskilled, he went to New Mexico Territory's Fort Sumner. There he worked as a wagon driver, a bartender, and at a hog farm. In 1880, after becoming a Sheriff and a Deputy U.S. Marshal, he captured Billy. In 1881, after Billy's jailbreak, he killed him. To profit from the killing, Garrett, with a ghostwriter, wrote an 1882 book, *The Authentic Life of Billy the Kid* 1896, he was hired by William Thornton, then

Governor and Catron's past law partner, to apprehend the murderers of Attorney Albert Jennings Fountain and his son. He was made Doña Ana County Sheriff. Accused was Catron's ranching competitor, Oliver Lee, and ranch hand, James Gilliland. On July 12th, 1898, Garrett ambushed Lee and his ranch hands. They killed his deputy. They were later acquitted of the Fountain murders. The deputy killing was called self-defense. On October 7th, 1899, Garrett killed an accused murderer named Norman Newman while assisting an Oklahoma sheriff in New Mexico. In 1901, Garrett was made El Paso Customs Collector by President Theodore Roosevelt, but was removed in 1906. He bought a New Mexico ranch. The rental of his land to a goat raiser named Wayne Brazel resulted in his murder by him on February 29th, 1908 in a heated altercation about selling the goats. Brazel was cleared by self-defense. *The Roswell Daily Record* front page of March 2nd, reported Garrett's death as: "Pat Garrett is Killed; Shot to death by his tenant Wayne Brazel after a quarrel on a highway; was a Roswell pioneer ... received greater notoriety for killing 'Billy the Kid' and causing other desperados to bite the dust; a famous character."

Garrett stayed connected to Catron by loans. His biographer, Leon Metz, in his 1974 book, *Pat Garrett: The Story of a Western Lawman*, cited his unpaid note of $500 from February 20th, 1901. On June 1st, 1904, Catron wrote to him with paternal benevolence reserved for his minions: "The time will come when there will be a reappointment, and then all these businessmen [to whom you are indebted] will turn loose against you, and you may find it somewhat difficult to get a party to stand by you."

Thug assassins were crucial to Ring cover-ups by plausible deniability. The higher-ups denied connection to the crimes done by the hitmen.

The Seven Rivers Ring rustlers were used as murderers in the Lincoln County War. They were indicted in the April, 1879 Lincoln County Grand Jury. By May 1st, Catron got them pardoned by misstating Governor Lew Wallace's Amnesty Proclamation.

On screen is Robert Olinger, the best known of the Seven Rivers rustler-murderers. **[FIGURE 42]** In 1879, he murdered fellow Seven Rivers rancher, John Jones. In the Lincoln County War period, he participated in every Ring killing. In 1880, he was

FIGURE 42. Deputy Robert "Bob" Olinger.
https://commons.wikimedia.org/wiki/File:Sheriff_Bob_Olinger.jpg

made a Deputy U.S. Marshal by the Secret Service to pursue Billy
Bonney. In 1881, Sheriff Pat Garrett made him a Deputy to guard
Billy, awaiting hanging in Lincoln's courthouse-jail. Billy killed
him during his April 28th, 1881 jailbreak. The May 3rd *Las Vegas
Morning Gazette* stated: "Bob Olinger was known all through
eastern New Mexico ... He was brave as a lion and a handy man
with a gun. ... He lived for a long time in Seven Rivers and was
known by all the stockmen in the Pecos Valley."

On screen is John Kinney. **[FIGURE 43]** He and his gang
from Mesilla were Ring rustlers. In 1878, they were Ring
murderers in the Lincoln County War. With Sheriff George
Peppin, he and his gang did its massacre at San Patricio. In 1881,
he was made a Deputy Sheriff to guard Billy Bonney
in his transport from his Mesilla hanging trial to Lincoln's
courthouse-jail.

FIGURE 43. John Kinney.
https://www.pinterest.com/pin/369013763201354984/

Kinney was born in about 1847 in Massachusetts, fought for the Union, and came to New Mexico Territory in 1868 in the 3rd U.S. Cavalry. Mustering out in 1873, in Las Cruces, he created a major rustling operation. In 1878, he was active in the Lincoln County War. In 1883, he was briefly jailed in Leavenworth for rustling. He then lived in Texas and Arizona. His August 29th, 1919 obituary in *The Daily Arizona Silver Belt* called him a "Pioneer of the border;" stating: "He started a civil career in New Mexico and came to be a deputy sheriff where he soon became known for his daring in running down bandits. Captain Kinney stepped aside to give Sheriff Pat Garrett of Lincoln county, this honor, but he kept in the saddle and performed equally daring deeds to wipe out the large criminal element."

Jessie Evans was involved in murdering John Tunstall and Huston Chapman. Billy Bonney, for his pardon bargain with Lew Wallace, testified against him for Chapman's murder.

Evans was born in 1853, in Missouri or Texas, into a criminal family. On June 26th, 1871, they were arrested in Kansas for passing counterfeit money. In 1872, he came to New Mexico Territory. First he rustled with John Kinney; then made his own gang. After his 1878 Lincoln County War involvement, he was arrested in 1879 by Governor Lew Wallace, with fellow Chapman murderers, James Dolan and Billy Campbell. He and Campbell escaped Fort Stanton incarceration on March 15th, with possible Ring assistance. In 1880, in Texas, he and his gang killed a Texas Ranger during their capture. Getting a 20 year sentence at Texas State Penitentiary, he escaped in 1882, disappearing from history.

Complicit press was indispensable for the Ring's cover-up propaganda.

The *Santa Fe New Mexican* was central. It was published by major Ringites, William Breeden and his law partner, Henry Waldo.

The *Las Vegas Gazette* was owned by John H. Koogler. He featured the outlaw myth of Billy the Kid. Billy himself ridiculed it in a December 12th, 1880 letter to Governor Lew Wallace. He wrote: "I noticed in the Las Vegas Gazette a piece which stated that, Billy "the" Kid ... was the captain of a Band of Outlaws .... There is no such Organization in Existence. So the Gentleman must have drawn very heavily on his Imagination." Koogler was controlled by Catron's loans. An example is his July 17th, 1889 letter to Catron, begging: "I wish you would send the money expected from the Marshall, Field and Company to me at Kansas City ... I will be quite short of funds unless I receive it."

The *Las Vegas Daily Optic* was owned by Russell A. Kistler. From 1880 to 1881, he backed Catron's Secret Service campaign to kill Billy the Kid. In a December 12th, 1891 letter, Kistler confidently asked Catron to retaliate against boycotters of his paper.

On screen is Ralph Emerson Twitchell. **[FIGURE 44]** An attorney and politician, he was the Ring's historian. In 1911, he published his five volume *Leading Facts in New Mexico History*. Hiding the Ring's part in the Lincoln County War, and using its outlaw myth of Billy the Kid, he wrote:

FIGURE 44. Ralph Emerson Twitchell.
https://commons.wikimedia.org/wiki/File:Ralph_Emerson_Twitche
ll.JPG

"In [Lincoln County] a feud was begun which, in the annals of New Mexico, is known as the 'Lincoln County War.' The cause of this trouble and era of crime can be traced to the rivalry existing between prominent cattlemen at the time living in Lincoln and the Pecos valley, respectively ... Others believe ... that the turbulence that terrorized the entire community, was the result of the outlawry established by such desperadoes as Billy the Kid." Twitchell died on August 26th, 1925. The August 31st, *Albuquerque Morning Journal* obituary called him an "historian and attorney, whose name for nearly half a century has been linked with every movement for the advancement of New Mexico."

Twitchell's letters show his political shenanigans for Catron. On October 22nd, 1892, with Catron running for Territorial Delegate, the Chairman of the Republican Central Committee contacted Twitchell about vote-buying; writing: "The democratic majority ... are Mexicans and a party will be sent there on the day of the election to change it. A little money will be necessary on the day of the election."

Over all these Ringite scoundrels was the protective umbrella of Washington enablers. Presidents, cabinet members, and senators colluded with co-boss S.B. Elkins - and at times with boss T.B. Catron directly. Relevant to Billy the Kid history were President Rutherford B. Hayes, Secretary of the Interior Carl Schurz, and Secretary of State William Evarts.

As we'll see in later talks, the flip side of cover-ups for Catron's minions, was creation of the Ring's outlaw myth of Billy the Kid to cover-up its own outlawry.

TALK 20:

THE SANTA FE RING'S OUTLAW MYTH OF BILLY THE KID

FROM BOOK: *THE SANTA FE RING VERSUS BILLY THE KID*

JANUARY 30, 2021

This talk presents the Santa Fe Ring's outlaw myth of Billy the Kid. The information is from my book, *The Santa Fe Ring Versus Billy the Kid: The Making of an American Monster.*

What most people think of as Billy the Kid history, is actually the Santa Fe Ring's outlaw myth of Billy the Kid. It crystallized into one person the Ring's customary ploy of outlawing opponents. It made Billy Bonney a dime novel desperado. It created the moniker Billy the Kid. It switched the Lincoln County War freedom fight into lawless troublemaking. And it hid the Ring.

The Ring's first outlaw myths were in response to New Mexico Territory's anti-Ring uprisings of the 1870's. In the 1872 Legislature Revolt, legislators passed acts to stop the Ring's malicious prosecutions of opponents. On April 3rd, 1873, Ringite Governor Marsh Giddings wrote to the Secretary of the Interior that it had been a, quote, "revolution" by Democrats, past corrupt officials, and the "vilest of the vile [Mexicans from] slums of vice" in Santa Fe.

In 1873, the Colfax County War began when Maxwell Land Grant settlers resisted the Ring's land-grab. The Ring called them outlaws, and used troops for their suppression.

By 1874, in Lincoln County, Territorial Ring boss, Thomas Benton Catron, tried to eliminate competitors of his developing mercantile and ranching monopolies. On January 10th, seeking troops, Ringite Judge, Warren Bristol, used the outlaw myth in a letter to Governor Giddings. He wrote: "[T]here are public disorders in Lincoln County ... [P]rompt and vigorous measures ought to be adopted to quell the disturbances and disarm the contending parties ... I see no way whereby this can be done effectively except by a sufficient military force."

In 1875, Governor Giddings died in office. He was replaced by Samuel Beach Axtell, who was bribed by the Ring. In an 1878 deposition, Colfax County attorney, Frank Springer, described Axtell's 1876 outlawing of the Colfax County War's anti-Ring opponents after they tried to arrest Ring murderers of their leader, Franklin Tolby. Springer stated: "[Axtell said] there were bad men there and that he intended to have them punished or compelled to leave the county if it took all the troops in New Mexico."

In 1877, Colfax County War firebrand, Mary McPherson, accused T.B. Catron to the federal Attorney General as heading the Ring, murdering Franklin Tolby, and conspiring with Governor Axtell to remove the courts to block prosecution of Tolby's murderers. Catron responded that she was a, quote, "crazy person," and, quote, "[the courts were removed] for the reason that lawlessness seemed to prevail in the county of Colfax at the time."

In February of 1878, in Lincoln County, boss Catron had his British competitor, John Tunstall, murdered. That started the anti-Ring Lincoln County War. Catron used the outlaw myth in a May 30th letter to complicit Governor Axtell to seek troops for its suppression. Lying that his murderous rustler henchmen were being attacked by the freedom fighting Regulators, he wrote: "[T]here seems to be an utter disregard of all law in [Lincoln] county ... I would most respectfully request that some steps be taken to disarm all parties carrying arms, and that the military be instructed to see that they all keep the peace."

Then a complication arose. On June 18th, Congress passed the Posse Comitatus Act, barring military intervention in civilian disputes. That made the Ring-beholden Commander of Fort Stanton, N.A.M. Dudley, hesitate to intervene in the Lincoln County War's final, six day battle. So Ringite Lincoln County Sheriff George Peppin used the outlaw myth. He wrote to Dudley: "Sir. If you could loan me a howitzer, I am sure that the parties for whom I have warrants would surrender. We are being attacked by a lawless mob. "

At the end of 1878, the outlaw myth was used in reports by Attorney Frank Warner Angel, investigating Tunstall's murder for Washington, D.C. His mission was covering-up the murderers' being U.S. public officials, and covering-up the Lincoln County War as being an anti-Ring freedom fight.

His October 4th, 1878 report was titled: "In the Matter of the Cause and Circumstances of the Death of John H. Tunstall, A British Subject." He used the outlaw myth by slyly focusing on the Ring's hitmen, Jessie Evans and his gang. And he made-up their motive as a grudge. Angel wrote: "Who shot Tunstall will never be known. But there is no doubt that William S. Morton, Jessie Evans and [Tom] Hill were the only persons present and saw the shooting, and that two of these persons murdered him ... For Tunstall was shot in two places – in the head and breast ... Of these persons Morton and Hill were afterwards killed, and the only survivor is Jessie Evans a notorious out-law ... Of these persons, Evans and Hill had been arrested at the instigation of Tunstall. They were at enmity with Tunstall, and enmity with them meant murder."

Another October 4th report by Angel was titled: "In the Matter of the Lincoln County Troubles." He used the outlaw myth to fake a conflict of local competing factions. He hid the Lincoln County War freedom fight. He shape-shifted Catron's rustling gangs, used against the freedom fighters, into random outlaws on both sides. Angel wrote: "The history of Lincoln County has been one of bloodshed from the day of its organization ... L.G. Murphy and Company had the monopoly of all business ... This has resulted in the formation of two parties, one led by Murphy and Company, and the other by McSween (now dead). [Note that Angel hid that Alexander McSween was murdered by the Ring in the final battle.] Both have done many things contrary to the law ... Bands of desperate characters who are ever found on the frontier ... have naturally gravitated to one or the other of these parties ... Governor Axtell appoints Peppin a leader of the Murphy and Company faction. As Sheriff, he comes to Lincoln accompanied by John Kinney and his notorious band of out-laws and murderers ... McSween then collects around himself an equally distinguished body ... A battle is fought – for five days it rages ... Both parties desire revenge and they are now ... collecting more desperate characters ... These out-laws who prowl the County with the avowed purpose of murder ... should be hunted down ... that the laws may be enforced and ... life and property protected."

Ring-shielding President Rutherford B. Hayes's response was scapegoating Governor Axtell by replacing him, on October 1st, with Civil War General, Lew Wallace. The Ring immediately presented Wallace with the outlaw myth.

On October 4th, the myth was used to stop convening of the October 1878 Lincoln County Grand Jury, because it would have indicted Ringites for murders and arson in that July's Lincoln County War Battle. Ringite Third Judicial District Judge Warren Bristol telegrammed Santa Fe's Ringite U.S. Marshal, John Sherman, claiming he could not get juries and, quote, "contending parties [were] ... each having in its employ professional assassins."

Two days later, on October 6th, Ringite Sherman manipulatively gave Wallace a list of mostly Regulators as so-called "worst outlaws" in the Territory. Number 14 was "The Kid" William Bonney," [wanted] for murder.

On November 13th, self-protectively hoping to avoid confronting the vindictive Ring, Lew Wallace made an Amnesty Proclamation for all non-indicted Lincoln County War participants, including troops.

It was not that simple. The final battle's Commander, N.A.M. Dudley, knowing he was responsible for treasonous murders and arson, likely advised by Catron, responded that pardoning implied wrongdoing. So he, or Catron, published an "Open Letter" to Wallace in the December 14th, *Santa Fe Weekly New Mexican*. It used the outlaw myth to fake Dudley's innocence; stating: "The Proclamation ... grants a pardon to officers who have on repeated occasions risked their lives, under fire at times, to aid and protect the women and children of Lincoln County against the outrages of armed organized bands of murderers, horse thieves, and convicted as well as unconvicted felons."

But this Ring cover-up was threatened. Alexander McSween's widow hired Attorney Huston Chapman to prosecute Dudley for the murder of her husband and arson of her home. So, on December 31st, local Ring boss James Dolan wrote the outlaw myth to Lew Wallace to attack Chapman. He stated: "He appears to be the only man in this County who is trying to continue the old feelings. I and many of our citizens feel confident that if this man was silenced, the troubles would end." When Wallace did nothing, on February 18th, 1879, Dolan, with Ring thugs Jessie Evans and Billy Campbell, murdered Chapman.

Then reality confronted the outlaw myth. On March 13th, Billy Bonney emerged. He wrote to Governor Wallace proposing a pardon bargain. He would testify against Chapman's murderers. He wrote: "I have indictments against me for things that happened in the late Lincoln County War and am afraid to give up because my Enimies would Kill me ... I was present when Mr. Chapman was murderded and know who did it and if it were not for these indictments I would have made it clear before now. if it is in your power to Annully those indictments I hope you will do so so as to give me a chance to explain." The next month, Billy testified. He got James Dolan, Billy Campbell, and Jessie Evans indicted.

And Susan McSween replaced Chapman with Attorney Ira Leonard. The Ring pushed back. Dudley, for his Court of Inquiry for possible court martial, was defended by Catron's past law firm member, Henry Waldo. And the Court was rigged by biased judges. Billy testified against Dudley, stating that, when escaping the burning McSween house, he saw three of Dudley's officers fire a volley at himself and others. That meant Dudley's attacking civilians as a partisan. So it was left to Waldo to use the outlaw myth in his closing argument to negate the truth. Waldo stated: "Then was brought forward William Bonney, alias "Antrim," alias "the Kid," a known criminal of the worst type although hardly up to his majority, murderer by profession, as records of this Court connect him with two atrocious murders, that of Roberts and the other of Sheriff Brady. Both of them are cowardly and atrocious assassinations. There were warrants enough for him, to the 19th of July last, to have plastered him from his head to his feet, yet he was engaged to do service as a witness." Dudley was exonerated.

Billy was now in the Ring's lethal sights. He'd gotten Huston Chapman's Ringite murderers indicted. In a fair Court, he would have gotten past Commander Dudley facing court martial. But there was an obstacle to murdering him. His anti-Ring partisans hid him. It was time for the big guns. Either Catron or his Washington co-boss, S.B. Elkins, contacted James Brooks, the Chief of the Secret Service, for a political assassination. In mid-September of 1880, Special Operative Azariah Wild was sent to the Territory. He stayed into December. Though counterfeiting was the Secret Service's focus, it investigated related crimes. It could justify any action, including killing. Lazy and lackluster Azariah Wild, would be manipulated by Catron's brother-in-law

Edgar Walz, local boss James Dolan, and Catron's agent, David Easton, into believing that Billy headed a huge counterfeiting-rustling gang out of Fort Sumner. Wild, in his daily reports to Chief Brooks, wrote fiction to hide that he uncovered nothing. He, thus, added to the outlaw myth of Billy the Kid. He also empowered Sheriff-elect Pat Garrett as a Deputy U.S. Marshal to capture or kill Billy with Texan posses, since New Mexicans refused.

In his report written on October 6th, 1880, Wild mentioned Billy for the first time. He wrote: "There is an outlaw in the mountains here who came here from Arizona after committing a murder there named William Antrom alias William Bonney alias Billy Kid with whom these cattle thieves meet, and by many it is believed that they ... receive the counterfeit money. I have found no evidence so far to support their suspicions." The use of the name "William Antrom" with murder, implies Catron's practice of using private detectives to dig dirt on adversaries. He likely discovered Billy's Arizona killing of Frank "Windy" Cahill as Henry Antrim.

For his report written on October 29th, tricked Wild wrote: "I am now perfectly confident that there is a counterfeiting gang here ... as I am of anything that I do not know absolutely certain, and that I have not seen with my own eyes ... The force of desperados now at Fort Sumner, the headquarters of the gang, numbers twenty six. They openly say that they number sixty two in Lincoln County and defy the authorities."

By his report written on November 7th, Wild's imaginary gang had swelled to 29 in Fort Sumner; and one of its leaders was "William Antrom alias "Billy Bony" [spelled B-O-N-Y] alias "Billy Kid."

Then the Ring launched a parallel press campaign against Billy. On December 3rd, 1880, leaked Azariah Wild reports were used about the fictional "Kid gang." The article was titled "Powerful Gang of Outlaws Harassing the Stockmen." It was by Ringite newspaper owner, J.H. Koogler, in his *Las Vegas Gazette*. It gave the outlaw myth of Billy the Kid. It also tried to get Billy lynched. Koogler wrote: "The gang includes forty to fifty men, all hard characters, the off scouring of society, fugitives from justice, and desperados by profession. Among them are men, with whose names and deeds the people of Las Vegas are perfectly familiar, such as 'Billy the Kid' ... and others of equally unsavory reputation ... The gang is under the leadership of "Billy the Kid," a desperate cuss ... They spend considerable time in enjoying themselves at the Portales ... They run stock from the Panhandle country into the White Oaks and from the Pecos country into the Panhandle ... Are the people of San Miguel county to stand for this any longer? Shall we suffer this hoard of outcasts and the scum of society, who are outlawed by a multitude of crimes, to continue their way to the very border of our county? We believe the citizens of San Miguel County to be order loving people, and call upon them to unite in forever wiping out this band to the east of us."

Billy's response should have been to leave the Territory. Instead, nine days later, on December 12th, he defiantly wrote to Governor Lew Wallace. He stated: "I noticed in the Las Vegas Gazette a piece which stated that, Billy "the" Kid, the name by which I am known in the Country was the captain of a Band of Outlaws who hold Forth at the Portales. There is no such Organization in Existence. So the Gentleman must have drawn very heavily on his Imagination."

On December 22nd, Wallace, having already betrayed their pardon bargain for fear of antagonizing the Ring, ignored him. He spitefully placed a $500 reward notice for Billy the Kid in the lying *Las Vegas Gazette*.

The same day, *The New York Sun* showed that it too had been sent the outlaw myth using leaked Secret Service reports. That resulted in tacking-on counterfeiting and famous counterfeiter, William Brockway. Its long headline was: "Outlaws of New Mexico, The Exploits of a Band Headed by a New York Youth, The Mountain fastness of the Kid and his Followers, War against a Gang of Cattle Thieves and Murderers, The Frontier Confederates of Brockway, the Counterfeiter." This launched Billy as a nationally famous, fictitious outlaw named Billy the Kid. And the Lincoln County War was shape-shifted to a dime novel fight between stockmen and the local Indian agent, during which soldiers, surrounding Billy the Kid in a burning house, were murdered by him while escaping. The long article, listed as from Las Vegas, was possibly written by J.H. Koogler, or even Catron himself. And it ultimately contaminated Billy's real history, distorting books and media to the present. As excerpted, it stated: "One hundred and twenty-seven miles southeast of Las Vegas, New Mexico, is Fort Sumner ... The property was condemned and sold to Pete Maxwell, a well-known ranchman of the section ... Until recently, on almost any fair day, there might have been seen lounging about the store or engaged in target practice four men, all of them young, neatly dressed, and of good appearance ... These men are the worst desperadoes in the West, and large parties of armed men are now scouring the country in pursuit of them. For a number of years the people of eastern New Mexico and Panhandle, Texas, have been harassed by a gang who have run off stock, burned ranches, and committed acts of violence and murder. It was only recently that the leaders and organization of the band were discovered. The leaders are Billy the Kid, so called from his youth; Dave Rudabaugh, Billy Wilson, and Tom O'Phallier [that meant Tom O'Folliard], the four loungers about Fort Sumner. The Kid is the captain of the gang. Their fastness is about thirty-five miles nearly due east from Fort Sumner, on the edge of the great Staked Plain. In that region there is a small lake called Las Portales ... This place the robbers selected ... on account of the opportunities it afforded them for stock thieving. No matter from what direction the storm came, it drove to the lake the herds of cattle which roam at large in the rich grazing country ... When supplies from roving herds ran short the desperadoes would make a raid on herds that were guarded, attacking ranches and killing or diving off the inmates. The people of the surrounding country finally found the existence of this band unendurable ... [I]t was resolved to organize several bands, who should cooperate in a campaign, which should end only when the outlaws were driven out of the country, or their capture, dead or alive, was effected ... The Panhandle Transportation Company, an association of stockmen of western Texas, banded together ... to organize an expedition against the outlaws. The White Oaks, a flourishing mining camp [in New Mexico], organized a band of rangers. Still another party of picked men, under the lead of Sheriff Pat Garrett of Lincoln County, who is considered one of the bravest and coolest men in the whole region, joined in the campaign ... The three parties are now engaged in scouting the country, and will not give up the chase till the country is rid of every one of the outlaws ... Government officials are now interested in the campaign, for, in addition to their other crimes, the outlaws have put in circulation a large quantity of the counterfeit money manufactured by William Brockway, the forger ...

"William Bonney, alias the Kid, the leader of the band, is scarcely over 20 years old. He is handsome and dresses well ... A beautiful bay mare, that he has carefully trained, is all that he seems to care for, unless he reserves some affection for his brace of six-shooters and Winchester rifle, which have helped him out of many a tight place ... He is considered a dead shot and much of his time is spent in target practice. He was born in New York State, but his parents removed to Indiana when he was quite small, and thence to Arizona. There in the Tombstone District the Kid killed his first man when he was only 17 years old, and was obliged to leave the country. He came to New Mexico, where he has since lived.

"About three years ago a difficulty arose in Lincoln County, New Mexico, between the stockmen and the Indian agent on the reservation. The trouble arose in regard to some cattle that had been purchased for the Indians. Nearly every man in the county was under arms, and the troops were called out by Governor Wallace to quell the disturbance. The Kid was mixed up in the affair, and had some narrow escapes. On one occasion he was hotly pursued and was obliged to take refuge in a house in Lincoln, which was surrounded by sixty solders. To the demand to surrender, he only laughed and shot down a soldier just to show that he was game. The house was set on fire, when the Kid, after loading up his Winchester Rifle, leaped from the burning building and made a dash for liberty. All the while he was running he kept firing from his Winchester, bringing down a number of his pursuers. Bullets whistled over his head, but he made his escape, and leaping on a horse was soon laughing at his pursuers. There is no telling how many men he has killed. He sets no value on human life, and has never hesitated at murder when it would serve his purpose. Governor Wallace a few days ago offered a reward of $500 for his capture, and prominent citizens would make up a handsome purse in addition.

"The career of the band is about run, for they are hotly pursued, and the chances are that before long they will be killed or captured. It is not expected that the Kid ... will be taken alive, as they will fight to the last."

On December 22nd, Pat Garrett captured Billy at Stinking Springs. The next step was a hanging trial.

Billy's venue had been changed to Doña Ana County's Mesilla by the Ring to avoid a Lincoln County Jury aware of the real Lincoln County freedom fight. To prejudice jurymen, newspaper owner, Simon Newman, in his April 2nd, 1881 *Newman's Semi-Weekly*, wrote an outlaw myth article titled "The Kid." It stated:

"[The Kid] is a notoriously dangerous character, [he] has on several occasions before escaped justice where escape appeared even more improbable than now, and has made his brags that he only wants to get free in order to kill three men – one of them being Governor Wallace. Should he break jail now, there is no doubt that he would immediately proceed to execute his threat ... We expect every day to hear of his escape and hope that legal technicalities may not be permitted to render escape more probable."

In Mesilla, the Ring succeeded in getting Billy a hanging sentence. But he escaped jail on April 28th, 1881. So Pat Garrett killed him in Fort Sumner that July 14th. That did not end the story as the Ring had hoped. They had accidentally created a media star.

Press reported the killing. The July 23rd *Las Cruces Rio Grande Republican* headlined: "Kid the Killer Killed, William Bonney alias Antrim, alias Billy the Kid, Fatally Meets Pat Garrett, the Lincoln County Sheriff." The outlaw myth was the history. It stated: "William Bonney, alias 'the Kid,' is dead. No report could have caused more general feeling of gratification than this, and when it was further announced that the faithful and brave Pat Garrett, he who had been the mainstay of law and order in Lincoln county ... has accomplished the crowning feat of his life by bringing down the fierce and implacable foe single-handed."

By the next year, Pat Garrett, with ghostwriter Ashmun "Ash" Upson, tried to cash in on the killing with an 1882 book: *The Authentic Life of Billy the Kid The Noted Desperado of the Southwest, Whose Deeds of Daring and Blood Made His Name a Terror in New Mexico, Arizona, and Northern Mexico*. As is obvious from the title, it was the outlaw myth. Its Billy the Kid is a criminal boy leading a senselessly rampaging and murderous gang. It stated: "The Kid had a devil lurking in him. It was a good-humored jovial imp, or a cruel and bloodthirsty fiend, as circumstances prompted. Circumstances favored the worser angel, and the Kid fell."

And, as will be seen in later talks, from 1881 to 1902, hypocritical Lew Wallace added to the outlaw myth in writings of his own to cover up his betrayal of his pardon bargain with Billy.

The Ring had its own historian named Ralph Emerson Twitchell. He was an attorney and boss Catron's political ally. In 1911, he published his five volume *Leading Facts in New Mexico History*. His Lincoln County War was pure Billy the Kid outlaw myth. And it hid the Ring. Twitchell wrote: "In [Lincoln county] a feud was begun which, in the annals of New Mexico, is known as the 'Lincoln County War.' The cause of this trouble and era of crime can be traced to the rivalry existing between prominent cattlemen at the time living in Lincoln and the Pecos valley, respectively. Both were furnishing cattle to the Mescalero Indian agent and each accused the other of stealing from their respective herds. This was the basis for the war ... Others believe ... that the turbulence that terrorized the entire community, was the result of the outlawry established by such desperadoes as Billy the Kid ... The beginning of the so-called Lincoln County War occurred when John H. Tunstel [misspelled throughout] was killed by a sheriff's posse seeking to levy an attachment upon property belonging to Tunstel. The latter had a friend and employee, William H. Bonney, later famous as "Billy the Kid" ... After the killing of Tunstel his sympathizers organized themselves into a party known as the McSwain [misspelled throughout] faction and a sort of guerrilla warfare continued for the following eighteen months until finally broken up by the civil authorities with the aid of the military."

In 1926, journalist, Walter Noble Burns, wrote the book: *The Saga of Billy the Kid*. He embellished Pat Garrett's book's fakery. He wrote: "[Billy the Kid] placed no value on human life ... He put a bullet through a man's heart as coolly as he perforated a tin can set upon a fence post ... After him came the great change ... Law and order came in on the flash and smoke of the six-shooter that with one bullet put an end to the outlaw and to outlawry."

Then came the scholarly historians of the second half of the 20th century. They did no better. They merely plastered their discoveries onto the original outlaw myth of Billy the Kid. Why? Possibly they didn't want to go head to head with the still-existing Santa Fe Ring.

Philip J. Rasch wrote articles from 1949 to 1970. They were compiled in a 1997 book titled *Gunsmoke in Lincoln County*. To Rasch, Billy was a quote, "psychopathic young rustler." And the Lincoln County War was a triumph of law. He wrote: "[Tunstall's and McSween's] failure to recognize that the society of Lincoln County was one that would respond to the symbols of legal chicanery with gunfire resulted in their own destruction and that of many of their followers."

William Keleher, a New Mexico lawyer, published a 1957 book, *Violence in Lincoln County 1869 to 1881*. It omitted the Santa Fe

Ring. Though Keleher knew about Billy's articulate pardon bargain letters, he called him "almost illiterate... a desperado, gunman and outlaw; a man who had not hesitated to take human life on more than one occasion."

Robert M. Utley, a popularizer, in his 1987 book, *High Noon in Lincoln: Violence in the Western Frontier*, denied the Santa Fe Ring's existence. Though backing the outlaw myth, he minimized Billy's role. He wrote: "By July of 1878 ... [s]ome of the Regulators turned toward good. The Kid turned the other way ... As for Billy the Kid's contribution to the Lincoln County War ... [h]ad he never found his way to Lincoln County – the course of the War would have almost certainly remained essentially as history has recorded it."

British Frederick Nolan, the most scholarly, in 1992 published *The Lincoln County War: A Documentary History*. The Santa Fe Ring plays no part. There are no anti-Ring uprisings. Nolan, missing the causal role of the Ring in the history, was left with only doubletalk nonsense to explain the Lincoln County War. He wrote: "Fueled by greed, propelled by religious and racial prejudice, by liquor, by firearms, and by some powerful American misbeliefs, the Lincoln County War was based on a whole catalog of self-deceptions. Each side believed it was 'us' against 'them' ... The Lincoln County War was a false premise pursued to an illogical conclusion." In Nolan's outlaw myth, Billy the Kid is a, quote, "callow youngster," a bit player, accidentally celebrated. Nolan wrote: "Indeed, those who savor the ironies of history may find a certain sweet justice in the fact that today, of all the powerful, rich, and famous men of his era, it is the Kid who is remembered best - and at that, for the things he never did." Thus for Nolan, Billy's pardon bargain letters, which risked his life to testify against Huston Chapman's Ringite murderers, became merely, quote: "the beginning of a correspondence unique in the annals of outlawry." Nolan used the Garrett-Upson outlaw myth book as authority. He wrote: "Upson's catalogue of the Kid's thievery is likely to be accurate as any other. It paints a believable picture of his activities, and confirms why he and his compadres were soon to be considered as big a menace as the original gang whose name they now bore - the Rustlers ... But the times at last were changing, and a cold new wind of law and order was beginning to blow."

Joel Jacobsen, a New Mexican politician-lawyer, published a 1994 book titled *Such Men as Billy the Kid: The Lincoln County*

War Reconsidered. It's mere Ring-denying outlaw myth. The title was even lifted from Susan McSween's court testimony recounting that Ringite Commander Dudley snidely refused her aid in the Lincoln County War Battle because she had, quote, "such men as Billy the Kid" in her house. For Jacobsen, Billy was a villainous murderer remembered only because he had a catchy nickname. Jacobsen said it was, quote: "a killer called Kid with a child's diminutive name."

It's finally time for the real history. It's time to abandon mythology shielding Santa Fe Ring victors. It's time to condemn Ring crimes, time to honor the anti-Ring freedom fighters, and time to credit the spectacular individual who made it all worth remembering: Billy Bonney.

TALK 21:
THE REAL LEW WALLACE
FROM BOOK: *THE LOST PARDON OF BILLY THE KID*
FEBRUARY 9, 2021

This talk gives my revisionist history perspective on Governor Lew Wallace, who betrayed his pardon bargain with Billy Bonney. The information is from my book, *The Lost Pardon of Billy the Kid: An Analysis Factoring in the Santa Fe Ring, Governor Lew Wallace's Dilemma, and a Territory in Rebellion.*

In late 1878, other than Billy Bonney, Lew Wallace was the most unusual man in New Mexico Territory. The coming together of Billy, as the Lincoln County War's last freedom fighter, and Wallace, as a Civil War General still fighting his own demons, had implications for Billy's pardon and the future of New Mexico Territory.

The complexity of new Territorial Governor, Lew Wallace, who replaced Santa Fe Ring-beholden Samuel Beach Axtell, must have confused one-dimensional Ringites. Their gluttonous goals were just money and power. He was a Civil War Major General; a graphic artist; a best-selling author of an historical novel, *The Fair God*, about conquistador Hernando Cortéz; and a prosecuting attorney who hanged Abraham Lincoln's murder conspirators. He was then writing a novel titled *Ben-Hur* about the coming of Jesus Christ.

On screen is Lew Wallace. **[FIGURE 45]** As Governor of New Mexico Territory from late 1878 to 1881, Lew Wallace could have changed the course of New Mexico history by fulfilling his 1879 pardon bargain with Billy Bonney. Granting it would have confirmed that Billy's Lincoln County War killings of William Brady, George Hindman, and Andrew "Buckshot" Roberts were justifiable in the Regulators' freedom fight against the Santa Fe Ring. Unfortunately, just then, that corrupt cabal was not only denying its role in the Lincoln County War, but also its very existence. Wallace realized the pardon would destroy his political career. He wrote to a Civil War friend on November 14th, 1878: "I came here and found a 'Ring' with a hand on the throat of the Territory. I refused to join them, and now they are proposing to fight me in the Senate [for removal as governor]."

FIGURE 45: LEW WALLACE: "Lew Wallace Dead." *New York Tribune*. February 16, 1905. Page 1. ChroniclingAmerica.loc.gov

In my novel, *Billy and Paulita*, I had Billy's fellow Tunstall employee, half-Chickasaw, Fred Waite, tell him: "Lincoln County is a moral proving ground. Evil here's so powerful it breaks people where they're weakest."

I'll present Lew Wallace's biography to show why he broke. Noteworthy, is that Wallace's psyche was surprisingly similar to Billy Bonney's, having been formed by traumas of early parental death, unusual talents, and abandonment; even though, from birth, Wallace and Billy were at opposite ends of America's class system. Their lives were a search for a father-figure and for acceptance.

Lew Wallace's affectionate biographers are Robert and Katherine Morsberger in their 1980 book, *Lew Wallace: Militant Romantic*. And Wallace's *Autobiography* was published posthumously in 1906.

Louis Wallace was born in Brookville, Indiana on April 10th, 1827 - 54 years plus one day before Billy Bonney's conviction for first degree murder for lack of his pardon. Wallace's West Point educated, lawyer father, David Wallace, became Indiana's Lieutenant Governor when Louis was five. There were three more brothers, with one of them dying in childhood.

Child Louis was a book-loving irresponsible dreamer. His unapproving cruel father punished him by whippings. His mother punished oddly by tying him to a bedframe and dressing him in her clothes. He was eight when she died; and his father abandoned him to a neighbor. At nine, he moved with his older brother to Crawfordsville, Indiana. His father then remarried without telling him. The traumas left Lewis resenting authority figures. And he identified with his sadistic father. So he later rebelled against orders and was pitiless to those in his power.

In 1837, when Lewis was 10, his father became Indiana's Governor, and moved the family to Indianapolis. By then, Louis enjoyed illustrating. David Wallace scorned it as effete. In 1838, David enabled massacre of 150 Potawatomis Indians, who refused illegal relocation. By the 1840's, David returned to private law practice, and abandoned Lewis to an aunt.

At 15, Louis wrote his first novel, set in Jerusalem during the crusades. His hero, after wartime heroism, is accepted by the heroine's father; as Louis longed for his father's acceptance.

At 16, Louis ran away to join a real war: Texas's War of Independence. Caught, he faced his furious father, who abandoned him again by cutting off all support. So Wallace took odd jobs.

At 17, he apprenticed as a lawyer. But, in two years, Mexican-American War fervor seized him, and he raised a company. In Mexico, he revealed his elitist prejudices. On March 26th, 1846, he wrote to his brother, William: "The native Mexican in his ignorance and mental imbecility bears the same relation to [Spaniards] as the imported African to us ... Their minds, like the Indian's, are entirely composed of cunning, low-trickery, and inclinations to deceit."

By 1847, Wallace was back in Indiana, without seeing battle. He wrote in his autobiography that he felt no qualms about the rightness of that war. His sole focus was himself. He wrote in his autobiography: "My nobelist dream of life has been one of fame."

In 1849, he got his law license. In 1852 he married wealthy Susan Elston from Crawfordsville, Indiana. Her never-wavering adulation of him matched his own.

In the 1850's, the Republican Party formed, with abolishing slavery as its cause. Though Wallace backed owners' rights, he joined the Union side. In 1856, he organized a Crawfordsville militia and was elected state senator. In 1859, seeing the Stephen A. Douglas and Abraham Lincoln debate, he chose Lincoln as a father-figure and became a Republican.

Wallace's benefactor was Indiana's governor, Oliver P. Morton. After the April 13th, 1861 attack on Fort Sumter, Morton made Wallace an Adjutant General in charge of raising troops. Wallace chose command as a Colonel of the 11th Regiment of Indiana Volunteers. And he renamed himself as Lew. By June, his regiment had a successful skirmish, which he initiated without orders, in Romney, West Virginia.

When his enlistment period ended, Wallace mustered a new regiment by August of 1861. He reported to Brigadier General Charles F. Smith. At 34, Wallace became a Brigadier General of volunteers. In 1862, he was promoted to Major General. Then Smith died on April 25th, 1862, after an accidental fall when visiting Wallace before the Battle of Shiloh. Smith was replaced by Ulysses S. Grant for that Tennessee battle.

It began on April 6th, 1862. It resulted in Wallace's unhealable trauma. On the first day of fighting, daydreamer Wallace got lost on the way to the battle at Pittsburg Landing, only a half mile away. He never arrived with his 7,500 troops. Grant and General William Tecumseh Sherman were under fierce attack by Confederate General Albert Sidney Johnston. The next day, Wallace arrived, and assisted victory. But Grant held him responsible for the Union's near loss and the battle's horrific total of 23,746 casualties. That exceeded the total casualties of the combined Revolutionary War, the War of 1812, and the Mexican-American War.

In June, Grant removed Wallace from any command. Wallace went back to Crawfordsville, humiliated, denying blame, and begging Grant for a pardon. In 17 years, he'd face Billy Bonney, petitioning for a pardon. His own pardon withheld, would combine with his sadistic power to repeat that injury on this dependent boy.

In August of 1862, Wallace's sympathetic backer, Indiana Governor Morton, got him sent, by himself, to Cincinnati, Ohio. Heading there coincidentally were also Confederate troops under General Kirby Smith. When Wallace found out, he made a proclamation forcing the inhabitants to defend their city. That worked. But it did not eradicate the curse of Shiloh. And he impulsively tried to hang some Cincinnati citizens he imagined as Confederate spies.

Through 1863, Wallace obsessively sought pardon from Grant. Only President Lincoln's intervention saved him from removal from service.

For Lincoln's 1864 reelection, Wallace was sent to Baltimore, Maryland, to "protect" poling places by his military presence. There, he hysterically tried to hang four, possibly innocent, men, whom he called Confederate spies. Lincoln stopped him.

In 1864, Wallace was directing secret aid to Mexican President Benito Juárez, fighting French colonizing forces. But Wallace additionally fantasized that the French were colluding with Texan Confederates to create an independent empire in Texas. So he drew up an Amnesty Proclamation for the Confederates, thinking he'd beat Grant in uniting the country. But it was rejected by the Confederates. And by May 26th, 1864, they surrendered anyway.

Then, on April 15th, 1865, President Lincoln was assassinated. New President, Andrew Johnson, appointed Wallace as a prosecutor for the conspirators' trial - the assassin, John Wilkes Booth, having been killed. In the trial, Wallace was accused of suppressing defense evidence and permitting perjury to attain the July 7th hangings of Lewis Powell; David Herold; George Atzerodt; and John Wilkes Booth's probably innocent, landlady, Mary Surratt - the first woman hanged by the federal government. And, before her hanging, Wallace cruelly rejected her pardon petition. He next succeeded in hanging the Confederate Andersonville prison camp's Captain Henry Wirz. And he tried to hang Confederate President Jefferson Davis.

On November 30th, 1865, Wallace left the army. To his killed wartime battle adversaries, he had added five hangings, while trying for many more. So in the War and its aftermath, Lew Wallace was connected to the killing of thousands. Sadistic power balanced Shiloh's impotence.

Wallace returned to Crawfordsville with limited finances and fear of failure at 40. In 1868, he tried politics; losing a seat in Congress amidst bad press about his hanging innocent Mary Surratt. And his enemy, Ulysses S. Grant, was by then President. In 1870, Wallace tried again for a seat in Congress, losing to attacks about Shiloh and Surratt.

In 1872, Wallace campaigned for Grant's re-election; though Grant ignored his continuing pleas for a Shiloh pardon. Grant also refused his request for an ambassadorship.

Wallace returned to writing. His historical novel, *The Fair God: A Tale of the Conquest of Mexico*, became a best-seller.

In 1876, Wallace campaigned for Republican presidential hopeful, Rutherford B. Hayes. Hayes defeated anti-Ring Democrat, Samuel Tilden, in a tainted election. Wallace was responsible. He was legal counsel for its Florida recount. Wallace got the canvassing board to throw out Tilden's leading votes to declare Hayes the winner. Wallace made Hayes President. The press called it the "Crime of '76." Wallace then asked Hayes for a pay-back of an exotic ambassadorship to Italy, Brazil, Spain, or Mexico. While waiting in Crawfordsville, he worked on his cathartic book, *Ben-Hur*, with its hero struggling to get a pardon from unjust accusation and enslavement by a high Roman official. Wallace was reworking Shiloh into a tale of salvation. In August of 1878, Hayes offered him a Bolivian ambassadorship. He refused it. That month, he submitted a plan to Secretary of War George McCrary for exterminating Native Americans, like his father's massacre of Potawatomis Indians. Possibly that appealed to Hayes, who offered him the Governorship of Territorial New Mexico that month. It was the remainder of removed Ringite Governor Samuel Beach Axtell's term. Wallace accepted. He had attained his father's level of public office. And it merged his airy fantasies of Old Mexico and the western frontier. The Territory's desperate Ring-tyrannized citizens would soon become just fodder for his continuing narcissistic saga of his own life.

Wallace was briefed in Washington on September 13th by Secretary of the Interior Carl Schurz, to whom he would report. And Investigator Frank Warner Angel, forced to cover-up the Santa Fe Ring in his 1878 reports about the Ring's part in murdering John Tunstall and in the Lincoln County War, secretly gave him his notebook listing Ringites, and an 1877 pamphlet by a Mary McPherson listing Thomas Benton Catron as Ring head, and the Ringites' crimes. But Wallace had no interest in laboring for justice. He intended rapid quieting of the Territory; keeping his wife, Susan, and son, Henry, amused in boring Santa Fe; finishing BEN-HUR; making some mining investments; and leaving quickly to an exotic ambassadorship.

Wallace arrived in Santa Fe on September 30th, 1878. He was sworn in as the Territory's 11th governor on October 1st. Immediately, he tried unsuccessfully to get Hayes to declare martial law so he could hang all troublemakers. He then focused on renovating his official residence, the Palace of the Governors, and completing *Ben-Hur*. He ignored annoying letters from an attorney named Huston Chapman, representing a widow named Susan McSween, against a Fort Stanton Commander, named N.A.M. Dudley, for arson and murder in the Lincoln County War. Wallace had no interest in visiting little Lincoln town's complaining citizens.

On November 13th, for a quick-fix, he issued an Amnesty Proclamation for non-indicted civilians and soldiers from the Lincoln County War. With his elitism, he even conferred with Catron himself, whose office was in the same plaza as the Palace of the Governors. Catron's henchman, U.S. Marshal John Sherman, had already provided Wallace with an outlaw list. It had mostly Regulators. Billy was number 14, as a murderer named " 'The Kid,' William Bonney." So as another quick fix, Wallace used troops to try and apprehend so-called "outlaws," whom he fabricated as causing the unrest. Billy evidently got extra Ring promotion. So Wallace offered an astronomical $1,000 dead or alive reward for him. That's almost $28,000 today.

Then came February 18th, 1879. The Ring murdered Huston Chapman in Lincoln to stop his prosecution of Dudley. In March, grudging Wallace arrived there. He tried another quick fix by removing Dudley as Fort Stanton's Commander. That didn't work. In Dudley's corner was Catron. Catron faked Dudley in the press as a noble officer insulted by Wallace. Dudley was no Grant, but to vulnerable Wallace, Shiloh's specter loomed again; with added anxiety about failure as governor in the eyes of father figures, Hayes and Schurz.

Right then, Wallace heard from teenaged Billy Bonney, cocky enough to propose a pardon deal, as part of his own compulsive quest for a father and acceptance. It was a March 13th letter, bargaining to give his eye-witness testimony against Chapman's murderers in exchange for a pardon for his Lincoln County War indictments for the Regulators' killings of Brady, Hindman, and Roberts. Wallace should have seen it as a godsend. And he had no qualms about giving pardons. He would soon turn a blind eye when boss Catron, colluding with Ringite Judge Warren Bristol, used his Amnesty Proclamation to pardon all Ringite murderers and arsonists, even though they were excluded from it by being indicted.

He met with Billy on March 17th, in the Lincoln home of Justice of the Peace John "Squire" Wilson. But there was a clash of personalities and politics. Billy was unintimidated by elitist Wallace. That brought out Wallace's sadism. And Wallace knew enough about the Lincoln County War to know Billy's pardon would pit him against the Santa Fe Ring. So he went through the motions, without intent. But Billy believed they had made a deal, and submitted to sham jailing in Lincoln. Housed next door, bored Wallace amused himself by interviewing Billy about local outlawry, avoiding questions about the Lincoln County War. But Billy followed up with a letter on the War's specifics. Then Billy testified against Chapman's murderers and got them indicted. No pardon followed.

Next, on his own, Billy testified for the prosecution in Commander Dudley's Court of Inquiry. Wallace, also testifying against Dudley, was exposed as an incompetent governor by Ringite defense attorney, Henry Waldo. As if reliving Shiloh, humiliated Wallace retreated to Santa Fe and thereafter ignored Lincoln County and Billy's pardon. Dudley was exonerated by the rigged Court. That furthered Wallace's avoidance of confronting the powerful Ring.

In January of 1880, hypocrite Wallace announced to the legislature that he had restored peace in Lincoln County. In truth, its citizens had sunk into hopeless silence, as the Ring flourished unchecked. And he completed BEN-HUR, an immediate best seller. In September of 1880, Wallace took a two month leave to campaign for James Garfield's presidential bid. On December

22nd, he placed a newspaper reward notice of $500 for Billy the Kid – what the Ring's outlaw myth had named Billy.

In 1881, elected Garfield offered Wallace the Ambassadorship to Turkey. Intending to escape his hated governorship early, Wallace still had to face his pardon promise to Billy. He had ignored captured Billy's January to March of 1881 pardon plea letters from the Santa Fe jail. He hoped to hide his betrayal by Billy's hanging death. On April 13th, he issued his own gubernatorial death sentence for Billy for Sheriff Pat Garrett. On April 28th, he gave a newspaper interview, lying that he didn't pardon Billy because it was undeserved. Coincidentally, Billy escaped jail that day. So, on May 3rd, Wallace made a second $500 newspaper reward offer for Billy the Kid.

But Wallace, unlike Ringites, had some conscience. Burying his guilt at betraying Billy, triggered his lifelong compulsive fictions outlawing Billy, and making himself the hero who was the object of outlaw Billy's murderous obsession. That projected his own wish to kill Billy. On May 16th, in the *St. Louis Daily Globe-Democrat*, Wallace published his bizarre, dime novel fantasy of Billy's outlaw gang; titled: "The Thug's Territory. Stage Robbers and Cut-Throats Have Things Their Own Way in New Mexico, General Lew Wallace Anxious to Punish the Crime That is So Prevalent – A Chapter About 'Billy the Kid.' "

On May 28th., Wallace left the Territory. But he could not escape his obsession with Billy. On June 18th, in the *Crawfordsville Saturday Evening Journal*, he presented: "Billy the Kid, General Wallace Tells Why the Young Desperado of New Mexico Wanted to Kill Him." By the end of June, Wallace and his wife were on a boat en route to Constantinople and his ambassadorship. Billy had two weeks left to live because of his betrayal.

From 1881 through 1885, Wallace entered his own romantic tales as Ambassador to Turkey. He toured Jerusalem, Cairo, and Rome.

On September 19th, 1881, President Garfield was assassinated. In 1884, Wallace, with his wife, took a leave to campaign for Republican James Blaine for president.

Then the ghost of Shiloh rose again. *Century* magazine ran articles on the Civil War. Ulysses S. Grant would cover Shiloh. Wallace again pleaded with him for its pardon. But Grant, dying of throat cancer, damned him with the magazine and his memoir. He wrote: "Wallace did not arrive in time to take part in the first day's fight. General Wallace has since claimed that the order delivered to him ... was simply to join the right of the army ... but this is not where I ordered him nor where I wanted him to go. I never could see, and do not know why, any order was necessary further than to direct him to come to Pittsburgh Landing."

In 1886, Wallace returned from Constantinople to Crawfordsville, Indiana. He toured the country giving talks on his romanticized adventures. In 1893, using his Near East experience, he wrote another best seller: *The Prince of India" Or Why Constantinople Fell.*

In 1893, Shiloh rose again. It was at a veterans' reunion, where Wallace gave a speech claiming he was unfairly blamed. In 1901, he went to Shiloh's battlefield and tried unsuccessfully to get the Shiloh Military Park Commission to present his version of the first day. He returned in 1903 for the 41st anniversary of the battle and gave a speech vindicating himself.

Likewise continuing into the 20th century, was Wallace's obsessive lying about Billy and the pardon in novella-like articles. He now admitted to the pardon promise. But he lied that Billy ruined the bargain by continued outlawry. On June 23rd, 1900, in *The Indianapolis Press,* was his "General Wallace's Feud with Billy the Kid, When the General Was Governor of New Mexico and Billy Bonne Was the Most Dangerous Western Outlaw." On June 8th, 1902, in the *New York World Magazine,* was his "General Lew Wallace Writes a Romance of 'Billy the Kid' Most Famous Bandit of the Plains: Thrilling Story of the Midnight Meeting Between General Wallace, Then Governor of New Mexico, and the Notorious Outlaw, in a Lonesome Hut in Santa Fe."

Billy also appeared in Wallace's late-life *Autobiography* as an outlaw obsessed with killing him in revenge for his denying the pardon. And, if death had not cut Wallace short in 1905, Billy the Kid would have likely become an outlaw and serial murderer in a novel on the Old West, in which Wallace himself was the hero. In the summer of 1904, Wallace was declining with stomach cancer. But he opposed a senate bill combining New Mexico and Arizona Territories, announcing hypocritically: "I love the people of New Mexico. I lived with them for two and a half years as their Governor, and I know their condition and their needs."

So Wallace broke where he was weakest: monumental selfishness. It topped off his elitism, racism, authoritarianism, narcissism, sadism, and hypocrisy. In an ironic twist that would have shocked him, the fame that he craved and got, ended up eclipsed by his homeless, penniless, low-class victim, Billy Bonney.

Wallace died on February 15th, 1905 at 77. His self-aggrandizing *Autobiography* was completed in 1906 by his wife.

As a postscript, Lew Wallace's wife, Susan, his son, Henry, and Henry's son, Lew Wallace Jr., preserved all his papers - including those of Billy the Kid. And when donating them as the Lew Wallace collection to the Indiana Historical Society and the Bloomington, Indiana, Lilly Library, Lew Wallace Jr. saved two items from the thousands of pages: Billy Bonney's first pardon plea letter of March 13th, 1879, and Billy's Santa Fe jail letter of March 2nd, 1881. Lew Wallace must have let it be known to his kin that there was something special about them. William N. Wallace, Lew Wallace's great-grandson and Lew Wallace Jr.'s son, sold those two letters to a historical museum in Lincoln, New Mexico.

That same William N. Wallace, in 2010, helped me stop a modern Santa Fe Ring Governor's publicity-stunt pardon for Billy the Kid to be granted to an old-timer, Billy the Kid imposter named Oliver "Brushy Bill" Roberts. So Lew Wallace's descendant helped me save Billy Bonney's history after his great-grandfather helped the Ring destroy Billy Bonney's life.

In upcoming talks, I'll discuss Billy Bonney's lost pardon. In later talks, I'll discuss the 20th century Billy the Kid imposter hoax of "Brushy Bill" Roberts, and its 21st century rerun by New Mexico's corrupt governor.

TALK 22:

BILLY BONNEY'S PARDON BARGAIN WITH LEW WALLACE

FROM BOOK: *THE LOST PARDON OF BILLY THE KID*

FEBRUARY 10, 2021

This talk presents my revisionist history of Billy Bonney's pardon bargain with New Mexico Territory Governor Lew Wallace. The information is from my book, *The Lost Pardon of Billy the Kid: An Analysis Factoring in the Santa Fe Ring, Governor Lew Wallace's Dilemma, and a Territory in Rebellion.*

A mystery has been why Billy Bonney didn't get his pardon from Governor Lew Wallace. He believed Wallace promised it to him in March of 1879. In a March 4th, 1881 letter from the Santa Fe jail, Billy wrote to Wallace: "I have done everything that I promised you I would, and you have done nothing that you promised me." It's remained a mystery because the answer is complex. It involves the nature of the pardon bargain; the psychology of Lew Wallace; the motives of the corrupt Santa Fe Ring controlling Territorial government; and the deficiency of Billy's attorney, Ira Leonard. Solving the mystery gives insight into Billy Bonney's courage and anti-Ring zeal; and to the Lincoln County War freedom fight, which the pardon would have vindicated, along with Billy himself.

The outcome of Billy Bonney's pardon bargain to Governor Lew Wallace depended on political and psychological factors beyond their control. It would alter both their lives, yielding Billy's death and Wallace's guilt-ridden obsession with hiding his betrayal. When Billy Bonney and Lew Wallace first crossed paths on March 13th, 1879, Billy was recently 19, and Wallace almost 52.

Each was in crisis. Billy, in the year past, had lost a life as a ranch owner and protégé of John Tunstall to become a hunted outlaw. Wallace, intending a quick fix to flee his backwater governorship, was mired in a military crisis that risked his future and flashed back to his Civil War scandal. That was the Battle of Shiloh, in which he got lost and missed the battle's first day. Each saw the other as famous, and needed the other. Risking hanging, Billy needed a pardon to free himself from Ring prosecution. Wallace needed to prove pacification of the Territory to escape its political quagmire and get rewarded by an exotic ambassadorship.

From opposite ends of the social spectrum, they were surprisingly similar. Both longed for unattained fatherly love, both had lost young mothers to tuberculosis, both were cast out too early and too harshly from home. Both felt wrongly outlawed: Billy by the Ring for rebelling, Wallace, by General Ulysses S. Grant, for Shiloh. Both had survived life's adversities by intellectual brilliance, tenacity, and bravado. Both were, at that moment, the most unusual people in the Territory. Their relationship would be a failure. By offering his pardon bargain to Lew Wallace, Billy could not know that he was heading into tragedy - where the only possible outcome was disaster.

The pardon bargain looked simple. Just weeks after the Ring murder of anti-Ring Attorney Huston Chapman in Lincoln, Billy approached Governor Lew Wallace. He knew that Wallace would recognize his name, since Wallace had placed an astronomical dead or alive reward of $1,000 on his head. That's about $28,000 today. Wallace had come to Lincoln to interview citizens. So Billy, by a letter to Wallace on about March 13th, offered to trade his eye-witness testimony in 1879's April Grand Jury against Chapman's murderers for a pardon for his Lincoln County War indictments for Regulator killings of William Brady, George Hindman, and Andrew "Buckshot" Roberts.

But, as I discussed in Talk 7 about my authenticating a new Billy the Kid letter, Billy's pardon request may have also been secretly backed by anti-Ring public officials, who saw him as the Lincoln County War's hero. They were Justice of the Peace John "Squire" Wilson and Jailor, Juan Patrón. They provided the fine stationery for some of Billy's pardon plea letters. Wilson gave his home for a Billy-Wallace meeting; and Patrón offered his home for Billy's sham jailing.

Adding complexity, is that Wallace was not really committed to the pardon. First of all, he knew about U.S. Attorney

T.B. Catron's federal indictment of Billy and the other Regulators for the "Buckshot" Roberts killing. He knew that only President Rutherford B. Hayes could issue that pardon. Wallace could only pardon for the Territorial indictments for the Brady and Hindman killings. Secondly, to avoid confronting the Ring, Wallace was using its outlaw myth to fake activity by pursuing past Regulators. Thirdly, he didn't like Billy. Billy's cocky attitude of being an equal to any man stimulated Wallace's competitive and sadistic feelings. Elitist Wallace required adulation - even from his wife and son. Lastly, Wallace knew the Ring wouldn't tolerate pardoning the last freedom fighter, who could renew anti-Ring rebellions. So Wallace let Billy's testify, but delayed action to assess his personal risk from pardoning. Then Wallace's betrayal crystallized by coincidence. The outcome of the Court of Inquiry against past Fort Stanton Commander N.A.M. Dudley was a Ring victory. Wallace, who testified against Dudley, realized the Ring was unbeatable.

Sadly, there was no way for Billy or his backers to anticipate betrayal. But once it became obvious, months hence, Billy's backers retreated into silence. Billy would ultimately have to face the Ring in court, unpardoned and alone, but defiant.

When Billy sent Wallace his letter of March 13th, there was reason for him to trust Wallace. Wallace represented the Regulator's only Lincoln County War victory: removal of Ringite Governor Samuel Beach Axtell. That was why Wallace got the job. So it was reasonable to assume that he cared about the freedom fight that made him Axtell's mid-term replacement.

There was reason for Billy to make a pardon request. Wallace's November 13th, 1878 Amnesty Proclamation had excluded those already indicted. And Billy may have gotten legal input from his backers, or even his new attorney, Ira Leonard. In his letter to Wallace, he correctly asked for annulling his indictments, not pardoning, which was after sentencing.

There was reason for Billy's audacious egalitarianism. As a teenager, he had become a wartime hero the year before. As an anti-Ring zealot, he was now continuing his agenda which already included his affidavit against John Tunstall's murderers, his being a deputy to serve arrest warrants on those murderers, his deposition on Tunstall's murder to Presidential Investigator Frank Warner Angel, and his risking death in every Lincoln County War encounter. Freed of his indictments, he could safely remain in the Territory. And he apparently also hoped that Wallace could become an ally in defeating the Ring.

Billy's March 13th, 1879 pardon bargain letter is presented in full in Talk 6. In his fine Spencerian script, it was downright brash. As to Wallace's huge, dead or alive reward, Billy airily dismissed it as negotiable. Billy wrote: "I have heard that You will give one thousand dollars for my body which as I can understand it means alive as a witness." That segued to his bargain's terms; quote: "I know it is as a witness against those that murdered Mr. Chapman. If it was so as that I could appear at Court, I could give the desired information ... I was present when Mr. Chapman was murdered and know who did it." That meant the exchange of his testimony for the annulling. Realistic about the murderous Ring, Billy added needing protection; writing that, quote: "my enemies would Kill me." The ball was then in Wallace's court. Billy wrote: "Please send me an annser telling me what you can do."

Wallace was suddenly offered a solution to his Chapman crisis, wrapped in romance of an outlaw boy of the wild frontier. And he had already arrested, and incarcerated, in Fort Stanton, the accused murderers: James Dolan, Billy Campbell, and Jessie Evans.

On March 15th, Lew Wallace, in full authoritarian mode, responded by letter to Billy, as the wily attorney who hanged John Wilkes Booth's innocent landlady in the trial against conspirators in Abraham Lincoln's assassination. Self-serving Wallace had the potential to get the boy's testimony, then hang him as a trophy in his fake war against so-called "outlaws." Pompously, Wallace even gave Billy directions around Lincoln: the town Billy obviously knew well, having been a Tunstall employee there and fighting in its War's Battle eight months earlier! And Wallace insultingly linked him to outlaw Jessie Evans, one of Tunstall's and Chapman's killers. Wallace wrote: "If you could trust Jesse Evans, you can trust me." More ominous was Wallace's trick wording, by writing: "I have the authority to exempt you from prosecution, if you will testify to what you say you know." Wallace may have had the authority, but he didn't promise to use it to pardon Billy! Further indicating trickery, as mentioned, is that he did not have the authority to pardon Billy for the federal indictment for the "Buckshot" Roberts killing. I take all this as proof that Wallace, even at the start, was merely setting a trap to capture Billy, and later decide his fate.

But was Wallace actually legally bound after Billy met the bargain's one condition? Wallace had repeated that condition in his letter, quote: "[I]f you will testify to what you say you know." And, as Governor, Wallace did have the power for Territorial pardons. So did Wallace's tricky wording void the bargain?

Leaving out that Wallace had no power to exempt Billy from the federal indictment, he could not wiggle out of the Territorial indictments' bargain by ambiguous wording. It was legally validated by tit-for-tat expectation. *Black's Law Dictionary* states that an "agreement" is "a manifestation of mutual assent by two or more persons ... The parties' actual bargain as found in their language or by ... course of ... performance." As to bargain, *Black's Law Dictionary* states it is "an agreement between parties for the exchange of promises or performances." So, if Billy testified, Wallace was legally required to pardon.

Also, layman Billy would have understood Wallace's March 15th letter as a "promise." In his March 4th, 1881 letter to Wallace from the Santa Fe jail, Billy wrote: "I have done everything that I promised you I would, and You have done nothing that You promised me." A promise, according to *Black's Law Dictionary,* is [t]he manifestation of an intention to act ... in a specified manner, conveyed in such a way that another is justified in understanding that a commitment has been made [or] a person's assurance that the person will ... do something." That concept of "promise" is strengthened by intertwined mutuality, as in: if I do this, you will do that. *Black's Law Dictionary* states about mutual promises: "Promises given simultaneously by two parties, each promise serving as a consideration for the other; [with consideration being] an act ... or a return promise."

So if Wallace reneged on annulling Territorial indictments after Billy testified, or later refused to pardon him after his 1881 sentencing, when even the federal indictment had been quashed, Wallace would betray not only Billy, but his legal obligation and integrity. But Wallace did betray the bargain. Billy did testify. Wallace issued no pardon. Since Wallace was no sociopath, like Ringites, his conscience tormented him for the rest of his life, though he hid his guilt in articles blaming outlaw Billy the Kid breaking the pardon bargain, not him.

There was more. In Billy's desperate March 2nd, 1881 letter from the Santa Fe jail (which particularly annoyed guilty Wallace as blackmail), Billy wrote: "I have some letters which date back two years and there are Parties who are very anxious to get them but I will not dispose of them until I see you. that is if you come immediately." Dating back two years, puts the letters in this 1879 pardon bargain period, implying Wallace had put the promise in writing. If so, Wallace, who kept copies of his correspondence with Billy, despicably expurgated this evidence. And Billy's originals are lost.

But there are other clues as to those lost letters. After Billy's April 28th, 1881 jailbreak, he first went to the ranch of a friend named John Meadows. Meadows's recollections were posthumously printed in a 2004 book titled *Pat Garrett and Billy the Kid as I Knew Them*. In it, Meadows referred to Billy's owning a letter from Wallace about the pardon promise. Though Meadows garbled the bargain as based on "standing trial," instead of "testifying in a trial," it repeats Billy's claim of having letters. Meadows wrote: "He had a letter which he showed me from the governor, Lew Wallace, which said that if he came in and stood his trial and was convicted, the governor would pardon him." And on June 8th, 1902, near the end of his life, Wallace published, in *New York World Magazine*, an article titled "General Lew Wallace Writes a Romance of 'Billy the Kid.'" In it, Wallace quoted himself from their meeting: "Testify ... before the Grand Jury and the trial court and convict the murderer of Chapman and I will let you go scot-free with a pardon in your pocket for all your misdeeds." That confirmed, after his decades of hiding it, that Wallace knew that he had made the pardon bargain.

Furthermore, another Wallace letter was revealed in 1880. That year, Secret Service Operative Azariah Wild was in the Territory. He was approached by Billy's attorney, Ira Leonard, about making a different pardon bargain. Wild, in his report, written on October 8th, referenced it. He wrote: "Governor Wallace has issued a proclamation granting immunity to those not indicted, but, as Antrom [meaning Billy] has been indicted, the proclamation did not cover his ... case." Then Wild mentioned the letter; stating: "Governor Wallace has since written Antrom's attorney on the subject saying he should be let go, but has failed to put it on shape that satisfied Judge Leonard, Antrom's attorney." This implies well-meaning but lackluster Attorney Leonard's failure. He apparently never petitioned in court for the pardon, to put Wallace on the spot to respond legally. And, unfortunately, this Wallace letter is also lost.

All this means that, by March 15th, 1879, Billy was correct to believe that he had a pardon bargain. For him, the issue was how to fulfill it without being murdered first by the Ring. In his letter of March 15th, Wallace proposed a meeting in Lincoln on the 17th, and stated: "The object of the meeting at Squire Wilson's is to arrange the matter in a way to make your life safe."

No transcript exists of this meeting. Its witness was Justice of the Peace John "Squire" Wilson, in whose house it occurred. Presumably, Wallace repeated his pardon promise. And he and Billy planned his sham arrest to conceal that he would be a witness for the prosecution.

But a calamity occurred on March 18th. Jessie Evans and Billy Campbell, two of the potential defendants, escaped from Fort Stanton. Remaining was James Dolan. That resulted in a March 20th flurry of letters as Billy tried to determine if the pardon bargain still existed.

Billy first wrote to Wilson, as "Friend Wilson," questioning if Wallace wanted to make, quote, "different arrangements" to the sham arrest plan, which he gave for the next day.

Wilson got it to Wallace, who wrote back to Wilson that Sheriff George Kimbrell should do the sham arrest. That implied that the bargain was still in effect.

Wallace also enclosed a letter for Billy. Only Wallace's draft of it exists. That's fortunate, because Wallace's cross-outs reveal his ongoing attempt at deceit. Wallace wrote: "The escape makes no difference in the arrangements." Then he crossed out: "I will comply with my part if you will with yours." Wallace was still trying to hedge his bets.

Billy responded to Wallace immediately, fine-tuning his dangerous arrest. He wrote: "I am not afraid to die like a man fighting but would not like to be killed like a dog unarmed." He assumed he would be held in Ring stronghold, Fort Stanton. So he wrote: "[A]ll I am afraid of is that in the Fort we might be poisoned or killed through a window at night. [B]ut You can arrange that all right … [T]here will be danger on the road of somebody waylaying us to kill us on the road to the Fort." Billy also changed the arrest site. And he made a bid in his search for a father-figure: He offered to help Wallace capture the escapees. He wrote: "You will never catch those fellows on the road. Watch Fritzes, Captain Bacas ranch, and the Brewery. They will either go to Seven Rivers or to Jicarillo Mountains. They will stay around close until the scouting parties come in. Give a spy a pair of glasses and let him get on the mountain back of Fritzes and watch, and if they are there there will be provisions carried to them. It is not my place to advise you, but I am anxious to have them caught, and perhaps know how men hide from soldiers, better than you." This joke was Billy's take-off on Wallace's failing to catch him with soldiers. Teasing Billy clearly thought a friendship was forming. He was wrong.

Billy's sham jailing was made safer by his friend: anti-Ring Jailor, Juan Patrón. Patrón offered his home for it, instead of dangerous Fort Stanton.

Lew Wallace kept in close touch with Secretary of the Interior Carl Schurz. In his own search for a father figure and for approval, he sent frequent self-congratulatory letters to him and to President Hayes. On March 21st, just after Billy was incarcerated, Wallace wrote a chilling letter to Schurz. Ominously, he mentions having gotten affidavits about Chapman's murder, but hides Billy's testifying role and pardon. Instead, he promoted his fake campaign against outlaws as, quote: "taking the head off the evil." He even enclosed Ringite U.S. Marshal John Sherman's outlaw list, which had " 'The Kid' William Bonney" as a murderer and number 14. But Wallace did mention Billy. He wrote: "To still further weaken my confidence in juries ... in this county ... everybody ... has in some way been committed to one side or the other in the recent war ... A precious specimen nick-named "The Kid," whom the Sheriff is holding here in the Plaza ... is an object of tender regard. I heard singing and music the other night; going to the door, I found the minstrels of the village actually serenading the fellow in his prison." So Billy appears as a random jailed outlaw, snidely called a "precious specimen," exemplifying factionalism that made such riff-raff an "object of tender regard." Proved is that Wallace was a treacherous hypocrite. Proved is that Billy had no hope.

Wallace's sadistic power over this trusting boy may also have stimulated his literary inspiration for his *Ben-Hur: A Tale of the Christ*, which he was then writing. Its theme was of unjustly enslaved hero, Judah Ben-Hur, seeking pardon. Wallace wrote: "Go now," [Arrius the slave master, who promised pardon] said, "and do not build upon what has passed between us. Perhaps I do but play with thee."

In later talks, I'll discuss how Lew Wallace's betrayal determined Billy Bonney's tragic fate.

TALK 23:
LEW WALLACE'S INTERVIEW OF BILLY BONNEY
FROM BOOK: *THE LOST PARDON OF BILLY THE KID*
FEBRUARY 17, 2021

This talk presents my revisionist history of Billy Bonney's interview with New Mexico Territory Governor Lew Wallace. The information is from my book, *The Lost Pardon of Billy the Kid: An Analysis Factoring in the Santa Fe Ring, Governor Lew Wallace's Dilemma, and a Territory in Rebellion.*

After Billy Bonney made his pardon bargain with Governor Lew Wallace in mid-March of 1879, he went into a sham imprisonment on March 21st, in the Lincoln home of his friend, Jailor, Juan Patrón. It was a life-saving ploy to trick the Santa Fe Ring by keeping secret that he'd be testifying in the April Grand Jury against Ring murderers of Attorney Huston Chapman in exchange for a pardon for his Lincoln County War murder indictments.

In Lincoln also was Lew Wallace, pretending to respond to the agitated citizens after yet another Ring murder in their town. Since Wallace had no intention to destroy his political future by confronting the Ring, he faked activity by interviewing locals about general outlawry and rustling. He was housed in the home of Jose Montaño, next door to Billy, so he included Billy in the interviewing on March 23rd.

Wallace took notes on Billy's responses, with headings for each topic. Noteworthy was that Wallace avoided questions about the Lincoln County War or Santa Fe Ring. Noteworthy also was Billy's tremendous knowledge of Territorial outlawry and geography. It showed why the Ring feared him as a future leader of another anti-Ring uprising. And it demonstrated his ability for meticulous observation that, in two months, would yield his devastating testimony against Commander NA.M. Dudley in his military Court of Inquiry. Also, Billy omitted mention of Regulators as outlaws, as was being promoted by Ring propaganda. And he slipped in Lincoln County War references, mentioning: the, quote, "Rustlers" gang that quote "had been with Peppin's posse;" the Owens gang, quote, "organized before the burning of McSween's home;" men going, quote, "thence to the Feliz where they took the Tunstall cattle;" and a certain man who, quote, "had no cattle when the War started." Billy was apparently delighted with Wallace as his new father-figure; so he followed-up with additional Lincoln County War information by letter the next day. It's covered in Talk 7 about my authenticating it.

One can guess that, in March of 1879, peripatetic Lew Wallace, stuck in one street Lincoln by Chapman's murder, was bored. Possible amusement was clever Billy Bonney, "jailed" just east of his Montaño's house lodging. Dreary interviewing of dreary townspeople, whose refusal to let sleeping dogs lie, was delaying his Palace of the Governors' renovation, his writing of BEN-HUR, and his amusing his equally bored wife and son in Santa Fe.

Billy was likely bored also, with the Grand Jury weeks away; though his sham jailing in friendly hospitality of Juan Patrón's home must have been pleasant; as must have been knowledge of Lew Wallace as a neighbor.

Wallace's writings about Billy in the 1900's imply that they had additional interviews. For example, Wallace knew that Billy was born in New York City and lived in Indiana as a child, before moving to New Mexico. And Wallace's described incident of asking Billy for a shooting demonstration could have happened in the back of Juan Patrón's house facing the south hills.

On his interview notes, Wallace wrote that they were of William Bonney, parentheses ("Kid"), as, quote, "relevant to arrangement with him." This is odd, since the arrangement was the pardon bargain for testifying, not giving interviews. Wallace titled it: "Statements by Kid, made Sunday night March 23rd, 1879."

Billy began with breathtaking detail. Wallace recorded: "There is a cattle trail beginning about 5 miles above Yellow Lake in a cañon, running a little west of north to Cisneza del Matcho, parenthesis (Mule Spring), and continuing around the point of the Capitan Mountains down toward Carrizozo in the direction of the Rio Grande. Frank Wheeler, Jake Owens and Dutch Chris are supposed to have used this trail taking a bunch of cattle over. Vansickle told K. so. They stopped and killed two beavers for Sam Corbett – hush money to Vansickle to whom they gave the beavers. Vansickle also said the Owens-Wheeler outfit mentioning 'Chris' Ladbessor using this trail for about a year, but that lately their horses had given out, and of 140 head which they started to work, they had only got through with 40. That now they were going to the Reservation to make a raid on the Indian horses to work on."

Under the topic, "the Rustlers," Billy referenced Seven Rivers boys. Wallace, missing their Ring participation in the War; wrote: " 'Kid says [the Rustlers] were organized in Fort Stanton. Before they organized as 'Rustlers' they had been with Peppin's posse. They came from Texas. Owens was conspicuous amongst them. They were organized before the burning of McSween's house, and after that they went on their first trip down the county as far as the Coe's ranch and thence to the Feliz where they took the Tunstall cattle." Billy then described other murders, rustling, robberies, and rape by them.

Under the topic "Shedd's Ranch," Billy referenced a Ringite holding camp for rustled stock. Wallace quoted him: "The trail used going from Seven Rivers to Shedd's was round the southwest part of the Guadalupe Mountains by a tank on the right hand of the trail. From Shedd's the drives would be over to Las Cruces." Billy mentioned Jessie Evans and his gang member, Frank Baker, who he said was killed; omitting that he and the Regulators killed him when Baker fled arrest for Tunstall's murder. Cattle were described as sold to a butcher in Las Cruces.

Under the topics "Mimbres" and "San Nicholas Spring," Billy cited outlaw and rustling gangs.

Under the topic "The Jones Family," Billy was quoted: "Came from Texas. Used to keep a saloon at Fort Griffin. The family consists of the father, Jim Jones, John Jones, boy about 10 years old, a girl about 13, and the mother. Marion Turner lives with the family, and he killed a Mexican man at Blazers Mill 'just to see him kick.' He had no cattle when the War started." That ended Wallace's interview notes.

It was not until June 23rd, 1900, in *The Indianapolis Press*, that Wallace mentioned a shooting demonstration by Billy during this period, which he calls the "confinement." It was in an article titled: "General Wallace's Feud with Billy the Kid, When the General Was Governor of New Mexico and Billy Bonne Was the Most Dangerous Western Outlaw." The event was titled: "Billy's Secret in Revolver Shooting." The location was fictionalized as Santa Fe, as were Billy's escape risk and clustered guards, as was Billy's gun aiming advice. So the whole incident may have been made-up. But it shows Wallace's ongoing fascination with Billy. He wrote:

"It was during this confinement that 'the Kid' gave the most phenomenal exhibition of shooting I have ever witnessed. I sent word to the jail to have him brought to my office.

" 'Billy,' I said, 'I am told you are a phenomenal shot. I wish you would give me an exhibition of your skill.'

" 'With pleasure, Governor. Have my pistols brought.'

" 'Here is a pistol, and a good one.'

" 'A violinist always wants his own bow, though another might be better. I want my own pistol.'

"His pistol was brought and we took him out into the big, open court. I ordered his chains taken from him. The guards whispered to me, 'For God's sake, Governor, do you know that you are giving him your life or his escape?'

"I knew that I was the last man in New Mexico Billy wanted to kill, for I was the only man that could give him a pardon.

"The guards stood with their weapons in their hands, ready to defend themselves ... Billy spied a small Boston bean can in the court. He ordered a guard to throw it high as he could. The can sailed in the air. Without taking aim, and seemingly without concern, he fired at it. The bullet passed through the center ...

" 'Billy,' said I, 'There is a trick in that, and I want to know it.'

" 'Yes,' he replied, 'there is a trick ... I put my index finger along the barrel, catch the trigger with my second finger and say, 'Why look at that, Billy,' and, pointing unconsciously at it, pull the trigger."

No matter what actually occurred, Billy wrongly thought that the interview cemented an alliance with Wallace. The next day, March 24th, he had delivered to Wallace a follow-up letter. It was on specially embossed stationery, which he got from Jailor, Juan Patrón. Only its last page exists. And it's signed only Billie, as

B-I-L-L-I-E. It shows not only that Billy spelled his name that way, but that he wanted to add Lincoln County War events to his information on outlaws. Since the stationery was in folio form - meaning folded like a greeting card – sadly missing might be at least four more pages. What is present in its two-sided last page indicates that Billy hoped to enlist Wallace in the anti-Ring crusade. Referenced is James Dolan no longer having the Pecos Cow Camp; Jessie Evans's gang; the rustlers selling cattle to merchants, John Riley and James Dolan, for their beef contract to the Mescalero Indian Reservation; the Seven Rivers boys rustling from John Chisum's herd; the killing of Seven Rivers rustler Robert Beckwith when the McSween house was burning down in the War; Robert and Wallace Olinger as being in the Seven River's rustling gang; the Regulators' Mescalero Indian Reservation encounter with "Buckshot" Roberts; and blaming Sheriff George Peppin for recruiting Seven Rivers boys by threatening that, if the War was lost, Chisum would take back his rustled cattle.

Unbeknownst to Billy, the chilling backdrop to his efforts was Lew Wallace's sadism and hypocrisy. In his BEN-HUR, which he was then writing, Wallace had a scene that may have been inspired by his power over Billy. He had his hero, Judah Ben-Hur, unjustly enslaved, being offered a pardon by the galley ship's slave master named Arrius. But Arrius adds: "Perhaps I do but play with thee." And, on March 21st, with Billy in sham jailing, Wallace had also written to Secretary of the Interior Carl Schurz, snidely ridiculing him as a random imprisoned outlaw, whose popularity with locals showed their debasement. He wrote: "A precious specimen nick-named "The Kid," whom the Sheriff is holding here in the Plaza ... is an object of tender regard." There was no mention that this boy was risking his life to testify against Huston Chapman's murderers in order to get a pardon promised by him.

Later talks will be about Billy fulfilling the pardon bargain, and Lew Wallace betraying it.

TALK 24:
BILLY BONNEY'S
FULFILLED PARDON BARGAIN
FROM BOOK: *THE LOST PARDON*
OF BILLY THE KID
FEBRUARY 22, 2021

This talk presents my revisionist history of Billy Bonney's fulfilled pardon bargain with New Mexico Territory Governor Lew Wallace. The information is from my book, *The Lost Pardon of Billy the Kid: An Analysis Factoring in the Santa Fe Ring, Governor Lew Wallace's Dilemma, and a Territory in Rebellion.*

In March of 1879, Billy Bonney made a bargain with Governor Lew Wallace. In exchange for his giving eye-witness testimony in that April's Lincoln County Grand Jury against the murderers of Huston Chapman, Wallace would pardon him for his Lincoln County War indictments for the Regulator killings of Sheriff William Brady; Deputy George Hindman; and Tunstall murder posseman, Andrew "Buckshot" Roberts.

It is known that Billy did testify. But the transcript is lost in likely expurgation of his damning evidence by the Santa Fe Ring, which orchestrated Chapman's murder. The judge was Ringite Warren Bristol. The District Attorney was Ringite William Rynerson. Billy got local Ring boss, James Dolan, indicted for first degree murder. He got Ring thug, Jessie Evans, indicted as an accessory. And he got Evans's gang member, Billy Campbell indicted for first degree murder.

Contemporary records prove Billy's testimony.

Attorney Ira Leonard, working with Governor Wallace, and aware of Billy's pardon bargain, confirmed Billy's testifying to

Wallace in an April 20th letter. He described Ring pressure, writing: "I tell you Governor that the prosecuting officer of this District [William Rynerson] is no friend to the enforcement of the law. He is bent on going for the Kid ... to destroy his testimony and influence, he is bent on pushing him to the wall. He is a Dolan man and is defending him by his conduct all he can." Billy's brave testimony likely inspired Leonard to become Billy's attorney.

That Billy achieved the indictments is proved by the April 28th filing by District Attorney Rynerson. It should be noted that Rynerson was required merely to record the Grand Jury's indictments; but not required to issue arrest warrants. Evans and Campbell had already escaped. And Dolan was never tried. This repeated the Ring's shielding of Dolan for his indictment as one of the murderers of John Tunstall the year before. Rynerson wrote: "The Grand Jurors for the Territory of New Mexico ... upon the oaths do present that James J. Dolan and William Campbell ... on the nineteenth [it was the eighteenth] day of February in the year of our Lord one thousand eight hundred and seventy nine ... with force and arms in and upon one Huston I. Chapman then and there being of their malice aforethought, unlawfully, feloniously, willfully, and from a premeditated design to effect the death of him ... did shoot and discharge ... leaden bullets ... in and upon the left breast of ... the said Huston I. Chapman ... the said Huston I. Chapman then and there instantly died ... And so the jurors ... do say that the said James J. Dolan and the said William Campbell the said Huston I. Chapman ... did kill and murder. And the jurors ... do further present that Jessie Evans ... did feloniously and maliciously unlawfully and from a premeditated design to effect the death of ... the said Huston I. Chapman, did incite move procure and counsel ... the said James J. Dolan and the said William Campbell."

Billy's Grand Jury testimony was also confirmed in the May 10th *Grant County Herald*. It stated: "At the recent term of court in Lincoln, about 200 indictments were found. Among them ... Dolan and Campbell for the Chapman murder, in which the Kid is the principal witness."

The first sign of Wallace's betrayal was that he did not pardon Billy after his successful testimony, which was the bargain's only condition. And Wallace didn't pardon Billy after the Ring made its move to kill him by hanging. On April 21ˢᵗ, District Attorney Rynerson, with Judge Warren Bristol, changed Billy's trial venue for his indictments to Doña Ana County's Mesilla court to guarantee hanging by a jury ignorant of Lincoln County War issues. Rynerson's request said: "[J]ustice cannot be done the said Territory on the trial of the said defendant William Bonney alias Kid alias William Antrim in the said County of Lincoln for the reason that jurors in attendance, and all those liable to be summoned for the trial of said defendant, by reason of partisanship in the late and existing troubles and lawlessness in said County have so prejudiced the said jurors that they cannot fairly and impartially try the said defendant."

Highlighting Wallace's betrayal, is that he permitted pardoning, on May 1ˢᵗ, 1879, of all Ringites already indicted for murder and arson in the Lincoln County War. This was achieved in court by Santa Fe Ring boss T.B. Catron; his law partner, William Thornton; and Ringite Attorneys Sidney Wilson and Simon B. Newcomb. (In 1881, Newcomb would be one of Billy's prosecuting attorneys in his Mesilla hanging trial). They audaciously presented to Ringite Judge, Warren Bristol, Wallace's Amnesty Proclamation, even though it specifically barred those indicted from using it! Catron and his cronies ignored that, declaring that its amnesty blocked prosecution of everybody he represented.

In fact, it was that exclusionary clause that forced Billy to propose his pardon bargain to Wallace. Billy had written: "[I]f it was so as that I could appear at Court, I could give the desired information. but I have indictments against me for things that happened in the late Lincoln County War." Billy and his lawyer, Ira Leonard, had taken Wallace at his word. They believed Billy was ineligible for the Amnesty Proclamation.

Billy and Ira Leonard were unaware that hypocrite Wallace, avoiding confrontation with the Santa Fe Ring, even rationalized Catron's misuse of his Proclamation in a June 11ᵗʰ, 1879 letter to Secretary of the Interior Carl Schurz by claiming that pardoning Ringites avoided costly trials. Wallace even pretended that had been his hope. He wrote: "[M]y amnesty proclamation has had exactly the effect intended; which was to shear the past off ... To illustrate, the grand jury empanelled for the recent county court was, with one or two exceptions, composed of men accounted of the McSween or anti-Dolan party, for it is undeniable that nearly all citizens eligible as grand-jurors are ... of that persuasion. They found nearly 200 indictments, the whole, with a few exceptions, against the Dolan people ... You cannot fail to see what would have come of the trial of the accused - how long they would have lasted - the expenses to a county which has nothing in its treasury ... As it was most of the indicted appeared in court and plead the amnesty in bar [of any prosecution]. Hereafter the labors of grand juries will be confined strictly to offences subsequent to my proclamation."

By July of 1879, Ringite Commander N.A.M. Dudley would be cleared by a corrupt military Court of Inquiry for the murder of Alexander McSween and the arson of his house. Ultimately only Billy was left unpardoned and with a hanging sentence. That's why he told a *Mesilla News* reporter on April 15th, 1881, after his hanging trial: "I think it hard that I should be the only one to suffer the extreme penalty of the law."

There remains a question about the injustice to Billy. Why didn't his attorney, Ira Leonard, do something? Leonard was present to aid the prosecution in that 1879 Grand Jury. But he didn't file a Petition for Billy's pardon, citing either amnesty in bar of prosecution used by Carton and associates, or citing Billy's own fulfilled bargain. By 1880, Leonard certainly did try to arrange a different pardon for Billy through Secret Service Operative Azariah Wild.

One can postulate that Leonard was too traumatized to function properly after just surviving his own Ring assassination attempt on April 25th, 1879 – just a month after his office mate, Huston Chapman's, actual Ring murder. And Leonard also backed away in 1881 after another likely Ring threat. When representing Billy at his Mesilla trial, Leonard had gotten quashed the "Buckshot" Roberts indictment, but then suddenly withdrew and departed.

One can also postulate that Leonard lacked legal sophistication to file for a Pardon Petition. As evidence, is his lackluster consulting with the prosecuting officer in the Dudley Court of Inquiry. Though nothing could have altered the corrupt outcome there, Leonard's tendency to rely on sincerity instead of savvy legal arguing was evident.

More realistic, however, is that Leonard was paralyzed by futility of fighting the Ring. Indicted Ringites could plead for amnesty and get pardoned. But if Billy had done that through Leonard, Judge Bristol would have simply rejected the Petition. Even more daunting would have been formulating that Petition's argument, since it needed anti-Ring contentions linking the killings of Roberts, Brady, and Hindman to mitigation of Billy's having been deputized for arrest of Tunstall's murderers, and the reasons for the Lincoln County War freedom fight. That would have risked Leonard's life, as well as being rejected by Judge Bristol anyway.

And yet more difficult, would have been revealing Wallace's bargain with Billy to argue pardon based on it. It was supposedly secret. It would have ended for Leonard any friendly relationship with Wallace. It would have tempted the Ring's murders of Leonard and Billy, and political revenge against Wallace. Only Billy, committed to the freedom fight against the Ring, had the stomach for such risk-taking.

But the outcome was clear: the only real chance Billy had with Wallace after testifying was Leonard's appealing to Wallace's conscience. And, for Wallace, protecting himself trumped conscience.

Having gone through the travesty of the 1879 Lincoln County Grand Jury which yielded indictments without consequences and all Ringites pardoned, Lew Wallace pretended success. On May 5th, 1879, omitting that he'd reduced Lincoln County citizens to legal impotence, Wallace fictionalized the outcome in a letter to Secretary of the Interior Carl Schurz. It makes clear that only 49 days after his March 17th pardon bargain meeting with Billy, and less than one month after Billy's Chapman testimony fulfilling that bargain, Wallace had no intention of honoring it. Wallace also knew, things were about to get worse. The Dudley Court of Inquiry was starting. So Wallace stuck to the outlaw myth for Schurz, stating: "I have the honor to inform you that all the recent reports, military and otherwise, justify me in saying Lincoln county is enjoying a term of peace … That it is due to the active measures taken [by me] against the outlaws the last month or two cannot be doubted."

Soon Wallace would single out one outlaw for literary impact: Billy the Kid. And in his subsequent years of obsessive articles about the pardon bargain, he would fabricate that the pardon was withheld because Billy had not fulfilled his part.

A future talk will be about Lew Wallace's testimony in the Court of Inquiry for possible court martial of past Fort Stanton Commander N.A.M. Dudley, in which his self-serving lies would be humiliatingly exposed by Dudley's Ringite, vicious, defense attorney, Henry Waldo, the best trial lawyer in the Territory.

TALK 25:
LEW WALLACE'S DUDLEY COURT OF INQUIRY DISASTER
FROM BOOK: *THE LOST PARDON OF BILLY THE KID*
MARCH 2, 2021

This talk gives my revisionist history of how Governor Lew Wallace's disastrous testimony against Fort Stanton's past Commander N.A.M. Dudley doomed his pardon bargain with Billy Bonney. The information is from my book, *The Lost Pardon of Billy the Kid: An Analysis Factoring in the Santa Fe Ring, Governor Lew Wallace's Dilemma, and a Territory in Rebellion.*

There were many reasons why Governor Lew Wallace betrayed his pardon bargain with Billy Bonney, after Billy fulfilled his part by testifying against the Santa Fe Ring murderers of Attorney Huston Chapman. As discussed in Talk 21, Wallace had many character flaws, including monumental selfishness. He also had an Achilles heel: As a Civil War Major General, he was disgraced for failing to arrive with his troops at Shiloh's first day of battle, almost causing the Union's defeat. He earned unforgiving hatred of its commander, General Ulysses S. Grant. It left Wallace obsessed with getting a pardon from Grant, and terrified of angering military brass. It impacted his pardon bargain with Billy Bonney by a coincidence.

Ongoing turmoil after the Lincoln County War, including Chapman's murder seven months after its end, focused citizens' rage at the final Battle's intervening Fort Stanton Commander, Nathan Augustus Monroe Dudley. They knew Chapman had been assassinated in Lincoln to stop his intended prosecution of Dudley for enabling the murder of Alexander McSween and arson of his home, thus aiding defeat of the anti-Ring freedom fighters.

Wallace had been made governor by President Rutherford B. Hayes to pacify the Territory. That caused his dilemma. To do it realistically, would have pitted him against the powerful and vindictive Santa Fe Ring controlling the Territory. They would have destroyed his political future. So, from his October 1st, 1878 arrival, to Chapman's February 18th, 1879 murder, Wallace avoided going to Lincoln. To fake action, he used troops to pursue so-called "outlaws," whom he fabricated as causing the unrest. Billy Bonney was one he pursued. Chapman's murder ended that ploy. Wallace was forced to go to Lincoln. He was forced to take action against Dudley. So he was forced to relive Shiloh's nightmare of conflict with military brass. He was forced to remove Dudley as Fort Stanton's Commander. That forced Wallace to testify against Dudley in his Court of Inquiry for possible court martial, while he still tried to appease the Ring. It failed. Dudley's Ringite lawyer trounced Wallace as an incompetent governor. Back came wounded pride of Shiloh. Back came his attempted escape by denying blame.

Wallace had sunk into his Dudley disaster like walking into quicksand. It started with his first attempt at a quick-fix of the Territorial troubles. On his 44th day as Governor, on November 13th, 1878, he issued an Amnesty Proclamation pardoning everyone in the Lincoln County War, except those indicted. Aware of Commander Dudley's illegal intervention in the final battle, he pardoned troops also. That was step one into the quagmire. Pardon implied wrongdoing. And if Dudley was labeled as guilty, so was the Ring that had used him.

Huston Chapman, as Susan McSween's lawyer, himself had started Wallace's disaster. On October 24th, 1878, he wrote to Wallace; stating: "I desire to call your attention to one person whose actions have been offensive in the extreme to a large number of the best citizens of that County, and that man is Colonel Dudley. I am in possession of facts which make Colonel Dudley criminally responsible for the killing of [Alexander] McSween." Wallace struggled to avoid siding against Dudley. He wrote to New Mexico Territory's Commander, Edward Hatch, that Chapman's accusations were, quote, "incredible;" meaning not believable. Then he blamed locals for wanting Dudley's removal as Commander, not himself. That ploy failed.

Hatch got Dudley to respond. On November 9th, Dudley, being prepared for litigation by the Ring, sent Wallace fake affidavits against Susan McSween's chastity to undermine her charges. Dudley, or Ring boss T.B. Catron writing for him, stated: "I am not here, quietly to submit, and allow such allegations against myself, as your Excellency has seen proper to forward to District Headquarters, without making an unqualified denial."

On November 14th, Wallace responded to Hatch. Trying to placate, he wrote that Dudley's response was, quote: "perfectly satisfactory." That would return to haunt him when he testified against Dudley. Dudley's Ringite lawyer would claim that he'd called the affidavits against Susan McSween "perfectly satisfactory," so had already exonerated Dudley.

On November 29th, Chapman wrote again to Wallace. He added the Ring; writing: "The McSween men are willing to stand their trial ... or to observe your proclamation, provided the other side or "ring" observe it, but they will never allow themselves to be arrested by murderers like Colonel Dudley ... I am now preparing a statement of facts for publication, which, I am sorry to say, will reflect upon you for not coming here in person." That hit Wallace. Father-figures President Hayes and Secretary of the Interior Carl Schurz would realize he was a failure.

Between the Devil and the deep blue sea, Wallace tried to placate Dudley. On November 30th, he proposed a private meeting to explain why he'd pardoned him. Like in Shiloh, Wallace missed the real battle: now it should have been against Dudley and the Ring.

By December 7th, Wallace tried another quick-fix. He wrote to Hatch requesting Dudley's removal as a local irritant. He again blamed complaining Lincolnites. Hatch ignored him.

On December 14th, the Ring sprang its trap in its *Santa Fe Weekly New Mexican*, under the headline "An Open Letter, By Lieutenant Colonel N.A.M. Dudley, 9th Cavalry, to His Excellency Governor Lew Wallace." To preempt accusations of Dudley, it publicly blamed Wallace as a bad governor, garbled the Lincoln County War, blamed so-called "outlaws," and had Dudley's officers vouch for him. Wallace folded. He refused to ruin his future ambitions. His humiliation was starting. Shiloh's specter was rising. His December 16th response was just a friendly invitation to Dudley's officers to meet with him for an explanation.

On December 21st, nervous Wallace did damage control by writing to Secretary of the Interior Carl Schurz. In this first battle with the Ring, Wallace lost. He discredited Huston Chapman, proving that he'd betray to save himself. He wrote: "An individual by the name of Chapman went to the ... town of Lincoln and tried to get up a disturbance, but failed." Wallace also whined that Dudley was upset with him. In three months, Billy Bonney's pardon would depend on this flawed man, whose sole loyalty was to himself.

By December 31st, Wallace had descended deeper into the quicksand. He was in trouble with soldiers - up to Secretary of War George McCrary. By requesting Dudley's removal, he'd inadvertently blamed Dudley's superiors for the charges: General Edward Hatch, Commanding District New Mexico; and above him Major General John Pope, Commanding the Department of Missouri. And the silly reason Wallace had given for insulting them all was Dudley's being irritating. And a removal request by a civilian was frowned-upon. So McCrary backed Dudley, and wrote that Wallace should offer real charges - if he had any.

The Ring read between the lines that Wallace wasn't backing Chapman. Local Ring boss, James Dolan, on December 31st, sent Wallace a letter; stating: "I and many of our Citizens feel Confident that if this man was silenced, the troubles would End." Unconsciously, Wallace agreed, and did nothing to protect Chapman.

What Wallace did do was travel to Colorado to meet his arriving wife and son at the railroad station, and start redecorating the Palace of the Governors. He also toyed with visiting Lincoln. On February 11th, he wrote to New Mexico's Chief Quartermaster, requesting a military escort. That may have accidentally sealed Chapman's assassination in seven days, since the Ring feared Wallace allying with him. On February 18th, Chapman was murdered in Lincoln by James Dolan and Ring thugs Jessie Evans and Billy Campbell.

Wallace's first response to Chapman's murder was blaming outlaws. His sources were an October 6th, 1878 "outlaw" list with Regulators sent to him by Ringite U.S. Marshal John Sherman; and input from James Dolan, whom he'd arrested and put in Fort Stanton. They accused William Bonney "the Kid," and his friend, Yginio Salazar. The Ring especially wanted them exterminated, since both teenagers were primed for anti-Ring rebellion. Wallace, with usual hyperbole, put a reward of $1,000 on "the Kid" -

presumably dead or alive." On February 20th, he ordered Lincoln County Sheriff George Kimbrell to pursue them. Utterly out-of-touch, he directed anti-Ring Kimbrell to use Fort Stanton troops - the same troops that Kimbrell knew had terrorized Lincoln seven months before. With macabre humor, even Commander Dudley joined the chase, reporting on February 24th that it was important to apprehend Bonney alias "Kid," since outlaws were causing, quote: "considerable fright."

On February 27th, Wallace finally reported Chapman's murder to Carl Schurz. Wallace's draft reveals him as an incompetent who lied to hide his mistakes. For Shiloh, he lied that he got wrong orders. The lie now was claiming Chapman's murder was by "notorious characters" and "outlaws." He asked for soldiers to pursue them. One should remember that Schurz and President Hayes knew the Ring was systematically murdering opponents. So Wallace and Washington were merely conducting a charade to keep the Ring secret. And fake outlaws would be scapegoated until only one was left to kill as Billy the Kid. So Wallace now floated to Schurz his fake plan of going to Lincoln to rid it of the "outlaws" causing "the troubles."

Lew Wallace didn't fool Grant County citizens. In 1876, they'd their own rebellion against the Ring. The March 1st *Grant County Herald* ridiculed Wallace for his interview in the *Denver Tribune* in which he said, quote: "he found the Territory in a state of anarchy and confusion ... [and] by systematic management ... he had brought about a state of prolonged peace." The article added snidely about Chapman: "In our telegraphic columns today, we publish an account of another murder committed upon the principal street of the town of Lincoln ... It is charitable to think that Governor Wallace ... supposed a good deal to have been accomplished ... but ... the whole affair looks very much as though he had tried to manufacture capital from misrepresentation." Lying Wallace could not escape mounting humiliation.

Arriving in Lincoln on March 5th, 1879, in what would be a stay till May 15th, Wallace faked action by chasing his so-called "outlaws."

But reality had already struck with Susan McSween's hiring of Attorney Ira Leonard to replace murdered Chapman to continue her litigation against N.A.M. Dudley. On March 4th, Leonard had filed charges against Dudley with Secretary of War George McCrary. And Dudley, under likely recommendation of boss Catron, who had represented him in his two past court martials, requested a military Court of Inquiry at Fort Stanton, assured that it would be rigged.

Wallace knew Ira Leonard from recommending him for a judgeship. Wallace's outlaw myths didn't trick him. On May 20th, 1879, Leonard would write to Wallace about local bosses James Dolan and Lawrence Murphy; quote: "They were a part and parcel of the Santa Fe Ring that has been so long an incubus on the government of this Territory."

On March 7th, Wallace wrote to General Hatch, asking for Dudley's removal as Commander. With Chapman's murder now hanging over him, Hatch complied. And Dudley requested the Court of Inquiry. It would last from May 2nd to July 8th.

On March 13th, Wallace got his only lucky break. He got Billy Bonney's pardon bargain letter, giving teeth to convicting Chapman's murderers by his eye-witness testimony.

On April 4th, Wallace did dishonest damage control by minimizing the looming Dudley Court of Inquiry to Carl Schurz as an "unfortunate" intrusion on his attention for April's Grand Jury to start in 10 days. In fact, Wallace was doing little preparation for either.

In the Grand Jury, Billy's testimony got indictments for Chapman's killers. Wallace not only issued no pardon, but also hid Billy's testimony from Hayes or Schurz. Billy, on his own, then testified against Dudley in the Court of Inquiry from May 28th to 29th. But Wallace never acknowledged that either.

On April 25th, James Dolan tried to assassinate Ira Leonard to hamper the Court of Inquiry beginning on May 2nd. Wallace did nothing. Like Chapman, Leonard annoyingly acted like the voice of conscience which Wallace didn't want to hear.

Wallace was focused on his own crisis: His request for Dudley's removal as Commander, allied him to the Court of Inquiry's prosecution. That meant his attacking a military officer and the Ring. It was the lowest point in his life other than the Battle of Shiloh. And in his corner would be mediocre military prosecutor, Captain Henry H. Humphreys, 15th Infantry at Fort Bliss, assisted by lackluster Ira Leonard. Dudley's attorney was the best trial lawyer in the Territory, Catron's law firm member, Henry Waldo. Unbeknownst to Wallace, the Chief Judge, of the three presiding, was Dudley's best friend, Galusha Pennypacker, from Fort Union.

Wallace testified four days: May 12th to 15th. It was a disaster. Though a witness for the prosecution, he tried to shield Dudley and the Ring. He even blamed the McSween side for causing the trouble. Revealed was that he'd gathered no evidence against Dudley. He hadn't even interviewed Susan McSween. Waldo made humiliatingly clear that he was an incompetent. Here are examples from the court transcript.

On the first day of testimony, May 12th, Prosecutor Henry Humphreys reasonably tried to get Wallace to state charges against Dudley. Asked to elaborate on his March 7th removal request stating that Dudley was an "active partisan," Wallace answered that local people had accused Dudley of killing Alexander McSween.

Waldo attacked. He said Wallace avoided the question. The Court agreed.

So Wallace spewed doubletalk. He said: "The charge is based upon certain acts of Colonel Dudley towards certain individuals, or supposed members of the so called ... McSween party."

Brought up was Wallace's November 14th, 1878 letter to General Hatch saying that Dudley's response to him had been "perfectly satisfactory." Wallace became defensive. He said the charges were by Huston Chapman, not him. He said "satisfactory" meant it was polite that Dudley wrote back to him. He said it didn't apply to Dudley's enclosed affidavits against Susan McSween's chastity.

The first day proved to Henry Waldo that Wallace would be a push-over.

The second day, May 13th, Prosecutor Humphreys questioned Wallace about Dudley's "Open Letter" to the press. Humphreys hoped to get Wallace to list charges that made him pardon Dudley. Instead, Wallace lied wildly. He said the "Open Letter" stopped his getting peace in Lincoln County because it mentioned the affidavits against Susan McSween. That made Chapman demand them from him. Because he refused to hand them over, Chapman made criminal charges against Dudley to rile up Lincolnites. And that caused Chapman's murder. Wallace was hiding the truth that the litigation was about Dudley's Lincoln County War crimes. Chapman was murdered to stop that litigation. The Open Letter was irrelevant. Wallace was betraying the prosecution to save himself.

The third day, May 14th, poor Prosecutor Henry Humphreys tried again to get Wallace to accuse Dudley, asking him what the military had done to make Wallace include them in his Amnesty Proclamation. Instead, Wallace despicably blamed Chapman and Susan McSween. He cast himself as protecting Dudley. He said: "It came to my knowledge, that it was the intention of certain parties living in Lincoln, who I had reason to believe were endeavoring to revive the McSween faction, intending commencement of prosecution of a criminal nature against Colonel Dudley. Mr. Chapman waited upon me in my office at Santa Fe, stated to me that he, amongst others, intended such a course, for which purpose it was his design to resort to the Grand Jury of the next Court. I remonstrated against such a course, but without effect. I then resolved that such should not be done if I could help it, or at least could furnish Colonel Dudley with a plea in case of such prosecution ... I did not stop to consider whether Colonel Dudley was guilty or not guilty in connection with the McSween killing affair. I foresaw if he were indicted, he would be put at a great cost, vexation and harassment, [and] I foresaw he might be confronted by a partisan jury ... I used the word officers, plural, to avoid mentioning specially and singly, Lieutenant Colonel Dudley's name, for that I thought would be offensive to him."

Poor Prosecutor Humphreys tried again. He asked Wallace to list the charges he made to Hatch on March 7th when asking for Dudley's removal. Wallace answered that he had written, quote: "that he, Colonel Dudley, is so compromised by connection with the troubles in the county, that his usefulness in the effort now making to restore order, is utterly gone." He blamed Lincolnites for dreading Dudley after the burning of the McSween house. But lawyer Wallace took no chance of sounding like an accuser. He added: "It was not then pretended that the charges were anything more than hearsay accusations." Wallace knew hearsay was of no legal value. Waldo, of course, objected to Wallace as giving hearsay. The Court upheld his objection.

Then came Henry Waldo's cross-examination. He went after Wallace's "perfectly satisfactory" statement, claiming it proved he backed the affidavits against Susan McSween. Wallace double-talked, and never said he knew they were false and she was credible.

Waldo then embarrassingly exposed Wallace's lack of preparation. Wallace couldn't recall a single report he'd supposedly read on Dudley, or how many.

Then Waldo questioned Wallace about not coming to Lincoln, heading to dereliction of duty (dangerously close to the wound of Shiloh). Waldo hissed, "Had you not been ... continuously in Santa Fe ... from the time of your arrival in the Territory of New Mexico, until the time of your departure for Lincoln?" When poor Prosecutor Humphreys tried to object that it was irrelevant, Waldo scornfully responded: "The witness has testified as to the effect of the open letter upon the people of Lincoln County ... 'T]he object of the question is to show that he had no opportunity of judging the effects of said letter not being present."

The fourth day, May 15th, Henry Waldo continued his cross-examination. Noting that Wallace blamed the "Open Letter" for agitating Susan McSween's friends and causing Chapman's murder, he demanded examples. Wallace repeated his hearsay claim. He said: "My knowledge ... is derived solely upon information received from others." He was intentionally betraying Susan McSween's case to save his skin.

Waldo stated: "In your examination in chief you state you made an investigation as to the situation of affairs in Lincoln County, and as a consequence thereof, reached the conclusion that a considerable portion of the people were suffering from intimidation caused by dread they had of Colonel Dudley. How long were you in the making of that investigation, and what was its extent and nature?" Wallace stated that he talked to people from his March 5th arrival. But everyone was too afraid to give affidavits. So he had none. (Here Wallace was lying. He was actually interviewing people about his outlaw fictions.) Waldo continued: "How many persons did you talk to about the situation of affairs in Lincoln County?" Wallace answered: "I found ... that people who I met, almost without exception, were in dread of the Military Commandant Colonel Dudley. Waldo asked for names. Wallace could only think of Juan Patrón, apparently because he'd been visiting Billy at his house during Billy's sham jailing. Waldo had made Wallace look like a liar or an incompetent.

Waldo then asked Wallace if he'd interviewed Dudley to get rebuttals. Looking stupid, Wallace answered: "I did not."

Then Henry Waldo went for the jugular. He circled back to Wallace's admission that he'd based the charges in his letter of March 7th to General Hatch on hearsay. He then asked if Wallace wanted Hatch to act based on that. Wallace feebly said yes. Waldo had made Wallace look like a fool: using hearsay evidence, having no affidavits, no recall of informers' names, and avoiding Lincoln County. It obviously meant that his testimony was worthless. This was a flash-back to Shiloh's utter failure. Waldo declared that he was finished with the witness.

Poor Prosecutor Humphreys, in redirect, tried to salvage anything. He asked Wallace about the statements he got from Lincolnites. Wallace made things worse. He answered: "I never reduced any of their statements to writing, or had them sworn to. These statements were given to me verbally." So lawyer Wallace had admittedly collected no legally usable evidence against Dudley!

After his testimony, Wallace retreated to Santa Fe; redecorating the Palace of the Governors; and writing *Ben-Hur*, about his hero's pardon from unjust accusation.

Present during Lew Wallace's wretched testimony, Attorney Ira Leonard stayed in touch with him. On June 6th, he wrote to him that he recognized the Court of Inquiry was rigged. He didn't guess that humiliated Wallace had abandoned him, Lincoln County "troubles," and Billy Bonney's pardon. Leonard wrote: "I am thoroughly and completely disgusted ... There is nothing to be looked or hoped from this tribunal, it is a farce on judicial investigation ... This evidence against Dudley would hang a man in any country where right and justice prevailed."

Ignoring Leonard, on June 11th, Wallace wrote to Carl Schurz, to spin boss Catron's misusing his Amnesty Proclamation in the April to May Grand Jury to block prosecution of all indicted Ringites. Hypocrite Wallace pretended it was his own cost-saving plan. He wrote: "This leaves me at liberty to repeat for your better understanding ... that the old factions known respectively as the "Murphy-Dolan" and the "McSween" are as dead organizations; to which may be added now, that my amnesty proclamation has had exactly the effect intended; which was to shear the past off ... To illustrate, the grand jury empanelled for the recent county court was ... composed of men accounted of the McSween or anti-Dolan party, for it is undeniable that nearly all citizens eligible as grand-jurors are ... of that persuasion. They found nearly 200 indictments, the whole, with a few exceptions, against the Dolan people ... You cannot fail to see what would have come of trial of the accused - how long they would have lasted - the expenses to a county ... As it was, most of the indicted appeared in court and plead the amnesty in bar [of further prosecution]. Hereafter the labors of grand juries will be confined strictly to offences subsequent to my proclamation." Then he used the outlaw myth; writing: "[T]he only ... disturbing element remaining to be grappled with is the confederacy of outlaws." Taking no chances with rumor of his stupid testimony, Wallace flippantly declared he didn't want to be involved in local military conflicts because; quote: "They get me into personal quarrels for which life is too short." He concluded with self-praise: "[I]t gives me great satisfaction to report the Territory elsewhere in a prosperous state."

Ira Leonard, unaware that he was abandoned, continued reporting to Wallace on the Court of Inquiry. On June 13th, he agonized that its out-of-control corruption was now blocking even his entering evidence against Dudley. He wrote: "If you ever saw three men [meaning the judges] who strained every effort to protect and shield an old scoundrel this Court have done it."

Since March 21st, Billy had been in his sham jailing in Juan Patrón's house, using that cover to testify against Chapman's murderers in the April Grand Jury to fulfill his pardon bargain with Lew Wallace. It got him no promised pardon. And Ringite District Attorney Rynerson, colluding with Ringite Judge Warren Bristol, changed his venue for his Lincoln County War indictments to Doña Ana County for certain hanging sentence. Nevertheless, for his own anti-Ring agenda, Billy stayed to testify on May 28th and 29th against Dudley at his Fort Stanton Court of Inquiry. On June 17th, certain that staying longer in Lincoln would be fatal, Billy simply left, apparently with Juan Patrón's blessing. Wallace would later lie that it was a jailbreak that proved Billy broke the pardon bargain.

On July 3rd, Wallace continued his mission of protecting himself. For the first time, he mentioned the Ring to Schurz, still nervous that they could injure him. He wrote: "The only thing worth attention is the development of the conspiracy of which I have had knowledge for some time, looking to removal of a number of federal appointees, including myself. It is the expiring flurry of the old ring." So Wallace - knowing that he'd left the Ring unchecked in Lincoln County - implied it was irrelevant since it was "expiring!" And Ring-enabling Schurz just played along. For the complicit Hayes administration, Wallace was achieving with finesse what brutal, removed Governor S.B. Axtell had failed: suppressing citizens without their realizing the malice.

Possibly Wallace's precaution with Schurz came from knowing that the Court of Inquiry was ending, and his disastrous testimony might be relayed to him and Hayes.

In fact, vicious Henry Waldo had a field day with it in his closing argument of July 5th. He certainly proved that the Ring was far from expiring, as Wallace had fabricated to Schurz. Waldo sealed Wallace's humiliation, thereby recycling Shiloh's. And he chillingly revealed that Wallace's secret communications about the Ring were known to its spies. Waldo jeered: "[T]he Governor was in great alarm about the awful 'bug bear' the 'Santa Fe Ring' preventing his confirmation. He wanted to manufacture some political thunder whose reverberation would resound in the halls of the Senate chamber in Washington."

Waldo continued ridiculing Wallace: "Nothing has been accomplished in the least that connects Colonel Dudley with anything which transpired in the town of Lincoln on the occasion of his presence there on the 19th and 20th day of July last, and all that has been truthfully told of his motives and actions reflects the highest credit upon him, as a man and as a soldier. Notwithstanding all this ... [h]e has been branded as a conspirator, a robber and a thief by no less a person than Governor Wallace ... to the Commander of the District.

"Look at this for a moment ... Governor Wallace had been in the county of Lincoln but one day, took no sworn or written testimony, never even inquired of the officers who were present with Colonel Dudley, when he was in Lincoln at the time mentioned.

"Language strong enough and severe enough cannot be employed in denunciation of the hideous and monstrous wickedness of these bad men who united in their efforts to disgrace and ruin a man who had never harmed either of them ... and that man an officer of high rank, and long and distinguished service in the Army ... Here, has Colonel Dudley been forced to submit to the humiliation and mortification of knowing that such charges had been lodged against him with the Department of War in Washington ... Lew Wallace and Ira E. Leonard are alone responsible for this ... harassing case. By their act, this disgrace has been brought upon a pure, humane, and just man ... Time does not remain to Colonel Dudley to clear away the stain, by them placed upon his name and character. The best years of his life are passed and gone, spent in the service of his country ..

"[Governor Wallace] did not come [to Lincoln] to learn the truth ... He came to accomplish the removal of Colonel Dudley ... even if he had to write as evil and malicious a letter as that upon which the removal was effected. Did Governor Wallace seek true knowledge of Colonel Dudley's relations to Lincoln County matters? Why did he not come to officers of the post? ... [H]e ... went directly to Lincoln, and talked with a few rabid and malignant partisans ...

"He wants somebody to lay the blame upon. [His Amnesty Proclamation] was a weak and ridiculous idea in the first place. What the villains who had made a hell of Lincoln County needed was a gallows, not a pardon. The whole truth about that proclamation ... is that just about the time the Governor was in great alarm about the awful "bug bear" the "Santa Fe Ring" preventing his confirmation. He wanted to manufacture some political thunder whose reverberation would resound in the halls of the Senate chamber in Washington ... He had been sent specifically to pacify the troubles in New Mexico. To this, his official announcement of the complete success of his efforts to pacification in Lincoln County is promulgated."

Waldo gloated theatrically: "The foul conspiracy to disgrace and ruin Colonel Dudley concocted by Lew Wallace, Ira E. Leonard, and Sue E. McSween has ended in utter and ignominious failure ... Colonel Dudley comes forth from this fiery ordeal unscathed. No blemish rests on his character, no cloud to darken his fame." So Wallace was once again branded with Shiloh-like accusation of "ignominious failure."

The same day, July 5th, 1879, Chief Judge Galusha Pennypaker, Dudley's best friend, with the other two judges, declared: "In view of the evidence adduced the Court is of the opinion that Lieutenant Colonel Dudley ... has not been guilty of any violation of law or orders, and that the act of proceeding to the town of Lincoln on the 19th day of July 1878 was prompted by the most humane and worthy motives and of good military judgment under exceptional circumstances. The Court is of the opinion that none of the allegations made against Lieutenant Colonel Dudley by His Excellency the Governor of New Mexico or by Ira E. Leonard have been sustained and that proceedings before a court martial are therefore unnecessary."

On July 30th, Wallace did damage control for himself with Carl Schurz. He wrote: "The Dudley investigation is at an end ... If what I hear is true, however, it must have been one of the most extraordinary tribunals ever assembled ... [T]he defense was permitted to prosecute me ... There is consequently no remedy left me but to request that the record be sent for by the Honorable Secretary of War ... and that such matters as may be there found affecting my personal or official honor, I may be furnished an opportunity for denial ... in case the record leaves a harmful doubt against me in the mind of the President."

On August 26th, Wallace got reassurance. Secretary of War George McCrary wrote: "[T]here is nothing in the proceedings of the Court to reflect injuriously upon the course pursued by Governor Wallace." In truth, as long as Wallace left the Santa Fe Ring alone, he satisfied Hayes and his cabinet.

By a September 15th letter to Carl Schurz, Wallace reduced Lincoln County's crisis to, quote, "the killing of outlaws by outlaws," needing no further official mention.

Ira Leonard, abandoned by Wallace, proceeded with Susan McSween's civil suit against Dudley for arson of her house and for libel by defamatory affidavits. But their venue had been changed by Ringite Judge Warren Bristol from knowledgeable Lincoln County to the November 1879 Doña Ana County Grand Jury in Mesilla. Ring death threats prevented Susan from traveling to appear, so Ira Leonard requested a continuance. Instead, on November 18th, Bristol declared her in contempt; forcing her to travel to Mesilla for a court appearance a week later. With Dudley's representation there by Catron's Ringite replacement as U.S. Attorney, Sidney Barnes, and with benefit of Dudley's having been exonerated by the military court, the jury found him not guilty of arson. The libel charge was abandoned. The Ringite *Mesilla News* of December 6th, wrote that after the verdict "a spontaneous outburst of applause came from the large audience."

As we will see in later talks, this would be the court, judge, and populace for jury selection that Billy Bonney, the only Lincoln County War participant without pardon, would face in 1881 to receive his intended Ring hanging sentence.

TALK 26:
BILLY THE KID'S
SECRET SERVICE PARDON BARGAIN
FROM BOOK: *THE LOST PARDON*
OF BILLY THE KID
MARCH 3, 2021

This talk presents my revisionist history of Billy Bonney's Secret Service pardon bargain. The information is from my book, *The Lost Pardon of Billy the Kid: An Analysis Factoring in the Santa Fe Ring, Governor Lew Wallace's Dilemma, and a Territory in Rebellion.*

By the end of May, 1879, Billy Bonney was likely number one on the Santa Fe Ring's hit list. In a Fort Stanton Court of Inquiry, he had just devastatingly testified against the Lincoln County War Battle's commander, N.A.M. Dudley, whose illegal intervention had been for the Ring. And the month before, he'd achieved indictments of Lincoln County's local Ring boss, James Dolan, and Ring hitmen, Jessie Evans and Billy Campbell, for the murder of anti-Ring Attorney Huston Chapman. The latter fulfilled Billy's pardon bargain with Governor Lew Wallace. If honored by Wallace, it would have freed Billy from his Lincoln County War indictments for the Regulator killings of William Brady, George Hindman, and Andrew "Buckshot" Roberts. Ring intimidation had halted Wallace's pardoning. So Wallace would have favored Billy's killing to hide his own betrayal.

Since most of the Regulators had fled the Territory after that lost War, the Ring was rightly suspicious of Billy's motives for testifying and staying. Billy, and his fellow Hispanic freedom fighters, were a good bet for future anti-Ring insurrections. In fact, the day before the Lincoln County War Battle, Billy had sent

what I named the "Regulator Manifesto" to Territorial Ring boss
T.B. Catron's brother-in-law. It stated: "[T]he man who plans
destruction shall have destruction measured on him. Steal from
the poorest or richest American or Mexican, and the full measure
of the injury you do, shall be visited upon the property of Mr.
Catron."

In fact, from the War's end in July of 1878 to his March of
1879 sham jailing for the pardon bargain, Billy had been doing
guerrilla rustling against the Ringites. After he departed the
sham jailing in June, he continued that rustling. Billy sold stock
to non-Ringites: Fort Sumner-area Dan Dedrick (also a
counterfeiter) and Three Rivers rustler and slaughter house
owner, Pat Coghlan. Billy also sold rustled horses in Tascosa,
Texas. His helpers were past Regulator friends Charlie Bowdre
and Tom O'Folliard; and career thieves: Dave Rudabaugh, Tom
Pickett, and Billy Wilson - likely met through Dan Dedrick, who
used Wilson and Pickett to pass fake bills.

Protected by his partisans, Billy avoided murder by the Ring
almost through 1880. That likely elicited use of Ring co-boss,
Stephen Benton Elkins, in Washington, D.C. In September of
1880, James Brooks, Chief of the Secret Service, was contacted.
The Secret Service was founded during the Civil War by President
Abraham Lincoln and Secretary of War Edward Stanton to combat
a counterfeit money problem. Added was power to pursue other
crimes, and even to kill. By September 10th, 1880, Special
Operative Azariah Wild, one of only 40 in the country, was sent to
New Mexico Territory. He was unaware that his real mission was
political assassination. He was sent to Lincoln, where his primary
minders would be Catron's brother-in-law, Edgar Walz; and local
Ring boss, James Dolan. Lazy and gullible Wild, doing minimal
personal investigation or even leaving Lincoln, would be tricked
by them that Billy headed a huge rustling and counterfeiting gang
out of Fort Sumner. That would result in Wild's backing Texan
posses under Sheriff-elect Pat Garrett, whom he made a Deputy
U.S. Marshal, to capture or kill Billy.

But the Ring's scheme almost failed. In Lincoln, Wild soon met
a relatively new resident: Attorney Ira Leonard. Leonard, after
assisting prosecution of past Commander N.A.M. Dudley in
nearby Fort Stanton, had remained there. He offered to help Wild
pursue counterfeiters.

Ira Leonard had become Billy's attorney after being impressed by his testimony in the 1879 Grand Jury in Lincoln and at Dudley's Court of Inquiry. Leonard had aided Billy's pardon bargain with Lew Wallace by updating Wallace about Billy's testimony. Wallace, fearing Ring backlash, nevertheless, had withheld the pardon.

So Leonard tried again to get a pardon for Billy. He offered to Azariah Wild the same bargain: Billy's eye-witness testimony against criminals in exchange for a pardon. Now the criminals were the counterfeiters. Also relevant to the outcome was that Leonard apparently told Billy about the Secret Service, and that Wild wrote daily reports to his Chief, James Brooks.

The counterfeiters were Dan Dedrick, located 12 miles south of Fort Sumner at his Bosque Grande Ranch, and his brothers, Mose and Sam, and a William West at a livery stable in White Oaks. Connected to the livery were Billy Wilson and Tom Pickett for passing bills. Dedrick also bought cattle with counterfeit bills, then resold them for good money. And his men also made purchases with bills in Lincoln. Billy's connection was using Dan Dedrick and the livery as outlets for rustled stock, and using Wilson and Pickett for rustling. Since Wild mentioned in a report that Dan Dedrick was rumored to have a press for printing bills, Billy may have also known about it.

Ira Leonard told Wild about Billy's pardon bargain with Lew Wallace, explaining Billy's exclusion in Wallace's Amnesty Proclamation. Wild was left poised to save Billy's life by a pardon which Wallace might have backed, since it freed him of its responsibility.

Wild described the new pardon option in his report to Chief Brooks on October 8th, 1880. He wrote: "In my report of October 5th, I spoke of an outlaw whose name was Antrom alias Billy Bonney. During the Lincoln County War he killed men on the Indian Reservation for which he has been indicted in the Territory and the United States Court." [Note that Wild garbled Leonard's information. The Territorial indictments were for the Regulator killings of William Brady and George Hindman. The "United States Court" or federal indictment, was for the Andrew "Buckshot" Roberts killing, made by U.S. Attorney Catron against the Regulators and claimed as occurring on federal land of the Mescalero Indian Reservation.] Wild continued: "Governor Wallace has issued a proclamation granting immunity to those not indicted, but as Antrom has been indicted, the proclamation did not cover his ... case and he ... has been in the mountains as an outlaw ever since ... Governor Wallace has since written Antrom's attorney on the subject saying he should be let go but has failed to put it on shape that satisfied Judge Leonard Antrom's attorney." [Note that Leonard confirmed that he had a letter from Wallace about the pardon, but it was somehow inadequate. This letter is lost. As to it being inadequate, Wild may be garbling that Wallace didn't file for the pardon in a court of law. In fact, as discussed in Talk 24, cagey Wallace avoided putting the full bargain in writing. Also revealed by Wild's statement is that loyal Leonard had continued to pursue Billy's pardon with Wallace. Also implied, is that Leonard may have been unaware of Catron's May 1st, 1879 court appearance, in which he simply ignored the Amnesty Proclamation's exclusion for those indicted, and got pardons for all Ringites indicted in the Lincoln County War. If Leonard had done that for Billy, Wallace may have let it go through, since he wouldn't be responsible.]

Wild also showed his early manipulations by his Ringite handlers; writing: "It is believed, and in fact is almost known that ... Antrom is one of the leading members of this gang."

Wild continued: "Antrom has recently written a letter to Judge Leonard which has been shown to me in confidence that leads me to believe that we can use Antrom in these cases provided Governor Wallace will make good his written promises, and the U.S. Attorney [Sidney Barnes] will allow the case pending in the U.S. Court to slumber and give ... Antrom one more chance to reform." [Note that Wild confirms written promises, and is prepared to get Wallace to grant Billy's pardon. Importantly, Wild realizes that Catron's federal indictment for the Roberts killing could not be pardoned by Wallace. It required a Presidential pardon. That's why Wild added that he could intervene to get federal prosecutor, U.S. Attorney Sidney Barnes, to simply ignore the federal case.]

Wild added: "I have promised nothing and will not except to receive any propositions ... Leonard and his client see fit to make ... Leonard has written Antrom to meet him ... The chances are that the conversation will take place within the next week when I will report fully to you and submit whatever propositions they see fit to make to US. Attorney Barnes for such action as he deems proper to take."

Reporting for October 9th, Wild provided a copy of his letter to U.S. Attorney Sidney Barnes with the new pardon bargain for Billy. He also revealed that Ira Leonard had given him information about the counterfeiters in White Oaks and at Dan Dedrick's ranch - likely from Billy to advertise his value for the new pardon bargain. Additionally, Billy wrote himself to confirm the bargain, and Wild answered it. [Note that Billy's letter and Wild's response are lost.] But Wild also reported negative Ringite input about Billy. This demonstrated that not-too-sharp Leonard had failed to inform Wild about the Ring, Billy's lawman or Regulator roles, or the Lincoln County War freedom fight. So Wild ended up informing the Ring, via U.S. Attorney Barnes, boss Catron's close associate, about Billy's new possible pardon. Wild wrote: "William Antrom alias Billy Kid is at Fort Sumner and is a member of the clan [meaning gang]. I have recently seen a letter written by him in which he expresses himself as being tired of challenging the officers. The letter has been answered and the chances are that I will meet with him under circumstances which may bring about good results ... [I]f able to use Antrom alias Billy Kid on reasonable terms ... I am satisfied full fifty arrests will follow." [Note that Ira Leonard had carelessly arranged a face-to-face meeting of Billy with Wild, leaving Billy open to capture.]

Reporting for October 11th, Wild revealed the Ring's push-back by naming Billy, and other Regulators, as outlaws. Wild wrote that he intended to arrest Billy, Charlie Bowdre, Josiah Scurlock, and Tom O'Folliard. To U.S. Attorney Barnes, Wild wrote: "It may be well to send down warrants for the other parties who stand indicted in U.S. Court, and who are making Fort Sumner their headquarters."

On October 16th, Billy, more canny than Leonard, intervened himself. He robbed the stagecoach carrying Wild's reports. He would have read October 11th's about arresting him and other Regulators. He realized the Wild meeting would be a trap. He backed out.

So the second pardon chance was lost because of Ira Leonard's failure to properly negotiate or to clarify Billy's anti-Ring role. Wild did not mention it again in his reports. Instead, he added stagecoach robbing to his fictional counterfeiting-rustling gang's crimes. Much like Lew Wallace, Wild, who was accomplishing nothing, needed "the Kid" to fake action.

For his report for October 20th, Wild reported Billy's mail theft. He requested a posse to seize the gang in Fort Sumner. Wild wrote: "In this mail I had several reports which if taken and read as they must have been as both mail pouches were cut open and the contents scattered about the ground. If this is as I believe it must be, the plans of our capture and my mission here is as well known to them as it is to myself. I have respectfully notified the U.S. Attorney [Sidney Barnes] of this gang of men, and their headquarters being at Fort Sumner. I have also asked for warrants to arrest these men and for Commissions for such men as are willing to assist me in the making of the arrests ... The parties Kid, Wilson, O'Follier [meaning O'Folliard] and Picket who are undoubtedly the ones who robbed the mail on the 17th [Wild meant the 16th] are out at a ranch twelve miles from Fort Sumner [referenced is Dan Dedrick's ranch] ... [They]can be taken at any time unless my reports taken from the mail frighten them away." Note that Billy is now listed first, as Wild lumps together Regulators with Dan Dedrick's counterfeiters.

For October 22nd, duped Wild was now writing about the "Wilson and Kid gang" linked to the mail theft. He wrote: "The man who was driving the mail back at the time it was robbed ... recognized several of the gang as being the Wilson and Kid gang who done the robbing of the mail on the night of the 16th instant."

So Billy lost his last chance at a pardon, and became the focus of duped Operative Azariah Wild's outlaw myth witch hunt, discussed in another talk.

TALK 27:
SECRET SERVICE PURSUIT OF BILLY THE KID
FROM BOOK: *THE LOST PARDON OF BILLY THE KID*
MARCH 6, 2021

This talk presents my revisionist history of the Secret Service's pursuit of Billy Bonney. The information is from my book, *The Lost Pardon of Billy the Kid: An Analysis Factoring in the Santa Fe Ring, Governor Lew Wallace's Dilemma, and a Territory in Rebellion.*

In July of 1878, after the corrupt political cabal of the Santa Fe Ring won the final battle of the Lincoln County War by partisan use of troops, it expected the anti-Ring fighters to flee the Territory. Planned was hiding the Ring's role and fabricating the freedom fight as just outlawry.

But the Ring's cover-up was jeopardized by teenaged zealot, Billy Bonney. In June of 1878, he'd given a deposition identifying Ringite murderers of his boss, John Tunstall, to Washington investigator Frank Warner Angel. By that October he was guerrilla rustling from Ringites, as he'd promised in his wartime "Regulator Manifesto" against Ring boss Thomas Benton Catron. It stated: "Steal from the poorest or richest American or Mexican, and the full measure of the injury you do, shall be visited upon the property of Mr. Catron." On October 24th, his bill of sale to a Henry Hoyt, in Tascosa, Texas, was for a sorrel horse named Dandy Dick. It had been Regulator-killed Ringite Sheriff William Brady's, and likely stolen by Billy from one of the Ring's Lincoln County ranches.

Boss Catron's biggest fear was of a Hispanic anti-Ring uprising. The Lincoln County War came close. Bi-cultural Billy and his Hispanic partisans were capable of doing another one.

By February of 1879, local Lincoln Ring boss, James Dolan, made strategic peace overtures to teenaged Billy. But hopes of quieting him ended at the night of their February 18th meeting, with a chance encounter in Lincoln's dark street of Attorney Huston Chapman. Chapman was initiating prosecution of Ringite Commander N.A.M. Dudley for enabling the Lincoln County War's murder of anti-Ring leader, Alexander McSween, and arson of his home. Eliminating Chapman was Dolan's priority. Billy thus was eye-witness to Chapman's murder by Dolan, and Ring thugs, Jessie Evans and Billy Campbell. Ended was any chance of reconciliation.

By March 13th, 1879, Billy offered new Governor, Lew Wallace, his testimony against Chapman's murderers in that April's Grand Jury in exchange for a pardon for his Lincoln County War indictments. He did testify, and, to the Ring's presumed horror, got Chapman's killers indicted. Not losing momentum, the next month, in May, Billy gave devastating testimony against Dudley in his Court of Inquiry for possible court martial. Then, before the Ring could transport him to Mesilla for a hanging trial, Billy departed his sham Lincoln jailing in his Wallace pardon bargain, and, once again, disappeared into secret safe havens of his partisans.

From the Ring's vantage, the sole good to come out of Billy's 1879 anti-Ring onslaught was confirmation that self-protecting Governor Wallace wouldn't pardon him. That stimulated the Ring's plot to capture Billy for hanging, or kill him outright. A complication was loyalist New Mexicans' refusal to join the hunt. But Catron had laid its groundwork with his June 21st, 1878 federal indictment Number 411 of Regulators: "The United States versus Charles Bowdre, Josiah Scurlock, Henry Brown, William Bonney alias Henry Antrim alias the Kid, John Middleton, Frederick Waite, Jim French, and George Coe for the murder of Andrew "Buckshot" Roberts."

In 1880, the Ring likely used its Washington, D.C. co-boss: Stephen Benton Elkins. At Catron's likely instigation, James Brooks, Chief of the Secret Service was contacted. As a Treasury Department branch, it focused on counterfeiting. So that was the claim. Reporting a few bad bills to Brooks was the Ring's Lincoln County sub-boss: James Dolan. Indicted for the murders of John

Tunstall and Huston Chapman, but never prosecuted, Dolan had taken over Tunstall's Lincoln store. It's possible that Chief Brooks knew the mission was political assassination. The Secret Service had broad powers to pursue other crimes, pay informers, and kill. But the assigned Special Operative, 45 year old Azariah Wild, was kept in the dark. Based in New Orleans, he had little knowledge of the West. He got the case on September 10th, and stayed in the Territory till December 23rd.

Lazy and gullible Wild did little investigating, as evidenced by his daily written reports to Chief Brooks. Instead, he stayed mostly in Lincoln, where he relied for information on Dolan; Catron's brother-in-law, Edgar Walz; and Catron's local agents. As discussed in Talk 26, through Billy Bonney's attorney, Ira Leonard, Wild initially considered a pardon bargain for Billy in exchange for his testimony against the counterfeiters. That ended when Wild told his Ring minders, including U.S. Attorney Sidney Barnes. Wild was then led to believe that Billy headed a huge rustling-counterfeiting gang out of Fort Sumner. So Wild farcically pursued this imaginary gang with men he appointed as Deputy U.S. Marshals, with Lincoln County Sheriff-elect Pat Garrett as leader. As Wild inflated gang numbers, he finally became paranoid that they were after him, and included famous outlaw, Jesse James.

The actual counterfeiters were Dan Dedrick, located 12 miles south of Fort Sumner in his Bosque Grande Ranch, and his partners in a White Oaks livery stable: his brothers, Mose and Sam, and a William West. From it also operated their distributors of fake bills: Billy Wilson, Thomas Cooper, and Tom Pickett. Dedrick's modus operandi was buying cattle with counterfeit bills, then reselling them for good money. His men also made occasional purchases with bills in Lincoln. Dedrick might also have had a printing press for bills, which Wild learned early-on, but abandoned when redirected to Billy. Billy's connection to the counterfeiters was using Dan Dedrick as one outlet for rustled stock, and using Wilson and Pickett for rustling. That rustling hook was also used by Catron to attack his ranching competition in the Tularosa Valley: Pat Coghlan. Coghlan was another non-Ring source used by Billy to sell stock. So, in one of his reports, tricked Wild said the "gang" had two ranches: one 75 five miles from Fort Sumner (that was Coghlan's), the other 12 miles from Fort Sumner (that was Dedrick's).

Key is that without Wild and his puppet lawman, Pat Garrett, using Secret Service-funded spies and Texan possemen, Billy would never have been captured for his Mesilla hanging trial. Wild sealed Billy's tragic and unjust fate.

One can trace Azariah Wild's hoodwinking in his reports to Chief Brooks.

Wild's earliest reports in the Territory show that he first correctly identified counterfeit bill distributors - whom he calls "passers of the queer" - as William Wilson and a Thomas Cooper.

For September 20th, Wild reported from Santa Fe, after meeting with Ringite U.S. Attorney Sidney Barnes and James Dolan, who came as the victimized Lincoln merchant who got a counterfeit $100 bill. They garbled the Lincoln County War to make Wild think the counterfeiters were responsible. Wild wrote: "Thomas Cooper and William Wilson are amongst the worst characters in Lincoln County where there have been over forty murders committed within the past two years, and not a single arrest made." Wild wrote that Dolan, quote: "has offered to render me any assistance possible, and has named several parties on whom I can rely to assist in making the arrests." By September 24th, Wild was introduced to Edgar Walz, Catron's brother-in-law. So, from arrival, Wild was controlled by the Ring.

On October 3rd, Wild met with James Dolan in Lincoln to see the counterfeit $100 bill. But he strayed enough to meet Attorney Ira Leonard in town. From that meeting, would soon come Leonard's ill-fated pardon attempt for Billy.

On October 4th, Wild reported that William Wilson had also passed a counterfeit $100 bill to a Lincoln merchant and to a Fort Stanton post trader firm.

On October 5th, Wild's manipulation, likely by Dolan, progressed to accusing Billy Wilson of rustling in addition to counterfeiting. Wilson was then linked to Billy. Wild wrote: "William Antrom alias William Bonney alias Billy Kid is an outlaw in the mountains here, who came here from Arizona after committing a murder there ... with whom these cattle thieves meet, and by many it is believed that they (the cattle thieves and shovers of the queer) receive the counterfeit money." Wild doubted, writing: "I have found no evidence so far to support their suspicions."

On October 8th, Wild reported Billy's pardon option to Chief Brooks. He explained that Governor Wallace's Amnesty

Proclamation excluded Billy, since he'd already been indicted. Wild also recognized that Wallace couldn't pardon Billy for Catron's federal indictment. But Wild was optimistic that a pardon could be worked out if U.S. Attorney Barnes simply ignored the federal indictment. Wild planned a meeting with Billy and Leonard. But he also met with Ringite William Delaney, Fort Stanton's post trader, as recommended by Edgar Walz. Colluding Delaney was cited by Wild: "[He] thinks Antrom alias Billy Bonney to be one of the gang."

On October 9th, Wild revealed information on actual counterfeiters from Ira Leonard, likely advertising Billy's knowledge, and showing a letter of intent by Billy. Wild also informed U.S. Attorney Barnes about the pardon plan.

On October 11th, Wild's report reflected Ring influence. He requested arrest warrants for Billy and other Regulators. By October 14th, Wild was tricked into believing that the counterfeiters were in a gang with Billy in Fort Sumner. He called them: "a terror to the whole country."

By October 16th, Billy, having determined the mail route for Wild's reports, robbed the stagecoach to get them. He would have read Wild' report for October 11th stating: "It may be well to send down warrants for the other parties who stand indicted in U.S. Court, and who are making Fort Sumner their headquarters." Billy realizing his meeting with Wild would be a trap, refused it.

On October 17th, still unaware of the mail theft, Wild, still in Lincoln, continued to report the Ring's focus on Billy. He noted: "William Antrom alias Billie Bonnie alias 'Billie Kid': Indicted in 3rd District of U.S. Court for the murder of the Indian Agent." This was Wild's garbling of the "Buckshot" Roberts killing within the Mescalero Indian Reservation. Wild added: "There are many more men connected with this gang whose names I have not learned but are making Fort Sumner and vicinity their headquarters."

On October 20th, Wild reported the mail theft, accusing Billy, Billy Wilson, Tom O'Folliard, and Tom Pickett. He wrote that reading of his reports meant; quote: "the plans of ... my mission here is as well known to them as it is to myself." He added that he'd been told that Lincoln County Sheriff George Kimbrell, quote, "played cards and drank with [Billy] repeatedly." And Wild named his imaginary band the "Wilson and Kid gang."

By October 22nd, Wild, still in Lincoln, to justify his fruitless investigation, now accepted any Ringite input to inflate his

"Wilson and Kid gang," which be blamed for any Territorial rustling.

For October 28th, still in Lincoln, duped Wild reported, quote: "I am now perfectly confident that there is a counterfeiting gang here who are making counterfeit $100 – and $50 – notes as I am of anything that I do not know absolutely certain, and that I have not seen with my own eyes ... The force of desperados now at Fort Sumner, the headquarters of the gang, numbers twenty six. They openly say that they number sixty two in Lincoln County and defy the authorities." Wild then fused the Dedrick counterfeiting with the Ring's outlaw fables. He wrote: "All the outlaws or nearly all, have been driven out of Texas and Arizona, and concentrated at Fort Sumner ... They have a band of their men out stealing horses, cattle, robbing mails ... whilst the balance of their force remain at the ranch guarding stock they have stolen." Note that Wild added "robbing the mails" to his fake gang's crimes, to cover Billy's seizing his reports. Wild also updated that mail robbery: "I am informed this day ... that a lady passenger who was along at the time the stage was robbed near Fort Sumner ... recognized [William Wilson] and William Antrom alias "Billy Bony" as two of the robbers who robbed her and the mails."

By his October 31st, report, still from Lincoln, Wild hysterically decided that he was in another Lincoln County War! And he revealed his power to kill. He wrote: "If things are not looked to [by arrests] ... soon it will end in another 'Lincoln County War.' " He added that once he got warrants, using White Oaks men, he could, quote: "arrest or kill the whole business."

The Ring had another problem. It needed a Ring-beholden Lincoln County Sheriff. Ringite George Peppin had quit after conducting the Lincoln County War. His replacement, George Kimbrell, was anti-Ring. Groomed by the Ring for 1880's upcoming election had been Pat Garrett, an unskilled, 30 year old, depressive, alcoholic, past murderer and ex-buffalo hunter living in Fort Sumner. To qualify, he'd resettled in Lincoln County's Roswell. Pre-election, Azariah Wild assisted in advertising him as a law-and-order candidate to new White Oaks settlers, unaware of Lincoln County War issues. When Garrett beat Kimbrell, Wild made him a Deputy U.S. Marshal to have Territory-wide jurisdiction to capture the "Kid gang." Since Garrett had known Billy in Fort Sumner since arriving there in early 1878, one can presume that he went along for the life-changing opportunity, but knew the gang was nonexistent.

Having recruited Pat Garrett and mob-mentality White Oaks residents, Azariah Wild decided to attack. For November 4th, still in Lincoln, he wrote to Chief Brooks: "I am now engaged in making preparations to get fifty men together to go to Fort Sumner and arrest this gang of men."

For his November 6th report, still in Lincoln, Wild was in a paranoid tizzy about his swelling gang, with its, quote, "leaders ... William Wilson and ... 'Billy Kid.' " And Ringite Judge Warren Bristol gleefully issued arrest warrants for this Secret Service dupe. Wild wrote: "From every indication there is no scare amongst this gang or they are calculating to make a stand at Fort Sumner and fight. They are known to be twenty nine in number ... Judge Bristol ...said he would issue warrants for parties who have been engaged in violating the United States law ... I will soon be in readiness to go to Fort Sumner ... The parties who robbed the mail or who were the leaders of it was William Wilson and William Antrom alias 'Billy Bony' alias 'Billy Kid.' "

Reporting for November 10th, still in Lincoln, Wild met with Garrett to plan the raid on Fort Sumner against, quote, "the worst ... gang of men that this country has."

For November 14th, still in Lincoln, Wild described using a White Oaks man, James Bell, "to make a deal with [a counterfeiter] if possible." (Note that, on the 28th, Bell would be a posseman involved in killing fellow posseman Jim Carlyle in friendly fire when ambushing Billy at Greathouse's ranch, and would then blame Billy for the killing. Bell was later deputized by Pat Garrett as Billy's pre-hanging guard in Lincoln, and was killed by Billy in his jailbreak.)

For November 18th and 20th, still in Lincoln, Wild reported hiring Garrett's friend, Barney Mason, Peter Maxwell's Fort Sumner foreman, to spy there. Importantly, Mason revealed an actual plot of counterfeiter, Dan Dedrick. It had nothing to do with Billy. But Wild added Billy by using Mason's input that Billy rustled with Billy Wilson. Wild wrote: "It appears from the statements of Garrett and Mason that ... Mason is an experienced stockman and is now ... in the employ of a man named Maxwell who resides at Fort Sumner. [Mason] states that a few days ago one Daniel Dedrick who resides at Bosque Grande, and who has an interest with his brother Samuel Dedrick and a [William] West in a livery stable at White Oaks came to him and proposed [to hire him to take $30,000 counterfeit money to Texas, buy cattle there, take them to a place near Mexico to Dedrick and West, then leave the country] ... Mason states that William Wilson boards at his house when at Fort Sumner ... [And Mason states] [t]hat William Wilson and Billy Kid left about the 15th instant with sixty head of stolen horses and went down the Canadian River to be gone two or three weeks ... [T]hey would probably return to his house when he would turn them over to Patrick F. Garrett Deputy U.S. Marshall and Sheriff."

Tricked White Oaks men, having gotten Pat Garrett elected Sheriff by their majority voting to eliminate "the Kid gang," were primed for action. But unaware, Billy still brought rustled horses to the Dedrick's livery there. The locals formed the White Oaks posse to capture him.

On November 22nd, they ambushed Billy and his companions near White Oaks at their Coyote Spring campsite; but firing wildly, they merely killed two of their horses.

Billy's group escaped to "Whiskey Jim" Greathouse's ranch, about 40 miles to the north. There, at November 28th, the posse ambushed them again. When Billy offered to negotiate, they sent in a Jim Carlyle. But Carlyle panicked, leapt out a window, and was killed in friendly fire as mistaken for Billy. The posse then retreated. But Billy finally realized his danger. The posse later burned down Greathouse's ranch, and blamed Carlyle's killing on Billy.

For November 23rd, Azariah Wild, having relocated to Pat Garrett's Roswell home, and never having gone to Fort Sumner, reported his fables to Chief Brooks. For the Coyote Spring ambush, his "Billy Kid" was now leader of the "Kid force," outnumbering White Oaks men. He snidely added: "There is talk of 'Judge Lynch' trying them at last account."

For November 26th, still in Garrett's house, Wild planned an imaginary battle, with Garrett using Texan possemen. Wild reported that they would, quote, "press the "Rustlers" from the White Oaks back into Fort Sumner and then surround the place with forces from above and below."

For his November 27th report, Wild, still at Garrett's Roswell house, had worked himself into terror of his imaginary gang. His only real information had come from Barney Mason, saying that

Dan Dedrick had backed out of the cattle-for-counterfeit-money deal. Wild, lost in paranoid fantasies, wrote to Chief Brooks: "I will respectfully state that I am very impatient to get away from here ... At the present time I am entirely cut off from reaching the rail road by these outlaws and will have to employ a guard unless

I remain until arrests are made and go along to Santa Fe with them."

For November 29th, still at Garrett's house, Wild wrote that he was setting out with, quote, "an armed and mounted force of twenty men under command of Deputy U.S. Marshal Garrett." With grim paranoia, he added: "It is believed that there will be blood shed when ever our men come up with the main gang."

For November 30th, still at Garrett's house, Wild reported the Greathouse ranch ambush, and embellished fabrications. He wrote: "Information has reached me this day that William Wilson et al of their gang numbering 17 were run into Greathouse's Ranch. That the house was surrounded by ... a posse numbering in all 13. One of the posse named Carlisle ... was one of the leaders ... and after a little talk with the parties on the inside of the house he was induced to go in. Soon as he was inside of the house he was murdered. Soon after Carlisle was murdered William Wilson and his gang made a rush out of the house, and made their escape under cover of the night."

For December 1st, Wild reported that he had actually remained in Garrett's Roswell house when Garrett left, quote, "with a posse to go to Fort Sumner."

For December 2nd, Wild hysterically decided that the gang had come to Roswell after him! He wrote: "Several of William Wilson gang of men have been seen near this place this day. It is feared trouble is brewing ... I am unable to get out of this place with safety."

On December 3rd, Wild, still in Garrett's house, reported ridiculously that Garrett was apparently arresting random people - like ones in, quote, "a cave some twenty miles from Fort Sumner." Lacking real arrests - or even a real gang - Wild whined to his Chief: "There has been cold weather and snow since the 20th of September to say nothing of being away from my family and almost severed from civilization. I ... hope you will ... not place the blame of the delay on me." Wild added that his work was appreciated by locals, unaware that the appreciation was by the Ring, now poised to kill Billy Bonney.

For December 5th, paranoid Wild, still in Garrett's house, reported: "The outlaws have divided up and have men on every road leading from Lincoln County to the rail road."

For December 7th, Wild, still in Garrett's house, tracked his phantom and migratory gang to Lincoln. He reported: "They left

going in the direction of the Capitan Mountains where it is believed their main force is."

For December 9th, Wild wrote that Garrett had captured "a large number of stolen horses and cattle." This was Wild's exaggeration of what Billy himself reported in a letter to Lew Wallace on December 12th: that two of his mules had been stolen by Garrett from the Fort Sumner area ranch of a Thomas Yerby. Garrett, unlike Wild, knew his job was to hunt just one man. Wild added to Chief Brooks: "[T]he "rustlers" ... have men on two out of three roads ... I am going to leave here for headquarters first occasion that presents itself to get away with safety."

By December 23rd, Wild was departing New Mexico Territory, en route to New Orleans, and reporting from Santa Fe about Garrett's pursuit of the, quote, "Kid and Wilson gang." For impact, he added Jesse James. He wrote: "Deputy Marshal P.F. Garrett has killed one of the Kid and Wilson gang, and badly wounded another in attempting to arrest them. He is still in pursuit of the balance of the outlaws: Jessie James is surely there under the name of Campbell."

On December 24th, Wild, in Santa Fe, met with Lew Wallace, his fellow outlaw fabricator, happy to piggy-back on Wild's concoctions. Wild wrote: "I called on Governor Wallace who was anxious to know the situation and stated such facts as I know. He at once said 'tell Mr Garrett to follow these men any place in the territory and tell him I say so.'"

On January 1st, 1881, back in New Orleans, Wild reported for December 24th: "I have this day received information ... that Deputy U.S. Marshal P.F. Garrett has the Kid and Wilson gang of outlaws at his mercy and that he will either kill or arrest them."

On January 2nd, from New Orleans, Wild wrote to Chief Brooks: "Information on the arrest of William Wilson, William Antrom alias Billy the Kid, with several members of their gang by Deputy U.S. Marshal Patrick F. Garrett has reached me."

Thus, in a little over three months from case assignment to departure from New Mexico Territory, Azariah Wild had collected only a few counterfeit $100 bills, had not pursued real counterfeiters or Dan Dedrick's printing press, had sabotaged real testimony against counterfeiters by Billy Bonney, and had never gone to Fort Sumner. He had merely manufactured an imaginary counterfeiting-rustling-mail-robbing mega-gang. Real counterfeiter, Dan Dedrick, had escaped to California. But foolish incompetent Wild had achieved the Ring's goal: empowering a lawman, Pat Garrett, to capture Billy Bonney, or give a gloss of legitimacy to murdering him.

Garrett, carrying out his real assignment of killing Billy, on December 19th, had ambushed Billy and his small group when they rode into Fort Sumner in a snowstorm. Garrett missed Billy, but fatally shot Tom O'Folliard. On December 21st, Garrett and a few possemen tracked them as they tried to escape the Territory. Billy's group stopped 16 miles from Fort Sumner at Stinking Springs's windowless, stacked stone, line cabin for Peter Maxwell's sheepherders. At dawn of the 22nd, Garrett shot dead Charlie Bowdre, thinking he was Billy when he emerged. Garrett then settled on capture, transporting Billy, Billy Wilson, Tom Pickett, and Dave Rudabaugh to the Las Vegas jail, on the way to the Santa Fe jail.

In later talks, I'll present Governor Lew Wallace's last chances to pardon Billy Bonney.

TALK 28:
BILLY BONNEY'S 1880 LETTER TO LEW WALLACE
FROM BOOK: *THE LOST PARDON OF BILLY THE KID*
MARCH 8, 2021

This talk presents my revisionist perspective on the only letter Billy Bonney sent to Governor Lew Wallace in 1880. The information is from my book, *The Lost Pardon of Billy the Kid: An Analysis Factoring in the Santa Fe Ring, Governor Lew Wallace's Dilemma, and a Territory in Rebellion.*

On December 12th, 1880, Billy Bonney sent a long, strange, and unique letter to New Mexico Territory Governor Lew Wallace. It sheds light on the real Billy the Kid.

The letter stemmed from Billy's March of 1879 letters and meetings with Wallace to make a pardon bargain for annulling his Lincoln County War indictments. He kept his part, which was testifying that April against murderers of Attorney Huston Chapman. But Wallace issued no pardon, as discussed in Talk 22 Worse, by 1880, Wallace was backing the Santa Fe Ring's Secret Service pursuit of Billy, as discussed in Talk 27.

By that December 12th, however, Billy knew only that a Secret Service Operative named Azariah Wild was in the Territory pursuing counterfeiters. Since he wasn't one, he didn't think Wild was after him. He'd learned about Wild, in October of 1880, through his attorney, Ira Leonard's, trying get him a new pardon bargain through Wild. It involved Billy's testifying against the counterfeiters in exchange for it. When Wild's Ring handlers found out, they convinced Wild that Billy was in the counterfeiting gang and should be arrested at the pardon meeting. Billy discovered that plot by robbing the mail coach of Wild's daily reports to the Secret Service. So he backed out of the pardon negotiation. But he must have been perplexed and angry about his fictionalized outlawry.

By November, ominous events were massing. But Billy was unaware they focused on him. Promoted by Azariah Wild, past buffalo hunter, Pat Garrett, won the Lincoln County Sheriff's election. Billy had met Garrett in Fort Sumner in 1878. He would have thought Garrett's jurisdiction was limited to Lincoln County. He didn't know that Wild also got Garrett appointed as a Deputy U.S. Marshal for Territory-wide power to capture or kill him. By November 22nd, White Oaks settlers, agitated by Wild's and Garrett's publicizing of a fictional Billy the Kid rustling-counterfeiting gang, made a posse. They ambushed Billy and his few companions at Coyote Spring near their town. Murderously shooting, they killed two of the group's horses. But the men escaped. They stopped at the ranch of "Whisky Jim" Greathouse. On November 28th, the posse ambushed them there. Jim Carlyle, a posseman who knew Billy, went in to negotiate surrender. In exchange, Greathouse went out to the possemen. But an accidental shot fired outside panicked Carlyle. He leapt out through a window. His men, mistaking him for Billy, killed him in friendly fire. Then they retreated. The posse later burned down Greathouse's ranch. And they lied that Billy had murdered Jim Carlyle. Billy apparently wracked his brains to comprehend this lethal pursuit.

On December 3rd, Billy read *Las Vegas Gazette* owner, J.H. Koogler's, article titled: "Powerful Gang of Outlaws Harassing the Stockmen." It gave the Santa Fe Ring's full-blown outlaw myth of Billy the Kid and his gang. That solved part of Billy's mystery of the pursuit. He was accused as a rustling gang leader. He should have fled the Territory - as most of the Regulators had done after the Lincoln County War. But he didn't. Instead, he wrote to Governor Lew Wallace.

The letter is strange because it is not about his pardon, which Billy certainly needed by that December 12th. It is strange because it shows that Billy was in denial that Wallace was betraying the bargain, since he still addressed Wallace as an ally and confidant.

From guilty and self-centered Lew Wallace's point of view, Billy's persistence must have seemed like taunting. In fact, while irrationally clinging to Wallace as a father-figure, Billy was trying to set things right - to be loved. It was the same course Wallace, with equally pathetic obstinacy, sought himself from General Ulysses S. Grant as pardon for his failure as a Major General in the 1862 Civil War Battle of Shiloh.

By the letter's December 12th date, Billy had endured more traumas: another lost pardon, two White Oaks posse ambushes, and false accusation as Jim Carlyle's killer. Possibly his teenaged lover, heiress Paulita Maxwell, in Fort Sumner, added to his determination to stay in the Territory. His letter gives "Fort Sumner" as his address. And he had no idea that his time as a free man was fast running out.

Seven days away was Pat Garrett's and his posse's ambush of Billy and his few companions at Fort Sumner's entrance corridor; shooting dead Tom O'Folliard, instead of intended Billy. Ten days away was Billy's capture at Stinking Springs by Garrett and his posse, with Garrett's shooting dead Charlie Bowdre, when mistaking him for Billy.

All Billy knew, as he complained in his letter to Wallace, was that Garrett had stolen two mules of his from the Thomas Yerby ranch. But he would have found it shocking that he was the object of Garrett's pursuit, or that Garrett had been made a Deputy U.S. Marshall by Secret Service Operative Azariah Wild to arrest or kill him anywhere in the Territory.

Billy's reason for the letter was rebuttal of J.H. Koogler's *Las Vegas Gazette* article nine days before. And adversity was transforming him since his last contact with Wallace. Raging at injustice, he was now famous; even with a flashy moniker, "Billy the Kid," to be nationally known in ten days in a *New York Sun* outlaw myth article. But not conceiving the magnitude of his adversaries, he blamed pursuit on the only person he knew was a traitor: the Territory's cattle king, John Chisum. Chisum had been trusted by John Tunstall, Billy's beloved employer. Tunstall had made Chisum President of his Lincoln Bank in his store. But when Tunstall and his Lincoln friend, Attorney Alexander McSween, were attacked by the Ring, Chisum gave no help. After Tunstall's Ring murder, and its precipitated Lincoln County War, Chisum withheld aid of his many cowboys. And he backed-out of his promise to pay Tunstall's men – including Billy – who then fought as anti-Ring Regulators. Billy may have rustled from Chisum in retribution. So Billy decided his trouble-making enemy was Chisum. All this added up to the bold familiarity of Billy's letter, with its message that justice was on his side, and assumption that Lew Wallace cared.

Wallace had also been writing self-justifying letters to one of his father-figures: Secretary of the Interior Carl Schurz. On December 7th, five days before he got Billy's letter, he'd dove-tailed his outlaw fabrications with Secret Service Operative Azariah Wild's, and had hidden Billy's new pardon-for-testimony bargain with Wild. And, while betraying Billy and Lincoln County citizens, Wallace reverted to his despotic nature and requested Schurz's aid in repealing the Posse Comitatus Act, so soldiers could hunt down citizens, like Billy – or repeat the Lincoln County War's annihilation.

Wallace's evil letter to Schurz must be read in perspective of what he knew. He knew that the murder and arson in the Lincoln County War Battle two years earlier had been by Fort Stanton's Ringite Commander, N.A.M. Dudley, violating the Posse Comitatus Act. He knew Lincolnites' fear of Dudley and his troops from Attorney Huston Chapman's letters. He knew Dudley and the Ring had Chapman murdered. He knew that Billy had fulfilled their pardon bargain. Truth and justice made no difference to self-serving Wallace. Wallace wrote: "From private advices received from Lincoln County last night, I have reason to believe a new trouble has broken out in Lincoln County. This time, however, it has one good feature – the civil officers of the county ... have taken the field to arrest outlaws, murderers, horse and cattle thieves, and counterfeiters ... [The affair] suggests the great need of speedy repeal by Congress of the law prohibiting the use of regular soldiers as posse comitati ... A large body of troops, including cavalry, is now quartered in Fort Stanton. If they were able to support the Sheriff, short work could be made of the pending trouble." This is what was in the mind of the man who would read Billy's letter in seven days.

On Sunday December 12th, 1880, Billy wrote to Lew Wallace with familiarity and equality.

On Screen is Billy Bonney's letter of December 12th, 1880 to Governor Lew Wallace. **[FIGURE 46]** To be noted is that its penmanship matched Billy's pardon bargain letters of March of 1879, as presented in Talk 6. I'll read it and add commentary.

Fort Sumner
Dec 12th 1880

Gov Lew Wallace

Dear Sir

I noticed in the Las Vegas Gazette a
peice which stated that, "Billy" the "Kid, the
name by which I am Known in the Country
was the Captian of a Band of Outlaws who
hold Forth at the Portales. There is no
Such Organization in Existence. so the Gentlewen
must have Drawn very heavily on his Imagination,
My bussioness at the White Oaks the time I was
waylaid and my horse Killed. was to See
Judge Leonard who has my Case in hand.
he had written to me to Come up. that he thought
he could get Everything Straightend up
   I did not find him at the Oaks & Should
have gone to Lincoln if I had met with no
accident, After mine and Billie Wilsons horses

2

were killed we both made our way to a
Station, forty miles from the Oaks kept by
Mr Greathouse. When I got up next morning
The house was Surrounded by an outfit led
by one Carlyle. Who came into the house and
demanded a Surrender. I asked for their
Papers and they had none. So I Concluded
it amounted to nothing more than a mob
and told Carlyle that he would have to
Stay in the house and lead the way out
that Night. Soon after a note was brought
in Stating that if Carlyle did not Come out
inside of five minutes they would kill the
Station keeper. (Greathouse) who had left the
house and was with them. in a Short time a
Shot was fired on the outside and Carlyle thinking
Greathouse was killed jumped through the
window. breaking the Sash as he went
and was killed by his own Party they thinking
it was me trying to make my Escape.
the Party then withdrew.

they returned the next day and burned an old
man named Spencer's house and Greathouses, also

3

I made my way to this Place afoot and
During my absence Weftily Sheriff Garrett
Acting under Chisums Orders went to the Portales
and found Nothing. on his way back he went
by Mr Yorbys ranch and took a pair of mules
of mine which I had left with Mr Bowdre
who is in charge of Mr Yorbys Cattle.
he (Garrett) Claimed that they were stolen
and even if they were not he had a right
to Confiscate any Outlaws property,
I have been at Summer Since I left
Lincoln making my living Gambling
the mules were bought by me the truth of which
I can prove by the best Citizens around Summer
J. S. Chisum is the man who got me into
Trouble. and was benifated Thousands by it
and is now doing all he can against me
There is no Doubt but what there is a great deal
of Stealing going on in the Territory. and a great
deal of the Property is taken accross the Plains as
it is a good outlet but so far as my being

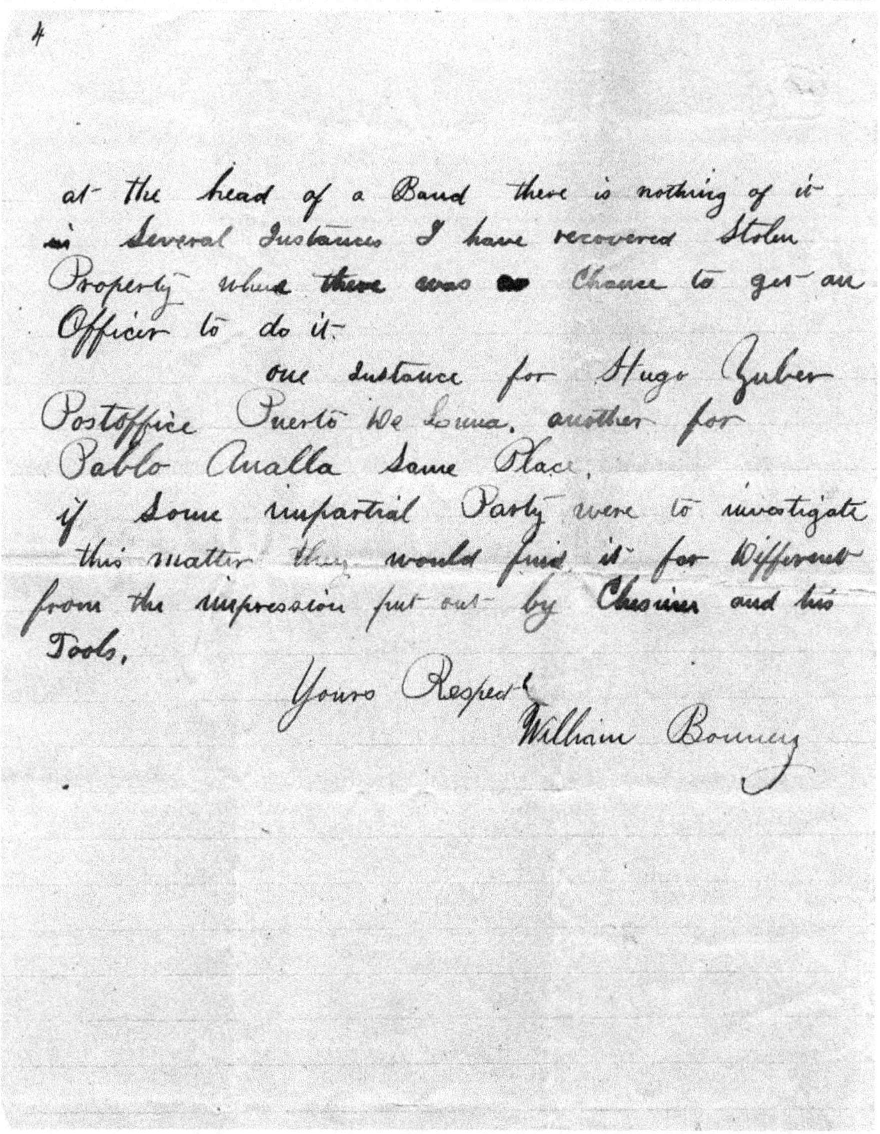

at the head of a Band there is nothing of it
in Several Instances I have recovered Stolen
Property when there was no Chance to get an
Officer to do it-

One Instance for Hugo Zuber
Postoffice Puerto De Luna, another for
Pablo Analla Same Place,

if Some impartial Party were to investigate
this matter they would find it far Different
from the impression put out by Chisum and his
Tools,

Yours Respec
William Bonney

FIGURE 46: December 12, 1880 Letter to Governor Lew Wallace
denying outlaw gang and the murder of Jim Carlyle. From
Indiana Historical Society, Indianapolis, Indiana, Lew Wallace
Collection

Giving his address as Fort Sumner, Billy wrote:

"I noticed in the Las Vegas Gazette a piece which stated that, Billy 'the' Kid, the name by which I am known in the Country was the captain of a Band of Outlaws who hold Forth at the Portales. There is no such Organization in Existence. So the Gentleman must have drawn very heavily on his Imagination. [Note that Billy not only ridicules his outlaw myth, but wrongly assumes that Lew Wallace believes him and cares about the injustice.] My business at the White Oaks at the time I was waylaid and my horse killed was to See Judge Leonard who has my case in hand. he had written me to come up, that he thought he could get Everything Straightened up I did not find him at the Oaks and Should have gone to Lincoln if I had met with no accident. [Note that Billy puts his Coyote Spring ambush of November 22nd in the context of meeting with his attorney, Ira Leonard, to end the injustice. Billy knew that Leonard had communicated with Wallace about his possible Secret Service pardon that October. He thought Wallace would sympathize.] After mine and Billie Wilsons horses were killed we both made our way to a Station, forty miles from the Oaks kept by Mr Greathouse. When I got up the next morning The house was Surrounded by an outfit led by one Carlyle, Who had come into the house and Demanded a Surrender. I asked for their Papers [that meant warrants] and they had none. So I concluded that it amounted to nothing more than a mob and told Carlyle that he would have to Stay in the house and lead the way out that night. Soon after a note was brought in Stating that if Carlyle did not come out inside of five minutes they would Kill the Station Keeper (Greathouse) who had left the house and was with them. in a Short time a Shot was fired on the outside and Carlyle thinking Greathouse was Killed jumped through the window breaking the Sash as he went and was killed by his own Party thinking it was me trying to make my Escape. the Party then withdrew. [Note that Billy described the Greathouse ranch ambush, making clear the men's mob illegality with no warrants. He was wrong to think Wallace would take his word that Carlyle was killed in friendly fire, not by him.] they returned the next day and burned an old man named Spencer's house and Greathouses also [Note that Billy presents the mob's lawless arson. He was wrong to think that Wallace cared.]

"I made my way to this Place afoot and During my absence Deputy Sheriff Garrett Acting under Chisum's orders went to the Portales and found Nothing. [Note that Billy again denies the *Las*

Vegas Gazette article's saying he had a gang headquartered in Portales.] on his way back he went by Mr Yerbys ranch and took a pair of mules of mine which I had left with Mr Bowdre who is in Charge of mr Yerby's cattle. he (Garrett) claimed that they were stolen and even if they were not he had a right to Confiscate any Outlaws property. [Note that Billy reports Garrett's harassment, but is unaware of the overall pursuit. And, using his legal experience, he adds that even an outlaw has rights; in this case, protection from theft. But in his agitation, he misstates it as; "even if they were not he had a right to Confiscate any Outlaws property." He meant to write: "even if they were stolen he had no right to Confiscate any Outlaws property." And he wrongly thought Wallace cared.]

"I had been at Sumner Since I left Lincoln making my living Gambling the mules were bought by me the truth of which I can prove by the best citizens around Sumner. [Note that Billy is claiming income by gambling, not rustling. And he is repeating a character reference offer like in his March 13th, 1879 pardon bargain letter, which stated: "As to my Character I refer to any of the Citizens. for the majority of them are my Friends and have been helping me all they could." Billy didn't guess that the last thing Wallace wanted was proof of his innocence. Wallace was framing Billy himself!] J.S. Chisum is the man who got me into Trouble and was benefited Thousands by it and is now doing all he can against me [Note that Billy had wrongly concluded that John Chisum was behind the attacks on him.] There is no Doubt but what there is a great deal of Stealing going on in the Territory. and a great deal of the Property is taken across the [Staked] Plains as it is a good outlet but so far as my being at the head of a Band there is nothing of it [Note that Billy yet again denies the outlaw myth.] in Several Instances I have recovered Stolen Property when there was no chance to get an Officer to do it. one instance for Hugo Zuber Post office Puerto de Luna. another for Pablo Analla Same Place. [Note that Billy presents his Robin Hood role, known to his partisans. He was wrong to think Wallace cared.]

"if Some impartial Party were to investigate this matter they would find it far Different from the impression put out by Chisum and his Tools." [Note that Billy hopes that Wallace will back him by investigation.] Billy signed as "William Bonney," realistic enough to pull back from the vulnerable Billie, as B-I-L-L-I-E, signature of his previous letter on March 24th, 1879.

In response to Billy's letter, Lew Wallace's sadism surged in mixed identification with his own sadistic father and rage at reminder of his moral failure as the pardon bargain's betrayer. He sought to silence this symbol of his hypocrisy by a hanging death. So, the next day, December 13th, Wallace requested from Territorial Secretary William Ritch a reward notice. Though other Regulators were on Lincoln County War indictments, Wallace focused just on Billy. He wrote: "Be good enough to prepare a draft of proclamation of reward $500 for the capture and delivery of William Bonney, alias Kid to the Sheriff of the County of Lincoln."

Nine days later, on December 22nd, Wallace placed it in the Ringite *Las Vegas Gazette*, whose outlaw myth of Billy the Kid article had precipitated Billy's cry for help letter. It appeared in a front page column titled: "BILLY THE KID, $500 REWARD." It stated: "I will pay $500 reward to any person or persons who will capture William Bonney, alias The Kid, and deliver him to any sheriff of New Mexico. Satisfactory proofs of identity will be required. Lew Wallace, Governor of New Mexico."

The day after Lew Wallace had requested his Billy the Kid reward notice, he implemented his own escape from the Territory and his failures, into his fantasy world of savior and salvation. On December 14th, 1880, he wrote to Secretary of the Interior Carl Schurz requesting leave to promote his book, *Ben-Hur: A Tale of the Christ*. And he continued his self-promoting outlaw myth by focus on Billy. He wrote: "I have intelligence to day from Lincoln County. The citizens are yet in the field under a very active and energetic deputy-sheriff [Pat Garrett], who has had several skirmishes [meaning Coyote Spring and Greathouse ranch ambushes] ... To stimulate them, I have made proclamation of $500 reward for the capture and delivery of the leader of the outlaws [Billy the Kid]."

The next day, December 15th, having relegated Billy to near certain death, Wallace callously wrote to his son, Henry, to check his *Ben-Hur* sales and his New Mexico Territory mining investments.

But fate would have it that Lew Wallace's hypocrisy would be tested to the end. He would next have to face captured Billy's letters from the Santa Fe jail, reminding him of their pardon bargain, Billy's fulfilling it, and his betrayal.

TALK 29:
BILLY BONNEY'S SANTA FE JAIL LETTERS
FROM BOOK: *THE LOST PARDON OF BILLY THE KID*
MARCH 17, 2021

This talk presents my revisionist history of Billy Bonney's Santa Fe jail letters to Governor Lew Wallace. The information is from my book, *The Lost Pardon of Billy the Kid: An Analysis Factoring in the Santa Fe Ring, Governor Lew Wallace's Dilemma, and a Territory in Rebellion.*

On December 22nd, 1880, Deputy U.S. Marshal and Sheriff-elect Pat Garrett, with back-up of the Santa Fe Ring, the Secret Service, and Texan possemen, captured Billy Bonney by an ambush at a Stinking Springs line cabin, about 16 miles from Fort Sumner. It's doubtful that Garrett, who'd known Billy since early 1878, believed he was an outlaw king, or that a huge gang of counterfeiter-rustlers were in the Territory. But he did know his mission was to kill Billy. He missed him in a Fort Sumner ambush that December 19th, killing Tom O'Folliard instead. At Stinking Springs, mistaking Charlie Bowdre for Billy, he shot him dead. Garrett then settled on Billy's capture, and an inevitable hanging trial. Captured with Billy were Billy Wilson, Tom Pickett, and "Dirty Dave" Rudabaugh.

Garrett was also backed by Governor Lew Wallace, who'd betrayed his pardon bargain with Billy. As Secret Service Operative, Azariah Wild, wrote in his December 23rd, 1880 report to his Chief: "I called on Governor Wallace [in Santa Fe] ... He at once said '[T]ell Mr. Garrett to follow these men any place in the territory and tell him I say so.'"

Garrett first transported his captives to Fort Sumner, then Las Vegas for a night in the jail, where Tom Pickett was released for lack of a warrant. Then Garrett took the others by train to the Santa Fe jail.

By then, Billy was the object of a media circus as an outlaw the Ring named "Billy the Kid." This negative press ultimately influenced his Mesilla trial's jury. On December 27th, the Ringite *Las Vegas Daily Gazette*, published editor Lucius "Lute" Wilcox's article about the Stinking Springs capture and prisoner transport to Las Vegas. It was titled: 'The Kid. Interview with Billy Bonney The Best Known Man in New Mexico." It showed that Billy's wit was unabated. About the gathered crowd and his defamatory press, Billy said: "Well, perhaps some of them will think me half man now; everyone seems to think I was some sort of animal."

On December 27th, Ringite Russell A. Kistler reported the capture in his *Las Vegas Daily Optic* as: "A Big Haul! Billy the Kid, Dave Rudabaugh, Billy Wilson and Tom Pickett in the Clutches of the Law, Notorious Gang of Outlaws Broken up, and the County Breathes Easier." Pure outlaw myth, it stated: "Our readers are familiar with the depredations committed in the lower country by a gang of daring desperadoes, under the leadership of Billy the Kid ... They have roamed over the country at will, placing no value upon human life, and appropriating the property of ranchmen and travelers without stint. Posses of men have been in hot pursuit of them for weeks ... However, the right boys started out, well mounted and heavily armed, and were successful in bagging their game.

"Yesterday afternoon, the town [of Las Vegas] was thrown into a fever of excitement by the announcement that the 'Kid' and other members of his gang of outlaws had been captured ... The rumor was soon verified by the appearance in town of a squad of men led by Pat Garrett, deputy sheriff of Lincoln county ... having in custody the Kid, Dave Rudabaugh, Billy Wilson and Tom Pickett. They were taken at once to the jail ...

"The party of men who risked their lives in the attempt to rid the country of this bloodthirsty gang of robbers and murderers are deserving of unbounded praise and should be rewarded handsomely ... They will undoubtedly obtain the reward of $500 offered by the Governor [Wallace] for the capture of the Kid ... [to] bring to justice one of the most desperate gangs of outlaws that ever terrorized the southwest ...

"Kid is about 24 years of age ... When interviewed between the bars at the [Las Vegas] jail this morning, he was in a talkative mood, but said that anything he might say would not be believed by the people. He laughed heartily when informed that the papers of the Territory had built him up a reputation second only to that of [Apache Chief] Victorio. Kid claims never to have had a large number of men with him, and that the few who were with him when captured were employed on a ranch. This is his statement and is taken for what it is worth."

On December 28th, Billy was again interviewed for the *Las Vegas Gazette* when inside the train departing to the Santa Fe jail. His banter reflected self-control when one realizes that, during his interview, his train was blocked by a mob on the tracks, with unclear intent either to lynch or to rescue him. He presented his Stinking Springs capture with a dime novel escape fantasy about jumping his famous bay mare out of the line cabin's doorway, obstructed by a dead horse, shot by Garrett. With the mob dispersed and the train finally departing, Billy avoided morbidity by jokingly inviting the reporter to visit him in Santa Fe.

Once in the Santa Fe jail, Billy immediately wrote to Lew Wallace. He was calling the bluff on his pardon. He would write four letters in his almost three month imprisonment, prolonged by the Ring's awaiting completion of tracks for railroad transport to prevent his partisan rescue. Billy's letters were demands. They likely contributed to guilty Lew Wallace's obsessive publishing of subsequent lying articles about the pardon bargain being betrayed by Billy.

Important to note is that handwriting in Billy's jail letters differs from his pardon bargain letters because he lacked a desk to enable proper Spencerian slant, as discussed in Talk 4. But he retained his alphabet, grammatical quirks, misspelling of answer as A-N-N-S-E-R, and his uniquely modified signatures.

Wallace answered none of Billy's jail letters. But he took them, with the rest of his Billy the Kid communications, when he left New Mexico Territory, and carefully preserved them.

On January 1st, 1881, four days after arriving, Billy wrote, giving the location as Santa Fe.

On screen is Billy's Santa Fe jail letter of January 1st, 1881 to, quote: "Governor Lew Wallace." **[FIGURE 47]** It stated: "Dear Sir, I would like to see you for a few moments if You can spare the time. Yours Respect. W.HBonney."

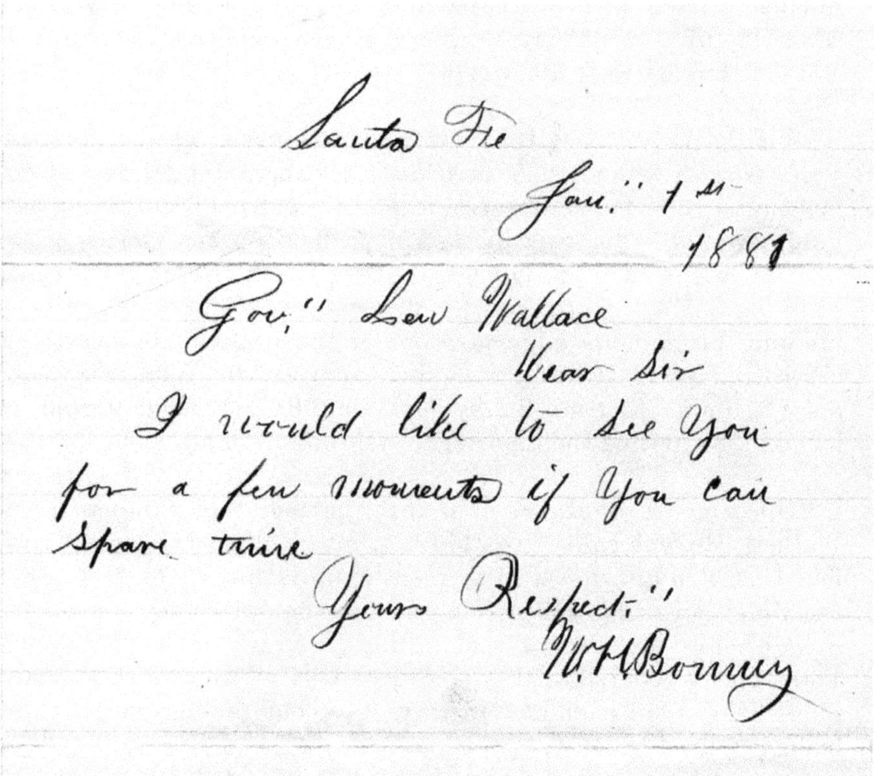

Santa Fe
Jan." 1st
1881
Gov." Lew Wallace
Dear Sir
I would like to see You
for a few moments if You can
Spare time
Yours Respect."
W.HBonney

[FIGURE 47] Santa Fe Jail letter of January 1, 1881. From Indiana Historical Society, Indianapolis, Indiana; from the Lew Wallace Collection

It should be noted that on February 28th, Billy and his cellmates almost succeeded in tunneling out of their cell. He was then put in solitary confinement for the rest of his jail stay.

Billy's next letter, dated March 2nd, 1881, angered Wallace. Billy implied he had letters from him confirming the pardon bargain. Wallace would later call it blackmail in his obsessive articles; but that threat must have alarmed that hypocrite counting the days till he could silence Billy's accusations by hanging.

On screen is Billy's Santa Fe jail letter of March 2nd, 1881. . [FIGURE 48] Billy gives his location as the "Santa Fe jail New Mex." Addressed to "Governor Lew Wallace,"

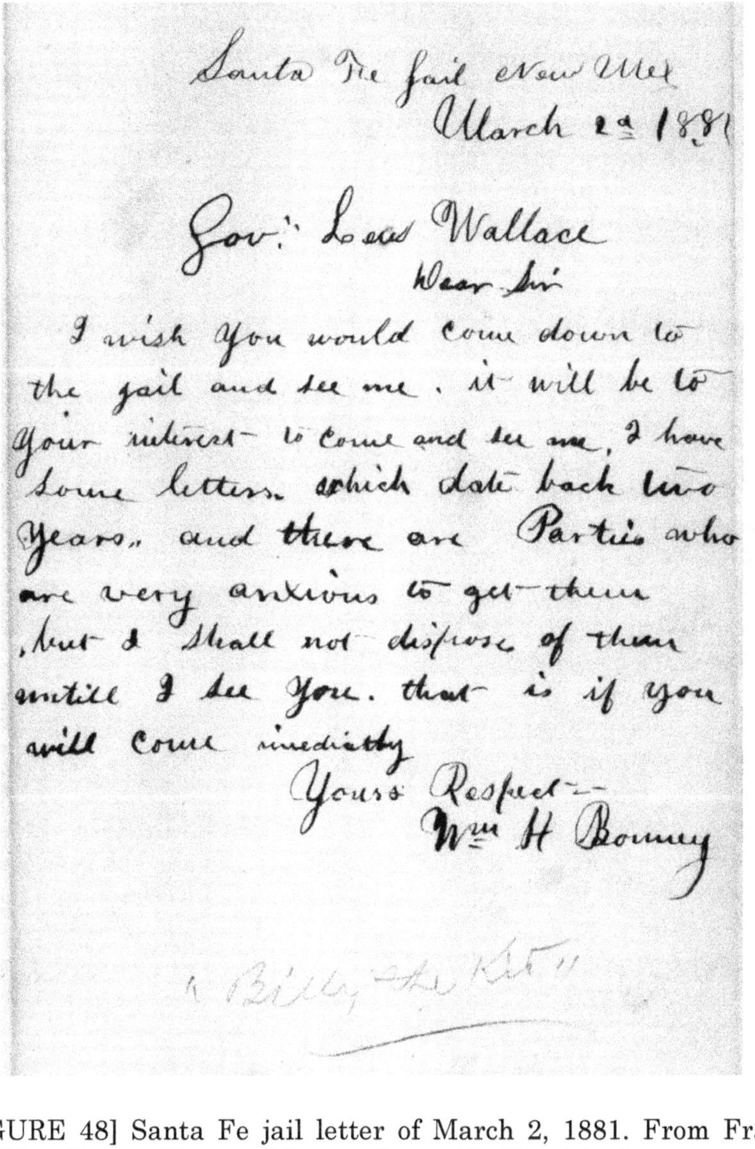

[FIGURE 48] Santa Fe jail letter of March 2, 1881. From Fray Angélico Chávez History Library, Santa Fe, New Mexico

Billy wrote: "Dear Sir, I wish you would come down to the jail to see me. it will be to your interest to come and see me. I have some letters which date back two years, and there are Parties who are very anxious to get them but I shall not dispose of them until I see you. that is if you will come immediately." It was signed: "Yours Respect, William H. Bonney."

Two days later, on March 4th, 1881, Billy wrote his third jail letter bitterly confirming the pardon's betrayal. He wrote: "I have done everything that I promised you I would, and You have done nothing that You promised me." He also threatened partisan rescue, giving a glimpse of his power as a rebel leader. He wrote: "I guess they mean to Send me up without giving me any Show. but they will have a nice time doing it I am not entirely without friends."

On screen is Billy's Santa Fe jail letter of March 4th, 1881. [FIGURE 49] He gives his location as "Santa Fe. In jail." Again it is to "Governor Lew Wallace," as "Dear Sir." As at his March 13th, 1879 start of pardon letters to Wallace, Billy addresses him as an equal. Now he rebukes him. Billy stated: "I wrote You a little note the day before yesterday but have received no annser. I Expect you have forgotten what you promised me, this Month two Years ago. but I have not, and I think You had ought to have come and seen me as I requested you to. I have done everything that I promised you I would, and You have done nothing that You promised me. I think when You think the matter over, You will come down and See me, and I can then Explain Everything to You. Judge Leonard, Passed through here on his way East in january and promised to come and See me on his way back. but he did not fulfill his Promise. it looks to me like I am getting left in the Cold. I am not treated right by [U.S. Marshal John] Sherman. he lets Every Stranger that comes to See me through Curiosity in to See me, but will not let a Single one of my friends in, not Even an Attorney. I guess they mean to Send me up without giving me any Show. but they will have a nice time doing it. I am not entirely without friends. I shall Expect to See you Sometime today Patiently Waiting I am Very truly Yours, Respect. William H. Bonney."

Santa Fe, in Jail
March 4th 1881

Gov. Lew Wallace

Dear Sir

I wrote you a little note
the day before yesterday, but have
received no answer, I Expect you have forgot
ten, what you promised me, this Month two
Years ago, but I have not, and I think You
had ought to have come and seen me as I
requested you to, I have done Everything that
I promised you I would, and you have done
nothing that You promised me,
I think when you think the matter over, you
will come down and see me, and I can then
Explain Everything to you,
Judge Leonard, Passed through here on
his way East, in January and promised to
Come and see me on his way back, but he did
not fulfill his Promise, it looks to me like I am
getting left in the Cold, I am not treated right

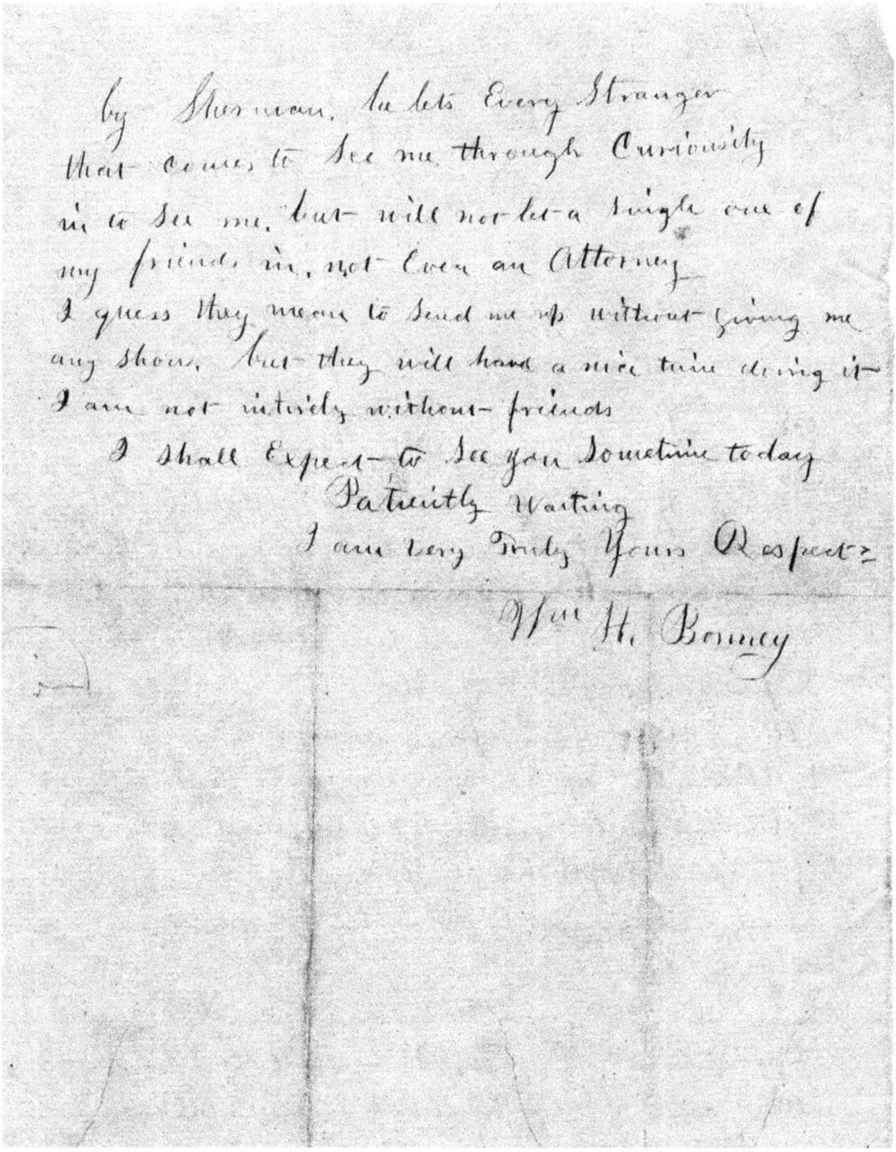

by Sherman, he lets Every Stranger
that comes to See me through Curiousity
in to See me, but will not let a single one of
my friends in, not Even an Attorney
I guess they mean to Send me up without giving me
any Show, but they will have a nice time doing it
I am not intirely without friends
I shall Expect to See you Sometime today
Patiently waiting
I am very truly Yours Respect=
Wm H. Bonney

[FIGURE 49] Santa Fe jail letter of March 4, 1881. From Indiana Historical Society, Indianapolis, Indiana; from the Lew Wallace Collection

On March 27th, 1881, Billy wrote to Wallace for the last time, emphasizing the pardon promise that his life now depended on, since he was about to be transported to his hanging trials. He may have clung to slim hope that Lew Wallace would issue the pardon at its technically proper time: after his sentencing in his Mesilla trials to come.

On screen is Billy's Santa Fe jail letter of March 27th, 1881. **[FIGURE 50]** He gives his location as "Santa Fe New Mexico." Again it is to "Governor Lew Wallace," as "Dear Sir." Billy wrote: "for the last time [underlined] I ask: Will you keep Your promise. I start below tomorrow. Send Annser by bearer." He signed: "Yours Respt, WBonney."

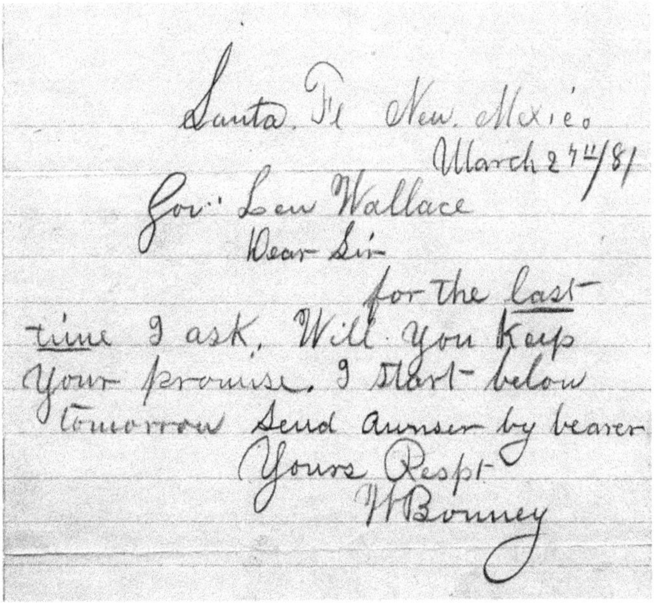

Santa Fe New Mexico
March 27th/81
Gov: Lew Wallace
Dear Sir
for the last time I ask, Will you Keep Your promise, I start below tomorrow Send Annser by bearer
Yours Respt
WBonney

FIGURE 50: Santa Fe jail letter of March 27, 1881. From Indiana Historical Society, Indianapolis, Indiana; from the Lew Wallace Collection

A later talk will analyze Billy Bonney's Mesilla hanging trials.

TALK 30:
THE HANGING TRIALS
OF BILLY THE KID
FROM BOOK: *THE LOST PARDON*
OF BILLY THE KID
MARCH 18, 2021

This talk presents my revisionist history of Billy Bonney's hanging trials in Mesilla. The information is from my book, *The Lost Pardon of Billy the Kid: An Analysis Factoring in the Santa Fe Ring, Governor Lew Wallace's Dilemma, and a Territory in Rebellion.*

Billy Bonney's Stinking Springs capture by Pat Garrett left him in the power of the Santa Fe Ring, now poised to kill him under guise of law by hanging. Governor Lew Wallace could have saved him by the promised pardon, but did not. Billy's indictments were for Regulator killings in the Lincoln County War of Sheriff William Brady, Deputy George Hindman, and posseman, Andrew "Buckshot" Roberts. Loyal Ira Leonard was Billy's defense attorney in the first trial. Then, likely Ring threat made him withdraw. So Billy was left with a Ringite Judge, Ringite prosecutors, court appointed prejudiced lawyers, press blaring outlaw myth propaganda, and an inevitable outcome.

Attorney Ira Leonard had protectively accompanied Billy from the Santa Fe jail on the Atchison, Topeka, and Santa Fe railroad, whose southward track construction had only reached the Rincón depot before the Ring got impatient to get Billy killed. Leonard stayed with Billy on the stagecoach to Las Cruces. With them were guards and fellow prisoner, Billy Wilson. At Las Cruces, a crowd had gathered to see the famous outlaw, Billy the Kid.

Someone asked which was Billy. As reported in the April 3rd, 1881 *Santa Fe Daily New Mexican* in "Something About the Kid," Billy teasingly pointed to bald, middle aged Leonard, and declared: "This is the man!" Billy also quipped: "At least two hundred men have been killed in Lincoln County during the past three years, but I did not kill all of them." Billy was brought to the Doña Ana County jail, adjacent to the courthouse in Mesilla's plaza.

On March 30th, 1881, under Ringite Judge Warren Bristol, the first case to be tried was the Regulators' April 4th, 1878 killing of John Tunstall murder posseman Andrew "Buckshot" Roberts. Santa Fe Ring boss Thomas Benton Catron, as U.S. Attorney, had written its June 21st, 1878 federal indictment: Case Number 411, for Billy and other Regulators. The Ring thought it was air-tight. And Wallace couldn't pardon a federal case - it needed the President. The prosecutor was Ringite U.S. Attorney Sidney Barnes, Catron's replacement.

But Attorney Ira Leonard surprised that court. He filed a motion to quash the indictment based on it being invalid! In the juryless hearing before Judge Bristol, with Prosecutor Barnes present, Leonard argued that Catron's indictment claimed federal jurisdiction by erroneously claiming that the Blazer's Mill killing site was part of the federally-controlled Mescalero Indian Reservation. Leonard stated that it was actually private property owned by a Dr. Joseph Blazer. Its being within the Reservation's perimeter was irrelevant. As private property, it came under Territorial law. Leonard was right. Judge Bristol was forced to withdraw the indictment. The Ring had underestimated Ira Leonard.

So the Ring reverted to its usual response to serious opposition: death threat. Leonard, having barely survived a Ring assassination on April 25th, 1879 - only 67 days after his office mate, Attorney Huston Chapman's, actual Ring killing - abruptly departed. Billy was left with court-appointed attorneys for his William Brady and George Hindman murder trials. They were Albert Jennings Fountain, who believed the Ring's outlaw myth; and boss Catron's business and political associate, John D. Bail.

To prejudice potential jurymen, Ring press spewed the outlaw myth. On April 2nd, 1881, *Newman's Semi-Weekly* ran an article titled "The Kid." It stated: "[The Kid] is a notoriously dangerous character ... [who] has made his brags that he only wants to get free in order to kill three men – one of them being Governor

Wallace. Should he break jail now, there is no doubt that he would immediately proceed to execute his threat ... We ... hope that legal technicalities may not be permitted to render escape more probable." The "legal technicalities" was a swipe at Ira Leonard, meaning the Ring would tolerate no courtroom truth to interfere with hanging.

The next trial was the Regulators' killing of Lincoln County's Sheriff: Case No. 532, New Mexico Territory versus William Bonney alias Kid alias Henry Antrim for the murder of William Brady. The prosecutor was Ringite District Attorney Simon Newcomb, one of the lawyers who'd freed, by habeas corpus, on April 13th, 1879, Lew Wallace's captured Ringite Seven Rivers rustler-murderers being held in Fort Stanton.

The transcript for that trial is lost, a likely Ring expurgation. But under Ringite Judge Bristol; with complicit defense attorneys Fountain and Bail; with no defense witnesses; and with Ringite prosecution witnesses James Dolan, Jacob Basil "Billy" Matthews, and Saturnino Baca - along with subpoenaed Lincoln merchant, Isaac Ellis - Billy had no chance.

Judge Bristol's prejudicial jury instructions do exist, and show that he made first degree murder the only possible verdict. Its only sentence was hanging. He told the jurymen: "There is no evidence before you showing that the killing of Brady is murder in any degree than the first ... [T]he punishment for murder in the 1st degree shall be death." Since first degree murder required "premeditated design," Bristol made that inevitable also; stating: "If the design to kill is completely formed in the mind but for a moment before inflicting the fatal wounds it would be premeditated and ... the same as though the design to kill had existed for a long time."

He continued: "In this case in order to justify you in finding this defendant guilty of murder in the 1st degree ... you should be satisfied and believe from the evidence to the exclusion of every reasonable doubt of the truth of several propositions.

"1st That the defendant either inflicted one or more of the fatal wounds causing Brady's death or that he was present at the time and place of the killing and encouraged – incited – aided in – abetted – advised or commanded such killing. [Note that aiding and abetting are actually a lesser degree. In 1879, Ring thug, Jessie Evans, got only accessory to murder in the Lincoln County Grand Jury for abetting the murder of Huston Chapman.]

"2nd That such killing was without justification or excuse. [Note that Billy had no defense witnesses or motivated defense attorneys to argue for his justification or excuse.]

"3rd That such killing of Brady was caused by inflicting upon his body a fatal gunshot wound. [Note that Brady had 8 gunshot wounds indicating multiple shooters.]

"And 4th that such fatal wound was either inflicted by the defendant upon a premeditated design to effect Brady's death or that he was present at the time and place of the killing of Brady and from a premeditated design to effect his death he ... encouraged – incited – aided in – abetted – advised or commanded such killing." [Note that this again lumps lesser offence of accessory with first degree murdering.] Bristol repeated this wrong instruction; stating: "If he was so present – encouraging – inciting – aiding in – abetting – advising – or commanding the killing of Brady he is as much guilty as though he fired the fatal shot." [Note again Jessie Evans's 1879 accessory to murder verdict for abetting Chapman's murder. And, in Texas, in 1880, Jessie and his gang had murdered a Texas Ranger. Jessie got second degree murder by being present but not actually killing – the opposite to Bristol's instruction.]

Bristol continued: "As to what would be or would not be reasonable doubt of guilt I charge you that belief in the guilt of the defendant ... does not require ... mathematical certainty ... as ... two and two are four ... Merely a vague conjecture or bare possibility that the defendant may be innocent is not sufficient to raise reasonable doubt of his guilt. [Note that Bristol removed all options for reasonable doubt of guilt.]

"Murder in the 1st degree is the greatest crime known to our laws ... [T]he punishment for murder in the 1st degree shall be death ...

"If you believe ... therefore from the evidence before you ... that the defendant is guilty of murder in the 1st degree then it will be your duty ... also saying in your verdict that the defendant shall suffer the punishment of death."

As discussed in Talk 11, Judge Warren Bristol's Ringite judicial corruption had been exposed during 1870's anti-Ring uprisings. In April of 1877, Colfax County War activist, Mary McPherson, sent charges against him and other Santa Fe Ring officials to President Rutherford B. Hayes. She wrote that Bristol, quote, "conspired together to corrupt and defraud justice and defeat the ends thereof" with U.S. Attorney Thomas B. Catron, Chief Justice Henry Waldo, and Governor Samuel B. Axtell. She enclosed a copy of February 18th, 1876's *Grant County Herald's* "Petition and Charges to Remove Judge Bristol." It stated: "We charge that Judge Bristol is guilty of manifest partiality, while acting in the trial of causes." That meant Bristol used his court to punish Ring opponents. Noteworthy, is that the Petition cited his obstructing witnesses for the defense. In one case, he, quote, "absolutely refused to the prisoner the right ... to procure witnesses in his behalf." It is known that Billy had no defense witnesses. There is no record of any being subpoenaed.

Also existing are the prejudicial jury instructions by Attorneys Albert Jennings Fountain and John D. Bail. It's known that Billy didn't testify on his own behalf. They may have discouraged him, though he was a master testifier. And they may have been to blame for not subpoenaing defense witnesses. Their paltry 312 word instructions were all that stood between Billy and Judge Bristol's noose. Yet they slyly backed Bristol's instruction that 1st degree murder was the only charge possible, by not informing the jurymen about lesser degrees of murder. They stated:

"The Court is asked to instruct the Jury as follows: to wit:

"1st Instructions asked – Under the evidence the Jury must either find the defendant guilty of Murder in the 1st degree, or acquit him. [Note that this repeats Bristol's wrong all-or-nothing instruction.]

"2nd Instruction asked – The jury will not be justified in finding the defendant guilty of Murder in the 1st degree unless they are satisfied, from the evidence, to the exclusion of all reasonable doubt, that the defendant actually fired the shot that caused the death of the deceased Brady, and that such shot was fired by the defendant with the premeditated design to effect the death of the deceased, or the defendant was present and actually assisted in firing the fatal shot or shots that caused the death of the deceased, and that he was present in a position to render such assistance and actually rendered assistance from a premeditated design to effect the death of the deceased. [Note that Fountain and Bail are listing degrees of murder, while calling them 1st degree murder guilt. They list: 1) firing the fatal shot; 2) firing it with premeditated intent to murder; 3) assisting in firing the shots; or 4) rendering assistance to murder. [Note again that the assisting options were lesser degrees. As mentioned, in Chapman's murder, abetting got Jessie Evans indicted as an accessory; as opposed to Chapman's fatal shooters, James Dolan and Billy Campbell, who got 1st degree murder indictments.]

"3rd Instruction asked – If the Jury are satisfied from the evidence to the exclusion of all reasonable doubt that the defendant was present at the time of the firing of the shot or shots that caused the death of the deceased Brady, yet, before they will be justified in finding the defendant guilty, they must be further satisfied from the evidence ... to the exclusion of all reasonable doubt, that the defendant either fired the shots that killed the deceased ... or that he assisted in firing said shot or shots ... or assisted the parties who fired the same either by his advice, encouragement procurement or command, from a premeditated design to effect the death of Brady. If the Jury entertains any reasonable doubt upon any of these points they must find a verdict of acquittal." [Note that this repeats degrees of participation, but gives only acquittal as an option. This removed jurymen's choosing a lesser, non-hanging, degree of murder; since Billy's presence was never denied.]

But were there defense arguments that could have saved Billy? Would Ira Leonard have dared to use them? There's no doubt he opposed the Ring. On May 20th, 1879, he'd written to Lew Wallace that the, quote, "Santa Fe Ring ... has been so long an incubus on the government of this Territory." And the real arguments required going head-to-head with the Ring. So here are hypothetical arguments not used by Fountain and Bail, who I'll simply cite as "Fountain."

Though the trial's transcript is lost, one can extrapolate from the jury instructions of Fountain that no correct defense was offered. Billy, however, was unaware of this betrayal, and subsequently tried to sell his bay racing mare to pay Fountain for his appeal. Nevertheless, one can show that evidence and argument could have established reasonable doubt against 1st degree murder verdict and its hanging penalty for the murder of William Brady.

The argument should have been for justifiable homicide for defense of another, as forcing the group of men - which included the Defendant - to use deadly force against Brady on April 1st, 1878 to stop his murdering Alexander McSween. If the group had responded to immediate threat - like seeing Brady attacking

McSween - it would be a complete defense for acquittal - comparable to self-defense.

But the time gap of about three hours between Brady's killing and McSween's arrival in Lincoln for his future Grand Jury trial required a mitigating defense based on Defendant William Bonney's certainty that Brady would kill McSween when McSween arrived. So trial evidence had to show why any reasonable person would think Brady was about to murder McSween.

First, there was evidence for William Brady as a murderer; as follows:

The posse under Brady had murdered McSween's friend, John Tunstall, just 42 days before Brady's own killing. And Brady had made a death threat to Tunstall in McSween's presence, stating: "I won't shoot you now, you haven't long to run."

Brady, as a rogue lawman beholden to the Ring, blocked arrest of Tunstall's killers, who were also Brady's deputies and possemen. And Brady illegally imprisoned the Defendant, on February 20th, 1878, to obstruct his arrest of Tunstall's murderers in his capacity as a Deputy Constable appointed by Justice of the Peace John Wilson.

Brady was a known threat to Alexander McSween, having maliciously harassed him by property attachment for his embezzlement case far in excess of the $8,000 set by Judge Bristol to satisfy a possible court judgment against him. Brady was a Ring agent, whose job was to kill McSween. McSween had gone into hiding because of certainty of Brady's murderous intent. And Las Vegas Deputy Sheriff Adolph Barrier had been so certain of McSween's murder risk from Brady, that he had kept McSween in his personal custody. On March 28th, 1878, Brady, brought Fort Stanton soldiers to the ranch of John Chisum, in failed attempt to apprehend, and likely kill, McSween. And just four days after that - the murder day - Brady knew that McSween would return to Lincoln for his Grand Jury trial and could be murdered then.

Importantly, there existed no legal way to stop Brady from murdering McSween, since, by a March 9th, 1878 illegal Proclamation, then Ringite Governor, S.B. Axtell, had removed Justice of the Peace Wilson, stating: "there are no Territorial Officers here to enforce [laws] except Sheriff Brady and his Deputies." Axtell himself was removed in late 1878 for that illegality.

Therefore, seeing themselves as McSween's sole protection, citizens, including the Defendant, came to Lincoln. They saw Brady and his deputies – all accused and indicted Tunstall murderers - heavily armed and positioning themselves for McSween's imminent arrival at the east end of town. Brady's murder intent was obvious.

Secondly, there was evidence for Defendant, William Bonney's, altruistic motive:

As to Defendant's character, he had been a ranch worker for murdered John Tunstall. He'd been deputized to serve warrants on Tunstall's murderers after Brady refused to do arresting - only losing his deputyship by its illegal removal by Governor Axtell. Defendant's commitment to law and order was further proved by his volunteering an eye-witness affidavit and a deposition about Tunstall's murder to bring Tunstall's assassins to justice.

On the murder day, Defendant was in a citizens' group having sole consensus that McSween would be killed by Brady upon arrival.

Furthermore, in that group, the Defendant had only a revolver, since Brady had confiscated his carbine; and all others had carbines. Defendant lacked the range to Brady's position; so could not have been Brady's shooter.

The Defendant's intent was to save McSween's life; and killing Brady was the only possible way to achieve that end.

There were other trial variables open to censure:

No translator was provided to the Spanish-speaking jury, except for jury instructions; even though a translator was required.

Defense witnesses should have included Billy himself; and subpoenaed Deputy Adolph Barrier, John "Squire" Wilson, and Juan Patrón. Prosecution witnesses James Dolan and Jacob Basil Matthews should have been impeached as being on Brady's murder posse, and themselves indicted for John Tunstall's murder.

Here is a hypothetical defense argument for a fair court:

Self-defense murder is legally blameless. So is defense of another from immediate death. The weight of the evidence has shown that Defendant William Bonney shared with his companions certainty that William Brady was about to kill

Attorney Alexander McSween, and that no recourse existed except to kill Brady to save McSween.

Defendant had no motive to kill Brady except in defense of McSween. To protect another from certain death is noble, and mitigates against a verdict of 1st degree murder, which is wanton and with malice aforethought.

The evidence has shown that after Brady's posse murdered John Tunstall, there was good reason for the Defendant to believe Brady would next kill Alexander McSween. It has been shown that McSween himself and Deputy Sheriff Barrier likewise believed that Brady would kill McSween. It has been shown that no legal recourse through public officials existed to stop Brady's murderous act.

Furthermore, the Defendant was not Brady's killer, since his revolver lacked range; and his companions had carbines which could attain the range to strike Brady. And the Defendant was not wanton or malicious, since his intent was to preserve McSween's life.

All the evidence therefore mitigates against a verdict of 1st degree murder, which requires hanging, and should be morally repugnant to declare against a reasonable man acting to save the life of another man.

And it is the burden of the Territory, not the Defendant, to prove beyond reasonable doubt that the Defendant did not act in defense of another. The prosecution, having used Brady's indicted fellow murderers as witnesses, has failed to do that. So, if you, the jurors, have reasonable doubt that the defendant acted in defense of another, you cannot find him guilty of 1st degree murder, and are free to find him not guilty - or, at most, guilty of a lesser degree of murder, which spares his life.

On April 9th, 1881, in Billy Bonney's real and corrupt trial of for William Brady's killing, the jury's inevitable verdict after Bristol's and Fountain's instructions was murder in the 1st degree. On April 13th, 1881, Bristol sentenced Billy to hang a month later - on May 13th - leaving little time to appeal.

It should be noted that if the Brady and Hindman indictments did not yield a hanging sentence, Bristol could have gotten a Territorial one against Billy for the Roberts killing.

Billy responded to the injustice in an interview published in the April 16th *Mesilla News*. In summary, he stated: "I think it hard that I should be the only one to suffer the extreme penalty of the law." He called his court "mob law;" ending with facetious "personal advice": "If mob law is going to rule, better dismiss judge and sheriff and let all take chances alike." He added Lew Wallace's pardon bargain betrayal by saying curtly: "Don't know that he will do it."

The article stated: "Well I had intended at one time not to say a word on my own behalf because persons would say, "Oh he lied." Newman, editor of the Semi-Weekly, gave me a rough deal; he created prejudice against me, and is trying to incite a mob to lynch me. He sent me a paper which showed it; I think it a dirty mean advantage to take of me, considering my situation and knowing that I could not defend myself by word or act. But I suppose he thought he would give me a kick down hill ... If mob law is going to rule, better dismiss judge and sheriff and let all take chances alike. I expect to be lynched going to Lincoln. Advise persons never to engage in killing. Considering the active part Governor Wallace took on our side and the friendly relations that existed between him and me, and the promise he made me, I think he ought to pardon me. Don't know that he will do it ... I think it hard that I should be the only one to suffer the extreme penalty of the law."

In darkness, on April 17th, 1881, Billy was secretly transported by wagon from the Mesilla jail to prevent rescue attempts. *Newman's Semi-Weekly* reported his departure, with Billy, as usual, joking: It stated: "On Saturday night about 10 o'clock Deputy U.S. Marshal Robert Ollinger with Deputy Sheriff David Woods and a posse of five men ... started for Lincoln with Henry Antrim alias the Kid. The fact that they intended to leave at that time had been purposely concealed and the report circulated that they would not leave before the middle of the week in order to avoid any possibility of trouble, it having been rumored that the Kid's band would attempt a rescue. They stopped in front of the Semi-Weekly office while we talked to them, and we handed the Kid an addressed envelope with some paper and he said he would write some things he wanted to make public. He appeared quite cheerful and remarked that he wanted to stay until their whiskey gave out, anyway. Said he was sure that his guard would not hurt him unless a rescue should be attempted and he was certain that it would not be done unless perhaps 'those fellows at White Oaks come out to take me,' meaning to kill him. It was, he said, about a stand-off whether he was hanged or killed in the wagon."

Having sacrificed Billy Bonney to save himself, Lew Wallace faced a golden future. On April 19th, 1881, he got a letter from a new father-figure, President James Garfield, praising his new book, BEN-HUR: A TALE OF THE CHRIST, and even being kind about the Battle of Shiloh. It led to Wallace's appointment to his coveted ambassadorship to Turkey. Garfield wrote: "Dear General, I have, this morning, finished reading 'Ben-Hur' – and I must thank you for the pleasure it has given me ... With this beautiful and reverent book you have lightened the burden of my daily life – and renewed our acquaintance which began at Shiloh – Very truly yours, J.A. Garfield."

A later talk will cover Billy's attempted appeal of his hanging sentence.

TALK 31:
BILLY BONNEY'S ATTEMPTED APPEAL
FROM BOOK: *THE LOST PARDON OF BILLY THE KID*
APRIL 6, 2021

This talk presents my revisionist history of Billy Bonney's attempted appeal of his hanging sentence. The information is from my book, *The Lost Pardon of Billy the Kid: An Analysis Factoring in the Santa Fe Ring, Governor Lew Wallace's Dilemma, and a Territory in Rebellion.*

On April 13th, 1881, Billy Bonney was sentenced to hang by Santa Fe Ring-beholden Judge Warren Bristol. But he continued to fight for justice. On April 15th, from the Mesilla jail, he wrote to a Santa Fe attorney named Edgar Caypless. He'd met Caypless in the Santa Fe jail, when Caypless was representing Billy's fellow Stinking Springs captives, Billy Wilson and Dave Rudabaugh. Billy became his client too; surprisingly, for a case of his own. He made a replevin (or rustling) case against Texan, Frank Stewart, one of Pat Garrett's possemen at the Stinking Springs ambush. Stewart had stolen Billy's famous bay mare after the capture. He then sold her in Las Vegas to Scott Moore, owner of Moore's Hotsprings Hotel. Moore gifted her to his wife, who named her Kid Stewart Moore. Caypless took Billy's case on contingency.

Billy had been fighting for justice since John Tunstall's Santa Fe Ring murder. He was a deputy to arrest Tunstall's murderers. He was a Regulator in the anti-Ring Lincoln County War. He fulfilled his pardon bargain with Governor Lew Wallace by testifying against the Ring murderers of Attorney Huston Chapman. And he testified in the Court of Inquiry against Ringite

Commander N.A.M. Dudley for murder and arson in the Lincoln County War Battle.

After Billy's hanging sentence, he turned to Edgar Caypless to help his appeal. Billy's attorneys had been Albert Jennings Fountain and John D. Bail. They'd been appointed by Judge Bristol after Billy's loyal attorney, Ira Leonard, suddenly quit after a likely Ring death threat. But, as discussed in Talk 30, Billy didn't recognize the inadequate defense made by these Ring-biased lawyers. Possibly to further impede him, Fountain then demanded money to do an appeal. So Billy turned to his replevin case to get money. And grounds for appeal were the lack of a translator for his Spanish-speaking jurymen.

Billy's April 15th letter to Edgar Caypless exists only as a copy. It's Billy's last known letter. He wrote: "Dear Sir. I would have written before this but could get no paper. My United States case was thrown out of court and I was rushed to trial on my Territorial charge. Was convicted of murder in the first degree and am to be hanged on the 13th day of May. Mr. A.J. Fountain was appointed to defend me and has done the best he could for me. He is willing to carry the case further if I can raise the money to bear his expense. The mare is about all I can depend on at present so hope you will settle the case right away and give him the money you get for her. If you do not settle the matter with Scott Moore and have to go to court about it either give him [Fountain] the mare or sell her at auction and give him the money. Please do as he wishes in the matter. I know you will do the best you can for me in this. I shall be taken to Lincoln tomorrow. Please write and direct care of Garrett, sheriff. Excuse bad writing. I have my handcuffs on. I remain as ever Yours respectfully, W.H. Bonney."

The letter proves that Billy never gave up. But abandonment is its sad subtext. He had no trial witnesses on his behalf. No partisan offered money for his appeal. And this letter, to save his own life, was almost impossible to write for lack of paper.

I'll comment on its content.

Billy's saying his United States case was thrown out, referred to Attorney Ira Leonard's quashing Santa Fe Ring boss and U.S. Attorney Thomas Benton Catron's federal indictment of him and his fellow Regulators on a technicality that it was actually a Territorial, not a federal, case. And the "Territorial charge" Billy referred to was the William Brady killing.

Billy reports his scheduled hanging for May 13th, implying urgency.

He describes Fountain's appointment, revealing unawareness of his poor defense by stating that he did, quote, "the best he could for me." Billy then reported, quote: "He is willing to carry the case further if I can raise the money to bear his expense."

Billy stated the mare was, quote, "all I can depend on." He doesn't mention Lew Wallace's promised pardon, finally resigned to its betrayal. He has to save himself. So he urges Caypless to settle the case with Scott Moore. But trusting no one now, he also instructs Caypless on alternatives of giving Fountain the mare or selling her at auction.

As contact information, Billy adds his transport to Lincoln, to Pat Garrett's custody.

Ever the perfectionist, even at death's door, Billy apologizes that his handcuffs interfered with writing his proper Spencerian script.

Caypless did win the replevin case, but after Billy's killing. He kept the money as his fee.

A later talk will discuss Billy's great escape from Lincoln's courthouse-jail, just 15 days before hanging.

TALK 32:

BILLY BONNEY'S GREAT ESCAPE
FROM BOOK: *THE LOST PARDON*
OF BILLY THE KID
APRIL 7, 2021

This talk presents my revisionist history of Billy Bonney's great escape from Lincoln's courthouse-jail. The information is from my book, *The Lost Pardon of Billy the Kid: An Analysis Factoring in the Santa Fe Ring, Governor Lew Wallace's Dilemma, and a Territory in Rebellion.*

Billy Bonney's great escape from Lincoln's courthouse-jail, 15 days before scheduled hanging, is famous; surpassed only by his killing by Pat Garrett, 78 days later. How Billy managed it, is a mystery examined here.

It's clear that Billy hadn't regarded his sentence as inescapable. On March 4th, 1881, from the Santa Fe jail, he'd written to Governor Lew Wallace an unanswered letter anticipating the outcome of his Mesilla trials. He stated: "I guess they mean to Send me up without giving me any Show. but they will have a nice time doing it. I am not entirely without friends."

Wallace's betrayal of their pardon bargain had left Billy facing hanging. Worse, Wallace wanted that, to silence Billy's accusations. In that same letter, Billy had written: "I have done everything that I promised you I would, and You have done nothing that You promised me."

On April 28th, 1881, Wallace gave the owner of the *Las Vegas Gazette*, J.H. Koogler, his "Interview with Governor Lew Wallace on 'The Kid.' " Wallace chose Santa Fe Ring-biased Koogler sadistically. On December 12th, 1880, Billy had written to Wallace exposing Koogler's lies; stating: "I noticed in the Las Vegas

Gazette a piece which stated that, Billy 'the' Kid, the name by which I am known in the Country was the captain of a Band of Outlaws who hold Forth at the Portales. There is no such Organization in Existence. So the Gentleman must have drawn very heavily on his Imagination."

Koogler now reported: "The conversation drifted into the sentence of 'the Kid.' 'It looks as though he would hang, Governor.' 'Yes, the chances seem good that the 13th of May would finish him.' 'He appears to look to you to save his neck.' 'Yes,' said Governor Wallace smiling, 'but I can't see how a fellow like him should expect any clemency from me.' Although not committing himself, the general tenor of the governor's remarks indicated that he would resolutely refuse to grant 'The Kid' a pardon. It would seem as though 'the Kid' had undertaken to bulldoze the governor, which has not helped his chances in the slightest."

That same April 28th, Billy escaped. But Wallace was unaware.

Up to that moment, Wallace had been covertly sadistic to Billy. Now, with his pardon denial public, Wallace's sadism became overt. He wanted to kill. On April 30th, as Governor, he wrote Billy's death warrant for Sheriff Pat Garrett. Wallace kept this murderous feeling for life, but projected it onto his fictional Billy the Kid as wanting to kill him!

Wallace wrote: "To the Sheriff of Lincoln County, New Mexico, Greeting: At the March term, A.D. 1881 of the District Court for the Third Judicial District of New Mexico, held at La Mesilla in the County of Doña Ana, William Bonney alias Kid, alias William Antrim, was duly convicted of the crime of murder in the First Degree; and on the fifteenth day of said term, the same being the thirteenth day of April, A.D. 1881 ... the said William Bonney, alias Kid, alias William Antrim, was adjudged and sentenced to be hanged by the neck until dead, by the Sheriff of the said County of Lincoln, within said county.

"Therefore, you the Sheriff of the said county of Lincoln, are hereby commanded that on Friday, the thirteenth day of May, A.D. 1881 ... you take the said William Bonney ... from the county jail of the county of Lincoln where he is now confined, to some safe and convenient place within the said county, and there, between the hours of ten o'clock, A.M. and three o'clock, P.M. ... you hang the said William Bonney ... by the neck until he is dead. And make due return of your acts hereunder."

On April 21st, Billy arrived in Lincoln to Pat Garrett's custody and to the new Lincoln courthouse with its second floor, makeshift jail. Symbolizing Santa Fe Ring triumph, it was the converted, two-story "House," the Ring's past, local, mercantile stronghold. It had been taken over from bankrupt James Dolan and John Riley by their backer: Ring boss Thomas Benton Catron. Catron had then sold it to the county.

Billy's two guards, deputized by Garrett, were Robert "Bob" Olinger and James W. Bell. Olinger had been a Ringite Seven Rivers rustler, taking part in all Lincoln County War murders. Bell had been a White Oaks posseman, and possible friendly-fire killer of Jim Carlyle at that posse's November 28th, 1880 Greathouse Ranch ambush of Billy and his companions.

Billy's hanging was 22 days away. He had no money to appeal. He was arm and leg shackled, chained to a metal fastener in the floor, and under 24 hour guard. On April 28th, his eighth day there, he escaped.

This is what's known.

Billy was not in a real jail cell, just a big, second story room, with windows at the north and east. In lieu of a chamber pot, he was taken to the outhouse behind the building. Billy's room opened at the west to Pat Garrett's office. There, or in the jail room, Deputy Bob Olinger kept his Whitney double barrel shotgun. Garrett's office opened to a north-to-south hallway. At its north end, were doors to a balcony, which lacked stairs and looked down on Lincoln's street. At the hall's northwest side was a room housing other prisoners. It led westward to a room which had been used for Masonic services. At the hall's southwest end was an armory room.

On April 27th, Garrett departed to White Oaks to collect taxes.

On April 28th, on Deputy James Bell's noon shift, Billy revealed that he had a revolver and was free of his wrist shackles. He offered to tie Bell; but Bell bolted down the stairway. Half-way down, he was shot through the chest by Billy. Bell staggered to the back door, was encountered by the building's caretaker, Gottfried Gauss, died in his arms, and was dragged to the back yard.

Somehow alerted, Deputy Bob Olinger ran from the Wortley Hotel, across the street, where he'd taken the other prisoners for lunch. He went to the courthouse's east side. There, from the second floor jail room's east window, Billy killed him with his own

Whitney double barrel shotgun. Then Billy smashed it and hurled the pieces onto Olinger's corpse.

Billy then demanded a miner's pick and a horse from Gauss, and addressed gathered townspeople from the balcony. No one tried to stop him, though breaking the leg chain with the miner's pick took a long time. Billy then rode away on County Clerk Billy Burt's pony.

Theories have claimed that Billy seized Bell's revolver or stole one from the armory. I favor the theory that Gottfried Gauss assisted him. Obviously, Gauss would have kept that secret.

This is my reconstruction. Gauss was no random caretaker. He'd been employed in the early 1870's to set up a brewery for "The House's" Ringite partners. But they cheated him out of his wages. He then became John Tunstall's cook. He would have met new ranch hand, Billy Bonney, in October of 1877. Gauss was present at Tunstall's Feliz River ranch during Tunstall's harassment by Ringite Sheriff William Brady's possemen for the property attachment in Alexander McSween's fake embezzlement case by the Ring. On February 18th, 1878, Gauss was left at that ranch when Tunstall took his men - including Billy - to herd his horses, which were immune to attachment, back to Lincoln. So Gauss saw Brady's rabid possemen arrive, looking for Tunstall; then he saw them return after murdering him. In the Lincoln County War that followed, Gauss would have personally known the Regulators - including Billy - as Tunstall's past ranch hands. He may have witnessed these Regulators' killings in Lincoln of Brady and his Deputy, George Hindman, to prevent their murdering Alexander McSween. He would have known about the Regulators' killing of Tunstall murder posseman, Andrew "Buckshot" Roberts in self-defense. He would have known about the final battle of the War's murders of Alexander McSween and his followers, and arson of his home. To Gauss, Billy would have been the Lincoln County War's hero. The next year, Gauss would have known about Attorney Huston Chapman's Ring murder on Lincoln's street. He would have been acquainted with Billy's loyal attorney, Ira Leonard, who'd moved to Lincoln. Through Leonard, Gauss might have heard about Governor Lew Wallace's betrayal of Billy's pardon bargain with him. So Gauss would have hated everything and everyone connected to Billy's intended hanging. It required that kind of passion to risk his life as an accessory to jailbreak and possible murder by providing its weapon. And

Pat Garrett, James Bell, and Bob Olinger, not from Lincoln, would have been unaware of Gauss's background and security risk.

Garrett, Bell, and Olinger would have also been unaware of Lincoln townspeople's hatred of the Santa Fe Ring. Most had fled town at the Lincoln County War's final battle from July 14th to 19th of 1878. Then they pressured new Governor, Lew Wallace, to remove Fort Stanton's Commander, N.A.M. Dudley, whose illegal invasion of their town to back the Ring had enabled murder, arson, and defeat of the freedom fight. In the April, 1879 Grand Jury, they had indicted 200, primarily Ringites, for that War's crimes. By May 1st, days later, in that same Grand Jury, boss Catron and other Ringite lawyers, representing those indicted Ringites, colluded with the Ringite judge to get them all pardoned by misuse of Lew Wallace's Amnesty Proclamation, which barred pardon to those indicted. That was the Grand Jury in which Billy's testimony got the Ringite murderers of Huston Chapman indicted. Lincolnites subsequently saw Chapman's indicted murderer and local Ring boss, James Dolan, shielded from prosecution by the Ring. Then Lincolnites saw treasonous Ringite Commander Dudley exonerated by a rigged military Court of Inquiry. So Lincolnites knew it was impossible to get justice. And they knew that Billy, their hero, now unjustly faced hanging.

The obvious weak link in Billy's captivity was the outhouse. It's part of the Gottfried Gauss-as-accomplice theory. As the building's caretaker, Gauss would have had access to Billy, albeit in the presence of his guards. Cryptic communication about the outhouse would have been possible. And Gauss could have gotten the revolver from the armory. He could have hidden it with the wrist shackle key in the outhouse. Presumably, the leg shackle key could not be found. And Gauss would know that the best time for an escape would be after Garrett left town.

Gottfried Gauss managed to stay free of suspicion. And Billy was killed by Garrett anyway 78 days later in Fort Sumner.

Gauss's version of the escape is known. On March 1st, 1890, he was interviewed by the *Lincoln County Leader*. Reading between-the-lines one can speculate that he directed Deputy Olinger to the courthouse-jail's east side, where Billy ambushed him; since there was no other reason for Olinger to go there. He also implied the enabling role of Lincolnites, who even shook hands with escaping Billy.

Gauss was quoted: "I was crossing the yard behind the courthouse, when I heard a shot fired, then a tussle upstairs in the courthouse, somebody hurrying downstairs, and deputy sheriff Bell emerging from the door running toward me. He ran right into my arms, expired the same moment, and I laid him down, dead. That I was in a hurry to secure assistance, or perhaps to save myself, everybody will believe.

"When I arrived at the garden gate leading to the street, in front of the courthouse, I saw the other deputy sheriff Olinger, coming out of the hotel opposite, with the four or five other county prisoners, where they had taken their dinner. I called to him to come quick. He did so, leaving his prisoners in front of the hotel. When he had come up close to me, and while I was standing not a yard apart, I told him that I was just after laying Bell dead on the ground in the courtyard behind. Before he could reply, he was struck by a well-directed shot fired from a window above us, and fell dead at my feet. I ran for my life to reach my room and safety, when Billy the Kid called to me: 'Don't run, I wouldn't hurt you - I am alone, and master not only of the courthouse, but also of the town, for I will allow nobody to come near us. You go,' he said, 'and saddle one of Judge (Ira) Leonard's horses, and I will clear out as soon as I have the shackles loosened from my legs.' With a little prospecting pick, I had thrown to him through the window, he was working for at least an hour, and could not accomplish more than to free one leg. He came to the conclusion to wait a better chance, tie one shackle to his waist-belt, and start out. Meanwhile I had saddled a small skittish pony belonging to Billy Burt (the county clerk), as there was no other horse available ...

"When Billy went down the stairs at last, on passing the body of Bell he said, 'I'm sorry I had to kill him but I couldn't help it.' On passing the body of Olinger he gave him a tip with his boot, saying, 'You are not going to round me up again.' And so Billy the Kid started out that evening, after he had shaken hands with everybody around, and having a little difficulty in mounting on account of the shackle on his leg, he went on his way rejoicing."

On April 30th, returned Pat Garrett got the humiliating news and had to report his failed assignment to kill Billy the Kid. He wrote on the back of Billy's court documents: "I certify that I received the within named William Bonny [misspelled as B-O-N-N-Y] into my custody on the 21st of April 1881. And I further certify that on April 28th he made his escape by killing his guards

James Bell and Robert Olinger ... Boarding Prisoner and two
Guards 8 days - $40.00. Guarding and transporting from Fort
Stanton - $69.00. Returning Writ - $.50. Total: $109.00 [Garrett
forgot to add the $.50. That's almost $13 today.]

Four days later, on May 3rd, Lew Wallace, now aware of the
escape, placed his second reward notice; this time in the *Santa Fe
Daily New Mexican*. It stated: "BILLY THE KID. $500 REWARD.
I will pay $500 reward to any person or persons who will capture
William Bonney, alias The Kid, and deliver him to any sheriff of
New Mexico. Satisfactory proofs of identity will be required.

At the escape, Billy was just 21, bi-cultural, and fluent in
Spanish. He could have ridden 150 miles south for a new life in
Mexico. But he refused to leave his Territory home and his
sweetheart, young Paulita Maxwell. So he rode 150 miles
northeast, to Fort Sumner. Known to its 200 residents since 1878,
he should have realized that, though most were his friends, hiding
there from Pat Garrett would be impossible. He had 78 days
to live.

Billy's friend, John Meadows, was at his Peñasco River ranch
when Billy arrived. That showed that Billy, after briefly staying
with his friend, Ygenio Salazar, in Las Tablas, on the north side of
the Capitan Mountains, first sensibly headed south towards
Mexico. Meadows, in his posthumous 2004 book, *Pat Garrett and
Billy the Kid As I Knew Them*, is quoted: "Old Man Salazar
[meaning Ygenio Salazar] let the Kid have a little sorrel horse ...
[O]ne night, after dark he showed up at Tom Norris' and my ranch
... and seeing there was nobody there but us two, whom he could
trust, he stepped to the door and said, 'Well, I've got you, haven't
I?' I said, 'Well, you have. So what are you going to do with us?' He
said, 'I'm going to eat supper with you.'

Unbeknownst to himself, Lew Wallace was no longer in control
of Billy's reputation. On May 4th, the day after Wallace's reward
notice, the *Santa Fe Daily New Mexican* reported Billy's jailbreak;
stating: "The above [account of the escape] is the record of as bold
a deed as those versed in the annals of crime can recall. It
surpasses anything of which the Kid had been guilty, so far that
his past offences lose much of their heinousness in comparison
with it, and it effectually settles the question of whether the Kid is
a cowardly cut-throat or a thoroughly reckless and fearless man."

Wallace likely read that article. On May 16th, it seems to have precipitated his retaliatory, first, full-blown, Billy the Kid outlaw myth. He used the *St. Louis Daily Globe-Democrat* for his article titled: "The Thugs Territory, Stage Robbers and Cut-Throats Have Things Their Own Way in New Mexico, General Lew Wallace Anxious to Punish Crime that is So Prevalent - A Chapter About "Billy the Kid." In it, Wallace lied that he withheld the pardon because Billy refused to reform. But with Billy now loose to expose him, Wallace's panic yielded his paranoid fantasy of Billy wanting to kill him, as well as hysterical defamations. Wallace wrote: "He stole, murdered, [and] ravished women ... It is claimed he has killed some forty men."

On May 28th, 1881, not waiting to complete his hated governorship, Wallace departed New Mexico Territory. Billy had 47 days left to live because of his treachery.

The real Billy Bonney, with his great escape, surpassed his outlaw myth by Ringite press and Lew Wallace. And it occurred against the backdrop of non-interference by Lincoln's townspeople, who finally won the Lincoln County War their own way.

A later talk will analyze Pat Garrett's Fort Sumner killing of Billy Bonney.

TALK 33:
THE KILLING OF BILLY THE KID
FROM BOOK: *THE LOST PARDON OF BILLY THE KID*
APRIL 8, 2021

This talk presents my revisionist history of Billy Bonney's killing by Sheriff Pat Garrett. The information is from my books, *The Lost Pardon of Billy the Kid* and *The Coroner's Jury Report of Billy the Kid*.

After Billy Bonney's odds defying jailbreak on April 28th, 1881, 15 days before scheduled hanging, his whereabouts were a mystery. In fact, he'd gone to Fort Sumner, and was hiding in the Maxwell family's sheep camps, with likely permission from Peter Maxwell and his mother Luz Maxwell. And Billy presumably continued his secret romance with Peter's sister, Paulita.

But New Mexico Territory's press went wild with bogus sightings and the Billy the Kid outlaw myth. On May 4th, the *Santa Fe Daily New Mexican*, published a letter to the editor from White Oaks, signed just "D." It was titled "More Killing by Kid, When But a Short Distance From Lincoln, He Meets One of His Old Enemies, and Kills Him and His Companion." It stated: "Information reaches us tonight ... to the effect that the 'Kid,' while escaping from justice, met Billy Matthews and an unknown party, and killed them both. The tragedy occurred a few miles from Lincoln. Matthews was one of Lincoln county's best men, and was always an enemy of the 'Kid's' ... having shot him through the thigh in the Lincoln County War."

On May 5th, the *Santa Fe Daily New Mexican* published two untitled stories. One stated: "Anything that the imagination can concoct in the way of murders and desperate deeds, may be heard upon the reports now in regard to Billy the Kid ... There was a report ... that the Kid was in Albuquerque, and was bound for Santa Fe. It was also said that he had killed another man near there." The other had Billy back at his Stinking Springs capture site. It stated: "Mr. Richard Dunham says that on the second instant he met the Kid at Stinking Springs ... The Kid said that he was going to Salt Lake, but that he intended doing up Santa Fe on his trip. He desired, he said, to pay his respects to Governor Wallace and U.S. Marshal Sherman, after which he would probably hunt up his old associates in Durango ... He says he has been badly treated and spoke as though he had no particular love to waste on anyone."

What was true was that 31 year old Pat Garrett, thus far, had failed his Santa Fe Ring mission to kill Billy. In 1880, when Lincoln County Sheriff-elect and working with Secret Service Operative Azariah Wild, who made him a Deputy U.S. Marshal for the task, Garrett first tried to kill Billy on December 19th, 1880 in a Fort Sumner ambush. But he accidentally shot dead Billy's companion, Tom O'Folliard, instead. On December 22nd, at the Stinking Springs ambush, Garrett mistook Billy's companion, Charlie Bowdre, for Billy, and killed him. Garrett then settled on taking Billy captive. Garrett's next chance to kill Billy was by hanging in Lincoln on May 13th. But Billy's jailbreak ended that option.

Pat Garrett's hunt for escaped Billy is in his 1882 ghostwritten book, titled: *The Authentic Life of Billy the Kid, The Noted Desperado of the Southwest, Whose Deeds of Daring and Blood Made His Name a Terror in New Mexico, Arizona, and Northern Mexico*. The hunt was also published by one of Garrett's deputies, John William Poe, in his 1933 book, *The Death of Billy the Kid*. It was first printed in 1922 by an E.A. Brininstool as a booklet titled: "The Killing of Billy the Kid."

In his book, Garrett wrote that he'd heard that Billy was hiding with the Maxwells' sheep-herders. Garrett wrote: "During the weeks following the Kid's escape, I was censured by some for my seeming ... inactivity ... [But] I was ... quietly at work seeking trustworthy information and maturing my plan of action." To be noted is that Garrett's being a Deputy U.S. Marshal gave him Territory-wide jurisdiction. He stated that he reused a spy from Billy's Stinking Springs capture, Fort Sumner area rancher

Manuel Brazil, who now informed that Billy was seen locally. Garrett enlisted two deputies, John William Poe and Thomas "Kip" McKinney. On July 13th, he, Poe, and McKinney arrived five miles south of Fort Sumner to meet with Brazil; but he backed out.

Garrett wrote that on the morning of July 14th, he told Poe to do reconnaissance as a stranger in Fort Sumner. Poe was then to go seven miles north to Sunnyside and check with its postmaster, Milnor Rudulph. That night, Poe met-up with Garrett and McKinney four miles north of Fort Sumner. He reported that Rudulph confirmed Billy's being in the area. Garrett wrote: "When I heard Poe's report, I concluded to go and have a talk with Peter Maxwell, in whom I felt sure I could rely." The three men went on foot through a peach orchard toward Maxwell's house. In the orchard, they saw a distant man standing up. Garrett wrote: "He wore a broad-brimmed hat, dark vest and pants, and was in his shirt sleeves ... [H]e went to the fence, jumped it, and walked down toward the Maxwell house. Little as we then expected it, this man was the Kid." Garrett added that, after the killing, he learned that Billy had been in the house of, quote, "a Mexican friend," where he took off his boots. He then asked for a butcher knife to go to Maxwell's and, quote, "get some beef," because he was hungry. Garrett wrote that Billy stayed in his sox because, quote: "Maxwell's house ... was but a few steps distant."

Garrett wrote that, at Maxwell's house, he left Poe and McKinney, quote: "at the end of the porch, about twenty feet from the door of Pete's bedroom, while I myself entered it. It was nearly midnight and Pete was in bed. I walked to the head of the bed and sat down near the pillow and beside Maxwell's head. I asked him as to the whereabouts of the Kid. He replied that the Kid certainly had been about, but he did not know whether he had left or not. At that moment, a man sprang quickly into the door, and, looking back, called twice in Spanish, 'Quien es? Quien es? (Who comes there?).' No one replied, and he came into the room. I could see that he was bareheaded, and from his tread I could perceive he was either barefooted or in stocking feet. He held a revolver in his right hand and a butcher knife in his left.

"He came directly towards the bed where I was sitting at the head of Maxwell's bed. Before he reached the bed, I whispered, 'Who is it, Pete?' but received no reply ... It struck me that he might be Pete's brother-in-law, Manuel Abreu, who had seen Poe and McKinney outside and wanted to know their business.

The intruder came close to me, leaned both hands on the bed, his right hand almost touching my knee, and asked in a low tone, 'Who are they, Pete?' At the same instant, Maxwell whispered to me, 'That's him!'

"Simultaneously the Kid must have seen or felt the presence of a third person at the head of the bed. He raised quickly his pistol - a self-cocker - within a foot of my breast. Retreating rapidly across the room, he cried, 'Quien es? Quien es? (Who's that? Who's that?)' ... As quickly as possible I drew my revolver and fired, threw my body to one side, and fired again. The second shot was useless. The Kid fell dead at the first one. He never spoke ...

"I went to the door, and met Poe and McKinney there. Maxwell ... rushed out the door past me and the others. Poe and McKinney drew their guns on him, but he shouted to them, 'Don't shoot.' I told my companions that I had got the Kid. They asked if I had shot the wrong man. I told them I had made no mistake, for I knew the Kid's voice too well."

Garrett explained: "To both of them the Kid was entirely unknown. They had seen him pass by them when they were sitting on the porch ... [H]e probably saw their guns, and thereupon threw down his own weapon as he sprang to the doorway, calling out, "Quien es?" Seeing a bareheaded, barefooted man, in his shirt sleeves, with a butcher knife in his hand, and hearing his hail in excellent Spanish, they naturally supposed him to be a Mexican and an attaché of the establishment; hence their suspicion that I had shot the wrong man.

"We now entered the room and examined the body. The ball had struck him just above the heart."

Poe's book described Garrett initially entering Maxwell's bedroom through, quote, "the open door (left open on account of the extremely warm weather)." He continued: "It was probably not more than thirty seconds after Garrett had entered Maxwell's room, when my attention was attracted ... to a man approaching me ... I observed he was only partially dressed and was both bareheaded and barefooted, or rather, had only socks on his feet, and it seemed to me he was fastening his trousers ... As Maxwell's place was the one place in Fort Sumner that I had considered above suspicion of harboring the Kid, I was entirely off my guard, the thought coming into my mind that the man approaching was either Maxwell or some guest of his ... Upon seeing me, he covered me with his six-shooter as quick as lightning, sprang onto the

porch, calling out in Spanish, 'Quien es? (Who is it?)' - at the same
time backing from me toward the door ... An instant after the man
left the door, I heard a voice inquire in a sharp tone, 'Pete, who are
those fellows on the outside?' An instant later a shot was fired in
the room ... A moment after Garrett came out of the door, Pete
Maxwell rushed squarely into me ... and I surely would have shot
him but for Garrett striking my gun down, saying, 'Don't shoot
Maxwell ... We afterward discovered that the Kid had frequently
been at his house after his escape from Lincoln, but Maxwell stood
in such terror of him that he did not dare inform against him."

Poe wrote that they looked into the bedroom through a
window, with a candle placed by Maxwell on its outside sill. They,
quote, "saw a man lying stretched upon his back dead, in the
middle of the room, with a six-shooter lying at his right hand and
a butcher-knife at his left. Upon examining the body, we found it
to be Billy the Kid."

There's no historical doubt that Pat Garrett killed Billy
Bonney that July 14th, 1881 night. But Garrett's coincidental
encounter tale, repeated by Poe and by Maxwell, is unconvincing.
I believe the tale kept secrets which can be deciphered.

First is the coincidental encounter itself. It required Garrett
and Billy to both intrude on presumably sleeping Peter Maxwell,
in the middle of the same night, for no urgent reason, and within
seconds of each other. Poe wrote, quote. "It was probably not more
than thirty seconds after Garrett had entered Maxwell's room,"
that the man who was Billy approached and entered the bedroom.
Poe continued: "An instant after the man left the door, I heard a
voice inquire ... 'Pete, who are those fellows on the outside?' An
instant later a shot was fired in the room." One can conclude that
the odds of this happening, as told, strain credulity.

In his lead-up, Garrett claimed that after Billy's jailbreak he
delayed for, quote, "maturing his plan of action." He admitted to
using a spy: Manuel Brazil. Brazil confirmed Billy being in Fort
Sumner's vicinity, but backed-out of further informing. Garrett
also had Poe use Sunnyside Postmaster, Milnor Rudulph. Poe's
long round trip of seven miles to get there from Fort Sumner
reconnaissance, and three miles back to Garrett's night-time
meeting point four miles north of Fort Sumner, may have been
justified by Rudulph's being a Ringite. In 1872, as Speaker of the

House, he'd helped crush an anti-Ring uprising in the Legislature. Ring-beholden Garrett likely knew Rudulph would betray anti-Ring Billy. And he did. So Garrett admittedly used spies.

But having Billy in the vicinity, doesn't get him into Maxwell's bedroom that night. Garrett tried to distract from that problem by an irrelevant story of not recognizing Billy as a distant man in the peach orchard.

Garrett got himself into Maxwell's bedroom by claiming he suddenly decided to check with him about Billy. But lacking urgent reason, it made no sense for him to barge into his bedroom near midnight. And, as happens with lying, truth creeps in. Garrett had Maxwell reply that, quote, "the Kid certainly had been about." That proved Maxwell was not only aware of Billy's presence, but willing to disclose it to the man obviously hunting him. I believe that this communication happened earlier, during Garrett's, quote, "maturing plan of action." In fact, Peter Maxwell was vulnerable to coercion. He'd already endured months of Ring press locating the fictional rustling-counterfeiting Billy the Kid gang to his town. That left him a target for the Ring's malicious prosecution for harboring criminals. He was also vulnerable to bribery. When his father, Lucien Bonaparte Maxwell, bought Fort Sumner in 1870 for $5,000, he got only the old Fort. Peter was then litigating for the property's 13,000 acres, with which he could have been bribed. One can conclude that Maxwell had been recruited as a traitor.

Noteworthy is that the coincidental encounter tale protests Maxwell's innocence too much. Garrett wrote that Maxwell, quote, "did not know whether [the Kid] had left or not." Poe wrote that it was his idea to check with Maxwell, because Garrett thought they were on a cold trial. But Garrett had written: "When I heard Poe's report [from Milnor Rudulph], I concluded to go and have a talk with Pete Maxwell." Poe had joined in: "Maxwell's place was the one place in Fort Sumner that I had considered above suspicion of harboring the Kid." For the killing, Garrett first wrote that Maxwell whispered, "That's him." But he then made himself the identifier by writing: "[Poe and McKinney] asked if I had shot the wrong man. I told them I had made no mistake, for I knew the Kid's voice too well." About Maxwell, Poe had added, "I learned afterward that [Maxwell] was at heart a well-meaning, inoffensive man, but very timid." Poe concluded: "We afterward discovered that the Kid had frequently been at his house after his escape ... but Maxwell stood in such terror of him that he did not dare inform against him." Garrett even used the press. The headline in July 21st's *Santa Fe Daily New Mexican* was: "Garrett Exonerates Maxwell." Garrett portrayed Maxwell as an accidental witness to the shooting. Garrett was quoted: "[H]e does not think that Maxwell was in with the Kid ... He says that Pete acknowledged that fear kept him from informing on the Kid." Poe's book stated: "There have been many wild and untrue stories of this affair, one of which was that we had in some way learned in advance that the Kid would come to Maxwell's residence that night, and had concealed ourselves there with the purpose of waylaying and killing him ... The actual facts, however, are as stated herein." At the inquest, Maxwell himself gave a witness statement. He stuck to the coincidental encounter tale; stating: "I being in my bed ... at about midnight on the 14th day of July, Pat F. Garrett came into my room and sat at the end on my bed to talk with me. A little while after Garrett sat down, William Bonney came in."

One can conclude that Maxwell needed to be concealed as a traitor for his own protection. Poe described danger to himself, Garrett, and McKinney from enraged townspeople. He wrote: "We spent the remainder of the night on the Maxwell premises, keeping constantly on our guard, as we were expecting to be attacked by the friends of the dead man."

But Maxwell enabling an ambush, doesn't get Billy into his bedroom that night. The coincidental encounter tale floats that Billy entered to check about strangers. But to wake the town's patrón to ask about visitors to his town, which commonly had visitors, isn't convincing. And alternatively, if Billy thought they were hunting him, he would have retreated from the property. Garrett was so defensive about this weak link in the tale, that he kept secret who Billy had been staying with. Garrett cited, a quote, "Mexican friend," where Billy took off his boots, felt hungry, got a butcher's knife, and walked to Maxwell's to, quote, "get some beef." Garrett explained his sox by saying, quote: "Maxwell's house ... was but a few steps distant." In fact, the so-called "Mexican friend" was Garrett's sister-in-law by marriage: Celsa Gutierrez, with her being Garrett's wife's sister. And her house, where she lived with her sheepherder husband, Sabal, was not "a few steps distant," but was on a diagonal across the 300 by 400 foot parade ground, around which stood the residentially converted past military buildings. Garrett, thus, shielded his relative from looking like the one who got Billy to the bedroom. And the "I'm-hungry" excuse for going to the side of beef, didn't get Billy into the bedroom anyway. It hung on Maxwell's north porch, as his courtesy to town residents. His bedroom was at the opposite side of his big mansion - the old Fort's converted officer's quarters - at its southeast corner. One can conclude that what got Billy into the bedroom was concealed.

A secret conspirator is implied. It's known that Billy stayed in the Maxwells' sheep camps. Telling Billy that the patrón wanted to see him on a specific night, or duping a friend of Billy's to give him that information, could get Billy into the bedroom. And during his late 1880 hunt for Billy, Garrett had used Maxwell's past foreman and his own friend, Barney Mason, as a spy. Mason could have named locals as potential traitors. One can conclude that the coincidental encounter tale was to hide participants.

Then there is the bedroom's darkness glitch in the coincidental encounter tale. Outside was almost light as day because the moon was almost full and hung low on the horizon. Poe wrote: "[T]he moon was shining very brightly." In fact, when outside, both Garrett and Poe had full visibility that night. For his peach orchard sighting, Garrett wrote about the distant man: "He wore a broad-brimmed hat, dark vest and pants, and was in his shirt sleeves ... [H]e went to the fence, jumped it, and walked down toward the Maxwell house." Poe wrote about the approaching man: "I observed that he was only partially dressed and was both bareheaded and barefooted, or rather, had only socks on his feet, and it seemed to me he was fastening his trousers."

But for the bedroom scene to work, absolute darkness is needed. Poe wrote that after Billy, quote, "disappeared into the room," he Poe couldn't see what took place inside, quote, "on account of its darkness." Key was that Billy had to be unable to see looming 6'4" Garrett sitting beside Maxwell's pillow, even when Billy was so close to Garrett that his hand on Maxwell's bed almost touched Garrett's knee! That degree of blindness would exceed Billy's incomplete light adaptation or shadowing from the overhanging porch. Worse, this absolute darkness didn't apply to the bedroom or to Garrett or to Maxwell. First of all, the room's door was open. As Poe said, it was, quote, "left open on account of the extremely warm weather." In fact, Fort Sumner in July has a high of 90 degrees Fahrenheit. So moonlight from that open door would have been illuminating, even if the windows had drawn curtains. And that moonlit room did let Garrett see Billy, though he himself had entered seconds earlier and would have had incomplete dark adaptation too. Garrett wrote: "I could see that he was bareheaded ... He held a revolver in his right hand and a butcher knife in his left." In fact, Garrett saw Billy so well that he shot him at a distance right in the heart. Garrett wrote: "Retreating rapidly across the room, he cried, 'Quien es?' ... As quickly as possible I drew my revolver and fired." And to account for Billy's bolting, the tale suddenly lets Billy see a third person, and point his revolver 12 inches from his chest. Garrett wrote: "[T]he Kid must have seen or felt the presence of a third person at the head of the bed. He raised quickly his pistol - a self-cocker - within a foot of my breast." Then the tale reverted to absolute darkness. Poe described needing candlelight. He wrote: "Looking through the window, with a candle placed by Maxwell on its outside sill, we saw a man lying stretched upon his back dead, in the middle of the room, with a six-shooter lying at his right hand and a butcher-knife at his left." But the window's candle added another glitch: proving its curtains were not drawn. So moonlight through that window, as well as through the open door, would have lit the room for entering Billy. One can conclude that the room was not too dark for Billy to see Garrett if he was positioned on Maxwell's bed.

Hearing was also a glitch for the coincidental encounter tale. From the outside porch, Poe could hear the man in the bedroom ask: "Pete, who are those fellows on the outside?" Inside, Garrett could even hear Billy's unshod footsteps; writing: "[F]rom his tread I could perceive he was either barefooted or in stocking feet." But Billy, almost touching Garrett and Maxwell on the bed, couldn't hear Garrett whisper, "Who is it, Pete?" One can conclude that Billy, beside the bed, would have heard Garrett and Maxwell if they conversed.

Then there is the coincidental encounter tale's near-shooting-of-Maxwell glitch. Garrett wrote: "Poe and McKinney drew their guns on [Maxwell], but he shouted to them, 'Don't shoot.' " Poe wrote: "A moment after Garrett came out of the door, Pete Maxwell rushed squarely into me ... and I surely would have shot him but for Garrett striking my gun down, saying, 'Don't shoot Maxwell." But Poe and McKinney were supposedly unaware that it was Billy the Kid who'd entered. Poe had written: "Maxwell's place was the one place in Fort Sumner that I had considered above suspicion of harboring the Kid." Poe claimed that he thought the entering man was, quote, "either Maxwell or some guest of his." All Poe and McKinney supposedly knew was that Garrett was checking with Maxwell. It's absurd that they'd try to kill an unrecognized man exiting. One can conclude that the Deputies were actually stationed by Garrett in a premeditated plan to shoot someone rushing out.

Then there is the coincidental encounter tale's glitch of Billy's revolver. Poe wrote: "Upon his seeing me, he covered me with his six-shooter." Garrett wrote: "He raised quickly his pistol - a self-cocker - within a foot of my breast." Later, looking into the candlelit room, Poe wrote that Billy was, quote, "dead, in the middle of the room, with a six-shooter lying at his right hand." But no gun was recovered. One can conclude that Billy's being armed was important to the tale, even if he wasn't armed.

Then there is the coincidental encounter tale's glitch of three shots heard. Poe wrote that right after Billy entered, quote, "a shot was fired in the room, followed immediately by what everyone within hearing distance thought was two shots fired, the third report, as we learned afterward, being caused by the rebound of the second bullet which had struck the adobe wall and rebounded against the headboard of the wooden bedstead." But that second bullet's rebound and strike would position firing Garrett across the room facing the bed, instead of being at the bed and firing into the room.

My conclusion is that this coincidental encounter tale was made-up to keep secret that Billy was intentionally ambushed by Garrett and his Deputies, with collusion of Peter Maxwell and an unknown conspirator, who directed Billy into the trap. I believe that Maxwell was in bed as a decoy, while Garrett hid across the room and facing the bed, where Billy would go. I believe there was enough light for Billy to notice hiding Garrett, but his bolting made Garrett immediately shoot. I don't believe that Billy had a revolver, because Garrett would have kept it. At Stinking Springs, Garrett took from Charlie Bowdre's body his bloody carte de visite showing him with his wife. Garrett likewise took Billy Wilson's Winchester carbine at that Stinking Springs capture. He would have kept dead Billy's gun. But it has never appeared. And the butcher's knife, belonging to Celsa and Sabal Gutierrez, which

Billy did have, is known to this day. The self-cocker or double action revolver, which Garrett did claim, was a well known, six shot, hide-away weapon: the Colt .41 Frontier. I believe the revolver fiction was intended to make the coincidental encounter tale appear as justifiable homicide by self defense, instead of murder by premeditated ambush. That was Garrett's presentation in his July 15th, 1881 letter, the day after the killing, to Acting-Governor William Ritch. It was published in July 23rd, 1881's *Las Cruces Rio Grande Republican* as "Kid the Killer Killed, William Bonney alias Antrim, alias Billy the Kid, Fatally Meets Pat Garrett, the Lincoln County Sheriff." It stated: "It was my desire to have been able to take him alive, but his coming upon me so suddenly and unexpectedly leads me to believe that he had seen me enter the room, or had been informed by someone of the fact; and that he came there armed with pistol and knife expressly to kill me if he could. Under that impression I had no alternative but to kill him or to suffer death at his hands." Furthermore, the near-shooting of Peter Maxwell by Deputies Poe and McKinney outside his bedroom door, shows that they were positioned to kill Billy if he escaped the ambush.

Nevertheless, this coincidental encounter tale doesn't remove the truth that Billy Bonney was killed by Pat Garrett on July 14th, 1881. He was 21 years, 7 months, and 22 days old.

Billy's corpse was profusely identified. First it was identified by Pat Garrett and Peter Maxwell, who knew him well.

Then Billy was identified by Fort Sumner's residents, who also knew him well. Poe wrote, "Within a very short time after the shooting, quite a number of native people had gathered around, some of them bewailing the death of their friend, while several of the women pleaded for permission to take charge of the body, which we allowed them to do. They carried it across the yard to a carpenter shop, where it was laid out on a workbench, the women placing lighted candles around it according to their ideas of properly conducting a 'wake' for the dead." So the women identified the body. Then up to 200 townspeople who attended the wake, with Billy laid out on the sheet-covered carpenter's bench, identified him.

Then Billy was identified by the Maxwell family's unemancipated Navajo slave, Deluvina, who was close to him. On June 4th, 1927, she was interviewed in Fort Sumner by historian

J. Evetts Haley. She stated: "I came here about [1869] and was here when Billy the Kid was killed. Billy the Kid was my compadre, my friend, poor Billy ... Pete Maxwell had told Billy he better go, as Pat Garrett was coming after him. Billy said he did not care, he was not afraid of Pat Garrett." [Note, as an aside, that this sounds like Maxwell tried to save Billy from the ambush, about which he knew.] Deluvina continued: "The night he was killed Billy came in hungry, went down with a butcher knife to get some meat at Pete Maxwell's ... After passing the men outside, he went into Maxwell's room where Garrett was and he shot him. The story is that I was there and went in with a candle to see if Billy was dead. I did not do it. Pete took a candle and held it around in the window ... When they saw he was dead, [Garrett and Maxwell] went in ... Most of the native people (Mexicans) who lived in town went to his funeral ... I did not see Billy the night after he was killed, but I saw him the following morning." Note that Deluvina confirmed the majority of the townspeople's witnessing the body, and her own identification. And, for years, she laid wildflowers on Billy's grave.

On July 15th, an inquest was held by Justice of the Peace Alejandro Segura. Segura appointed six jurymen, with Sunnyside Postmaster Milnor Rudulph as President. Segura wrote their Coroner's Jury Report in Spanish for Santa Fe's District Attorney of the First Judicial District, which included San Miguel County's Fort Sumner. Peter Maxwell was the witness. He stated: "I being in my bed in my room, at about midnight on the 14th day of July, Pat F. Garrett came into my room and sat at the end on my bed to talk with me. A little while after Garrett sat down, William Bonney came in and got close to my bed with a gun in his hand and asked me 'Who is it? Who is it?' and then Pat F. Garrett fired two shots at the said William Bonney and the said Bonney fell near my fire place and I went out of the room and when I came in again about three or four minutes after the shots the said Bonney was dead." The six jurymen identified the body and gave their verdict. They stated: "We the jury unanimously find that William Bonney has been killed by a bullet in the left breast in the region of the heart, the same having been fired from a pistol in the hand of Pat F. Garrett, and our verdict is that the act of said Garrett was justifiable homicide."

On February 18th, 1882, Pat Garrett, through an act of the legislature, was granted Lew Wallace's $500 Billy the Kid reward because of certainty that he had killed Billy Bonney.

Later talks will discuss Billy Bonney's Coroner's Jury Report in detail, and will also show how Lew Wallace, the man responsible for Billy's death, spent the rest of his life writing outlaw myth articles about Billy the Kid to bury his guilt.

TALK 34:
LEW WALLACE'S OUTLAW MYTH OF BILLY THE KID
FROM BOOK: *THE LOST PARDON OF BILLY THE KID*
APRIL 20, 2021

This talk presents my revisionist history of Lew Wallace's outlaw myth of Billy the Kid. The information is from my book, *The Lost Pardon of Billy the Kid* and *The Coroner's Jury Report of Billy the Kid*.

One can say that so-called "history" of Billy the Kid is partly the outlaw myth creation of a guilty conscience in a creative writer. Best-selling novelist and New Mexico Territory Governor Lew Wallace's betrayal of his 1879 pardon bargain with Billy Bonney yielded 20 years of his publishing fables covering-up his guilt by making himself the hero and Billy the villain. Talks 21 to 29 analyze Wallace's pardon betrayal.

In Lew Wallace's Billy the Kid outlaw myth, Billy was a murderous outlaw obsessed with killing him, while he futilely offered a pardon to reform the incorrigible desperado. Wallace's lies hid that Billy fulfilled the bargain's sole condition of testifying in the Grand Jury to indict Huston Chapman's murderers. Wallace even hid that their pardon bargain meeting was in Lincoln, switching it to Santa Fe. He hid the Lincoln County War, with Billy as a freedom fighter. He hid the corrupt Santa Fe Ring, which intimidated him into refusing the pardon.

Lew Wallace's outlaw myth is particularly obnoxious because he knew Billy through letters and meetings; so lied maliciously. Billy's risking his life to get justice was undeniable. But Wallace merely lifted the life story Billy told him - like being born in

New York City and living in Indiana - to build his fictional evil Billy the Kid.

When the Santa Fe Ring was pursuing Billy with its own outlaw myth, Billy even personally denied it to Wallace. On December 12th, 1880, he wrote: "I noticed in the Las Vegas Gazette a piece which stated that Billy 'the' Kid, the name by which I am known in the Country was the captain of a Band of Outlaws who hold Forth at the Portales. There is no such Organization in Existence. So the Gentleman must have drawn very heavily on his Imagination."

Wallace's December 22nd response was publishing, in that Las Vegas Gazette, a $500 reward for "Billy the Kid," the Ring's moniker for Billy. That's equal to about $13,000 today.

After Wallace issued his Billy the Kid reward, he wrote to Secretary of the Interior Carl Schurz to fuse his outlaw myth to the Ring's. He wrote: "I have intelligence to day from Lincoln County. The citizens are yet in the field under a very active and energetic deputy-sheriff [Pat Garrett] ... To stimulate them, I have made proclamation of $500 reward for the capture and delivery of the leader of the outlaws [Billy the Kid]."

That December 22nd, Billy was captured at Stinking Springs. From the Santa Fe jail, he wrote pardon plea letters to Wallace. The one of March 2nd, 1881 stated: "it will be to your interest to come and see me. I have some letters which date back two years, and there are Parties who are very anxious to get them but I shall not dispose of them until I see you." Guilty Wallace would later call it blackmail. On March 4th, 1881, Billy wrote: "I have done everything that I promised you I would, and You have done nothing that You promised me." Wallace never responded.

Billy's first hanging trial in Mesilla was on March 30th. His attorney, Ira Leonard, got him off on a technicality. On April 2nd, Newman's Semi-Weekly ran an article titled "The Kid." Wallace may have provided its lie about Billy wanting to kill him. Simon Newman wrote: "[The Kid] is a notoriously dangerous character ... [who] has made his brags that he only wants to get free in order to kill three men - one of them being Governor Wallace."

On April 13th, 1881, in the William Brady killing trial, Billy was sentenced to hang on May 13th. No pardon came. On April 28th, Billy escaped from Lincoln's courthouse-jail.

That same April 28th, unaware of Billy's jailbreak, the Las Vegas Gazette's owner, J.H. Koogler, printed "Interview with Governor Lew Wallace on 'The Kid.' " Koogler wrote: "The conversation drifted into the sentence of 'The Kid.' 'It looks as though he would hang, governor ... He appears to look to you to save his neck.' 'Yes,' said Governor Wallace smiling, 'but I can't see how a fellow like him should expect any clemency from me.' "

Wallace wanted Billy's dead to hide the truth. On April 30th, he wrote Billy's death warrant for Pat Garrett.

Then Wallace learned about Billy's jailbreak. On May 3rd, he placed a second reward notice; this time in the *Santa Fe Daily New Mexican*. It stated: "BILLY THE KID. $500 REWARD. I will pay $500 reward to any person or persons who Will capture William Bonney, alias The Kid, and deliver him to any sheriff of New Mexico."

On May 16th, Wallace published his first outlaw myth article in the *St. Louis Daily Globe-Democrat*, even though leaving his governorship in 12 days. It was titled: "The Thugs Territory, Stage Robbers and Cut-Throats Have Things Their Own Way in New Mexico, General Lew Wallace Anxious to Punish Crime that is So Prevalent - A Chapter About 'Billy the Kid.' " Wallace lied that Billy lost the pardon by continued outlawry. He made-up a monster Billy the Kid as a serial murderer of 40 victims, a rapist, a highwayman, and a rustler.

The excerpted article stated: "Your correspondent visited ... Santa Fe and the Governor gave a very interesting sketch of the life of 'Billy the Kid,' the most noted and desperate character in New Mexico ... Governor Wallace has offered a reward of $500 for his recapture ... 'I deem him,' said the Governor, 'the most dangerous man at large, and I hope I will have the pleasure of seeing him meet his just deserts for the many crimes he has committed.' "

"Billy, he said, was born in the East, and for some years lived in Indianapolis, Indiana. He is 21 years of age, and came to New Mexico with his head crammed with dime novel stories. His ambition was to become one of the most noted outlaws he had read so much of. He settled down in Lincoln ... [making] his name in the terror of the inhabitants. He stole, murdered, ravished women, and at one time stole a herd of cattle consisting of 300 head ... It is claimed he has killed some forty men, and it is positively known that he killed at least five or six in Mexico alone. Some two years ago a murder was committed in New Mexico and Governor Wallace was positive that Billy had a hand in the deed... [H]e learned that he was in the mountains a short distance from

Santa Fe, and sent a messenger with a note ... saying that if he ... was willing to give his evidence before the Grand Jury, he would grant him a pardon, providing he also led a different life. Billy was to meet him at a certain house in Santa Fe ... At the appointed time ... a knock was heard at the door and in walked 'Billy the Kid.' A long talk followed, and it was agreed that the Sheriff should arrest him to protect him from the pals of the murderer. The Governor's idea in granting a pardon to Billy was to capture the leader and break up the gang ... Billy... was brought before the Grand Jury, testified, and two of the men were sentenced to be hanged ... Since the day Billy received the Governor's letter he has been leading the life of a murderer, stage robber, etc., and felt that the letter would forever shield him from the law ... At length Billy committed one murder too many, was arrested, and sentenced to be hanged on the 13th instant at Santa Fe, but escaped by killing two of the guards. While in jail he wrote two letters to the Governor, demanding a pardon, and threatening to expose him should he not do as requested. The Governor remembered the letter, and sent word to Billy's lawyer that he might do him a favor by publishing it. This was too much for the outlaw, and he ... openly avowed that Lew Wallace would die by his hands ... But the Governor does not fear him, and as soon as the outlaw is within two days ride of Santa Fe, Wallace himself will start the pursuit."

This claptrap was recycled and embellished as Wallace's lying formula for the next 20 years. He was as much writing the hero myth of Lew Wallace, as the outlaw myth of Billy the Kid.

On June 15th, 1881, Russ Kistler's *Las Vegas Daily Optic* published an odd outlaw myth article titled: "The Land of the Petulant Pistol, Scenes where Life and Land are Cheap ... Billy the Kid as a Killer." It's odd, because Lew Wallace may have authored it. Its by-line cited a Jap Turpen of the *Indianapolis Saturday Review*. Wallace was then back home in Indiana; and, three days later, on June 18th, he published, in the *Crawfordsville Saturday Evening Journal,* his own outlaw myth article, also with "The Land of the Petulant Pistol" in its title.

Kistler's excerpted article stated: "A young man by the name of Lute Wilcox, city editor of the "Daily Optic," [came by] ... [I said] 'Tell me something of Billy the Kid.' 'Of all the killers in that country the 'Kid' is the most successful. He has slain 36, and wants to wind up with Governor Wallace. The Governor has offered a reward of $500 for his apprehension ... He had been in New Mexico about four years. At first he was only a herder, and got his hands in by killing Mexicans. His last triumphant escape was about three months ago ... Two officers were on duty, one a deputy United States marshal by the name of Bell, in the room with him. A pistol shot was heard. 'The Kid has tried to escape,' said one of the officers who at the time was upon the street, 'and Bell has shot him.' The room was in the second story of the building. Saying this he opened the door and walked in ... 'Billy the Kid' stood at the head of the stairs and shot him down. He had worked his bracelet off and snatched the officer's pistol. Billy then ... shuffled ... to a blacksmith shop. The smith cut his irons, and he compelled another man to saddle him a fleet horse ... He is now in the San Juan country, collecting ... a large party of killers ... [An] officer ... at the insistence of Governor Wallace, started in search of him."

On June 18th, was Wallace's admitted article. Back in Crawfordsville only 11 days, he had just gotten his desired ambassadorship to Turkey. The *Crawfordsville Saturday Evening Journal* had: "Billy the Kid, General Wallace Tells Why the Young Desperado of New Mexico Wanted to Kill Him. A Dashing and Daring Career in the Land of the Petulant Pistol." This version adds Huston Chapman, with Jesse James as one of his murderers. It lies that Billy's pardon bargain was to indict Chapman's killers, then to testify in their trials; but Billy broke it by leaving before the trials. This Billy escapes a burning house as an outlaw exploit. Lifted from real Billy's December 12th, 1881 letter to Wallace, is cattle king, John Chisum, fictionalized as Billy's employer against whom vicious Billy had a murder vendetta for unpaid wages.

Excerpted, it stated: "[A]ccounts of the exploits of 'Billy the Kid,' the New Mexico outlaw, have made him the chief among frontier desperados ... In Crawfordsville additional interest in him is created by the fact that he is the same who swore to kill General Wallace, late Governor of New Mexico. His real name is William Bonne, and he was born in New York, which place he left when a small boy with his widowed mother, for Indiana ... and four years ago went to the Territory of New Mexico ... He now ... lives in the mountains to evade the edicts of the law ... being under sentence for death for murder. He has killed ... thirty-nine men, and is still not satisfied. He worked for John Chisum, the cattle dealer, in the late Lincoln county trouble, and claiming he has never received the promised $5 per day for his services, he is ... killing Chisum's herdsmen, and giving their employer credit for $5 for each man killed.

"It is only recently that he killed two guards of the Lincoln county jail ... It was during this confinement that he swore to kill Governor Wallace. Given in the following narrative, which a reporter of "The Journal" got from General Wallace ... is the cause of Billy's anger at the Governor: A young lawyer named Chapman was murdered in Lincoln county, and for this were arrested four men, among whom was the notorious Jesse James ... Governor Wallace heard that the 'kid' saw the murder ... [and] sent him a note requesting a conference with him at midnight at a certain house ... The note assured the 'kid' that if he ... would testify before the grand jury ... the Governor would pardon him for crimes for which he had been indicted, provided he would leave the Territory for good. [P]romptly at midnight ... 'Billy the Kid' ... walked in ... Governor Wallace asked Billy to tell what he knew ... The Governor asked him if he would go before the grand jury and tell the same thing. Billy's reply was that he would not dare to do it voluntarily, as the criminals' friends would kill him. The Governor suggested ... permitting himself to be captured.

"This was agreed upon ... He went before the grand jury and by his evidence the criminals were indicted for murder. But before the trial in which he was to appear as a witness for the prosecution, he tired of jail life, and ... took to the mountains. Billy was ... informed that he had not complied with all the conditions of the promise. This greatly enraged the young outlaw ... While under sentence of death he swore to kill three men ... Governor Wallace, John Chisum ... and Pat Garrett ... [H]e gained liberty by killing his two guards ... Governor Wallace felt no particular alarm and was more anxious to find Billy than Billy was to find him ...

"There was once a three day siege of a house in which were Billy and a party ... [W]hen Billy was a prisoner [General Wallace] had him to tell of the workings on the inside. The besieging party finally succeeded in firing the house and those inside were driven ... to the kitchen ... One by one those attacked ... ran out the door ... Each fell ... until the 'Kid' ... escaped without a scratch."

Lew Wallace actually had two obsessions about the pardon bargain. One was hiding his betrayal, the other was repairing his self-esteem as its betrayer. The latter yielded December 10th, 1893's *San Francisco Chronicle's* article titled: "Lew Wallace's Foe, Threatened by 'Billy the Kid,' The Writing of 'Ben-Hur' Interrupted, An Incident of the Soldier-Author's Career in New Mexico." By then, Wallace was also competing with Billy's rising fame, calling him: "the illustrious 'Billy the Kid.' " The pardon was omitted. There is just hero Wallace capturing outlaw Billy the Kid, Billy's jailbreak, and Billy's obsession with killing Wallace.

The excerpted article stated: "General Wallace was once Governor of the Territory of New Mexico ... [His] enemy was ... the illustrious 'Billy the Kid' ... [N]o man had ever excited more terror on the frontier ... He boasted that he had killed more men than he was years of age and would shoot a man ... 'just to see him kick.' [Note that Wallace lifted that phrase from Billy's March 23rd, 1879 interview with him about a murderer named Marion Turner.] ...

"Governor Wallace offered a reward for his capture ... [T]he result ... was that ... 'Billy the Kid' was surrounded by overwhelming numbers and forced to surrender ... Enraged at having been trapped, the outlaw swore that ... he would kill three men. One was a judge who had passed sentence upon him, one was Pat Garrett ... and the third was Governor Lew Wallace ...

"This seemed idle boasting ... He was in the custody of Sheriff Garrett in the County Jail of Lincoln ... Garrett appointed as guards ... Bob Ollinger [sic] and John [it was James] Bell ... One day when Ollinger [sic] had gone across the street to a restaurant, Bell took the 'Kid' from his cell to an up-stairs room in the little two-story adobe jail. [He unfastened his cuff for him to eat] ... [T]he 'Kid' ... dealt him a rap on the head with the handcuffs ... and ... snatched the revolver from the holster and sent a bullet through Bell's body ... Ollinger [sic] ... heard the shot. The outlaw seized a double-barreled shotgun and ran out on the front balcony ... [B]efore [Olinger's] foot struck the steps he fell with a load of buckshot in his heart ...

" 'Billy the Kid' ... then ... rode out of town ... saying ... 'Now for the Governor' ...

"It soon became known that .... Governor Wallace [was] improving himself as a pistol shot preparatory to an impromptu duel with 'Billy the Kid' ...

"Pat Garrett was in hot pursuit of 'Billy the Kid.' ... The announcement finally came from Fort Sumner that Garrett had forever rid the country of the 'Kid.' He had tracked him to the house of Peter Maxwell, near Fort Sumner, and, concealing himself in one of the rooms, had fired one shot ... [It] passed through the desperado's heart and he fell dead in his tracks."

On January 6th, 1894, Wallace gave a Billy the Kid interview to the *Weekly Crawfordsville Review* as "Street Pickings." Omitting the pardon bargain, he fabricated himself as the object of Billy's vengeance and as an expert marksman.

The excerpted article stated: "General Lew Wallace is a dead-shot with the pistol. Speaking of how and why he acquired such expert marksmanship, the renowned author-soldier said ... 'When I was governor of New Mexico that territory was ... terrorized by bands of daring and murderous outlaws, at the head of whom was the famous border desperado, 'Billy the Kid.' By virtue of my office I became this man's deadliest enemy ... He had openly boasted that he killed nearly fifty men and enjoyed shooting a man down 'just to see him kick.' I determined to rid the territory of this scourge and offered a large reward for his capture ... [A]fter a most exciting chase the outlaw was surrounded by overwhelming numbers and compelled to surrender at the point of fifty guns after shooting down three of his pursuers. He was taken to Lincoln county ... to answer an unusually flagrant murder. He was wildly enraged at having been trapped and swore that the moment he got free he would ... shoot me down ...

" 'I determined in order to be safer, to begin pistol practice ... [O]ne day at Santa Fe we got the alarming news that 'Billy the Kid' had murdered his two jailors, stolen a horse and had started for Santa Fe with the open threat, 'Now for the governor' ...

" 'Finally, one day there rode up to my residence a travel-stained six-footer ... I met him on the front step ... 'I am Pat Garrett, governor, and have just shot 'Billy the Kid' out here at Fort Sumner' ... He had come up with the desperado heading for Santa Fe to end me ... and ... shot him through the heart.' "

A new century didn't dampen Lew Wallace's obsession with defaming Billy and promoting himself. On June 23rd, 1900, for *The Indianapolis Press*, he embellished his outlaw myth in "General Wallace's Feud with Billy the Kid, When the General Was Governor of New Mexico and Billy Bonne Was the Most Dangerous Western Outlaw, He Was a Waif and was Reared in Indiana." For it, Wallace made-up the tally of killing a man for each of his 22 years - later changed to 21. He also apparently used Pat Garrett's 1882 book, *The Authentic Life of Billy the* Kid, for his own fiction of Billy's death. And he repeated his lie that the pardon bargain required testifying in the trials after indicting Chapman's murderers.

The excerpted article stated: " 'Yes, he killed a man for every one of the twenty-two years he lived' ... General Lew Wallace ... said: 'I will never lose the image of Billy the Kid, as I saw him that midnight in old Santa Fe, back in 1879 ... The door flew open and there stood the most feared ... man in New Mexico, hunted by every limb of the law ... The room was covered by a Winchester rifle held in one hand. In the other was a Colt's revolver ... "Your note gave me the promise of protection," he said. 'There is no one here but us three,' replied I, pointing to the owner of the cottage. Billy ... came straight to the table near which I sat' ...

"The General ... said: 'Billy the Kid, the New Mexican outlaw that attracted the attention of a nation, and under whose fearful vendetta I was placed while Governor of New Mexico, was a New York waif whose name was William Bonne. He was brought to Indiana when he was a small boy ... He was about 17 years old in 1876, when he went West ...

" 'Billy the Kid' became the most daring and notorious of desperadoes ... He started ... by taking employment of John Chisum ... the 'Cattle King' ... [who] disputed Billy's account. The latter swore that he would square matters by killing Chisum's herdsmen: that for each man he killed he would credit the cattleman with $5, but if he killed Chisum himself then the whole account would be wiped out.

" 'A young lawyer named Chapman was murdered at Lincoln. Four men were arrested, among them the notorious Jesse James ... I had been sent to pacify the country ... I heard that Billy the Kid had witnessed the murder. In the outskirts of Santa Fe lived an old 'squire,' who was one of Billy's friends. [Note that Wallace lifted Justice of the Peace John Wilson's nickname of "Squire," in whose Lincoln house he and Billy had actually met.] I ... told him I wanted the young outlaw to meet me promptly at midnight ... In [a] note I said ... if he would appear before the Grand Jury and court and convict them I would pardon him for all his crimes.

" 'The midnight meeting was as I have described. When he heard from my lips my proposition he said: 'My God, Governor, they would kill me.' 'But that can be arranged,' I replied. It was decided that Billy was to be taken the next morning ...

" 'It was during this confinement that 'the Kid' gave the most phenomenal exhibition of shooting ... [Wallace then made-up that

Billy told him the trick to aiming was laying his index finger along the barrel and pretending to point at the target.]

" 'It was a week before the trial ... [H]e said [to his guards] ... '[T]ell the Governor that I am tired' ... [U]nhitching a horse, [he] dashed out of town ...

" 'Later Billy was arrested for a series of murders. He had kept my note offering pardon ... He had been in jail a week when he addressed me: 'Governor, why haven't you come to see me?' ... A few days later there was a second note: 'Governor, I have some papers you would not want to see displayed. Come to the jail.' I knew what he meant. I sent a copy ... over to the paper and it was published ... It was then that he swore his vendetta on my life ...

" 'He was convicted for murder and sentenced to be hanged ...

" 'He had gone through many a danger. At one time, surrounded in a Mexican house, 'the Kid' fought nine men. The house was set on fire, and he ... escaped through all the musketry ...

" 'From his trial," continued General Wallace, 'Billy was taken back to jail ... A day before the execution, nine guards were watching him. At dinner time all but one left ... As the guard stood to place the [dinner] tray on the floor, Billy the Kid struck him ... with the handcuffs, crushing the skull. Then he took the guard's revolver, routed all the other guards ... forced a blacksmith ... to break the handcuffs, mounted a good horse ... and rode away ...

" 'It is needless to touch upon my danger under the vendetta ... Sufficient it is to say that he started for Santa Fe at once, and, determined to have a shot in return, I started out to meet him, but for some reason he never reached the point.

" 'Sheriff Pat Garrett was the only man in New Mexico not afraid of Billy ... Pat received information that Billy had gone back to an old fort in the mountains to see his sweetheart. Garrett journeyed there. He lay in wait in the dooryard of Billy's love, and finally saw the door open one night and a man come out in stocking feet ... Garrett walked in and covered the girl's father with a gun. 'Not a word,' he whispered, as he passed behind the headboard of the bed with gun in hand. The door opened again. Billy seemed to smell danger ... He cried to the old man in Spanish, 'Who's there?' ... Garrett raised his revolver. There were two reports ... There were two bullet holes through his heart ... [H]e was only twenty-two.' "

On June 8th, 1902, Wallace published his last Billy the Kid outlaw myth article, his lying silenced, in about 2½ years, by his cancer death. Novella-like, it was in *New York World Magazine*, almost 21 years after Billy died because of his betrayed pardon. It was titled "General Lew Wallace Writes a Romance of 'Billy the Kid,' Most Famous Bandit of the Plains, Thrilling Story of the Midnight Meeting Between General Wallace, Then Governor of New Mexico, and the Notorious Outlaw, in a Lonesome Hut at Santa Fe." The text came from Wallace's manuscript for his autobiography, which he was then writing.

The excerpted article stated: "General Lew Wallace, author of 'Ben Hur,' is completing his autobiography ... The most thrilling chapter ... tells of the midnight meeting ... between General Wallace, at the time Governor of the Territory of New Mexico, and 'Billy the Kid,' the most notorious outlaw the far West has ever produced ... General Wallace conceived the idea that he might gain certain important information by a face-to-face talk ...

"On the night of the meeting [Wallace and the owner] sat ... in the hut ... which was on the outskirts of Santa Fe ... The door flew open and, standing ... was 'Billy the Kid.' In his left hand he carried a Winchester rifle. In his right was a revolver ... He had killed scores of men: he was the quarry of every sheriff ...

"General Wallace was able to effect an important arrangement with the outlaw, of which he gives the details ... 'Shortly before I had become Governor of New Mexico, Chapman, a young attorney in Lincoln, had been murdered ... [Note that Wallace is self-protectively lying. Because Chapman was murdered over 4½ months after his arrival as Governor, he was accused of ignoring the troubles.] When I reached New Mexico it was declared ... that 'Billy the Kid' had been a witness .... I had been sent to ... pacify the territory ... Therefore I arranged the meeting ... 'Testify,' I said, 'before the Grand Jury and the trial court and convict the murderer of Chapman and I will let you go scot-free with a pardon in your pocket for all your misdeeds' ... 'Governor,' said he, 'if I were to do what you ask they would kill me.' 'We can prevent that,' said I ... To all appearances, his capture was to be genuine. To this he agreed ... [He was] confined in the Lincoln County jail.'

"It was here that General Wallace, in spite of the fears of the guards, permitted the outlaw to give an exhibition of his skill with the revolver and the rifle ...

"Billy ... did not remain long confined. One morning [he told his guards] 'Boys ... [t]ell the Governor I'm tired' ... [and he rode off] ... "He was arrested soon afterward for a series of murders, and was brought again to the Lincoln County Jail. Patrick Garrett was Sheriff ... [Billy] must have considered himself in desperate straits. [T]he outlaw sent [Governor Wallace] a note. [It] said: 'Come to the jail. I have some papers you would not want to see displayed.' 'I knew what he meant,' said General Wallace ... 'He referred to the note he received from me in response to which he appeared in the hut on the mesa ... I thwarted his purpose by giving a copy of the latter, and a narrative of the circumstances connected with it, to the paper published in the town ...

" '[T]he desperado was convicted and sentenced to be hanged ... Nine men were put on guard ... On the day before that set for his execution one man sat in front of Billy while he ate his dinner ... [Billy] ... dashed his brains out with his handcuffs. He seized the dead guard's revolver and ... routed all the other guards ... He forced a blacksmith to break the manacle chains, seized a good horse ... and rode away ...

" 'Patrick Garrett ... received information that Billy had gone back to an old fort in the mountains to see his sweetheart ... [Garrett] lay in wait in the dooryard of the home of Billy's love, and finally ... he saw the door open one night and a man step out ... [Garrett] covered the girl's father with his gun. 'Not a word,' he said, and slid behind the headboard of the bed. The door opened again and 'Billy the Kid' entered ... [I]nstinct taught him that something was wrong. He cried to the cowering old man in Spanish: 'Who's here?' ... Garrett raised his revolver; two shots rang out ... A form tottered, then crashed to the floor. In the nerveless hand was a smoking revolver ... the notorious New Mexican outlaw had missed his aim ... But there were two bullet wounds in the body of 'Billy the Kid,' and both pierced the heart ...

" 'Las Cruces [actually Fort Sumner] possesses the final resting place of the worst bad man that ever infested the Southwestern border. An ancient Mexican, who sometimes shows this grave to visitors [responded when asked] 'And how old was Billy when he died?' 'Twenty-one, senor,' replied the ancient ... 'How many, amigo, had this man killed?' ... 'He had killed ... twenty-one men, one for each year of his age' ... said the Mexican.' [Note that Wallace's fake tally is inscribed on one of Billy's Fort Sumner gravestones.]

"General Wallace also tells in his autobiography how and why 'Billy the Kid' started on his career of crime: 'The man whose deeds of blood had drawn upon him the eyes of an entire nation, was born a New York waif. Before he was more than ten years of age he was brought to Indiana ... In 1876, when he was about seventeen years old, he suddenly left his home ...to the country of the men of his kind – the frontier of the far West.

" 'Billy began his career with an oath to kill John Chisum, his first employer ... Chisum and the 'Kid' had been unable to agree on terms of settlement for a season's work. The result was the lad's fearful vendetta, sworn not only against Chisum, but against all of Chisum's other employees as well ... Then his bloody career began. It was not long until William Bonne ... became the most feared man in the Southwest.' "

Lew Wallace also created an enduring secondary myth: that Billy was short. Wallace's December 10th, 1893 *San Francisco Chronicle* article titled "Lew Wallace's Foe," stated: "Garrett appointed as guards over the 'Kid' Bob Ollinger [sic] and John [it was James] Bell ... who towered over their diminutive prisoner." In fact, Billy, at 5'8 or 9", was almost the same height as Wallace at 5'10", both above their day's average of 5'6". The December 27th, 1880, *Las Vegas Daily Gazette*, in "The Kid. Interview with Billy Bonney," had stated: "He is about five feet, eight or nine inches tall ... weighing about 140." Frank Coe, Billy's fellow Regulator, as an old-timer wrote to a William Steele Dean, on August 3rd, 1926, that Billy was, quote: "5ft 8in, weight 138 lb." Sexist Wallace also demeaned Billy as effeminate. In *The Indianapolis Press's* June 23rd, 1900's "General Wallace's Feud with Billy the Kid," he stated: "I was not expecting to see a stripling, with rounded shoulders, slightly stooping stature ... effeminate physique ... His voice was as musical as that of a society belle." For June 8th, 1902's *New York World Magazine's* "General Lew Wallace Writes a Romance of 'Billy the Kid,'" Wallace declared that Billy left the sham jailing for lack of masculine endurance. He wrote: "[T]he desperado drawled in the feminine voice that was a part and parcel of his character: 'Tell the Governor I'm tired.' " In fact, December 27th, 1880's *Las Vegas Daily Gazette's* article, "The Kid. Interview with Billy Bonney," stated: "[O]ne would scarcely mistrust that he was the hero of the 'Forty Thieves' romance ... He is ... quite a handsome looking fellow." Frank Coe had written in his 1926 letter, that Billy "stood straight as an Indian" and was a "fine looking ... lad."

But was there more to Lew Wallace's outlaw myth? I believe he planned to use Billy in a Western novel. He'd used his Turkey ambassadorship to write his 1893 bestseller: *The Prince of India or Why Constantinople Fell.*

Wallace dropped clues in interviews. In January 16th, 1886's *Crawfordsville Saturday Evening Journal,* he claimed two books in progress. One was *The Prince of India.* He added, quote, "the other is wholly American." Was that a book on Billy?

In a February 10th, 1894 *Cincinnati Post* editorial, he declared that he'd surpassed Charles Dickens, who only wrote about, quote, "trifling, frivolous, or bad, cheap people;" while he wrote about famous people. Billy the Kid was certainly famous.

On October 5th, 1894, on a lecture tour of western states, Wallace was interviewed by the *St. Paul, Minnesota Dispatch.* He reported a, quote, "new novel ... in course of preparation."

The same month, on the 14th, the *Tacoma, Washington, Daily Ledger's* reporter wrote: "[Wallace] said ... he is preparing to write another book ... [He said] '[The subject] I prefer to keep to myself ... If I were to make public my subject, why a dozen fellows might write a dozen books on the same and publish them before I had half completed mine.' "

On April 15th, 1902, the *Cincinnati Commercial Tribune* printed: "General Lew Wallace ... is Working on New Book." Wallace was quoted: "I have been employed for the past four years on a ... book ... I do not care to say what the title or character ... will be. It is manifestly bad policy, for the financial and from every other standpoint."

There's another clue. When Lew Wallace departed New Mexico Territory on May 28th, 1881, he stole the official documents of his governorship - to the anger of archivists to this day. To them he added documents of a civilian: Billy Bonney. In fact, he had enough research to write a novel on the West. And he'd developed its plot with 20 years of Billy the Kid outlaw myth articles. That has an irony. Billy Bonney's letters and interview, preserved by Wallace, reveal the real Billy the Kid, whom he'd tried so hard to hide.

A later talk will discuss Billy Bonney's enemies' branding him with the outlaw myth moniker: "Billy the Kid."

TALK 35:
THE BILLY THE KID MONIKER
FROM BOOK: *THE LOST PARDON OF BILLY THE KID*
APRIL 21, 2021

This revisionist history talk is about the "Billy the Kid" moniker, invented by Billy Bonney's enemies for his outlaw myth. The information is from my book, *The Lost Pardon of Billy the Kid* and *The Coroner's Jury Report of Billy the Kid*.

A misconception is that "Billy the Kid" was Billy Bonney's alias. That implies that he used it himself. It was actually devised by his Santa Fe Ring enemies; promoted by his pardon's betrayer, Lew Wallace; and used by his killer, Pat Garrett to sell his 1882 book: *The Authentic Life of Billy the Kid*. For real Billy, the moniker would have been an anathema: a symbol of his unjust outlawing.

Billy's real alias was William Bonney. His names reflect his traumatic life. He was possibly the illegitimate child of a Michael McCarty, and was called Henry McCarty till he was 13½. Then his mother, Catherine, whose last name is unknown, married a William Henry Harrison Antrim in Santa Fe. Billy became Henry Antrim. Heartless Antrim, however, abandoned him to homelessness when his mother died of T.B. the following year. As Billy wrote to Governor Lew Wallace, on March 13th, 1879, in his first pardon plea letter: "I am called Kid Antrim but Antrim is my stepfathers name." He created his identity-hiding alias, William Henry "Billy" Bonney, after his August 17th, 1877 killing of a bullying blacksmith in Arizona, and flight back to New Mexico Territory. Bonney may have been his Irish mother's maiden name.

Billy knew the Billy the Kid moniker was used against him. In his December 12th, 1880 letter to Governor Lew Wallace, he wrote: "I noticed in the Las Vegas Gazette a piece which stated that, Billy 'the' Kid, the name by which I am known in the Country was the captain of a Band of Outlaws ... There is no such Organization in Existence."

The moniker's root was benign. When Billy came to Lincoln County in October of 1877 to work as a ranch hand for John Tunstall, he was just 17. So other employees called him "Kid."

Governor Lew Wallace started its darker use in his March 31st, 1879 letter to Secretary of the Interior Carl Schurz. Though Wallace had just made the pardon bargain with Billy, which included sham imprisonment, he likely intended its betrayal. So he portrayed Billy as a random criminal. He wrote: "A precious specimen nick-named "The Kid," whom the Sheriff is holding here in the Plaza ... is an object of tender regard. I heard singing and music the other night ... I found the minstrels of the village actually serenading the fellow in his prison."

The full moniker, "Billy the Kid," appeared first in the 1879 Fort Stanton military Court of Inquiry of Fort Stanton Commander N.A.M. Dudley for illegal intervention in the Lincoln County War Battle causing murder of Alexander McSween and arson of his home.

On May 23rd, Susan McSween, who'd filed the charges, testified that she heard him say "Billy the Kid." Since Dudley was Ring-beholden, he must have heard the Ring's early outlaw myth. Susan described going to his camp to plead for protection. She stated: "He then got very angry and said ... that he would send his soldiers where he pleased, that I have no such business to have such men as Billy the Kid ... in my house."

On May 28th, Billy testified about seeing Dudley's soldiers fire a volley at him and others fleeing the burning McSween house. He showed his confusion about the new moniker. His questioning by the prosecutor is as follows: " 'What is your name and place of residence?' ... 'My name is William Bonney' ... 'Are you known or called Billy Kidd [spelled K-I-D-D], also Antrim?' 'Yes Sir.' " Dudley's attorney later questioned: " '[A]re you also known as the 'Kid?' 'I have already answered that question, Yes Sir, I am, but not 'Billy Kid' that I know of.' "

In late 1880, Billy was pursued by a Secret Service Operative named Azariah Wild. Wild was fed the outlaw myth by Ringite handlers, who told him that Billy headed a counterfeiting-rustling gang. On October 5th, Wild garbled the moniker in his report to his Chief; writing: "William Antrom alias William Bonney alias Billy Kid is an outlaw in the mountains here, who came here from Arizona after committing a murder there." Wild left the Territory in late December, but, by January 2nd, 1881, his report from New Orleans showed he'd mastered the moniker. He wrote: "Information on the arrest of William Wilson, William Antrom alias Billy the Kid, with several members of their gang by Deputy U.S. Marshal Patrick F. Garrett has reached me."

On December 3rd, 1880, the Ring began its outlaw myth press against Billy using leaked information from Operative Wild. The *Las Vegas Gazette* article was by owner-editor, J.H. Koogler, and titled "Powerful Gang of Outlaws Harassing the Stockmen." It stated: "The gang includes forty to fifty men ... The gang is under the leadership of 'Billy the Kid,' a desperate cuss, who is eligible for the post of captain in any crowd, no matter how mean and lawless."

Billy read that article. On December 12th, he wrote to Lew Wallace denying its lies. He showed that, by then, he knew the moniker, calling it: "Billy 'the' Kid, the name by which I am known in the Country."

On December 22nd, when Lew Wallace placed his first reward offer in the *Las Vegas Gazette*, it was for "Billy the Kid," proving he believed the moniker's universal recognition by then. He wrote: "BILLY THE KID, $500 REWARD."

That same December 22nd, Billy gained national fame as Billy the Kid in a Ringite *New York Sun* article titled: "Outlaws of New Mexico, The Exploits of a Band Headed by a New York Youth, The Mountain Fastness of the Kid and his Followers." It stated: "The leaders are Billy the Kid, so called from his youth; Dave Rudabaugh, Billy Wilson, and Tom O'Phallier [meaning O'Folliard]."

On December 27th, the Ringite *Las Vegas Gazette's* article by Lucius "Lute" Wilcox was about Billy's Stinking Springs capture.

It was titled "The Kid. Interview with Billy Bonney, The Best Known Man in New Mexico." [Described was Billy and the other captives getting new clothes at the Las Vegas jail.] It stated: " 'Billy the Kid,' and Billy Wilson ... stood patiently while a blacksmith took off their shackles and bracelets to allow them an opportunity to make a change of clothing."

The same December 27th, Ringite Russell A. Kistler reported the capture in his *Las Vegas Daily Optic* as: "A Big Haul! Billy the Kid, Dave Rudabaugh, Billy Wilson and Tom Pickett in the Clutches of the Law, Notorious Gang of Outlaws Broken up." It stated: "Our readers are familiar with the depredations committed ... by a gang of daring desperados, under the leadership of Billy the Kid."

On April 3rd, 1881, the *Santa Fe Daily New Mexican,* in "Something About the Kid," described Billy's transport from the Santa Fe jail to Mesilla. It gave an anecdote with Billy joking about the moniker. At Las Cruces, a crowd gathered around the stagecoach. It stated: "[S]omeone asked which is 'Billy the Kid.' The Kid himself answered by placing his hand on [his attorney] Judge Leonard's shoulder and saying 'this is the man.' " Billy's attorney, Ira Leonard, was, in fact, bald and middle-aged.

On May 3rd, after Billy's April 28th, 1881 jailbreak, Lew Wallace repeated his reward offer, this time in the *Santa Fe Daily New Mexican,* again for "Billy the Kid."

On May 16th, 1881, Wallace published a *St. Louis Daily Globe-Democrat* article: "The Thugs Territory." The interviewer stated: "[T]he Governor gave a very interesting sketch of the life of 'Billy the Kid,' the most noted and desperate character in New Mexico."

On June 18th, 1881, the *Crawfordsville Saturday Evening Journal* published Wallace's article titled: "Billy the Kid, General Wallace Tells Why the Young Desperado of New Mexico Wanted to Kill Him. A Dashing and Daring Career in the Land of the Petulant Pistol." It stated: "[N]ewspaper accounts of the exploits of 'Billy the Kid,' the New Mexico outlaw, have made him the chief among frontier desperados."

In 1882, Billy's killer, Pat Garrett, featured the then famous moniker and outlaw myth to sell his book, titled: *The Authentic Life of Billy the Kid*.

The December 10th, 1893 *San Francisco Chronicle* carried a Lew Wallace interview titled: "Lew Wallace's Foe." It stated: "The Governor's enemy was no less a personage than the illustrious 'Billy the Kid,' than whom no man had ever excited more terror on the frontier."

On January 6th, 1894, Wallace gave a *Weekly Crawfordsville Review* interview as "Street Pickings." It stated: "When I was governor of New Mexico that territory was ... terrorized by bands of daring and murderous outlaws, at the head of whom was the famous border desperado, 'Billy the Kid.' "

On June 23rd, 1900, for *The Indianapolis Press*, Wallace presented "General Wallace's Feud with Billy the Kid, When the General Was Governor of New Mexico and Billy Bonne Was the Most Dangerous Western Outlaw." Wallace stated: "I will never lose the image of Billy the Kid, as I saw him that midnight in old Santa Fe, back in 1879 ... It was not long until 'Billy the Kid' became the most daring and notorious of desperadoes."

On June 8th, 1902, for *New York World Magazine*, Wallace was interviewed for "General Lew Wallace Writes a Romance of 'Billy the Kid.' " It stated: "The most thrilling chapter in [Lew Wallace's autobiography, then in progress] ... tells of the midnight meeting ... between General Wallace, at the time Governor of the Territory of New Mexico, and 'Billy the Kid,' the most notorious outlaw the far West has ever produced."

Lew Wallace died in 1905. His wife completed his autobiography in 1906. She inserted her May 11th, 1879 letter to their son, Henry, parroting Wallace's outlaw myth. She wrote: "[W]e hold our lives at the mercy of desperados and outlaws, chief among them Billy the Kid, whose boast is that he has killed a man for every year of his life."

In 1927, Pat Garrett's *The Authentic Life of Billy the Kid* was republished. By the 1930's, the "Billy the Kid" moniker was synonymous with Billy, being used by anyone writing about him.

In 1934, George Coe, Billy's friend and fellow Regulator, as an old-timer published *Frontier Fighter: The Autobiography of George Coe, Who Fought and Rode With Billy the Kid*. In 1955, as an old-timer, "Teddy Blue" Abbott, who never met Billy, published *We Pointed Them North: Recollections of a Cowpuncher*. He wrote: "The Lincoln County troubles was still going on, and you had to be either for Billy the Kid or against him."

Later talks exposing Billy the Kid imposter hoaxes, will show how lying old-timers claiming to be Billy called themselves Billy the Kid, ignorant of what that hated symbol of the outlaw myths meant to real Billy Bonney.

TALK 36:
BILLY THE KID'S CORONER'S JURY REPORT
FROM BOOK: *THE CORONER'S JURY REPORT OF BILLY THE KID*
APRIL 27, 2021

This talk presents my revisionist history of Billy Bonney's Coroner's Jury Report. The information is from my book: *The Coroner's Jury Report of Billy the Kid: The Inquest That Sealed the Fame of Billy Bonney and Pat Garrett.*

Arguably the most famous Old West killing was of Billy Bonney by Pat Garrett on July 14th, 1881, in the Maxwell family's Fort Sumner mansion. It's discussed in Talk 33. The next day, July 15th, there was an inquest, yielding the six jurymen's Coroner's Jury Report. It identified the victim as William Bonney, had a witness statement by Peter Maxwell, and called the shooting by Garrett justifiable homicide.

Billy Bonney's killing occurred right after New Mexico Territory's 1870's decade of bloody grass-roots uprisings against the lethal, land-grabbing, political-economic cabal of the Santa Fe Ring. In the most famous rebellion, the 1878 Lincoln County War, teenaged Billy became the people's hero, ending up outlawed by the Ring as "Billy the Kid." The Ring's attempt to eliminate him by hanging for that war's Regulator killings failed with his escape on April 28th, 1881 from Sheriff Pat Garrett's custody in Lincoln County's courthouse-jail. So Garrett was just completing his killing task 78 days later.

Billy's Coroner's Jury Report was filed with the correct authority to validate it. He was the District Attorney of the First

Judicial District, which included Fort Sumner's San Miguel County. And because Pat Garrett additionally claimed the Billy the Kid reward, that Report ended up validated by the Territory's other high public officials for its granting.

As will be seen in later talks, that Coroner's Jury Report was the bugaboo of 20th century, old-timer, Billy the Kid imposters and their huckster promoters, who lied that Billy survived Pat Garrett's shooting. Of necessity, they also lied that the Report didn't exist, so the body wasn't identified. Or they lied that Garrett wrote the Report to hide that he killed an innocent victim, not Billy. Or they lied that Jury President, Milnor Rudulph, wasn't present, so the Report was faked.

Billy's Coroner's Jury Report of July 15th, 1881 is a three page document written by Justice of the Peace Alejandro Segura in that day's legal Spanish. He forwarded it to the proper District Attorney: William Breeden. It began: "To the District Attorney of the First Judicial District of the Territory of New Mexico, Greetings."

Segura, as ex officio coroner by virtue of being Justice of the Peace, chose the jurymen. He wrote: "[I]mmediately upon receiving said information [of a murder] I proceeded to the said place and named Milnor Rudulph, Jose Silva, Antonio Saavedra, Pedro Antonio Lucero, Lorenzo Jaramillo and Sabal Gutierres a jury to investigate the case."

Segura confirmed identification of the body and its fatal wound. He wrote: "[The jurymen] found the body of William Bonney alias 'Kid' with a shot in the left breast."

Segura provided Peter Maxwell's eye-witness account; stating: "Pat F. Garrett fired two shots at the said William Bonney and the said William Bonney fell near my fire place and I went out of the room and when I came in again about three or four minutes after the shots the said William Bonney was dead."

Segura gave the jurymen's verdict. He wrote: "[T]he deed of said Garrett was justifiable homicide."

Segura gave the jurymen's recommendation: "[He] is worthy of being rewarded."

On screen is the three page Spanish Coroner's Jury Report of July 15th, 1881 for William H. Bonney, in Precinct Number 27, in the County of San Miguel. **[FIGURE 51]** Translated, it stated:

"To the District Attorney of the First Judicial District of the Territory of New Mexico, Greetings:

"On this 15th day of July, A.D. 1881, I, the undersigned, Justice of the Peace of the above named precinct, received information that a murder had taken place in Fort Sumner, in said precinct, and immediately upon receiving said information I proceeded to the said place and named Milnor Rudulph, Jose Silva, Antonio Saavedra, Pedro Antonio Lucero, Lorenzo Jaramillo and Sabal Gutierres a jury to investigate the case and the above jury convened in the home of Luz B. Maxwell and proceeded to a room in the said house where they found the body of William Bonney alias 'Kid' with a shot in the left breast and having examined the body they examined the evidence of Pedro Maxwell, which evidence is as follows:

" 'I being in my bed in my room, at about midnight on the 14th day of July, Pat F. Garrett came into my room and sat at the end on my bed to talk with me. A little while after Garrett sat down, William Bonney came in and got close to my bed with a gun in his hand and asked me 'Who is it Who is it?' and then Pat F. Garrett fired two shots at the said William Bonney and the said Bonney fell near my fire place and I went out of the room and when I came in again about three or four minutes after the shots the said Bonney was dead.'

"The jury has found the following verdict: We the jury unanimously find that William Bonney has been killed by a bullet in the left breast in the region of the heart, the same having been fired from a pistol in the hand of Pat F. Garrett, and our verdict is that the act of said Garrett was justifiable homicide and we are unanimous in the opinion that the gratitude of all the community is due to the said Garrett for his deed and [he] is worthy of being rewarded.

"[The jurymen signed as] M. Rudulph, President; Antonio Saavedra; Pedro Antonio Lucero; Jose Silva, signed with an X; Sabal Gutierrez, signed with an X; and Lorenzo Jaramillo; signed with an X.

"All which information I put at your disposal. [Signed] Alejandro Segura Justice of the Peace."

Territorio de Nuevo Méjico ⎰ Precinto No 27.
Condado de San Miguel ⎱ Del ~~Pcino~~ y Distrito judicial
          Al Procurador ~~General~~ del Territorio de Nuevo
Méjico   Salud.

        Este dia 15 de Julio, A.D. 1881, reciví
yo, el abajo firmado, Juez de Paz del Precinto arriba
escrito, informacion que habia habido una muerte
en Fuerte Sumner en dicho precinto é immediata
mente al recivir la informacion procedí al
dicho lugar y nombré á Milnor Rudulph,
José Silva, Antonio Saavedra, Pedro Antonio
Lucero, Lorenzo Jaramillo y Sabal Gutierrez
un ju   do para averiguar el asunto y venir
nier   el dicho jurado en la casa de
Luz 10   axwell procedieron á un cuarto
en dicha casa donde hallaron el cuerpo
de William Bonney alias "Kid" con un bala
zo en el pecho en el lado yzquierdo del pecho
y habiendo esaminado el cuerpo ecsaminaron
la evidencia de Pedro Maxwell cuya eviden
cia es como sigue "Estando yo acostado en

mi cama en mi cuarto a cosa de media noche
El dia 14 de Julio entró á mi cuarto Pat. F.
Garrett y se sentó en la orilla de mi cama á
platicar conmigo. A poco rato que Garrett
se sentó entró William Bonney y se arrimó
á mi cama con una pistola en la mano y
me preguntó "Who is it? Who is it?" y entónces
Pat. F. Garrett le tiró dos balazos á dicho
William Bonney y se cayó el dicho Bonney
en un lado de mi fogon y yo salí del cuarto
cuando volví á entrar ya as en tres ó cuatro
minutos despues de los balazos estaba muerto dicho Bonney."

El jurado há hallado el siguiente
dictámen "Nosotros los del jurado u-
nanimente hallamos que William Bonney há sido muerto por un balazo en el
pecho yzquierdo en la region del Corazon
tirado de una pistola en la mano de Pat.
F. Garrett y nuestro dictámen es que
el hecho de dicho Garrett fué homicidio
justificable y estamos unánines en
opinion que la gratitud de toda la

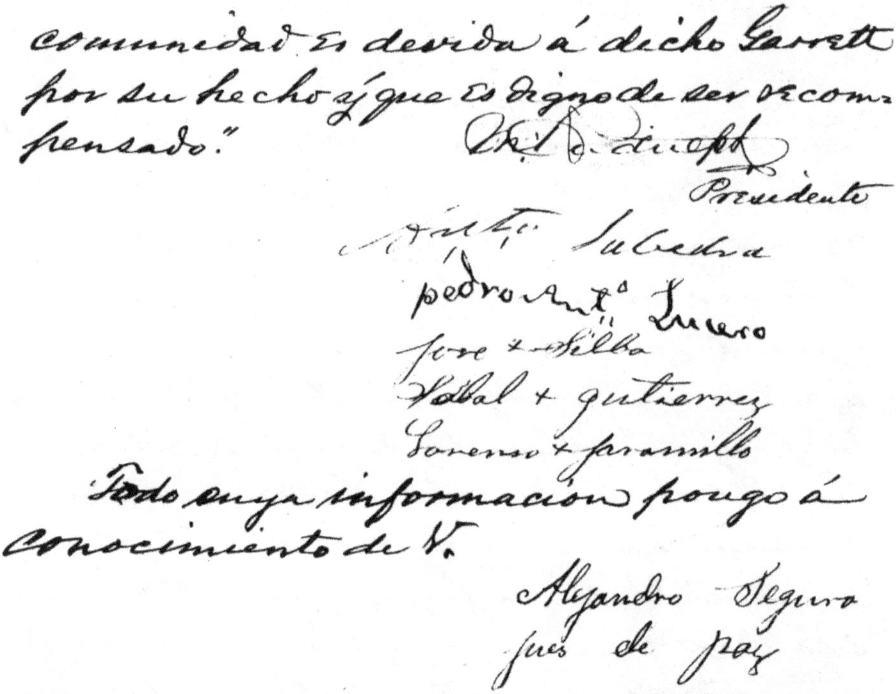

[handwritten Spanish text:]

comunidad Es devida á dicho Garrett por su hecho y que Es digno de ser recompensado."

M. B. Rudulph
Presidente

Anto. Sabedra
pedro Anto. Lucero
jose + Silba
Noval + gutierrez
Lorenzo + jaramillo

Todo cuya información pongo á conocimiento de V.

Alejandro Segura
juez de paz

FIGURE: 51. Original Spanish Coroner's Jury Report of July 15, 1881 for William H. Bonney aka Kid (Courtesy of the Indiana Historical Society, Lew Wallace Collection)

The "Brushy Bill" Roberts Billy the Kid imposter hoax fabricated that Jury President, Milnor Rudulph, was not present, so the Report was fake. But Rudulph's signature on the Report, with its unique Spencerian penmanship flourishes, matches Rudulph's signature on his May 18th, 1879 letter to Territorial Secretary William G. Ritch, proving his presence.

On screen is Milnor Rudulph's signature on the July 15th, 1881 Coroner's Jury Report, and his matching signature on his May 18th, 1879 letter to Territorial Secretary William G. Ritch **[FIGURE 52]**, proving his presence at the inquest by his signing the Report.

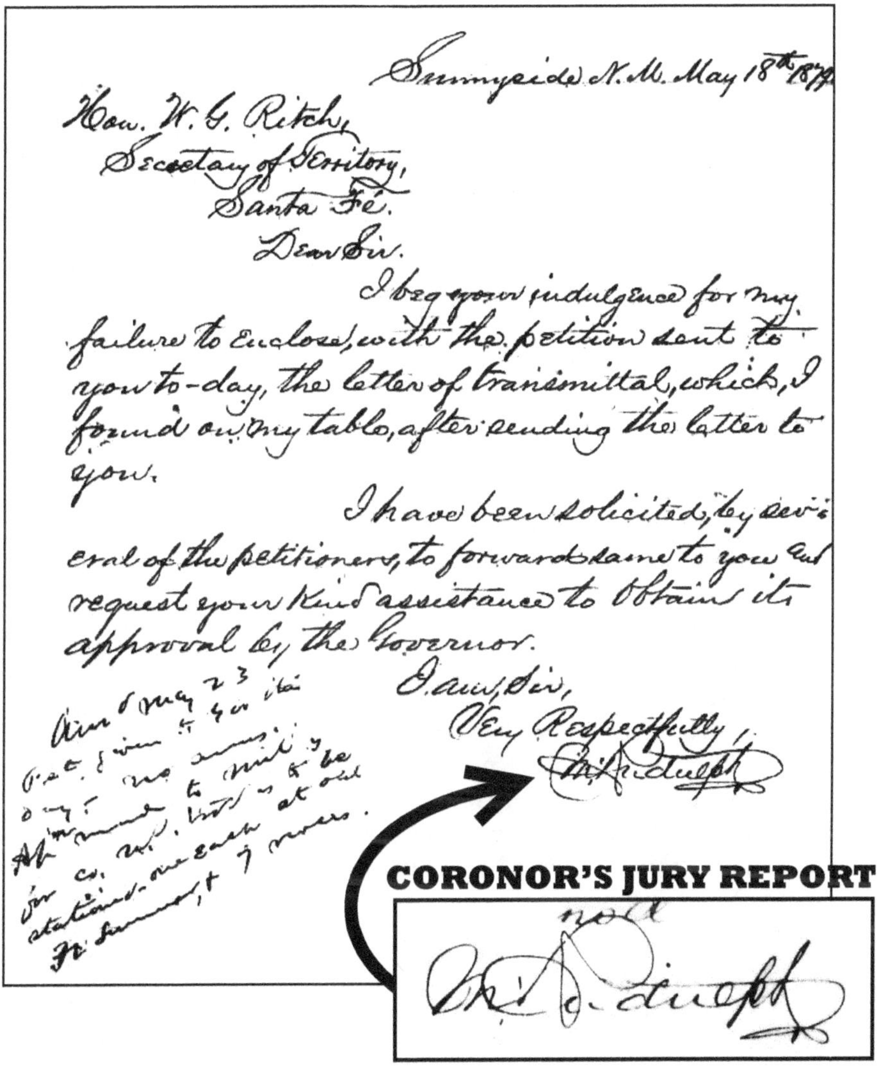

Sunnyside N. M. May 18th 1879

Hon. W. G. Ritch,
Secretary of Territory,
Santa Fé.
Dear Sir.

I beg your indulgence for my failure to enclose, with the petition sent to you to-day, the letter of transmittal, which, I found on my table, after sending the letter to you.

I have been solicited, by several of the petitioners, to forward same to you and request your kind assistance to obtain its approval by the Governor.

I am, Sir,
Very Respectfully,
M. Rudulph

FIGURE: 52. Letter of May 18, 1879 from Milnor Rudulph to Territorial Secretary William G. Ritch to show that his signature matched the one on the Coroner's Jury Report. (Courtesy Territorial Archives of New Mexico Microfilm, Albuquerque Genealogical Library Microfilm)

Milnor Rudulph's presence explains the jurymen's conclusion, which was unexpected given their friendship with Billy. The Report stated: "[W]e are unanimous in the opinion that the gratitude of all the community is due to the said Garrett for his deed and [he] is worthy of being rewarded." Rudulph was Postmaster of Sunnyside, seven miles north of Fort Sumner. A loyal Ringite, he'd helped boss Thomas Benton Catron and his Santa Fe Ring take over the Legislature in 1872 to block anti-Ring bills. That caused the first anti-Ring, freedom fight, which I named the Legislature Revolt. Ringite Governor Marsh Giddings used troops to suppress the anti-Ring legislators and cancel their bills. Rudulph's threatening presence apparently influenced Alejandro Segura's writing of the Report. His frightened juryman had no alternative but to sign the conclusion the day after Ring terrorism had invaded their town.

Another ploy of the "Brushy Bill" hoax was claiming the Coroner's Jury Report's signers didn't exist or weren't local men. But the census for 1880, the year before they signed, shows all being in San Miguel County.

Another ploy of the "Brushy Bill" hoax, was claiming that Pat Garrett wrote the Report. But Justice of the Peace Alejandro Segura identified himself as the author; writing it in the first person, as translated: "On this 15th day of July, A.D. 1881, I, the undersigned, Justice of the Peace ... proceeded to the said place and named [the jurymen]." He concluded for the District Attorney recipient: "All which information I put at your disposal." He signed as "Alejandro Segura Justice of the Peace."

Additionally, Segura wrote the Report with script idiosyncrasies compatible with a native-speaking writer, like him, and unknown to Pat Garrett.
Furthermore, the name Pat F. Garrett, as written in the Report, doesn't match how Garrett wrote his name. If he wrote the Report, his own name would match his handwriting.

On screen is the Pat Garrett name as written in the Coroner's Jury Report. It's followed by his actual, non-matching signature on his December 13th, 1901 letter to his wife. **[FIGURE 53]**

NAME IN THE REPORT

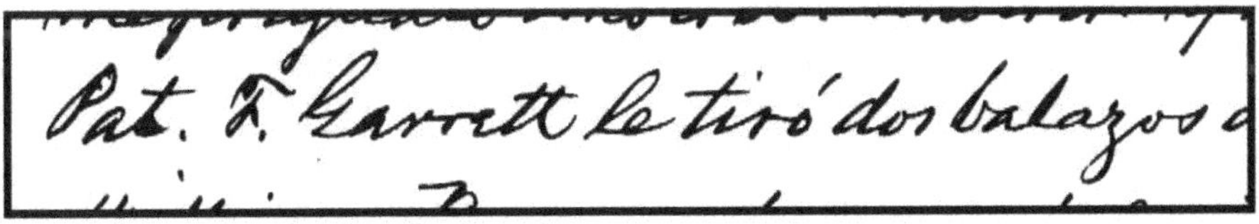

ACTUAL SIGNATURE ON LETTER

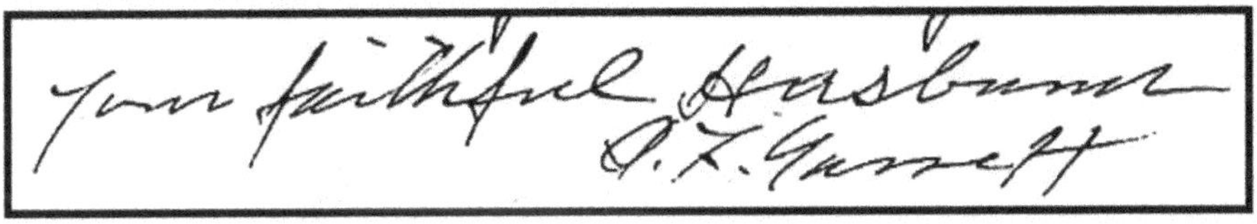

FIGURE: 3. Comparison of Pat Garrett's written name. (Signature from Pat Garrett's December 13, 1901 letter to his wife, courtesy of historian, David G. Thomas)

Another ploy of the "Brushy Bill" hoax, was claiming the Report didn't exist because it wasn't in Alejandro Segura's files. But it wasn't supposed to be there. Segura complied with the Territory's *General Laws of New Mexico* under the Act of January 30th, 1867, "Article XV, Chapter XL, Constables, Coroners, and Inquests." It stated: "[T]he verdict of the jury shall be in writing, which shall be signed by the justice of the peace and each one of the jury, and so recorded in the office of the probate judge of the county in which the inquest was held." But probate judge filing didn't apply to Billy, who had no estate or assets. So Segura sent the Report of this high-profile killing to, quote: "[T]he District Attorney of the First Judicial District." As prosecutor, this official could vouch for the verdict of justifiable homicide of the identified victim, Billy Bonney.

That July 15th, 1881, Pat Garrett sent a letter, with enclosed copy of that Coroner's Jury Report, to the Territory's Acting-Governor, William Ritch, to claim past Governor Lew Wallace's Billy the Kid reward. The actual Governor, Lionel Sheldon, was on leave from the Territory. Garrett confirmed his killing of Billy and its self-defense nature. It was quoted in July 23rd, 1881's

Las Cruces Rio Grande Republican in "Kid the Killer Killed, William Bonney alias Antrim, alias Billy the Kid, Fatally Meets Pat Garrett, the Lincoln County Sheriff." It stated: "Below is given Sheriff Garrett's report as made to Acting Governor Ritch which contains also the verdict of the coroner's jury [explained as its translation]."

The excerpted article stated: "William Bonney, alias 'the Kid,' is dead. No report could have caused more general feeling of gratification than this ... The following is Sheriff Garrett's official report to the chief executive of the territory ...

" 'To his Excellency the Governor of New Mexico:

" 'I have the honor to inform your Excellency that I had received several communications from persons in and about Fort Sumner, that William Bonney, alias the Kid, had been there ...

" 'In view of these reports I deemed it my duty to go there ... all the time doubting their accuracy; but on Monday, July 11, I left home, taking with me John W. Poe and T.L. McKinney ... and arrived just below Fort Sumner, on Wednesday, 13th [note that it was Thursday the 14th]. I ... entered the fort about midnight, and went to Mr. P. Maxwell's room. I found him in bed, and had just commenced talking to him about the object of my visit ... when a man entered the room in stockinged feet, with a pistol in one hand and a knife in the other. He came and placed his hand on the bed just beside me, and in a low whisper, 'who is it?' ... he asked Mr. Maxwell.

" 'I ... knew he was the Kid, and reached behind me for my pistol, feeling almost certain of receiving a ball from his ... as I felt sure he had now recognized me, but fortunately he drew back from the bed ... and, although he had his pistol pointed at my breast, he delayed to fire, and asked me in Spanish, "Quien es? Quien es?" This gave me time to bring mine to bear on him, and the moment I did so I pulled the trigger and he received his death wound ... It was my desire to have been able to take him alive, but his coming upon me so suddenly and unexpectedly leads me to believe that he had seen me enter the room, or had been informed by someone of the fact; and that he came there armed with pistol and knife expressly to kill me if he could. Under that impression I had no alternative but to kill him or to suffer death at his hands.

" 'I herewith annex a copy of the verdict rendered by the jury called in by the justice of the peace (ex officio coroner), the original of which is in the hands of the prosecuting attorney of the first judicial district.' "

[The article translated the Report stating that William Bonney was fatally shot by Pat Garrett in justifiable homicide and he deserved to be rewarded. It named the signers.]

This July 15th letter to Acting-Governor Ritch confirmed that the original Coroner's Jury Report went to the District Attorney for the First Judicial District, which included the San Miguel County killing site of Fort Sumner. Garrett stated: "I herewith annex a copy of the verdict rendered by the jury called in by the justice of the peace, the original of which is in the hands of the prosecuting attorney of the first judicial district."

That meant recipient District Attorney William Breeden checked the "justifiable homicide" verdict. His filing no murder charge against Garrett, confirmed he agreed with self-defense. And Acting-Governor Ritch showed agreement by facilitating Garrett's reward payment.

It's important to note that William Breeden was a major Santa Fe Ringite. He would have been pleased at the death of the Territory's last Regulator. Politically powerful, he had aided the Ring's 1866 founding by its bosses: Thomas Benton Catron and Steven Benton Elkins.

In 1874, Breeden was made Attorney General by Ringite Governor Marsh Giddings. That automatically made him District Attorney for the First Judicial District under an 1863 Territorial statute. In 1876 and 1878, Breeden was reappointed by Ringite Governor S.B. Axtell.

In 1875, Breeden was elected to the Legislature's Council from Santa Fe County, and re-elected in 1878.

From 1878 through 1880, Henry Waldo, Breeden's Ringite law partner and boss Catron's past law firm member, was Attorney General. In 1881, Breeden was re-appointed as Attorney General by Ringite Governor Lionel Sheldon, Lew Wallace's replacement. That also made Breeden District Attorney for the First Judicial District of Santa Fe, which included San Miguel County's Fort Sumner; which made him the correct recipient of Billy's Coroner's Jury Report. He served until 1889. He was also President of the New Mexican Printing and Publishing Company, which published the Ringite newspaper: the *Santa Fe New Mexican*.

So Breeden's backing the Coroner's Jury Report represented its Ring approval.

An additional consideration is that a 21st century Billy the Kid imposter hoax, which will be exposed in later talks, besides lying that the Coroner's Jury Report didn't exist, lied that a real murder case could be filed in 2003 against dead Pat Garrett for murdering an innocent victim instead of Billy Bonney. But the Coroner's Jury Report dated the killing to July 14th, 1881. There was a ten year statute of limitations on murder, established in the 1876 *Acts of the Legislative Assembly of the Territory of New Mexico*. So the last year that Garrett could have been prosecuted for murder in that case was 1891.

The original Coroner's Jury Report can be traced from its July 15th, 1881 recipient, District Attorney William Breeden, to its chance finding in 1932 by a government employee named Harold Abbott. Abbott was employed in Santa Fe at the State Land Office from 1931 to 1933. He found the Report with San Miguel County court records, in the state capitol's basement. He made copies and included his brother George. Harold died in 1937.

So George Abbott made the front page of November 30th, 1950's *Alamogordo News* in "Sumner Jury Thought The Kid Had Been Killed." The article debunked the "Brushy Bill" Roberts imposter hoax, then in the news. It stated: "Although the perennial controversy over whether the infamous Billy the Kid still lives ... George Abbott ... of Alamogordo has in his office at the Pioneer Abstract Company a photostatic copy of the verdict of the coroner's jury which viewed the remains of the late William Bonney. Some twenty years ago, when the late Harold Abbott, brother of George, was an employee of the state land office in Santa Fe, he, with other employees, were going over some old records in the basement of the state capitol. There they ran across, in the San Miguel court records, the original copy of the coroner's jury, dated July 15, 1881, and written in Spanish. The document covered three pages of which they made photostatic copies ... [T]he six men serving on the jury and the Justice of the Peace who empanelled them, seemed convinced that William Bonney, known as 'Kid,' was quite dead, and that he had been killed by Pat Garrett." A translation of the Report was provided.

George Abbott's Coroner's Jury Report copy also appeared in February, 1951's *New Mexico Magazine* under "Glimpses of History," to rebut the "Brushy Bill" hoax. The reporter wrote: "Interest in Billy the Kid - New Mexico's most notorious outlaw - was revived a few weeks ago when an old timer appeared ... to claim the identity of the Kid ... [with] an assertion that a coroner's inquest report was not legally on file ... However, a photostatic copy of the report has been located by New Mexico Magazine in Alamogordo. The photostat is owned by George Abbott, who said his brother had the copy made about 20 years ago." [It was partly reproduced for the article.]

On August 5th, 1951, Billy the Kid historian, Maurice Garland Fulton, responding to the "Brushy Bill" hoax, relocated the Report. He published an article in *The El Paso Times* titled "Coroner's Report Proves Billy the Kid is Dead, Historian Asserts, Researcher Discovers Document." The article had Fulton's photostatic copy of the Report. It stated: "Billy the Kid is dead. The famed outlaw met death at the business end of Pat Garrett's flaming pistol in July of 1881. So says Colonel Maurice G. Fulton ... former custodian of the Lincoln County Museum ... Colonel Fulton ... said: 'We are lucky to have a report in this instance, for coroner's jury reports are hard to find.' " End quote. Fulton had donated a copy to the Indiana Historical Society, stamped with legal certification of authenticity on January 18th, 1951. That's the Report I showed earlier in this talk.

One can trace the Coroner's Jury Report's storage in the state's successive Capitol Buildings. First was William Breeden's Palace of the Governors office. He apparently stored it, in his capacity as District Attorney for the First Judicial District, under San Miguel County court records, since this Fort Sumner killing was in that county.

On screen is Attorney General William Breeden's office space in Santa Fe's Palace of the Governors capitol building, shown as rooms 5, 6, and 8. Breeden used that office till 1889. **[FIGURE 54]** It was then used by the State Land Office. Apparently they stored their records with Breeden's.

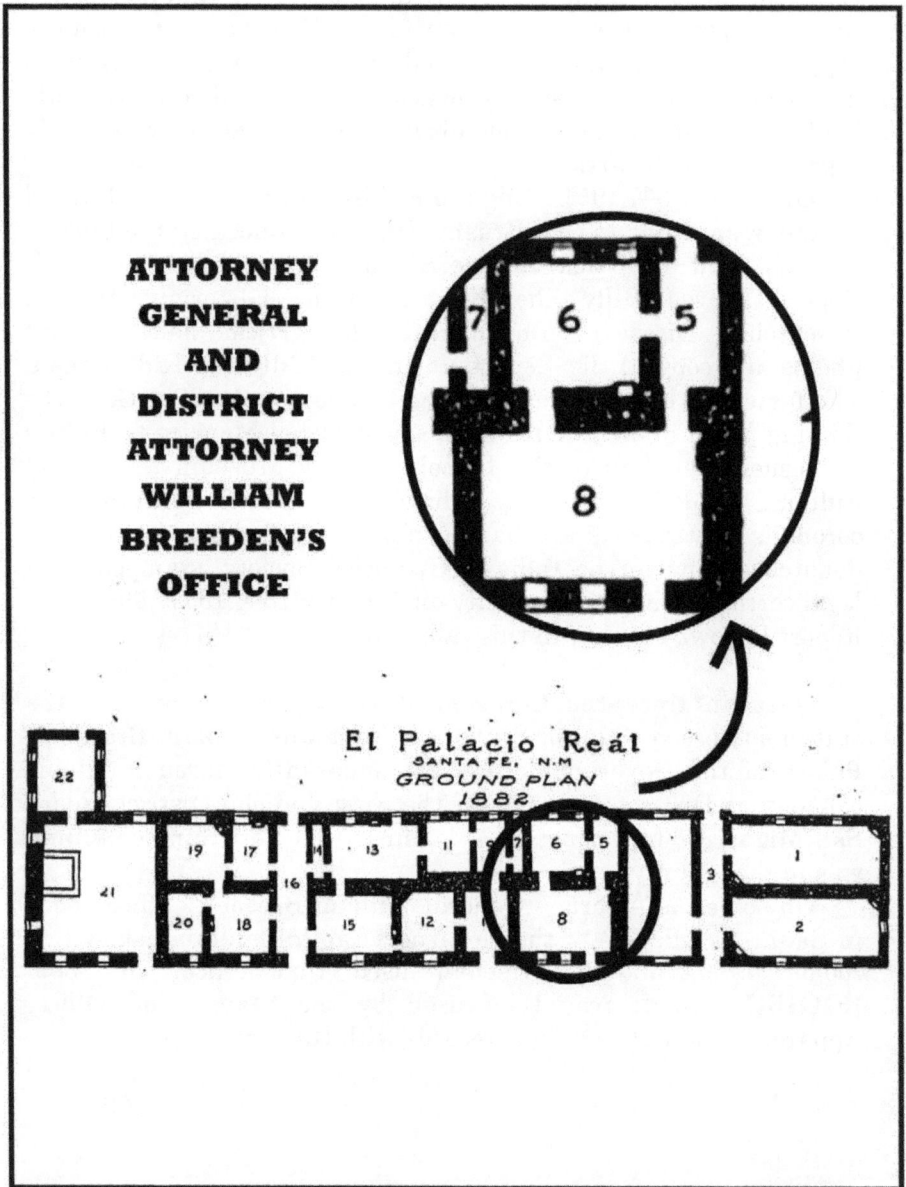

FIGURE: 54 Palace of the Governors in 1882, showing Attorney General William Breeden's office as rooms 5, 6, and 8. (From Clinton P. Anderson's 1944 *New Mexico Historical Review* article titled "The Adobe Palace," Page 110)

The records were moved with relocations of the capitol building. In 1932, as Harold Abbott stated, he, with other State Land Office employees, were searching old records in the basement of the capitol building. His finding of Breeden's San Miguel court records with them indicates that they'd stayed together with the Land Office ones since their Palace of the Governors storage.

There were several subsequent capitol buildings. From 1850 to 1886 one was under construction, but ended up as the Territorial Courthouse. In 1886, another building became the capitol, but burned down on May 12th, 1892, though its archives were saved. Then the Territorial Courthouse became the temporary capitol building, until another was completed in 1900. It was used for 66 years, until today's capitol building, "the Roundhouse," was dedicated in 1966.

So by Harold Abbott's 1932 finding of the Coroner's Jury Report in his day's capitol building's basement, the old Palace of the Governors records might have been moved multiple times. Demonstrated is that governmental personnel had done a good job of preserving old records. The Coroner's Jury Report of Billy the Kid proves their achievement!

A later talk will discuss additional witnesses who identified the body of Billy Bonney.

TALK 37:
WITNESSES OF
BILLY THE KID'S BODY
FROM BOOK: *THE CORONER'S JURY REPORT OF BILLY THE KID*
MAY 3, 2021

This talk presents identifications of Billy the Kid's body, adding to those of his Coroner's Jury Report. The information is from my book: *The Coroner's Jury Report of Billy the Kid: The Inquest That Sealed the Fame of Billy Bonney and Pat Garrett.*

One could say that Billy Bonney's July 14th, 1881 killing by Pat Garrett was the best documented death in the Old West. Billy's July 15th Coroner's Jury Report is presented in Talk 36. Witnesses of his body are also discussed in Talk 33 about the killing. As will be discussed in later talks on Billy the Kid imposter hoaxes, Billy's old-timer impersonators and their fraudster promoters hid the huge number of corpse identifications, adding to that of the Report's witness, Peter Maxwell, and its six jurymen. Additionally, killing Billy the Kid was major national news.

For the Coroner's Jury Report, witness Peter Maxwell had stated: "I being in my bed in my room, at about midnight on the 14th day of July, Pat F. Garrett came into my room and sat down. William Bonney came in and got close to my bed with a gun in his hand and asked me 'who is it' and then Pat F. Garrett fired two shots at the said William Bonney and the said William Bonney fell near my fire place and I went out of the room and when I came in again about three or four minutes after the shots the said William Bonney was dead."

Pat Garrett, the obvious witness as killer, wrote, on July 15ᵗʰ, 1881, to Acting-Governor William Ritch, as excerpted here: "[A] man entered the room in stockinged feet, with a pistol in one hand and a knife in the other. He came and placed his hand on the bed just beside me, and in a low whisper, 'who is it?' ... he asked Mr. Maxwell. I ... knew he was the Kid, and reached behind me for my pistol ... he drew back from the bed at noticing my movement ... and asked me in Spanish, 'Quien es? Quien es?' This gave me time to bring mine to bear on him, and the moment I did so I pulled the trigger and he received his death wound."

Pat Garrett also gave his account of the killing in his 1882 book, *The Authentic Life of Billy the Kid*, ghostwritten with his journalist boarder, Ashmun "Ash" Upson. Both men knew Billy. Upson had been a border with his family in Silver City. Garrett had met Billy in early 1878, and certainly knew the specifics of his own tracking, capturing, jailing, and killing of him. Garrett's lethality was indisputable. He first killed two of Billy's companions in his attempt to kill him. On December 19ᵗʰ, 1880, he and his Texan posse ambushed Billy's group returning to Fort Sumner. Tom O'Folliard was fatally shot. At the December 22ⁿᵈ, 1881 Stinking Springs capture, Garrett fatally shot Charlie Bowdre by mistaking him for Billy.

As to his killing of Billy, Garrett's book described his coming to Fort Sumner with his Deputies, John William Poe and Thomas "Kip" McKinney; and, late that moonlit night of July 14ᵗʰ, 1881, stationing them on the porch of the Maxwell family's mansion, while he went inside Peter Maxwell's dark bedroom, to ask about Billy's whereabouts. The excerpted book stated: "At that moment, a man sprang quickly in the door, and looking back, called twice in Spanish, 'Quien es? Quien es? (Who comes there?)' No one replied, and he came into the room. I could see he was bareheaded, and from his tread ... he was either barefooted or in his stocking feet. He held a revolver in his right hand and a butcher knife in his left. He came directly towards me while I was sitting at the head of Maxwell's bed ... [He] leaned both hands on the bed ... and asked in a low tone 'Who are they, Pete?' At the same instant Maxwell whispered to me, 'That's him!' Simultaneously the Kid must have seen or felt the presence of a third person at the head of the bed. He raised quickly his pistol - a self-cocker - within a foot of my breast. Retreating rapidly across the room, he cried, 'Quien es? Quien es? (Who is that? Who is that?)' ... As quick as possible

I drew my revolver and fired, threw my body to one side, and fired again. The second shot was useless. The Kid fell dead at the first one."

Pat Garrett's Deputy, John William Poe, also wrote a book. A past buffalo hunter, like Garrett, he'd been a Deputy U.S. Marshal and a Deputy Sheriff in Texas. In late 1880, he was hired by the Canadian River Cattlemen's Association to combat rustling centered in New Mexico, and had moved there to White Oaks. After Billy's killing, Poe was elected Lincoln County Sheriff the next year, serving until 1885; then did ranching and later moved to Roswell, operating a store and founding the Bank of Roswell and the Citizen's Bank of Roswell.

Poe's book, *The Death of Billy the Kid*, was first printed as an article, then as a booklet by an E.A. Brininstool in 1922. In 1933, it was published as a book. Poe did not know Billy. But the multiple victim identifications left him certain that Billy was the victim. His excerpted book stated: "As Maxwell's was the one place in Fort Sumner that I had considered above suspicion of harboring the Kid, I was entirely off my guard, the thought coming into my mind that the man approaching was either Maxwell or some guest of his ... Upon seeing me, he covered me with his six-shooter ... sprang onto the porch, calling out in Spanish, 'Quien es' (Who is it?) ... As I moved toward him trying to reassure him, he backed up into the doorway of Maxwell's room ... An instant after the man left the door, I heard a voice inquire in a sharp tone, 'Pete, who are those fellows on the outside?' An instant later a shot was fired in the room, followed immediately by what everyone within hearing distance thought were two other shots [but it was a rebound of the second shot] ... An instant later, Garrett came out ... He ... said to me, 'that was the Kid that came in there onto me, and I think I have got him.' I said, 'Pat, the Kid would not come to this place; you have shot the wrong man.' Upon my saying this, Garrett seemed to be in doubt himself ... but quickly spoke up and said, 'I am sure that was him, for I know his voice too well to be mistaken.' We afterwards discovered that the Kid had frequently been at [Maxwell's] house after his escape from Lincoln ...[Maxwell then got a candle ... and placed it on the window-sill from the outside.] [W]e saw a man lying stretched upon his back dead, in the middle of the room, with a six-shooter lying at his right hand and a butcher knife at his left. Upon examining the body, we found it to be that of Billy the Kid. Garrett's first shot had penetrated his breast just above the heart."

After his jailbreak on April 28th, 1881, Billy picked Fort Sumner for two reasons: his secret young lover, Paulita Maxwell, was there; and he trusted protection by the Maxwell family and Fort Sumner's 200 residents, who knew him since early 1878. These townspeople's response to Billy's killing was described by Poe in his 1933 book, *The Death of Billy the Kid*. He wrote: "Within a short time after the shooting, quite a number of the native people gathered around, some of them bewailing the death of their friend, while several women pleaded for permission to take charge of the body, which we allowed them to do. They carried it across the yard to a carpenter shop, where it was laid out on a workbench, the women placing lighted candles around it according to their ideas of properly conducting a 'wake' for the dead ... We spent the remainder of the night on the Maxwell premises, keeping constantly on our guard, as we were expecting to be attacked by friends of the dead man."

So further identification of Billy was by women talking his body and by the townspeople at his wake. And they were so certain of his identity that they presented a risk to his killers.

Another witness was Deluvina Maxwell, an unemancipated Navajo slave, bought as a child by Lucien Bonaparte Maxwell, owner first of the two million acre Maxwell Land Grant, then of Fort Sumner. Attached to Billy, for decades she laid wildflowers on his Fort Sumner grave.

Her eye-witness confirmation of Billy's body, and her confirmation that the majority of the townspeople had also identified it, was given in Fort Sumner in a June 24th, 1927 interview to historian, J. Evetts Haley. She stated: "I came here about [1869] and was here when Billy the Kid was killed. Billy the Kid was my compadre, my friend, poor Billy ... The night he was killed Billy came in hungry, went down with a butcher knife to get some meat at Pete Maxwell's ... After passing the men outside, he went into Maxwell's room where Garrett was and he shot him ... Pete took a candle and held it around in the window ... When they saw he was dead, they both went in ... Most of the native people (Mexicans) who lived in town went to his funeral ... I did not see Billy the night after he was killed, but I saw him the following morning."

Billy's Fort Sumner friend, A.P. "Paco" Anaya, had his memoir published posthumously in 1991 as *I Buried Billy*. He was in the night vigil for Billy's body. He wrote: "I ... and my brother ... and several others of those that were there, dressed Billy ... then we laid him on a high bed [note that it was a carpenter's bench] ... [A]nd on the next day we buried him."

There was also front page, national press about Billy the Kid's killing; with no reason to fabricate it; with Billy portrayed as an outlaw-murderer, whose death was a public relief. Discussed in Talk 36, was the July 23rd, 1881 *Las Cruces Rio Grande Republican's* "Kid the Killer Killed, William Bonney alias Antrim, alias Billy the Kid, Fatally Meets Pat Garrett, the Lincoln County Sheriff," which used Pat Garrett's letter to the Acting-Governor on the killing and the Coroner's Jury Report.

Here are other Territorial examples:

On July 18th, *The Las Vegas Daily Optic's* headline was: " 'The Kid' Killed! He Meets His Death at the Hands of Sheriff Pat Garrett, of Lincoln County." It stated: "An inquest was held on his body ... and the verdict of the jury was 'justifiable homicide' and that Pat Garrett ought to receive the thanks of the whole community ... and that he is truly worthy of a handsome reward."

The July 22nd *Las Vegas Daily Gazette*, in "Words of Commendation and Encouragement," stated: "Immediately on the receipt of the news of the killing of Billy 'the Kid' by Sheriff Garrett, prominent citizens of Roswell and the lower Pecos wrote us giving particulars and expressing satisfaction."

Here are some national examples.

The July 20th *Chicago Daily Tribune* had "Account of the Manner in Which 'Billy the Kid' Was Killed." It stated: "[Garrett], who had taken advantage of the dim, uncertain light to get his weapon ready for use, brought it to bear on the Kid, shooting him through the heart at the first pull of the trigger."

July 23rd's *The Weekly Gazette* of Colorado Springs had "Billy the Kid, At Last the Bullet Finds its Billet, New Mexico's Noted Outlaw Shot by a Sheriff." It stated: "The Gazette has positive information ... from Fort Sumner of the death of 'Billy the Kid.' This noted desperado was killed at Fort Sumner ... on the 14th by Pat Garrett, sheriff of Lincoln county."

On July 26th was the "Savannah Morning News's" "Billy the Kid, A Youth With Nineteen Murders to His Account – The Inhabitants of New Mexico Overawed by a Boy of Twenty-One,

Who Was Killed at Sight." It stated: "Pat [Garrett] ... started on Billy's trail a few weeks ago, meeting with success ... as the telegraph informs us of Billy's death by his hands."

August 10th's *The New York Sun* article was reprinted in August 12th's *The Lancaster Intelligencer* as "Billy the Kid, His Name Was Billy McCarthy and He was Born in New York, Murdering a Man at the Age of Sixteen – ... Under Sentence of Death – Killing Two Men in Thirty Seconds – The Kid Killed." It stated: "Shortly before midnight Garrett went to Maxwell's, and had just seated himself in the dark on the side of Maxwell's bed when the door opened, and in walked the Kid ... [He] leveled his pistols, exclaiming: "Quien es? Quien es? But his delay of asking was fatal. Before the words were off his lips Pat Garrett's bullet was through his heart, and 'Billy the Kid,' the terror of New Mexico, lay a gasping, quivering corpse."

A later Talk will give further confirmation of the corpse's identity as Billy Bonney by the Territorial Legislature's granting to Pat Garrett the reward for killing of Billy the Kid.

TALK 38:
PAT GARRETT'S BILLY THE KID REWARD
FROM BOOK: *THE CORONER'S JURY REPORT OF BILLY THE KID*
May 7, 2021

This revisionist history talk discusses Pat Garrett's reward for killing Billy the Kid. The information is from my book: *The Coroner's Jury Report of Billy the Kid: The Inquest That Sealed the Fame of Billy Bonney and Pat Garrett.*

On July 15th, 1881, the day after he killed Billy Bonney, Pat Garrett sent a letter, with enclosed copy of that day's Coroner's Jury Report, to the Territory's Acting-Governor, William Ritch. It gave the circumstances of the killing. It's discussed in Talk 37.

That letter was quoted in the July 23rd *Las Cruces Rio Grande Republican* as "Kid the Killer Killed, William Bonney alias Antrim, alias Billy the Kid, Fatally Meets Pat Garrett, the Lincoln County Sheriff."

It stated: "Below is given Sheriff Garrett's report as made to Acting Governor Ritch which contains also the verdict of the coroner's jury." [Stated was that the article had translated the Report from the original Spanish.] Garrett's letter's purpose was justifying his getting the $500 Billy the Kid award offered by past Governor Lew Wallace. That's almost $13,000 today. A sticking point, which Garrett anticipated, was the killing. Wallace's last offer, published in May 3rd, 1881's *Santa Fe Daily New Mexican* after Billy's jailbreak, was for capture, not killing. It stated: "BILLY THE KID. $500 REWARD. I will pay $500 reward to any person or persons who will capture William Bonney, alias The Kid, and deliver him to any sheriff of New Mexico. Satisfactory proofs of identity will be required." Lew Wallace, Governor of New Mexico."

To be noted is that there was no dispute of, quote, "proofs of identity" of the victim as Billy Bonney. The July 15th, 1881 Coroner's Jury Report confirmed that. Garrett's letter also addressed the identity issue by confirming that the original Report was sent to the District Attorney of the First Judicial District; and enclosing its copy for Acting-Governor Ritch.

Garrett's letter to Ritch justified killing instead of capture. He claimed self-defense. Garrett wrote: "It was my desire to have been able to take him alive, but his coming upon me so suddenly and unexpectedly leads me to believe that he had seen me enter the room, or had been informed by someone of the fact; and that he came there armed with pistol and knife expressly to kill me if he could. Under that impression I had no alternative but to kill him or to suffer death at his hands." The enclosed Coroner's Jury Report copy gave the jurymen's verdict of "justifiable homicide" because of that self-defense killing. A bonus was the jurymen's backing the reward as, quote: "[H]e deserves to be compensated."

But a technicality delayed Garrett's receiving the reward. To be noted, the "Brushy Bill" imposter hoax of Billy the Kid, which is covered in later talks, made-up that Garrett wasn't given the reward because the Coroner's Jury Report didn't exist, so the body was never identified. It alternatively made-up that Garrett did get the reward through the legislature because the corrupt Santa Fe Ring intervened to cover-up no victim identification.

In reality, the complication was that Lew Wallace had left his governorship and the Territory on May 28th, 1881. The reward was apparently his private offer. So Acting-Governor William Ritch was uneasy about simply paying it with Territorial funds. No concern was ever raised about the victim's identity or the reward's not being a dead-or-alive offer.

Ritch sought legal opinion about Wallace's private reward offer from William Breeden. Breeden was the proper prosecutor as District Attorney of the First Judicial District, and had received the Coroner's Jury Report from Justice of the Peace Alejandro Segura, who wrote it. So Breeden had already agreed that Garrett's killing was in self-defense.

Breeden was also Territorial Attorney General, so he could advise on converting the private reward to a Territorial one. His being a major Ringite would have ensured his having been satisfied by the Coroner's Jury Report that anti-Ring fighter Billy Bonney was dead.

Garrett also met personally with Acting-Governor Ritch on July 20th, as reported by July 21st's *Santa Fe Daily New Mexican*. It described Garrett as accompanied by, quote, "Honorable T.B. Catron." Apparently Ring boss Catron was the attorney representing Garrett for the reward. Ritch, himself a Ringite, was quoted as "willing to pay the amount." The article confirmed that Ritch had delayed payment to follow proper procedure. There was no question of victim identity.

Acting-Governor William Ritch recorded William Breeden's input in his July 21st, 1881 *Executive Record Book 2* entry. It stated: "In the matter of the application by Patrick F. Garrett for a reward claimed to have been offered May-1881 for the capture of William Bonney alias 'the Kid.' " Ritch wrote that he'd confirmed the existence of Wallace's reward offer by getting an affidavit of its publication by Charles H. Greene, the editor and manager of the *Santa Fe Daily New Mexican*. (As an aside, the "Brushy Bill" imposter hoax lied wildly that Charles Greene was Garrett's lawyer for reward collection, who hid the Report's not existing by writing it himself.) In reality, Ritch, in his entry, confirmed the Coroner's Jury Report's existence and Garrett's statement to his office.

Ritch then quoted Breeden's opinion. Breeden had stated: "This certainly appears to be the personal offer of Governor Wallace, and it seems he did nothing to indicate that it was intended as an executive act on behalf of, and to bind the Territory. If the reward should be paid, it is very probable that the Legislature would approve the payment if so desired, and that no objection would be raised, or that it will provide for its payment if it remained unpaid, at the next session thereof; but if the Governor [meaning Ritch] should now direct the payment of the claim, he would doubtless expose himself to the charge of misappropriation of the Territorial funds." So Breeden agreed it was Wallace's private offer and believed the Legislature would convert it to a Territorial reward for payment, but felt Ritch had to wait for the legislative act to avoid issuing Territorial funds himself, before legislative permission.

Ritch concluded by concurring. He stated: "The opinion of the Attorney General appearing to be consistent with the law and the facts, decision is rendered accordingly and the Governor [meaning himself as stand-in] declines to allow the reward at this time. Believing however, that Mr. Garrett has an equitable claim against the Territory for said reward, the action at this office will simply be suspended until the case can properly be represented to the next Legislative Assembly." So Ritch concluded that he had to delay paying until the deserved reward was converted by the Legislature to a Territorial reward.

It may be noted that Ritch apparently forgot that he had recorded Wallace's reward notice eight months earlier, when he was Territorial Secretary. On December 13th, 1880, Wallace had presented it to him by letter. Wallace had written: "Be good enough to prepare a draft of proclamation of reward $500 for the capture and delivery of William Bonney, alias the Kid to the Sheriff of the County of Lincoln."

Ritch, on behalf of Wallace, then made its December 13th, 1880 entry in *Executive Record Book 2* He wrote: "Whereas William Bonney, alias 'The Kid' charged under indictment issued from the District Court in and for the county of Lincoln of the crime of murder committed in said county: And whereas the said William Bonney, alias 'The Kid' is a fugitive from justice, Now Therefore Lewis Wallace, Governor of the Territory, by virtue of the power and authority vested in me by law and believing the ends of justice will be served thereby do hereby offer a reward of five hundred dollars ($500) for the apprehension and arrest of said William Bonney, alias 'The Kid' and for his delivery to the Sheriff of Lincoln County at the county seat of said county." Nonetheless, it was still debatably Wallace's private offer. So Ritch's precaution of legislative intervention made the reward air-tight.

On February 18th, 1882, the legislative "Act for the Relief of Pat. Garrett" was passed. It attributed delay to mere "technicality." It stated: "Garrett is justly entitled to the above reward, and payment thereof has been refused [by Acting-Governor Ritch] upon a technicality." (Note that the "Brushy Bill" hoax lied that payment was refused for no corpse identification.)

The Act stated:

"WHEREAS, The Governor of New Mexico did, on or about the 7th day of May, A.D., 1881 [it was May 3rd, 1881], issue certain proclamation in words and figures as follows, to-wit: 'I will pay five hundred dollars reward to any person or persons who will capture William Bonney, alias 'The Kid,' and deliver him to any sheriff of New Mexico. Satisfactory proof of identity will be required' ...

"AND, WHEREAS, Pat. Garrett was at that time sheriff of Lincoln county, and did, on or about the month of August [it was July], 1881, in pursuance of the above reward, and by virtue of a warrant placed in his hands for the purpose, attempted to arrest said William Bonney, and in said attempt did kill said William Bonney at Fort Sumner, in the county of San Miguel, in the Territory of New Mexico, and wherefore, said Garrett is justly entitled to the above reward, and payment thereof has been refused upon a technicality. Therefore

"Be it enacted by the Legislative Assembly of the Territory of New Mexico [that] ...

"The Territorial Auditor is hereby authorized to draw a warrant upon the Territorial Treasurer ... in favor of Pat. Garrett for the sum of five hundred dollars ... in payment of the reward of five hundred dollars heretofore offered by his Excellency, Governor Lew. Wallace, for the arrest of William Bonney, alias 'The Kid.' "

Ironically, when Governor Lionel Sheldon returned to the Territory, he sent a February 14th, 1882, letter to the Legislature, saying he himself would have paid Garrett's reward outright. He wrote: "The case under consideration is too notorious and remarkable to be made a precedent for the refusal to pay for services performed substantially in compliance with the provisions of high authority. It is a claim which I think I should have paid if it had not been understood that the matter was to be referred to the legislature before it came into my hands."

As mentioned, the "Brushy Bill" imposter hoax, without understanding the Santa Fe Ring, lied that it helped Garrett get the reward despite no Coroner's Jury Report proving victim identity, since they controlled the Legislature. The reverse was true. The Ring would have wanted Garrett rewarded precisely because he killed Billy. The Ring had wanted that anti-Ring Regulator dead as risking another Hispanic uprising, like the past Lincoln County War Battle. Since 1878, it had tried to kill him. Boss Catron's 1878 federal indictment of Billy for the murder of Andrew "Buckshot" Roberts was to block any Territorial governor's pardon and hang him. Garrett's 1880 election as Sheriff was to capture or kill him. Garrett's 1880 Secret Service elevation to Deputy U.S. Marshal was to give him Territory-wide power to kill Billy. Billy's 1881 trial under Ringite Judge Warren Bristol sentenced him to death by hanging. And aiding Garrett's reward collection was Ring boss Catron, as his attorney, and Ringite William Breeden, as Attorney General. Proved was that the Coroner's Jury Report got the highest level of Ring approval. Trying to fool Catron and Breeden about the victim's identity would have been lethal, as Garrett, working for the Ring, would have known!

So the issue of Pat Garrett's collecting Lew Wallace's Billy the Kid reward ended up getting additional validation of the Coroner's Jury Report for William Bonney by the head of the Santa Fe Ring, the Acting-Governor, the Territorial Attorney General, the Governor, and the Territorial Legislature; with all agreeing that Pat Garrett killed Billy Bonney.

Later talks will discuss old-timer Billy the Kid imposter hoaxes, desperately lying in attempt to jump the impassable hurdles of William Bonney's Coroner's Jury Report and Pat Garrett's collection of his reward for killing Billy the Kid.

TALK 39:

BILLY THE KID DOCUFICTION NOVEL
FROM BOOK: *BILLY AND PAULITA*
MAY 10, 2021

This talk is about my Billy the Kid docufiction novel that brings to life my revisionist history. The book's title is: *Billy and Paulita: The Saga of Billy Bonney, Paulita Maxwell, and the Santa Fe Ring*.

The first Billy the Kid history book I wrote is titled BILLY AND PAULITA. It's a docufiction novel. My goal was creating a virtual world, with chapters titled by dates, so a reader could enter the 19th century reality. It used extensive research, over 300 expert consultants - from firearms to astronomy - and visits to the historic sites. It's a story of how the West was stolen, ending America's dream of a frontier with limitless freedom.

It's America's Romeo and Juliet, with the teenaged romance of homeless Billy Bonney and heiress, Paulita Maxwell. Their love was star-crossed by the Santa Fe Ring: the land-grabbing, murderous, political cabal taking over New Mexico Territory.

Paulita's parents were Ring victims. Its bosses cheated her parents, Lucien Bonaparte Maxwell and Luz Beaubien, out of their fabled 2 million acre land grant, encompassing northern New Mexico and southern Colorado. Her family was exiled to the desert wasteland of Fort Sumner, a past military outpost with dark history as a concentration camp for Navajos and Apaches. There, Lucien soon died. There, in the Maxwell family mansion, the converted past commanding officer's quarters, Billy would be killed by Pat Garrett in an ambush abetted by Paulita's brother.

Billy was a Ring target as the bi-cultural, freedom-fighting, Regulator hero of the Lincoln County War - the last and bloodiest of the grass roots anti-Ring rebellions in the 1870's. He was a fearless testifier against Ring criminals: like the murderers of John Tunstall and Huston Chapman; and Commander N.A.M. Dudley, who marched on Lincoln. And, with other Regulators in that War, Billy had shot down Ringite murderers. He was also a rustler against Ringites, a reminder that he could instigate another uprising. The Ring outlawed him as Billy the Kid. It blocked his pardon from Governor Lew Wallace. It pursued him with the Secret Service. It made Pat Garrett a Sheriff and Deputy U.S. Marshal to kill or capture him. It tried him in a rigged hanging court.

The backdrop is the tsunami of profiteering racist greed flooding the nation. Hispanic land grant owners were robbed of their land. Native Americans were hunted in genocidal Indian Wars and imprisoned on reservations. Sixty million buffalos were slaughtered by hunters like Billy's eventual killers: Pat Garrett and John William Poe.

Billy was converted from dangerous delinquent to the last of the anti-Ring freedom fighters by martyrdoms of his employer, John Tunstall, and Lincoln County War leader, Alexander McSween; by the revolutionary spirit of the War's Hispanic fighters; by the wisdom of past slave, George Washington; by the courage of Fort Stanton's black cavalrymen testifying against their treasonous Commander; by newspaper accounts of rebel Apache Chief Victorio, slaughtered with his band soon before Billy's killing; and by never-emancipated Navajo slave, Deluvina, owned by the Maxwell family, who loved Billy like a mother or a spiritual guide.

A mystical subtext is the cosmic battle of light and darkness, of good and evil. Billy, having fought the Ring for freedom, having escaped an inescapable jail and hanging for freedom, finds ultimate freedom in the current carrying him back to Fort Sumner, to Paulita, and to the destiny of his choosing. Paulita won't force him to flee the Territory - though she'd go with him - and accepts their victory as refusal to yield to the Ring. Billy's death merges him forever with the young hope of the frontier. And his fame lives on to expose the Ring to history's judgment.

And Paulita, pregnant with Billy's child, forced into marriage, escaped it in five years. Staying in Fort Sumner, where Billy was buried, she never remarried. When she died, she fulfilled her dream during Billy's long imprisonment, in which she and Billy were separated by a raging torrent, giving way to a calm shallow river, easily crossable in forty strides. Now she lies in the

Maxwell family's cemetery, separated from Billy's grave by that short distance.

The conclusion harks back to half-Chickasaw Fred Tecumseh Waite's observation to Billy, his fellow past Tunstall employee. Waite said: "Lincoln County's a moral proving ground. Evil here's so powerful it breaks people where they're weakest." Billy and Paulita didn't break. They are still powerful enough to break the still-existing Santa Fe Ring.

TALK 40:
REAL BILLY THE KID HISTORY SUMMARY
MAY 13, 2021

This talk summarizes my revisionist history of Billy the Kid, as presented in Talks 1 to 39.

The overview of my revisionist history of Billy the Kid is in Talk 1. Presented was how teenaged Billy Bonney became the nemesis of the Santa Fe Ring, which targeted him for killing as the outlaw Billy the Kid.

The Santa Fe Ring - started in 1866 by attorney partners, Thomas Benton Catron and Steven Benton Elkins - was a corrupt land-grabbing cabal controlling New Mexico Territory politics and law enforcement. Grass roots rebellions against it in the 1870's were crushed with increasing savagery and terrorism. The Lincoln County War of 1878 was the last and bloodiest.

Billy Bonney was a violent delinquent, who escaped Silver City jailing at 15 for robbery and burglary; and, at 17, killed a blacksmith named Frank "Windy" Cahill in Arizona. He was converted to an anti-Ring zealot in 1877, when a Lincoln County ranch hand for John Tunstall.

After Tunstall's 1878 Ring murder, Billy became a Regulator and a deputy to arrest the murderers. With other Regulators, he was involved in killing two of them - Frank Baker and William "Buck" Morton - when they fled arrest. He also gave a deposition to a presidential investigator against Tunstall's other murderers. He then fought in the Lincoln County War, in which he was in Regulator groups which killed Tunstall murderers: Sheriff William Brady; his Deputy, George Hindman; and his posseman, Andrew "Buckshot" Roberts. Bi-cultural Billy was further politicized by the Ring's retaliative San Patricio massacre of his anti-Ring Hispanic friends. In the Lincoln County War's final Battle, Billy fought to protect anti-Ring leader, Alexander McSween, in his besieged Lincoln house. That War, lost by Ring treachery and murder of McSween and other followers, further politicized him.

In 1879, Billy fought the Ring on his own by a pardon bargain with Governor Lew Wallace to free himself from his Lincoln County War indictments in exchange for testifying against Ring murderers of anti-Ring Attorney Huston Chapman. He also testified against Ringite Fort Stanton Commander N.A.M. Dudley, whose illegal intervention in the Lincoln County War Battle enabled Ring victory. His testifying against Ringites, his allegiance to the Ring-oppressed Hispanic populace, and his guerilla rustling from Ringites fueled Ring motivation for his killing. Pressured by the Ring, Wallace betrayed their pardon bargain, which could have saved him.

In 1880, as the Ring publicized Billy in an outlaw myth, he was almost killed by a bounty hunter named Joe Grant, whom he killed in self-defense.

To kill Billy, the Ring used the Secret Service and complicit Sheriff-elect and Deputy U.S. Marshall Pat Garrett. Garrett's ambushes missed Billy, but killed his companions: Tom O'Folliard and Charlie Bowdre. Garrett then settled on capturing Billy.

In 1881, after being held in the Santa Fe jail, Billy was tried in Mesilla by a Ringite judge and sentenced to hang. Billy rightly claimed to the press that he was, unjustly, the only War participant to be sentenced. Almost 200 Ringite Lincoln County War murderers and arsonists had been indicted in the 1879 Grand Jury, but the Ring manipulated Lew Wallace's Amnesty Proclamation to get all pardoned. And Huston Chapman's murderer, local Ring boss James Dolan, indicted by that Grand Jury also, was later shielded from prosecution by the Ring.

Incarcerated in Lincoln awaiting hanging, Billy escaped; killing his Deputy guards, James Bell and Bob Olinger. Instead of fleeing to Old Mexico and a long life, he defiantly went to Fort Sumner, to his sweetheart, Paulita Maxwell. Using spies, Pat Garrett located him there. Aided by Paulita's treacherous brother, Peter, on July 14th, 1881, Garrett fatally shot Billy in Peter's bedroom in the Maxwell family's Fort Sumner mansion.

Billy's body was identified by Pat Garrett; Peter Maxwell; up to 200 townspeople at his wake; the six coroner's jurymen at the inquest; and the Maxwell family's Navajo servant, Deluvina.

Because of Garrett's reward needing a legislative act, Billy's Coroner's Jury Report, identifying him, was further approved by the District Attorney of the First Judicial District, the Attorney General, the Acting-Governor, the Governor, and the legislature.

Billy was buried in the Maxwell family's cemetery beside Pat Garrett's other Regulator victims: Charlie Bowdre and Tom O'Folliard. The inscription on one of Billy's tombstones - as killing a man for each of his 21 years - was made-up by his pardon's betrayer, Lew Wallace. Billy's final tally was nine, all arguably justifiable.

The triumphant Santa Fe Ring wrote the history to conceal its role and itself. Untouched by justice, it still exists in New Mexico as malignant cronyism contaminating government, law enforcement, and history books.

The Ring's one mistake was underestimating Billy Bonney. His fame eclipsed his death. With him, he dragged the Ring into history's glaring judgment. As famous freedom-fighting Mexican President Benito Juárez wrote in 1864: "It is given a man ... to attack the rights of others, seize their goods ... make of their virtues crimes, and one's vices a virtue, but there is one thing beyond that perversity: the tremendous judgment of history."

As will be seen in later talks, this revisionist perspective helps to crack Billy the Kid history hoaxes that have plagued the real history from the 1930's to the present.

TALK 41:
RESEARCHING REAL BILLY THE KID HISTORY SUMMARY
MAY 17, 2021

This talk is about how I researched the real history of Billy the Kid.

History exists as facts and their interpretation. This is how I developed my revisionist history of Billy the Kid.

My approach relied on primary sources, meaning original documents. Fortunately, for Billy Bonney's history, they're profuse. They're collected papers of people like Lew Wallace, in the Indiana Historical Society; or Thomas Benton Catron, in the University of New Mexico's Center for Southwest Research. And Billy Bonney's words are saved in his letters retained by Lew Wallace, and in his deposition and Court of Inquiry testimony in the National Archives.

My strategy was to visit collections, and look at every page in every archival box. It takes weeks. Though collections are indexed, documents can be mislabeled or missed. That's how I authenticated Billy's wrongly dated letter in the Lew Wallace Collection, and how I found Wallace's secret letter to Absalom Markland confirming his fear of the Santa Fe Ring. Archivists can also miss papers accidentally mixed with others. In that way, in Ring boss Thomas Benton Catron's papers, I located two of his undiscovered cipher-code lists for secret letters and telegrams. Increasingly available are also digitized antique newspapers.

Most important, is that I get a copy of every document even remotely connected to the history. Some collections I copy completely - like the National Archives' Departments of Justice and the Interior records of Frank Warner Angel, or the National Archives' Department of the Treasury Secret Service Reports of

Azariah Wild, or the Herman Weisner collection in New Mexico State University Library at Las Cruces. That's how I made my own library of thousands of reference documents for ongoing research. They also empower my books' readers by being quoted in my texts and listed in my bibliographies.

But the sources alone can't tell the real history. For example, Billy the Kid history is heavily distorted by outlaw myths created by the Santa Fe Ring and Lew Wallace. Deciphering truth is where historical research becomes an art. Sources must be weighed against each other to establish credibility, and to eliminate hearsay and biased fakery. And one must formulate the big picture of an individual or an occurrence, to check claims. For example, in my revisionist history, I see the Santa Fe Ring as precipitating events. Sources that hide it, are obviously suspect to me. I also researched history beyond immediate Lincoln County War events. That enabled me to expose the pattern of Territorial anti-Ring uprisings that culminated in that War. And researching Thomas Benton Catron's entire life, enabled me to confirm his monopolistic mercantile motives and his responsibility for Lincoln County assassinations.

I also used 300 expert consultants - specializing, for example, in firearms, cattle drives, geology, astronomy, weather conditions, period clothing, tintype photography, and 19th century military - to gain perspective on events.

Adding to reality are historical sites. For Billy the Kid history, one is fortunate. New Mexico's economic depression, arguably a product of ongoing Santa Fe Ring corruption, has minimized development. Conrad Keeler Naegle, in his 1943 doctoral thesis, *The History of Silver City, New Mexico 1870-1886*, concluded that the Ring had, quote, "retarded progress in New Mexico" by purging New Mexico's valuable and honorable citizens by murder and forced flight, and draining public resources for private gain. So most historic sites are untouched from the days of Billy Bonney. At them, one can experience the events, or test them. For example, I went to the John Tunstall murder site, taking the same dirt trail he himself and his men, including Billy, rode through the forested land. Off that trail, at the spot he was murdered, I lay on the cold red earth, to merge, for a moment, with him. And 600 yards away, as the trail climbs, is a clearing, sheltered by a rock-studded embankment, where his escaping men stopped and realized he wasn't with them. I had a friend fire a period revolver at the killing site. I could hear it from that bowl - as did Billy.

As he testified in his June 8th, 1878 deposition to Investigator Frank Warner Angel, quote: "Deponent, Widenmann, and Brewer rode over a hill towards an other which was covered with large rocks and trees in order to defend themselves and make a stand. But the attacking party, undoubtedly seeing Tunstall, left off pursuing deponent and the two with him ... Shortly afterwards we heard two or three separate and distinct shots and the remark was then made by Middleton that they, the attacking party, must have killed Tunstall." And, in Lincoln, where that historic town is intact, I sat on the deep ledge of the courthouse-jail's second floor east window, exactly where and how Billy must have sat, and pointed my imaginary Whitney double barrel shotgun to the stone plaque in the ground marking where hated Ringite rustler-murderer, Deputy guard Bob Olinger, fell, fatally struck by buckshot of his own weapon.

Then there are the books published on Billy, with the first by his killer, Pat Garrett, and ongoing to the present. I read them, and found most parroting the outlaw myth of Billy the Kid, and missing the role of the Santa Fe Ring.

There are only a few I'd recommend. The most scholarly are by British Frederick Nolan, who used a research team, and discovered the Frank Warner Angel reports. His books are: 1965's *The Life and Death of John Henry Tunstall*, 1992's *The Lincoln County War: A Documentary History,*, and 1998's *The West of Billy the Kid*. The first reproduces John Tunstall's letters to his London family, allowing one to see his innocence and integrity, which changed Billy's life. Nolan's other two books are an unmatchable compendium of individuals, documents, events, period photographs, and bibliographic references. However, as I discussed in Talk 20, Nolan's historical analysis is diminished by his reliance on the outlaw myth to denigrate Billy Bonney and by his missing the causative role of the Santa Fe Ring.

In my opinion, the only historian to uncover the real Billy Bonney is Jerry Weddle, in his meticulously researched and sensitive 1993 book, *Antrim is my Stepfather's Name*, about Billy's early adolescence in Silver City and Arizona Territory.

Deserving mention is Norman Cleaveland, a Santa Fe Ring-exposing author and great-grandson of the Colfax County War's anti-Ring firebrand, Mary McPherson. His 1971 book, *The Morley's: Young Upstarts on the Southwest Frontier*, in a homespun ironic way, exposes early anti-Ring uprisings and Ring terrorism endured by his grandparents. He wrote: "When my grandparents, William Raymond Morley and Ada McPherson Morley, pioneer New Mexicans, were in their twenties they were confronted with an establishment known as the Santa Fe Ring. By comparison, present-day establishments would rate rather as societies of butterfly collectors."

And a budding and brave historian in the 1940's, named Conrad Keeler Naegle, took on the original Ring, when doing that required moxie. Researching early anti-Ring rebellions in the Santa Fe legislature and Silver City, he wrote his unvarnished University of New Mexico 1943 doctoral thesis titled *The History of Silver City, New Mexico 1870-1886*; and a 1968 article in *Arizona and the West: A Quarterly Journal of History* titled "The Rebellion of Grant County, New Mexico in 1876."

As will be seen, real Billy the Kid history has another problem as big as its historians missing its point. It's a near century of Billy the Kid hoaxes, hijacking the history, by attention-craving, old-timer, Billy the Kid imposters and their profiteering promoters, impersonating historians. Upcoming talks will hoaxbust all of them.

愉•愉

THESE YOUTUBE TALKS CONTINUE
WITH VIDEO PLAYLIST TALK 43
IN THE BOOK:
GALE COOPER'S REAL BILLY THE KID
HOAXBUSTING

ANNOTATED BIBLIOGRAPHY

COMPREHENSIVE REFERENCES

Nolan, Frederick. *The   War: A Documentary History*. Norman: University of Oklahoma Press. **1992**.
_____. *The West of Billy the Kid*. Norman: University of Oklahoma Press. **1998**.

LEGAL REFERENCES FOR PARDON AND CRIMINAL CASES

Prince, Hon. L. Bradford, Chief Justice of the Supreme Court of New Mexico. *The General Laws of New Mexico Including All the Unrepealed General Laws From the Promulgation of the "Kearney Code" in 1846, to the End of the Legislative Session of 1880*. Albany, New York: W.C. Little & Co. Law Publishers. 1880.

Victory, John P., Edward L. Bartlett, Thomas N. Wilkerson, Commission. *Compiled Laws of New Mexico in Accordance With an Act of the Legislature, Approved March 16ᵗʰ 1897, Including the Constitution of the United States, the Treaty of Guadalupe Hidalgo, the Gadsdon Treaty, the Original Act Organizing the Territory, the Organic Acts as Now in Force, the Original Kearny Code, and a List of Laws Enacted Since the Compilation of 1884, as Well as Those in that Work*. Santa Fe, New Mexico: New Mexico Printing Company. 1897. (**Page 857. Section 3457. Governor's discretion as to pardon.**)

New Mexico Rules Annotated (NMRA), Criminal Code. UJI 14-5172. "Justifiable Homicide; Defense of Another." (**Jury instructions**)

Territory v. Baker, 4 N.M. 236, Supreme Court of the Territory of New Mexico (1887) 4 Gild. 236, 13 P. 30, 4 Johnson 117, 1887-NMSC- 021 (**Jury instructions**)

HISTORICAL ORGANIZATIONS (PERIOD)

NORTH CAROLINA REGULATORS, 18ᵗʰ CENTURY

HISTORY OF 18ᵗʰ CENTURY REGULATORS

Hudson, Arthur Palmer . "Songs of the Carolina Regulators." *William and Mary Quarterly*. 4. No. 4 (1947): Page 146.

Kars, Marjoline. *Breaking Loose Together: The Regulator Rebellion in Pre-Revolutionary North Carolina*. Chapel Hill and London: The University of North Carolina Press. 2002.

Maier, Pauline. *From Resistance to Revolution: Colonial radicals and the development of American opposition to Britain, 1765-1776*. New York and London: W.W. Norton & Company. 1991.

LINCOLN COUNTY REGULATORS, 19ᵗʰ CENTURY

AMERICAN INDEPENDENCE DOCUMENTS

Vincent, Wilson, Jr. *The Book of Great American Documents*. Brookville, Maryland: American History Research Associates. 1993.

REGULATOR MANIFESTO (BY BILLY BONNEY)

Regulator. "Mr. Walz. Sir ..." Letter to Edgar Walz. July 13, 1878. Adjutant General's Office. File 1405 AGO 1878. (Quoted in Maurice Garland Fulton, *History of the*

446

Lincoln County War. Tucson: University of Arizona Press. 1975. pages 246-247, and Frederick Nolan, *The Lincoln County War: A Documentary History*, page 310.)

SANTA FE RING

GENERAL BOOKS ON ORGANIZED CRIME

Ackerman, Kenneth D. *Boss Tweed: The Rise and Fall of the Corrupt Pol Who Conceived the Soul of Modern New York*. New York: Carroll & Graff Publishers. 2005.

Critchley, David. *The Origin of Organized Crime in America: The New York Mafia, 1891-1931*. New York, London: Routledge, Taylor & Francis Group. 2009.

Reppetto, Thomas. *American Mafia: A History of Its Rise to Power*. New York: Henry Holt and Company. 2004.

Short, Martin. *The Rise of the Mafia: The Definitive Story of Organized Crime*. London: John Blake Publishing Ltd. 2009.

MODERN SOURCES

Cleaveland, Agnes Morley. *No Life for a Lady*. Boston: Houghton Mifflin. 1941.

_____. *Satan's Paradise: From Lucien Maxwell to Fred Lambert*. Boston: Houghton Mifflin Company. 1952.

Cleaveland, Norman, *Colfax County's Chronic Murder Mystery*. Santa Fe: New Mexico. The Rydel Press. 1977.

_____. *A Synopsis of the Great New Mexico Cover-up*. Self-printed. 1989.

_____. *Some Comments Norman Cleveland May Make to the Huntington Westerners on Sept. 19, 1987*. Unpublished.

_____. *Some Highlights of William R. Morley's Contribution to the Pioneer Development of the Southwest*. Self-printed. No Date.

_____. *The Great Santa Fe Cover-up*. Based on a Talk given Before the Santa Fe Historical Society on November 1, 1978. Self-printed. 1982.

Cleaveland, Norman and George Fitzpatrick. *The Morleys - Young Upstarts on the Southwest Frontier*. Albuquerque, New Mexico: Calvin Horn Publisher, Inc. 1971.

Cooper, Gale. *The Santa Fe Ring Versus Billy the Kid: The Making of An American Monster*. Albuquerque, New Mexico: Gelcour Books. 2018.

Klasner, Lilly. Eve Ball. Ed. *My Girlhood Among Outlaws*. Tucson, Arizona: The University of Arizona Press. 1972. Klasner, Lilly. Eve Ball. Ed. *My Girlhood Among Outlaws*. Tucson, Arizona: The University of Arizona Press. 1972. **(John Chisum's in jail write-up about Santa Fe Ring injustices to himself)**

Lamar, Howard Robert N. *The Far Southwest 1846 – 1912: A Territorial History*. New Haven and London: Yale University Press. 1966. **(Chapter 6 covers the Santa Fe Ring))**

Meinig, D. W. *The Shaping of America. A Geographical Perspective on 500 Years of History. Vol. 3. Transcontinental America 1850 - 1915*. New Haven and London: Yale University Press. 1998. **(Pages 127 and 132 are on the Santa Fe Ring.)**

Montoya, María E. Translating Property. The Maxwell Land Grant and the Conflict Over Land in the American West, 1840-1900. Berkeley and Los Angeles: University of California Press. 2002.

Naegle, Conrad Keeler. *The History of Silver City, New Mexico 1870-1886*. University of New Mexico Bachelor of Arts thesis. Pages 30-60. Unpublished. 1943. Collection of the Silver City Museum, Silver City, New Mexico. **(Grant County rebellion)**

_____. "The Rebellion of Grant County, New Mexico in 1876." *Arizona and the West: A Quarterly Journal of History*. Autumn, 1968. Volume 10. Number 3. Tucson, Arizona: The University of Arizona Press. 1968. Pages 225-240. **(Grant County rebellion against Santa Fe Ring)**

Newman, Simeon Harrison III. "The Santa Fe Ring." *Arizona and the West*. Volume 12. Autumn 1970. Pages 269-288.

Otero, Miguel A. *My Life on the Frontier, 1882-1897: Incidents and Characters of the period when Kansas, Colorado, and New Mexico were Passing Through the Last of their Wild and Romantic Years.* New York: The Press of the Pioneers. 1935. Pages 232-233. (Quoted by Victor Westphall, *Thomas Benton Catron and His Era.* Page 188*)* (**Quote: "the 'Santa Fe Ring,' the real machine controlling the political situation in New Mexico."**)

Pearson, Jim Berry. *The Maxwell Land Grant.* Norman: University of Oklahoma Press. 1961.

Taylor, Morris F. *O.P. McMains and the Maxwell Land Grant Conflict.* Tucson, Arizona: The University of Arizona Press. 1979. (**Traces origins of the Santa Fe Ring**)

Theisen, Lee Scott. "Frank Warner Angel's Notes on New Mexico Territory, 1878." *Arizona and the West: A Quarterly Journal of History.* Winter 1976. Volume 18. Number 4. Pages 333-370. (**About the Angel notebook given to Lew Wallace and listing names of Santa Fe Ring members**)

Westphall, Victor. *Thomas Benton Catron and His Era.* Tucson, Arizona: University of Arizona Press. 1973. (**Ring-denier, who cites sources exposing the Ring**)

CONTEMPORARY SOURCES (CHRONOLOGICAL)

No Author. *Diario del Consejo der Territorio de Neuvo Mejico, Session de 1871-1872.* *Santa Fe New Mexican.* **January 8, 1872.** Santa Fe: A.P. Sullivan. 1872. Pages 144-154. New Mexico Supreme Court Library. Santa Fe, New Mexico. (**A Ring expurgated document, with copy found in 1942 by Conrad Naegle; confirms troops used by Ring to suppress 1872 Legislature Revolt**)

No Author. *Diario del Consejo der Territorio de Neuvo Mejico, Session de 1871-1872.* Las Cruces *Borderer.* **January 24, 1872.** Pages 110-113. (**President of the Council Don Diego Archuleta objects to troops in legislature**)

No Author. *Journal of the House of Representatives of the Territory of New Mexico, Session of 1871-1872.* Santa Fe: A.P. Sullivan. **1872.** Pages 144-154. (**Confirms troops used by Ring to suppress the Legislature Revolt of 1872**)

Mills, Melvin W. "Thought I would write you how things are running." Letter to Robert H. Longwill. **December 5, 1873.** "Exhibit A" in the August 9, 1878 deposition of Frank Springer to Investigator Frank Warner Angel. Frank Warner Angel report titled *In the Matter of the Investigation of the Charges Against S.B. Axtell Governor of New Mexico.* October 3, 1878. Interior Department Papers 1850-1907; Appointments Division and Subsequent Actions. Microfilm Case File No. 44-4-8-3. Record Group 48. Microfilm Roll M750. National Archives and Records Administration. U.S. Department of Interior. Washington, D.C. (**About Catron and Ring empowerment**)

Bristol Warren. "From sources of information that I deem perfectly reliable I am satisfied that there are public disorders in Lincoln County ..." Letter to Governor Marsh Giddings. **January 10, 1874.** Herman B. Weisner Papers, ca. 1957-1992. New Mexico State University Library at Las Cruces. Rio Grande Historical Collections. Accession No. Weisner Ms 0249. Box 4/39. Folder D-4. Folder Name: "Judge Bristol's letter." (**Santa Fe Ring's outlaw myth and proposed use of military intervention**)

No Author. "Ring influence [in the Territorial legislature is] being actively used against every measure that tends to do justice" [in Grant and Doña Counties]." *Grant County Herald.* **August 8, 1875.** Quoted by Conrad Keeler Naegle in *The History of Silver City, New Mexico 1870-1886,* doctoral thesis. Page 39.

Morley, William Raymond and Frank Springer. On Oscar McMains's citizen's Meeting. *Cimarron News and Press.* **November 10, 1875.** In Mary McPherson, Letters and Petitions to President Rutherford B. Hayes re: Removal Governor Axtell and the Santa Fe Ring. 1977. Interior Department Papers 1850-1907; Appointments Division and Subsequent Actions. Microfilm File Case Number 44-4-8-3. **Record**

Group 48. Microfilm Roll M750. National Archives and Records Administration. (**Colfax County citizens meeting on F.J. Tolby murder by Santa Fe Ring.**)

_____. " 'The Territory of Elkins.' Assassination of Supposed Sun Correspondent. The Murder of the Rev. F.J. Tolby in New Mexico. A Probate Judge Accused of Complicity in the Crime. Indignation Meeting." *New York Weekly Sun.* **December 22, 1875.** Interior Department Papers 1850-1907; Appointments Division and Subsequent Actions. Microfilm Roll M750. National Archives and Records Administration. Record Group 48. Microfilm Case File Number 44-4-8-3. U.S. Department of Interior. Washington, D. C. (**From May 1, 1877 submission to President Rutherford B. Hates as "Mary E. McPherson and W.B. Matchett 'Make certain charges against the U.S. Officials in the Territory of New Mexico.' "**)

A.C.L. Editorial. "New Mexico, A Sorry Showing for a Would-be State, Tweed's Disciples Preying on the Populace, How the Territorial Ring is Run, Why the Territory Should Not Be Made a State. **March 13, 1876.** *The Boston Daily Globe.* Volume IX, Number 62. Newspaperarchive.com.

Middaugh, Asa F. Deposition. **March 31, 1876.** "Exhibit B" in the August 9, 1878 deposition of Frank Springer to Investigator Frank Warner Angel. Frank Warner Angel report titled *In the Matter of the Investigation of the Charges Against S.B. Axtell Governor of New Mexico.* October 3, 1878. Interior Department Papers 1850-1907; Appointments Division and Subsequent Actions. Microfilm Case File No. 44-4-8-3. Record Group 48. Microfilm Roll M750. National Archives and Records Administration. U.S. Department of Interior. Washington, D.C. (**About Catron's malicious prosecution of Ada McPherson Morley**)

No Author. "A Contemplated Political Change." Grant County *Herald.* **September 16, 1876.** Quoted by Conrad Keeler Naegle in *The History of Silver City, New Mexico 1870-1886* doctoral thesis. Pages 39-40. (**Listing reasons to escape the Ring by seceding to Arizona Territory**)

No Author. [Grant County should not] "sort o' wait and hear from Santa Fe ... before taking action." Tucson *Arizona Citizen.* **September 23, 1876.** Quoted by Conrad Keeler Naegle in *The History of Silver City, New Mexico 1870-1886* doctoral thesis. Page 41. (**Arizona encourages escape from Santa Fe Ring**)

No Author. Grant County *Herald.* **September 30, 1876.** (**"Annexation Meeting" announced**)

No Author. "Proceedings of Grant County Annexation Meeting." Grant County *Herald.* **Saturday October 7, 1876.** Page 2. Columns 1 and 2. Collection of the Silver City, New Mexico, Museum. (**Anti-Santa Fe Ring "Grant County Declaration of Independence" published**)

No Author. Grant County *Herald.* " 'Petition to Remove Judge Bristol. We the undersigned citizens of the Third Judicial District of the Territory of New Mexico, without regard to party, would respectfully request and petition for the removal of Judge Warren Bristol ...' " No date. **1876 or 1877.**(Quoted in "W.B. Matchett and Mary E. McPherson 'Make certain charges against the U.S. Officials in the Territory of New Mexico.' " Letter to President Rutherford B. Hayes. Received and filed May 1, 1877. Interior Department Papers 1850-1907; Appointments Division and Subsequent Actions. Microfilm File Case Number 44-4-8-3. Record Group 48. Microfilm No. M750. Roll 1. National Archives and Records Administration. U.S. Department of Justice. Washington, D.C.) (**Anti-Santa Fe Ring article**)

No Author. Report on murder trial for Franklin Tolby. Pueblo, *Colorado Chieftain.* **May 25, 1876.** Quoting *Daily New Mexican,* May 1, 1876. From Morris F. Taylor. *O.P. McMains and the Maxwell Land Grant Conflict.* Tucson, Arizona: The University of Arizona Press. 1979. Page 49. (**Ring-biased jury instructions by Judge Henry Waldo to protect Ring murderers of Tolby**)

McPherson, Mary. "Charges against Thomas B. Catron, U.S. Attorney, and Others." **February 7, 1877.** Letter to Attorney General Alphonso Taft. Interior Department Papers 1850-1907; Appointments Division and Subsequent Actions.

Microfilm File Case Number 44-4-8-3. Record Group 48. Microfilm Roll M750. National Archives and Records Administration. U.S. Department of Justice. Washington, D.C.

Catron, Thomas Benton. "Answering Charges of Mary E. McPherson." **February 24, 1877.** Letter to Attorney General Alphonso Taft. Interior Department Papers 1850-1907; Appointments Division and Subsequent Actions. Microfilm File Case Number 44-4-8-3. Record Group 48. Microfilm Roll M750. National Archives and Records Administration. U.S. Department of Justice. Washington, D.C.

Morley William Raymond. "I was astonished beyond measure at your proceedings, and have fears as to the result ..." Letter to Mary McPherson. **March 6, 1877.** McPherson, Mary E. Letters and Petitions to President Rutherford B. Hayes re: Removal Governor Axtell and the Santa Fe Ring. Interior Department Papers 1850-1907; Appointments Division and Subsequent Actions. File Case Number 44-4-8-3. Record Group 48. Microfilm Roll M750. National Archives and Records Administration. U.S. Department of Justice. Washington, D. C. (**Hopes she can help fight against Santa Fe Ring; enclosed in Mary McPherson's addendum to her "Certain Charges against U.S. Officials in the Territory of New Mexico."**)

Morley William Raymond. "I was astonished beyond measure at your proceedings, and have fears as to the result ..." Letter to Mary McPherson. **March 6, 1877.** McPherson, Mary E. Letters and Petitions to President Rutherford B. Hayes re: Removal Governor Axtell and the Santa Fe Ring. Interior Department Papers 1850-1907; Appointments Division and Subsequent Actions. Microfilm File Case Number 44-4-8-3. Record Group 48. Microfilm Roll M750. National Archives and Records Administration. U.S. Department of Justice. Washington, D. C. (**Hopes she can help fight against Santa Fe Ring; enclosed in Mary McPherson's "Charges Against U.S. Officials in the Territory of New Mexico."**)

Morley, Ada. "Yes, we have received all your letters at Vermejo here but we have hesitated about replying ..." Letter to Mary McPherson. **March 7, 1877.** McPherson, Mary E. Letters and Petitions to President Rutherford B. Hayes re: Removal Governor Axtell and the Santa Fe Ring. Interior Department Papers 1850-1907; Appointments Division and Subsequent Actions. Microfilm File Case Number 44-4-8-3. Record Group 48. Microfilm Roll M750. National Archives and Records Administration. U.S. Department of Justice. Washington, D. C. (**Fears about her fight against Santa Fe Ring; oddly this private letter was in her mother's governmental file**)

Lambert, J.J. "At It Again." Pueblo, Colorado, *Enterprise and Chronicle*. **April 21, 1877.** Interior Department Papers 1850-1907; Appointments Division and Subsequent Actions. Microfilm File Case Number 44-4-8-3. Record Group 48. Microfilm No. M750. Roll 1. National Archives and Records Administration. U.S. Department of Justice. Washington, D.C. (**Description of Santa Fe Ring control of courts and malicious prosecution of opponents like Oscar McMains in the Franklin Tolby murder; used in: "W.B. Matchett and Mary E. McPherson 'Make Certain Charges Against the U.S. Officials in the Territory of New Mexico.' " Letter to President Rutherford B. Hayes. Received and filed May 1, 1877. Interior Department Papers 1850-1907; Appointments Division and Subsequent Actions. Microfilm File Case Number 44-4-8-3. Record Group 48. Microfilm No. M750. Roll 1. National Archives and Records Administration. U.S. Department of Justice. Washington, D.C.**)

Matchett, W.B. and Mary E. McPherson. "W.B. Matchett and Mary E. McPherson 'Make Certain Charges Against the U.S. Officials in the Territory of New Mexico.' " Letter to President Rutherford B. Hayes. Received and filed **May 1, 1877.** Interior Department Papers 1850-1907; Appointments Division and Subsequent Actions. Microfilm File Case Number 44-4-8-3. Record Group 48. Microfilm No. M750. Roll 1. National Archives and Records Administration. U. S. Department of

Justice. Washington, D.C. (**Sent to President Rutherford B. Hayes and Secretary of the Interior Carl Schurz 141 pages of letters, affidavits, petitions, newspaper articles, itemized requests for removal of Governor Samuel Beach Axtell and District Judge Warren Bristol, documentation of use of the military against civilians, documentation of the Ring murder of Ring opponent Reverend F.J. Tolby, and identification of the Santa Fe Ring and Elkins and Catron as its leaders.**)

McPherson, Mary and W.B. Matchett. "To the President. Please make the enclosed a part of the evidence in the case of "Charges Against New Mexican Officials" Letter to President Rutherford B. Hayes. **May 3, 1877**. McPherson, Mary E. Letters and Petitions to President Rutherford B. Hayes re: Removal Governor Axtell and the Santa Fe Ring. Interior Department Papers 1850-1907; Appointments Division and Subsequent Actions. Microfilm File Case Number 44-4-8-3. Record Group 48. Microfilm Roll M750. National Archives and Records Administration. U.S. Department of Justice. Washington, D.C. (**Addendum to their May, 1877 "Certain Charges Against U.S. Officials in New Mexico Territory."**)

McPherson, Mary and W.B. Matchett. "The Secretary of the Interior, Sir - Accompanying please find copy of charges, &c., against S.B. Axtell, Governor, and other New Mexican Officials ..." "Charges Against New Mexican Officials." Letter to Secretary of the Interior Carl Schurz. **May 5, 1877**. McPherson, Mary E. Letters and Petitions to President Rutherford B. Hayes re: Removal Governor Axtell and the Santa Fe Ring. Interior Department Papers 1850-1907; Appointments Division and Subsequent Actions. Microfilm File Case Number 44-4-8-3. Record Group 48. Microfilm Roll M750. National Archives and Records Administration. U.S. Department of Justice. Washington, D. C.

McPherson, Mary E. Letters and Petitions to President Rutherford B. Hayes re: Removal Governor Axtell and the Santa Fe Ring. **1977**. Interior Department Papers 1850-1907; Appointments Division and Subsequent Actions. Microfilm File Case Number 44-4-8-3. Record Group 48. Microfilm Roll M750. National Archives and Records Administration.

McPherson, Mary and W.B. Matchett. "We have respectfully to request that the following named records, documents, papers, communications and correspondence be supplied ..." Records Request to Secretary of the Interior Carl Schurz. **July 26, 1877**. Interior Department Papers 1850-1907; Appointments Division and Subsequent Actions. Microfilm File Case Number 44-4-8-3. Record Group 48. Microfilm No. M750. Roll 1. National Archives and Records Administration. U. S. Department of Justice. Washington, D.C. (**Requesting records of the Santa Fe Ring, Carton, Elkins, and Axtell**)

McPherson, Mary. "Please place before the Attorney General ..." Letter to President Rutherford B. Hayes. **August 23, 1877**. Interior Department Papers 1850-1907; Appointments Division and Subsequent Actions. Microfilm File Case Number 44-4-8-3. Record Group 48. Microfilm No. M750. Roll 1. National Archives and Records Administration. U.S. Department of Justice. Washington, D.C. (**Requesting that her "Charges vs. New Mexico Officials" go to the Attorney General.**)

McPherson, Mary and W.B. Matchett. *"In the Matter of Charges vs. Gov. S.B. Axtell and Other New Mexico Officials. Submitted to the Departments of the Interior and Justice.* **August, 1877**. Printed as a 31 page booklet. No publisher listed. Indiana Historical Society. Lew Wallace Collection. M0292. Box 3. Folder 20. (**Exposé of Santa Fe Ring, Catron, and Elkins; in Lew Wallace's possession**)

McPherson, Mary. "I desire to know when I can be heard ..." Letter to Secretary of Interior Carl Schurz. **September 30, 1977**. Interior Department Papers 1850-1907; Appointments Division and Subsequent Actions. Microfilm File Case Number 44-4-8-3. Record Group 48. Microfilm No. M750. Roll 1. National Archives and Records Administration. U. S. Department of Justice. Washington, D.C. (**Wants meeting on her charges against Ring officials**)

Angel, Frank Warner. "To Gov. Lew Wallace, Santa Fe, N. M., 1878." Notebook. **1878**. Indiana Historical Society. Lew Wallace Collection. M0292. Microfilm No. F372. (**Original missing, copy on microfilm; Notebook prepared for Lew Wallace listing names in Lincoln County and the Santa Fe Ring**)

Tunstall, John Henry. "A Taxpayer's Complaint ... January 18, 1878." Mesilla *Independent*. **January 26, 1878**. (**Exposé of William Brady, James Dolan, and John Riley for tax fraud and use of public money to purchase cattle; and T.B. Catron then paid that bill**)

Dolan, James J. "Answer to A Taxpayer's Complaint." Mesilla *Independent*. **January 29, 1878**. (**Response to J.H. Tunstall's exposé of him, William Brady, and John Riley for tax fraud and use of public money to purchase cattle; and T.B. Catron then paid that bill**)

Springer, Frank. "I hope you have received a full account of the Troubles in Lincoln County from your nephew ..." Letter to Senator Rush Clark. **April 9, 1878**. Herman B. Weisner Papers, ca. 1957-1992. New Mexico State University Library at Las Cruces. Rio Grande Historical Collections. Accession No. Weisner Ms 0249. Box 4/39. Folder D-6. Folder Name "Frank Springer Letter to Rush Clark." (**Links Santa Fe Ring to murder of J.H. Tunstall**)

Leonard, Ira. "When you left here I promised to write you concerning events transpiring here ..." Letter to Lew Wallace. **May 20, 1878 [sic - 79]**. Indiana Historical Society. Lew Wallace Collection. M0292. Box 4. Folder 10. (**With quote: "the Santa Fe Ring that has been so long an incubus on the government of this territory"**)

Morley, William Raymond. "Your letter of the 7th came last night and it was a good long newsy letter ..." Letter to wife, Ada McPherson Morley. **August 15, 1878**. Collection of Norman Cleaveland. Quoted in Norman Cleaveland, *The Morleys: Young Upstarts in the Southwest*. Albuquerque, New Mexico: Calvin Horn Publisher, Inc. 1971. Pages 152-155. (**About possible betrayal by Angel's reports; about the Santa Fe Ring, T.B. Catron, S.B. Elkins, S.B. Axtell, and Henry Waldo; and the Lincoln County War**)

Angel, Frank Warner. *Examination of Charges Against F. C. Godfroy, Indian Agent, Mescalero, N. M.* **October 2, 1878**. (Report 1981, Inspector E. C. Watkins; Cited as Watkins Report). M 319-20 and L147-44-4-8. Record Group 075. National Archives and Records Administration. U.S. Department of Justice. Washington, D.C.

Morley, William Raymond. Deposition to Investigator Frank Warner Angel. August 9, 1878. Frank Warner Angel report titled *In the Matter of the Investigation of the Charges Against S.B. Axtell Governor of New Mexico*. **October 3, 1878**. Interior Department Papers 1850-1907; Appointments Division and Subsequent Actions. Microfilm Case File No. 44-4-8-3. Record Group 48. Microfilm Roll M750. National Archives and Records Administration. U.S. Department of Interior. Washington, D.C. (**Mentions Catron, Elkins, and the Santa Fe Ring, and provided Exhibits of letters exposing Catron's evil.**)

Angel, Frank Warner. *In the Matter of the Investigation of the Charges Against S.B. Axtell Governor of New Mexico*. **October 3, 1878**. Frank Warner Angel report. Interior Department Papers 1850-1907; Appointments Division and Subsequent Actions. Microfilm Case File No. 44-4-8-3. Record Group 48. Microfilm Roll M750. National Archives and Records Administration. U.S. Department of Interior. Washington, D.C. (**Mentions Santa Fe Ring**)

_____. *In the Matter of the Investigation of the Charges Against S. B. Axtell Governor of New Mexico*. **October 3, 1878**. Angel Report. Microfilm File No. 44-4-8-3. Record Group 48. Roll M750. National Archives. U.S. Department of Interior. Washington, D.C.

_____. *In the Matter of the Examination of the Causes and Circumstances of the Death of John H. Tunstall a British Subject*. **October 4, 1878**. Angel Report. Microfilm File Case Number 44-4-8-3. Record Group 48. Microfilm No. M750.

Roll 1. National Archives and Records Administration. U.S. Department of Justice. Washington, D.C.

_____. *In the Matter of the Lincoln County Troubles. To the Honorable Charles Devens, Attorney General.* **October 4, 1878.** Angel Report. Microfilm Case File No. 44-4-8-3. Record Group 48. Microfilm Roll M750. National Archives and Records Administration. U.S. Department of Justice. Washington, D.C.

Wallace, Lew. "Our mutual friend, M. Hinds, who will hand you this ..." Letter to A.H. Markland. **November 14, 1878.** Indiana Historical Society. Lew Wallace Collection. M0292. Box 3. Folder 17. **(Aware of the Santa Fe Ring and its attempt to remove him as governor)**

No Author. *Proceedings of a Court of Inquiry in the Case of Lt. Col. N.A.M. Dudley.* **May 2, 1879 – July 5, 1879.** File No. QQ1284. (Boxes 3304, 3305, 3305A); Court Martial Files 1809-1894. Records of the Office of the Judge Advocate General – Army. Record Group 153. Old Military and Civil Branch. National Archives and Records Administration. Washington, D.C.

Leonard, Ira E. "When you left here I promised to write you concerning events transpiring here ..." Letter to Lew Wallace. **May 20, 1878 [sic - 79].** Indiana Historical Society. Lew Wallace Collection. M0292. Box 4. Folder 10. **(Has quote on the Murphy-Dolan party as: "part and parcel of the Santa Fe ring that has been so long an incubus on the government of this territory.")**

_____. "I write to you with pencil because I am laboring for breath ..." Letter to Lew Wallace. **May 23, 1879.** Indiana Historical Society. Lew Wallace Collection. M0292. Box 4. Folder 11. **(With quote "we are pouring the 'hot shot' into Dudley." With enclosed letter of May 20, 1879)**

_____. "Yours of the 7th inst reached me ..." Letter to Lew Wallace. **June 13, 1879.** Indiana Historical Society. Lew Wallace Collection. M0292. Box 4. Folder 11. **(Important quotes: "... they would not enter our objections ..." "... would not allow us to show the conspiracy formed with Dolan beforehand ..." "I tell you Governor as long as the present incumbent occupies the bench all that Grand Juries may do to bring to justice these men every effort will be thwarted by him and the sympathizers of that side.")**

Elkins, Stephen Benton. "I have waited some time to reply to your lengthy letter ..." Letter to T.B. Catron. **August 15, 1879.** West Virginia & Regional History Center. West Virginia University Libraries, Morgantown, W. Va. Stephen B. Elkins Papers (A&M 53). Box 1. Folder 1. **(Reveals he prevented Catron's dismissal and indictment from Angel's report)**

Wallace, Lew. "I have the honor to inform you that the Legislature of this Territory adjourned ..." **February 16, 1880.** Letter to Carl Schurz. Indiana Historical Society. Lew Wallace Collection. M0292. Box 4. Folder 14. **(Important documentation of Catron as head of the Santa Fe Ring, and Wallace's Ring opposition)**

No Author. "White Cap's Proclamation." *Las Vegas Optic.* **March 12, 1880.** **(Manifesto against land-grabbing Catron and the Ring)**

No Author. "The Santa Fe Ring is the most corrupt combination that ever cursed any country or community." Las Cruces *Thirty-Four Newspaper.* **October 27, 1880.** From Victor Westphall, *Thomas Benton Catron and His Era.* Page 186. **(Article on Santa Fe Ring abuses urging voters to oppose Ring candidates)**

No Author. "A man named Springer is in Washington trying to defeat the nomination of Governor Axtell. Springer is a friend of the thugs and thieves of Colfax County." *Santa Fe New Mexican.* **July 6, 1882.** **(Santa Fe Ring re-instatement of S.B. Axtell to public office)**

No Author. " 'Chief Justice Axtell' is a bitter pill for the Raton *News and Press*." *Santa Fe New Mexican.* **July 18, 1882.** **(Santa Fe Ring re-instatement of S.B. Axtell as Chief Justice)**

No Author. "The Ring must soon discover that the time has passed in New Mexico when men can be herded like so many sheep ..." *Albuquerque Daily Democrat.* **March 4, 1884.** Quoted by Victor Westphall, *Thomas Benton Catron and His Era.* Page 191. (**About Santa Fe Ring control of appointments to legislature**)

No Author. *Santa Fe Weekly New Mexican Review.* **March 13, 1884.** *Santa Fe Weekly New Mexican Review.* (**Accusation of Catron and the Ring of controlling grand juries and bribery**)

Thornton, W.T. "Your favors received. We will try and have the matter of Mrs. Wilson's estate at Albuquerque attended to for your Bates County friends." Letter to John J. Cockrell, Esq. **January 16, 1886.** Herman B. Weisner Papers, ca. 1957-1992. New Mexico State University Library at Las Cruces. Rio Grande Historical Collections. Accession No. Weisner Ms 0249. Box 12. Folder S-5. Folder Name: "Catron, Thornton, & Clancy Letterhead." (**Catron's law partner discloses Ring planned malicious prosecution in Lincoln County**)

Borrego, Francisco Gonzales y. "dear Sir I have the honor to report to you that I have two men that they have agreed to come to the Republican party ... they want $10.00 each ..." **July 23, 1890.** Letter to Thomas Benton Catron. Catron Papers 102, Box 8. Quoted by Victor Westphall, *Thomas Benton Catron and His Era.* Page 268. (**Revealing Catron's Ringite vote-buying and loyalty to Ring agents**)

Valdez, Jose and Enrique Mares. "Scorching Letter, The Knights of Labor Send a Communication to Powderly! Politicians Arraigned! The Boldest Document Ever Issued in the Territory." **August 18, 1890.** *Las Vegas Democrat.* Volume 1. Center for Southwest Studies. Thomas B. Catron Papers, MSS 29, Series 102, Box 8, Folder 4. (**Gives history of Santa Fe Ring with T.B. Catron as head**)

Chavez, Juliana V. "Mr. Catron, you are not above suspicion of knowing more about the assassination of my son than you have found it convenient to reveal ..." Letter of Juliana Chavez to T.B. Catron. Reprinted in *Santa Fe Weekly New Mexican.* **March 8, 1894.** Quoted in Victor Westphall, *Thomas Benton Catron and his Era.* Page 226. (**Accusing Catron as accomplice to murder of Francisco Chavez, with implication of Santa Fe Ring**)

No author. "T.B. Catron's reputation now being "smirched" by evidence that he was a briber and too dishonest even to practice law ..." *Las Vegas Independent Democrat.* 1895; quoting from *Las Vegas Optic.* **September 2, 1884.** From Victor Westphall. *Thomas Benton Catron and His Era.* Pages 105-106. (**About Catron's and Elkins's dishonesty, the Santa Fe Ring, and disbarring Catron from law practice in New Mexico**)

Catron, Thomas Benton (As "Anonymous"). "Is it honesty or partisanship?" Letter to the Editor, Thomas Hughes. *Albuquerque Daily Citizen.* **October 9, 1895.** (**Defamation of his disbarment Judge Thomas J. Smith**) Cited by Victor Westphall, *Thomas Benton Catron and His Era.* Page 246. Thomas B. Catron Papers. University of New Mexico Center for Southwest Studies. University Library. MSS 29 BC.

_____. "[Y]ou must absolutely stand pat and not give away any information that will injure me ..." Letter to Editor of the *Albuquerque Daily Citizen* Thomas Hughes. **October 10, 1895.** Catron Papers. 801. Box 1. Quoted by Victor Westphall, *Thomas Benton Catron and His Era.* Page 247. (**Catron influencing the Ringite newspaper editor to prevent his own disbarment by the New Mexico Supreme Court**)

_____. "Editor of the Citizen: I have noticed an article in the Citizen of the 9th inst., which seems to reflect on Chief Justice Smith ..." Letter to Editor of the *Albuquerque Daily Citizen* Thomas Hughes. **October 10, 1895.** Catron Papers 801. Box 1. Quoted by Victor Westphall, *Thomas Benton Catron and His Era.* (page 248) (**Catron lying in letter to complicit Ringite editor to conceal his own authorship of the newspaper's article accusing his Supreme Court disbarment judge of bias**)

_____. "[Chief Justice] Tom Smith, son of "Extra Billy" Smith, brother of ... the embezzler, who fled from justice in Arizona, and brother of the other Smith who took a prominent part in the murder of Dave Broderick ..." "[Judge] Hamilton should ... see that the decision is an absolute, complete, unconditional vindication. This is what I ask him. He can afford to give it." Letter to *Socorro Chieftain* publisher S.W. Williams. **October 25, 1895**. Catron Papers. 105. Vol. 13. Quoted by Victor Westphall, *Thomas Benton Catron and His Era*. Page 251. **(Example of Catron's vicious defamation of his Supreme Court disbarment Chief Judge Thomas Smith in Ringite collusion with the press, and use of illegal influence on another judge)**

Hamilton, Humphrey. *Majority Opinion* in disbarment case against Thomas Benton Catron. "[T]he low moral character and poor reputation for veracity of the prosecution witnesses rendered their testimony beyond belief." **October 25, 1895**. Catron Papers. 801. Box 1. Quoted by Victor Westphall, *Thomas Benton Catron and His Era*. Page 251. **(Ring colluding judge vindicating Catron from disbarment by blocking prosecution evidence)**

Catron, Thomas Benton. "His [Chief Justice Thomas Smith] skin is so thin that the slightest attack punctures him. I think the papers should now puncture him so much ..." Letter to T.W. Collier. **November 11, 1895**. Catron Papers. 105. Vol. 13. Quoted by Victor Westphall, *Thomas Benton Catron and His Era*. Page 249. **(Example of Catron's vicious Ringite harassment of an opponent)**

_____. "The letter of Gov. Thornton [in the September 11, 1896 of the *Santa Fe Daily New Mexican* and exposing his defamation plot] is regarded here by all good citizens as being ... calculated to bring about a state of unrest and possible bloodshed." **September 16, 1896**. Letter to President Grover Cleveland. Catron Papers 801, Box 1. Quoted by Victor Westphall, *Thomas Benton Catron and His Era*. Pages 269-270. **(Catron's paranoid accusations against Thornton)**

Wallace, Lew. "I have your several letters, including the last one of the 3rd inst." Letter to Eugene Fiske. **November 6, 1897**. Indiana Historical Society. Lew Wallace Collection. AC233. Box 1. Folder 7. (part of 1981 addition) **(About T.B. Catron's control over New Mexicans)**

No Author. *Los Angeles Times*. **1899**. Undated clipping, Laughlin Papers, State Records Center, Santa Fe, New Mexico. Quoted by Victor Westphall, *Thomas Benton Catron and His Era*. Page 285. **(Joking article about the Santa Fe Ring)**

Catron, Thomas Benton. "[Otero backers] have made a very villainous, mean ugly fight against me." **September 20, 1902**. Letter to Dave Winters. Catron Papers 105, Volume 20. Quoted by Victor Westphall, *Thomas Benton Catron and His Era*. Pages 291. **(Catron's accusing of rival, Governor Miguel Otero, of his own ring-style criminality)**

Cutting, Bronson. "Catron was the boss of the Territory ..." Letter to James Roger Addison. **December 11, 1911**. Cited by Victor Westphall in *Thomas Benton Catron and His Era* from his citation: Lincoln County Manuscripts Division. Box 12. Courtesy of David Stratton. **(Catron as head of the Santa Fe Ring)**

(SEE: Thomas Benton Catron; Stephen Benton Elkins; Mary McPherson, Frank Warner Angel, Legislature Revolt, Grant County Rebellion, Colfax County War, Lincoln County War)

EXPOSÉS OF (CONTEMPORARY)

COMPLAINT ABOUT TO PRESIDENT RUTHERFORD B. HAYES

Matchett, W.B. and Mary E. McPherson. " W.B. Matchett and Mary E. McPherson 'Make certain charges against the U.S. Officials in the Territory of New Mexico.' " Letter to President Rutherford B. Hayes. Received and filed **May 1, 1877**. Interior Department Papers 1850-1907; Appointments Division and Subsequent Actions. Microfilm File Case Number 44-4-8-3. Record Group 48. Microfilm No. M750.

Roll 1. National Archives and Records Administration. U. S. Department of Justice. Washington, D.C.

McPherson, Mary and W.B. Matchett. "To the President. Please make the enclosed a part of the evidence in the case of "Charges Against New Mexican Officials" Letter to President Rutherford B. Hayes. **May 3, 1877.** McPherson, Mary E. Letters and Petitions to President Rutherford B. Hayes re: Removal Governor Axtell and the Santa Fe Ring. Interior Department Papers 1850-1907; Appointments Division and Subsequent Actions. Microfilm File Case Number 44-4-8-3. Record Group 48. Microfilm Roll M750. National Archives and Records Administration. U.S. Department of Justice. Washington, D.C. (**Addendum to their May, 1877 "Certain Charges Against U.S. Officials in New Mexico Territory."**)

_____. "The Secretary of the Interior, Sir – Accompanying please find copy of charges, &c., against S.B. Axtell, Governor, and Other New Mexican Officials ..." "Charges Against New Mexican Officials." Letter to Secretary of the Interior Carl Schurz. **May 5, 1877.** McPherson, Mary E. Letters and Petitions to President Rutherford B. Hayes re: Removal Governor Axtell and the Santa Fe Ring. Interior Department Papers 1850-1907; Appointments Division and Subsequent Actions. Microfilm File Case Number 44-4-8-3. Record Group 48. Microfilm Roll M750. National Archives and Records Administration. U.S. Department of Justice. Washington, D. C.

_____. "*In the Matter of Charges vs. Gov. S.B. Axtell and Other New Mexico Officials. Submitted to the Departments of the Interior and Justice.* **August, 1877.** Printed as a 31 page booklet. No publisher listed. Indiana Historical Society. Lew Wallace Collection. M0292. Box 3. Folder 20. (**In Lew Wallace's personal possession; about the Santa Fe Ring, Catron, and Elkins**)

McPherson, Mary. "Please place before the Attorney General ..." Letter to President Rutherford B. Hayes. **August 23, 1877.** Interior Department Papers 1850-1907; Appointments Division and Subsequent Actions. Microfilm File Case Number 44-4-8-3. Record Group 48. Microfilm No. M750. Roll 1. National Archives and Records Administration. U. S. Department of Justice. Washington, D.C.

Springer, Frank. Deposition to Investigator Frank Warner Angel for the Departments of Justice and the Interior. **August 9, 1878.** Frank Warner Angel report titled *In the Matter of the Investigation of the Charges Against S.B. Axtell Governor of New Mexico.* October 3, 1878. Interior Department Papers 1850-1907; Appointments Division and Subsequent Actions. Microfilm Case File No. 44-4-8-3. Record Group 48. Microfilm Roll M750. National Archives and Records Administration. U.S. Department of Interior. Washington, D.C.

(SEE: Thomas Benton Catron)

SECRET SERVICE, 19th CENTURY

Bowen, Walter S. and Harry Edward Neal. *The United States Secret Service.* Philadelphia and New York: Chilton Company Publishers. 1960.

Brooks, James J. *1877 Report on Secret Service Operatives.* (September 26, 1877). "On Azariah Wild." p.392. Department of the Treasury. United States Secret Service. Washington, D.C.

Burnham, George P. *American Counterfeits. How Detected, And How Avoided. Comprising Sketches of Noted Counterfeiters, and Their Allies, Of Secret Agents, and Detectives; Authentic Accounts of the Capture of Forgers, Defaulters, and Swindlers; With Rules for Deciding Good and Counterfeit Notes, or United States Currency; A List of Terms and Phrases in Use Among This Fraternity of Offenders, &c., &c.* Springfield, Massachusetts: W. J. Holland. 1875.

_____. *Memoirs of the United States Secret Service With Accurate Portraits of Prominent Members of the Detective Force, Some of Their Most Notable Captures,* and a Brief Account of the Life of Col. H. C. Whitley, Chief of the Division. Boston: Lee, Shepard. 18??.

_____. Three Years With Counterfeiters, Smugglers, and Boodle Carriers; With Accurate Portraits of the Prominent Members of the Detective Force in The Secret Service. Boston: John P. Dale & Co. 18??.

Johnson, David R. Illegal Tender. Counterfeiting and the Secret Service in Nineteenth Century America. Washington and London: Smithsonian Institution Press. 1995.

Wild, Azariah F. "Daily Reports of U. S. Secret Service Agents, Azariah F. Wild. Microfilm T-915. Record Group 87. Rolls 306 (June 15, 1877 - December 31, 1877), 307 (January 1, 1878 - June 30, 1879), 308 (July 1, 1879 - June 30, 1881), 309 (July 1, 1881 - September 30, 1883), and 310 (October 1, 1883 - July 31, 1886). National Archives and Records Department. Department of Treasury. United States Secret Service. Washington, D. C.

WHITE CAPS (LAS GORRAS BLANCAS) (1880)

No Author. "White Cap's Proclamation." Las Vegas Optic. March 12, 1880. **(Manifesto against land-grabbing Catron and the Ring)**

NEW MEXICO TERRITORY REBELLIONS AGAINST THE SANTA FE RING (CHRONOLOGICAL)

LEGISLATURE REVOLT (1872)

No Author. Journal of the House of Representatives of the Territory of New Mexico, Session of 1871-1872. Santa Fe: A.P. Sullivan. **1872**. Pages 144-154. **(Confirms troops used by Ring to suppress the Legislature Revolt of 1872)**

No Author. "Our Own Dear Steve, How Elkins Made His Influence Felt in New Mexico – The Ring in Which a Judge Figured – Politics in 1870. Las Vegas Daily Optic. **September 2, 1884.** (Reprinted from the Omaha Herald) Front Page. Volume V, Number 258, Column 4. Newspaperarchive.com. **(Exposing the Ring in the 1872 Legislature Revolt)**

GRANT COUNTY REBELLION (1876)

MODERN SOURCES

Naegle, Conrad Keeler. The History of Silver City, New Mexico 1870-1886. University of New Mexico Bachelor of Arts thesis. Pages 30-60. Unpublished. 1943. Collection of the Silver City Museum, Silver City, New Mexico.

_____. "The Rebellion of Grant County, New Mexico in 1876." Arizona and the West: A Quarterly Journal of History. Autumn, 1968. Volume 10. Number 3. Tucson, Arizona: The University of Arizona Press. 1968. Pages 225-240. **(Rebellion against Santa Fe Ring)**

CONTEMPORARY SOURCES (CHRONOLOGICAL)

No Author. "Diario del Consejo der Territorio de Neuvo Mejico, Session de 1871-1872." Santa Fe New Mexican. **January 8, 1872.** Santa Fe: A.P. Sullivan. 1872. Pages 144-154. New Mexico Supreme Court Library. Santa Fe, New Mexico. **(A Ring expurgated document, with a copy found in 1942 by Conrad Naegle; confirming troops used by Ring to suppress Territorial legislature)**

No Author. "Diario del Consejo der Territorio de Neuvo Mejico, Session de 1871-1872. Las Cruces Borderer. **January 24, 1872.** Pages 110-113. **(Don Diego Archuleta, President of the Council, gives speech objecting to troops in legislature)**

No Author. "Ring influence [in the Territorial legislature is] being actively used against every measure that tends to do justice" [in Grant and Doña Ana Counties]." *Grant County Herald.* **August 8, 1875.** Quoted by Conrad Keeler Naegle in *The History of Silver City, New Mexico 1870-1886,* doctoral thesis. Page 39.

No Author. "A Contemplated Political Change." Grant County *Herald.* **September 16, 1876.** Quoted by Conrad Keeler Naegle in *The History of Silver City, New Mexico 1870-1886* doctoral thesis. Pages 39-40. **(Listing reasons to escape the Ring by annexing to Arizona Territory)**

No Author. [Grant County should not] "sort o' wait and hear from Santa Fe ... before taking action." Tucson *Arizona Citizen.* **September 23, 1876.** Quoted by Conrad Keeler Naegle in *The History of Silver City, New Mexico 1870-1886* doctoral thesis. Page 41. **(Arizona encourages escape from Santa Fe Ring)**

No Author. Grant County *Herald.* **September 23, 1876. (Need for school system stressed.)**

No Author. Grant County *Herald.* **September 30, 1876. ("Annexation Meeting" announced)**

No Author. "Proceedings of Grant County Annexation Meeting." Grant County *Herald.* **Saturday October 7, 1876.** Page 2. Columns 1 and 2. Collection of the Silver City, New Mexico, Museum. **(Anti-Santa Fe Ring "Grant County Declaration of Independence" published)**

No Author. Grant County *Herald.* " 'Petition to Remove Judge Bristol. We the undersigned citizens of the Third Judicial District of the Territory of New Mexico, without regard to party, would respectfully request and petition for the removal of Judge Warren Bristol ...' " No date. **1876 or 1877.**(Quoted in "W.B. Matchett and Mary E. McPherson 'Make certain charges against the U.S. Officials in the Territory of New Mexico.' " Letter to President Rutherford B. Hayes. Received and filed May 1, 1877. Interior Department Papers 1850-1907; Appointments Division and Subsequent Actions. Microfilm File Case Number 44-4-8-3. Record Group 48. Microfilm No. M750. Roll 1. National Archives and Records Administration. U.S. Department of Justice. Washington, D.C.) **(Anti-Santa Fe Ring article)**

(SEE: Santa Fe Ring; Thomas Benton Catron; Stephen Benton Elkins)

COLFAX COUNTY WAR (1877)

MODERN SOURCES

Caffey, David L. *Frank Springer and New Mexico: From the Colfax County War to the Emergence of Modern Santa Fe.* Texas A and M. University Press. 2007.

Cleaveland, Norman. *The Morleys - Young Upstarts on the Southwest Frontier.* Albuquerque, New Mexico: Calvin Horn Publisher, Inc. 1971.

Dunham, Harold H. "New Mexican Land Grants with Special Reference to the Title Papers of the Maxwell Grant." *New Mexico Historical Review.* (January 1955) Volume 30, Number 1. Pages 1 - 23.

Keleher, William A. *The Maxwell Land Grant. A New Mexico Item.* Albuquerque, New Mexico: University of New Mexico Press. 1964.

Lamar, Howard Roberts. *The Far Southwest 1846 - 1912. A Territorial History.* New Haven and London: Yale University Press. 1966.

Montoya, María E. *Translating Property. The Maxwell Land Grant and the Conflict Over Land in the American West, 1840-1900.* Berkeley and Los Angeles, California: University of California Press. 2002.

Murphy, Lawrence R. *Lucien Bonaparte Maxwell. Napoleon of the Southwest.* Norman: University of Oklahoma Press. 1983.

Pearson, Jim Berry. *The Maxwell Land Grant.* Norman: University of Oklahoma Press. 1961.

Poe, Sophie. *Buckboard Days.* Albuquerque, New Mexico: University of New Mexico Press. 1964.

Taylor, Morris F. *O.P. McMains and the Maxwell Land Grant Conflict.* Tucson, Arizona: The University of Arizona Press. 1979.

CONTEMPORARY SOURCES (CHRONOLOGICAL)

Morley, William Raymond and Frank Springer. On Oscar McMains's citizen's Meeting. *Cimarron News and Press.* **November 10, 1875.** In Mary McPherson, Letters and Petitions to President Rutherford B. Hayes re: Removal Governor Axtell and the Santa Fe Ring. 1977. Interior Department Papers 1850-1907; Appointments Division and Subsequent Actions. Microfilm File Case Number 44-4-8-3. Record Group 48. Microfilm Roll M750. National Archives and Records Administration. **(Colfax County citizens meeting on F.J. Tolby murder by Santa Fe Ring.)**

No author. "Anarchy at Cimarron." *Santa Fe Weekly New Mexican.* **November 16, 1875. (Ringite backing of Axtell's use of troops in the Colfax County War)**

Morley, William Raymond and Frank Springer. " 'The Territory of Elkins.' Assassination of Supposed Sun Correspondent. The Murder of the Rev. F.J. Tolby in New Mexico. A Probate Judge Accused of Complicity in the Crime. Indignation Meeting." *New York Weekly Sun.* **December 22, 1875.** Interior Department Papers 1850-1907; Appointments Division and Subsequent Actions. Microfilm Roll M750. National Archives and Records Administration. Record Group 48. Microfilm Case File Number 44-4-8-3. U. S. Department of Interior. Washington, D. C.**(From May 1, 1877 complaint to President Rutherford B. Hayes as "Mary E. McPherson and W.B. Matchett 'Make certain charges against the U.S. Officials in the Territory of New Mexico.' ")**

Dawson, Will. Editorial. *Cimarron News and Press.* **December 31, 1875. (Ring-biased editorial by temporary editor blaming citizens for unrest)**

No Author. Report on murder trial for Franklin Tolby. Pueblo, *Colorado Chieftain.* **May 25, 1876.** Quoting *Daily New Mexican,* May 1, 1876. From Morris F. Taylor. *O.P. McMains and the Maxwell Land Grant Conflict.* Tucson, Arizona: The University of Arizona Press. 1979. Page 49. **(Ring-biased jury instructions by Judge Henry Waldo to protect Ring murderers of Tolby)**

Morley William Raymond. "I was astonished beyond measure at your proceedings, and have fears as to the result ..." Letter to Mary McPherson. **March 6, 1877.** McPherson, Mary E. Letters and Petitions to President Rutherford B. Hayes re: Removal Governor Axtell and the Santa Fe Ring. Interior Department Papers 1850-1907; Appointments Division and Subsequent Actions. Microfilm File Case Number 44-4-8-3. Record Group 48. Microfilm Roll M750. National Archives and Records Administration. U.S. Department of Justice. Washington, D. C. **(Hopes she can help fight against Santa Fe Ring; enclosed in Mary McPherson's "Charges Against U.S. Officials in the Territory of New Mexico.")**

Lambert, J.J. "At It Again." Pueblo, Colorado, *Enterprise and Chronicle.* **April 21, 1877.** Interior Department Papers 1850-1907; Appointments Division and Subsequent Actions. Microfilm File Case Number 44-4-8-3. Record Group 48. Microfilm No. M750. Roll 1. National Archives and Records Administration. U.S. Department of Justice. Washington, D.C. **(Description of Santa Fe Ring control of courts and malicious prosecution of opponents like Oscar McMains in the Franklin Tolby murder; used in: "W.B. Matchett and Mary E. McPherson 'Make Certain Charges Against the U.S. Officials in the Territory of New Mexico.' " Letter to President Rutherford B. Hayes. Received and filed May 1, 1877. Interior Department Papers 1850-1907; Appointments Division and Subsequent Actions. Microfilm File Case Number 44-4-8-3. Record Group 48. Microfilm No. M750. Roll 1. National Archives and Records Administration. U. S. Department of Justice. Washington, D.C.)**

Matchett, W.B. and Mary E. McPherson. "Make Certain Charges Against the U.S. Officials in the Territory of New Mexico." To the President. **April, 1877.** Microfilm

File Case Number 44-4-8-3. Record Group 48. Microfilm No. M750. Roll 1. National Archives and Records Administration. U. S. Department of Justice. Washington, D.C. (**Sent to President Rutherford B. Hayes and Secretary of the Interior Carl Schurz 141 pages of letters, affidavits, petitions, newspaper articles, itemized requests for removal of Governor Samuel Beach Axtell and District Judge Warren Bristol, documentation of use of the military against civilians, documentation of the Ring murder of Ring opponent Reverend F.J. Tolby, and identification of the Santa Fe Ring.**)

McPherson, Mary and W.B. Matchett. "To the President. Please make the enclosed a part of the evidence in the case of "Charges Against New Mexican Officials" Letter to President Rutherford B. Hayes. **May 3, 1877**. McPherson, Mary E. Letters and Petitions to President Rutherford B. Hayes re: Removal Governor Axtell and the Santa Fe Ring. Interior Department Papers 1850-1907; Appointments Division and Subsequent Actions. Microfilm File Case Number 44-4-8-3. Record Group 48. Microfilm Roll M750. National Archives and Records Administration. U.S. Department of Justice. Washington, D.C. (**Addendum to their May, 1877 "Certain Charges Against U.S. Officials in New Mexico Territory."**)

McPherson, Mary and W.B. Matchett. "The Secretary of the Interior, Sir - Accompanying please find copy of charges, &c., against S.B. Axtell, Governor, and other New Mexican Officials ..." "Charges Against New Mexican Officials." Letter to Secretary of the Interior Carl Schurz. **May 5, 1877**. McPherson, Mary E. Letters and Petitions to President Rutherford B. Hayes re: Removal Governor Axtell and the Santa Fe Ring. Interior Department Papers 1850-1907; Appointments Division and Subsequent Actions. Microfilm File Case Number 44-4-8-3. Record Group 48. Microfilm Roll M750. National Archives and Records Administration. U.S. Department of Justice. Washington, D. C.

McPherson, Mary and W.B. Matchett. "We have respectfully to request that the following named records, documents, papers, communications and correspondence be supplied ..." Records Request to Secretary of the Interior Carl Schurz. **July 26, 1877**. Interior Department Papers 1850-1907; Appointments Division and Subsequent Actions. Microfilm File Case Number 44-4-8-3. Record Group 48. Microfilm No. M750. Roll 1. National Archives and Records Administration. U.S. Department of Justice. Washington, D.C. (**Requesting records of the Santa Fe Ring, Carton, Elkins, and Axtell**)

McPherson, Mary E. and W.B. Matchett. "In the Matter of the Charges vs. Gov. S. B. Axtell and Other New Mexico Officials; Submitted to the Departments of the Interior and of Justice. Governor of New Mexico." **August, 1877**. Printed as a 31 page booklet. No publisher listed. Indiana Historical Society. Lew Wallace Collection. M0292. Box 3. Folder 20. (**Focus on the Santa Fe Ring**)

McPherson, Mary. "I desire to know when I can be heard ..." Letter to Secretary of Interior Carl Schurz. **September 30, 1977**. Interior Department Papers 1850-1907; Appointments Division and Subsequent Actions. Microfilm File Case Number 44-4-8-3. Record Group 48. Microfilm No. M750. Roll 1. National Archives and Records Administration. U. S. Department of Justice. Washington, D.C. (**Requesting audience on charges against Ring officials**)

Springer, Frank. "I endorse herewith, directed to the President ..." Letter to Secretary of the Interior Carl Schurz. June 10, 1878. Microfilm File Case Number 44-4-8-3. Record Group 48. Microfilm No. M750. Roll 1. National Archives and Records Administration. U.S. Department of Justice. Washington, D.C.

_____. "The undersigned, a citizen of the County of Colfax ..." To His Excellency, the President of the United States. Enclosed in letter to Secretary of the Interior Carl Schurz. June 10, 1878. Microfilm File Case Number 44-4-8-3. Record Group 48. Microfilm No. M750. Roll 1. National Archives and Records Administration. U.S. Department of Justice. Washington, D.C.

_____. Deposition to Investigator Frank Warner Angel. August 9, 1878. Frank Warner Angel report titled *In the Matter of the Investigation of the Charges*

460

Against S.B. Axtell Governor of New Mexico. October 3, 1878. Interior Department Papers 1850-1907; Appointments Division and Subsequent Actions. Microfilm Case File No. 44-4-8-3. Record Group 48. Microfilm Roll M750. National Archives and Records Administration. U.S. Department of Interior. Washington, D.C. **(Mentions Catron, Elkins, and the Santa Fe Ring; with Exhibits of letters)**

Morley, William Raymond. "Your letter of the 7th came last night and it was a good long newsy letter ..." Letter to wife, Ada McPherson Morley. **August 15, 1878.** Collection of Norman Cleaveland. Quoted in Norman Cleaveland, *The Morleys: Young Upstarts in the Southwest.* Albuquerque, New Mexico: Calvin Horn Publisher, Inc. 1971. Pages 152-155. **(About possible betrayal by Angel's reports; about the Santa Fe Ring, T.B. Catron, S.B. Elkins, S.B. Axtell, and Henry Waldo; and the Lincoln County War)**

Springer, Frank. Deposition to Investigator Frank Warner Angel. **August 9, 1878.** Frank Warner Angel report titled *In the Matter of the Investigation of the Charges Against S.B. Axtell Governor of New Mexico.* October 3, 1878. Interior Department Papers 1850-1907; Appointments Division and Subsequent Actions. Microfilm Case File No. 44-4-8-3. Record Group 48. Microfilm Roll M750. National Archives and Records Administration. U.S. Department of Interior. Washington, D.C. **(Mentions Catron, Elkins, and the Santa Fe Ring; with Exhibits of letters)**

SEE ALSO: Santa Fe Ring; Thomas Benton Catron; Stephen Benton Elkins

LINCOLN COUNTY WAR (1878)

MODERN SOURCES

Cramer, T. Dudley. *The Pecos Ranchers in the Lincoln County War.* Orinda, California: Branding Iron Press. 1996.

Fulton, Maurice Garland. Robert N. Mullin. Ed. *History of the Lincoln County War.* Tucson, Arizona: The University of Arizona Press. 1997.

Jacobsen, Joel. *Such Men as Billy the Kid. The Lincoln County War Reconsidered.* Lincoln and London: University of Nebraska Press. 1994.

Keleher, William A. *The Fabulous Frontier: Twelve New Mexico Items.* Albuquerque, New Mexico: The University of New Mexico Press. 1962.

_____. *Violence in Lincoln County 1869-1881.* Albuquerque, New Mexico: University of New Mexico Press. 1957.

Mullin, Robert N. Re: Frank Warner Angel Meeting with President Hayes. August, 1878. Binder RNM, VI, M. Midland, Texas: Nita Stewart Haley Memorial Library and J. Evetts Haley History Center. (Unpublished).

Nolan, Frederick W. *The Life and Death of John Henry Tunstall.* Albuquerque, New Mexico: The University of New Mexico Press. 1965.

_____. *The Lincoln County War: A Documentary History.* Norman: University of Oklahoma Press. 1992.

_____. *The West of Billy the Kid.* Norman: University of Oklahoma Press. 1998.

Rasch, Philip J. *Gunsmoke in Lincoln County.* Laramie, Wyoming: National Association for Outlaw and Lawmen History, Inc. with University of Wyoming. 1997.

_____. Robert K. DeArment. Ed. *Warriors of Lincoln County.* Laramie: National Association for Outlaw and Lawmen History, Inc. with University of Wyoming. 1998.

Utley, Robert M. *High Noon in Lincoln. Violence on the Western Frontier.* Albuquerque, New Mexico: University of New Mexico Press. 1987.

Wilson, John P. *Merchants, Guns, and Money: The Story of Lincoln County and Its Wars.* Santa Fe, New Mexico: Museum of New Mexico Press. 1987.

No Author. "Disturbances in the Territories, 1878 - 1894. Lawlessness in New Mexico." Senate Documents. 67th Congress. 2nd Session. December 5, 1921 - September 22, 1922. pp. 176 - 187. Washington, D.C.: Government Printing Office. 1922.

CONTEMPORARY SOURCES (CHRONOLOGICAL)

No Author. "Brady Inventory McSween Property." **February, 1878.** Herman B. Weisner Papers, ca. 1957-1992. New Mexico State University Library at Las Cruces. Rio Grande Historical Collections. Accession No. Weisner Ms 0249. Box 10. Folder M15. Folder Name. "Will and Testament A. McSween."

No Author. "Amnesty for Matthews and Long in the Third Judicial Court April Term 1879." **April, 1879.** Herman B. Weisner Papers, ca. 1957-1992. New Mexico State University Library at Las Cruces. Rio Grande Historical Collections. Accession No. Ms 0249. Box 1. Folder 4. Folder Name. "Amnesty."

No Author. "Charges against Jessie Evans and John Kinney." Doña Ana County Civil and Criminal Docket Book. **August 18, 1875 to November 7, 1878.** Herman B. Weisner Papers, ca. 1957-1992. New Mexico State University Library at Las Cruces. Rio Grande Historical Collections. Accession No. Ms 0249. Box 13. Folder V 3. Folder Name. "Venue, Change Of."

No author. "Why Axtell Wanted Troops." **July 31, 1878.** Santa Fe. Newspaper unknown. Enclosed in report of Frank Warner Angel: *In the Matter of the Examination of the Causes and Circumstances of the Death of John H. Tunstall a British Subject.* Report filed October 4, 1878. Interior Department Papers 1850-1907; Appointments Division and Subsequent Actions. Microfilm File Case Number 44-4-8-3. Record Group 48. Microfilm No. M750. Roll 1. National Archives and Records Administration. U.S. Department of Justice. Washington, D.C. **(Enclosed with letter to the President, from a John G. Hubbard of August 1, 1878.).**

No Author. "Dismissal of Cases Against Dolan, Matthews, Peppin, October 1879 District Court." **October, 1879.** Herman B. Weisner Papers, ca. 1957-1992. New Mexico State University Library at Las Cruces. Rio Grande Historical Collections. Accession No. Ms 0249. Box 13. Folder V3. Folder Name: "Venue, Change Of."

No Author. "Killers of Tunstall. February 18, 1879." Herman B. Weisner Papers, ca. 1957-1992. New Mexico State University Library at Las Cruces. Rio Grande Historical Collections. Accession No. Ms 0249. Box 12. Folder T1. Folder Name: "Tunstall, John H."

No Author. "Lincoln County Indictments **July 1872 - 1881.**" Herman B. Weisner Papers, ca. 1957-1992. New Mexico State University Library at Las Cruces. Rio Grande Historical Collections. Accession No. Ms 0249. Box 8. Folder L11. Folder Name. "Lincoln Co. Indictments."

Ealy, Mrs. Taylor. Ed. Haniel Long. "New Mexico Writers: The Lincoln County War Part 1. *The New Mexico Sentinel.* **October 5, 1937.** Volume 1, Number 45, Page 8. New York Public Library. **(Eye-witness of Lincoln County War; describes mutilation of John Tunstall's face)**

_____. Ed. Haniel Long. "New Mexico Writers: The Lincoln County War Part 2. *The New Mexico Sentinel.* **October 12, 1937.** Volume 1, Number 46, Page 6. New York Public Library. **(Eye-witness of Lincoln County War)**

Corbet, Sam. "Sam Corbet Writes of Slayings." *The New Mexico Sentinel.* **July 17, 1938.** Volume 2, Number 33. Angelo State University Library. West Texas Collection, New York Public Library. **(Eye-witness of Lincoln County War)**

_____. "Tunstall's Father Learns of the Raids." *The New Mexico Sentinel.* **July 17, 1938.** Volume 2, Number 33. Angelo State University Library. West Texas Collection, New York Public Library. **(Sam Corbet's letter as eye-witness of Lincoln County War)**

HISTORY OF WILLIAM HENRY BONNEY
(WILLIAM HENRY McCARTY, HENRY ANTRIM,
AKA BILLY THE KID)

BIOGRAPHICAL SOURCES

Abbott, E.C. ("Teddy Blue") and Helena Huntington Smith. *We Pointed Them North: Recollections of a Cowpuncher*. Norman, Oklahoma: University of Oklahoma Press. 1955. (**Billy the Kid's multi-culturalism, Page 47.**)

Anaya, A.P. "Paco." *I Buried Billy*. College Station, Texas: Creative Publishing Company. 1991.

Ball, Eve. *Ma'am Jones of the Pecos*. Tucson, Arizona: The University of Arizona Press. 1969.

Bell, Bob Boze. *The Illustrated Life and Times of Billy the Kid*. Cave Creek, Arizona: Boze Books. 1992. (Frank Coe quote about the Kid's cartridge use, Page 45.)

Bell, Bob Boze. *The Illustrated Life and Times of Billy the Kid*. Second Edition. Phoenix, Arizona: Tri Star-Boze Publications, Inc. 1996.

Burns, Walter Noble. *The Saga of Billy the Kid*. Stamford, Connecticut: Longmeadow Press. 1992. (Original printing: 1926, Doubleday.)

_____. *"I also know that the Kid and Paulita were sweethearts."* Unpublished letter to Jim East. **June 3, 1926.** Robert N. Mullin Collection. File RNM, IV, NM, 116-117. Nita Stewart Haley Memorial Museum, Haley Library. Midland, Texas.

Coe, George with Doyce B. Nunis, Jr. Ed. *Frontier Fighter. The Autobiography of George Coe Who Fought and Rode With Billy the Kid*. Chicago: R. R. Donnelley and Sons Company. **1984.**

Cooper, Gale. *Billy the Kid's Writings, Words, and Wit*. Gelcour Books: Albuquerque: New Mexico. 2012.

_____. *Billy and Paulita: The Saga of Billy the Kid, Paulita Maxwell, and the Santa Fe Ring*. Gelcour Books: Albuquerque: New Mexico. **2012.**

_____. *The Lost Pardon of Billy the Kid: An Analysis Factoring in the Santa Fe Ring, Governor Lew Wallace's Dilemma, and a Territory in Rebellion*. Gelcour Books: Albuquerque: New Mexico. 2017.

_____. *The Santa Fe Ring Versus Billy the Kid: The Making of an American Monster*. Gelcour Books: Albuquerque: New Mexico. 2018.

Garrett, Pat F. *The Authentic Life of Billy the Kid The Noted Desperado of the Southwest, Whose Deeds of Daring and Blood Made His Name a Terror in New Mexico, Arizona, and Northern Mexico*. Santa Fe, New Mexico: New Mexico Printing and Publishing Co. 1882. (Edition used: Edited by Maurice Garland Fulton. New York: The Macmillan Company. 1927)

Hoyt, Henry. *A Frontier Doctor*. Boston and New York: Houghton Mifflin Company. 1929. (**Describes Billy's superior abilities. Pages 93-94, including fluency in Spanish.**)

Jacobsen, Joel. *Such Men as Billy the Kid. The Lincoln County War Reconsidered*. Lincoln and London: University of Nebraska Press. 1994.

Kadlec, Robert F. *They "Knew" Billy the Kid. Interviews with Old-Time New Mexicans*. Santa Fe, New Mexico: Ancient City Press. 1987.

Keleher, William A. *The Fabulous Frontier: Twelve New Mexico Items*. Albuquerque, New Mexico: The University of New Mexico Press. 1962.

_____. *Violence in Lincoln County 1869-1881*. Albuquerque, New Mexico: University of New Mexico Press. 1957.

Koop, W.E. *Billy the Kid: The Trail of a Kansas Legend*. Self Published. **1965.**

McFarland, David F. Reverend. *Ledger: Session Records 1867-1874. Marriages in Santa Fe New Mexico. "Mr. William H. Antrim and Mrs. Catherine McCarty." March 1, 1873*. Santa Fe, New Mexico: First Presbyterian Church of Santa Fe.

Meadows, John P. "Billy the Kid to John P. Meadows on the Peñasco, May 1-2, 1881." *Roswell Daily Record.* **February 16, 1931**. Page 6.

_____. "Story of Billy the Kid, His Life and Death, as Told Here by John Meadows, Friend of the Kid." *Roswell Daily Record.* **March 2, 1931**. Page 6.

_____. "Oldtimer, Friend of the Billy the Kid, Tells of the Kid's Capture After Many Killings." *Roswell Daily Record.* **March 3, 1931**. Page 6.

_____. "Oldtimer Pays Tribute to Sheriff Pat Garrett in Final Chapter of Billy the Kid." *Roswell Daily Record.* **March 4, 1931**. Page 6.

_____. Ed. John P. Wilson. *Pat Garrett and Billy the Kid as I Knew Them: Reminiscences of John P. Meadows.* Albuquerque: University of New Mexico Press. **2004**.

Mullin, Robert N. *The Boyhood of Billy the Kid.* Monograph 17, Southwestern Studies 5(1). El Paso, Texas: Texas Western Press. University of Texas at El Paso. 1967.

Nolan, Frederick. Personal communication agreeing Stinking Springs capture was on December 22, 1880 not December 23, 1880. **2008**.

Poe, John W. *The Death of Billy the Kid.* (Introduction by Maurice Garland Fulton). Boston and New York: Houghton Mifflin Company. **1933**.

_____. "The Killing of Billy the Kid." (a personal letter written at Roswell, New Mexico to Mr. Charles Goodnight, Goodnight P.C., Texas) **July 10, 1917**. Earle Vandale Collection. 1813-946. No. 2H475. Center for American History. University of Texas at Austin.

Rakocy, Bill. *Billy the Kid.* El Paso, Texas: Bravo Press. **1985**.

Rasch, Phillip J. *Trailing Billy the Kid.* Laramie, Wyoming: National Association for Outlaw and Lawman History, Inc. with University of Wyoming. **1995**.

Russell, Randy. *Billy the Kid. The Story - The Trial.* Lincoln, New Mexico: The Crystal Press. 1994.

Siringo, Charles A. *The History of Billy the Kid.* Santa Fe: New Mexico. Privately Printed. 1920.

Tuska, Jon. *Billy the Kid. His Life and Legend.* Westport, Connecticut: Greenwood Press. 1983.

Utley, Robert M. *High Noon in Lincoln. Violence on the Western Frontier.* Albuquerque, New Mexico: University of New Mexico Press. 1987.

_____. *Billy the Kid. A Short and Violent Life.* Lincoln and London: University of Nebraska Press. 1989.

Weddle, Jerry. *Antrim is My Stepfather's Name. The Boyhood of Billy the Kid.* Monograph 9, Globe, Arizona: Arizona Historical Society. 1993.

No Author. "The Prisoners Who Saw the Kid Kill Olinger." April 28, 1881. Herman B. Weisner Papers, ca. 1957-1992. New Mexico State University Library at Las Cruces. Rio Grande Historical Collections. Accession No. Ms 0249. Box 30 T. Folder 8.

WORDS OF (CHRONOLOGICAL)

SPENCERIAN PENMANSHIP

Spencer, Platt Rogers. *Spencerian Penmanship.* New York: Ivison, Phinney, Blakemont Co. **1857**.

_____. *Spencerian System of Practical Penmanship.* New York: Ivison, Phinney, Blakemont Co. **1864**. (Reprinted by Milford, Michigan: Mott Media, Inc. 1985.)

Cooper, Gale. *Billy the Kid's Writings, Words, and Wit.* Albuquerque, New Mexico: Gelcour Books. **2012**.

464

HOYT BILL OF SALE

Bonney, W H. "Know all persons by these presents ..." Thursday, **October 24, 1878.** Collection of Panhandle-Plains Historical Museum, Canyon, Texas. Item No. X1974-98/1. **(Hoyt Bill of Sale)**

LETTERS TO LEW WALLACE

Bonney, W H. "I have heard you will give one thousand $ dollars for my body which as I see it means alive ..." **March 13(?), 1879.** Fray Angélico Chávez Historical Library, Santa Fe, New Mexico. Lincoln County Heritage Trust Collection. (AC481).

_____. "I will keep the keep the appointment ..." **March 20, 1879.** Indiana Historical Society. M0292.

_____. "... on the Pecos." ("Billie" letter fragment). **March 24(?), 1879.** Indiana Historical Society. Lew Wallace Collection. M0292. Box 4. Folder 7.

_____. "I noticed in the *Las Vegas* Gazette a piece which stated that 'Billy the Kid' ..." **December 12, 1880.** Indiana Historical Society. Lew Wallace Collection. M0292.

_____. "I would like to see you ..." **January 1, 1881.** Indiana Historical Society. Lew Wallace Collection. M0292.

_____. "I wish you would come down to the jail and see me ..." **March 2, 1881.** Fray Angélico Chávez Historical Library, Santa Fe, New Mexico. Lincoln County Heritage Trust Collection. (AC481).

_____. "I wrote you a little note day before yesterday ..." **March 4, 1881.** Indiana Historical Society. Lew Wallace Collection. M0292.

_____. "For the last time I ask ..." **March 27, 1881.** Indiana Historical Society. Lew Wallace Collection. M0292.

(SEE: Lew Wallace response letters to)

LETTER TO SQUIRE WILSON

Bonney, W H. "Friend Wilson ..." **March 18, 1879.** Indiana Historical Society. Lew Wallace Collection. M0292. **(For pardon negotiation with Lew Wallace)**

LETTER TO EDGAR CAYPLESS

Bonney, W H. "I would have written before ..." **April 15, 1881.** Copy in William Kelleher's *Violence in Lincoln County;* originally reproduced in Griggs *History of the Mesilla Valley.* **(Original lost)**

REGULATOR MANIFESTO LETTER

Regulator. "Mr. Walz. Sir ..." Letter to Edgar Walz. **July 13, 1878.** Adjutant General's Office. File 1405 AGO 1878. (Quoted in Maurice Garland Fulton, *History of the Lincoln County War.* Tucson: University of Arizona Press. 1975. Pages 246-247.)

DEPOSITION OF

Bonney, William Henry. Deposition to Frank Warner Angel. **June 8, 1878.** Frank Warner Angel report, Pages 314-319 from *In the Matter of the Examination of the Causes and Circumstances of the Death of John H. Tunstall a British Subject.* Report filed October 4, 1878. Angel Report. Records of the Justice Department. Record Group 60. Class 44 Litigation Files. Container 21. National Archives and Records Administration. U.S. Department of Justice. Washington, D.C. or Angel Report in Interior Department Papers 1850-1907; Appointments Division and Subsequent Actions. Microfilm File Case Number 44-4-8-3. Record Group 48. Microfilm No. M750. Roll 1. National Archives and Records Administration. U.S. Department of Justice. Washington, D.C.

COURT TESTIMONY OF

Rynerson, William. "The Grand Jurors for the Territory of New Mexico taken from the body of the good and lawful men of the County of Lincoln ..." Indictments of the April, Lincoln County Grand Jury. **April 28, 1879.** Herman B. Weisner Papers, ca. 1957-1992. New Mexico State University Library at Las Cruces. Rio Grande Historical Collection. Accession No. Ms 0249. Box 4/39. Folder E-Z. Folder Name: "Jessie Evans Accessory to Murder." **(Billy's testimony for pardon bargain)**

Bonney, William Henry. Testimony in Court of Inquiry for N.A.M. Dudley. **May 28-29, 1879.** *Proceedings of a Court of Inquiry in the Case of Lt. Col. N.A.M. Dudley (May 2,1879 – July 5, 1879).* File No. QQ1284. (Boxes 3304, 3305, 3305A); Court Martial Files 1809-1894. Records of the Office of the Judge Advocate General - Army. Record Group 153. Old Military and Civil Branch. National Archives and Records Administration. Washington, D. C.

Waldo, Henry. "Then was brought forward William Bonney, alias "Antrim," alias "the Kid," a known criminal of the worst type ..." Closing argument on Billy Bonney's testimony in Court of Inquiry for N.A.M. Dudley. **July 5, 1879.** *Proceedings of a Court of Inquiry in the Case of Lt. Col. N.A.M. Dudley (May 2,1879 – July 5, 1879).* File No. QQ1284. (Boxes 3304, 3305, 3305A); Court Martial Files 1809-1894. Records of the Office of the Judge Advocate General – Army. Record Group 153. Old Military and Civil Branch. National Archives and Records Administration. Washington, D. C.

INTERVIEW WITH LEW WALLACE OF

Wallace, Lew. "Statements by Kid, made Sunday night **March 23, 1879.**" (Cover sheet reads: "Fort Stanton, March 20, 1879. William Bonney ("Kid") relative to arrangement with him." Indiana Historical Society. Lew Wallace Collection. M0292. Box 4. Folder 6.

NEWSPAPER INTERVIEWS BY

Wilcox, Lucius "Lute" M. (city editor, owner, J.H. Koogler). "The Kid. Interview with Billy Bonney The Best Known Man in New Mexico." *Las Vegas Gazette.* **December 27, 1880. (Mentions that Billy Bonney has squirrel-like incisors)**
_____. Interview, at train depot. *Las Vegas Gazette.* **December 28, 1880.**

No Author. "Something about the Kid." *Santa Fe Daily New Mexican.* **April 3, 1881. (Billy's quote: "two hundred men have been killed ... he did not kill all.")**

No Author. "I got a rough deal ..." *Mesilla News.* **April 15, 1881.**

Newman, Simon N. Ed. Interview with "The Kid." *Newman's Semi-Weekly.* **April 15, 1881.**
_____. Departure from Mesilla. *Newman's Semi-Weekly.* **April 20, 1881.** Pages 1, 3. https://chroniclingamerica.loc.gov/ **(Reporting for April 16th, listing the transport guards and their positions in the vehicle)**

FEDERAL INDICTMENT OF

Catron, Thomas Benton. "Case No. 411. The United States vs. Charles Bowdry [Bowdre], Doc Scurlock, Henry Brown, Henry Antrim alias "Kid," John Middleton, Stephen Stevens, John Scroggins, George Coe and Frederick Waite." **June 21, 1878.** Herman B. Weisner Papers, ca. 1957-1992. New Mexico State University Library at Las Cruces. Rio Grande Historical Collections. Accession No. Ms 0249. Box 1. B-Folder 4. Name: Andrew Roberts Indictment.

GENERAL LETTERS ABOUT

Kimbrell, George. "I have the honor to request that you will furnish me a posse ..." Letter to Lieutenant Millard Filmore Goodwin. **February 20, 1879.** Indiana

Historical Society. Lew Wallace Collection. Box 4, Folder 3. (**For pursuit of William Bonney and Yginio Salazar**)

Goodwin, Millard Filmore. ""I have the honor to submit the following report regarding my duties performed ..." Letter to Fort Stanton Post Adjutant John Loud. **February 23, 1879**. Indiana Historical Society. Lew Wallace Collection. Box 4. Folder 3. (**Assisting pursuit of William Bonney and Yginio Salazar**)

Dudley, Nathan Augustus Monroe. "I enclose herewith report of 2nd Lieut. M.F. Goodwin ..." Letter to Acting Assistant Adjutant General at Headquarters. **February 24, 1879**. Indiana Historical Society. Lew Wallace Collection. M0292. Box 4, Folder 3. (**Documents military pursuit of William Bonney**)

Leonard, Ira. "The air is filled tonight with 'rumors of wars ... Letter to Lew Wallace. **April 20, 1879**. Indiana Historical Society. Lew Wallace Collection. M0292. Box 4. Folder 9. (**About DA Rynerson: "He is bent on going for the Kid"**)

East, James H. "Jim." "I wish to say that I appreciate your courtesy ..." Letter to William B. Burgess. **May 20, 1926**. C.L. Sonnichsen Papers, MS 141. C.L. Sonnichsen Special Collections Department. University of Texas El Paso Library. Box 92. Folder 386. (**About Paulita Maxwell as Billy's lover**)

Hoyt, Henry F. "This time it is me who is apologizing for the long delay in answering ..." (Letter to Lew Wallace Jr.) **April 27, 1927**. Indiana Historical Society. Lew Wallace Collection. M0292. Box 14, Folder 11. (**About having a sample of Billy's handwriting in his Bill of Sale**)

_____. "Copy of a bill of sale written by Wm H. Bonney ..." Letter to Lew Wallace Jr. **April 27, 1927**. Indiana Historical Society. Lew Wallace Collection. M0292. Box 14, Folder 11. (**Calls Billy Bonney "a natural leader of men"**)

SECRET SERVICE REPORTS ABOUT

Wild, Azariah F. "Daily Reports of U. S. Secret Service Agents, Azariah F. Wild." Microfilm T-915. Record Group 87. Rolls 308 (July 1, 1879 - June 30, 1881) National Archives and Records Department. Department of the Treasury. United States Secret Service. Washington, D. C.

LEW WALLACE WRITINGS TO AND ABOUT

WALLACE'S LETTERS TO (CHRONOLOGICAL)

Wallace, Lew. "Come to the house of Squire Wilson ..." Letter to W H. Bonney. **March 15, 1879**. Indiana Historical Society. Lew Wallace Collection. M0292. Box 4. Folder 6.

_____. "The escape makes no difference in arrangements ..." Letter to W.H. Bonney. **March 20, 1879**. Indiana Historical Society. Lew Wallace Collection. M0292. Box 4. Folder 6.

WALLACE'S LETTERS ABOUT (CHRONOLOGICAL)

Wallace, Lew. "I have just ascertained that 'The Kid' is at a place called Las Tablas ..." Letter to Edward Hatch. **March 6, 1879**. Indiana Historical Society. Lew Wallace Collection. Box 9, Folder 10. (**Written on dead John Tunstall's stationery**)

_____. "I beg to submit to you a list of persons whom it is necessary, in my judgment, to arrest ..." Letter to Henry Carroll. **March 11, 1879**. Indiana Historical Society. Lew Wallace Collection. M0292. Box 4. Folder 5. (**Sherman outlaw list with "The Kid" – William Bonney**)

_____. "I enclose a note for Bonney." Letter to John "Squire" Wilson. **March 20, 1879**. Indiana Historical Society. Lew Wallace Collection. M0292. Box 4. Folder 6.

_____. "My time has been so constantly occupied in getting my work into operation ..." Letter to Carl Schurz. **March 21, 1879**. Indiana Historical Society. Lew Wallace Collection. M0292. Box 4. Folder 7. (**Progress report with** multiple enclosures; one listing "The Kid -William Bonney in anti-outlaw campaign of "taking the head off the evil.")

_____. "To day I forwarded a telegram to you, with another to the President ..." Letter to Carl Schurz. **March 31, 1879**. Indiana Historical Society. Lew Wallace Collection. M0292. Box 4. Folder 7. (**Mention of "precious specimen nicknamed 'The Kid' "**)

REWARD NOTICES FOR

Wallace, Lew. "Be good enough to prepare a draft of proclamation of reward $500 for the capture and delivery of William Bonney, alias the Kid ..." Letter to Territorial Secretary William Ritch. **December 13, 1880**. Herman B. Weisner Papers, ca. 1957-1992. New Mexico State University Library at Las Cruces. Rio Grande Historical Collections. Accession No. Ms 0249. Box W3. Folder 13. Folder Name: "Wallace, Gov. N.M." From Lew Wallace Papers. New Mexico State Records Center. Santa Fe, New Mexico. (**Wallace's first reward for Billy the Kid**)

_____. "Billy the Kid: $500 Reward." *Las Vegas Gazette*. **December 22, 1880**.

_____. "Billy the Kid. $500 Reward." **May 3, 1881**. *Daily New Mexican*. Volume X, Number 33, Page 1, C 3.

REWARD POSTERS FOR

Greene, Chas. W. "To the New Mexican Printing and Publishing Company." **May 20, 1881**. Indiana Historical Society. Lew Wallace Collection. M0292. Box 4, Folder 17. (**Printer's bill to Lew Wallace for Reward posters for "Kid"**)

_____. "I enclose a bill ..." Letter to Lew Wallace for "Kid" wanted posters. **June 2, 1881**. Indiana Historical Society. Lew Wallace Collection. M0292. Box 4, Folder 18.

DEATH WARRANT FOR

Wallace, Lew. "To the Sheriff of Lincoln County, Greeting ..." **April 30, 1881**. Indiana Historical Society. Lew Wallace Collection. M0292. Box 9, Folder 11.

CORONER'S JURY REPORT FOR, AND LATER LOCATION OF (CHRONOLOGICAL)

Segura, Alejandro. Coroner's Jury Report for William Bonney alias "Kid." **July 15, 1881**. Original in Spanish. Indiana Historical Society. Lew Wallace Collection. M0292. Box 9. Folder 11. (**Certified photocopy donated by Maurice Garland Fulton in 1951 of Spanish Coroner's Jury Report, July 15, 1881 - matches photo in William Kelleher's** *Violence in Lincoln County*, **Pages 306-307**)

_____. Coroner's Jury Report for William Bonney alias "Kid." **July 15, 1881**. English translation. The Mullin Collection, RNM, VI, J - Legal Papers and Documents. Midland, Texas: Nita Stewart Haley Memorial Library and J. Evetts Haley History Center.

_____. Coroner's Jury Report for William Bonney alias "Kid." **July 15, 1881**. English translation. William A. Keleher. *Violence in Lincoln County 1869-1881*. Pages 343-344.

Ritch, William G. "In the matter of the application by Patrick F. Garrett for a reward claimed to have been offered May-1881 for the capture of Wm Bonney alias "the Kid." *Executive Record Book Number 2*. July 25, 1867-November 8, 1882. **July 21, 1881**. Pages 533-535. New Mexico Secretary of State Records. Collection 1971-001, Series 1; Records of the Secretary of the Territory. (Accessed from Albuquerque Public Library Microfilm, Territorial Archives of New Mexico, Roll 21.) (**Demonstrating that Acting-Governor Ritch agreed with the reward, and cited the Coroner's Jury Report's identification of William Bonney**)

No Author. *Executive Record Book Number 2*. July 25, 1867-November 8, 1882. **July 21, 1881**. Pages 533-535. New Mexico State Records Center and Archives,

468

Santa Fe. New Mexico Secretary of the State Records Series 1. Records of the Secretary of the Territory. (**About granting Garrett's reward, citing copy of Coroner's Jury Report**)

No Author. "Kid the Killer Killed, Wm. Bonney alias Antrim, alias Billy the Kid, Fatally Meets Pat Garrett, the Lincoln County Sheriff." Las Cruces *Rio Grande Republican.* **July 23, 1881.** Page 2. Volume 1, Number 10. NewspaperArchive.com. (**Copy of Pat Garrett's letter to Acting Governor William Ritch confirming that the original Coroner's Jury Report was sent to District Attorney of the First Judicial District, and copy of it was included in this letter to the Governor; this was later found in 1932 with the papers of the Secretary of State in the state Capitol Building**)

Prince, L. Bradford, Ed. *The General Laws of New Mexico; Including All the Unrepealed Laws From the Promulgation of the 'Kearney Code' in 1846, to the End of the Legislative Session of 1880. With Supplement, Including the Session of 1882.* Albany, New York: W.C. Little & Co., Law Publishers. **1882.**

No Author. The Western Survey Company. *New Mexico: The Last Great West.* Chicago: Rand McNally & Co. **1917.** (**States that the State Land Office was housed in the Capital Building – the future Bataan Memorial Building**)

No Author. "Call for Bids." *Santa Fe New Mexican.* **May 26, 1932.** Page 6, Column 4. (**Showing that the Secretary of State's office was in the state Capitol Building, where Pat Garrett's letter to Acting-Governor Ritch was found**)

No Author. "Local Items." *Alamogordo News.* **February 12, 1933.** Volume 37, Number 8. Page 4. Column 1. (**Harold Abbott, finder of the original Report in state capitol basement while working for the State Land Office**)

King, Frank M. *Wranglin' the Past: Reminiscences of Frank M. King.* "Chapter xix, The Kid's Exit." Pasadena, California: Trail's End Publishing Company. **1935 and 1946.** (**Describes recent location of Pat Garrett's report to the Governor about the killing of Billy the Kid, which had a copy of the Coroner's Jury Report, Page 171**)

Anderson, Clinton P. "The Adobe Palace." *New Mexico Historical Review.* **1944.** Volume 19, Number 2. Pages 97-122. (**Diagram showing that William Breeden's office was later used by the State Land Office, Pages 110-111**)

No Author. "Fort Sumner Jury Thought the Kid Had Been Killed." *Alamogordo News.* **November 30, 1950.** Volume 53, Number 48. .NewspaperArchive.com. (**Harold Abbott's finding the Coroner's Jury Report in 1932**)

No Author. "Glimpses of History." **February, 1951.** *New Mexico Magazine.* Volume 29, Number 2, Pages 26, 54. (**Reprinting the Harold Abbott Coroner's Jury Report copy**)

Keleher, William A. *Violence in Lincoln County 1869-1881.* Albuquerque, New Mexico: University of New Mexico Press. **1957.** (**Photocopy of Spanish Coroner's Jury Report, July 15, 1881. Pages 306-308; Keleher's English translation, Pages 343-344; Harold Abbott's finding it, Page 343.**)

Nusbaum, Rosemary. *The City Different and the Palace, The Palace of the Governors: Its Role in Santa Fe History.* Santa Fe: Sunstone Press. **1978.**

No Author. "Obituaries." *Alamogordo Daily News.* **January 22, 2006.** Page 7A. (**Death announcement for George Abbott, who got a copy of the Coroner's Jury Report from his brother, Harold Abbott, in 1932**)

No Author. *Texas, Death Certificates. 1903-1982.* Provo, Utah. Ancestry.com. Operations, Inc. **2013.** (**Death certificate of Harold Abbott, who located the Report in 1932 in the State Land Office basement in the Capitol Building**)

Stangl, Karin. Ed. "New Mexico State Land Office." *State Land Office 2011-2012 Annual Report.* Santa Fe. 2013. nmstatelands.org. (**Function of Office**)

Taylor, Aaron. Expert consultation on the orthography of the Coroner's Jury Report. Consultation with author, April, 2020. (**Confirming the Report was written with stylistic idiosyncrasies of the later 1880's and by a native Spanish speaker like Alejandro Segura**)

CERTIFIED COPY OF

Segura, Alejandro, Milnor. Coroner's Jury Report for William Bonney alias "Kid." **July 15, 1881.** Indiana Historical Society. Lew Wallace Collection. M0292. Box 9. Folder 11. Accession Number 1951.0104 from Maurice G. Fulton. (**Photostatic copy of original Spanish Coroner's Jury Report, certified on January 18, 1951, donated by Maurice Garland Fulton - matches photo in William Kelleher's** *Violence in Lincoln County* **copy; identifying the body of Billy Bonney**)

No Author. "Coroner's Report Proves Billy the Kid is Dead, Historian Asserts, Researcher Discovers Document." **August 5, 1951.** *The El Paso Times.* Number 217, Page 13. (**M. G. Fulton finds and publishes its certified copy**)

CONFIRMING SIGNERS OF REPORT

Rudulph, Milnor. " I beg your indulgence for ..." Letter to William G. Ritch. **May 18, 1879.** Albuquerque and Bernalillo County Public Library. Genealogical Center. MS. Territorial Archives of New Mexico Microfilm. Roll 99. Image 10. (**Rudulph's signature matches his signature on the Coroner's Jury Report.**)

No Author. **Census 1880 for Alejandro Segura and Sabal Gutierrez.** Place: *Cabra Arenoso, Fort Sumner, San Miguel, New Mexico*; Roll: *803*; Page: *434B*; Enumeration District: *037*. Ancestry.com and The Church of Jesus Christ of Latter-day Saints. *1880 United States Federal Census* [database on-line]. Lehi, UT, USA: Ancestry.com Operations Inc, 2010. 1880 U.S. Census Index provided by The Church of Jesus Christ of Latter-day Saints © Copyright 1999 Intellectual Reserve, Inc. Original data: Tenth Census of the United States, 1880. (NARA microfilm publication T9, 1,454 rolls). Records of the Bureau of the Census, Record Group 29. National Archives, Washington, D.C. (**Confirmed as local residents**)

No Author. **Census 1880 for Milnor Rudulph and Jose Silva.** Place: *Sunnyside, Fort Sumner, San Miguel, New Mexico*; Roll: *803*; Page: *435C*; Enumeration District: *037*.Ancestry.com and The Church of Jesus Christ of Latter-day Saints. *1880 United States Federal Census* [database on-line]. Lehi, UT, USA: Ancestry.com Operations Inc, 2010. 1880 U.S. Census Index provided by The Church of Jesus Christ of Latter-day Saints © Copyright 1999 Intellectual Reserve, Inc. Original data: Tenth Census of the United States, 1880. (NARA microfilm publication T9, 1,454 rolls). Records of the Bureau of the Census, Record Group 29. National Archives, Washington, D.C. (**Confirmed as local residents**)

No Author. **Census 1880 for Lorenzo Jaramillo and Antonio Saavedra.** Place: *Fort Sumner, San Miguel, New Mexico*; Roll: *803*; Page: *436A*; Enumeration District: *037*. Ancestry.com and The Church of Jesus Christ of Latter-day Saints. *1880 United States Federal Census* [database on-line]. Lehi, UT, USA: Ancestry.com Operations Inc, 2010. 1880 U.S. Census Index provided by The Church of Jesus Christ of Latter-day Saints © Copyright 1999 Intellectual Reserve, Inc. Original data: Tenth Census of the United States, 1880. (NARA microfilm publication T9, 1,454 rolls). Records of the Bureau of the Census, Record Group 29. National Archives, Washington, D.C. (**Confirmed as local residents**)

No Author. **Census 1880 for Pedro Antonio Lucero.** Place: *San Miguel, New Mexico*; Roll: *803*; Page: *381B*; Enumeration District: *035*. Ancestry.com and The Church of Jesus Christ of Latter-day Saints. *1880 United States Federal Census* [database on-line]. Lehi, UT, USA: Ancestry.com Operations Inc, 2010. 1880 U.S. Census Index provided by The Church of Jesus Christ of Latter-day Saints © Copyright 1999 Intellectual Reserve, Inc. All rights reserved. Original data: Tenth Census of the United States, 1880. (NARA microfilm publication T9, 1,454 rolls). Records of the Bureau of the Census, Record Group 29. National Archives, Washington, D.C. (**Confirmed as local resident**)

(SEE: William Breeden)

OUTLAW MYTH ARTICLES ABOUT (CHRONOLOGICAL)

GENERAL ARTICLES (CHRONOLOGICAL)

No Author. Grant County *Herald.* **May 10, 1879**. Results of the Lincoln County Grand Jury. (**Also published in the Mesilla** *Thirty Four.* **Confirmation of the Billy's testimony and indictments, from Page 224 of William Kelleher,** *Violence in Lincoln County.*)

Koogler, John H. Editorial. "Desperadoe's Stronghold, An Organized Gang Assisted by Nature and Defiantly Reckless, Who Terrorize the Country to the East of Us." *Las Vegas Morning Gazette.* **December 3, 1880**. Volume 2, Number 120. https://chroniclingamerica.loc.gov. (**Calling Billy an outlaw leader; motivating his denial letter of December 12, 1880 to Governor Lew Wallace.**)

No Author. "Outlaws of New Mexico, The Exploits of a Band Headed by a New York Youth, The Mountain Fastness of the Kid and His Followers - War Against a Gang of Cattle Thieves and Murderers - The Frontier Confederates of Brockway, the Counterfeiter." *The Sun.* New York. **December 22, 1880**. Volume XLVIII, Number 118, Page 3, Columns 1-2.

No Author. "A Big Haul! Billy Kid, Dave Rudabaugh, Billy Wilson and Tom Pickett in the Clutches of the Law." *The Las Vegas Daily Optic.* Monday, **December 27, 1880**. Volume 2, Number. 45. Page 4, Column 2. chroniclingamerica.loc.gov.

No Author. "A Bay-Mare. Everyone who has heard of Billy 'the kid' has heard of his beautiful bay mare." *Las Vegas Morning Gazette.* Tuesday, **January 4, 1881**.

No Author. "The Kid. Billy 'the Kid' and Billy Wilson were on Monday taken to Mesilla for Trial." *Las Vegas Morning Gazette.* Tuesday, **March 15, 1881**.

Newman, Simon. "In the Name of Justice! In the Case of Billy Kid." *Newman's Semi-Weekly.* Saturday, **April 2, 1881**.

No Author. "Billy the Kid. Seems to be having a stormy journey on his trip Southward." *Las Vegas Morning Gazette.* Tuesday, **April 5, 1881**.

No Author. "The Kid." *Santa Fe Daily New Mexican.* **May 1, 1881**. Volume X, Number 32, Page 1, Column 2.

No Author. "Billy Bonney. Advices from Lincoln bring the intelligence of the escape of 'Billy the Kid.'" *Las Vegas Daily Optic.* Monday, **May 2, 1881**.

No Author. "The Kid's Escape." *Santa Fe Daily New Mexican.* Tuesday Morning, **May 3, 1881**. Volume X, Number 33, Page 1, Column 2.

No Author. "The above is the record of as bold a deed ..." *Santa Fe Daily New Mexican.* **May 4, 1881**. (**About Billy's great escape jailbreak**)

No Author. "Dare Devil Desperado. Pursuit of 'Billy the Kid' has been abandoned." *Las Vegas Daily Optic.* **May 4, 1881**.

No Author. "More Killing by Kid, When But a Short Distance From Lincoln, He Meets one of His Old Enemies, and Kills Him and His Companion. Two More Victims." Editorial. *Santa Fe Daily New Mexican.* **May 4, 1881**. Volume X, No. 34, Page 1, Column 2. Newspaperarchive.com. (**Claims Kid killed Billy Matthews**)

No Author. No headline. "Anything that the imagination can concoct ..." *Santa Fe Daily New Mexican.* **May 5, 1881**. Volume X. Page 4, Column 1. Newspaperarchive.com. (**Claims Kid was in Albuquerque**)

No Author. No headline. Mr. Richard Dunham says ..." *Santa Fe Daily New Mexican,* **May 5, 1881**, Volume X. Page 4, Column 3. Newspaperarchive.com. (**Claims Kid was in Stinking Springs**)

No Author. "Richard Dunham's May 2, 1881 encounter with Billy the Kid.", *Santa Fe Daily New Mexican,* **May 5, 1881**, Page 4, Column 3. (private collection)

No Author. "The question if how to deal with desperados who commit murder has but one solution - kill them." *Las Vegas Daily Optic.* Tuesday, **May 10, 1881**.

No Author. "Billy 'the Kid.'" *Las Vegas Gazette.* Thursday, **May 12, 1881**.

No Author. "The Kid was in Chloride City ..." *Santa Fe Daily New Mexican.* **May 13, 1881**. Page 4, Column 3.

No Author. "Billy 'the Kid' is in the vicinity of Sumner." *Las Vegas Gazette*. Sunday, **May 15, 1881**.

No Author. "The Kid is believed to be in the Black Range ..." *Santa Fe Daily New Mexican*. **May 19, 1881**. Page 4, Column 1.

No Author. "Billy the Kid was last seen in Lincoln County ..." *Santa Fe Daily New Mexican*. **May 19, 1881**. Page 4, Column 1.

No Author. (O.L. Houghton's Conversation with Lew Wallace, before May 26, 1881), *The Las Vegas Daily Optic*, **May 26, 1881**, p.4, c.4. Indiana Historical Society. Lew Wallace Collection. M0292.

No Author. " 'Billy the Kid' has been heard from again." *Las Vegas Daily Optic*. Friday, **June 10, 1881**.

No Author. " 'Billy the Kid,' He is Reported to Have Been Seen on Our Streets Saturday Night." *Las Vegas Daily Optic*. Monday Evening, **June 13, 1881**. Volume 2, Number 188, Page 4, Column 2.

Wilcox, Lute, Ed. "Billy the Kid would make an ideal newspaper-man in that he always endeavors to 'get even' with his enemies." *Las Vegas Daily Optic*. Monday Evening, **June 13, 1881**. Volume 2, Number 188, Page 4, Column 1.

No Author. "Land of the Petulant Pistol, "Scenes" where Life and Land are Cheap ... 'Billy the Kid' as a Killer." *Las Vegas Daily Optic*. Wednesday Evening, **June 15, 1881**. Front Page. 1, Volume 2, Number 190, Columns 1-2. (Possibly contributed to by Lew Wallace, who published with a similar title in the Crawfordsville *Saturday Evening Journal* on June 18, 1881)

No Author. "Barney Mason at Fort Sumner states the 'Kid' is in Local Sheep Camps." *Las Vegas Morning Gazette*. **June 16, 1881**.

No Author. "The Kid." *Santa Fe Daily New Mexican*. **June 16, 1881**. Volume X, Number 90, Page 4, Column 2.

No Author. "Billy the Kid." *Las Vegas Daily Optic*. Thursday, June 28, 1881.

No Author. " 'The Kid' Killed! He Meets His Death at the Hands of Sheriff Pat Garrett, of Lincoln County. The Particulars of the Affair as Poured into the Ears of Eager Reporters. *The Las Vegas Daily Optic*. **July 18, 1881**. Volume 2, Number 217. Newspaperarchives.com. (**Confirming Pat Garrett's killing of Billy the Kid**)

No Author. "Words of Commendation and Encouragement." *Las Vegas Daily Gazette*. **July 22, 1881**. Volume 3. Number 15. Newspapers.com. (**Confirming Pat Garrett's killing of Billy the Kid**)

No Author. No title. **Thursday, July 28, 1881**. Pueblo, Colorado, *Colorado Chieftain*. www.coloradohistoricnewspapers.org. (**Quoting from the New York *Tribune* on killing of "Tiger in human form known as "Billy the Kid"**)

No Author. "The Life of Billy the Kid. His Name Was Billy McCarthy, and He was Born in New York." *The New York Sun*. (From *The St. Louis Globe-Democrat*) **August 10, 1881**. Volume XLIII, Number 314. Newspapers.com. (**Confirming Pat Garrett's killing of Billy the Kid**)

Gauss, Gottfried. Interview with *Lincoln County Leader*. **November 21, 1889. (About Billy Bonney's Lincoln jailbreak)**

LEW WALLACE'S ARTICLES

Koogler, John H. "Interview with Governor Lew Wallace on 'The Kid.'" *Las Vegas Gazette*. **April 28, 1881**.

No Author. "The Thug's Territory. Stage Robbers and Cut-Throats Have Things Their Own Way in New Mexico. Gen. Lew Wallace Anxious to Punish the Crime That is So Prevalent – A Chapter About 'Billy the Kid' – The Governor has a Narrow Escape From Being Spanked." *St. Louis Daily Globe-Democrat*. Monday Morning, **May 16, 1881**. Page 2, Columns 5 and 6. (private collection)

No Author. (Lew Wallace interview) "Billy the Kid. General Wallace Tells Why the Young Desperado of New Mexico Wanted to Kill Him, A Dashing and Daring Career in the Land of the Petulant Pistol." (Lew Wallace interviewed on June 13,

1881), Crawfordsville *Saturday Evening Journal,* **June 18, 1881.** Indiana Historical Society. The Papers of Lew and Susan Wallace. Microfilm Edition. Indianapolis, Indiana: Indiana Historical Society Press. 2008.

No Author. (Lew Wallace interview) "Lew Wallace's Foe. Threatened by 'Billy the Kid.' The Writing of 'Ben Hur' Interrupted. An Incident of the Soldier-Author's Career in New Mexico. *San Francisco Chronicle.* December 10, 1893. Indiana Historical Society. Lew Wallace Collection. M0292. Box 14. Folder 11. (Lew Wallace creating outlaw myth of outlaw Billy the Kid")

No Author. "Street Pickings," Weekly *Crawfordsville Review - Saturday Edition,* **January 6, 1894.** Indiana Historical Society. The Papers of Lew and Susan Wallace. Microfilm Edition. Series I. Reel 27. Indianapolis, Indiana: Indiana Historical Society Press. 2008.

No Author. "An Old Incident Recalled." Crawfordsville *Weekly News-Review.* **December 20, 1901.** Indiana Historical Society. The Papers of Lew and Susan Wallace. Microfilm Edition. Series I. Reel 27. Indianapolis, Indiana: Indiana Historical Society Press. 2008.

Lewis, E.I. "Gen. Wallace's Feud with Billy the Kid, When the General Was Governor of New Mexico and Billy Bonne Was the Most Dangerous Western Outlaw. He Was a Waif and Was Reared in Indiana. *The Indianapolis Press.* Saturday, **June 23, 1900.** Page 7. Lew Wallace Collection. Indiana Historical Society. M0292. Box 14. Folder 11. (photocopy) (Original article is in OMB 23, Box 1. Folder 5) (**Creating self-serving myth of outlaw Billy the Kid**")

Wallace, Lew. "General Lew Wallace Writes a Romance of 'Billy the Kid' Most Famous Bandit of the Plains: Thrilling Story of the Midnight Meeting Between Gen Wallace, Then Governor of New Mexico, and the Notorious Outlaw, in a Lonesome Hut in Santa Fe." *New York World Magazine.* Sunday, **June 8, 1902.** Lew Wallace Collection. Indiana Historical Society. M0292. . Box 14. Folder 11.

OTHER HISTORICAL FIGURES (PERIOD)

ANGEL, FRANK WARNER

PRESIDENT HAYES MEETING BY

Mullin, Robert N. Re: Frank Warner Angel Meeting With President Hayes August, 1878. Binder RNM, VI, M. (Unpublished). Midland, Texas: Nita Stewart Haley Memorial Library and J. Evetts Haley History Center. (Undated).

LETTERS BY

Angel, Frank Warner. "I am in receipt of your favor of the 12th ..." Letter to Samuel Beach Axtell. **August 13, 1878.** Interior Department Papers 1850-1907; Appointments Division and Subsequent Actions. Microfilm Roll M750. National Archives and Records Administration Record Group 48. Microfilm Case Number 44-4-8-3. U.S. Department of Interior. Washington D.C.

_____. "I enclose copies of letters received by me from Gov Axtell ..." Letter to Secretary of the Interior Carl Schurz. **August 24, 1878.** (Enclosing copy of letter to him from Governor S.B. Axtell of August 12, 1878; and Angel's response to Axtell of August 13, 1878.) Microfilm File Case Number 44-4-8-3. Record Group 48. Microfilm No. M750. Roll 1. National Archives and Records Administration. U.S. Department of Justice. Washington, D.C.

_____. "I have just been favored by a call from W.L. Rynerson ..." Letter to Secretary of Interior Carl Schurz. **September 6, 1878.** Microfilm. Case Number 44-4-8-3. Record Group 48. Microfilm No. M750. Roll 1. National Archives and Records Administration. U.S. Department of Justice. Washington, D.C.

REPORTS BY

Angel, Frank Warner. *Examination of charges against F. C. Godfroy, Indian Agent, Mescalero, N. M.* **October 2, 1878.** (Report 1981, Inspector E.C. Watkins; Cited as Watkins Report). M319-20 and L147, 44-4-8. Record Group 075. National Archives and Records Administration. U.S. Department of Justice. Washington, D. C.

_____. *In the Matter of the Investigation of the Charges Against S.B. Axtell Governor of New Mexico. Report and Testimony.* **October 3, 1878.** Angel Report. Interior Department Papers 1850-1907; Appointments Division and Subsequent Actions. Microfilm Case File No. 44-4-8-3. Record Group 48. Microfilm Roll M750. National Archives and Records Administration. U.S. Department of Interior. Washington, D.C. (**Mentions Santa Fe Ring**)

_____. *In the Matter of the Examination of the Causes and Circumstances of the Death of John H. Tunstall a British Subject.* Report filed **October 4, 1878.** Angel Report. Interior Department Papers 1850-1907; Appointments Division and Subsequent Actions. Microfilm File Case Number 44-4-8-3. Record Group 48. Microfilm No. M750. Roll 1. National Archives and Records Administration. U.S. Department of Justice. Washington, D.C.

_____. *In the Matter of the Lincoln County Troubles. To the Honorable Charles Devens, Attorney General.* **October 4, 1878.** Angel Report. Microfilm Case File No. 44-4-8-3. Record Group 48. Microfilm Roll M750. National Archives and Records Administration. U.S. Department of Justice. Washington, D.C.

NOTEBOOK ON SANTA FE RING MEMBERS BY

Angel, Frank Warner. "To Gov. Lew Wallace / Santa Fe, N. M., 1878." Notebook. **1878.** Indiana Historical Society. Lew Wallace Collection. M0292. Microfilm No. F372. (**Original missing, prepared for Lew Wallace listing Ringites**)

Theisen, Lee Scott. "Frank Warner Angel's Notes on New Mexico Territory, 1878." *Arizona and the West: A Quarterly Journal of History.* Winter 1976. Volume 18. Number 4. Pages 333-370. (**About the red Angel notebook**)

AXTELL, SAMUEL BEACH

CONTEMPORARY SOURCES (CHRONOLOGICAL)

No author. "Anarchy at Cimarron." *Santa Fe Weekly New Mexico.* **November 16, 1875.** (**Ringite justifying Governor S.B. Axtell calling in troops in the Colfax County War after murder of Reverend Franklin Tolby**)

Axtell, Samuel B. "The Legislature to Assess Property. *Message of Gov. Samuel B. Axtell to the Legislative Assembly of New Mexico, Twenty-second Session.* Page 4. Manderfield & Tucker, Public Printers: Santa Fe, New Mexico. **1875 or 1876.** Interior Department Papers 1850-1907; Appointments Division and Subsequent Actions. Microfilm File Case Number 44-4-8-3. Record Group 48. Microfilm No. M750. Roll 1. National Archives and Records Administration. U.S. Department of Justice. Washington, D.C.

Elkins, Stephen B. "I trouble you to say a word in behalf of Gov. Axtell ..." Letter to President Rutherford B. Hayes. **June 11, 1877.** Interior Department Papers 1850-1907; Appointments Division and Subsequent Actions. Microfilm Roll M750. National Archives and Records Administration Record Group 48. Microfilm Case Number 44-4-8-3. U. S. Department of Interior. Washington D. C. (**Ring head trying to prevent Axtell's removal as governor after Frank Warner Angel Report condemning him**)

Axtell, Samuel B. "I have today mailed to you a reply to the charges on file in your Dept against me." Letter to Secretary of the Interior Carl Schurz. **June 15, 1877.** Interior Department Papers 1850-1907; Appointments Division and Subsequent Actions. Microfilm Roll M750. National Archives and Records Administration Record Group 48. Microfilm Case Number 44-4-8-3 U.S. Department of Interior. Washington D.C. (**Refuting charges made in Colfax County**).

Isaacs, I. and G.N. Coe. "Charges Against S.B. Axtell, Governor of New Mexico." **June 22, 1878.** Interior Department Papers 1850-1907; Appointments Division and Subsequent Actions. Microfilm File Case Number 44-4-8-3. Microfilm No. M750. Roll 1. National Archives and Records Administration. Record Group 48. U.S. Department of Justice. Washington, D.C.

Routt, John C. "I am here on a visit to my daughter and have more by accident than otherwise heard statements ..." Letter to President Rutherford B. Hayes. **August 29, 1878.** Interior Department Papers 1850-1907; Appointments Division and Subsequent Actions. Microfilm File Case Number 44-4-8-3. Microfilm No. M750. Roll 1. National Archives and Records Administration. U.S. Department of Justice. Washington, D.C. (**Ringite letter opposing removal of Governor Axtell and U.S. Attorney Catron.**)

Schurz, Carl. "I transmit herewith an order from the President ..." **September 4, 1878.** Letter to Lew Wallace. Indiana Historical Society. Lew Wallace Collection. M0292. Box 3. Folder 14. (**Suspension of Governor S.B. Axtell and Wallace's appointment as new Governor**)

Elkins, Stephen Benton. "To the President. Referring to a conversation had with you last week ..." Letter to President James Abram Garfield. **March 17, 1881.** (Received Executive Mansion April 6, 1881). Interior Department Papers 1850-1907; Appointments Division and Subsequent Actions. Microfilm Roll M750. National Archives and Records Administration Microfilm Roll M750. National Archives and Records Administration Record Group 48. Microfilm Case Number 44-4-8-3. U.S. Department of Interior. Washington D.C. Microfilm Case Number 44-4-8-3. U.S. Department of Interior. Washington D.C. (**Request for re-appointment of Axtell as Territorial New Mexico Governor**)

Bradstreet, George P. "Referring to the nomination of Sam'l B. Axtell of Ohio to be Chief Justice of the Supreme Court of New Mexico ... he is alleged to have been removed by President Hayes ..." Letter to Judiciary Committee of the U.S. Senate. **June 22, 1882.** Interior Department Papers 1850-1907; Appointments Division and Subsequent Actions. Microfilm Roll M750. National Archives and Records Administration Microfilm Roll M750. National Archives and Records Administration Record Group 48. Microfilm Case Number 44-4-8-3. U.S. Department of Interior. Washington D.C.

No Author. " 'Chief Justice Axtell' is a bitter pill for the Raton *News and Press.*" *Santa Fe New Mexican.* **July 18, 1882.** (**Santa Fe Ring instatement of S.B. Axtell as Chief Justice**)

(SEE: Mary Tibbles McPherson, Frank Warner Angel for exposés about)

BACA, SATURNINO

BIOGRAPHICAL SOURCES

Charles, Tom. (Edited by Mrs. Tom Charles) "The Father of Lincoln County." *More Tales of Tularosa.* 1961. (unpublished manuscript)

Jonathan (no last name given). "About Saturnino Baca." July 23, 2001. http://www.genealogy.com/forum/surnames/topics/baca/509/

Nolan, Frederick. "New and Updated Biographies." *The Lincoln County War: A Documentary History. Revised Edition.* .Santa Fe: Sunstone Press. 2009.

LETTERS FROM AND ABOUT (CHRONOLOGICAL)

Baca, Saturnino. "When I sent in my bid for the hay contract ..." Letter to Quartermaster Captain A.J. McGonigle. **July 19, 1871.** University of New Mexico Library. Center for Southwest Studies. Thomas B. Catron Papers, MSS 29, Series 803, Box 1, Folder 25. (**About hay contract to Fort Stanton**)

Kantz, August V. "I learn from Col. Fritz that you are under the impression ..." Letter to Quartermaster Captain A.J. McGonigle. **July 20, 1871.** University of New Mexico Library. Center for Southwest Studies. Thomas B. Catron Papers, MSS 29, Series 803, Box 1, Folder 25. (**Emil Fritz pressures Fort Stanton to take bottom hay - which would allow Baca to fill his contract - and Kantz warns that Fritz and Murphy will get hay monopoly**)

Carey, A.B. "Letter of Saturnino Baca, dated Fort Stanton ..." Letter to Quartermaster Captain A.J. McGonigle. **July 20, 1871.** University of New Mexico Library. Center for Southwest Studies. Thomas B. Catron Papers, MSS 29, Series 803, Box 1, Folder 25. (**Baca declines his contract to supply grama hay**)

McGonigle, A.J.M. "I have the honor to forward enclosed herewith ..." Letter to Quartermaster General M.C. Meigs. **September 24, 1871.** University of New Mexico Library. Center for Southwest Studies. Thomas B. Catron Papers, MSS 29, Series 803, Box 1, Folder 25. (**Wants Baca barred from hay contracts**)

BAIL, JOHN D.

BIOGRAPHICAL SOURCE

No Author. *Minutes of the New Mexico Bar Association at its Regular Annual Session 1904.* Obituary. Santa Fe: New Mexico Publishing Company. 1904.

LETTERS BY (CHRONOLOGICAL)

Bail, John D. "Did you call Mr. Catron's attention ..." Letter to F.W. Clancy. **June 8, 1889.** University of New Mexico Library. Center for Southwest Studies. Thomas B. Catron Papers, MSS 29, Series 102, Box 1, Folder 2.

_____. "I am in receipt of your letter of 11th inst..." Letter to T.B. Catron. **May 14, 1890.** University of New Mexico Library. Center for Southwest Studies. Thomas B. Catron Papers, MSS 29, Series 102, Box 7, Folder 2.

BONNEY, WILLIAM HENRY
(See History of William Henry Bonney)

BOWDRE, CHARLES

CONTEMPORARY SOURCES (CHRONOLOGICAL)

Wallace, Lew. "Please select ten of your Rangers ..." Letter to Juan Patrón. **March 3, 1879.** Indiana Historical Society. Lew Wallace Collection. M0292. Box 4. Folder 4. (**To arrest "Scurlock and Bowdre"**)

_____. "I have reliable information that J.G. Scurlock and Charles Bowdre are now at a ranch called Taiban ..." Letter to Edward Hatch. **March 6, 1879.** Indiana Historical Society. Lew Wallace Collection. Box 4, Folder 4.

BRADY, WILLIAM

BIOGRAPHICAL SOURCE

Lavash, Donald R. *Sheriff William Brady. Tragic Hero of the Lincoln County War.* Santa Fe, New Mexico: Sunstone Press. 1986.

CONTEMPORARY SOURCES (CHRONOLOGICAL)

Brady, William. Affidavit of **July 2, 1876** concerning appointment as Administrator for the Emil Fritz Estate. Copied from the original District Court Record. (private collection)

_____. Affidavit of **August 22, 1876** documenting business debts to L. G. Murphy and Co. pertaining to the Emil Fritz Estate. Copied from the original District Court Record. (private collection)

_____. Affidavit of **July __, 1876** of Resignation as Emil Fritz Estate Administrator. Copied from the original District Court Record. (private collection.)

_____. Affidavit of **August 22, 1876** confirming giving Alexander McSween the books of the L.G. Murphy Company for the purpose of making business debt collections. Copied from the original District Court Record. (private collection)

Tunstall, John Henry. "A Taxpayer's Complaint ... January 18, 1878." Mesilla *Independent.* **January 26, 1878. (Exposé of William Brady embezzling tax money to buy cattle for "The House;" and Catron then paid that bill)**

Dolan, James J. "Answer to A Taxpayer's Complaint." Mesilla *Independent.* **January 29, 1878. (Response to J.H. Tunstall's exposé)**

Bristol, Warren. "Action of Assumpsit to command Sheriff Brady of Lincoln County to attach goods of Alexander A. McSween." **February 7, 1878.** District Court Record. (private collection). **(Used for malicious prosecution of John Tunstall by the false claim that he was McSween's partner)**

_____. Preprinted form for "Writ of Attachment" (Printed and sold at the office of the Mesilla News) filled out to command the Sheriff of Lincoln County to attach goods of Alexander McSween for a suit of damages for ten thousand dollars. **February 7, 1878.** District Court Record. (private collection).

Brady, William. "List of Articles Inventoried by Wm Brady sheriff in the suit of Charles Fritz & Emilie Scholand vs A.A. McSween now in the dwelling house belonging to A.A. McSween." (undated, but in **February of 1878**) (private collection)

BREEDEN, WILLIAM (CHRONOLOGICAL)

BIOGRAPHICAL SOURCES

Breeden, William. "I read your speech yesterday ..." **May 31, 1874.** Letter to S.B. Elkins. West Virginia & Regional History Center. West Virginia University Libraries, Morgantown, West Virginia. Stephen B. Elkins Papers (A&M 53). Box 1, Folder 1. **(Connection to Elkins and Catron since 1866)**

No Author. *Acts of the Legislative Assembly of the Territory of New Mexico, Twenty-Second Session, Convened at the Capitol, at the City of Santa Fe on Monday the 6th day of December, 1875, and adjourned on Friday the 14th day of January, 1876. Santa Fe: Manderfield & Tucker.* **1876. (Breeden is listed under "Territorial Officers" as both Attorney General and District Attorney for the First Judicial District, Page 13)**

Speer, William S. and John Henry Brown, eds. *The Encyclopedia of the New West, Containing Fully Authenticated Information of the Agricultural, Mercantile, Commercial, Manufacturing, Mining and Grazing Industries, and Representing the Character, Development, Resources and Present Development of Texas, Arkansas, Colorado, New Mexico and Indian Territory, Also Biographical Sketches of Their Representative Men and Women.* Marshall, Texas: The United States Biographical Publishing Company. **1881.**

No Author. *Acts of the Legislative Assembly of the Territory of New Mexico, Twenty-Sixth Session, Convened at the Capitol, at the City of Santa Fe on Monday the 18th day of February, 1884, and adjourned on Thursday, the 3rd day of April, 1884.* Santa Fe: New Mexican Printing Co. **1884. (Attorney General is listed as** *ex officio* District Attorney for the First Judicial District, as did Breeden since 1881)

Prince, L. Bradford, Ed. *The General Laws of New Mexico; Including All the Unrepealed Laws From the Promulgation of the 'Kearney Code' in 1846, to the End of the Legislative Session of 1880. With Supplement, Including the Session of 1882.* Albany, New York: W.C. Little & Co., Law Publishers. "Article VI, Chapter X, Attorney General, District Attorneys, and Attorneys." 1882. Pages 56-57. **(Inquest law for writing a Coroner's Jury Report, as followed by Alejandro Segura)**

Ritch, William. Ed. *The Legislative Blue-Book of the Territory of New Mexico.* Santa Fe. Charles W. Greene Publisher. 1882. **(With listing of Breeden as Attorney General in the "Official Register")**

Ayer, N.W. and Son. eds. *N.W. Ayer & Son's American Newspaper Annual Containing a Catalogue of American Newspapers.* Philadelphia: N.W. Ayer & Son. 1888. **(Listing Breeden's and Henry Waldo's New Mexico Printing Company as publishing *The Santa Fe New Mexican*)**

No Author. "Obituary Notes." *The New York Times.* January 29, 1913. Page 11, Column 5. Newspaperarchive.com.

Twitchell, Ralph Emerson. *The Leading Facts of New Mexico History.* Volume III. Cedar Rapids: The Torch Press. 1917. **(Breeden biography)**

Anderson, Clinton P. "The Adobe Palace." *New Mexico Historical Review.* 1944. Volume 19, Number 2. Pages 97-122.

Nusbaum, Rosemary. *The City Different and the Palace, The Palace of the Governors: Its Role in Santa Fe History.* Santa Fe: Sunstone Press. 1978.

BRISTOL, WARREN HENRY

BIOGRAPHICAL SOURCES

Thompson, Mark. "Judge Warren Henry Bristol: A Man of his Time and Place? January 3, 2012. https://www.leg.state.mn.us/archive/LegDB/Articles/11430Essay.

Twitchell, Ralph Emerson. *The Leading Facts of New Mexico History.* Vol. II. Page 420, Note 247. Santa Fe: Sunstone Press. 2007. (Reprinted from 1912 edition)

CONTEMPORARY SOURCES (CHRONOLOGICAL)

Bristol Warren. "From sources of information that I deem perfectly reliable I am satisfied that there are public disorders in Lincoln County ..." Letter to Governor Marsh Giddings. January 10, 1874. Herman B. Weisner Papers, ca. 1957-1992. New Mexico State University Library at Las Cruces. Rio Grande Historical Collections. Accession No. Weisner Ms 0249. Box 4/39. Folder D-4. Folder Name: "Judge Bristol's letter." **(Creating Ring's outlaw myth)**

No Author. Grant County *Herald.* " 'Petition to Remove Judge Bristol. We the undersigned citizens of the Third Judicial District of the Territory of New Mexico, without regard to party, would respectfully request and petition for the removal of Judge Warren Bristol ...' " No date. **1876 or 1877.**(Quoted in "W.B. Matchett and Mary E. McPherson 'Make certain charges against the U.S. Officials in the Territory of New Mexico.' " Letter to President Rutherford B. Hayes. Received and filed May 1, 1877. Interior Department Papers 1850-1907; Appointments Division and Subsequent Actions. Microfilm File Case Number 44-4-8-3. Record Group 48. Microfilm No. M750. Roll 1. National Archives and Records Administration. U.S. Department of Justice. Washington, D.C.) **(Exposing him as a corrupt Santa Fe Ring member)**

Bristol, Warren. "Writ of Embezzlement." December 21, 1877. Herman B. Weisner Papers, ca. 1957-1992. New Mexico State University Library at Las Cruces. Rio

Grande Historical Collections. Accession No. Ms 0249. Box 10. Folder M-13. Folder Name. "Will and Testament A. McSween."

_____. "Action of Assumpsit to command Sheriff Brady of Lincoln County to attach goods of Alexander A. McSween." **February 7, 1878**. District Court Record. (private collection).

_____. Preprinted form for "Writ of Attachment" (Printed and sold at the office of the Mesilla News) filled out to command the Sheriff of Lincoln County to attach goods of Alexander McSween for a suit of damages for ten thousand dollars. **February 7, 1878**. District Court Record. (private collection).

_____. "My reasons for not holding October term of Court ..." Telegram to U.S. Marshal John Sherman. **October 4, 1878**. Indiana Historical Society. Lew Wallace Collection. M0292. Box 3. Folder 15.

_____. *Instructions to the Jury*. District Court 3rd Judicial. District Doña Ana. Filed **April 9, 1881**. Writ of Embezzlement. New Mexico State University Library at Las Cruces. Rio Grande Historical Collection. Accession No. Ms 0249. Box 1. Folder 14C. Folder Name: "Billy the Kid Legal Documents."

CATRON, THOMAS BENTON

BIBLIOGRAPHICAL SOURCES

Cleaveland, Norman, *A Synopsis of the Great New Mexico Cover-up*. Self-printed. 1989.

_____. *The Great Santa Fe Cover-up. Based on a Talk given Before the Santa Fe Historical Society on November 1, 1978*. Self-printed. 1982.

_____. *The Morleys - Young Upstarts on the Southwest Frontier*. Albuquerque, New Mexico: Calvin Horn Publisher, Inc. 1971. (**Page 93 gives Catron's vindictive indictment of Cleaveland's grandmother, Ada Morley, for mail theft as revenge denying him use of a Maxwell Land Grant buggy.**

Dodge, Andrew R., and Betty K. Koed, eds. *Biographical Directory of the United States Congress 1774-2005*. Washington, D.C.: United States Government Printing Office. 2005

Dunham, Harold H. "New Mexican Land Grants with Special Reference to the Title Papers of the Maxwell Grant." *New Mexico Historical Review*. (January, 1955) Vol. 70. No. 1. pp. 1 - 23.

Hefferan, Vioalle Clark. *Thomas Benton Catron*. Albuquerque, New Mexico: University of New Mexico. Zimmerman Library. Unpublished Thesis for the Degree of Master of Arts. 1940. .(**In praise of Catron; includes railroad involvement, Page 35; First National Bank stockholder from 1871 to 1907, Page 28**)

Keleher, William A. *The Maxwell Land Grant. A New Mexico Item*. Albuquerque, New Mexico: University of New Mexico Press. 1964.

Klasner, Lilly. Eve Ball. Ed. *My Girlhood Among Outlaws*. Tucson, Arizona: The University of Arizona Press. 1972.

Lamar, Howard Robert N. *The Far Southwest 1846 – 1912: A Territorial History*. New Haven and London: Yale University Press. 1966. (**Chapter 6 covers the Santa Fe Ring)**)

Montoya, María E. *Translating Property. The Maxwell Land Grant and the Conflict Over Land in the American West, 1840-1900*. Berkeley and Los Angeles: University of California Press. 2002.

Mullin, Robert N. "A Specimen of Catron's Dirty Work. Sworn Affidavit of Samuel Davis." October 1, 1878. Binder RNM IV, EE. (Unpublished). Midland, Texas: Nita Stewart Haley Memorial Library and J. Evetts Haley Historical Center.

_____. "Catron Embarrassed Throughout His Life by an Affliction." (Date Unknown). Binder RNM, IV, M. (Unpublished). Midland, Texas: Nita Stewart Haley Memorial Library and J. Evetts Haley Historical Center. Robert Mullin Papers. Binder RNM IV, EE (Unpublished).

_____. "Prior to Lincoln County War Catron Had Defended Colonel Dudley." (No Date). Notes from "Lincoln County War Cast of Characters." Midland, Texas: Nita Stewart Haley Memorial Library and J. Evetts Haley Historical Center.

Murphy, Lawrence R. *Lucien Bonaparte Maxwell. Napoleon of the Southwest.* Norman: University of Oklahoma Press. 1983.

Otero, Miguel A. *My Life on the Frontier, 1882-1897: Incidents and Characters of the period when Kansas, Colorado, and New Mexico were passing through the last of their Wild and Romantic Years.* New York: The Press of the Pioneers. 1935. Pages 232-233. (Quoted by Victor Westphall, *Thomas Benton Catron and His Era.* Page 188) **(Quote: "the 'Santa Fe Ring,' the real machine controlling the political situation in New Mexico.")**

Pearson, Jim Berry. *The Maxwell Land Grant.* Norman: University of Oklahoma Press. 1961.

Routt, John C. "I am here on a visit to my daughter and have more by accident than otherwise heard statements ..." Letter to President Rutherford B. Hayes. August 29, 1878. Interior Department Papers 1850-1907; Appointments Division and Subsequent Actions. Microfilm File Case Number 44-4-8-3. Microfilm Roll M750. National Archives and Records Administration Record Group 48. U.S. Department of Interior. Washington D.C. **(In opposition to removal of Governor Axtell and U.S. Attorney Thomas Benton Catron.)**

Sluga, Mary Elizabeth. *Political Life of Thomas Benton Catron 1896-1912.* Albuquerque, New Mexico: University of New Mexico. Zimmerman Library. Unpublished Thesis for the Degree of Master of Arts. 1941. **(Thesis in praise of Catron for an M.A.)**

Taylor, Morris F. *O.P. McMains and the Maxwell Land Grant Conflict.* Tucson, Arizona: The University of Arizona Press. 1979. **(Traces origins of the Santa Fe Ring with T.B. Catron and S.B. Elkins)**

Westphall, Victor. *Thomas Benton Catron and His Era.* Tucson, Arizona: University of Arizona Press. 1973.

_____. "Fraud and Implications of Fraud in the Land Grants of New Mexico." *New Mexico Historical Review.* 1974. Vol. XLIX, No. 3. 189 - 218.

Wooden, John Paul. *Thomas Benton Catron and New Mexico Politics 1866-1921.* Albuquerque, New Mexico: University of New Mexico. Zimmerman Library. Unpublished Thesis for the Degree of Master of Arts. 1959. **(M.A. thesis praising Catron)**

CONTEMPORARY EXPOSÉS OF (CHRONOLOGICAL)

Middaugh, Asa F. Deposition. **March 31, 1876.** "Exhibit B" in the August 9, 1878 deposition of Frank Springer to Investigator Frank Warner Angel. Frank Warner Angel report titled *In the Matter of the Investigation of the Charges Against S.B. Axtell Governor of New Mexico.* October 3, 1878. Interior Department Papers 1850-1907; Appointments Division and Subsequent Actions. Microfilm Case File No. 44-4-8-3. Record Group 48. Microfilm Roll M750. National Archives and Records Administration. U.S. Department of Interior. Washington, D.C. **(About Catron's malicious prosecution of Ada McPherson Morley)**

Springer, Frank. Deposition to Investigator Frank Warner Angel. **August 9, 1878.** Frank Warner Angel report titled *In the Matter of the Investigation of the Charges Against S.B. Axtell Governor of New Mexico.* October 3, 1878. Interior Department Papers 1850-1907; Appointments Division and Subsequent Actions. Microfilm Case File No. 44-4-8-3. Record Group 48. Microfilm Roll M750. National Archives and Records Administration. U.S. Department of Interior. Washington, D.C. **(Mentions Catron, Elkins, and the Santa Fe Ring, and provided Exhibits of letters exposing Catron's evil.)**

Morley, William Raymond. "Your letter of the 7th came last night and it was a good long newsy letter ..." Letter to wife, Ada McPherson Morley. **August 15, 1878.**

Collection of Norman Cleaveland. Quoted in Norman Cleaveland, *The Morleys: Young Upstarts in the Southwest*. Albuquerque, New Mexico: Calvin Horn Publisher, Inc. 1971. Pages 152-155. **(About possible betrayal by Angel's reports; about the Santa Fe Ring, T.B. Catron, S.B. Elkins, S.B. Axtell, and Henry Waldo; and the Lincoln County War)**

No Author. "White Cap's Proclamation." *Las Vegas Optic*. **March 12, 1880. (Manifesto against land-grabbing Catron and the Ring)**

Wallace, Lew. "I have the honor to inform you that the Legislature of this Territory adjourned ..." **February 16, 1880.** Letter to Carl Schurz. Indiana Historical Society. Lew Wallace Collection. M0292. Box 4. Folder 14. **(Important documentation of Catron as head of the Santa Fe Ring, and Wallace's Ring opposition)**

No Author. "The Santa Fe Ring is the most corrupt combination that ever cursed any country or community." Las Cruces *Thirty-Four Newspaper*. **October 27, 1880.** From Victor Westphall, *Thomas Benton Catron and His Era*. Page 186. **(Article summarizing Ring abuses in urging voters to oppose Ring candidates)**

No Author. "The Ring must soon discover that the time has passed in New Mexico when men can be herded like so many sheep ..." *Albuquerque Daily Democrat*. **March 4, 1884.** Quoted by Victor Westphall, *Thomas Benton Catron and His Era*. Page 191. **(About Santa Fe Ring control of appointments to legislature)**

No Author. *Santa Fe Weekly New Mexican Review*. **March 13, 1884.** *Santa Fe Weekly New Mexican Review*. **(Accusation of Catron and the Ring of controlling grand juries and bribery)**

Valdez, Jose and Enrique Mares. "Scorching Letter, The Knights of Labor Send a Communication to Powderly! Politicians Arraigned! The Boldest Document Ever Issued in the Territory." **August 18, 1890.** *Las Vegas Democrat*. Volume 1. Center for Southwest Studies. Thomas B. Catron Papers, MSS 29, Series 102, Box 8, Folder 4. **(Gives history of Santa Fe Ring with T.B. Catron as head)**

No Author. "Catron and the Laboring Men." Unknown newspaper. **1892?** University of New Mexico Library. Center for Southwest Studies. Thomas B. Catron Papers, MSS 29, Series 401, Box 1, Folder 3. **(Opposition to Catron as Delegate to Congress as "the biggest corporation man in New Mexico")**

Victory, John P. "No Consistent Democrat Should Vote for T.B. Catron, John P. Victory in Forcible and Cogent Language Gives Answerable Reasons." —, **1895.** Printed broadside. University of New Mexico Library. Center for Southwest Studies. Thomas B. Catron Papers, MSS 29, Series 409, Box 1, Folder 3.

Wallace, Lew. "I have your several letters, including the last one of the 3rd inst." Letter to Eugene Fiske. **November 6, 1897.** Indiana Historical Society. Lew Wallace Collection. AC233. Box 1. Folder 7. (part of 1981 addition) **(About Catron's control over New Mexicans)**

Cutting, Bronson. "Catron was the boss of the Territory ..." Letter to James Roger Addison. **December 11, 1911.** Cited by Victor Westphall in *Thomas Benton Catron and His Era* from his citation: Lincoln County Manuscripts Division. Box 12. Courtesy of David Stratton. **(Catron as head of the Santa Fe Ring)**

Johnson, E. Dana. "[H]e ruled with a rod of iron ..." Editorial. *Santa Fe New Mexican*. **May 16, 1921.** Catron Papers 801, Box 1. Quoted by Victor Westphall, *Thomas Benton Catron and His Era*. Pages 394-395. **(Tactics of "boss" Catron without using the words Santa Fe Ring)**

(SEE: William Raymond Morley, Mary Tibbles McPherson, Franklin Tolby, Oscar McMains, Frank Warner Angel)

SECRET CIPHER-CODE OF

McSween, Alexander. "Catron being "Grapes ..." **June 6, 1878.** Deposition to Frank Warner Angel. Pages 5-183 of Frank Warner Angel report *In the Matter of the Examination of the Causes and Circumstances of the Death of John H. Tunstall a*

British Subject. Report filed **October 4, 1878**. Angel Report. Microfilm File Case Number 44-4-8-3. Record Group 48. Microfilm No. M750. Roll 1. National Archives and Records Administration. U.S. Department of Justice. Washington, D.C. (**Ring code book discovered on February 14, 1878 from John Riley**)

Elkins, Stephen Benton. "Elkins - Telegraph Cipher, Cipher with Catron." Sent to Thomas Benton Catron. ——, **1978?** University of New Mexico Library. Center for Southwest Studies. Thomas B. Catron Papers, MSS 29, Series 108, Box 1, Folder 4. (**Code reference to "Angel" dates codes to 1878**)

Catron, Thomas Benton. "Waldo ... Robinson, Newcomb ... Turner ..." To unknown recipient(s). ____, **1881 ?**. University of New Mexico Library. Center for Southwest Studies. Thomas B. Catron Papers, MSS 29, Series 804, Box 1, stored with T.B. Catron's pocket notebooks dated 1869 to 1886. (**Santa Fe Ring code-cipher key**)

Elkins, Stephen Benton. "Elkins – Telegraph Cipher, Cipher with Catron." Mailing to T.B. Catron. ___ **1878?** University of New Mexico Library. Center for Southwest Studies. Thomas B. Catron Papers, MSS 29, Series 108, Box 1, Folder 4. (**Ring code-cipher key about T.B. Catron's resignation as U.S. Attorney; code reference to "Angel" dates codes to 1878**)

Dame, W.E. "We earnestly request you to give the Honorable T.B. Catron ..." Letter to the President. **May ___, 1905.** University of New Mexico Library. Center for Southwest Studies. Thomas B. Catron Papers, MSS 29, Series 103, Box 22, Folder 5. (**"Dame" was used in a cipher-code message)**)

Catron, Thomas Benton. "I have yours of Aug. 1st. I never contributed ..." **August 11, 1908.** Letter to Ralph Emerson Twitchell. University of New Mexico Library. Center for Southwest Studies. Thomas B. Catron Papers, MSS 29, Series 105, Volume 28, Page 9. (**Part of the money transaction continuing to August 14, 1908 apparently using cipher-code**)

_____. "Yours of the 13th at hand ..." **August 14, 1908.** Letter to Ralph Emerson Twitchell. University of New Mexico Library. Center for Southwest Studies. Thomas B. Catron Papers, MSS 29, Series 105, Volume 28, Page 20. (**Part of the money transaction of August 11, 1908 apparently using cipher-code "display of apples"**)

FEDERAL INDICTMENT OF REGULATORS BY

Catron, Thomas Benton. "Case No. 411. The United States vs. Charles Bowdry [Bowdre], Doc Scurlock, Henry Brown, Henry Antrim alias "Kid," John Middleton, Stephen Stevens, John Scroggins, George Coe and Frederick Waite." **June 21, 1878.** Herman B. Weisner Papers, ca. 1957-1992. New Mexico State University Library at Las Cruces. Rio Grande Historical Collections. Accession No. Ms 0249. Box 1. Folder B-4. Folder Name: Andrew Roberts Indictment.

RESIGNATION AS TERRITORIAL U.S. ATTORNEY BY

Elkins, Stephen Benton. "Elkins – Telegraph Cipher, Cipher with Catron." Sent to T.B. Catron. ___ **1878?** University of New Mexico Library. Center for Southwest Studies. Thomas B. Catron Papers, MSS 29, Series 108, Box 1, Folder 4. (**Ring code-cipher key about T.B. Catron's resignation as U.S. Attorney**)

_____. "Asking delay of action upon charges against U.S. Atty. Catron ..." **September 24, 1878.** Angel Report. Microfilm File Case No. 44-4-8-3. Record Group 48. National Records and Archives Administration. Microfilm No. M750. Roll 1. U.S. Department of Justice. Washington, D. C.

_____. "Regarding Attorney General's decision on T.B. Catron." Letter. **September___, 1878.** Angel Report. Microfilm File Case No. 44-4-8-3. Record Group 48. National Records and Archives Administration. Microfilm No. M750. Roll 1. U.S. Department of Justice. Washington, D.C.

Catron, Thomas Benton. "In accordance with a purpose long entertained ....." Letter to Charles Devens. **October 10, 1878.** Angel Report. Microfilm File Case No. 44-4-8-3. Record Group

48. National Records and Archives Administration. Microfilm No. M750. Roll 1. U.S. Department of Justice. Washington, D.C. (**Resignation as U.S. Attorney**)

Devens, Charles. "Your resignation of the office of United States Attorney ..." Letter to T.B. Catron. **October 19, 1878**. Angel Report. Microfilm File Case No. 44-4-8-3. Record Group 48. National Records and Archives Administration. Microfilm No. M750. Roll 1. U.S. Department of Justice. Washington, D. C.

Catron, Thomas Benton. "Please change my resignation ...." **November 4, 1878.** Telegram to Charles Devens. Angel Report. Microfilm File Case No. 44-4-8-3. Record Group 48. National Records and Archives Administration. Microfilm No. M750. Roll 1. U.S. Department of Justice. Washington, D. C. (**Resignation as U.S. Attorney**)

Devens, Charles. "Your resignation of the office of United States Attorney ..." Letter to T.B. Catron. **November 12, 1878**. Angel Report. Microfilm File Case No. 44-4-8-3. Record Group 48. National Records and Archives Administration. Microfilm No. M750. Roll 1. U.S. Department of Justice. Washington, D.C.

Elkins, Stephen Benton. "Relative to resignation of T. B. Catron U. S. Attorney." Letter to Charles Devens. **November 10, 1878**. Angel Report. Microfilm File Case No. 44-4-8-3. Record Group 48. National Records and Archives Administration. Microfilm No. M750. Roll 1. U.S. Department of Justice. Washington, D.C.

Devens, Charles. "To honorable S. B. Elkins re. T. B. Catron continuing to act as U.S. Attorney ..." Letter to Stephen B. Elkins. **November 12, 1878**. Angel Report. Microfilm File Case No. 44-4-8-3. Record Group 48. National Records and Archives Administration. Microfilm No. M750. Roll 1. U.S. Department of Justice. Washington, D.C.

Barnes, Sidney M.. "I Sidney M. Barnes do solemnly swear ..." Swearing in as U.S. Attorney. **January 20, 1879**. Angel Report. Microfilm File Case No. 44-4-8-3. Record Group 48. National Records and Archives Administration. Microfilm No. M750. Roll 1. U.S. Department of Justice. Washington, D.C. (**Catron replaced by Ringite attorney Sidney Barnes**)

Elkins, Stephen Benton. "I have waited some time to reply to your lengthy letter ..." Letter to T.B. Catron. **August 15, 1879**. West Virginia & Regional History Center. West Virginia University Libraries, Morgantown, W. Va. Stephen B. Elkins Papers (A&M 53). Box 1. Folder 1. (**Reveals he prevented Catron's dismissal and indictment from Angel's report**)

Clancy, Frank W. "From something I have heard ..." Letter to T.B. Catron. **September 20, 1892**. University of New Mexico Library. Center for Southwest Studies. Thomas B. Catron Papers, MSS 29, Series 102, Box 16, Folder 2. (**Warning Catron that opponents are seeking the Angel Report to use against his campaign for Delegate, but Elkins is making obstacles**)

_____. "I am much surprised at what you say in your letter ..." Letter to T.B. Catron. **December 2, 1896**. University of New Mexico Library. Center for Southwest Studies. Thomas B. Catron Papers, MSS 29, Series 106, Box 1, Folder 6. (**Surprise that Catron now wants to be U.S. Attorney again**)

OWNERSHIP FILING ON CARRIZOZO CATTLE COMPANY

Catron, Thomas Benton.. Statement of Sole ownership of Carrizozo Ranch in Tax Dispute Case. No date. Herman B. Weisner Papers, ca. 1957-1992. New Mexico State University Library at Las Cruces. Rio Grande Historical Collections. Accession No. Ms 0249. Box. 2. Folder C-8. Folder Name "T.B. Catron Tax Troubles." (**One of Catron's Lincoln County holdings**)

AZTEC MINE OWNERSHIP OF

Catron, Thomas Benton. "I have disposed of the Aztec mine ..." Letter to Charles C. Catron. **September 30, 1914.** University of New Mexico Library. Center for

Southwest Studies. Thomas B. Catron Papers, MSS 29, Series 107, Box 1, Folder 3. **(Sale of Aztec mine reported to son)**

EXPURGATING OFFICE FIRE OF 1888 OF

Smith, Derwent H. "I have a letter from Geo. W. Knaebel; in which he mentions the destruction of your office ..." Letter to Frank W. Clancy. **July 29, 1888.** University of New Mexico Library. Center for Southwest Studies. Thomas B. Catron Papers, MSS 29, Series 102, Box 1, Folder 1. **(Gives the July 20, 1888 date of the record expurgating fire)**

Beatty, Denson & Oatman. "... We have noticed in the papers, with very much concern for yourselves ..." Letter to Catron, Knaebel, and Clancy. **July 30, 1888.** University of New Mexico Library. Center for Southwest Studies. Thomas B. Catron Papers, MSS 29, Series 102, Box 1, Folder 1. **(Provides the July 20, 1888 date of the record-expurgating fire)**

PECOS RIVER COW CAMP OF (CHRONOLOGICAL)

Riley, John H. Letter to N.A.M. Dudley. **May 19, 1878. (Fabricated Regulator theft of Catron's cattle from the Dolan Pecos Cow Camp)** Cited by Victor Westphall, Page 87.

Catron, Thomas Benton. Catron letter to Governor S. B. Axtell to intervene in Lincoln County. **May 30, 1878.** Midland, Texas: Nita Stewart Haley Memorial Library and J. Evetts Haley Historical Center. Robert Mullin Papers. Binder RNM IV, EE (Unpublished). **(Fabricated attack of Regulators on his cow camp workers)** Cited by Victor Westphall, Page 89-90.

SELLING AND BUYING LAND BY

Catron, Thomas Benton. Letter to a Don Matais Contreras. **July 30, 1896. (On acquiring land grants by bartering attorney's fees)** Cited in John Paul Wooden's unpublished masters thesis, Page 11.

(SEE: Land-grab exposés of Mary McPherson)

POSSIBLE VOTE BUYING AND POLITICAL PAY OFFS BY

Otero, Miguel A. "At the time of the Rep. Convention in this City ..." Letter to T.B. Catron. **October 25, 1888.** University of New Mexico Library. Center for Southwest Studies. Thomas B. Catron Papers, MSS 29, Series 102, Box 1, Folder 5. **(Documents a pay off to remove a candidate for a clerkship)**

Gonzales y Borrego, Francisco. "I have the honor to Report to you that I have two men ..." Letter to T.B. Catron. **July 23, 1890.** University of New Mexico Library. Center for Southwest Studies. Thomas B. Catron Papers, MSS 29, Series 102, Box 8, Folder 2. **(Documents T.B. Catron's vote buying)**

Lucero, Jose A. "the Democrats are making a desperate fight and I been oblige to meet them ..." Letter to T.B. Catron. **October 29, 1890.** University of New Mexico Library. Center for Southwest Studies. Thomas B. Catron Papers, MSS 29, Series 102, Box 9, Folder 3. **(Requests more money for vote apparent buying of Democrats and necessary secrecy about it)**

Carley, R.M. "The following is a list of men that voted ..." Letter to E.L. Bartlett. for T.B. Catron **November 5, 1890.** University of New Mexico Library. Center for Southwest Studies. Thomas B. Catron Papers, MSS 29, Series 102, Box 9, Folder 3. **(Reporting on voters for Catron)**

Martinez, D. "I most heartily have the honor to congratulate you ..." Letter to T.B. Catron. **August 30, 1892.** University of New Mexico Library. Center for Southwest Studies. Thomas B. Catron Papers, MSS 29, Series 102, Box 15, Folder 5. **(Getting voters by paying their poll taxes)**

Santistevan, Juan. "I had delayed the answer to your esteemed favor ..." Letter to T.B. Catron. **April 9, 1892.** University of New Mexico Library. Center for Southwest Studies. Thomas B. Catron Papers, MSS 29, Series 102, Box 14, Folder 3. **(Possible vote fixing)**

Gregg, George W. "I have your letter from parties in this county ..." **October 22, 1892.** Letter to R.E. Twitchell. University of New Mexico Library. Center for Southwest Studies. Thomas B. Catron Papers, MSS 29, Series 401, Box 1, Folder 3. **(Planning possible vote buying for Catron's campaign for Delegate)**

Hunt, Charles F. "I returned from Colfax County yesterday ..." Letter to T.B. Catron. **October 29, 1892.** University of New Mexico Library. Center for Southwest Studies. Thomas B. Catron Papers, MSS 29, Series 102, Box 16, Folder 5. **(Vote buying by exchange for free naturalization certificates)**

Amires, Jesucita. "I write you a short letter. ..." Letter to T.B. Catron. **November 4, 1892.** University of New Mexico Library. Center for Southwest Studies. Thomas B. Catron Papers, MSS 29, Series 102, Box 16, Folder 5. **(Wants money in exchange for vote-getting)**

Martin, T.P. "Our campaign committee has just arrived from the north ..." — **1896.** Letter to T.B. Catron. University of New Mexico Library. Center for Southwest Studies. Thomas B. Catron Papers, MSS 29, Series 103. Box 11, Folder 4. **(Wants $250 "to buy enough votes ... to carry the county)**

Santistevan, P.J. "I am doing the possible for your Election ..." Letter to T.B. Catron. **October 12, 1896.** University of New Mexico Library. Center for Southwest Studies. Thomas B. Catron Papers, MSS 29, Series 401, Box 1, Folder 7. **(Wants possible vote buying money)**

Catron, Thomas B. "I am entitled to same from a political standpoint ... having made the race paying all the expenses ..." Letter to Joshua S. Reynolds. **December 16, 1897.** Quoted in Mary Elizabeth Sluga's masters thesis, Page 53.

Mills, Melvin W. "There are a few men who are candidates [for Senator] that I guess have some money ..." Letter to T.B. Catron. **September 12, 1911.** Catron Papers 103, Box 37. Quoted by Victor Westphall, *Thomas Benton Catron and His Era.* Page 350. **(Revealing possible bribery for legislators' vote)**

ALLEGED ASSASSINATION ATTEMPT ON

Elkins, Stephen Benton. "I was shocked this morning on reading of the attempted assassination of you ..." Letter to T.B. Catron. **February 7, 1891.** University of New Mexico Library. Center for Southwest Studies. Thomas B. Catron Papers, MSS 29, Series 102, Box 10, Folder 5.

Francolon, J.B. "Please accept my hearty congratulations on your happy narrow escape ..." Letter to T.B. Catron. **February 7, 1891.** University of New Mexico Library. Center for Southwest Studies. Thomas B. Catron Papers, MSS 29, Series 102, Box 10, Folder 4.

Broad, W.E. "Since reading the account of the attempted assassination ..." Letter to T.B. Catron. **January 2, 1891.** University of New Mexico Library. Center for Southwest Studies. Thomas B. Catron Papers, MSS 29, Series 102, Box 10, Folder 3. **(Catron's Ringite agent for the Tierra Amarilla Grant, setting up malicious prosecution of rebellious settlers, primarily Refugio Martinez.)**

_____. "Since reading the account of the attempted assassination ..." Letter to T.B. Catron. **February 9, 1891.** University of New Mexico Library. Center for Southwest Studies. Thomas B. Catron Papers, MSS 29, Series 102, Box 11, Folder 4. **(Catron's Ringite agent for the Tierra Amarilla Grant, setting up malicious prosecution of Refugio Martinez as an alleged White Cap attempted assassin of Catron.)**

Wright, John M.. "Ancheta is talking very hard about Catron ..." Letter to R.E. Twitchell. **September 12, 1892.** University of New Mexico Library. Center for Southwest Studies. Thomas B. Catron Papers, MSS 29, Series 401, Box 1,

Folder 11. (**Letter from Silver City operative to Ringite informer Twitchell about rumor that Catron faked the assassination plot**)

TERRITORIAL DELEGATE ELECTIONS RUNNING FOR

Mills, Melvin W. "Yours of recent date at hand." Letter to T.B. Catron. **August 2, 1892.** University of New Mexico Library. Center for Southwest Studies. Thomas B. Catron Papers, MSS 29, Series 102, Box 15, Folder 3. (**Discourages his running for Delegate because of White Cap opposition**)

Catron, Thomas Benton. "A short time since I wrote you with reference to the position of Chief Justice ..." Letter to Stephen Benton Elkins. **August 15, 1892.** University of New Mexico Library. Center for Southwest Studies. Thomas B. Catron Papers, MSS 29, Series 401, Box 1, Folder 3.

No Author. "Catron and the Laboring Men." **September ? __, 1892.** Printed opposition advertisement. Unknown publication. Center for Southwest Studies. Thomas B. Catron Papers, MSS 29, Series 401, Box 1, Folder 3. (**Opposition to Catron as Delegate to Congress as "the biggest corporation man in New Mexico"**)

No Author. "One of the Ablest and Most Brainy Men in New Mexico, He Should Be Elected." **September 8, 1892.** *The Daily New Mexican.* Front Page. Column 3. https://chroniclingamerica.loc.gov/ (**On behalf of Catron for Delegate**)

Clancy, Frank W. "From something I have heard ..." Letter to T.B. Catron. **September 20, 1892.** University of New Mexico Library. Center for Southwest Studies. Thomas B. Catron Papers, MSS 29, Series 102, Box 16, Folder 2. (**Warning Catron that opponents are seeking the Angel Report to use against his campaign for Delegate, but Elkins is making obstacles**)

No Author. *Las Vegas Daily Optic* . **September 30, 1896.** (**Stating Catron had been an incompetent Delegate to Congress**)

Clancy, Frank W. "I am much surprised at what you say in your letter ..." Letter to T.B. Catron. **December 2, 1896.** University of New Mexico Library. Center for Southwest Studies. Thomas B. Catron Papers, MSS 29, Series 106, Box 1, Folder 6. (**Surprise that Catron now wants to be U.S. Attorney again; and that he lost as Delegate because of his enemies**)

BORREGO MURDER CASE BY

Gonzales y Borrego, Francisco. "I have the honor to Report to you that I have two men ..." Letter to T.B. Catron. **July 23, 1890.** University of New Mexico Library. Center for Southwest Studies. Thomas B. Catron Papers, MSS 29, Series 102, Box 8, Folder 2. (**Documents T.B. Catron's vote buying**)

Frost, Max. "Matters are progressing well here ..." Letter to Judge A.L. Morrison. **September 26, 1892.** University of New Mexico Library. Center for Southwest Studies. Thomas B. Catron Papers, MSS 29, Series 401, Box 1, Folder 3. (**States that Catron and Sheriff Charles Conklin are rumored as Francisco Chavez's murderers**)

Chavez, Juliana V. "Mr. Catron, you are not above suspicion of knowing more about the assassination of my son than you have found it convenient to reveal ..." Letter of Juliana Chavez to T.B. Catron. Reprinted in *Santa Fe Weekly New Mexican.* **March 8, 1894.** Quoted in Victor Westphall, *Thomas Benton Catron and his Era.* Page 226. (**Open letter from mother of Francisco Chavez implicating Catron in his murder**)

Hudson, Richard. "In talking with a Santa Fe man a few days ago in regard to the trial of the men whom you are defending ..." Letter to T.B. Catron. **May 14, 1995.** University of New Mexico Library. Center for Southwest Studies. Thomas B. Catron Papers, MSS 29, Series 102, Box 25, Folder 4. (**Feigned warning about Sheriff Cunningham being a danger to the Borrego case defendants by a Ringite lackey**)

Catron, Thomas Benton. "[The Francisco Chavez murder case] has left me more prostrated than any case I have ever had." Letter to wife, Julia Catron. **June 1, 1895.** C.P. 105, Vol. 12. Quoted in Victor Westphall, *Thomas Benton Catron and His Era.* Page 228. **(Catron implicated in political murder)**

Laughlin, Napoleon B. "In the Supreme Court of the Territory of New Mexico, In re Thomas B. Catron and Charles A. Spiess, Dissenting Opinion of Associate Justice N.B. Laughlin." **December 20, 1895.** University of New Mexico Library. Center for Southwest Studies. Thomas B. Catron Papers, MSS 29, Series 801, Box 1, Folder 8. **(Confirms that victim Sheriff Francisco Chavez was a political enemy of Catron's, implying that Catron may have instigated his murder using the Borregos)**

Catron, Thomas Benton. "... I wrote you a short time ago that I thought arrangements ought to be made ..." Letter to Charles A. Spiess. **January 22, 1897.** University of New Mexico Library. Center for Southwest Studies. Thomas B. Catron Papers, MSS 29, Series 103, Box 2, Folder 3. **(Trying to prevent Borregos' hanging by using political favors)**

No Author. "The Borregos Respited. The President Grants a Respite to the Condemned Men Until March 23. Telegram from Attorney-General." _____, **1897.** Unknown newspaper. University of New Mexico Library. Center for Southwest Studies. Thomas B. Catron Papers, MSS 29, Series 103, Box 2, Folder 3.

Catron, Thomas Benton. "Francisco Gonzales y Borrego, Antonio Gonzales y Borrego, Lauriano Alarid and Patricia Valencia are present under sentence of death ..." Letter to President Grover Cleveland. **February 16, 1897.** University of New Mexico Library. Center for Southwest Studies. Thomas B. Catron Papers, MSS 29, Series 106, Box 2, Folder 2. **(Request for commuting to life sentence)**

No Author. "The Borregos Respited, The President Grants a Respite to the Condemned Men Until March 23." — **1897.** Unknown newspaper clipping. University of New Mexico Library. Center for Southwest Studies. Thomas B. Catron Papers, MSS 29, Series 103, Box 2, Folder 3.

Mills, Melvin W. "Up at the Court House today the question of the power of the President to respite the Borregos ..." Letter to T.B. Catron. **February 22, 1897.** University of New Mexico Library. Center for Southwest Studies. Thomas B. Catron Papers, MSS 29, Series 106, Box 2, Folder 4. **(Helping in Borrego case)**

Gortner, Robert C. "I have your letter of Feb. 25th ..." Letter to T.B. Catron. **March 3, 1897.** University of New Mexico Library. Center for Southwest Studies. Thomas B. Catron Papers, MSS 29, Series 106, Box 2, Folder 6. **(Law partner helping in Borrego case)**

Catron, Thomas Benton. "Yours of the 4th instant at hand ..." Letter to Melvin W. Mills. **March 8, 1897.** University of New Mexico Library. Center for Southwest Studies. Thomas B. Catron Papers, MSS 29, Series 106, Box 2, Folder 7. **(Gives political maneuvering connecting to Borrego case)**

DISBARMENT CASE NO. 637 FOR (CHRONOLOGICAL)

Crist, Jacob. "In the Supreme Court of the Territory of New Mexico, at the July Term, A.D. 1895. Case No. 637." **August 20, 1895.** University of New Mexico Library. Center for Southwest Studies. Thomas B. Catron Papers, MSS 29, Series 801, Box 1, Folder 8. **(Filed information about unprofessional conduct)**

Victory, John P. "In the Supreme Court of the Territory of New Mexico, In the matter of the information concerning Thomas B. Catron and Charles A. Spiess." **August 31, 1895.** University of New Mexico Library. Center for Southwest Studies. Thomas B. Catron Papers, MSS 29, Series 801, Box 1, Folder 7. **(Committee appointed by Supreme Court lists misconduct)**

Catron, Thomas Benton. "In the Supreme Court of the Territory of New Mexico, In the matter of Thomas B. Catron and Charles A. Spiess." **July Term, 1895.** University of New Mexico Library. Center for Southwest Studies. Thomas B.

Catron Papers, MSS 29, Series 801, Box 1, Folder 7. (**Response to the Supreme Court denying the charges**)

Spiess, Charles A. "In the Supreme Court of the Territory of New Mexico, In the matter of charges and specifications against Charles A. Spiess." **July Term, 1895.** University of New Mexico Library. Center for Southwest Studies. Thomas B. Catron Papers, MSS 29, Series 801, Box 1, Folder 7. (**Response to the Supreme Court denying the charges**)

Committee Appointed by Supreme Court. "In the Supreme Court of the Territory of New Mexico, In the matter of the Information concerning Thomas B. Catron and Charles A. Spiess." **August 31, 1895.** University of New Mexico Library. Center for Southwest Studies. Thomas B. Catron Papers, MSS 29, Series 801, Box 1, Folder 8. (**Based on information filed by Prosecutor Jacob Crist in the Supreme Court on August 20, 1895 as Case No. 637**)

No author. *Las Vegas Independent Democrat.* ___ 1895; based on *Las Vegas Optic.* September 2, 1884. (**About disbarring Catron**)

Field, Neil B. "I received this morning papers from Springer ..." **September 7, 1895.** Letter to T.B. Catron. University of New Mexico Library. Center for Southwest Studies. Thomas B. Catron Papers, MSS 29, Series 801, Box 1, Folder 7. (**Sends copies of legal defense answers written by Attorney Frank Springer**)

Elkins, Stephen Benton. "Mr. Catron's prominence in the capital territory and his leadership ..." Letter to Gideon B. Bantz. **September 9, 1895.** Quoted in John Paul Wooden's unpublished thesis, Page 32. (**Corrupt influencing of Supreme Court judge not to disbar Catron**)

No Author. "In the Supreme Court of the Territory of New Mexico, In the matter of the charges and specifications against Thomas B. Catron and Charles A. Spiess – Unprofessional Conduct." Transcript of Supreme Court testimony. **October, 1895.** University of New Mexico Library. Center for Southwest Studies. Thomas B. Catron Papers, MSS 29, Series 801, Box 2, Folder 22. (**With testimony on Catron trying to get false affidavits by having a refusing woman witness beaten**)

Springer, Frank. "In the Matter of Thomas B. Catron and Charles A. Spiess." Response of Respondents. **October, 1895.** University of New Mexico Library. Center for Southwest Studies. Thomas B. Catron Papers, MSS 29, Series 801, Box 1, Folder 7. (**On behalf of Catron and Spiess moves for all evidence given by prosecution witnesses to be stricken from the record based on alleging that they had bad moral and no credibility**)

_____. "In the Matter of Thomas B. Catron and Charles A. Spiess." Moving to find then not guilty. **October, 1895.** University of New Mexico Library. Center for Southwest Studies. Thomas B. Catron Papers, MSS 29, Series 801, Box 1, Folder 7.

Crist, Jacob. "Mr. Crist Speaks Out. Makes a Clean Breast of the Davis Communication – Served as Attorney and Was Paid For it. What's Catron's Case to Do With it? Invites the Bar Association to Investigate." *The Daily New Mexican.* **October 5, 1895.** Letter to the Editor. University of New Mexico Library. Center for Southwest Studies. Thomas B. Catron Papers, MSS 29, Series 801, Box 1, Folder 8. (**Makes clear that testimony to the Supreme Court will support the disbarment charges for the Borrego Case**)

Hamilton, Humphrey B. "In the Supreme Court of the Territory of New Mexico, In the matter of the charges and specifications against Thomas B. Catron and Charles A. Spiess – Unprofessional Conduct." Majority Opinion. **October 25, 1895.** University of New Mexico Library. Center for Southwest Studies. Thomas B. Catron Papers, MSS 29, Series 801, Box 1, Folder 8. (**Corrupt Supreme Court's vindication of Catron and Spiess from disbarment**)

Laughlin, Napoleon B. "In the Supreme Court of the Territory of New Mexico, In re Thomas B. Catron and Charles A. Spiess, Dissenting Opinion of Associate Justice N.B. Laughlin." **December 20, 1895.** University of New Mexico Library. Center for Southwest Studies. Thomas B. Catron Papers, MSS 29, Series 801, Box 1, Folder 8. (**Dissenting opinion: favoring disbarment**)

Keleher, William A. *The Fabulous Frontier: Twelve New Mexico Items*. Pages 128-129. Albuquerque, New Mexico: The University of New Mexico Press. 1962. (**Ring-biased historian's distortion of Catron's disbarment case**)

ALBUQUERQUE DAILY CITIZEN ANONYMOUS LETTER PLOT AGAINST CHIEF JUSTICE THOMAS SMITH TO SABOTAGE DISBARMENT CASE BY

Twitchell, Ralph Emerson. ""I enclose you herewith a letter from Mr. Hughes, the editor of the Citizen ...." **September 26, 1892.** Letter to T.B. Catron. University of New Mexico Library. Center for Southwest Studies. Thomas B. Catron Papers, MSS 29, Series 401, Box 1, Folder 3. (**Advising a pay-off of editor Hughes**)

Catron, Thomas Benton (As "Anonymous"). "Is it honesty or partisanship?" Letter to the Editor, Thomas Hughes. *Albuquerque Daily Citizen*. **October 9, 1895.** Thomas B. Catron Papers. University of New Mexico Center for Southwest Studies. University Library. Center for Southwest Research, University Libraries, University of New Mexico. (Selectively quoted by Victor Westphall, *Thomas Benton Catron and His Era*. Page 246.) (**Catron's defamation of his disbarment Judge Thomas J. Smith to block a disbarment decision**)

_____. "Editor of the Citizen: I have noticed an article in the Citizen of the 9th inst., which seems to reflect on Chief Justice Smith ..." Published letter to Editor of the *Albuquerque Daily Citizen* Thomas Hughes. **October 10, 1895.** Catron Papers 801. Box 1. Folder 8. (Selectively quoted by Victor Westphall, *Thomas Benton Catron and His Era*. Page 248) (**Catron's lying Letter to the Editor to Thomas Hughes to conceal his own authorship of the editorial**)

_____. "The editorial in your paper came to hand today and the democrats and members of the Supreme Court are very indignant ..." Real letter to the Editor, Thomas Hughes. **October 10, 1895.** University of New Mexico Library. Center for Southwest Studies. Thomas B. Catron Papers, MSS 29, Series 801. Box 1, Folder 8. (Selectively quoted by Victor Westphall, *Thomas Benton Catron and His Era*. Page 248.) (**Catron's coercing Hughes not to reveal him as the anonymous "Is it honesty or partisanship?" letter.**)

Hobart, D.C. "As I was returning home yesterday (on the train) ..." Letter to T.B. Catron. **October 14, 1895.** University of New Mexico Library. Center for Southwest Studies. Thomas B. Catron Papers, MSS 29, Series 102, Box 27, Folder 1. (**Warning Catron that he is identified as the *Albuquerque Citizen* anonymous writer, and that editor, Hughes, would be prosecuted**)

Catron, Thomas Benton. "Tom Smith, son of "Extra Billy" Smith, brother of ... the embezzler, who fled from justice in Arizona ..." "[Judge] Hamilton should ... see that the decision is an absolute, complete, unconditional vindication. This is what I ask him." Letter to *Socorro Chieftain* publisher S.W. Williams. **October 25, 1895.** Catron Papers. 105. Vol. 13. Quoted by Victor Westphall, *Thomas Benton Catron and His Era*. Pages 251-254. (**Defamation of his disbarment Chief Judge Thomas Smith; and illegal influence on another judge**)

_____. "[Smith], thank heaven, took the diarrhoea from the article published in the 'Citizen' and was soon after thrown into a congestive chill ..." Letter to Walter C. Hadley. **October 29, 1895.** (**Gloating over his sadistic attack on his disbarment judge, Thomas Smith**) Quoted by Victor Westphall, *Thomas Benton Catron and His Era*. Page 259.

_____. "His skin is so thin that the slightest attack punctures him. I think the papers should now puncture him ..." Letter to T.W. Collier. **November 11, 1895.** Catron Papers. 105. Vol. 13. (**Sadistic attack on his disbarment judge, Thomas Smith**) Quoted by Victor Westphall, *Thomas Benton Catron and His Era*. Page 249.

_____. First National Bank check to T. Hughes for $350.00. **July 11, 1896.** Check to Thomas Hughes. University of New Mexico Library. Center for Southwest Studies. Thomas B. Catron Papers, MSS 29, Series 805, Box 1, Bunch 1. (**Catron's pay-off check to Thomas Hughes**)

(SEE: Thomas Hughes)

CONGRATULATIONS FOR AVOIDING DISBARMENT TO

Helm, T.J. "Will you allow me to extend my harty congratulations ..." **October 28, 1895.** Letter to T.B. Catron. University of New Mexico Library. Center for Southwest Studies. Thomas B. Catron Papers, MSS 29, Series 801, Box 1, Folder 9. (**Decision against disbarment**)

Elkins, Stephen Benton. "We reached home yesterday at noon ..." Letter to T.B. Catron. **October 30, 1895.** University of New Mexico Library. Center for Southwest Studies. Thomas B. Catron Papers, MSS 29, Series 102, Box 26, Folder 2. (**Congratulating on not being disbarred**)

Ashenfelter, Singleton M. "I congratulate you on the result of the Supreme Court Inquiry ..." **November 1, 1895.** Letter to T.B. Catron. University of New Mexico Library. Center for Southwest Studies. Thomas B. Catron Papers, MSS 29, Series 801, Box 1, Folder 9. (**Decision against disbarment**)

Rudulph, Charles. "Allow me to congratulate you on your recent great victory. **November 5, 1895.** Letter to T.B. Catron. University of New Mexico Library. Center for Southwest Studies. Thomas B. Catron Papers, MSS 29, Series 102, Box 27, Folder 2. (**Son of Milnor Rudulph, Billy Bonney's Ringite President of his Coroner's Jury who wrote its Report praising Pat Garrett**)

REVENGE FOR DISBARMENT CASE BY

ATTACKING PROSECUTOR JACOB CRIST BY

Broad, W.E. "Replying to that part of your letter of the 3rd inst ..." Letter to T.B. Catron. **December 6, 1890.** University of New Mexico Library. Center for Southwest Studies. Thomas B. Catron Papers, MSS 29, Series 102, Box 9, Folder 5. (**Ringite agent reporting to Catron about Jacob H. Crist**)

Crist, Jacob. "Mr. Crist Speaks Out. Makes a Clean Breast of the Davis Communication – Served as Attorney and Was Paid For it. What's Catron's Case to Do With it? Invites the Bar Association to Investigate." *The Daily New Mexican.* **October 5, 1895.** Letter to the Editor. University of New Mexico Library. Center for Southwest Studies. Thomas B. Catron Papers, MSS 29, Series 801, Box 1, Folder 8. (**Makes clear that testimony to the Supreme Court will support the disbarment charges for the Borrego Case**)

Johnson, Charles A. "I am in receipt of your favor of 27th ultimo re. Crist matter ..." Letter to T.B. Catron. **October 3, 1895.** University of New Mexico Library. Center for Southwest Studies. Thomas B. Catron Papers, MSS 29, Series 102, Box 27, Folder 1. (**Catron's investigator to find dirt on Jacob H. Crist**)

_____. "I am in receipt of your favor of the 24th ultimo regarding the Crist matter." Letter to T.B. Catron. **November 4, 1895.** University of New Mexico Library. Center for Southwest Studies. Thomas B. Catron Papers, MSS 29, Series 102, Box 27, Folder 3.(**About Catron's revenge pursuit of Crist**)

ATTACKING DISSENTING SUPREME COURT JUDGE NAPOLEON BONAPARTE LAUGHLIN BY

Catron, Thomas Benton. "This man [Judge] Laughlin ... tried to disbar me and when he could not do it he wrote a filthy, dirty, dissenting opinion ..." Letter to William J. Mills. **July 18, 1896.** Catron Papers. 105. Vol. 13. Quoted by Victor Westphall,

Thomas Benton Catron and His Era. Page 258. (**Trying to destroy reputation of disbarment judge, Napoleon B. Laughlin**)

ALBUQUERQUE CITIZEN ANONYMOUS "POKER BILL" ATTACK ON GOVERNOR WILLIAM THORNTON BY

Catron, Thomas Benton (as Anonymous, "XXX"). "Severe Criticism, Gov. Thornton Charged With Prostituting His Office." *Albuquerque Daily Citizen.* **September 5, 1896.** (With reprinted letter dated September 4, 1896) Vol. 10, No. 276. Page 2. Center for Southwest Research Collection, University Libraries, University of New Mexico. Zim CSWR oversize AN2, A411 January – June 1896, July – December 1896. Reprinted September 11, 1896 in the *Santa Fe Daily New Mexican.* University of New Mexico Library. Center for Southwest Studies. Thomas B. Catron Papers, MSS 29, Series 801, Box 2, Folder 13. (**Catron's anonymous attack on Governor William Thornton**)

Thornton, William T. "The following is an extract from a communication from Santa Fé which appeared in last Saturday's issue of the Albuquerque Citizen under the nom de plum of XXXX ..." Letter to T.B. Catron. **September 10, 1896.** University of New Mexico Library. Center for Southwest Studies. Thomas B. Catron Papers, MSS 29, Series 801, Box 2, Folder 13. (**Responding to Catron's anonymous defamatory "Poker Bill" letter published in the *Albuquerque Daily Citizen***)

_____. "Open Letter to T.B. Catron." *Santa Fe Daily New Mexican.* **September 11, 1896.** Front Page. University of New Mexico Library. Center for Southwest Studies. Thomas B. Catron Papers, MSS 29, Series 801, Box 2, Folder 13. (Quoted by Victor Westphall, *Thomas Benton Catron and His Era.* Page 262.) (**Reprinting his own letter of September 10, 1896 to Catron debunking Catron's anonymous defamatory "Poker Bill" letter of September 4, 1896 to the Editor of the *Albuquerque Daily Citizen***)

Catron, Thomas Benton. "I am this morning in possession of your communication of the 10th inst., written from the "Office of the Executive" ... Letter to William T. Thornton. **September 16, 1896.** University of New Mexico Library. Center for Southwest Studies. Thomas B. Catron Papers, MSS 29, Series 801, Box 2, Folder 13. (Quoted by Victor Westphall, *Thomas Benton Catron and His Era* Page 263.) (**Catron's paranoid and violent letter against Thornton**)

_____. "You will recognize me as the Delegate from New Mexico ..." Letter to President Grover Cleveland. **September 16, 1896.** University of New Mexico Library. Center for Southwest Studies. Thomas B. Catron Papers, MSS 29, Series 801, Box 2, Folder 13. (Quoted by Victor Westphall, *Thomas Benton Catron and His Era.* Pages 269-270*)* (**Catron's attempted revenge on Governor William Thornton**)

_____. "Enclosed I send you copies of two letters ..." Letter to Stephen Benton Elkins. **September 16, 1896.** University of New Mexico Library. Center for Southwest Studies. Thomas B. Catron Papers, MSS 29, Series 801, Box 2, Folder 13. (**Denying the "Poker Bill" plot to Elkins**)

Thornton, William T. "Catron Begs the Question – Replies to Gov. Thornton's Open Letter – But Does Not Deny That the Anonymous Screed Emanated from His Office." **September 17, 1896.** *Santa Fe Daily New Mexican.* University of New Mexico Library. Center for Southwest Studies. Thomas B. Catron Papers, MSS 29, Series 106, Box 2, Folder 2.

Catron, Thomas Benton. "Yours of the 18th instant at hand. Thornton's trial came out about as I expected ..." Letter to Max Frost. **February 23, 1897.** University of New Mexico Library. Center for Southwest Studies. Thomas B. Catron Papers, MSS 29, Series 106, Box 2, Folder 4. (**Still denying his anonymous letter plots in the *Albuquerque Daily Citizen***)

PURSUIT OF OLIVER LEE USING PAT GARRETT BY

Bryan, John D. "On yesterday indictments were returned by our Grand Jury against Oliver M. Lee ..." Letter to Thomas Benton Catron. **October 1, 1898.** University of New Mexico Library. Center for Southwest Studies. Thomas B. Catron Papers, MSS 29, Series 103, Box 6, Folder 2. (**Reporting to Catron on malicious prosecution of Oliver Lee**)

Barnes, R.P. "I have spent a couple of days down here on the Fountain cases ..." Letter to T.B. Catron. **May 21, 1899.** University of New Mexico Library. Center for Southwest Studies. Thomas B. Catron Papers, MSS 29, Series 103, Box 7, Folder 5. (**Update on Pat Garrett on the Fountain murder cases to get conviction of Oliver Lee**

CAMPAIGN SPEECH BY

Catron, Thomas Benton. "Speech of Thomas B. Catron, delivered before the Bernalillo County Republican Convention at Albuquerque." **October 26, 1898.** University of New Mexico Library. Center for Southwest Studies. Thomas B. Catron Papers, MSS 29, Series 401, Box 1, Folder 9.

Fergusson, Harvey B. "Speech of H.G. Fergusson, Santa Fe N.M." **October 29, 1898.** University of New Mexico Library. Center for Southwest Studies. Thomas B. Catron Papers, MSS 29, Series 401. Box 1, Folder 9. (**Alluding to Santa Fe Ring tactics in response to Catron's October 26, 1898 speech**)

ATTACKS ON GOVERNOR MIGUEL OTERO BY

Elkins, Stephen Benton. "Your letter from Las Vegas received ..." Letter to T.B. Catron. **June 14, 1901.** University of New Mexico Library. Center for Southwest Studies. Thomas B. Catron Papers, MSS 29, Series 103, Box 13, Folder 1. (**Informing him that Miguel Otero was appointed governor despite his efforts to the contrary**)

Catron, Thomas Benton. "[Otero backers] have made a very villainous, mean ugly fight against me." **September 20, 1902.** Letter to Dave Winters. Catron Papers 105, Volume 20. Quoted by Victor Westphall, *Thomas Benton Catron and His Era.* Pages 291. (**Catron's accusing political rival, Governor Miguel Otero, of his own ring-style criminality**)

Miller, Fred and W.E. Dame. "We earnestly request you to give the Honorable T.B. Catron, formerly Delegate to Congress from New Mexico ..." **May __, 1905.** Letter to Theodore Roosevelt. University of New Mexico Library. Center for Southwest Studies. Thomas B. Catron Papers, MSS 29, Series 103, Box 22, Folder 5. (**"Dame" is a name which appeared in a Catron cipher-code letter**)

MAYOR OF SANTA FE OF

Montenie, L.F. "The City of Santa Fe, Office of the City Clerk, Certificate of Election." **April 3, 1906.** University of New Mexico Library. Center for Southwest Studies. Thomas B. Catron Papers, MSS 29, Series 801, Box 2, Folder 17.

SENATORSHIP OF

Mills, Melvin W. "There are a few men who are candidates [for Senator] that I guess have some money ..." Letter to T.B. Catron. **September 12, 1911.** Catron Papers 103, Box 37. Quoted by Victor Westphall, *Thomas Benton Catron and His Era.* Page 350. (**Revealing possible bribery for legislators' vote**)

Catron, Thomas Benton. "I am informed that you have been elected a member of the House Of Representatives ..." Form letter from T.B. Catron to legislators. **November 15, 1911.** University of New Mexico Library. Center for Southwest Studies. Thomas B. Catron Papers, MSS 29, Series 511, Box 1, Folder 5. (**Soliciting votes for himself for Senator**)

LETTERS FROM, TO, ABOUT (CHRONOLOGICAL)

FROM SATURNINO BACA

Baca, Saturnino. "Which if anything has been done in regard to the claim of Francisco Baca ..." Letter to T.B. Catron. **March 28, 1892.** University of New Mexico Library. Center for Southwest Studies. Thomas B. Catron Papers, MSS 29, Series 102, Box 14, Folder 2.

TO AND FROM JOHN D. BAIL

Catron, Thomas Benton et al. "Can you give us any information in regard to A.M. Connor, whom we are informed is living in Silver City ..." Letter to John D. Bail. **December 28, 1888.** University of New Mexico Library. Center for Southwest Studies. Thomas B. Catron Papers, MSS 29, Series 101, Volume 1, Page 250. **(Using Bail as a spy for his law firm)**

Bail, John H. "Yes I will do so ..." Telegram to T.B. Catron. **August 20, 1889.** University of New Mexico Library. Center for Southwest Studies. Thomas B. Catron Papers, MSS 29, Series 102, Box 4, Folder 5.

_____. "I will attend to the Hughes case ..." Letter to T.B. Catron. **August 21, 1889.** University of New Mexico Library. Center for Southwest Studies. Thomas B. Catron Papers, MSS 29, Series 102, Box 4, Folder 5.

_____. "I send you a print ..." Letter to T.B. Catron. **April 19, 1892.** University of New Mexico Library. Center for Southwest Studies. Thomas B. Catron Papers, MSS 29, Series 102, Box 14, Folder 3.

_____. "I have received your letter..." Letter to T.B. Catron. **February 6, 1893.** University of New Mexico Library. Center for Southwest Studies. Thomas B. Catron Papers, MSS 29, Series 102, Box 17, Folder 4.

Catron, Thomas Benton. First National Bank check to John D. Bail for $250.00 **July 15, 1896.** Check to J.D. Bail. University of New Mexico Library. Center for Southwest Studies. Thomas B. Catron Papers, MSS 29, Series 805, Box 1, Bunch 1. **(Payment to attorney who had been Billy Bonney's court appointed defense lawyer in Mesilla in 1881)**

FROM AND ABOUT JOSEPH BLAZER

Easton, David M. "I am in receipt of a letter from Maj Llewellyn ..." Letter to T.B. Catron. **May 15, 1890.** University of New Mexico Library. Center for Southwest Studies. Thomas B. Catron Papers, MSS 29, Series 102, Box 7, Folder 3. **(Easton in trying to sell all his Mescalero property to Catron, mentions that John Riley and William Rynerson are part owners of Joseph Blazer's mill property in Mescalero)**

FROM CHARLES C. CATRON

Catron, Charles C. "My father probably spent over a million dollars in following up his hobby [of politics]." Letter to Major Harry F. Cameron. **June 3, 1921.** Catron Papers 101, Box 29. Quoted by Victor Westphall, *Thomas Benton Catron and His Era.* Page 387. **(Revealing possible political bribery)**

FROM, TO, ABOUT JAMES J. DOLAN

Dolan, James J. "I want to borrow from you about one thousand dollars ..." Letter to T.B. Catron. **December 14, 1889.** University of New Mexico Library. Center for Southwest Studies. Thomas B. Catron Papers, MSS 29, Series 102, Box 5, Folder 5.

_____. "I wish you would try & carry that note ..." Letter to T.B. Catron. **July 9, 1890.** University of New Mexico Library. Center for Southwest Studies. Thomas B. Catron Papers, MSS 29, Series 102, Box 8, Folder 1.

_____. "Will you do me the kindness to send me a personal letter to S.B. Elkins ..." Letter to T.B. Catron. **October 15, 1891**. University of New Mexico Library. Center for Southwest Studies. Thomas B. Catron Papers, MSS 29, Series 102, Box 12, Folder 2.

_____. "It looks like we may be left ..." Letter to T.B. Catron. **November 26, 1892**. University of New Mexico Library. Center for Southwest Studies. Thomas B. Catron Papers, MSS 29, Series 102, Box 16, Folder 7.

_____. "I met with Curry on the street this Evening ..." Letter to T.B. Catron. **October 6, 1894**. University of New Mexico Library. Center for Southwest Studies. Thomas B. Catron Papers, MSS 29, Series 401, Box 1, Folder 5. (**Dolan as Catron's Lincoln spy**)

_____. "You no doubt have noticed that cowardly slanderous article against me ..." Letter to T.B. Catron. **June 11, 1995**. University of New Mexico Library. Center for Southwest Studies. Thomas B. Catron Papers, MSS 29, Series 102, Box 25, Folder 6. (**Using Catron to prosecute his political enemies**)

Dolan, James J. "Your favor of the 2nd ins't received, I have delayed answering it until after my trip to Lincoln ..." Letter to T.B. Catron. **February 23, 1897**. University of New Mexico Library. Center for Southwest Studies. Thomas B. Catron Papers, MSS 29, Series 106, Box 2, Folder 4. (**Attacking Lincoln County War politician Florencio Gonzales**)

FROM AND ABOUT DAVID M. EASTON AND WIFE

Easton, David M. "While in Santa Fe I several times sought an opportunity to see you ..." Letter to T.B. Catron. **April 8, 1889.** University of New Mexico Library. Center for Southwest Studies. Thomas B. Catron Papers, MSS 29, Series 102, Box 3, Folder 4. (**About being in debt to Catron and wanting Catron to make him Mescalero Indian Reservation Agent to pay it back; and entanglement with William Rynerson and John Riley**)

_____. "I would like to know about time you can come up ..." Letter to W.H.H. Llewellyn. **April 17, 1890.** University of New Mexico Library. Center for Southwest Studies. Thomas B. Catron Papers, MSS 29, Series 102, Box 7, Folder 2. (**Trying to settle business with Catron**)

_____. "I am in receipt of a letter from Maj Llewellyn ..." Letter to T.B. Catron. **May 15, 1890.** University of New Mexico Library. Center for Southwest Studies. Thomas B. Catron Papers, MSS 29, Series 102, Box 7, Folder 3. (**Easton in trying to sell all his Mescalero property to Catron, mentions that John Riley and William Rynerson are part owners of Joseph Blazer's mill property in Mescalero**)

_____. "Maj Llewellyn informed me personally ..." Letter to T.B. Catron. **November 15, 1891.** University of New Mexico Library. Center for Southwest Studies. Thomas B. Catron Papers, MSS 29, Series 102, Box 12, Folder 4. (**Still trying to get an answer of resolving his loan to Catron**)

Easton, Lizzie A. "Mr. Easton is absent from home ..." Letter to T.B. Catron. **April 2, 1894.** University of New Mexico Library. Center for Southwest Studies. Thomas B. Catron Papers, MSS 29, Series 102, Box 21, Folder 4.

Easton, Davin M. "Your letter of the 13th inst in answer ..." Letter to T.B. Catron. **July 24, 1894.** University of New Mexico Library. Center for Southwest Studies. Thomas B. Catron Papers, MSS 29, Series 102, Box 22, Folder 3. (**Catron sadistically toyed with Easton about the land deal**)

_____. "As you have failed to make a legal appraisement ..." Letter to W.H.H. Llewellyn. **July 25, 1894.** University of New Mexico Library. Center for Southwest Studies. Thomas B. Catron Papers, MSS 29, Series 102, Box 22, Folder 3. (**Easton fired appraiser Llewellyn**)

Galleger, __. "I am about to buy the farm of Dave Easton's ..." Letter to T.B. Catron. **April 11, 1898.** University of New Mexico Library. Center for Southwest Studies.

Thomas B. Catron Papers, MSS 29, Series 103, Box 5, Folder 1. **(Shows Easton had Catron as mortgage holder)**

FROM AND TO STEPHEN BENTON ELKINS

Elkins, Stephen Benton. "I beg to acknowledge the receipt of yours of the 15th inst. ..." Letter to T.B. Catron. **August 19, 1892.** University of New Mexico Library. Center for Southwest Studies. Thomas B. Catron Papers, MSS 29, Series 102, Box 15, Folder 5. **(Confirming his directing the requested appointment; and advising Catron that becoming Senator was more important than becoming Territorial Delegate)**

_____. "Kerens sent me your letter. Letter to T.B. Catron. **December 4, 1897.** University of New Mexico Library. Center for Southwest Studies. Thomas B. Catron Papers, MSS 29, Series 103, Box 4, Folder 2. **(Tried to influence the President and Attorney General to get Catron appointed U.S. Attorney)**

_____. "Your letter from Las Vegas received ..." Letter to T.B. Catron. **June 14, 1901.** University of New Mexico Library. Center for Southwest Studies. Thomas B. Catron Papers, MSS 29, Series 103, Box 13, Folder 1. **(Informing that Miguel Otero was appointed governor despite Elkins's efforts to the contrary)**

Catron, Thomas Benton. "I understand from the press dispatches last night that the bill for the admission of New Mexico ..." **February 1, 1910.** Letter to S.B. Elkins. University of New Mexico Library. Center for Southwest Studies. Thomas B. Catron Papers, MSS 29, Series 105, Volume 29, Pages 374-376. **(Using Elkins as a Washington insider source to block federal control of New Mexico's public lands and irrigation)**

_____. "I have your letter and am sorry to hear that you are not feeling well ..." **September 19, 1910.** Letter to S.B. Elkins. University of New Mexico Library. Center for Southwest Studies. Thomas B. Catron Papers, MSS 29, Series 105, Volume 30, Page 116. **(Feels his chances for senatorship are good)**

(SEE: Stephen Benton Elkins; Thomas Benton Catron topics on U.S. Attorney resignation, assassination attempt on, disbarment attempt on)

ABOUT BY MARSH GIDDINGS

Giddings, Marsh. "To defeat Catron's confirmation [as U.S. Attorney] a grossly false affidavit [by August Kirchner] has been sent to Senator [Lyman Trumbull]." **Month (?) 1872.** Telegram from Governor Marsh Giddings to Washington, D.C. Attorney General George H. Williams. From Victor Westphall. *Thomas Benton Catron and His Era.* Page 107. **(About the 1872 legislature's actions against Palen and Catron)**

TO JAMES J. HAGERMAN

Catron, Thomas Benton. "[If your son] is to be appointed, I shall be very pleased ... if he will take immediate steps to have the "Augean stables" cleaned ..." Letter to James J. Hagerman. **November 22, 1905. (Wanting appointment as Attorney General to maliciously prosecute opponents)** Quoted in Mary Elizabeth Sluga's masters thesis, Pages 87-88.

FROM JOHN H. KOOGLER

Koogler, John H. "I will start for Kansas City to-morrow ..." Letter to T.B. Catron. **July 17, 1889.** University of New Mexico Library. Center for Southwest Studies. Thomas B. Catron Papers, MSS 29, Series 102, Box 4, Folder 3. **(Pleading for money)**

_____. "I wrote you before I left Las Vegas ..." Letter to T.B. Catron. **July 29, 1889**. University of New Mexico Library. Center for Southwest Studies. Thomas B. Catron Papers, MSS 29, Series 102, Box 4, Folder 4. (**Pleading for money**)

_____. "Mr. Gorther in sending me the balance of the testimony in the case of Doloritas Martin ..." Letter to T.B. Catron. **August 14, 1890**. University of New Mexico Library. Center for Southwest Studies. Thomas B. Catron Papers. MSS 29, Series 102, Box 8, Folder 4. (**About fees for legal work for Catron**)

FROM JACOB BASIL "BILLY" MATTHEWS

Matthews, Jacob Basil. "I congratulate you upon your nomination ..." Letter to T.B. Catron. **August 30, 1892**. University of New Mexico Library. Center for Southwest Studies. Thomas B. Catron Papers, MSS 29, Series 102, Box 16, Folder 1.

TO MARY McPHERSON COMPLAINT

Catron, Thomas Benton. "Answering Charges of Mary E. McPherson." **February 24, 1877**. Letter to Attorney General Alphonso Taft. Interior Department Papers 1850-1907; Appointments Division and Subsequent Actions. Microfilm File Case Number 44-4-8-3. Record Group 48. Microfilm Roll M750. National Archives and Records Administration. U.S. Department of Justice. Washington, D.C. (**Letter denying McPherson's charges**)

ABOUT LAWRENCE GUSTAV MURPHY

Gilliam, W.J. " I have been told you were administrator of Murphys estate. ..." Letter to T.B. Catron. **April 24, 1895**. University of New Mexico Library. Center for Southwest Studies. Thomas B. Catron Papers, MSS 29, Series 102, Box 25, Folder 3.

FROM MELVIN WHITSON MILLS

Mills, Melvin W. "Would you take a little of the political situation as we have it here ..." Letter to T.B. Catron. **February 1, 1889**. University of New Mexico Library. Center for Southwest Studies. Thomas B. Catron Papers, MSS 29, Series 102, Box 2, Folder 4.

_____. "Yours of recent date at hand." Letter to T.B. Catron. **August 2, 1892**. University of New Mexico Library. Center for Southwest Studies. Thomas B. Catron Papers, MSS 29, Series 102, Box 15, Folder 3. (**Coaching and advising Catron for Delegate election**)

_____. "Will you go over to Mora Court ..." Letter to T.B. Catron. **October 13, 1892**. University of New Mexico Library. Center for Southwest Studies. Thomas B. Catron Papers, MSS 29, Series 102, Box 16, Folder 4. (**Political machinations with Catron and Frank Springer**)

_____. "Up at the Court House today the question of the power of the President to respite the Borregos ..." Letter to T.B. Catron. **February 22, 1897**. University of New Mexico Library. Center for Southwest Studies. Thomas B. Catron Papers, MSS 29, Series 106, Box 2, Folder 4. (**Helping in Borrego case**)

_____."There are a few men who are candidates [for Senator] that I guess have some money ..." Letter to T.B. Catron. **September 12, 1911**. Catron Papers 103, Box 37. Quoted by Victor Westphall, *Thomas Benton Catron and His Era*. Page 350. (**Revealing possible bribery for legislators' vote**)

FROM, TO, ABOUT MIGUEL OTERO

Otero, Miguel A. "At the time of the Rep. Convention in this City ..." Letter to T.B. Catron. **October 25, 1888.** University of New Mexico Library. Center for Southwest Studies. Thomas B. Catron Papers, MSS 29, Series 102, Box 1, Folder 5.(**Documents a pay off to remove a candidate for a clerkship**)

Catron, Thomas Benton. "You must see that Otero is not reappointed ..." Letter to Stephen Benton Elkins. **November 11, 1901.** Quoted in Mary Elizabeth Sluga's masters thesis, Page 79.

_____. "[Otero backers] have made a very villainous, mean ugly fight against me." **September 20, 1902.** Letter to Dave Winters. Catron Papers 105, Volume 20. Quoted by Victor Westphall, *Thomas Benton Catron and His Era.* Pages 291. (**Accusing Governor Otero of his own Ring-style criminality**)

FROM, TO, ABOUT JOHN HENRY RILEY

Riley, John H. "Today mailed Senator Edmunds my affidavit corroborated by Dolan against Fiske ..." Letter to T.B Catron. **February 5, 1890.** University of New Mexico Library. Center for Southwest Studies. Thomas B. Catron Papers, MSS 29, Series 102, Box 6, Folder 1.

_____. "Ought you not see to the matter of the Wilson Waddingham tract of land ..." Letter to T.B. Catron. **June 19, 1890.** University of New Mexico Library. Center for Southwest Studies. Thomas B. Catron Papers, MSS 29, Series 102, Box 7, Folder 4. (**Lookout for land for Catron**)

_____. "Rynerson and I wish to talk with you ..." Letter to T.B. Catron. **December 19, 1891.** University of New Mexico Library. Center for Southwest Studies. Thomas B. Catron Papers, MSS 29, Series 102, Box 12, Folder 6.

_____. "I can now recommend to you a foreman ..." Letter to T.B. Catron. **January 27, 1892.** University of New Mexico Library. Center for Southwest Studies. Thomas B. Catron Papers, MSS 29, Series 102, Box 13, Folder 2.

_____. "Rynerson and I called on Hughes (Levi) last night ..." Letter to T.B. Catron. **February 9, 1892.** University of New Mexico Library. Center for Southwest Studies. Thomas B. Catron Papers, MSS 29, Series 102, Box 13, Folder 4.

_____. "Yours notifying me of having drawn on me favor ..." Letter to T.B. Catron. **May 13, 1894.** University of New Mexico Library. Center for Southwest Studies. Thomas B. Catron Papers, MSS 29, Series 102, Box 21, Folder 6.

FROM WILLIAM LOGAN RYNERSON

Rynerson, William. "I notice what you say in relation to having mutual understanding ..." Letter to T.B. Catron. **November 11, 1888.** University of New Mexico Library. Center for Southwest Studies. Thomas B. Catron Papers, MSS 29, Series 102, Box 2, Folder 1.

_____. "I was close after you ..." Letter to T.B. Catron. **December 28, 1888.** University of New Mexico Library. Center for Southwest Studies. Thomas B. Catron Papers, MSS 29, Series 102, Box 2, Folder 3. (**Shoes that Rynerson traveled to Washington for the Ring, meeting Elkins and influencing the** *New York Tribune*)

_____. "Riley is away over at Lincoln ..." Letter to T.B. Catron. **April 13, 1891.** University of New Mexico Library. Center for Southwest Studies. Thomas B. Catron Papers, MSS 29, Series 102, Box 10, Folder 7.

FROM AND TO RALPH EMERSON TWITCHELL

Twitchell, Ralph Emerson. "I enclose you herewith a letter from Mr. Hughes, the editor of the Citizen ...." **September 26, 1892.** Letter to T.B. Catron. University of New Mexico Library. Center for Southwest Studies. Thomas B. Catron Papers, MSS 29, Series 401, Box 1, Folder 3. **(Advising a pay-off of press owner Hughes)**
Gregg, George W. "I have your letter from parties in this county ..." **October 22, 1892.** Letter to R.E. Twitchell. University of New Mexico Library. Center for Southwest Studies. Thomas B. Catron Papers, MSS 29, Series 401, Box 1, Folder 3. **(Planning possible vote buying for Catron)**

Riley, John H. "I suggest you get out in Spanish a number of copies of your letter ..." Letter to Ralph E. Twitchell. **October 24, 1907.** University of New Mexico Library. Center for Southwest Studies. Thomas B. Catron Papers, MSS 29, Series 401-409, Box 1, Folder 3. **(Using Twitchell to fix votes for Catron)**

FROM EDGAR WALZ

Walz, Edgar. "I have often while in New Mexico heard ..." Letter to T.B. Catron. **June 8, 1897.** University of New Mexico Library. Center for Southwest Studies. Thomas B. Catron Papers, MSS 29, Series 103, Box 3, Folder 1.

ABOUT LEW WALLACE

Catron, Thomas Benton. "He [Lew Wallace] and I were not on friendly terms while he was governor." Letter to Stephen Benton Elkins. **August 4, 1897.** **(About Wallace's opposition to his reappointment as U.S. Attorney)** Quoted in Mary Elizabeth Sluga's masters thesis, Page 50.

OBITUARIES FOR

Johnson, E. Dana. "[H]e ruled with a rod of iron ..." Editorial Obituary. *Santa Fe New Mexican.* **May 16, 1921.** Catron Papers 801, Box 1. Quoted by Victor Westphall, *Thomas Benton Catron and His Era.* Pages 394-395. **(Hinted at tactics of "boss" Catron without using the words Santa Fe Ring)**
Pritchard, George W. "Eulogy." **May 17, 1921.** University of New Mexico Library. Center for Southwest Studies. Thomas B. Catron Papers, MSS 29, Series 104. Box 1, Folder 3. **(**Quoted by Victor Westphall, *Thomas Benton Catron and His Era.* Pages 393-394.**) (Cover-up of his Ring and his atrocities)**

(SEE: Stephen Benton Elkins; Santa Fe Ring, Mary Tibbles McPherson, Lincoln County War)

CHAPMAN, HUSTON INGRAM

CONTEMPORARY SOURCES (CHRONOLOGICAL)

Wallace, Lew. "I enclose you a copy of a letter from Las Vegas ..." Letter to Edward Hatch. **October 28, 1878.** Indiana Historical Society. Lew Wallace Collection. M0292. Box 3. Folder 16. **(Forwards Chapman's letter to Hatch)**
_____. "In a communication, dated October 28. inst., I requested, for reasons stated, a safe-guard for Mrs. McSween ..." Letter to Edward Hatch. **November 9, 1878.** Indiana Historical Society. Lew Wallace Collection. M0292. Box 3. Folder 17.
No Author. (signed E.). "Death of Chapman." *Las Vegas Gazette.* **March 1, 1879.** From *Proceedings of a Court of Inquiry in the Case of Lt. Col. N.A.M. Dudley (May 2,1879 – July 5, 1879).* File No. QQ1284. (Boxes 3304, 3305, 3305A); Court Martial Files 1809-1894. Records of the Office of the Judge Advocate General – Army.

Record Group 153. Old Military and Civil Branch. National Archives and Records Administration. Washington, D. C.

No Author. "Wallace and Lincoln County." Grant County *Herald*. **March 1, 1879**. Indiana Historical Society. The Papers of Lew and Susan Wallace. Microfilm Edition. Indianapolis, Indiana: Indiana Historical Society Press. 2008.

Chapman, W.W. "Yours of the 1ˢᵗ inst. came ..." Letter to Ira E. Leonard. **March 20, 1879**. Indiana Historical Society. Lew Wallace Collection. M0292. Box 4. Folder 6.

Rynerson, William. "The Grand Jurors for the Territory of New Mexico taken from the body of the good and lawful men of the County of Lincoln ..." Indictments of the April, Lincoln County Grand Jury. **April 28, 1879**. Herman B. Weisner Papers, ca. 1957-1992. New Mexico State University Library at Las Cruces. Rio Grande Historical Collection. Accession No. Ms 0249. Box 4/39. Folder E-Z. Folder Name: "Jessie Evans Accessory to Murder." (**Billy's testimony indicts J.J. Dolan, Billy Campbell, and Jessie Evans fulfilling his pardon bargain**)

Chapman, W.W. "Since receiving yours of the 1ˢᵗ March ..." Letter to Ira Leonard. **May 8, 1879**. Indiana Historical Society. Lew Wallace Collection. M0292. Box 4. Folder 10.

LETTERS BY

Chapman, Huston I. "You will please pardon me for presuming so much upon your kindness ..." Letter to Lew Wallace. **October 24, 1878**. Indiana Historical Society. Lew Wallace Collection. M0292. Box 3. Folder 16. (**Makes clear N.A.M. Dudley's danger to Susan McSween**)

_____. *'You attach much importance to the awe-inspiring influence of the military* ..." Letter to Lew Wallace. **November 25, 1878**. From Frederick Nolan, *The Lincoln County War,* p. 359.

_____. "You must pardon me for so often presuming upon your kindness ..." Letter to Lew Wallace. **November 29, 1878**. Indiana Historical Society. Lew Wallace Collection. M0292. Box 3. Folder 18.

CHISUM, JOHN SIMPSON

Hinton, Harwood P., Jr. "John Simpson Chisum, 1877-84." *New Mexico Historical Review* 31(3) (July 1956): 177 - 205; 31(4) (October 1956): 310 - 337; 32(1) (January 1957): 53 - 65.

Klasner, Lilly. Eve Ball. Ed. *My Girlhood Among Outlaws*. Tucson, Arizona: The University of Arizona Press. 1972. (**Contains John Chisum's in jail write-up about Santa Fe Ring injustices to himself**)

COE FAMILY

BIOGRAPHICAL SOURCES

Coe, George. Doyce B. Nunis, Jr. Ed. *Frontier Fighter. The Autobiography of George Coe Who Fought and Rode With Billy the Kid.* Chicago: R. R. Donnelley and Sons Company. 1984.

Coe, Wilbur. *Ranch on the Ruidoso. The Story of a Pioneer Family in New Mexico, 1871 - 1968.* New York: Alfred A. Knopf. 1968.

DEDRICK BROTHERS

BIOGRAPHICAL SOURCES

Upham, Elizabeth. (Related by marriage to Daniel Dedrick). Personal interviews. 1998.

Upham, Marquita. (Relative by marriage to Daniel Dedrick). Personal interview. 1998.

CONTEMPORARY SOURCES (CHRONOLOGICAL)

Dedrick, Dan. "I have been under an arrest for six days ..." **April 5, 1879**. Letter to Lew Wallace. Indiana Historical Society. Lew Wallace Collection. M0292. Box 4. Folder 8. **(Says he was not told his arrest charges)**

No Author. "Arrests of Dedricks. Legal Documents." Herman B. Weisner Papers, ca. 1957-1992. New Mexico State University Library at Las Cruces. Rio Grande Historical Collections. Accession No. Ms 0249. Box 1. Folder B-8. Folder Name: "Lincoln County Bonds."

DOLAN, JAMES JOSEPH

BIOGRAPHICAL SOURCE

Slates, Thomas. "The James J. Dolan House, Lincoln New Mexico." *New Mexico Architecture* 11. 8/9 (1969). pp. 17-20.**(With Dolan biography)**

CONTEMPORARY SOURCES BY AND ABOUT (CHRONOLOGICAL)

Tunstall, John Henry. "A Taxpayer's Complaint ... January 18, 1878." Mesilla *Independent*. **January 26, 1878. (Exposé of William Brady, James Dolan, and John Riley for tax fraud and use of public money to purchase cattle; and T.B. Catron then paid that bill)**

Dolan, James J. "Answer to A Taxpayer's Complaint." Mesilla *Independent*. **January 29, 1878. (Response to J.H. Tunstall's exposé of him, William Brady, and John Riley for tax fraud and use of public money to purchase cattle; and T.B. Catron then paid that bill)**

McSween, Alexander. "It looks as though the agent were the property of J.J. Dolan & J.H. Riley, known here as Dolan & Co." Letter to Secretary of Interior Carl Schurz. **February 11, 1878**. From Frederick Nolan. *The Life and Death of John Henry Tunstall*. Albuquerque, New Mexico: The University of New Mexico Press. 1965. Page 266.

Rynerson, William. "Friends Riley & Dolan, Lincoln N.M. I have just received letters from you mailed 10th inst." **February 14, 1878**. Letter to James Dolan and John Riley. Copy as Exhibit B in June 6, 1878 deposition of Alexander McSween. Frank Warner Angel report. *In the Matter of the Examination of the Causes and Circumstances of the Death of John H. Tunstall a British Subject.* Report filed October 4, 1878. Frank Warner Angel report. Interior Department Papers 1850-1907; Appointments Division and Subsequent Actions. Microfilm File Case Number 44-4-8-3. Record Group 48. Microfilm No. M750. Roll 1. National Archives and Records Administration. U.S. Department of Justice. Washington, D.C. (James J. Dolan Deposition. June 20, 1878. Pages 235-247.) **(Implying planned killing of J.H. Tunstall)**

Wilson, John, George B. Barker, Robert M. Gilbert, John Newcomb, Samuel Smith, Benjamin Ellis. "We the undersigned Justice of the Peace and Coroners Jury who sat upon the inquest held this 19th day of February 1878 on the body of John H. Tunstall ..." Coroner's Jury Report for John Tunstall. **February 19, 1878. (Naming the murderers as, among others, James Dolan, Frank Baker, Jessie Evans, William Morton, and George Hindman)**

Dolan, James. "On my arrival at Fort Stanton, I repeated Your Explanation &c to the Comd'g Officer (Gen'l Dudley) ..." Letter to Lew Wallace. **December 31, 1878**. Indiana Historical Society. Lew Wallace Collection. M0292. Box 3. Folder 19.

Rynerson, William. "The Grand Jurors for the Territory of New Mexico taken from the body of the good and lawful men of the County of Lincoln ..." Indictments of the April, Lincoln County Grand Jury. **April 28, 1879**. Herman B. Weisner Papers, ca. 1957-1992. New Mexico State University Library at Las Cruces. Rio Grande Historical Collection. Accession No. Weisner MS 249. Box 4/39. Folder E-Z.

Folder Name: "Jessie Evans Accessory to Murder." **(Billy Bonney's testimony indicts J.J. Dolan, Billy Campbell, and Jessie Evans for pardon bargain)**

Leonard, Ira E. "When you left here I promised to write you concerning events transpiring here ..." Letter to Lew Wallace. **May 20, 1878 [sic - 79]**. Indiana Historical Society. Lew Wallace Collection. M0292. Box 4. Folder 10. **(Has quote on the Murphy-Dolan party as: "part and parcel of the Santa Fe ring that has been so long an incubus on the government of this territory.")**

_____. "Yours of the 7th inst reached me ..." Letter to Lew Wallace. **June 13, 1879**. Indiana Historical Society. Lew Wallace Collection. M0292. Box 4. Folder 11. **(Important quotes: "... they would not enter our objections ..." "... would not allow us to show the conspiracy formed with Dolan beforehand ..." "I tell you Governor as long as the present incumbent occupies the bench all that Grand Juries may do to bring to justice these men every effort will be thwarted by him and the sympathizers of that side.")**

No Author. "Dismissal of Cases Against Dolan, Matthews, Peppin, October 1879 District Court." **October, 1879**. Herman B. Weisner Papers, ca. 1957-1992. New Mexico State University Library at Las Cruces. Rio Grande Historical Collections. Accession No. Ms 0249. Box 13. Folder V3. Folder Name: "Venue, Change Of."

No Author. "Lincoln County Indictments **July 1872 - 1881**." Herman B. Weisner Papers, ca. 1957-1992. New Mexico State University Library at Las Cruces. Rio Grande Historical Collections. Accession No. Ms 0249. Box 8. Folder L11. Folder Name. "Lincoln Co. Indictments."

Wild, Azariah F. "Daily Reports of U. S. Secret Service Agents, Azariah F. Wild." Microfilm T-915. Record Group 87. Rolls 307 (January 1,1878 - June 30, 1879) and 308 **(July 1, 1879 - June 30, 1881)**. National Archives and Records Department. Department of the Treasury. United States Secret Service. Washington, D. C. **(Dolan as an informer against "the Kid gang")**

LETTERS BY (CHRONOLOGICAL)

LETTERS TO THOMAS BENTON CATRON (SEE THOMAS BENTON CATRON)

LETTERS TO LEW WALLACE

Dolan, James J. "On my arrival at Fort Stanton, I repeated Your Explanation &c to the Comd'g Officer (Gen'l Dudley) ..." Letter to Lew Wallace. **December 31, 1878**. Indiana Historical Society. Lew Wallace Collection. M0292. Box 3. Folder 19.

_____. "Attorney Wilson told me yesterday that 'your life was threatened' ..." Letter to Lew Wallace. **December 31, 1878**. Indiana Historical Society. Lew Wallace Collection. M0292. Box 4. Folder 7.

_____. "I hear from reliable authority that it has been reported to you that I was one of a party ..." Letter to Lew Wallace. **March 14, 1879**. Indiana Historical Society. Lew Wallace Collection. M0292. Box 4. Folder 5.

DUDLEY, NATHAN AUGUSTUS MONROE

BIOGRAPHICAL SOURCES

Kaye, E. Donald. *Nathan Augustus Monroe Dudley: Rogue, Hero, or Both?* Parker, Colorado: Outskirts Press, Inc. 2007.

Oliva, Leo E., *Fort Union and the Frontier Army in the Southwest*. Southwest Cultural Resource Center, Professional Papers No. 41, National Park Service, 1993, Pages 488-489, 550, 574, 624-626, 656-659 are on Dudley. **(Quoted to E. Donald Kaye: "I guess you heard that Dudley made Colonel. The army bureaucracy is like a giant cesspool, where the biggest chunks rise to the top.")**

POSSE COMITATUS ACT ISSUE FOR

No Author. *Regulations of the Army of the United States,* Washington, D.C.: Government Printing Office. 1891.

No Author. "The Army as a Posse Comitatus." *The Internal Revenue and Customs Journal.* October 14, 1878. New York: C.&F.P. Church. 1878.

MILITARY COURT OF INQUIRY FOR

Leonard, Ira E. "*Charges and specifications against Lieutenant Colonel N.A.M. Dudley, Commander at Fort Stanton, New Mexico.*" **March 4, 1879**. Letter to Secretary of War George McCrary. *Proceedings of a Court of Inquiry in the Case of Lt. Col. N.A.M. Dudley (May 2,1879 - July 5, 1879).* File No. QQ1284. (Boxes 3304, 3305, 3305A); Court Martial Files 1809-1894. Records of the Office of the Judge Advocate General - Army. Record Group 153. Old Military and Civil Branch. National Archives and Records Administration. Washington, D. C. (**Charges against Dudley for murders of A.A. McSween and H.I. Chapman and arson of McSween's house**)

No Author. *Proceedings of a Court of Inquiry in the Case of Lt. Col. N.A.M. Dudley (May 2,1879 – July 5, 1879).* File No. QQ1284. (Boxes 3304, 3305, 3305A); Court Martial Files 1809-1894. Records of the Office of the Judge Advocate General - Army. Record Group 153. Old Military and Civil Branch. National Archives and Records Administration. Washington, D. C.

OTHER CONTEMPORARY SOURCES FOR (CHRONOLOGICAL)

Dudley, Nathan Augustus Monroe. "I am in receipt of a copy of letter written by one H.I. Chapman, calling himself the Attorney ..." **November 9, 1878**. Letter to Lew Wallace. From *Proceedings of a Court of Inquiry in the Case of Lt. Col. N.A.M. Dudley (May 2,1879 – July 5, 1879).* File No. QQ1284. (Boxes 3304, 3305, 3305A); Court Martial Files 1809-1894. Records of the Office of the Judge Advocate General – Army. Record Group 153. Old Military and Civil Branch. National Archives and Records Administration. Washington, D.C. (**Forwarding the Susan McSween affidavits in answer to the charges made by Chapman**)

Wallace, Lew. "I am in receipt of Col. Dudley's reply to the charges against him ..." Letter to Edward Hatch. **November 14, 1878**. Indiana Historical Society. Lew Wallace Collection. M0292. Box 3. Folder 17. (**Has quote: "the "reply is perfectly satisfactory"**)

_____. "I am constrained to request that Lieut Col. N.A.M. Dudley, Commanding at Fort Stanton, be relieved ..." Letter to Edward Hatch. **December 7, 1878**. Indiana Historical Society. Lew Wallace Collection. M0292. Box 3. Folder 18.

Dudley, Nathan Augustus Monroe. "An Open Letter, By Lieut. Col. N.A.M. Dudley, 9th Cavalry, to His Excellency Governor Lew Wallace." Letter to Lew Wallace. Santa Fe *Weekly New Mexican.* **December 14, 1878**. Reprinted in *Mesilla News.* December 21, 1878. As Exhibit 13 from *Proceedings of a Court of Inquiry in the Case of Lt. Col. N.A.M. Dudley (May 2,1879 – July 5, 1879).* File No. QQ1284. (Boxes 3304, 3305, 3305A); Court Martial Files 1809-1894. Records of the Office of the Judge Advocate General – Army. Record Group 153. Old Military and Civil Branch. National Archives and Records Administration. Washington, D.C.

_____. "I have the honor to repeat the request made on a former occasion that Lt. Col. N.A.M. Dudley be relieved of the command ..." Letter to Edward Hatch. **March 7, 1879**. Indiana Historical Society. Lew Wallace Collection. M0292. Box 4, Folder 4.

Hatch, Edward. "Lieutenant Colonel N.A.M. Dudley is hereby relieved from command and duty ..." Special Field Order 2. **March 8, 1879**. Indiana Historical Society. Lew Wallace Collection. M0292. Box 4, Folder 4. (**Wallace succeeds in removing Dudley**)

Wallace, Lew. "I have official information that a court of inquiry for Col. Dudley has been ordered ..." Letter to Carl Schurz. **April 4, 1879**. Indiana Historical Society. Lew Wallace Collection. M0292. Box 4. Folder 8.

Purington, George Augustus. "The District Court adjourned on Thursday ..." **May 3, 1879**. Letter to Adjutant General. Indiana Historical Society. Lew Wallace Collection. M0292. Box 4. Folder 10.

No Author. Verdict on Civil Cause 298 for arson of Susan McSween's house. *Mesilla News*. **December 6, 1879**. Unpublished. personal communication from Frederick Nolan. July 29, 2005. **(Dudley exonerated)**

ELKINS, STEPHEN BENTON

BIOGRAPHICAL SOURCES

Cleaveland, Norman, *A Synopsis of the Great New Mexico Cover-up*. Self-printed. 1989.
_____. *The Great Santa Fe Cover-up. Based on a Talk given Before the Santa Fe Historical Society on November 1, 1978*. Self-printed. 1982.
_____. *The Morleys - Young Upstarts on the Southwest Frontier*. Albuquerque, New Mexico: Calvin Horn Publisher, Inc. 1971.

Lamar, Howard Robert N. *The Far Southwest 1846 – 1912: A Territorial History*. New Haven and London: Yale University Press. 1966. **(Chapter 6 on Santa Fe Ring)**

Lambert, Oscar Doane. *Stephen Benton Elkins. American Foursquare*. Pittsburgh, Pennsylvania: University of Pittsburg Press. 1955.

Montoya, María E. *Translating Property. The Maxwell Land Grant and the Conflict Over Land in the American West, 1840-1900*. Berkeley and Los Angeles: University of California Press. 2002.

Taylor, Morris F. *O.P. McMains and the Maxwell Land Grant Conflict*. Tucson, Arizona: The University of Arizona Press. 1979. **(Traces origins of the Santa Fe Ring with T.B. Catron and S.B. Elkins)**

Westphall, Victor. *Thomas Benton Catron and His Era*. Tucson, Arizona: University of Arizona Press. 1973.

SECRET CODE WITH T.B. CATRON BY

Elkins, Stephen Benton. "Elkins – Telegraph Cipher, Cipher with Catron." Mailed to T.B. Catron. ___ 1878? University of New Mexico Library. Center for Southwest Studies. Thomas B. Catron Papers, MSS 29, Series 108, Box 1, Folder 4. **(Ring code-cipher key about T.B. Catron's resignation as U.S. Attorney)**

LETTERS TO, FROM, ABOUT THOMAS BENTON CATRON BY (SEE THOMAS BENTON CATRON)

VOTE FIXING BY

Elkins, Stephen Benton. "I have just seen the Probate Judge of Valencia County about the throwing out of the vote of that County ..." **October 8, 1873**. Letter to W.G. Ritch. University of New Mexico Library. Center for Southwest Studies. Thomas B. Catron Papers, MSS 29, Series 409, Box 1, Folder 2. **(Vote manipulation)**

INTERVENING WITH FRANK WARNER ANGEL REPORT AND CATRON'S U.S. ATTORNEY DISMISSAL BY (CHRONOLOGICAL)

Elkins, Stephen Benton. "Asking delay of action upon charges against U.S. Atty. Catron ..." Letter about Angel Report. **September 24, 1878**. Angel Report. Microfilm File Case No. 44-4-8-3. Record Group 48. National Records and Archives Administration. Microfilm No. M750. Roll 1. U.S. Department of Justice. Washington, D. C.
_____. "Regarding Attorney General's decision on T.B. Catron." Letter. **September___, 1878**. Angel Report. Microfilm File Case No. 44-4-8-3. Record

Group 48. National Records and Archives Administration. Microfilm No. M750. Roll 1. U.S. Department of Justice. Washington, D.C.

_____. "Relative to resignation of T. B. Catron U. S. Attorney." Letter. **November 10, 1878**. Angel Report. Microfilm File Case No. 44-4-8-3. Record Group 48. National Records and Archives Administration. Microfilm No. M750. Roll 1. U.S. Department of Justice. Washington, D. C.

Devens, Charles. "To honorable S. B. Elkins re. T. B. Catron continuing to act as U.S. Attorney." Letter to Stephen B. Elkins. **November 12, 1878**. Angel Report. Microfilm File Case No. 44-4-8-3. Record Group 48. National Records and Archives Administration. Microfilm No. M750. Roll 1. U.S. Department of Justice. Washington, D. C.

Elkins, Stephen Benton. "I have waited some time to reply to your lengthy letter ..." Letter to T.B. Catron. **August 15, 1879**. West Virginia & Regional History Center. West Virginia University Libraries, Morgantown, W. Va. Stephen B. Elkins Papers (A&M 53). Box 1. Folder 1. (**Reveals he prevented Catron's dismissal and indictment from Angel's report**)

ATTEMPTING REINSTATEMENT OF S.B. AXTELL BY

Elkins, Stephen Benton. "To the President. Referring to a conversation had with you last week ... Hon S. Elkins favors appointment Axtell, Ex Gov. as Gov'r of New Mexico". Letter to President James Abram Garfield. **March 17, 1881**. (Received Executive Mansion April 6, 1881). Interior Department Papers 1850-1907; Appointments Division and Subsequent Actions. Microfilm Roll M750. National Archives and Records Administration Record Group 48. Microfilm Case Number 44-4-8-3. U.S. Department of Interior. Washington D.C. (**Requesting S.B. Axtell reappointment as Territorial New Mexico Governor**)

_____. "I trouble you to say a word in behalf of Gov. Axtell ..." Letter to President Rutherford B. Hayes. **June 11, 1877**. (Referred by direction of President to the Secretary of the Interior June 13, 1877.) Interior Department Papers 1850-1907; Appointments Division and Subsequent Actions. Microfilm File Case No. 44-4-8-3. Record Group 48. National Records and Archives Administration. Microfilm No. M750. Roll 1. U.S. Department of Justice. Washington, D. C.

EXPOSÉS OF (CONTEMPORARY)

COMPLAINT ABOUT TO PRESIDENT RUTHERFORD B. HAYES

Matchett, W.B. and Mary E. McPherson. " W.B. Matchett and Mary E. McPherson 'Make certain charges against the U.S. Officials in the Territory of New Mexico.' " Letter to President Rutherford B. Hayes. Received and filed **May 1, 1877**. Interior Department Papers 1850-1907; Appointments Division and Subsequent Actions. Microfilm File Case Number 44-4-8-3. Record Group 48. Microfilm No. M750. Roll 1. National Archives and Records Administration. U. S. Department of Justice. Washington, D.C. (**Sent to President Rutherford B. Hayes and Secretary of the Interior Carl Schurz 141 pages of letters, affidavits, petitions, newspaper articles, itemized requests for removal of Governor Samuel Beach Axtell and District Judge Warren Bristol, documentation of use of the military against civilians, documentation of the Ring murder of Ring opponent Reverend F.J. Tolby, and identification of the Santa Fe Ring and Elkins and Carton as its leaders.**)

McPherson, Mary and W.B. Matchett. "To the President. Please make the enclosed a part of the evidence in the case of "Charges Against New Mexican Officials" Letter to President Rutherford B. Hayes. **May 3, 1877**. McPherson, Mary E. Letters and Petitions to President Rutherford B. Hayes re: Removal Governor Axtell and the Santa Fe Ring. Interior Department Papers 1850-1907; Appointments Division and Subsequent Actions. Microfilm File Case Number 44-4-8-3. Record Group 48.

Microfilm Roll M750. National Archives and Records Administration. U.S. Department of Justice. Washington, D.C. (**Addendum to their May, 1877 "Certain Charges Against U.S. Officials in New Mexico Territory."**)

McPherson, Mary and W.B. Matchett. "The Secretary of the Interior, Sir – Accompanying please find <u>copy</u> of charges, &c., against S.B. Axtell, Governor, and Other New Mexican Officials ..." "Charges Against New Mexican Officials." Letter to Secretary of the Interior Carl Schurz. **May 5, 1877**. McPherson, Mary E. Letters and Petitions to President Rutherford B. Hayes re: Removal Governor Axtell and the Santa Fe Ring. Interior Department Papers 1850-1907; Appointments Division and Subsequent Actions. Microfilm File Case Number 44-4-8-3. Record Group 48. Microfilm Roll M750. National Archives and Records Administration. U.S. Department of Justice. Washington, D. C.

McPherson, Mary. "Please place before the Attorney General ..." Letter to President Rutherford B. Hayes. **August 23, 1877**. Interior Department Papers 1850-1907; Appointments Division and Subsequent Actions. Microfilm File Case Number 44-4-8-3. Record Group 48. Microfilm No. M750. Roll 1. National Archives and Records Administration. U. S. Department of Justice. Washington, D.C. (**Requesting that her "Charges vs. New Mexico Officials" go to the Attorney General.**)

Morley, William Raymond. "Your letter of the 7th came last night and it was a good long newsy letter ..." Letter to wife, Ada McPherson Morley. **August 15, 1878**. Collection of Norman Cleaveland. Quoted in Norman Cleaveland, *The Morleys: Young Upstarts in the Southwest*. Albuquerque, New Mexico: Calvin Horn Publisher, Inc. 1971. Pages 152-155. (**About possible betrayal by Angel's reports; about the Santa Fe Ring, T.B. Catron, S.B. Elkins, S.B. Axtell, and Henry Waldo; and the Lincoln County War**)

COMPLAINT ABOUT TO DEPARTMENTS OF INTERIOR AND JUSTICE

McPherson, Mary and W.B. Matchett. *"In the Matter of Charges vs. Gov. S.B. Axtell and Other New Mexico Officials. Submitted to the Departments of the Interior and Justice.* **August, 1877.** Printed as a 31 page booklet. No publisher listed. Indiana Historical Society. Lew Wallace Collection. M0292. Box 3. Folder 20. (**About the Santa Fe Ring, Catron, and Elkins; in Lew Wallace's personal possession**)

Springer, Frank. Deposition to Investigator Frank Warner Angel for the Departments of Justice and the Interior. **August 9, 1878**. Frank Warner Angel report titled *In the Matter of the Investigation of the Charges Against S.B. Axtell Governor of New Mexico*. October 3, 1878. Interior Department Papers 1850-1907; Appointments Division and Subsequent Actions. Microfilm Case File No. 44-4-8-3. Record Group 48. Microfilm Roll M750. National Archives and Records Administration. U.S. Department of Interior. Washington, D.C. (**Mentions Catron, Elkins, and the Santa Fe Ring, and provided Exhibits of letters exposing Catron's evil.**)

PUBLIC RECORDS REQUEST ABOUT

McPherson, Mary and W.B. Matchett. "We have respectfully to request that the following named records, documents, papers, communications and correspondence be supplied ..." Records Request to Secretary of the Interior Carl Schurz. **July 26, 1877**. Interior Department Papers 1850-1907; Appointments Division and Subsequent Actions. Microfilm File Case Number 44-4-8-3. Record Group 48. Microfilm No. M750. Roll 1. National Archives and Records Administration. U. S. Department of Justice. Washington, D.C. (**Requesting records of the Santa Fe Ring, Carton, Elkins, and Axtell**)

ARTICLES ABOUT (CHRONOLOGICAL)

Morley, William Raymond and Frank Springer. On Oscar McMains's citizen's Meeting. *Cimarron News and Press.* **November 10, 1875.** In Mary McPherson, Letters and Petitions to President Rutherford B. Hayes re: Removal Governor Axtell and the Santa Fe Ring. 1977. Interior Department Papers 1850-1907; Appointments Division and Subsequent Actions. Microfilm File Case Number 44-4-8-3. **Record Group 48.** Microfilm Roll M750. National Archives and Records Administration. (**Colfax County citizens meeting on F.J. Tolby murder by Santa Fe Ring.**)

No Author. " 'The Territory of Elkins.' Assassination of Supposed Sun Correspondent. The Murder of the Rev. F.J. Tolby in New Mexico. A Probate Judge Accused of Complicity in the Crime. Indignation Meeting." *New York Weekly Sun.* **December 22, 1875.** Interior Department Papers 1850-1907; Appointments Division and Subsequent Actions. Microfilm Roll M750. National Archives and Records Administration. Record Group 48. Microfilm Case File Number 44-4-8-3. U. S. Department of Interior. Washington, D.C. (**In May 1, 1877 complaint to President Hayes as "Mary E. McPherson and W.B. Matchett 'Make certain charges against the U.S. Officials in the Territory of New Mexico.' "**)

No Author. "Elkins would probably have been Garfield's Secretary of the Interior ..." *New York Sun.* **June 13, 1881.** Quoted by Oscar Doane Lambert. *Stephen Benton Elkins: American Foursquare.* Page 89. (**Political influence of**)

Faulkner, C.J. "I will tell you the secret of Elkins' political as well as business success." Baltimore, Maryland *The Sun.* **December 17, 1891.** Quoted by Oscar Doane Lambert. *Stephen Benton Elkins: American Foursquare.* Page 141. (**Elkins's success from loyalty to friends**)

No Author. "T.B. Catron's reputation now being "smirched" by evidence that he was a briber and too dishonest even to practice law ..." *Las Vegas Independent Democrat.* **1895**; quoting from *Las Vegas Optic.* September 2, 1884. From Victor Westphall. *Thomas Benton Catron and His Era.* Pages 105-106. (**About Catron's and Elkins's dishonesty, the Ring, and disbarring Catron**)

No Author. "It seems that Senator Elkins was one of the five stockholders in the North American Commercial Company that had leased from the United States the sea Islands of Alaska." Cincinnati, Ohio *Commercial Tribune.* **June 8, 1897.** Quoted by Oscar Doane Lambert. *Stephen Benton Elkins: American Foursquare.* Pages 224-225. (**Elkins's tax violation cover-up**)

No Author. "He is the biggest man ... the State of West Virginia has ever had in the Senate of the United States." West Virginia *St. Mary's Journal.* **June 22, 1906.** From Oscar Doane Lambert. *Stephen Benton Elkins.* Page 286.

LETTERS TO, FROM, ABOUT (SEE: Thomas Benton Catron)

TO PRESIDENT RUTHERFORD B. HAYES

Elkins, Stephen Benton. "Axtell Gov. New Mexico: A strong protest against his removal by S.B. Elkins who says the charges against him are vague & irresponsible." To the President. **June 11, 1877.** Microfilm File Case Number 44-4-8-3. Record Group 48. Microfilm No. M750. Roll 1. National Archives and Records Administration. U.S. Department of Justice. Washington, D.C. (**Against removal of Ringite Governor S.B. Axtell**)

_____. "To the President. Referring to a conversation had with you last week ... " Letter to President Rutherford B. Hayes. **March 17, 1881.** (Received Executive Mansion April 6, 1881). Microfilm Roll M750. National Archives and Records Administration. Record Group 48. Microfilm Case File Number 44-4-8-3. U.S. Department of Interior. Washington, D.C. (**Reappointing Axtell**)

ELLIS, ISAAC

Ellis, Isaac. "We are two residents of Lincoln County ..." Letter written with George Coe to President Rutherford B. Hayes. **June 22, 1878**. In Angel Report papers. Microfilm File Case Number 44-4-8-3. Record Group 48. Microfilm No. M750. Roll 1. National Archives and Records Administration. U.S. Department of Justice. Washington, D.C.

_____. Affidavit of Isaac Ellis. **March ?, 1879**. Indiana Historical Society. Lew Wallace Collection. M0292. Box 4, Folder 7.

EVANS, JESSIE

BIOGRAPHICAL SOURCE

McCright, Grady E. and James H. Powell. *Jessie Evans: Lincoln County Badman.* College Station, Texas: Creative Publishing Company. 1983.

CONTEMPORARY SOURCES (CHRONOLOGICAL)

Wilson, John, George B. Barker, Robert M. Gilbert, John Newcomb, Samuel Smith, Benjamin Ellis. "We the undersigned Justice of the Peace and Coroners Jury who sat upon the inquest held this 19th day of February 1878 on the body of John H. Tunstall ..." Coroner's Jury Report for John Tunstall. **February 19, 1878**. **(Naming as murderers, among others, James Dolan, Frank Baker, Jessie Evans, William Morton, and George Hindman)**

Wallace, Lew. "I have information that William Campbell, J.B. Matthews, and Jesse Evans were of the party engaged in the killing ..." Letter to Edward Hatch. **March 5, 1879**. Indiana Historical Society. Lew Wallace Collection. M0292. Box 4, Folder 4. **(Murder of Huston Chapman)**

_____. "Under the circumstances, particularly in the absence here of suitable cells for safekeeping of Jesse Evans, Jacob B. Matthews and William Campbell ..." Letter to Henry Carroll. **March 10, 1879**. Indiana Historical Society. Lew Wallace Collection. M0292. Box 4. Folder 4.

_____. "Upon reflection, I am of opinion that if Col. Dudley is really going to Fort Union ..." Letter to Henry Carroll. **March 11, 1879**. Indiana Historical Society. Lew Wallace Collection. M0292. Box 4. Folder 5. **(Advises not to send Evans, Campbell, Matthews, and Dolan to Fort Union because of N.A.M. Dudley being there)**

_____. "I beg to submit to you a list of persons whom it is necessary, in my judgment, to arrest ..." Letter to Henry Carroll. **March 11, 1879**. Indiana Historical Society. Lew Wallace Collection. M0292. Box 4. Folder 5. **(Lists Jessie Evans, "The Kid" – William Bonney, Yginio Salazar)**

_____. "Be good enough to send word to all your men to turn out soon as possible ..." Letter to Juan Patrón. **March 19, 1879**. Indiana Historical Society. Lew Wallace Collection. M0292. Box 4. Folder 6. **(Reports escape of Jessie Evans and Billy Campbell from Fort Stanton; $1000 reward)**

_____. "With Evans and Campbell at large ..." Letter to Henry Carroll. **March 19, 1879**. Indiana Historical Society. Lew Wallace Collection. M0292. Box 4. Folder 6.

Rynerson, William. "Indictments of the April, Lincoln County Grand Jury." **April 28, 1879**. Herman B. Weisner Papers, ca. 1957-1992. New Mexico State University Library at Las Cruces. Rio Grande Historical Society Collection. Accession No. Ms 0249. Box 4/39. Folder E-Z. Folder Name: "Jessie Evans Accessory to Murder." **(Billy's testimony indicts Dolan, Campbell, and Evans for his pardon)**

Purington, George Augustus. "The District Court adjourned on Thursday ..." **May 3, 1879**. Indiana Historical Society. Lew Wallace Collection. M0292. Box 4. Folder 10. **(Letter to Adjutant General on Grand Jury indictments of the**

Murphy-Dolans - including Evans for the H.I. Chapman murder - and N.A.M. Dudley; copy sent to Lew Wallace)

No Author. "Charges against Jessie Evans and John Kinney." Doña Ana County Criminal Docket Book. **August 18, 1875 to November 7, 1878.** Herman B. Weisner Papers, ca. 1957-1992. New Mexico State University Library at Las Cruces. Rio Grande Historical Collections. Accession No. Ms 0249. Box No. 13. Folder V3. Folder Name: "Venue, Change of."

FOUNTAIN, ALBERT JENNINGS

BIBLIOGRAPHICAL SOURCE

Gibson, A. M. *The Life and Death of Colonel Albert Jennings Fountain.* Norman: University of Oklahoma Press. 1965.

CONTEMPORARY SOURCE

Fountain, Albert Jennings, Attorney and J.D. Bail. "Instructions Asked for by Defendants Counsel. April 9, 1881. Herman B. Weisner Papers, ca. 1957-1992. New Mexico State University Library at Las Cruces. Rio Grande Historical Society Collection. Accession No. Ms 0249. Box 1. Folder 14-D. Folder Name: "Billy the Kid Legal Documents."

Fountain, Albert Jennings. "Please send me this case ..." Telegram to T.B. Catron. September 16, 1890. University of New Mexico Library. Center for Southwest Studies. Thomas B. Catron Papers. MSS 29, Series 102, Box 8, Folder 5. **(Did legal cases with Catron)**

FRITZ FAMILY (EMIL AND CHARLES FRITZ AND EMILIE FRITZ SCHOLAND)

Fritz, Charles. Affidavit of **September 18, 1876** claiming that Emil Fritz had a will. Probate Court Record. (private collection)

_____. Affidavit of **September 26, 1876** Authorizing Alexander McSween to Receive Payments for the Emil Fritz Estate. Probate Court Record. (private collection)

Scholand, Emilie and Charles Fritz. Affidavit of **September 26, 1876** appointing McSween to collect debts for the Emil Fritz Estate. Copied from the original District Court Record. (private collection)

Fritz, Charles. Affidavit of **December 7, 1877** to order Alexander McSween to pay the Emil Fritz insurance policy money. Probate Court Record. (private collection)

Scholand, Emilie. Affidavit of **December 21, 1877** Accusing Alexander McSween of Embezzlement. Copied from the original District Court Record. (private collection)

Bristol Warren. "Writ of Embezzlement." **December 21, 1877.** Herman B. Weisner Papers, ca. 1957-1992. New Mexico State University Library at Las Cruces. Rio Grande Historical Collections. Accession No. Ms 0249. Box 10. Folder M-13. Folder Name. "Will and Testament A. McSween." **(Emilie Fritz Scholand's sworn complaint against Alexander McSween)**

Fritz, Charles. Affidavit sworn before John Crouch, Clerk of Doña Ana District Court, for Writ of Attachment issued against property of Alexander A. McSween. Probate Court Record. **February 6, 1878.** (private collection)

_____ and Emilie Scholand. Attachment Bond sworn before John Crouch, Clerk of Doña Ana District Court, against Alexander A. McSween for indebtedness to them. **February 6, 1878.** (private collection).

No Author. Diagram showing parcels of land to each of the heirs of Emil Fritz. Herman B. Weisner Papers, ca. 1957-1992. New Mexico State University Library at Las Cruces. Rio Grande Historical Collections. Accession No. Ms 0249. Box P1. Folder 11. Folder Name. "Charles Fritz Estate."

GARRETT, PATRICK FLOYD

AUTOBIOGRAPHICAL SOURCE

Garrett, Pat F. *The Authentic Life of Billy the Kid The Noted Desperado of the Southwest, Whose Deeds of Daring and Blood Made His Name a Terror in New Mexico, Arizona, and Northern Mexico.* Santa Fe, New Mexico: New Mexico Printing and Publishing Co. 1882. (Edition used: Edited by Maurice Garland Fulton. New York: The Macmillan Company. 1927)

BIBLIOGRAPHICAL SOURCES

Glen, Skelton. "Pat Garrett As I Knew Him on the Buffalo Ranges." (**1890**, Unpublished). Binder RNM, III B, 20. Nita Stewart Haley Memorial Museum. Haley Library. Midland, Texas. (**His killing of Joe Briscoe is recounted as willful murder**)

Metz, Leon C. *Pat Garrett. The Story of a Western Lawman.* Norman: University of Oklahoma Press. 1974.

Mullin, Robert N. "Killing of Joe Briscoe." Letter to Eve Ball. January 31, 1964. (Unpublished). Binder RNM, VI, H. Nita Stewart Haley Memorial Museum. Haley Library. Midland, Texas.

_____. "Pat Garrett. Two Forgotten Killings." *Password.* X(2) (Summer 1965). pp. 57 - 65.

REWARD FOR KILLING BILLY THE KID

No Author. No title. *Santa Fe Daily New Mexican.* **July 21, 1881.** Volume X, Number 120, Page 4. Column 1. NewspaperArchive.com. (**Pat Garrett's meeting with Acting Governor Ritch about the Billy the Kid reward.**)

Ritch, William G. "In the matter of the application by Patrick F. Garrett for a reward claimed to have been offered May-1881 for the capture of Wm Bonney alias "the Kid." *Executive Record Book Number 2.* July 25, 1867-November 8, 1882. **July 21, 1881.** Pages 533-535. New Mexico Secretary of State Records. Collection 1971-001, Series 1; Records of the Secretary of the Territory. (Accessed from Albuquerque Public Library Microfilm, Territorial Archives of New Mexico, Roll 21.) (**Presentation of Garret's bill for the reward, showing that Acting-Governor Ritch agreed with the reward, but legal opinion from Attorney General William Breeden necessitated getting a legislative act to convert Wallace's private reward to Territorial**)

No Author. "Kid the Killer Killed, Wm. Bonney alias Antrim, alias Billy the Kid, Fatally Meets Pat Garrett, the Lincoln County Sheriff." Las Cruces *Rio Grande Republican.* **July 23, 1881.** Page 2. Volume 1, Number 10. NewspaperArchive.com. (**Copy of Pat Garrett's letter to Acting Governor William Ritch confirming that the original Coroner's Jury Report was sent to District Attorney of the First Judicial District, and copy of it was included in this letter to the Governor**)

Sheldon, Lionel. "In the Matter of the Claim of Sheriff Pat Garrett." Letter to the Legislature. **February 14, 1882.** Territorial Archives of New Mexico. Microfilm Roll 5, Frame 765. (**As Governor, approving Garrett's reward and stating he would have granted it outright had it not already been sent to the Legislature by Acting-Governor Ritch for an act**)

No Author. "An Act for the Relief of Pat. Garrett." *1882 Acts of the Legislative Assembly of the Territory of New Mexico, Twenty-Fifth Session. Convened at the Capitol, at the City of Santa Fe, on Monday, the 2d day of January, 1882, and adjourned on Thursday, the 2d day of March, 1882.* **February 18, 1882.** Chapter 101. Page 191. (**Granting Pat Garrett's reward for Billy the Kid, confirming it had been withheld on a technicality**)

Fulton, Maurice Garland. "I think I have solved the puzzle of the reward offers ..." October 28, 1951. Letter to Robert N. Mullin. Nita Stewart Haley Memorial Library and J. Evetts Haley History Center, Midland, Texas. Mullin Collection. Series RNM, VI, J, Legal Papers and Documents. "William Bonney, Reward for Death, Lincoln Notes." (**Confirming Attorney General's opinion to Acting Governor William Ritch about conversion of reward by legislative act**)

_____. "The rewards for the Kid give a clue to Catron's participation ..." **November 26, 1951.** Letter to Robert N. Mullin. Nita Stewart Haley Memorial Library and J. Evetts Haley History Center, Midland, Texas. Mullin Collection. Series RNM, VI, J, Legal Papers and Documents. "William Bonney, Rewards." (**Contemplating Catron's participation for the reward**)

_____. "Ritch was governor for the time-being ..." **March 15, 1953.** Letter to Robert N. Mullin. Nita Stewart Haley Memorial Library and J. Evetts Haley History Center, Midland, Texas. Mullin Collection. Series RNM, VI, J, Legal Papers and Documents. "William Bonney, Rewards." (**Confirming Attorney General's opinion to Acting Governor William Ritch about conversion of reward by legislative act**)

OTHER CONTEMPORARY SOURCES (CHRONOLOGICAL)

No Author. "Garrett Exonerates Maxwell." *Santa Fe Daily New Mexican.* **July 21, 1881.** Volume X, Number 120. NewspaperArchive.com. (**Denial that Peter Maxwell was complicit in Billy Bonney's ambush**)

Wild, Azariah F. "Daily Reports of U. S. Secret Service Agents, Azariah F. Wild." Microfilm T-915. Record Group 87. Roll 308 (**July 1, 1879 - June 30, 1881**). National Archives and Records Administration. Department of the Treasury. United States Secret Service. Washington, D. C. (**Capture of Billy Bonney**)

GAUSS, GOTTFRIED

Gauss, Gottfried. Interview with *Lincoln County Leader.* **November 21, 1889.** (**About Billy Bonney's Lincoln jailbreak**)

GIDDINGS, MARSH

CONTEMPORARY SOURCES (CHRONOLOGICAL)

No Author. *Diario del Consejo der Territorio de Neuvo Mejico, Session de 1871-1872.* *Santa Fe New Mexican.* **January 8, 1872.** Santa Fe: A.P. Sullivan. 1872. Pages 144-154. New Mexico Supreme Court Library. Santa Fe, New Mexico. (**Confirms Giddings's use of troops for Ring suppression in 1872 Legislature Revolt**)

No Author. *Diario del Consejo der Territorio de Neuvo Mejico, Session de 1871-1872.* Las Cruces *Borderer.* **January 24, 1872.** Pages 110-113. (**President of the Council Don Diego Archuleta gives speech objecting to Giddings's bringing troops into legislature**)

No Author. *Journal of the House of Representatives of the Territory of New Mexico, Session of 1871-1872.* Santa Fe: A.P. Sullivan. **1872.** (**Covers 1872 Legislature Revolt: Pages 86-91 on Giddings's veto of House acts; Pages 144-154 on Giddings's use of troops for suppression**)

Catron, Thomas B., M.A. Breeden, William Breeden, José D. Sena, J.G. Palen, T.F. Conway. "We have just learned that the character of the Adjutant General of New Mexico has been attacked at Washington ..." Letter to Senator Thomas W. Ferry. **March 26, 1873.** Interior Department Papers 1850-1907; Appointments Division and Subsequent Actions. Microfilm File Case Number 44-4-8-3. Record Group 48. Microfilm No. M750. Roll 1. National Archives and Records Administration. U.S. Department of Justice. Washington, D.C. (**Ringmen supporting Marsh Giddings's appointing his son as Adjutant General**)

Gallegos, Jose M. "My people are extremely anxious to have Governor Giddings removed as Governor ..." Letter to President Ulysses S. Grant. **March 13, 1873.** Interior Department Papers 1850-1907; Appointments Division and Subsequent Actions. Microfilm File Case Number 44-4-8-3. Record Group 48. Microfilm No. M750. Roll 1. National Archives and Records Administration. U.S. Department of Justice. Washington, D.C. **(Movement to remove Governor Marsh Giddings)**

Giddings, Marsh. "A transfer of Territorial officers from the State Dept. to the Dept of the interior ..." Letter to Secretary of the Interior. **April 3, 1873.** Interior Department Papers 1850-1907; Appointments Division and Subsequent Actions. Microfilm File Case Number 44-4-8-3. Record Group 48. Microfilm No. M750. Roll 1. National Archives and Records Administration. U.S. Department of Justice. Washington, D.C. **(Responses to charges against him)**

_____. "By the enactment of these laws in the last two days of the session our securities doubled in value within six months ..." Letter to Secretary of the Interior. **April 20, 1873.** Interior Department Papers 1850-1907; Appointments Division and Subsequent Actions. Microfilm File Case Number 44-4-8-3. Record Group 48. Microfilm No. M750. Roll 1. National Archives and Records Administration. U.S. Department of Justice. Washington, D.C. **(About charges)**

_____. "I have the honor to inform you that ... there have been disturbances between the Mexicans and Texans ..." Letter to Secretary of Interior C. Delano. **January 12, 1874.** Interior Department Papers 1850-1907; Appointments Division and Subsequent Actions. Microfilm File Case Number 44-4-8-3. Record Group 48. Microfilm No. M750. Roll 1. National Archives and Records Administration. U.S. Department of Justice. Washington, D.C. **(Creating outlaw myth to justify military intervention against Ring opponents)**

HAYES, RUTHERFORD BIRCHARD

BIOGRAPHICAL SOURCES

Davison, Kenneth E. *The Presidency of Rutherford B. Hayes.* Westport, Connecticut: Greenwood Press, Inc. 1972.

Hoogenboom, Ari. *Rutherford B. Hayes. Warrior and President.* Lawrence, Kansas: University Press of Kansas. 1995.

Mullin, Robert N. Re: Frank Warner Angel Meeting With President Hayes August, 1878. Binder RNM, VI, M. (Unpublished). Midland, Texas: Nita Stewart Haley Memorial Library and J. Evetts Haley History Center. (Undated).

Williams, Charles Richard. *The Life of Rutherford Birchard Hayes. Nineteenth President of the United States. Vol. I.* Boston and New York: Houghton Mifflin Co. 1914.

_____. The Life of Rutherford Birchard Hayes. Nineteenth President of the United States. Vol. II. Boston and New York: Houghton Mifflin Co. 1914.

PROCLAMATION BY

Hayes, Rutherford B. "By the President of the United States of America: A Proclamation." **October 7, 1878.** Indiana Historical Society. Lew Wallace Collection. OMB 0023. Box 1. Folder 1; and Senate Documents. 67th Congress. 2nd Session. December 5, 1921 - September 22, 1922. Washington: Government Printing Office. 1922.

LETTERS TO

Leverson, Montague R. "His Excellency Rutherford B. Hayes. President of the United States. Excellency! Since my last letter to your Excellency on the state of affairs in this Territory ..." Letter to Rutherford B. Hayes. **March 16, 1878.** Microfilm M750. National Archives and Records Administration. Record Group 60. Microfilm Case No. 44-4-8-3. U.S. Department of Interior. Washington, D.C

Isaacs, J. and J. N. Coe. "We are two residents of Lincoln Co. who after incurring the greatest peril at the hands of thieves and murderers when the Governor and the U.S. troops aided ..." Letter to Rutherford B. Hayes. **June 22, 1878**. Frank Warner Angel File. Microfilm Roll M750. National Archives and Records Administration. Record Group 60. Microfilm Case Number 44-4-8-3. U.S. Department of Interior. Washington, D.C.

McSween, A. A. "The undersigned have the Honor of transmitting you as requested a copy of the proceeds of a meeting held by the Citizens of Lincoln County, N. Mex. relative to the late troubles ..." Letter to Rutherford B. Hayes. **April 26,1878**. Frank Warner Angel File. Microfilm Roll M750. National Archives and Records Administration. Record Group 060. Microfilm Case Number 44-4-8-3. U.S. Department of Interior. Washington, D.C.

Elkins, Stephen B. "To the President referring to a conversation ..." Letter titled "Hon. S. R. Elkins favors appointment Axtell, ExGov. as Gov'r of New Mexico. **March 23, 1881**. (Received Executive Mansion April 6, 1881) Microfilm Roll M750. National Archives and Records Administration. Record Group 60. Microfilm Case File Number 44-4-8-3. U.S. Department of Interior. Washington, D.C.

LETTERS TO AND FROM LEW WALLACE

Wallace, Lew. "I avail myself of your request this morning. It is hardly necessary to give reasons for a preference of the Italian mission ..." Letter to Rutherford B. Hayes. **March 9, 1877**. Indiana Historical Society. Lew Wallace Collection. M0292. Box 3. Folder 13. **(Desired ambassadorships)**

_____. "The feuds recently in Lincoln county, New Mexico, left a large many thieves and murderers, who, with others of like class since added to their number, are now confederated for plunder." Letter to Rutherford B. Hayes. **March 31, 1879**. Indiana Historical Society. Lew Wallace Collection. M0292. Box 4. Folder 7. **(Wants martial law against confederacy of outlaws)**

Hayes, Rutherford B. "We are greatly obliged by your kindness." Letter to Lew Wallace. **January 9, 1881**. Indiana Historical Society. Lew Wallace Collection. M0292. Box 4. Folder 16. **(Thanking for gift of *Ben- Hur*)**

HOYT, HENRY F.

AUTOBIOGRAPHICAL SOURCE

Hoyt, Henry. *A Frontier Doctor*. Boston and New York: Houghton Mifflin Company. 1929. **(Describes Billy Bonney's superior abilities, pp. 93-94.)**

CONTEMPORARY SOURCES (CHRONOLOGICAL)

Bonney, William H. Bill of Sale to Henry Hoyt. **October 24, 1878**. Collection of Panhandle-Plains Historical Museum. Canyon, Texas. (Item No. X1974-98/1)

Hoyt, Henry F. "This time it is me who is apologizing ..." Letter to Lew Wallace Jr. (Lew Wallace's grandson) **April 27, 1927**. Indiana Historical Society. Lew Wallace Collection. M0292. Box 14, Folder 11.

_____. "Copy of a bill of sale written by Wᵐ H. Bonney ..." Letter to Lew Wallace Jr. **April 27, 1927**. Indiana Historical Society. Lew Wallace Collection. M0292. Box 14, Folder 11.

KIMBRELL, GEORGE

Kimbrell, George. "I have the honor to request that you will furnish me a posse ..." Letter to Lieutenant Millard Filmore Goodwin. **February 20, 1879**. Indiana Historical Society. Lew Wallace Collection. Box 4, Folder 3.

KINNEY, JOHN

BIOGRAPHICAL SOURCE

Mullin, Robert N. "Here Lies John Kinney." *Journal of Arizona History.* 14 (Autumn 1973). Pages 223 - 242.

CONTEMPORARY SOURCES (CHRONOLOGICAL)

No Author. "Charges against Jessie Evans and John Kinney." Doña Ana County Criminal Docket Book. **August 18, 1875 to November 7, 1878.** Herman Weisner Collection. New Mexico State University Library at Las Cruces. Rio Grande Historical Collections. Accession No. Ms 0249. Box 13. Folder V-3. Folder Name: "Venue, Change of."

No Author. "Obituary of John Kinney." *Prescott Courier.* **August 30, 1919.** Obituary Section.

No Author. Obituary. "Over the Range Goes Another Pioneer." *Journal Miner.* Tuesday Morning, **August 26, 1919.**

No Author. "Captain Kinney Dead." *The Daily Arizona Silver Belt.* August 29, 1919. Page 2. NewspaperArchive.com.

KISTLER, RUSSELL A.

LETTERS ABOUT

Elston, J.A. "Mr. Kistler of the "Optic" of Las Vegas, your territory, referred me to you ..." Letter to T.B. Catron. **December 16, 1889.** University of New Mexico Library. Center for Southwest Studies. Thomas B. Catron Papers, MSS 29, Series 102, Box 5, Folder 4.

Mills, William J. "Kistler has been in to see me ..." Letter to T.B. Catron. **December 12, 1891.** University of New Mexico Library. Center for Southwest Studies. Thomas B. Catron Papers, MSS 29, Series 102, Box 12, Folder 6. **(About a boycott attempting to have Kistler removed from the *Optic*)**

Gould, George T. "Replying to yours of a recent date ..." Letter to T.B. Catron. **August 19, 1899.** University of New Mexico Library. Center for Southwest Studies. Thomas B. Catron Papers, MSS 29, Series 103, Box 8, Folder 3. **(Confirming that Frank Springer, among others, bought Kistler's *Optic*)**

BILLY THE KID ARTICLES BY (SEE: William H. Bonney's *Las Vegas Optic* articles)

KOOGLER, JOHN H.

LETTERS ABOUT AND FROM

Koogler, John H. "Affidavit of publication." **March 9, 1876.** University of New Mexico Library. Center for Southwest Studies. Thomas B. Catron Papers, MSS 29, Series 103, Box 26, Folder 2. **(For case with Catron representing the plaintiffs.)**

Wilcox, Lucius "Lute" M. (city editor; owner, J.H. Koogler). "The Kid. Interview with Billy Bonney The Best Known Man in New Mexico." *Las Vegas Gazette.* **December 28, 1880. (Has Billy Bonney's quote that "the laugh's on me this time")**

_____. Interview, at train depot. *Las Vegas Gazette.* **December 28, 1880. (Has Billy Bonney's "adios" quote.)**

Catron, Thomas Benton. "Paid Koogler for Paper & advertisement ..." **August 14, 1881.** Pocket notebook kept by T.B. Catron. University of New Mexico Library. Center for Southwest Studies. Thomas B. Catron Papers, MSS 29, Series 804, Box 1. **(Demonstrating Catron's paying *Las Vegas Gazette* editor, J.H. Koogler, who published Ring-biased articles on Billy the Kid)**

Koogler, John H. "I will start for Kansas City to-morrow ..." Letter to T.B. Catron. **July 17, 1889**. University of New Mexico Library. Center for Southwest Studies. Thomas B. Catron Papers, MSS 29, Series 102, Box 4, Folder 3. (**Pleading for money**)

_____. "I wrote you before I left Las Vegas ..." Letter to T.B. Catron. **July 29, 1889**. University of New Mexico Library. Center for Southwest Studies. Thomas B. Catron Papers, MSS 29, Series 102, Box 4, Folder 4. (**Pleading for money**)

_____. "Mr. Gorther in sending me the balance of the testimony in the case of Doloritas Martin ..." Letter to T.B. Catron. **August 14, 1890**. University of New Mexico Library. Center for Southwest Studies. Thomas B. Catron Papers. MSS 29, Series 102, Box 8, Folder 4. (**About fees for legal work for Catron**)

ARTICLES PUBLISHED BY (CHRONOLOGICAL)

No Author. (signed E.). "Death of Chapman." *Las Vegas Gazette*. **March 1, 1879**. From *Proceedings of a Court of Inquiry in the Case of Lt. Col. N.A.M. Dudley (May 2,1879 – July 5, 1879)*. File No. QQ1284. (Boxes 3304, 3305, 3305A); Court Martial Files 1809-1894. Records of the Office of the Judge Advocate General – Army. Record Group 153. Old Military and Civil Branch. National Archives and Records Administration. Washington, D. C.

LEONARD, IRA E.

BIOGRAPHICAL SOURCE

Nolan, Frederick. Biography and photograph of Ira Leonard. Unpublished. personal communication. July 29, 2005.

COURT OF INQUIRY OF N.A.M. DUDLEY BY (SEE: Nathan Augustus Monroe Dudley Court of Inquiry)

LETTERS TO AND FROM

HUSTON CHAPMAN'S FATHER TO

Chapman, W.W. "Yours of the 1st inst. came ..." Letter to Ira E. Leonard. **March 20, 1879**. Indiana Historical Society. Lew Wallace Collection. M0292. Box 4. Folder 6.

_____. "Since receiving yours of the 1st March ..." Letter to Ira Leonard. **May 8, 1879**. Indiana Historical Society. Lew Wallace Collection. M0292. Box 4. Folder 10.

LEW WALLACE TO AND FROM

Wallace, Lew. "I enclose a paper, signed by all the leading attorneys ..." Letter to Carl Schurz. **November 13, 1878**. Indiana Historical Society. Lew Wallace Collection. M0292. Box 3. Folder 17. (**Urging judgeship for Ira Leonard**)

Leonard, Ira E. "Dear Gov. You have undoubtedly learned ere this of the assassination ..." Letter to Lew Wallace. **February 24, 1879**. Indiana Historical Society. Lew Wallace Collection. M0292. Box 4. Folder 3. (**On Chapman murder.**)

Wallace, Lew. "It is important to take steps to protect the coming court ..." Letter to Ira Leonard. **April 6, 1879**. Indiana Historical Society. Lew Wallace Collection. M0292. Box 4. Folder 8.

_____. "Your favors both received. The arrest of Wilson was a blow at the right time ..." **April 9, 1879**. Indiana Historical Society. Lew Wallace Collection. M0292. Box 4. Folder 9. (**With quote: "To work trying to do a little good, but with the world against you, requires the will of a martyr"**)

Leonard, Ira E. "I was disappointed in not seeing you ..." Letter to Lew Wallace. **April 12, 1879**. Indiana Historical Society. Lew Wallace Collection. M0292. Box 4. Folder 9. (**Saw rough men in town before his Ring assassination attempt**)

Wallace, Lew. "Your favor, with the prisoner received." Letter to Ira Leonard. **April 13, 1879**. Indiana Historical Society. Lew Wallace Collection. M0292. Box 4. Folder 9. **(About writs of habeas corpus to free his Fort Stanton prisoners)**

Leonard, Ira. "The air is filled tonight with 'rumors of wars ... Letter to Lew Wallace. **April 20, 1879**. Indiana Historical Society. Lew Wallace Collection. M0292. Box 4. Folder 9. **(About District Attorney Rynerson in the Grand Jury: "He is bent on going for the Kid")**

_____. "When you left here I promised to write you concerning events transpiring here ..." Letter to Lew Wallace. **May 20, 1878 [sic - 79]**. Indiana Historical Society. Lew Wallace Collection. M0292. Box 4. Folder 10. **(Has quote on the Murphy-Dolan party as: "part and parcel of the Santa Fe ring that has been so long an incubus on the government of this territory.")**

_____. "I write to you with pencil because I am laboring for breath ..." Letter to Lew Wallace. **May 23, 1879**. Indiana Historical Society. Lew Wallace Collection. M0292. Box 4. Folder 11. **(With quote "we are pouring the 'hot shot' into Dudley." (With enclosed letter of May 20, 1879)**

_____. "Dudley commenced on the defense Thursday afternoon ..." Letter to Wallace. **June 6, 1879**, Indiana Historical Society. Lew Wallace Collection. M0292. Box 4. Folder 11. **(About disgust at Court.")**

_____. "Yours of the 7th inst reached me ..." Letter to Lew Wallace. **June 13, 1879**. Indiana Historical Society. Lew Wallace Collection. M0292. Box 4. Folder 11. **(about Court of Inquiry bias)**

LEVERSON, MONTEGUE

CONTEMPORARY SOURCES (CHRONOLOGICAL)

Leverson, Montegue. "I earnestly entreat you to read the enclosed letter and hand it to the president ..." Letter to Secretary of Interior Carl Schurz. **March 16, 1878**. Part of file of report of October 4, 1878. Angel Report. Microfilm File Case Number 44-4-8-3. Record Group 48. Microfilm No. M750. Roll 1. National Archives and Records Administration. U.S. Department of Justice. Washington, D.C.

_____. "Affairs of Lincoln County." Letter to Secretary of Interior Carl Schurz and President Rutherford B. Hayes. **June 28, 1878**. Part of file of report of October 4, 1878. Angel Report. Microfilm File Case Number 44-4-8-3. Record Group 48. Microfilm No. M750. Roll 1. National Archives and Records Administration. U.S. Department of Justice. Washington, D.C. **(About Santa Fe Ring)**

_____. "I send you herewith a copy of a letter I have published ..." Letter to Secretary of Interior Carl Schurz. **July 12 (?), 1878**. Part of file of report of October 4, 1878. Angel Report. Microfilm File Case Number 44-4-8-3. Record Group 48. Microfilm No. M750. Roll 1. National Archives and Records Administration. U.S. Department of Justice. Washington, D.C. **(About opposing Thomas Benton Catron and the Ring)**

_____. "I enclose you a letter I have just received ..." Letter to President Rutherford B. Hayes. **July 30, 1878**. Part of file of report of October 4, 1878. Angel Report. Microfilm File Case Number 44-4-8-3. Record Group 48. Microfilm No. M750. Roll 1. National Archives and Records Administration. U.S. Department of Justice. Washington, D.C. **(About murder of Alexander McSween and Frank MacNab by the Ring – blaming Hayes)**

MARKLAND, ABSALOM HANKS

BIOGRAPHICAL SOURCE

Perret, Geoffrey. *Ulysses S. Grant: Soldier and President*. New York: Random House. 1997. **(Pages 16, 467, 471)**

CONTEMPORARY SOURCES (CHRONOLOGICAL)

Grant, Ulysses. Presentation of the Grimsby Saddle to Colonel Absalom Markland. **May 19, 1865.** *The Papers of Ulysses S. Grant: May 1-December 31, 1865.* Carbondale, Illinois: Southern Illinois University Press. 1967 - 2009.

Wallace, Lew. "Our mutual friend, M. Hinds, who will hand you this ..." Letter to A.H. Markland. **November 14, 1878.** Indiana Historical Society. Lew Wallace Collection. M0292. Box 3. Folder 17. **(About Santa Fe Ring attempting to remove him as governor)**

MATTHEWS, JACOB BASIL "BILLY"

BIOGRAPHICAL SOURCE

Fleming, Elvis E. *J.B. Matthews. Biography of a Lincoln County Deputy.* Las Cruces, New Mexico: Yucca Tree Press. 1999.

CONTEMPORARY SOURCES (CHRONOLOGICAL)

Wallace, Lew. "Under the circumstances, particularly in the absence here of suitable cells for safekeeping of Jesse Evans, Jacob B. Matthews and William Campbell ..." Letter to Henry Carroll. **March 10, 1879.** Indiana Historical Society. Lew Wallace Collection. M0292. Box 4. Folder 4.

_____. "Upon reflection, I am of opinion that if Col. Dudley is really going to Fort Union ..." Letter to Henry Carroll. **March 11, 1879.** Indiana Historical Society. Lew Wallace Collection. M0292. Box 4. Folder 5. **(Advises not to send Evans, Campbell, Matthews, and Dolan to Fort Union)**

No Author. "Amnesty for Matthews and Long in the Third Judicial Court April Term 1879." **April, 1879.** Herman B. Weisner Papers, ca. 1957-1992. New Mexico State University Library at Las Cruces. Rio Grande Historical Collections. Accession No. Ms 0249. Box 1. Folder 4. Folder Name. "Amnesty." **(Catron got all indicted Ringite Lincoln County War murderers and arsonists pardoned)**

(SEE: Letter to Thomas Benton Catron)

MAXWELL, DELUVINA

Maxwell, Deluvina. "I came here after Lucien Maxwell was already here...." Letter to J. Evetts Haley. June 24, 1927. Nita Stewart Haley Memorial Library and J. Evetts Haley History Center, Midland, Texas. J. Evetts Haley Collection, JEH, J-I – Maxwell, Deluvina. **(Confirming Billy Bonney's killing)**

MAXWELL FAMILY

Cleaveland, Agnes Morley. *No Life for a Lady.* Boston: Houghton Mifflin. 1941.

_____. *Satan's Paradise: From Lucien Maxwell to Fred Lambert.* Boston: Houghton Mifflin Company. 1952.

Cleaveland, Norman. *The Morleys - Young Upstarts on the Southwest Frontier.* Albuquerque, New Mexico: Calvin Horn Publisher, Inc. 1971.

Dunham, Harold H. "New Mexican Land Grants with Special Reference to the Title Papers of the Maxwell Grant." *New Mexico Historical Review.* (January 1955) Volume 30, Number 1, Pages 1 - 23.

East, James H. "Jim." "I wish to say that I appreciate your courtesy ..." Letter to William B. Burgess. **May 20, 1926.** C.L. Sonnichsen Papers, MS 141. C.L. Sonnichsen Special Collections Department. University of Texas El Paso Library. Box 92. Folder 386. **(About Paulita Maxwell as Billy's lover)**

Freiberger, Harriet. *Lucien Maxwell: Villain or Visionary.* Santa Fe, New Mexico: Sunstone Press. 1999.

Keleher, William A. *The Maxwell Land Grant. A New Mexico Item.* Albuquerque, New Mexico: University of New Mexico Press. 1964.

Lamar, Howard Roberts. *The Far Southwest 1846 - 1912. A Territorial History.* New Haven and London: Yale University Press. 1966.

Miller, Kenny. Descendant of Lucien Bonaparte Maxwell. Personal communication. 2011 to 2012.

Montoya, María E. *Translating Property. The Maxwell Land Grant and the Conflict Over Land in the American West, 1840-1900.* Berkeley and Los Angeles, California: University of California Press. 2002.

Murphy, Lawrence R. *Lucien Bonaparte Maxwell. Napoleon of the Southwest.* Norman: University of Oklahoma Press. 1983.

Pearson, Jim Berry. *The Maxwell Land Grant.* Norman: University of Oklahoma Press. 1961.

Poe, Sophie. *Buckboard Days.* Albuquerque, New Mexico: University of New Mexico Press. 1964.

Taylor, Morris F. *O. P. McMains and the Maxwell Land Grant Conflict.* Tucson, Arizona: The University of Arizona Press. 1979. (**Origins of Santa Fe Ring**)

No Author. "Mrs. Paula M. Jaramillo, 65 Died Here Tuesday." *The Fort Sumner Leader.* Official Newspaper County of De Baca. December 20, 1929. No. 1158, Page 1, Column 1. (**Billy Bonney's sweetheart, Paulita Maxwell**)

McMAINS, OSCAR P.

BIOGRAPHICAL SOURCES FOR

Cleaveland, Norman. *The Morleys - Young Upstarts on the Southwest Frontier.* Albuquerque, New Mexico: Calvin Horn Publisher, Inc. 1971.

Taylor, Morris F. *O.P. McMains and the Maxwell Land Grant Conflict.* Tucson, Arizona: The University of Arizona Press. 1979. (**Traces origins of the Santa Fe Ring with T.B. Catron and S.B. Elkins**)

McPHERSON, MARY E. TIBBLES

BIOGRAPHICAL SOURCES

Cleaveland, Agnes Morley. *No Life for a Lady.* Boston: Houghton Mifflin. 1941.

_____. *Satan's Paradise: From Lucien Maxwell to Fred Lambert.* Boston: Houghton Mifflin Company. 1952.

Cleaveland, Norman, *A Synopsis of the Great New Mexico Cover-up.* Self-printed. 1989.

_____. *The Great Santa Fe Cover-up. Based on a Talk given Before the Santa Fe Historical Society on November 1, 1978.* Self-printed. 1982.

_____. *The Morleys - Young Upstarts on the Southwest Frontier.* Albuquerque, New Mexico: Calvin Horn Publisher, Inc. 1971.

Taylor, Morris F. *O.P. McMains and the Maxwell Land Grant Conflict.* Tucson, Arizona: The University of Arizona Press. 1979.

Tibbles, Thomas Henry. Editor Vivian K. Barris. *Buckskin and Blanket Days: Memoirs of a Friend of the Indians.* Written in 1905. Published by Garden City, New York: Doubleday & Company, Inc. in 1957. (**Brother of Mary Tibbles McPherson**)

McPHERSON'S SANTA FE RING EXPOSÉS

McPherson, Mary. "Charges against Thomas B. Catron, U.S. Attorney, and Others." **February 7, 1877.** Letter to Attorney General Alphonso Taft. Interior Department Papers 1850-1907; Appointments Division and Subsequent Actions. Microfilm File Case Number 44-4-8-3. Record Group 48. Microfilm Roll M750. National Archives and Records Administration. U.S. Department of Justice. Washington, D.C.

Catron, Thomas Benton. "Answering Charges of Mary E. McPherson." **February 24, 1877.** Letter to Attorney General Alphonso Taft. Interior Department Papers 1850-1907; Appointments Division and Subsequent Actions. Microfilm File Case Number 44-4-8-3. Record Group 48. Microfilm Roll M750. National Archives and Records Administration. U.S. Department of Justice. Washington, D.C.

Matchett, W.B. and Mary E. McPherson. "W.B. Matchett and Mary E. McPherson 'Make Certain Charges Against the U.S. Officials in the Territory of New Mexico, Together With Corroboration Evidence.' " Letter to President Rutherford B. Hayes. Received and filed **May 1, 1877.** Interior Department Papers 1850-1907; Appointments Division and Subsequent Actions. Microfilm File Case Number 44-4-8-3. Record Group 48. Microfilm No. M750. Roll 1. National Archives and Records Administration. U. S. Department of Justice. Washington, D.C.

McPherson, Mary and W.B. Matchett. "To The President. Please make the enclosed a part of the evidence in the case of "Charges Against New Mexican Officials" Letter to President Rutherford B. Hayes. **May 3, 1877.** McPherson, Mary E. Letters and Petitions to President Rutherford B. Hayes re: Removal Governor Axtell and the Santa Fe Ring. Interior Department Papers 1850-1907; Appointments Division and Subsequent Actions. Microfilm File Case Number 44-4-8-3. Record Group 48. Microfilm Roll M750. National Archives and Records Administration. U.S. Department of Justice. Washington, D. C. (**Addendum to their May, 1877 "Certain Charges Against U.S. Officials in New Mexico Territory."**)

McPherson, Mary and W.B. Matchett. "The Secretary of the Interior, Sir - Accompanying please find copy of charges, &c., against S.B. Axtell, Governor and other New Mexico Officials ..." "Charges Against New Mexican Officials." Letter to Secretary of the Interior Carl Schurz. **May 5, 1877.** McPherson, Mary E. Letters and Petitions to President Rutherford B. Hayes re: Removal Governor Axtell and the Santa Fe Ring. Interior Department Papers 1850-1907; Appointments Division and Subsequent Actions. Microfilm File Case Number 44-4-8-3. Record Group 48. Microfilm Roll M750. National Archives and Records Administration. U.S. Department of Justice. Washington, D. C.

McPherson, Mary and W.B. Matchett. "We have respectfully to request that the following named records, documents, papers, communications and correspondence be supplied ..." Records Request to Secretary of the Interior Carl Schurz. **July 26, 1877.** Interior Department Papers 1850-1907; Appointments Division and Subsequent Actions. Microfilm File Case Number 44-4-8-3. Record Group 48. Microfilm No. M750. Roll 1. National Archives and Records Administration. U.S. Department of Justice. Washington, D.C. (**Requesting records of the Santa Fe Ring, Carton, Elkins, and Axtell**)

McPherson, Mary. "Please place before the Attorney General ..." Letter to President Rutherford B. Hayes. **August 23, 1877.** Interior Department Papers 1850-1907; Appointments Division and Subsequent Actions. Microfilm File Case Number 44-4-8-3. Record Group 48. Microfilm No. M750. Roll 1. National Archives and Records Administration. U. S. Department of Justice. Washington, D.C. (**Requesting that her "Charges" go to the Attorney General.**)

McPherson, Mary and W.B. Matchett. "*In the Matter of Charges vs. Gov. S.B. Axtell and Other New Mexico Officials. Submitted to the Departments of the Interior and Justice.* **August, 1877.** Printed as a 31 page booklet. No publisher listed. Indiana Historical Society. Lew Wallace Collection. M0292. Box 3. Folder 20.

McPherson, Mary. "I desire to know when I can be heard ..." Letter to Secretary of Interior Carl Schurz. **September 30, 1977.** Interior Department Papers 1850-1907; Appointments Division and Subsequent Actions. Microfilm File Case Number 44-4-8-3. Record Group 48. Microfilm No. M750. Roll 1. National Archives and Records Administration. U. S. Department of Justice. Washington, D.C.

518

CONTEMPORARY SOURCES (CHRONOLOGICAL)

Morley, William Raymond and Frank Springer. On Oscar McMains's citizen's Meeting. *Cimarron News and Press.* **November 10, 1875.** In Mary McPherson, Letters and Petitions to President Rutherford B. Hayes re: Removal Governor Axtell and the Santa Fe Ring. 1977. Interior Department Papers 1850-1907; Appointments Division and Subsequent Actions. Microfilm File Case Number 44-4-8-3. **Record Group 48.** Microfilm Roll M750. National Archives and Records Administration. **(Colfax County citizens meeting on F.J. Tolby murder by Santa Fe Ring.)**

Morley, William Raymond and Frank Springer. " 'The Territory of Elkins.' Assassination of Supposed Sun Correspondent. The Murder of the Rev. F.J. Tolby in New Mexico. A Probate Judge Accused of Complicity in the Crime. Indignation Meeting." *New York Weekly Sun.* **December 22, 1875.** Interior Department Papers 1850-1907; Appointments Division and Subsequent Actions. Microfilm Roll M750. National Archives and Records Administration. Record Group 48. Microfilm Case File Number 44-4-8-3. U.S. Department of Interior. Washington, D. C.**(Submitted to President Hayes in May 1, 1877's "Mary E. McPherson and W.B. Matchett 'Make certain charges against the U.S. Officials.")**

Morley William Raymond. "I was astonished beyond measure at your proceedings, and have fears as to the result ..." Letter to Mary McPherson. **March 6, 1877.** McPherson, Mary E. Letters and Petitions to President Rutherford B. Hayes re: Removal Governor Axtell and the Santa Fe Ring. Interior Department Papers 1850-1907; Appointments Division and Subsequent Actions. Microfilm File Case Number 44-4-8-3. Record Group 48. Microfilm Roll M750. National Archives and Records Administration. U.S. Department of Justice. Washington, D.C. **(Hopes she can help fight against Santa Fe Ring)**

Morley, Ada. "Yes, we have received all your letters at Vermejo here but we have hesitated about replying ..." Letter to Mary McPherson. **March 7, 1877.** McPherson, Mary E. Letters and Petitions to President Rutherford B. Hayes re: Removal Governor Axtell and the Santa Fe Ring. Interior Department Papers 1850-1907; Appointments Division and Subsequent Actions. Microfilm File Case Number 44-4-8-3. Record Group 48. Microfilm Roll M750. National Archives and Records Administration. U.S. Department of Justice. Washington, D.C. **(Fears about her fight against Santa Fe Ring)**

McSWEEN, ALEXANDER

Bristol Warren. "Writ of Embezzlement." **December 21, 1877.** Writ of Embezzlement. New Mexico State University Library at Las Cruces. Rio Grande Historical Collections. Lincoln County Papers. New Mexico State University Library at Las Cruces. Rio Grande Historical Collections. Accession No. Ms 0249. Box No. 10. Folder M-13. "Will and Testament A. McSween." **(Emilie Fritz Scholand's sworn complaint against Alexander McSween)**

Fritz, Charles. Affidavit sworn before John Crouch, Clerk of Doña Ana District Court, for Writ of Attachment issued against property of Alexander A. McSween. Probate Court Record. **February 6, 1878.** (private collection).

Bristol, Warren. Action of Assumpsit to command Sheriff of Lincoln County to attach goods of Alexander A. McSween. **February 7, 1878.** District Court Record. (private collection).

_____. Preprinted form in his name for "Writ of Attachment" (Printed and sold at the office of the Mesilla News) filled out to command the Sheriff of Lincoln County to attach goods of Alexander McSween for a suit of damages for ten thousand dollars. **February 7, 1878.** (private collection).

McSween, Alexander. "It looks as though the agent were the property of J.J. Dolan & J.H. Riley, known here as Dolan & Co." Letter to Secretary of Interior Carl Schurz. **February 11, 1878.** From Frederick Nolan. *The Life and Death of John*

Henry Tunstall. Albuquerque, New Mexico: The University of New Mexico Press. 1965. Page 266.

_____. "Will and Testament A. McSween." **February 25, 1878**. Herman B. Weisner Papers, ca. 1957-1992. New Mexico State University Library at Las Cruces. Rio Grande Historical Collections. Accession No. Ms 0249. Box 10. Folder M15. Folder Name. "Will and Testament A. McSween."

_____. and B.H. Ellis. Secretaries. "The undersigned have the Honor of transmitting you, as requested, a copy of the proceedings of a meeting held by the citizens of Lincoln County ..." Letter to President Rutherford B. Hayes; with attached proceedings of the April 1878 Lincoln Grand Jury. **April 26, 1878**. Microfilm File Case Number 44-4-8-3. Record Group 48. Microfilm No. M750. Roll 1. National Archives and Records Administration. U.S. Department of Justice. Washington, D.C.

_____. Deposition to Frank Warner Angel. **June 6, 1878**. Pages 5-183 of Frank Warner Angel report *In the Matter of the Examination of the Causes and Circumstances of the Death of John H. Tunstall a British Subject.* Report filed **October 4, 1878**. Angel Report. Microfilm File Case Number 44-4-8-3. Record Group 48. Microfilm No. M750. Roll 1. National Archives and Records Administration. U.S. Department of Justice. Washington, D.C. (**Reports secret**

Angel, Frank Warner. *In the Matter of the Lincoln County Troubles. To the Honorable Charles Devens, Attorney General.* **October 4, 1878**. Angel Report. Microfilm File Case Number 44-4-8-3. Record Group 48. Microfilm No. M750. Roll 1. National Archives and Records Administration. U.S. Department of Justice. Washington, D.C.

McSWEEN, SUSAN

BIOGRAPHICAL SOURCE FOR

Chamberlain, Kathleen P. *In the Shadow of Billy the Kid: Susan McSween and the Lincoln County War.* Albuquerque: University of New Mexico Press. 2013.

CONTEMPORARY SOURCES ABOUT (CHRONOLOGICAL)

Dudley, Nathan Augustus Monroe. "I am in receipt of a copy of letter written by one H.I. Chapman, calling himself the Attorney ..." **November 9, 1878**. Letter to Lew Wallace. From *Proceedings of a Court of Inquiry in the Case of Lt. Col. N.A.M. Dudley (May 2,1879 – July 5, 1879).* File No. QQ1284. (Boxes 3304, 3305, 3305A); Court Martial Files 1809-1894. Records of the Office of the Judge Advocate General - Army. Record Group 153. Old Military and Civil Branch. National Archives and Records Administration. Washington, D.C. (**Answer to charges, with attached defamatory affidavits against Susan McSween**)

McSween, Susan. Testimony in Court of Inquiry for Lieutenant Colonel N.A.M. Dudley. **May 23-24, 26, 1879**. *Proceedings of a Court of Inquiry in the Case of Lt. Col. N.A.M. Dudley (May 2,1879 – July 5, 1879).* File No. QQ1284. (Boxes 3304, 3305, 3305A); Court Martial Files 1809-1894. Records of the Office of the Judge Advocate General – Army. Record Group 153. Old Military and Civil Branch. National Archives and Records Administration. Washington, D.C.

No Author. Verdict on Civil Cause 298 for arson of Susan McSween's house. *Mesilla News.* **December 6, 1879**. Unpublished. personal communication from Frederick Nolan. July 29, 2005. (**Dudley exonerated**)

MEADOWS, JOHN P.

Meadows, John P. "Billy the Kid to John P. Meadows on the Peñasco, May 1-2, 1881." *Roswell Daily Record.* **February 16, 1931**. Page 6.

_____. "Story of Billy the Kid, His Life and Death, as Told Here by John Meadows, Friend of the Kid." *Roswell Daily Record.* **March 2, 1931**. Page 6.

_____. "Oldtimer, Friend of the Billy the Kid, Tells of the Kid's Capture After Many Killings." *Roswell Daily Record.* **March 3, 1931.** Page 6.

_____. "Oldtimer Pays Tribute to Sheriff Pat Garrett in Final Chapter of Billy the Kid." *Roswell Daily Record.* **March 4, 1931.** Page 6.

_____. Ed. John P. Wilson. *Pat Garrett and Billy the Kid as I Knew Them: Reminiscences of John P. Meadows.* Albuquerque: University of New Mexico Press. 2004.

Meadows, John P. Ed. John P. Wilson. *Pat Garrett and Billy the Kid as I Knew Them: Reminiscences of John P. Meadows.* Albuquerque: University of New Mexico Press. 2004.

MURPHY, LAWRENCE GUSTAV

Murphy, Lawrence G. "Will of Lawrence G. Murphy." Herman B. Weisner Papers, ca. 1957-1992. New Mexico State University Library at Las Cruces. Rio Grande Historical Collections. Accession No. Ms 0249. Box 11. Folder P15. Folder Name: "Murphy, Lawrence G."

Murphy, Lawrence G. "Will of Lawrence G. Murphy." Herman B. Weisner Papers, ca. 1957-1992. New Mexico State University Library at Las Cruces. Rio Grande Historical Collections. Accession No. Ms 0249. Box 11. Folder P15. Folder Name: "Murphy, Lawrence G."

PATRÓN, JUAN

Wallace, Lew. "Be good enough to send word to all your men to turn out soon as possible ..." Letter to Juan Patrón. **March 19, 1879.** Indiana Historical Society. Lew Wallace Collection. M0292. Box 4. Folder 6.

Patrón, Juan. First letter to Lew Wallace on **March 29, 1879.** Indiana Historical Society. Lew Wallace Collection. M0292. Box 4, Folder 7.

_____. Second letter to Lew Wallace on **March 29, 1879.** Indiana Historical Society. Lew Wallace Collection. M0292. Box 4, Folder 7.

PENNYPACKER, GALUSHA

BIOGRAPHICAL SOURCE

Heitman, Francis B. *Historical Register and Dictionary of the United States Army, From Its Organization, September 29, 1789, to March 2, 1903.* (Pennypacker, Pages 782-7830.) Washington, D.C.: Government Printing Office. 1903.

CONTEMPORARY SOURCE

No Author. *Proceedings of a Court of Inquiry in the Case of Lt. Col. N.A.M. Dudley (May 2,1879 – July 5, 1879).* File No. QQ1284. (Boxes 3304, 3305, 3305A); Court Martial Files 1809-1894. Records of the Office of the Judge Advocate General - Army. Record Group 153. Old Military and Civil Branch. National Archives and Records Administration. Washington, D.C. **(Chief Judge in Court of Inquiry)**

PEPPIN, GEORGE

No Author. "Old Citizen Gone." *Capitan News.* **September 23, 1904.** Volume 5. Number 29. Page 4. Center for Southwest Research. Microfilm AN2.L52a.

POE, JOHN WILLIAM

Poe, John W. "The Killing of Billy the Kid." (a personal letter written at Roswell, New Mexico to Mr. Charles Goodnight, Goodnight P.C., Texas) July 10, 1917.

_____. *The Death of Billy the Kid.* (Introduction by Maurice Garland Fulton). Boston and New York: Houghton Mifflin Company. 1933.

Poe, Sophie. *Buckboard Days.* Albuquerque, New Mexico: University of New Mexico Press. 1964. **(Biographical)**

PURINGTON, GEORGE AUGUSTUS

BIOGRAPHICAL SOURCES

Caldwell, Clifford R. *John Simpson Chisum: Cattle King of the Pecos Revisited.* Santa FE: Sunstone Press. 2010.

Coffey, David. "Hatch, Edward." *Encyclopedia of North American Indian Wars, 1607-1890: A Political, Social, and Military History.* Ed. Spencer C. Tucker. Volume 1. Santa Barbara: ABC-CLIO. 2010.

Trapp, Dan L. *Encyclopedia of Frontier Biography.* Volume 3. Spokane: University of Nebraska Press. 1988.

LETTER TO ADJUTANT GENERAL FROM

Purington, George Augustus. "The District Court adjourned on Thursday ..." **May 3, 1879.** Indiana Historical Society. Lew Wallace Collection. M0292. Box 4. Folder 10. (**Documenting Grand Jury indictments**)

RILEY, JOHN HENRY

CONTEMPORARY SOURCES ABOUT

Tunstall, John Henry. "A Tax-payer's Complaint, Office of John H. Tunstall, Lincoln, Lincoln Co., N.M., January 18, 1878, 'The Present Sheriff of Lincoln County Has Paid Nothing During His Present Term of Office.' Governor's Message for 1878." Mesilla *Independent.* **January 26, 1878.** Volume 1, Number 32. NewspaperArchive.com. (**Exposé of William Brady and John Riley for embezzling tax money to buy cattle; and T.B. Catron then paid that bill**)

Dolan, James J. "Answer to A Taxpayer's Complaint." Mesilla *Independent.* **January 29, 1878.** (**Response to J.H. Tunstall's exposé of embezzlement of tax money to buy cattle**)

McSween, Alexander. "It looks as though the [Indian] agent were the property of J.J. Dolan & J.H. Riley, known here as Dolan & Co." Letter to Secretary of Interior Carl Schurz. **February 11, 1878.** From Frederick Nolan. *The Life and Death of John Henry Tunstall.* Albuquerque, New Mexico: The University of New Mexico Press. 1965. Page 266.

_____. Deposition to Frank Warner Angel. **June 6, 1878.** Pages 5-183 of Frank Warner Angel report *In the Matter of the Examination of the Causes and Circumstances of the Death of John H. Tunstall a British Subject.* Report filed **October 4, 1878.** Angel Report. Microfilm File Case Number 44-4-8-3. Record Group 48. Microfilm No. M750. Roll 1. National Archives and Records Administration. U.S. Department of Justice. Washington, D.C.

No Author. "John Riley Dead." *Deming Graphic.* February 25, 1916. Page 2. Column 1. http://chroniclingamerica.loc.gov.

LETTERS FROM, TO, ABOUT (CHRONOLOGICAL)

TO AND FROM THOMAS BENTON CATRON
(SEE: T.B. Catron)

TO N.A.M DUDLEY

Riley, John H. Letter to N.A.M. Dudley. **May 19, 1878.** (**Fabricated Regulator theft from Catron-Dolan Pecos Cow Camp**) Cited by Victor Westphall, *Thomas Benton Catron and His Era,* Page 87.

FROM WILLIAM L. RYNERSON

Rynerson, William. "Friends Riley & Dolan, Lincoln N.M. I have just received letters from you mailed 10th inst." **February 14, 1878**. Letter to James Dolan and John Riley. Copy as Exhibit B in June 6, 1878 deposition of Alexander McSween. Frank Warner Angel report. *In the Matter of the Examination of the Causes and Circumstances of the Death of John H. Tunstall a British Subject.* Report filed October 4, 1878. Interior Department Papers 1850-1907; Appointments Division and Subsequent Actions. Microfilm File Case Number 44-4-8-3. Record Group 48. Microfilm No. M750. Roll 1. National Archives and Records Administration. U.S. Department of Justice. Washington, D.C. (James J. Dolan Deposition. June 20, 1878. pp. 235-247.) **(Planned killing of J.H. Tunstall)**

RUDULPH, MILNOR

Rudulph, Milnor. " I beg your indulgence for ..." Letter to William G. Ritch. **May 18, 1879**. Albuquerque and Bernalillo County Public Library. Genealogical Center. MS. Territorial Archives of New Mexico Microfilm. Roll 99. Image 10. **(Rudulph's signature matches his signature on the Coroner's Jury Report.)**

Keleher, William A. *Violence in Lincoln County 1869-1881.* **Pages 350-351. Albuquerque, New Mexico: University of New Mexico Press. 1957.**

(SEE: William H. Bonney Coroner's Jury Report)

RYNERSON, WILLIAM LOGAN

BIOGRAPHICAL SOURCES

Miller, Darlis A. "William Logan Rynerson in New Mexico. 1862-1893." *New Mexico Historical Review* 48 (April 1973) pp. 101-131.

No Author. "A Brief History of the Rynerson House." Las Cruces: Del Valle Design & Imaging. No copyright. https://delvalleprintinglc.com/rynerson-house/.

CONTEMPORARY SOURCES BY AND ABOUT (CHRONOLOGICAL)

Rynerson, William L "Indictments of the April, Lincoln County Grand Jury." **April 28, 1879**. Herman B. Weisner Papers, ca. 1957-1992. New Mexico State University Library at Las Cruces. Rio Grande Historical Society Collection. Accession No. Ms 0249. Box 4/39. Folder E-Z. Folder Name: "Jessie Evans Accessory to Murder." **(Indictments of Dolan, Campbell, and Evans)**

_____. "Friends Riley & Dolan, Lincoln N.M. I have just received letters from you mailed 10th inst." Letter to James Dolan and John Riley. **February 14, 1878**. Copy as Exhibit B in June 6, 1878 deposition of Alexander McSween. Frank Warner Angel report. *In the Matter of the Examination of the Causes and Circumstances of the Death of John H. Tunstall a British Subject.* Report filed October 4, 1878. Interior Department Papers 1850-1907; Appointments Division and Subsequent Actions. Microfilm File Case Number 44-4-8-3. Microfilm No. M750. Roll 1. National Archives and Records Administration. U.S. Department of Justice. Washington, D.C. (James J. Dolan Deposition. June 20, 1878. Pages 235-247.) **(Planned killing of J.H. Tunstall)**

Angel, Frank Warner. "I have just been favored by a call from W.L. Rynerson ..." Letter to Secretary of Interior Carl Schurz. **September 6, 1878**. Microfilm File Case Number 44-4-8-3. Record Group 48. Microfilm No. M750. Roll 1. National Archives and Records Administration. U. S. Department of Justice. Washington, D.C.

Rynerson, William. Venue Change. **April 21, 1879**. Herman B. Weisner Papers, ca. 1957-1992. New Mexico State University Library at Las Cruces. Rio Grande

Historical Collection. Accession No. Ms 0249. Box 1. Folder 14-D. Folder Name: "Billy the Kid Legal Documents." **(Change of Billy Bonney's trial venue from Lincoln County to Doña Ana County to insure a hanging trial by prevent Lincoln County citizens knowledgeable about the War being jurors)**

(SEE: Letters for Thomas Benton Catron, John H. Riley)

SALAZAR, YGINIO

Kimbrell, George. "I have the honor to request that you will furnish me a posse ..." Letter to Lieutenant Millard Filmore Goodwin. **February 20, 1879.** Indiana Historical Society. Lew Wallace Collection. Box 4, Folder 3. **(For pursuit of Yginio Salazar and William Bonney)**

Goodwin, Millard Filmore. ""I have the honor to submit the following report regarding my duties performed ..." Letter to Fort Stanton Post Adjutant John Loud. **February 23, 1879.** Indiana Historical Society. Lew Wallace Collection. Box 4, Folder 3. **(Assisting pursuit of William Bonney and Yginio Salazar)**

Wallace, Lew. "I beg to submit to you a list of persons ... to arrest ..." Letter to Henry Carroll. **March 11, 1879.** Indiana Historical Society. Lew Wallace Collection. M0292. Box 4. Folder 5. **(Lists Ygenio Salazar and "the Kid)**

Salazar, Joe. (Grandson of Yginio Salazar). Personal Interviews 1999-2001 about Ygenio.

SHERMAN, JOHN

Sherman, John. Letter to Governor Lew Wallace. **October 6, 1878.** Indiana Historical Society. Lew Wallace Collection. M0292. Box 3, Folder 15. **(Outlaw list of Regulators with first reference to Billy Bonney, to Governor Wallace.)**

SPRINGER, FRANK

Springer, Frank. Deposition to Investigator Frank Warner Angel. August 9, 1878. Frank Warner Angel report titled *In the Matter of the Investigation of the Charges Against S.B. Axtell Governor of New Mexico.* October 3, 1878. Interior Department Papers 1850-1907; Appointments Division and Subsequent Actions. Microfilm Case File No. 44-4-8-3. Record Group 48. Microfilm Roll M750. National Archives and Records Administration. U.S. Department of Interior. Washington, D.C. **(Mentions Catron, Elkins, and the Santa Fe Ring; with Exhibits of letters)**

THORNTON, WILLIAM TAYLOR

(SEE: Thomas Benton Catron letters to and from, and Catron's "Poker Bill" Plot)

TOLBY, FRANKLIN J.

BIOGRAPHICAL SOURCES

Cleaveland, Norman. *The Morleys - Young Upstarts on the Southwest Frontier.* Albuquerque, New Mexico: Calvin Horn Publisher, Inc. 1971.

Taylor, Morris F. *O.P. McMains and the Maxwell Land Grant Conflict.* Tucson, Arizona: The University of Arizona Press. 1979. **(Origins of the Santa Fe Ring)**

CONTEMPORARY SOURCES (CHRONOLOGICAL)

Morley, William Raymond and Frank Springer. On Oscar McMains's citizen's Meeting. *Cimarron News and Press.* **November 10, 1875.** In Mary McPherson, Letters and Petitions to President Rutherford B. Hayes re: Removal Governor Axtell and the Santa Fe Ring. 1977. Interior Department Papers 1850-1907; Appointments Division and Subsequent Actions. Microfilm File Case Number 44-4-8-3. **Record Group 48.** Microfilm Roll M750. National Archives and Records Administration.

_____. "The Territory of Elkins.' Assassination of Supposed Sun Correspondent. The Murder of the Rev. F.J. Tolby in New Mexico. A Probate Judge Accused of Complicity in the Crime. Indignation Meeting." New York *Weekly Sun*. **December 22, 1875.** Interior Department Papers 1850-1907; Appointments Division and Subsequent Actions. Microfilm Roll M750. National Archives and Records Administration. Record Group 48. Microfilm Case File Number 44-4-8-3. U.S. Department of Interior. Washington, D. C. **(From May 1, 1877 submission to President Hates as "Mary E. McPherson and W.B. Matchett 'Make certain charges against the U.S. Officials")**

No Author. Report on murder trial for Franklin Tolby. Pueblo, Colorado *Chieftain*, May 25, 1876 quoting from *Daily New Mexican*, **May 1, 1876.** From Morris F. Taylor. *O.P. McMains and the Maxwell Land Grant Conflict*. Tucson, Arizona: The University of Arizona Press. 1979. Page 49. **(Ring-biased jury instructions by Judge Henry Waldo)**

No Author. (Editorial). **May 15, 1876.** *The Daily New Mexican*. Volume 9. http://chroniclingamerica.loc.gov. **(Ringite article covering up guilt of Mills with Longwill in murder of Franklin Tolby as just "rumor")**

(SEE: Mary Tibbles McPherson, Oscar McMains)

TUNSTALL, JOHN HENRY

BIOGRAPHICAL SOURCES

Nolan, Frederick W. *The Life and Death of John Henry Tunstall*. Albuquerque, New Mexico: The University of New Mexico Press. 1965.

CONTEMPORARY SOURCES (CHRONOLOGICAL)

Tunstall, John Henry. "A Tax-payer's Complaint, Office of John H. Tunstall, Lincoln, Lincoln Co., N.M., January 18, 1878, 'The Present Sheriff of Lincoln County Has Paid Nothing During His Present Term of Office.' Governor's Message for 1878." Mesilla *Independent*. **January 26, 1878.** Volume 1, Number 32. NewspaperArchive.com. **(Exposé of William Brady and John Riley for embezzling tax money to buy cattle; and T.B. Catron then paid that bill)**

Dolan, James J. "Answer to A Taxpayer's Complaint." Mesilla *Independent*. **January 29, 1878. (Response to J.H. Tunstall's exposé of embezzlement of tax money to buy cattle)**

Rynerson, William. "Friends Riley & Dolan, Lincoln N.M. I have just received letters from you mailed 10th inst." Letter to James Dolan and John Riley. **February 14, 1878.** Copy as Exhibit B in June 6, 1878 deposition of Alexander McSween. Frank Warner Angel report. *In the Matter of the Examination of the Causes and Circumstances of the Death of John H. Tunstall a British Subject*. Report filed October 4, 1878. Interior Department Papers 1850-1907; Appointments Division and Subsequent Actions. Microfilm File Case Number 44-4-8-3. Record Group 48. Microfilm No. M750. Roll 1. National Archives and Records Administration. U. S. Department of Justice. Washington, D.C. (James J. Dolan Deposition. June 20, 1878. pp. 235-247.) **(Planned killing of J.H. Tunstall)**

Wilson, John, George B. Barker, Robert M. Gilbert, John Newcomb, Samuel Smith, Benjamin Ellis. "We the undersigned Justice of the Peace and Coroners Jury who sat upon the inquest held this 19th day of February 1878 on the body of John H. Tunstall ..." Coroner's Jury Report for John Tunstall. **February 19, 1878.** **(Naming Tunstall's murderers)**

Springer, Frank. "I hope you have received a full account of the Troubles in Lincoln County from your nephew ..." Letter to Senator Rush Clark. **April 9, 1878.** Herman B. Weisner Papers, ca. 1957-1992. New Mexico State University Library at Las Cruces. Rio Grande Historical Collections. Accession No. MS 0249.

Box 4/39. Folder D-6. Folder Name "Frank Springer Letter to Rush Clark." (**Links Santa Fe Ring to murder of J.H. Tunstall**)

No Author. "Killers of Tunstall. **February 18, 1879**." Herman B. Weisner Papers, ca. 1957-1992. New Mexico State University Library at Las Cruces. Rio Grande Historical Collections. Accession No. Ms 0249. Box 12. Folder T1. Folder Name: "Tunstall, John H."

Ealy, Mrs. Taylor. Ed. Haniel Long. "New Mexico Writers: The Lincoln County War Part 1. *The New Mexico Sentinel.* **October 5, 1937**. Volume 1, Number 45, Page 8. New York Public Library. (**Eye-witness of Lincoln County War; describes mutilation of head of murdered Tunstall**)

(SEE: Frank Warner Angel)

TWITCHELL, RALPH EMERSON

BOOKS BY

Twitchell, Ralph Emerson. *The Leading Facts of New Mexico History.* Vol. I-II. Santa Fe: Sunstone Press. 2007. (Reprinted from a 1912 edition) (**Ring cover-up historian**)

LETTERS TO, FROM, AND ABOUT (CONTEMPORARY)

Wright, John M. "Ancheta is talking very hard about Catron ..." Letter to Ralph E. Twitchell. **September 12, 1892**. University of New Mexico Library. Center for Southwest Studies. Thomas B. Catron Papers, MSS 29, Series 401, Box 1, Folder 11. (**Twitchell as Catron's political agent**)

Twitchell, Ralph Emerson. "I enclose you herewith a letter from Mr. Hughes, the editor of the Citizen ..." Letter to T.B. Catron. **September 26, 1892**. University of New Mexico Library. Center for Southwest Studies. Thomas B. Catron Papers, MSS 29, Series 401, Box 1, Folder 3.

Frost, Max. "Matters are progressing well here ..." Letter to Ralph E. Twitchell as "Judge". **September 26, 1892**. University of New Mexico Library. Center for Southwest Studies. Thomas B. Catron Papers, MSS 29, Series 401, Box 1, Folder 3.

Twitchell, Ralph Emerson. "I enclose you herewith a letter from Mr. Hughes, the editor of the Citizen ..." Letter to T.B. Catron. **September 26, 1892**. University of New Mexico Library. Center for Southwest Studies. Thomas B. Catron Papers, MSS 29, Series 401-409, Box 1, Folder 3. (**Twitchell involved with Hughes**)

Catron, Thomas Benton. I wired Hughes ..." Letter to Ralph E. Twitchell. **October 16, 1892**. University of New Mexico Library. Center for Southwest Studies. Thomas B. Catron Papers, MSS 29, Series 401, Box 1, Folder 3. (**Catron's campaign**)

Gregg, G.W. "I have your letter from parties in this county ..." Letter to Ralph E. Twitchell. **October 22, 1892**. University of New Mexico Library. Center for Southwest Studies. Thomas B. Catron Papers, MSS 29, Series 401, Box 1, Folder 3.

Riley, John. "I suggest you get out in Spanish a number of copies of your letter ..." Letter to Ralph E. Twitchell. **October 24, 1907**. University of New Mexico Library. Center for Southwest Studies. Thomas B. Catron Papers, MSS 29, Series 401, Box 1, Folder 3.

(SEE: Correspondence with Thomas Benton Catron)

UNDERWOOD (NATHAN) AND NASH (JOSIAH "JOE")

MODERN SOURCES

Armes, George A. *Ups and Downs of an Army Officer.* Washington, D.C. No Publisher listed. 1900. Page 464.

Klasner, Lilly. Eve Ball ed. *My Childhood Among Outlaws.* Tucson: The University of Arizona Press. 1972.

Dearen, Patrick. *A Cowboy of Pecos.* Guilford, Connecticut: Lone Star Books. 2017.

Haley, J. Evetts. J. Phelps White Interview." March 2, 1933. Roswell, New Mexico. Nita Stewart Haley Memorial Library. Midland Texas. Page 101. (**Dates the Underwood and Nash cattle partnership to pre-1875, Page 76**)

"James P. Jones Interview." January 13-14, 1927. Rocky Arroyo, New Mexico. *Notes on the History of Southeastern New Mexico.* Nita Stewart Haley Memorial Library. Midland Texas. Page 101.

"W.R. Owen Interview." March 2, 1933. Carlsbad, New Mexico. Nita Stewart Haley Memorial Library. Midland Texas. Pages 86, 95.

CONTEMPORARY SOURCE

Tunstall, John Henry. "A Tax-payer's Complaint, Office of John H. Tunstall, Lincoln, Lincoln Co., N.M., January 18, 1878, 'The Present Sheriff of Lincoln County Has Paid Nothing During His Present Term of Office.' Governor's Message for 1878." Mesilla *Independent.* **January 26, 1878.** Volume 1, Number 32. NewspaperArchive.com. (**Exposé of William Brady and John Riley for embezzling tax money to buy cattle from Underwood and Nash; T.B. Catron then paid that bill**)

VICTORIO

Ball, Eve and James Kaywaykla. *In the Days of Victorio. Recollections of a Warm Springs Apache.* Tucson, Arizona: The University of Arizona Press. 1997.

Thrapp, Dan L. *Victorio and the Mimbres Apaches.* Norman: University of Oklahoma Press. 1974.

No Author. "Glory! Hallelujah!! Victorio Killed." Wednesday, October 20, 1880. *Thirty-Four Newspaper.* Las Cruces, New Mexico. Page 1, Column 4.

WALDO, HENRY

BIOGRAPHICAL SOURCES

Speer, William S. and John Henry Brown, eds. *The Encyclopedia of the New West, Containing Fully Authenticated Information of the Agricultural, Mercantile, Commercial, Manufacturing, Mining and Grazing Industries, and Representing the Character, Development, Resources and Present Development of Texas, Arkansas, Colorado, New Mexico and Indian Territory, Also Biographical Sketches of Their Representative Men and Women.* Marshall, Texas: The United States Biographical Publishing Company. 1881.

Twitchell, Ralph Emerson. *The Leading Facts of New Mexico History.* Volume III. Cedar Rapids: The Torch Press. 1917.

CONTEMPORARY SOURCES (CHRONOLOGICAL)

Waldo, Henry. *Proceedings of a Court of Inquiry in the Case of Lt. Col. N.A.M. Dudley (May 2,1879 – July 5, 1879).* File No. QQ1284. (Boxes 3304, 3305, 3305A); Court Martial Files 1809-1894. Records of the Office of the Judge Advocate General - Army. Record Group 153. Old Military and Civil Branch. National Archives and Records Administration. Washington, D.C. (**Defense attorney for Dudley**)

Ayer, N.W. and Son. eds. *N.W. Ayer & Son's American Newspaper Annual Containing a Catalogue of American Newspapers.* Philadelphia: N.W. Ayer & Son. **1888.** (**Listing Waldo's and Breeden's New Mexico Printing Company as publishing *The Santa Fe New Mexican*)**

Waldo, Henry L. "Yours at hand ..." Letter to T.B. Catron. **December 24, 1890.** University of New Mexico Library. Center for Southwest Studies. Thomas B. Catron Papers, MSS 29, Series 102, Box 10, Folder 1.

No Author. "Death of Judge Waldo." *Santa Fe Magazine.* **August, 1915.** Volume IX, Number 9, Page 50.

(SEE: Mary Tibbles McPherson, N.A.M. Dudley)

WALLACE, LEW

AUTOBIOGRAPHICAL SOURCES

Wallace, Lew. *An Autobiography. Vol. I.* New York and London: Harper and Brothers Publishers. 1997.
_____. *An Autobiography. Vol. II.* New York and London: Harper and Brothers Publishers. 1997.

BIOGRAPHICAL SOURCES

Grant, Ulysses S. "General Lew Wallace and General McCook at Shiloh: Memoranda on the Civil War." *Battles and Leaders of the Civil War. Century* magazine. 30 [n.s. 8], 776. August, 1885. Vol. I, Page 468. **(Quote damning Wallace for Shiloh)**
_____. *Personal Memoirs.* New York: Charles L. Webster. 1885. **(Same quote from *Century* magazine damning Lew Wallace for Shiloh)**
Jones, Oakah L. "Lew Wallace: Hoosier Governor of Territorial New Mexico. 1878-81." *New Mexico Historical Review. 59(1)* (January, 1984).
Morsberger, Robert E. and Katherine M. Morsberger. *Lew Wallace: Militant Romantic.* New York: McGraw-Hill Book Company. 1980.
Paarlberg, Larry. Height of Lew Wallace. (Personal communication. Head of Lew Wallace Museum, Crawfordsville, Indiana. 2014) **(Height from Civil War Records is 5'10" - 5'11")**
Perret, Geoffrey. *Ulysses S. Grant: Soldier and President.* New York: Random House. 1997. **(Pages 170-171, 185, 188, 191)**
Stephens, Gail. "Shadow of Shiloh: Major General Lew Wallace in the Civil War." Indianapolis: Indiana Historical Society Press. 2010.

NOVELS BY

Wallace, Lew. *Commodus: An Historical Play.* **1872.** Unpublished manuscript. Wallace MSS., Lilly Library, Indiana University, Bloomington, Indiana.
_____. *The Fair God: A Tale of the Conquest of Mexico.* **1873.** Manuscript. Wallace MSS., Lilly Library, Indiana University, Bloomington, Indiana.
_____. *Ben-Hur: A Tale of the Christ.* New York: Harper & Brothers, Franklin Square. **1880.**
_____. *Prince of India: Or Why Constantinople Fell.* **1893.** Manuscript. Wallace MSS., Lilly Library, Indiana University, Bloomington, Indiana.

COLLECTED PAPERS OF

Wallace, Lew. Collected Papers. Microfilm Project Sponsored by the National Historical Publications Commission. Microfilm Roll No. 99. Santa Fe, New Mexico: State of New Mexico Records Center and Archives. 1974.
_____. Lew and Susan Wallace Collection. Indiana Historical Society. M0292.
_____. Collected Papers. Lilly Library. Bloomington, Indiana.

SECRET ANGEL NOTEBOOK ON SANTA FE RING FOR

Angel, Frank Warner. "To Gov. Lew Wallace, Santa Fe, N. M., 1878." Notebook. **1878.** Indiana Historical Society. Lew Wallace Collection. M0292. Microfilm No. F372. **(Original missing, copy on microfilm; Notebook prepared for Lew Wallace listing names for Lincoln County and the Santa Fe Ring)**

Theisen, Lee Scott. "Frank Warner Angel's Notes on New Mexico Territory, 1878." *Arizona and the West: A Quarterly Journal of History*. Winter 1976. Volume 18. Number 4. Pages 333-370. (**About the Angel notebook**)

SECRETLY RECEIVED BOOKLET ON SANTA FE RING FOR

McPherson, Mary and W.B. Matchett. *"In the Matter of Charges vs. Gov. S.B. Axtell and Other New Mexico Officials. Submitted to the Departments of the Interior and Justice.* **August, 1877.** Printed as a 31 page booklet. No publisher listed. Indiana Historical Society. Lew Wallace Collection. M0292. Box 3. Folder 20. (**Exposé about Santa Fe Ring, Catron, and Elkins; in Lew Wallace's possession**)

OATH OF OFFICE OF

Wallace, Lew. "Oath of Office, Governor, New Mexico Territory. **October 1, 1878.** Indiana Historical Society. Lew Wallace Collection. DNA; RG 48, M364. [Copy in New Mexico Archives: Records of Secretary of Territory of New Mexico (Acc# 1971-001), Series B-02: Executive Record Book 2, 1867-1882.]

AMNESTY PROCLAMATION OF

Wallace, Lew. "Proclamation by the Governor." **November 13, 1878.** Indiana Historical Society. Lew Wallace Collection. M0292. Box 3. Folder 17. (**Amnesty Proclamation for Lincoln County War fighters**)

PARDON BARGAIN WITH BILLY BONNEY (See History of William Henry Bonney)

LETTERS TO AND FROM WILLIAM BONNEY (SEE: William H. Bonney)

INTERVIEW NOTES ON BILLY BONNEY BY (SEE: William H. Bonney)

REWARD NOTICES AND POSTERS FOR WILLIAM BONNEY BY (SEE: William H. Bonney)

DEATH WARRANT FOR BILLY THE KID BY (SEE: William H. Bonney)

PARDONS TO RINGITES ISSUED AS GOVERNOR BY

Wallace, Lew. "Pardon of Jacob B. Matthews, William B. Powell, John Long, and John Hurlie et al." April, 1879 District Court. Filed **May 1, 1879.** (Under Attorneys S.B. Newcomb, Sidney Wilson, and Catron & Thornton). Herman B. Weisner Papers, ca. 1957-1992. New Mexico State University Library at Las Cruces. Rio Grande Historical Society Collection. Accession No. Ms 0249. Box 1. Folder 4. Folder Name: "Amnesty. (**Condoned Catron's using his Amnesty Proclamation to pardon indicted Ringmen, even though the Proclamation barred the indicted, and resulted in no Ringites prosecuted for the War's murders and arson**)
_____. Pardon of Marian Turner. April, 1879 District Court. Filed **May 1, 1879.** (Under Attorneys Catron & Thornton and S.B. Newcomb). Herman B. Weisner Papers, ca. 1957-1992. New Mexico State University Library at Las Cruces. Rio Grande Historical Society Collection. Accession No. Ms 0249. Box 1. Folder 4. Folder Name: "Amnesty." (**Condoned Catron's using his Amnesty Proclamation to pardon indicted Ringmen, even though the Proclamation barred the indicted, and resulted in no Ringites prosecuted for the War's murders and arson**)

DUDLEY COURT OF INQUIRY TESTIMONY BY

Wallace, Lew. Testimony in Court of Inquiry for Lieutenant Colonel N.A.M. Dudley. **May 12-15, 1879.** *Proceedings of a Court of Inquiry in the Case of Lt. Col. N.A.M. Dudley (May 2,1879 – July 5, 1879).* File No. QQ1284. (Boxes 3304, 3305, 3305A); Court Martial Files 1809-1894. Records of the Office of the Judge Advocate General – Army. Record Group 153. Old Military and Civil Branch. National Archives and Records Administration. Washington, D.C.

LETTERS BY AND TO

TO GENERAL ULYSSES S. GRANT

Wallace, Lew. "About a year after the battle of Pittsburgh Landing ..." **February 28, 1868.** Letter to Ulysses S. Grant. Indiana Historical Society. Lew Wallace Collection. M0292. Box 3. Folder 4. (**Wallace trying to get pardoned for the Battle of Shiloh**)

TO HENRY HOLT (*BEN HUR* PUBLISHER)

Wallace, Lew. "How are the books selling?" December 15, 1880. **December 14, 1880.** Indiana Historical Society. Lew Wallace Collection. M0292. Box 4. Folder 15. (**About** *Ben-Hur*)

TO CAPTAIN HENRY CARROLL

Wallace, Lew. "Under the circumstances, particularly in the absence here of suitable cells for safekeeping of Jesse Evans, Jacob B. Matthews and William Campbell ..." Letter to Henry Carroll. **March 10, 1879.** Indiana Historical Society. Lew Wallace Collection. M0292. Box 4. Folder 4.

_____. "J.J. Dolan was down here tonight. Arrest him upon his return ..." Letter to Henry Carroll. **March 10, 1879.** Indiana Historical Society. Lew Wallace Collection. M0292. Box 4. Folder 4.

_____. "I beg to submit to you a list of persons whom it is necessary, in my judgment, to arrest ..." Letter to Henry Carroll. **March 11, 1879.** Indiana Historical Society. Lew Wallace Collection. M0292. Box 4. Folder 5. (**U.S. Marshal John Sherman's outlaw list, with 14, "The Kid."**)

_____. "I sent you herewith a complete copy of all the cattle brands regularly recorded in the clerk's office of Lincoln County." **March 10, 1879.** Indiana Historical Society. Lew Wallace Collection. M0292. Box 4. Folder 5.

_____. "With Evans and Campbell at large ..." Letter to Henry Carroll. **March 19, 1879.** Indiana Historical Society. Lew Wallace Collection. M0292. Box 4. Folder 6.

FROM, TO, AND ABOUT ATTORNEY HUSTON CHAPMAN

Chapman, Huston I. "You will please pardon me for presuming so much upon your kindness ..." **October 24, 1878.** Indiana Historical Society. Lew Wallace Collection. M0292. Box 3. Folder 16.

Wallace, Lew. "I enclose you a copy of a letter from Las Vegas ..." Letter to Edward Hatch. **October 28, 1878.** Indiana Historical Society. Lew Wallace Collection. M0292. Box 3. Folder 16.

Chapman, Huston I. "You must pardon me for so often presuming upon your kindness ..." **November 29, 1878.** Indiana Historical Society. Lew Wallace Collection. M0292. Box 3. Folder 18.

FROM JAMES JOSEPH DOLAN (SEE: James J. Dolan)

TO AND FROM COMMANDER N.A.M. DUDLEY

Dudley, Nathan Augustus Monroe. "I am in receipt of a copy of letter written by one H.I. Chapman, calling himself the Attorney ..." **November 9, 1878.** Letter to Lew Wallace. From *Proceedings of a Court of Inquiry in the Case of Lt. Col. N.A.M. Dudley (May 2,1879 – July 5, 1879).* File No. QQ1284. (Boxes 3304, 3305, 3305A); Court Martial Files 1809-1894. Records of the Office of the Judge Advocate General – Army. Record Group 153. Old Military and Civil Branch. National Archives and Records Administration. Washington, D.C. **(Forwarding the Susan McSween affidavits in answer to the charges made by Chapman)**

Wallace, Lew. "Your favor containing the duplicate accounts of the messenger who posted the President's Proclamation ..." Letter to N.A.M. Dudley. **November 30, 1878.** Indiana Historical Society. Lew Wallace Collection. M0292. Box 3. Folder 18.

Dudley, Nathan Augustus Monroe. "An Open Letter, By Lieut. Col. N.A.M. Dudley, 9th Cavalry, to His Excellency Governor Lew Wallace." Letter to Lew Wallace. Santa Fe *Weekly New Mexican.* **December 14, 1878.** Reprinted in *Mesilla News.* December 21, 1878. As Exhibit 13 from *Proceedings of a Court of Inquiry in the Case of Lt. Col. N.A.M. Dudley (May 2,1879 - July 5, 1879).* File No. QQ1284. (Boxes 3304, 3305, 3305A); Court Martial Files 1809-1894. Records of the Office of the Judge Advocate General - Army. Record Group 153. Old Military and Civil Branch. National Archives and Records Administration. Washington, D.C. **(Attacks Wallace's Amnesty Proclamation as applying to the military)**

Wallace, Lew. "The public interests with which I am charged make it, in my judgment, exceedingly improper for me to answer publicly your letters in the New Mexican ..." Letter to N.A.M. Dudley and other Fort Stanton officers. **December 16, 1878.** Indiana Historical Society. Lew Wallace Collection. M0292. Box 3. Folder 19.

Dudley, Nathan Augustus Monroe Dudley. "This being regular report day, I respectfully state ..." **March 1, 1879.** Indiana Historical Society. Lew Wallace Collection. M0292. Box 4. Folder 4. **(Blaming Lincoln County "troubles" on rustlers)**

FROM PRESIDENT JAMES ABRAM GARFIELD

Garfield, James Abram. "I have, this morning, finished reading "Ben-Hur" ...." Letter to Lew Wallace. **April 19, 1881.** Indiana Historical Society. Lew Wallace Collection. M0292. Box 4. Folder 17.

TO SHERIFF PATRICK F. GARRETT

Wallace, Lew. "To the Sheriff of Lincoln County, New Mexico, Greeting ..." **April 30, 1881.** Indiana Historical Society. Lew Wallace Collection. M0292. Box 9. Folder 11. **(Death Warrant for William Bonney)**

TO AND FROM GENERAL EDWARD HATCH

Wallace, Lew. "I think all that is needed now for the thorough pacification of Lincoln County is ..." Letter to Edward Hatch. **October 26, 1878.** Indiana Historical Society. Lew Wallace Collection. M0292. Box 3. Folder 16. **(wants to use troops to pacify Lincoln County)**

_____. "In a communication, dated October 28. inst., I requested, for reasons stated, a safe-guard for Mrs. McSween ..." Letter to Edward Hatch. **November 9, 1878.** Indiana Historical Society. Lew Wallace Collection. M0292. Box 3. Folder 17.

_____. "I am in receipt of Col. Dudley's reply to the charges against him ..." Letter to Edward Hatch. **November 14, 1878.** Indiana Historical Society. Lew Wallace Collection. M0292. Box 3, Folder 17. **(Has quote: "the "reply is** perfectly satisfactory," which was later used in the Dudley Court of Inquiry claiming he had already exonerated Dudley)

_____. "I am constrained to request that Lieut Col. N.A.M. Dudley, Commanding at Fort Stanton, be relieved ..." **December 7, 1878.** Indiana Historical Society. Lew Wallace Collection. M0292. Box 3, Folder 18. **(Removal of Dudley requested but denied)**

Wallace, Lew. "In your communication today, speaking of the arrest of Campbell ..." Letter to Edward Hatch. **March 6, 1879.** Indiana Historical Society. Lew Wallace Collection. M0292. Box 4, Folder 4. **(arrest of Huston Chapman's murderer)**

_____. "I have reliable information that J.A. Scurlock and Charles Bowdre are now at a ranch called Taiban ..." **March 6, 1879.** Indiana Historical Society. Lew Wallace Collection. M0292. Box 4, Folder 4. **(pursuing Regulators with troops as outlaws)**

_____. "I have just ascertained that 'The Kid' is at a place called Las Tablas ..." **March 6, 1879.** Indiana Historical Society. Lew Wallace Collection. M0292. Box 9, Folder 10. **(pursuing Billy Bonney with troops as an outlaw)**

_____. "I have the honor to repeat the request made on a former occasion that Lt. Col. N.A.M. Dudley be relieved of the command ..." **March 7, 1879.** Letter to Edward Hatch. Indiana Historical Society. Lew Wallace Collection. M0292. Box 4, Folder 4. **(repeat request to remove Commander Dudley)**

Hatch, Edward. "Lieutenant Colonel N.A.M. Dudley is hereby relieved from command and duty ..." Special Field Order 2. **March 8, 1879.** Indiana Historical Society. Lew Wallace Collection. M0292. Box 4, Folder 4. **(Dudley removed)**

TO AND FROM PRESIDENT RUTHERFORD B. HAYES

Wallace, Lew. "I avail myself of your request this morning. It is hardly necessary to give reasons for a preference of the Italian mission ..." Letter to Rutherford B. Hayes. **March 9, 1877.** Indiana Historical Society. Lew Wallace Collection. M0292. Box 3. Folder 13. **(Desired ambassadorships)**

_____. "The feuds recently in Lincoln county, New Mexico, left a large many thieves and murderers, who, with others of like class since added to their number, are now confederated for plunder." Letter to Rutherford B. Hayes. **March 31, 1879.** Indiana Historical Society. Lew Wallace Collection. M0292. Box 4. Folder 7. **(Wants martial law against confederacy of outlaws)**

Hayes, Rutherford B. "We are greatly obliged by your kindness." Letter to Lew Wallace. **January 9, 1881.** Indiana Historical Society. Lew Wallace Collection. M0292. Box 4. Folder 16. **(Thanking for gift of *Ben-Hur*)**

TO LINCOLN COUNTY SHERIFF GEORGE KIMBRELL

Wallace, Lew. "The duty of keeping the peace in the county and arresting offenders is devolved by the law upon you ..." **April 2, 1879.** Indiana Historical Society. Lew Wallace Collection. Box 4, Folder 8.

TO AND FROM IRA E. LEONARD (SEE: Ira Leonard)

TO COLONEL ABSALOM H. MARKLAND

Wallace, Lew. "Our mutual friend, M. Hinds, who will hand you this ..." Letter to A.H. Markland. **November 14, 1878.** Indiana Historical Society. Lew Wallace Collection. M0292. Box 3. Folder 17. **(proves that Wallace was fully aware of the Santa Fe Ring, his refusal to join, its attempt to remove him as governor, and the cause of his avoiding any confrontation of the Ring while in the Territory)**

FROM SECRETARY OF WAR GEORGE W. McCRARY

McCrary, George W. "This will be presented to you by Gen. Lew Wallace, the newly appointed Governor of New Mexico ..." Letter given to Lew Wallace to present to General Edward Hatch. **September 18, 1878**. Indiana Historical Society. Lew Wallace Collection. M0292. Box 3. Folder 14.

Wallace, Lew. "By the statute now in force ..." **October 4, 1878**. Indiana Historical Society. Lew Wallace Collection. M0292. Box 3. Folder 15. (**Requesting arms from the Secretary of War**)

McCrary, George W. "I have the honor to acknowledge the receipt of your letter..." **November 23, 1878**. Indiana Historical Society. Lew Wallace Collection. M0292. Box 3. Folder 17. (**About Wallace requesting arms to fight "outlaws"**)

Wallace, Lew. "I have the honor to acknowledge the receipt of two communications from you..." Letter to George McCrary. **November 23, 1878**. Indiana Historical Society. Lew Wallace Collection. M0292. Box 3. Folder 18. (**Refuses to post personal bond for arms**)

McCrary, George W. "I have the honor to acknowledge the receipt of your letter..." **August 26, 1879**. Indiana Historical Society. Lew Wallace Collection. M0292. Box 4. Folder 12.(**Freeing Wallace from responsibility for Dudley Court of Inquiry outcome**)

Bell, A. "Referring to your letter of the 30th ultimo ..." **August 29, 1879**. Letter to Lew Wallace about George McCrary. Indiana Historical Society. Lew Wallace Collection. M0292. Box 4. Folder 12. (**Acting Secretary of the Interior and Secretary of War placate Wallace about Court of Inquiry outcome**)

TO LINCOLN JAILOR JUAN PATRÓN

Wallace, Lew. "Please select ten of your Rangers ..." Letter to Juan Patrón. **March 3, 1879**. Indiana Historical Society. Lew Wallace Collection. M0292. Box 4. Folder 4. (**To arrest "Scurlock and Bowdre"**)

_____. "Please report to Sheriff Kimbrell ..." Letter to Juan Patrón. **March 3, 1879**. Indiana Historical Society. Lew Wallace Collection. M0292. Box 4. Folder 4.

_____. Wallace, Lew. "Be good enough to send word to all your men to turn out soon as possible ..." Letter to Juan Patrón. **March 19, 1879**. Indiana Historical Society. Lew Wallace Collection. M0292. Box 4. Folder 6. (**Reports escape of Jessie Evans and Billy Campbell from Fort Stanton**)

FROM LIEUTENANT GEORGE PURINGTON

Purington, George Augustus. "The District Court adjourned on Thursday ..." **May 3, 1879**. Indiana Historical Society. Lew Wallace Collection. M0292. Box 4. Folder 10. (**Letter to Adjutant General on Grand Jury indictments of the Murphy-Dolans and N.A.M. Dudley; copy sent to Lew Wallace**)

TO AND FROM SECRETARY OF INTERIOR CARL SCHURZ

Wallace, Lew. "I have the honor to inform you ..." Letter to Carl Schurz. **October 1, 1878**. Indiana Historical Society. Lew Wallace Collection. M0292. Box 3. Folder 15. (**Informing Schurz that he informed Axtell of suspension and that he now qualified as Governor, and wanted "extreme measures"**)

_____. "I have the honor to enclose herewith a requisition ..." **October 4, 1878**. Letter to Carl Schurz. Indiana Historical Society. Lew Wallace Collection. M0292. Box 3. Folder 15. (**About arms from Secretary of War**)

_____. "As the basis of the request which I have to prefer relative to the affairs in the county of Lincoln ..." Letter to Carl Schurz. **October 5, 1878**. Indiana Historical Society. Lew Wallace Collection. M0292. Box 3. Folder 15. (**Requesting President to declare martial law**)

_____. "In further exemplification of affairs in Lincoln county accept extract received ..." Letter to Carl Schurz. **October 5, 1878**. Indiana Historical Society. Lew Wallace Collection. M0292. Box 3. Folder 15. (**N.A.M. Dudley's report of "Wrestlers" raping in Lincoln County**)

No signatures. (But in Lew Wallace's handwriting). "Yesterday, at the request of Governor Wallace the undersigned, physicians ...." Letter to Carl Schurz. **October 23, 1878**. Indiana Historical Society. Lew Wallace Collection. M0292. Box 3. Folder 16. (**Focus on need to refurbish the Palace of the Governors**)

Schurz, Carl. "I acknowledge the receipt of your letter of the 13th instant ..." Letter from Carl Schurz. **November 23, 1878**. Indiana Historical Society. Lew Wallace Collection. M0292. Box 3. Folder 18. (**Amnesty Proclamation, has approval of President**)

_____. "I have received your letter ..." Letter to Lew Wallace. **December 9, 1878**. Indiana Historical Society. Lew Wallace Collection. M0292. Box 3. Folder 19. (**Answer denying he would be removed**)

Wallace, Lew. "I have the honor to report that affairs of the Territory are moving on quietly ..." Letter to Carl Schurz. **December 21, 1878**. Indiana Historical Society. Lew Wallace Collection. M0292. Box 3. Folder 19. (**N.A.M. Dudley's indignation about the Amnesty Proclamation**)

_____. "One H.I. Chapman, lawyer, was assassinated ...." Letter to Carl Schurz. **February 27, 1879**. Indiana Historical Society. Lew Wallace Collection. M0292. Box 4. Folder 3. (**Reacting to Chapman murder by using troops to track "outlaws" – meaning the Regulators.**)

_____. "My time has been so constantly occupied in getting my work into operation ..." Letter to Carl Schurz. **March 21, 1879**. Indiana Historical Society. Lew Wallace Collection. M0292. Box 4. Folder 7. (**Progress report with enclosure of Sherman's outlaw list with "The Kid," and outlaw myth**)

_____. "To day I forwarded a telegram to you, with another to the President ..." Letter to Carl Schurz. **March 31, 1879**. Indiana Historical Society. Lew Wallace Collection. M0292. Box 4. Folder 7. (**Mention of "precious specimen nicknamed 'The Kid' "**)

_____. "I have official information that a court of inquiry for Col. Dudley has been ordered ..." Letter to Carl Schurz. **April 4, 1879**. Indiana Historical Society. Lew Wallace Collection. M0292. Box 4, Folder 8.

_____. "I have the honor to inform you that affairs in Lincoln County are progressing favorably ..." Letter to Carl Schurz. **April 18, 1879**. Indiana Historical Society. Lew Wallace Collection. M0292. Box 4, Folder 9.

_____. "I have the honor to inform you that all the recent reports, military and otherwise, justify me in saying Lincoln County is enjoying a term of peace." Letter to Carl Schurz. **May 5, 1879**. Indiana Historical Society. Lew Wallace Collection. M0292. Box 4. Folder 10.

_____. "Enclosed please find a copy of the report of the commandant at Fort Stanton." Letter to Carl Schurz. **June 11, 1879**. Indiana Historical Society. Lew Wallace Collection. M0292. Box 4. Folder 11. (**Self-serving progress report of quelling disturbances**)

_____. "The accompanying document received from Fort Stanton which will explain itself." Letter to Carl Schurz. **July 30, 1879**. Indiana Historical Society. Lew Wallace Collection. M0292. Box 4. Folder 12. (**Claims he pacified the Territory**)

_____. "In reply to the communication of Acting Secretary Bell ..." **September 15, 1879**. Letter to Carl Schurz. Indiana Historical Society. Lew Wallace Collection. M0292. Box 4. Folder 13. (**On Bob Olinger killing John Jones; calling Olinger a "bloody ... Bandit of the Pecos."**)

_____. "I have the honor to inform you ..." **February 16, 1880**. Letter to Carl Schurz. Indiana Historical Society. Lew Wallace Collection. M0292. Box 4, Folder 14. (**Reports Catron as head of Ring**)

_____. "From private advices received from Lincoln county ..." **December 7, 1880**. Indiana Historical Society. Lew Wallace Collection. M0292. Box 4. Folder 15. (**Reports pursuit of outlaws by people in Lincoln County**)

_____. "I have private business urgently requiring my presence in New York City ..." Letter to Carl Schurz. **December 14, 1880**. Indiana Historical Society. Lew Wallace Collection. M0292. Box No. 4. Folder 15. (**Mention's Billy as leader of the outlaws**" [Billy] for whom he has set a "**$500 reward.**")

TO AND FROM JUSTICE OF THE PEACE JOHN B. WILSON

Wallace, Lew. "I hasten to acknowledge receipt of your favor of the 11th Jan. ult. ..." **January 18, 1879**. Indiana Historical Society. Lew Wallace Collection. M0292. Box 4. Folder 1. (**Lincoln County as carrying on a revolution**)

_____. "Your favors are both in hand and place me under renewed obligation. ..." **February 6, 1879**. Indiana Historical Society. Lew Wallace Collection. M0292. Box 4. Folder 2.

Wilson, John B. Letter to Lew Wallace. Unsigned but noted as from "Sqr. Wilson by Wallace. Undated, but likely **March, 1879**. Indiana Historical Society. Lew Wallace Collection. M0292. Box 4, Folder 7. (**On Lady Liberty stationery**)

_____. Affidavit of John Wilson. **March ?, 1879**. Indiana Historical Society. Lew Wallace Collection. M0292. Box 4, Folder 7.

Wallace, Lew. "I understand that affidavits will be filed with you against the prisoners. ..." Letter to John B. Wilson. **March 8, 1879**. Indiana Historical Society. Lew Wallace Collection. M0292. Box 4. Folder 4.

_____. "I enclose a note for Bonney." Letter to John "Squire" Wilson. **March 20, 1879**. Indiana Historical Society. Lew Wallace Collection. M0292. Box 4. Folder 6. (**The pardon negotiation for Billy Bonney**)

Wilson, John B. Signed JBW. **April 8, 1879**. Indiana Historical Society, Lew Wallace Collection. M0292. Box 4, Folder 8. (**Notes on rustling**)

_____. Letter to Lew Wallace. **May 18, 1879**. Indiana Historical Society. Lew Wallace Collection. M0292. Box 4, Folder 5.

ARTICLES ABOUT WILLIAM BONNEY BY (SEE: William H. Bonney)

WALZ, EDGAR A.

No Author. *The American Book of Biography: Men of 1912*. Chicago: American Publishers Association. 1913. Page 614.

No Author. "Edgar A. Walz Dead: Expert on credit, Founder of The Travelers Hotel Credit Corporation – Managed New Mexico Ranch in Youth." *The New York Times*. **April 5, 1935**. Volume LXXXIV, Number 28,195. Page 24.

WILD, AZARIAH

BIOGRAPHICAL SOURCE

Nolan, Frederick. "Biography of Azariah Wild." Unpublished and personal communications, June 11, 2005 and October 9, 2005.

CONTEMPORARY SOURCES (CHRONOLOGICAL)

Brooks, James J. *1877 Report on Secret Service Operatives*. "On Azariah Wild." **September 26, 1877**. Page 392. Department of the Treasury. United States Secret Service. Washington, D.C.

Wild, Azariah F. "Daily Reports of U. S. Secret Service Agents, 1875-1937." Record Group 87. Microfilm T-915. Microfilm Rolls 306 (June 15, 1877 - December 31, 1877), 307 (January 1,1878 - June 30, 1879), 308 (July 1, 1879 - June 30, 1881; October 4, 1880, Pages 330-333; October 5, 1880, Pages 336-339; November 11,

1880, Pages 484-488), 309 (July 1, 1881 - September 30, 1883), 310 (October 1, 1883 - July 31, 1886). National Archives and Records Department. Department of the Treasury. Secret Service Division. Washington, D.C.

WILSON, JOHN B. "SQUIRE"

CORONER'S JURY REPORT FOR JOHN H. TUNSTALL BY

Wilson, John, George B. Barker, Robert M. Gilbert, John Newcomb, Samuel Smith, Benjamin Ellis. "We the undersigned Justice of the Peace and Coroners Jury who sat upon the inquest held this 19th day of February 1878 on the body of John H. Tunstall ..." Coroner's Jury Report for John Tunstall. **February 19, 1878**. **(Naming as murderers, among others, James Dolan, Frank Baker, Jessie Evans, William Morton, and George Hindman)**

LETTERS FROM

Wilson, John B. Letter to Lew Wallace. Unsigned but noted as from "Sqr. Wilson by Wallace. Undated, but likely **March, 1879**. Indiana Historical Society. Lew Wallace Collection. M0292. Box 4, Folder 7. **(On Lady Liberty stationery)**
_____. Affidavit of John Wilson. **March ?, 1879**. Indiana Historical Society. Lew Wallace Collection. M0292. Box 4, Folder 7.
_____. Signed JBW. **April 8, 1879**. Indiana Historical Society, Lew Wallace Collection. M0292. Box 4, Folder 8. **(Notes on rustling)**
_____. Letter to Lew Wallace. **May 18, 1879**. Indiana Historical Society. Lew Wallace Collection. M0292. Box 4, Folder 5.

LETTERS TO

Bonney, W H. "Friend Wilson ..." **March 18, 1879**. Indiana Historical Society. Lew Wallace Collection. M0292. **(For his pardon negotiation with Lew Wallace)**
Wallace, Lew. "I enclose a note for Bonney." Letter to John "Squire" Wilson. **March 20, 1879**. Indiana Historical Society. Lew Wallace Collection. M0292. Box 4. Folder 6. **(The pardon negotiation for Billy Bonney)**

INDEX

542

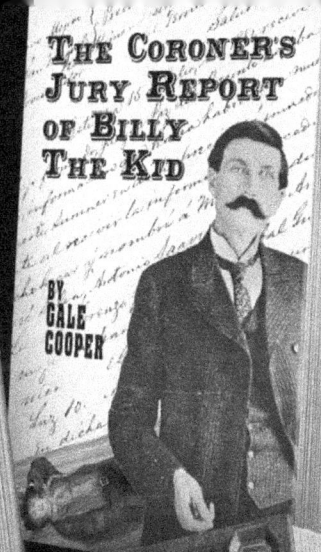

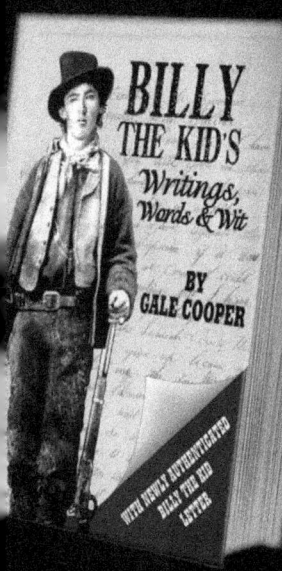

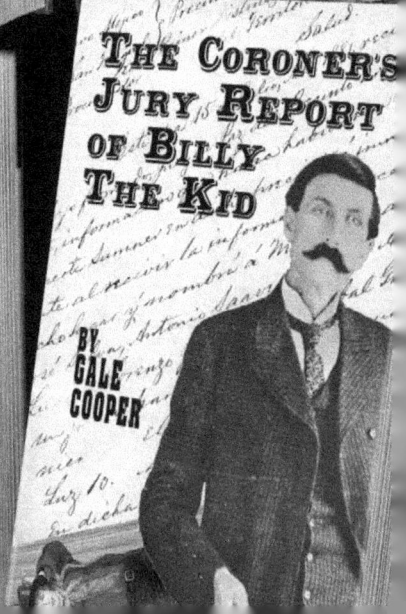

www.ingramcontent.com/pod-product-compliance
Lightning Source LLC
Chambersburg PA
CBHW032037090426
42744CB00004B/40